Creating Justice in a Multiracial Democracy

New Will for Evidence-Based Policies That Work

Edited by
Alan Curtis

Foreword by
Wes Moore

TEACHERS COLLEGE PRESS
TEACHERS COLLEGE | COLUMBIA UNIVERSITY
NEW YORK AND LONDON

Published by Teachers College Press,˙ 1234 Amsterdam Avenue, New York, NY 10027

Copyright © 2024 by Teachers College, Columbia University

Chapter 3 adapted excerpt reprinted from *The Big Myth* © 2023 by Naomi Oreskes and Erik M. Conway, with permission from Bloomsbury Publishing Inc.

All rights reserved. No part of this publication may be reproduced or transmitted in any form or by any means, electronic or mechanical, including photocopy, or any information storage and retrieval system, without permission from the publisher. For reprint permission and other subsidiary rights requests, please contact Teachers College Press, Rights Dept.: tcpressrights@tc.columbia.edu

Library of Congress Cataloging-in-Publication Data is available at loc.gov

ISBN 978-0-8077-6994-2 (paper)
ISBN 978-0-8077-6995-9 (hardcover)
ISBN 978-0-8077-8251-4 (ebook)

Printed on acid-free paper
Manufactured in the United States of America

To Ying, the love of my life.

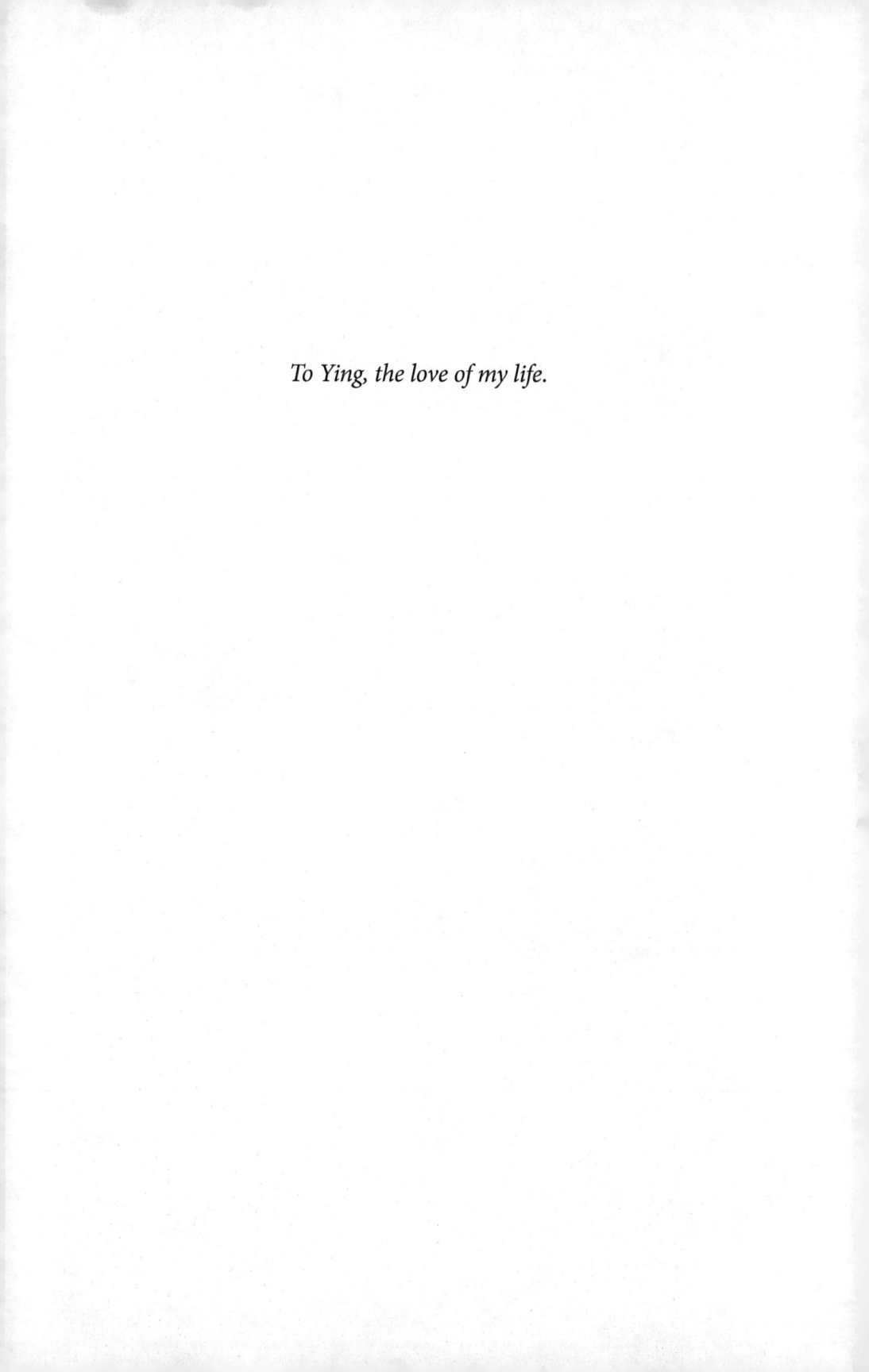

Contents

Foreword   xi
    Wes Moore
    Governor of Maryland

Acknowledgments   xv

Introduction   xvii
    Alan Curtis
    President and CEO
    Eisenhower Foundation

PART I: WHAT EVIDENCE-BASED POLICY WORKS?

Economic and Employment Policy   3

1. Should the Federal Government Play a Role in Racial Equity? Of Course   5
    Jared Bernstein

2. The New Economics and the Rebalancing of Power   11
    Felicia Wong and Matt Hughes

3. Guidez-Faire: Why Capitalism Needs Effective Governance   22
    Naomi Oreskes and Erik M. Conway

4. Worker-Centered and Race-Conscious Policies Are Essential for Equity and Economic Justice   36
    Valerie Wilson and Adewale Maye

Education and Youth Development Policy   49

5. The Long Quest for Equitable Educational Opportunity   51
   Linda Darling-Hammond

6. Building Loving Systems to Create One America for All Children   62
   John H. Jackson and Zakiyah Ansari

7. A New Great Society   73
   Randi Weingarten

8. Action to Reaffirm: Equity, Racial Justice, and the Future of College Admissions   86
   Dwayne Kwaysee Wright and Michael Feuer

9. Act Now! Invest in America's Youth   96
   Dorothy Stoneman with Mary Ellen Sprenkel

Crime Prevention and Criminal Justice Policy   107

10. Police Reform: Where Do We Go From Here?   109
    Neil Gross

11. Race, Transparency and Policing: Practical Advice From One Pracademic's Point of View   122
    Branville Bard Jr.

12. Two Justice Systems—Separate and Unequal   133
    Kim Taylor-Thompson

13. One in Five: Progress and Pushback in Lowering the Lifetime Likelihood of Imprisonment for Young Black Men   143
    Nazgol Ghandnoosh

14. Violence in Post-Pandemic America: Hard Truths and Enduring Lessons   157
    Elliott Currie

Housing and Neighborhood Investment Policy   167

15. Scaling Economic and Housing Justice   169
    Lisa Rice, Michael Akinwumi, and Nikitra Bailey

16. What the Kerner Commission Got Wrong and How
    We Can Get It Right: Remedying Segregation
    Requires Recognizing Its True Origins   186
    Leah Rothstein and Richard Rothstein

Public Health Policy   197

17. An Accidental Public Health Manifesto   199
    Michelle A. Williams

18. U.S. Health Care Policy, the Evidence, and the Will for Change: What
    Will It Take to Transform Decades of Evidence Regarding U.S. Race
    and Income Based Health Disparities to a "Will for Change"?   213
    Herbert C. Smitherman Jr. and Anil N. F. Aranha

Latino, Native American, and Asian American Policy Perspectives   239

19. The Power of Stories   241
    Janet Murguía

20. E Pluribus Unum: Out of Many, [We Are] One   252
    Sindy M. Benavides

21. Kerner Commission Report: 21st-Century
    Native American Perspective   263
    Judith LeBlanc

22. United Against Hate: How Asian America Is Standing Up   278
    George Huynh

PART II: HOW TO CREATE NEW WILL?

Dr. King, Economic Justice, and Moral Fusion   291

23. Reviving the Heart of Democracy   293
    Rev. William Barber II

24. An Email and an Epistle for American Democracy   302
    Cornell William Brooks

Persuasion, Democracy, and Voter Rights — 313

25. Values, Villain, Vision: Messaging to Mobilize Our Base and Persuade the Conflicted — 315
Anat Shenker-Osorio

26. A New North Star to Lead Us to a Representative Democracy That Is Just and Equitable for All — 326
LaTosha R. Brown

27. Calling In as Compassionate Activism — 336
Loretta J. Ross

Media, Evidence, and Misinformation — 345

28. When Our "Truth-Tellers" Won't Tell Us the Truth: Looking Back at the Kerner Commission Report and Ahead to a Transformed Media Landscape — 347
Ray Suarez

29. "Little Brother Is Watching Big Brother": The Flawed Media Lens on Policing and Racism — 359
Julian E. Zelizer

30. Race and Media in a Polarized Society — 370
Robert Faris

31. Toward a More Evidence-Based Policy Agenda — 380
Justin Milner

The Visual Arts, Monuments, and the Performing Arts — 397

32. Carry History, Hold Truth: Art in the Public Realm — 399
Rocío Aranda-Alvarado, Margaret S. Morton, and Lena Sze

33. Healing Toward New Will — 412
Claudia Peña

34. Art as Translation — 418
Carlton Mackey

35. Regenerating the Body of Culture	429
brooke smiley	
36. The Art Will . . . A Musing on Life in the Performing Arts: A Case Study for NEW WILL	440
Lisa Richards Toney	
Index	**448**
About the Editor and Contributors	**471**

Foreword

The National Guard has been activated around a dozen times at the federal level since our nation's founding. More than half of those instances have involved racial conflict.[1] Men and women join the Guard with the expectation that they will devote their time to helping Americans recover from hurricanes and earthquakes. But more often, they find themselves in the streets of our communities patching up the undressed wounds of racial tension.

In 2015, the National Guard came to Baltimore City. Violence had broken out in the wake of the death of Freddie Gray, who passed away in police custody on April 19, 2015. Guardsmen lined up in front of City Hall to staunch the unrest and enforce a strict curfew. I walked the streets of the city and saw row after row of American soldiers patrolling neighborhoods consumed by conflict. I had learned about this kind of military intervention in books about the Civil Rights Era, but I had never experienced it first-hand.

One simple thought rang in my head: "Why is this still happening?"

Cycles of tragedy, unrest, and armed response dot many chapters of the American story, from our founding to today. The delicate threads of cause and effect that drive these cycles and systems are neither simple nor straightforward. But in the soundbite culture of modern politics, those strands of nuance are easily overlooked—even ignored. When horror strikes, we look for someone to blame, and then we move on. If we marshal the courage to offer solutions, they often amount to little more than band-aids to issues so deep that they require stitches—or even surgery.

But occasionally, an individual or group helps us break from the simplicity with which pundits talk about the challenges we face and guides us toward the complexity with which people experience those challenges. There have been few greater examples of this kind of visionary leadership than in the case of the 1968 Kerner Commission.

President Lyndon Johnson formed the Kerner Commission in response to the Watts riots in California, and he directed the team to answer three basic questions about the violence that had swept the nation—both in Watts and in other communities across the country:

"What happened?"

"Why did it happen?"

"What can be done to prevent it from happening again and again?"[2]

The members of the Kerner Commission could have easily pulled together public data, leaned back on tested and tired talking points, and concluded their report with a full-throated endorsement of President Johnson's Great Society programs. Instead, the Commission did what few had done before and few have done after: They engaged in an honest, thorough investigation of the truth.

This ragtag crew of tested political minds and establishment hands rejected the ease of simplicity. They chose to embrace complexity, study the systems in which they worked, and look under the hood of American life. They gifted the nation with a blueprint for a kind of politics that accepts nuance as a prerequisite for leadership. To read the Kerner Commission today is to come face-to-face with a treatise on political honesty. And in an age of half-truths and false choices, we deserve leaders who draw their strength from the same commitment to uncovering real answers that inspired the members of the Commission decades ago.

The conclusions of the Commission should no longer shock us. We know that the unique challenges that festered in low-income, predominantly Black communities during the 1950s and 1960s—which helped drive unrest and violence—did not magically appear. They were created. Policies like redlining, predatory lending, mass incarceration, forced segregation, over-policing, and the underfunding of education and transportation have walled off opportunity to Black families for generations and wreak havoc to this day. Low achievement in African American neighborhoods isn't a function of low intelligence or low ambition on the part of any individual within a community—but rather, a function of broken policies implemented by those outside the community. We accept these premises.

But in 1968, the notion of institutional racism hadn't yet entered the mainstream. The members of the Kerner Commission performed an act of intellectual daring: they sought to share wisdom that lay beyond the overused and underdeveloped explanations for violence and discord. Instead, they took a hard look at the forces that exist at the center of our society.

Members of the Commission expressed the relationship between bad policies of white institutions and bad outcomes within Black communities in direct, unflinching terms: "What white Americans have never fully understood—but what the Negro can never forget—is that white society is deeply implicated in the ghetto. White institutions created it, white institutions maintain it, and white society condones it."[3]

The members of the Commission were all white men, most of whom held elected office during their tenure of service to the project. They understood that they worked at the pleasure of President Johnson, who established the Commission by executive order. Still, they had the moral courage to seek truth instead of papering over it—even if it meant defying the source of their own authority. Truth overruled political grace.

And just as the members of the Kerner Commission had the courage to assemble a nuanced view of civil unrest that defied established views, so too did they take a nuanced view of the solutions to civil unrest. Among the authors' most innovative recommendation is the call for a "New Will." The idea is simple, but powerful:

> The need is not so much for the Government to design new programs as it is for the Nation to generate new will. Private enterprise, labor unions, the churches, the foundations, the universities–all our urban institutions–must deepen their involvement in the life of the city and their commitment to its revival and welfare.[4]

Members of the Kerner Commission insisted that efforts to heal racial wounds, soothe racial tensions, and disrupt patterns of violence could only be achieved through a symphony of action stretching beyond the federal government. If the challenges we face are multidetermined, then so too are the solutions. Partnership drives change. And not just partnership between individuals, but also partnership between institutions that occupy different sectors of our society.

The Kerner Commission challenges us to think beyond this false choice between a do-nothing government and a do-everything government. "New Will" cannot exist exclusively inside or outside of the institutions of the state. Rather, "New Will" can flourish only when everyone agrees to be a part of the solution to the thorniest issues of our time.

In my State of Maryland, we have taken this notion of "New Will" and implemented it through policy. Partnership is not simply something to which we aspire—it is a governing philosophy by which we lead. In 2024, we rolled out the ENOUGH Act, our most successful effort yet to operationalize the kind of robust, organized, and intentional partnership that the authors of the Kerner Commission encouraged.

Our legislation aims to break down cycles of intergenerational poverty by engaging neighborhoods, nonprofits, organizations, unions, governments, and households. Our approach centers on both a renewed focus on poverty and also a new way of governing. Government can provide resources, expertise, and collaboration. But you need to recruit people on the ground to fully address complex challenges like poverty.

The ENOUGH Act doesn't throw money blindly at communities that need it. Instead, we are calling on community leaders to come together and create comprehensive plans on how to make their neighborhoods better. These proposals will give us a framework for progress that's written *by* our communities and not simply *for* our communities. The premise is simple: local leaders will provide the vision, and state government will provide the support. We will fund winning proposals with a mix of public and private money and engage directly with Marylanders whose proposals we agree to finance.

Our legislation provides a model for how "New Will" can manifest in 2024. And by working together to solve big problems, we stand a chance of restoring many of the social and civic bonds that have frayed over time. People who serve together stick together, and by building up strong relationships, we can start to break down social divisions. Moving in partnership is both meaningful as a means toward an end and as an end in itself.

Our legislation is the first of its kind in the nation, but it doesn't have to be the last. We can begin to view one another as partners instead of adversaries. We can begin to pass legislation that empowers people to step up and serve. We can work together to find a shared sense of unity—not because it sounds good, but because when everyone has a seat at the table, you deliver better results. We can begin to look beyond the simple explanations we've been handed and instead embrace complexity as a precondition for progress.

Change takes time. I'm not naive about the wide distance between where we are now and where we need to go. But while progress isn't preordained, progress is possible.

We can start to see glimmers of hope at the margins of America: the returning citizen who spends their time helping kids learn to put down guns; the police officer who runs a holiday toy drive for families living in poverty; the minister who uses her house of worship to bring together dueling factions in a neighborhood; the union leader who sits down with their local alderman to hash out differences in policy; the teacher who runs for school board because she has a vision for change. These are the seeds of partnership that can one day grow into a "New Will" that brings our country together again.

In the months following Freddie Gray's killing, Baltimore was a city divided against itself. Marylanders were left reeling from the emotional toll of what had transpired—not just in the days after Gray's death, but also in the years that had preceded it. For weeks, it was hard to tell which of the wrecked stores and rowhouses had been looted during the outbreak of violence and which had been falling apart for decades. Some questioned if the city should be saved at all.

But nearly a decade later, the city is bouncing back. We've broken the fever of record-high homicides. Baltimore is considered one of the fastest-growing economies in the country. You can spot cranes on nearly every city block, lifting steel into the sky as new buildings emerge from the ground. Even in the aftermath of the collapse of the Francis Scott Key Bridge, we remain Maryland Tough and Baltimore Strong.

We earned this moment by following the spirit of the authors of the Kerner Commission: We are unafraid to study complexity, and we are ready to do more than simply pave over the cracks of broken systems. We maintain a healthy skepticism of the very institutions we work within, but never allow our skepticism to fester into cynicism. We cherish our shared dedication to moving in partnership toward shared goals. We've wrapped our arms around each other: small businesses and labor leaders, state's attorneys and public defenders, elected officials and village elders, police officers and the communities they protect. We stand undaunted by the hard problems, unwilling to slow our pace, and unwavering in our commitment to progress.

Together, with the values and vision of the Kerner Commission as helpful guides, we can—and we will—build the kind of society that those who came before us dreamed of and that those who come after us deserve.

Wes Moore
Governor of the State of Maryland

NOTES

1. Chelsey Cox, "Fact Check: National Guard Was Activated Most Often During the Civil Rights Era," *USA Today,* June 17, 2020, https://www.usatoday.com/story/news/factcheck/2020/06/14/fact-check-national-guard-activated-16-times-us/5319853002/.

2. The National Advisory Commission on Civil Disorders, *The Kerner Report* (introduction by Julian E. Zelizer) (Princeton: Princeton University Press, 2016), 479, https://doi.org/10.2307/j.ctvcszz6s.9.

3. *The Kerner Report*, 2.

4. *The Kerner Report*, 413.

Acknowledgments

We are proud that *Creating Justice in a Multiracial Democracy* is sponsored by the Eisenhower Foundation, whose mission embraces the priorities of both the 1967–1968 Kerner Commission and the 1968–1969 National Commission on the Causes and Prevention of Violence.

To Tracey Felder, vice president for operations at the Eisenhower Foundation, our deep gratitude for managing the day-to-day production of the book, communicating with all the authors and orchestrating our many Kerner forums and panels before and after publication.

In 2023, on the exact day of the 55th anniversary of the Kerner Commission Report, we held our Nelson Mandela United Nations Anniversary Forum and Dinner, which was superbly organized by Lin Gao, Sophia Sun, and Ying Wang. The Mandela event and its United Nations awardees launched *Creating Justice in a Multiracial Democracy*.

Special thanks to Council of Economic Advisors Chairman Jared Bernstein, Senator Cory Booker, Professor Elizabeth Hinton, Governor Wes Moore, and Congressman Robert C. Scott for engaging the legacy of the Kerner Commission during these times so crucial to the future of American democracy.

All the chapter authors of *Creating Justice in a Multiracial Democracy* diligently identified the meaning of Kerner today and integrated their wisdom with evidence-based commonsense recommendations for action. Linda Darling-Hammond, William Barber, Dorothy Stoneman, Elliott Currie, Cornell Brooks, Michelle Williams, and Felicia Wong provided especially helpful guidance as the book developed.

Brian Ellerbeck, Allison Scott, Alyssa Jordan, Lori Tate, Julie Kerr, Nancy Power, Abigail Naqvi, and their colleagues at Teachers College Press were always there for us and infused courageous energy into this book and its companion volume, the reissuance of the original 1968 Kerner Report.

As we continue the movement begun so many decades ago, we dedicate *Creating Justice in a Multiracial Democracy* to David Ginsburg, who was Executive Director of the Kerner Commission and taught us the New Deal, and A. Leon Higginbotham Jr., who guided the Violence Commission and Foundation and taught us *In The Matter of Color*.

Introduction

Alan Curtis

Creating Justice is part of a movement that offers hope for multiracial democracy based on creating new will to scale up evidence-based solutions that work.

To keep the page length of *Creating Justice* manageable, the full introduction is available online at https://www.tcpress.com/creating-justice-in-a-multiracial-democracy-9780807769942. (See also the QR code at the end of this introduction on page xliv.) What follows below is a summary of the introduction. We encourage the reader to review the full online introduction because it synthesizes the 36 chapters in *Creating Justice*, adds a great deal of new material, and provides detail on programs and policies that work.

The 2024 and 1968 election years had at least some things in common. There were deep divisions in America. Students protested on college campuses. Political violence shocked the nation. Class and race were important issues. The incumbent president chose not to run for reelection.

Spanning 1968 to 2024, the Eisenhower Foundation is the private sector continuation of the National Advisory Commission on Civil Disorders—known as the Kerner Commission, after its chair, Otto Kerner, then-governor of Illinois. The 1968 Kerner Commission was formed by President Lyndon Johnson after over 150 urban disturbances in the 1960s. Whites tended to call the disturbances riots. Blacks called them protests. Most members of the Commission were privileged white men, yet they concluded in 1968 that the underlying cause of the protests was "white racism" and that America was heading toward "two societies, black and white, separate and unequal." One of the Commission's most famous statements was, "What white Americans never fully understood—but what the Negro can never forget—is that white society is deeply implicated in the ghetto. White institutions created it, white institutions maintain it, and white society condones it." The Kerner Report urged, "It is time to make good the promises of American democracy to all citizens—urban and rural, white and black, Spanish-surname, American Indian, and every minority group."[1]

There have been criticisms of the composition of the Commission. Yet, in some ways, the Commission's privileged white maleness adds credibility today to its conclusions on "white racism."

Both Dr. Martin Luther King Jr. and Senator Robert F. Kennedy endorsed the Kerner Report in 1968—and then they were assassinated.

The Eisenhower Foundation periodically updates the Kerner Commission. *Creating Justice*, the present update, builds upon recommendations at the Eisenhower Foundation's Nelson Mandela Forum at the United Nations in 2023 that celebrated the 55th anniversary of the Kerner Report. Black Americans were disproportionately involved in the urban protests of the 1960s, and so the original Kerner Report focused its recommendations on them. We do the same in *Creating Justice*—but, also following the Kerner Commission's concern for all people of color, we have included chapters in *Creating Justice* by and for Latinos, Native Americans, and Asian Americans. In addition, the present volume is being accompanied by republication of the original 1968 Kerner Report.

The Kerner Commission was as much about class as race—and so is *Creating Justice*. The Kerner framing of class and race was in sync with how, at the time of the Commission in 1968, Dr. King was transitioning the civil rights movement into an economic justice movement. Reducing racial injustice, economic inequality, and poverty were outcomes of co-importance to Dr. King, as they are to us.[2]

Framing Kerner in terms of both class and race is historically accurate based on the teachings of King and Kerner. But such framing also strengthens our pushback today against deniers who spread misinformation claiming that Kerner is about race only.

Why is it important to continue to update the Kerner Commission? Surely we can recognize progress since the 1960s—like people of color as president and vice president, a Native American cabinet secretary, 21 Latino cabinet members, the significant increase in Black and Latino elected officials, and the expansion of the Black and Latino middle classes.

Yet there has been no or insufficient progress in many areas since the Kerner Commission—while in other ways things have gotten worse. What are some examples?

Wealth and income inequality have increased since Kerner. Today, median family wealth is $188,200 for whites and $24,100 for Blacks. A Black family with a college-educated head of household is, on average, less wealthy than a white family whose head did not graduate from high school. And the median Black household income has been roughly 60% of the median white household income since the early 1970s.[3] We need to recognize here the affirmative action of generational wealth.

As estimated by official federal government poverty measures, there has been little sustained improvement in the poverty rate from Kerner to the present—with the rate moving up and down over the decades, through recessions and boom years and through the administrations of both major parties.* In the United States, a larger share of working-age people (aged 18 to 65) lives in poverty than in any other nation belonging to the Organization for Economic Cooperation and Development (OECD). And while the child poverty rate was cut in half during the pandemic, this was reversed when Congress failed to make the legislation permanent.[4]

Since the Kerner Commission, the increase in wealth and income inequality has been dramatic—and coterminous with significant reductions in taxes paid by the richest Americans and by corporations—as Figures I.1 and I.2 strikingly show. With well-paid lawyers, the tax rate for the 400 richest Americans now is lower than the tax rate for the

---

* However, when one includes all cash and noncash benefits provided to low-income households, the poverty rate has fallen since the Kerner Commission.

Figure I.1. The Falling Tax Rate for the Richest Americans

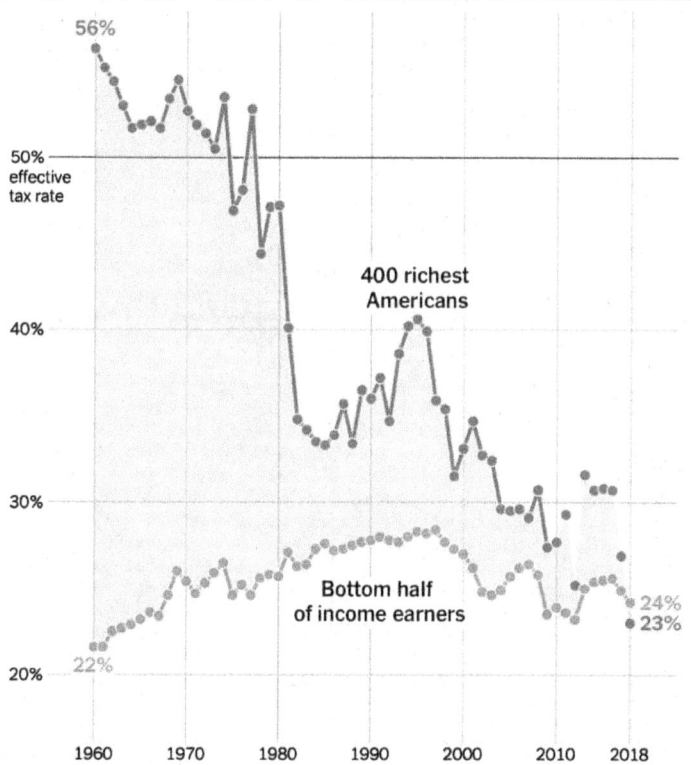

Source: Emmanuel Saez and Gabriel Zucman • Note: Tax rates shown include levies paid at all levels of government. Government transfers such as Social Security benefits have not been subtracted.

bottom half of American income earners. Taxes on the rich and on corporations were much higher during the Eisenhower Administration in the 1950s than they are today.[5]

During the time of the Kerner Commission, CEOs received about 20 times as much as their workers. Today, they receive over 320 times as much. Corporate opposition to unions has had a powerful impact. The private sector union membership rate was 30% during the late 1960s and is 10% today—even though 68% of Americans approve of unions.[6]

Hourly wages for Blacks have been persistently lower than for whites since the Kerner Commission. The wage disparity grew from about 17% in 1979 to about 26% percent in 2019. Unemployment rates have been consistently double for Blacks compared to whites since the late 1970s.[7]

Other illustrations of lack of progress or negative trends since Kerner include the failure to implement the Fair Housing Act of 1968; the growing crisis in the availability of affordable housing; the apartheid resegregation of public schools; the expanding Black–white school achievement gap; the police killings of George Floyd, Breonna Taylor, and Sonya Massey (among many others); the lack of police reform, the dramatic increase in mass incarceration that disproportionately targets people of color; our carceral environment

Figure I.2 The Corporate Income Tax Rate, 1954–2022

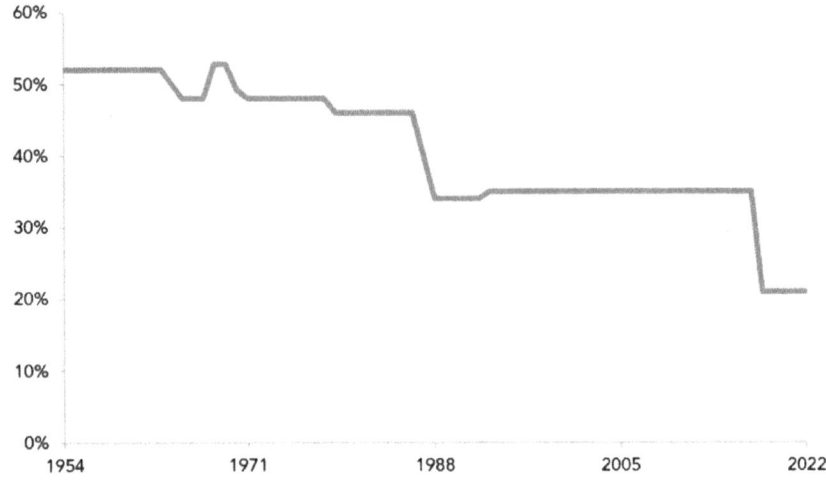

in which one in three Black male children in America can be expected to spend time in jail or prison; a reported national homicide rate that is almost the same today as it was in the 1960s; endemic violence in many poor urban neighborhoods; the outperformance of the United States by other advanced democracies in almost every measure of health and well-being; an increase from 80 million guns in civilian hands to over 400 million guns in civilian hands; the January 6, 2021 white supremacist insurrection at the U.S. Capitol; the campaign to suppress voting rights; the politicalization of the Supreme Court; and failures to reform the Electoral College, gerrymandering, campaign finance and the Senate filibuster. An underlying theme has been denial by naysayers that these failures even exist—and denial that many Americans polled oppose naysayer views.[8]

In terms of class and race, then, fulfillment of the Kerner legacy has only just begun.

The Kerner Commission concluded that we know the evidence-based policy needed—but that "new will" was required to invest in what works "at a scale equal to the dimensions of the problem."[9]

The same remains true today. We now know much more about what works—based on facts and scientific evidence and not on ideology, misinformation, and disinformation. But we have not scaled up—and we still need new will to make reform happen.

Creating Justice therefore is organized around two themes—identifying evidence-based policy that works and creating new will to scale it up. With the future of democracy at stake, we hope to cut through political and media rhetoric to further the policy narrative and public discourse in a constructive and objective way.

Introduction

IDENTIFYING EVIDENCE-BASED POLICY THAT WORKS

Table I.1 summarizes what doesn't work and what does work today among policies of relevance to the priorities of the 1968 Kerner Commission.

Table I.1. A Summary of What Doesn't Work and What Does

What Doesn't Work	What Works
Basing policy on ideology, misinformation, and disinformation.	Basing policy on evidence and science.
Failing to recognize that Kerner is about both class and race.	Recognizing that the Kerner legacy is about both class and race.
Reducing taxes on the rich and corporations.	Increasing taxes on the rich and corporations.
Believing in the myth of market fundamentalism.	Exposing the myth of market fundamentalism.
Pursuing trickle-down policy that benefits the rich and corporations.	Moving forward with bubble-up policy that benefits the poor, workers and the middle class.
Returning to "zombie economics" that repeat past failures.	Continuing new industrial policy that builds on Franklin Roosevelt and John Maynard Keynes.
Claiming that trickle-down enterprise, empowerment, and opportunity zones work.	Scaling up nonprofit community development corporations to lead place-based economic and community development in the spirit of Franklin Thomas, Jane Jacobs, Geno Baroni, and Pablo Eisenberg.
Disempowering labor unions.	Empowering labor unions.
Reducing child tax credits.	Increasing child tax credits and legislating paid family leave.
Eliminating affirmative action.	Continuing reframed affirmative action.
Lobbying for private school vouchers.	Prioritizing public K–12 schools.
Failing to provide preschool to all eligible children.	Scaling up preschool for all eligible.
Failing to continue investments in mentoring and tutoring that close the pandemic-created achievement gap between students of color and whites.	Continuing those investments.
Failing to acknowledge that school teachers should be valued more than hedge and equity fund billionaires.	Significantly increasing teacher salaries.
Failing to reform police culture in response to the murders of George Floyd, Breonna Taylor, Sonya Massey, and many others.	Reforming police culture and significantly expanding evidence-based partnerships between nonprofit organizations and police.

(continued)

Table I.1. (*continued*)

What Doesn't Work	What Works
Ending the present decline in the prison population.	Accelerating the present decline in the prison population.
Failing to address endemic violence in America.	Acting to prevent endemic violence in poor urban communities.
Failing to act on guns.	Banning assault weapons and limiting handguns.
Failing to implement the Fair Housing Act of 1968.	Significantly increasing low income rental housing and providing housing vouchers to all eligible families.
Continuing the present public health system.	Reforming the public health system, giving priority to prevention and providing adequate health insurance for all.
Continuing to exploit citizens and denying the exploitation.	Reversing denial and exploitation. Making the privileged uncomfortable.
Failing to recognize the need for "moral fusion."	Investing in "moral fusion" and speaking with Birmingham-jail-like outrage.
Restricting voter rights.	Expanding voter rights.
Resisting partnerships among the poor, workers, Gen Z, women, and people of color.	Strengthening those partnerships.
Ignoring the need for media reform. Allowing misinformation and disinformation to spread further.	Scaling up model programs that reduce misinformation and disinformation. Investing in nonprofit media.
Failing to challenge universities and students to do more for their country.	Encouraging universities and students to better ask what they can do for their country.
Failing to create new university degree programs that heal our divided society and partner with nonprofit organizations.	Creating such commonsense degree programs and community outreach partnerships.
Failing to recognize the importance of the visual and performing arts in motivating "new will" to scale up what works.	Embracing how the arts can better create "new will" and build on the examples of William Barber, Hank Willis Thomas, and Marc Bamuthi Joseph.

With this summary table of *Creating Justice* as a guide, below we briefly set forth evidence-based economic, education, criminal justice, housing, and public health policies consonant with the Kerner legacy that we conclude are needed today.

Economic Policy

As its highest priority, the Kerner Commission called for "compassionate, massive, and sustained" national action led by Keynesian macroeconomic policy, with Franklin

Roosevelt-style commitment to expanding and funding government. Over a few years after Kerner, there was economic progress for the truly disadvantaged. But for most of the 55-plus years after Kerner and especially beginning in the 1980s, the nation accepted the myth of market fundamentalism—trickle down and deregulated economic policy, primacy to the profit-driven private sector, receptiveness to private equity and hedge funds, hostility to labor unions, and the above-illustrated tax breaks to corporations and the rich.[10]

In *Creating Justice*, Felicia Wong, Matt Hughes, Naomi Oreskes, and Erik Conway document how market fundamentalism did not work, creating massive income and wealth inequality. Compared to New Deal policies, market fundamentalism failed to generate greater economic growth and stability. This failure most clearly expressed itself in the Great Recession and meltdown of 2007–2008. Nobel Laureate Paul Krugman calls market fundamentalism "zombie economics"—because trickle-down has kept on coming back from the dead in spite of its failure. For Kerner constituencies, the evaluated failures of "welfare reform" (Temporary Assistance to Needy Families) and of "empowerment," "enterprise" and "opportunity" zones have illustrated such zombie economics.[11]

New Economic Policy That Invests in Workers

But in recent years a new, promising economic opportunity policy has begun to emerge. It is bubble-up, not trickle-down. It features significant Roosevelt-style government and Keynesian fiscal and monetary policy. The new paradigm is based on empowering the poor, the working class, and the middle class. The policy is a function of democratic values and public investment in workers.[12]

In response to the pandemic and the unemployment it created, the $1.9T American Rescue Plan Act provided direct payments and tax cuts—disproportionately to middle class, working class, and low income Americans. It also extended unemployment insurance. Accompanying the full-employment success, the stock market has soared while labor unions have been strengthened.[13]

The American Rescue Plan revived the economy faster than anyone could have imagined as America faced COVID-19 and a dramatic economic downturn. In the words of Krugman, "the U.S. economy is a remarkable success story," and that assessment has been shared by the World Bank and the International Monetary Fund.[14]

Industrial policy is integral to the bubble-up success of the economic opportunity framework that has been emerging. Industrial policy is being implemented to create jobs and bring manufacturing back to America from countries like China. As part of industrial policy, the Inflation Reduction Act is investing in clean energy and the CHIPS and Science Act is investing in semiconductor manufacturing in the United States, as well as in research and development.[15] There is a need, however, to better ensure that low income workers of color benefit from training and the jobs created—see Dorothy Stoneman's discussion in Chapter 9.[16]

In discussing the emerging economic policy, Felicia Wong, Matt Hughes, Valerie Wilson and Adewale A. Maye also point to the need for higher minimum wages, reinstatement of the Child Tax Credit that cut poverty but then tragically was allowed to expire after the pandemic, investment in child care and family leave, and anti-monopoly and anti-trust checks against private and corporate domination over the public interest.[17]

Industrial policy needs to be carried out with an awareness that the United States is facing a dramatic labor shortfall and constantly must expand legal immigration in targeted locations and sectors of the economy, as Sindy Benavides points out in Chapter 20.[18] Contrary to disinformation that has been spread, the evidence is that immigrants are not taking jobs from Black workers.[19] And contrary to other disinformation, the evidence is that immigrants commit less crime than U.S.-born people.[20]

To continue moving from failed trickle-down to promising bubble-up in a way that reinforces Kerner priorities, the tax cuts on highest earners and corporations that were legislated in 2017 and that were unpopular with the American public should be allowed to expire and the tax code should be reformed to increase taxes on corporations and people making over $400,000. Nobel Laureate Joseph Stiglitz has called for such tax increases on the rich to reduce economic inequality.[21]

Education Policy

We made progress in Kerner-relevant K–12 education policy in the late 1960s and the 1970s. The War on Poverty, the Elementary and Secondary Education Act of 1965, school desegregation, and school finance reform helped reduce educational inequality. Reading and math achievement gaps between students of color and whites diminished. Child poverty rates declined in the 1960s.[22]

But in the 80s and 90s, federal courts released school districts from obligations to desegregate. School segregation increased steadily. Today, America's public schools are more segregated than any time since the late 1960s. The growing number of apartheid schools has almost exclusively served students of color from low-income families. Often these schools have been severely under-resourced. The pandemic exacerbated K–12 education disparities, especially for low-income children and families of color. The achievement gap between Black and white students grew wider. Careful evaluation evidence showed school vouchers raised the risk of harm to students, did little to expand opportunity, and cut funding to public schools.[23] Yet billionaires and market fundamentalists continue to lobby for vouchers–an illustration of zombie education policy.

Kerner Education Policy Today

As Linda Darling-Hammond, Randi Weingarten, John Jackson, and Zakiyah Ansari review in Chapters 5–7, today K–12 policy in support of Kerner priorities includes education funding based on student life status (like poverty and homelessness) rather than a function of property wealth status in local communities; federal leadership in reversing growing school segregation; universal prekindergarten for 3- and 4-year-olds; the scaling up of nonprofit evidence-based mentoring, tutoring, and life skills models like Community Schools, the Harlem Children's Zone and Quantum Opportunities that close the school achievement gap; a reformed strategy to prevent school gun violence; and increased teacher recruitment and pay to address the national teacher shortage.[24] The online introduction discusses these and related policies.

Introduction   xxv

Kerner-relevant policy in higher education needs to address the backlash against civil rights legislation illustrated by the Supreme Court's 2023 ruling denying race-based affirmative action at universities. We can work toward future Supreme Court majorities reversing that decision, but at present one of the most important strategies is to use socioeconomic disadvantage as a basis for preferences in competitive college admissions. See the online introduction and Chapter 8 by Dwayne Kwaysee Wright and Michael Feuer for more on the future of college admissions.[25]

Most students attend colleges where three-quarters of all applicants are accepted. That means the pressing need for Kerner constituencies is to invest in facilities at these institutions, improve the quality and number of teachers, and expand Pell Grants to all students who qualify, among a host of reforms. This strategy holds the possibility of advancing racial equity and addressing Kerner priorities more than admission decisions by top-ranked schools.[26] For such a strategy, we need much greater federal, state, and philanthropic funding of historically Black colleges and universities (HBCUs). Recent Bloomberg Philanthropies funding of Black medical school endowments is an outstanding example of moving forward.[27]

Crime Prevention, Criminal Justice and Drug Policy

There are many difficulties in measuring crime. The most accurately reported crime is homicide. The reported homicide rate today is roughly the same as it was in the years around the Kerner Commission. Reported homicide rates in America are much higher than in other industrialized democracies.[28] Over the 55-plus years since the Kerner Commission, it is reasonable to question the effectiveness and morality of the billions of dollars spent on the racially biased American criminal justice and mass incarceration system. During the pandemic, America became an even deadlier and less equal place. There was an unprecedented surge in gun related violence in low income neighborhoods of people of color. Young Black men in the United States are among the most endangered groups for violent deaths anywhere in the world.[29]

Endemic Violence

In Chapters 12 and 14 Elliott Currie and Kim Taylor-Thompson warn that, instead of recognizing the endemic violence that was present at the time of the Kerner Commission and remains today, there recently has been a punitive turn in the policy narrative—renewed calls for "get tough" policies that we have encountered time and again in the past.[30] Instead, the nation needs to better understand how disconnected policy is from what we have learned over decades about the root origins of America's endemic violence. Policy needs to build on bubble-up economics, keep unemployment low, scale up evidence-based models like YouthBuild that integrate job training and placement for high-risk youth and scale up many of the same kinds of nonprofit mentoring, tutoring and life skills models that are needed to close the education achievement gap—as discussed above. The role of nonprofit organizations needs to be enhanced. Currently popular nonprofit "violence interrupter" programs may also qualify as solutions to scale up, although more evaluation evidence is needed.[31]

Firearms Control

Endemic violence is propagated by guns, yet guns are "normal" for much of the United States, which is home to nearly half of all the civilian-owned firearms in the world.[32]

California and New Jersey have the strictest gun laws in the nation and are among the states with the lowest gun homicide rates. Policy that incorporates Kerner priorities needs to support the scaling up of these evidence-based state models, which include bans on assault weapons. We hope that, as a result of the 2024 presidential candidate assassination attempt, the federal ban on assault weapons that was in place between 1994 and 2004 can be renewed and improved upon. Sixty-one percent of Americans support an assault weapons ban. But it is imperative to also keep in mind that most people killed by guns are killed by handguns. This is very much the case in poor urban areas. Handguns will be significantly impacted by new regulations recently finalized by the Department of Justice. The new rules close a loophole that allowed people to sell firearms online, at gun shows, and at other informal venues without conducting background checks on those who purchase them. The Justice Department has estimated that over 20% of Americans have obtained guns without a background check.[33] The online Introduction has more on the need to significantly reduce guns in America as part of a Kerner strategy.

Police Reform

The Kerner Report concluded in 1968 that police had often sparked the protests of the 1960s and overreacted after the protests began. The commission found that racial tensions frequently reflected low income community grievances with the police and the rest of the criminal justice system:[34]

> The police are not merely a "spark" factor. To some Negroes police have come to symbolize white power, white racism and white repression. . . . The atmosphere of hostility and cynicism is reinforced by a widespread belief among Negroes in the existence of police brutality and in a "double standard" of justice and protection—one for Negroes and one for whites."

Yet in the decades after Kerner was released a policy of zero tolerance policing developed in many police departments. Today, there is broad evidence that zero tolerance was ineffective in reducing crime and destructive to low income communities of color—from Rodney King's Los Angeles to Michael Brown's Ferguson, Missouri, to George Floyd's Minneapolis to Breonna Taylor's Louisville to Sonya Massey's Springfield, Illinois.[35]

The George Floyd Justice in Policing Act was proposed in 2021 to increase police accountability and reform police culture, but the legislation never passed in Congress. Nor have proposals been successful in eliminating "qualified immunity," which long has been used to shield officers from the consequences of their actions.[36] Nonetheless, advocacy on police reform must remain a leading long term Kerner priority. Innovative police chiefs need the courage to scale up the models of nonprofit organization–police partnerships that already exist. Police are discussed in more detail in the online introduction—and in Chapters 10 and 11 by Neil Gross and Branville Bard Jr.

Deincarceration and Drug Policy Reform

According to a top White House aide, in the late 1960s and early 70s the White House "had two enemies: the anti-war left and Black people." Politically, the criminalization of drugs became a way to discredit both groups—creating the War on Drugs and mass incarceration.[37]

The Kerner Commission did not anticipate mass incarceration. Between 1972 and 2009, the prison population in the United States increased by almost 700%—from about 200,000 to over 1,400,000. Then, from the peak incarceration year of 2009 to the present, the United States experienced a decline in its prison population of well over 20%. While notable, the prison population decline is insufficient given the dramatic earlier increase. So, for example, the prison and jail incarceration rate in the United States today is between 5 and 8 times the rates in France, Canada, and Germany.[38]

Rigorous evaluations have shown that mass incarceration has not worked as an effective system of crime and drug prevention. But it has been an extremely effective system of racial social control.[39] Large numbers of people of color have been placed under the jurisdiction of the criminal justice system and saddled with criminal records for life. In 2021, Black Americans were imprisoned at 5 times the rate of whites, Native Americans 4.2 times the rate of whites and Latinos 2.4 times.[40]

However, Nazgol Ghandnoosh reminds us in Chapter 13 that, in part because of advocacy by nonprofit organizations with policies complementary to Kerner, racial disparities in drug sentencing have been reduced (though not eliminated) in recent years. For the first time in decades, the federal Office of National Drug Control Policy today spends slightly more on prevention and treatment than on law enforcement and interdiction.[41] Now we need to eliminate all racial disparities in the criminal justice system. We need to scale up the evidence-based Bard Prison Initiative, which allows people in prison to study for college degrees. And we need to fund evaluations that provide solid evidence on the treatment and re-entry strategies that are most effective. Those strategies need to be carefully linked to reliable, permanent investments in jobs, education, housing, and health. Yet continued progress is precarious, given the current retreat back to the failed punitive polices of the past. American remains in an era of mass incarceration that betrays the values of the Kerner Commission.[42]

Housing Policy

The Kerner Commission recognized decades of underfunded federal housing programs as a chronic problem for disadvantaged households. The Commission recommended that 6 million new low- and moderate income rental units be built by 1973. But by 2024 we have barely reached the 6-million-unit goal.[43]

For a while after the Kerner Commission there was slow progress on affordable housing, led by partnerships between the federal government and private institutions like the Local Initiatives Support Corporation, ShoreBank, the Community Preservation Corporation, and Enterprise Community Partners. But the trickle-down market fundamentalism of the 1980s led the federal government to stop building affordable housing. Instead, the Department of Housing and Urban Development turned to distributing housing vouchers on a very limited basis to help cover the cost of rental housing. As a result, in 2024 there is only enough housing voucher funding for one in four households that qualify, and not all owners accept vouchers. By 2024, nearly two-thirds of renters in the bottom fifth of the income distribution faced "severe cost burdens"—meaning they spend more than half their income on shelter. This is a record high, and it coincides with record levels of homelessness. The evidence is clear that public and private sector resistance to housing aid involves race—the more that housing programs are perceived as favoring people of color, the less political support they attract.[44]

Affordable Housing Policy Today

We need to preserve the affordable housing rental homes that already exist, build new housing, and significantly expand vouchers to all eligible households—bridging the gap between incomes and rent. New legislation needs to better protect voucher holders from discrimination. Local governments should be required to eliminate restrictive zoning rules that increase the cost of development and limit housing supply. To build that housing, we need to return to the earlier successful partnerships between the federal government and entities like the Local Initiatives Support Corporation, above. And we need to scale up the adequately funded bipartisan rental program implemented since 2008 by the Department of Housing and Urban Development and the Department of Veterans Affairs that has reduced the number of unhoused veterans by half.[45]

The financing of affordable housing needs to begin by acknowledging the nation's class-and-race-based inequality. The federal government today spends less on subsidizing housing for low-income Americans than on subsidizing housing for better-off Americans.[46]

Fair Housing Policy Today

At the same time, given that we now are more segregated residentially than during the Kerner 1960s, the federal government needs to finally and comprehensively enforce the Fair Housing Act of 1968. As Leah and Richard Rothstein document in Chapter 16, the overwhelming evidence is that federal, state, and local governments in collaboration with the private sector have facilitated conscious, purposeful segregation in metropolitan areas across the nation. The discriminatory policies created distinct advantages for white families, leading to the massive homeownership, wealth, and credit gaps that persist today. See the fair housing policy proposals of Lisa Rice, Michael Akinwumi, and Nikitra Bailey in Chapter 15.[47]

The federal government needs to require state and local governments receiving federal money to direct significant housing into healthier neighborhoods where residents are provided access to transportation, jobs and decent schools. This is extremely difficult to do in our divided society. But there are existing models of success that we need to scale up—like the Rand Corporation-evaluated Montgomery County, Maryland strategy that requires developers to set aside units for low income families, the Chicago Gatreaux program and the federal Moving to Opportunity program. Both "mobility" and "place based" action led by citizens and nonprofit organizations at the grassroots are needed,

Introduction

and the nineteen seventies Office of Neighborhoods at the Department of Housing and Urban Development needs to be recreated and adequately funded to assist local non-profit work integrating housing.[48]

Public Health Policy

The Kerner Report did not include a section on public health policy. But the Commission concluded, "The residents of the racial ghetto are significantly less healthy than most other Americans. They suffer from higher morality rates, higher incidence of major diseases, and lower availability and utilization of medical services." This remains true today, and the pandemic heightened the health disparities between people of color and whites. Poor people can expect to die 12 to 13 years sooner than rich people in the United States. The death rate gap between rich and poor has increased by 570% since 1980.[49]

The Affordable Health Care Act

In 2010, the Affordable Health Care Act brought health insurance to almost 20 million previously uninsured adults—with the biggest beneficiaries being people of color, who obtained insurance coverage through the law's Medicaid expansion. The evidence is that states which accepted the Medicaid expansion saw a drop in disease-related deaths, and there were measurable decreases in some racial health disparities. The percentage of Americans without health insurance has fallen by almost half since 2010. Nonetheless, some states have refused to participate in Medicaid expansion. And naysayers who originally opposed the Affordable Health Care Act continue to try to repeal the legislation. This is one of the clearest examples of how, notwithstanding overwhelming evidence of success, many in the Kerner-related policy debate make assertions based on ideology, supposition and denial.[50]

As of 2022, there were over 25 million nonelderly uninsured Americans, almost 10% of the population. Over 41% of the American population consists of people of color, but they account for over 58% of the uninsured population. Many proposals for health insurance reform have been made, but the most comprehensive and Kerner-relevant proposal is universal coverage that is automatic and free, providing basic medical care (rather than a high-end experience).[51] That is our recommendation in *Creating Justice*. Today, all industrialized democracies except the United States have guaranteed health care for all citizens.

Prevention and Primary Care

Beyond universal coverage, in Chapters 17 and 18, Michelle Williams, Herbert Smitherman and Anil Aranha advocate for how we need to shift our health policy mindset from treatment to prevention and primary care. They consider public health as including not only care in doctor's offices and hospitals but also in terms of making sure that all people can live in safe communities, access sufficient nutrition, attend good schools, and pursue gainful employment—among other critical factors that contribute to our overall health. The goal is to holistically improve the well-being of all people.

While some deniers actually oppose the words "public health," we believe these words can, as necessary, be easily reframed as "improving the lives of children." Some governors already have successfully used such alternative framing.[52]

CREATING NEW WILL FOR JUSTICE

In order to legislate, fund and implement policies like the ones just proposed, the Kerner Commission cautioned that "new will" was needed from the American people. But since Kerner there has been limited progress. That is why *Creating Justice* sets out the following strategies for how to generate new will. We need to:

- Strengthen voter democracy
- Integrate both class and race into campaign messaging
- Strategically mobilize Kerner constituencies in those campaigns
- Advance structural reform in the democratic system
- Establish a federal Department of Democracy
- Create a third wave of moral fusion and coalition building
- Expose exploitation and denial by the privileged with more intensity
- Reinforce the movement for evidence-based policy
- Combat disinformation and significantly expand nonprofit media
- Mobilize universities to more effectively ask what they can do for their country
- Enhance how the visual and performing arts can better support Kerner-aligned action

Strengthen Voter Democracy

If more people with Kerner priorities vote and elect more Kerner-supportive candidates, new will potentially can be generated over time by the legislative, executive, and judicial branches of government. More and better financed nonprofit and related organizations are needed to strengthen the voting process.

Yet over recent years lawmakers in 39 states have introduced more than 400 bills designed to restrict, dilute, and undermine the votes of people of color—along with the votes of poor and low-income people, women, youth, and seniors, among others. A naysaying coalition has continued to pass significant voter restrictions. Billionaire-backed advocacy groups have been lobbying for new state-level legislation. In 2024, the well-funded movement to restrict voting rights gained new momentum via a powerful network of lawyers and activists planning to contest elections, delay vote counts, allow challenges after votes are cast, and refuse certification if results are not in their favor.[53]

However, a counter-movement with new laws making voting more accessible has emerged in some states since 2020. Examples of new state laws increasing accessibility include restoring felon voting rights, expanding early and mail voting opportunities, and providing more time for voters to fix errors on ballots. These are new will-generating changes that could allow for more Kerner-focused legislation. As Robert Kuttner concludes, on balance electoral democracy is better defended today than in 2020. But voting

Introduction

rights activists and litigators need to be vigilant. The thousands of sophisticated nonprofit and related organizations needed for voting rights advocacy nationally and locally include organized labor, longstanding groups like Common Cause and the League of Women Voters, and relatively new nonprofit entities like Black Voters Matter.. In coordination, the Department of Justice needs to use all its authorities to combat the new wave of restrictive voting laws—and every level of government needs to reinforce voter rights.[54]

Integrate Both Class and Race in Campaign Messaging

What new will-focused messaging can increase the likelihood that citizens will vote for Kerner-supportive candidates? In Chapter 25, Anat Shenker-Osorio shares the effective Kerner-relevant messaging strategy she developed in Minnesota in recent elections. She found that messaging integrating both class and race worked better with voters than other messaging that was tested.[55] The findings held for people of color as well as for whites. This is powerful evidence for *Creating Justice* because such integration validates what Dr. Martin Luther King Jr. was advocating in 1968 at the time of the Kerner Commission—that the civil rights movement needed to transform into a movement for economic justice.

The Shenker-Osorio class and race messaging was based on several principles. One was to be positive—to set forth very specific policies in a campaign. Another principle was to paint a "beautiful tomorrow," offering people a sense of what the world would be like if Kerner-relevant and related policies were put into practice. The narrative clearly stated outcomes that the evidence-based policy would deliver. A final principle was to identify who was responsible for the problem that the policies were trying to solve.[56]

Shenker-Osorio found that failing to identify who was responsible could lead to blaming the victim—to voter assumptions that people experiencing poor outcomes were the ones responsible. In the context of Kerner, there has been a long history of politicians and academics blaming victimized people of color. But the class-and-race campaigns in Minnesota created winning values-based narratives that called out the politics of cruelty and enticed multiracial coalitions to come together for the better.[57] Details of this John Lewis style "good trouble" strategy are found in the online introduction and in Chapter 25. The Minnesota strategy for new will needs to be scaled up.

Strategically Mobilize Kerner Constituencies in Election Campaigns

There is evidence that Minnesota-style class and race messaging can generate support within the American middle class. Other overlapping voter constituencies that are especially important for advocating Kerner new will include poor- and low-income voters, the white working class, interracial coalitions of poor and working-class people, coalitions of people of color, women, younger voters, and seniors—as follows:

In Chapter 23, William Barber shows us how poor citizens and near-poor low-income people of color are potential mass mobilization catalysts for new will. The poor and near-poor make up a third of the U.S. electorate and 40% in swing states. Yet their turnout has been disappointing—because politicians have not been sufficiently willing to work with them. Organizing and mobilizing this constituency around issues like increasing the minimum wage, raising teacher salaries, controlling guns, and reforming police will advance Kerner new will.[58]

National polls have shown that white workers are concerned and angry over how corporations have been inflating prices, wealthy corporate CEOs and billionaires aren't paying what they should in taxes, and the richest 1% is gaming the system.[59] These are top Kerner issues that need to be better communicated to working-class Americans—especially to men who disproportionately have been voting against Kerner values. Working class Americans were left behind economically when manufacturing jobs declined, and many are homeless and addicted. As we have said earlier, for Kerner class is as important as race. We need to act on Franklin Roosevelt's 1932 speech hailing "the forgotten man at the bottom of the economic pyramid."[60]

The poverty rate is higher for Blacks than for whites, but the number of people in poverty is higher for whites than for Blacks—poverty is a common bond cutting across race in ways that Dr. King recognized with his focus on economic justice. Importantly, today William Barber's Poor People's Campaign is leading the advocacy for such racial bonding on poverty among poor, near poor and working class Americans.[61]

Women's pro-choice rights are supported by majorities of women of color and white women. This is a crucial Kerner priority, and the multipronged attack on reproductive freedom in the naysaying Project 2025 report is deeply unpopular with women.[62]

National polling consistently shows that Gen Z is receptive to Kerner-related issues like investments in human capital, strengthened voter rights, replication of education models that work, expansion of affordable housing, and control of guns. The first person from Generation Z elected to Congress has evolved through his gun control advocacy and personal experience with gun violence. More savvy messaging on Kerner issues framed by Gen Z–relevant culture and with Gen Z–relevant language is needed—though social media disinformation needs to be countered, as we discuss later.[63]

Seniors are in support of Kerner-related policies like an improved public health system and more extensive reductions in prescription costs.[64]

All of these constituencies need to be better organized and mobilized by a fresh wave of better-financed nonprofit and related organizations in support of candidates with Kerner values. The mobilization needs to motivate more Americans to run for office. After the Kerner Commission, one of the most effective national nonprofit organizations training Kerner-supportive people for public office was Wellstone Action, formed by the late Senator Paul Wellstone. Wellstone Action created "leadership pipelines" by partnering with local nonprofit organizations to recruit indigenous community leaders to run for office. A high priority was placed on recruiting people of color, women, young Americans, and members of the LGBTQIA+ community. Wellstone Action sought out individuals who were effective in building trust. Candidates and their teams were equipped with the skills, tactics, and confidence to run and win. The training combined grassroots organizing, public policy, electoral strategy, and digital technology. Wellstone Action trained thousands.[65] However, the organization has changed its name and mission. Today, there are some organizations with Kerner values that carry on the training of candidates—like Arena, Run for Something, the Zinc Collective, Higher Heights for America, the Latino Victory Project, and EMILYS List. But American philanthropy needs to substantially increase support for the original vision of Wellstone Action. A sea change increase in resources could make a big difference in enhancing new will.

Advance Structural Reform to the Democratic System

To encourage more people to vote—and to vote in concert with Kerner priorities—we need to reform the Electoral College, pass the John R. Lewis Voting Rights Advancement Act, modify the Senate filibuster, legislate automatic and compulsory voting, eliminate gerrymandering, reconstruct campaign finance, pass the Freedom to Vote Act, and create regular turnover on the Supreme Court. These are difficult issues, but the generation of new will in America depends on upgrading more effective advocacy, however long it takes:

Electoral College Reform

The Electoral College has led candidates to focus on battleground states. This neglects noncompetitive states and the concerns of Kerner constituencies in them. It undermines the democratic ideal of representing the interests of all citizens, irrespective of their backgrounds. The need to fairly represent all the people in national elections has led to longstanding advocacy to abolish the Electoral College or to modify it with a more democratic system.[66]

The John R. Lewis Voting Rights Advancement Act

The 1965 Voting Rights Act required that counties with a history of racial discrimination at the polls needed to obtain permission from the Justice Department before changing local voting laws or procedures. In 2013, in its *Shelby County v Holder* decision, the Supreme Court effectively killed this part of the Voting Rights Act. Passage of the John R. Lewis Voting Rights Advancement Act today is very much needed to reinstate the full 1965 Voting Rights Act.[67] As part of the Lewis Act, the Native American Voting Rights Act is crucial legislation aimed at addressing the unique challenges faced by Native Americans, as articulated in Chapter 21 by Judith LeBlanc—who shows how the Kerner Commission failed to formulate effective solutions in Indian Country.[68]

Filibuster Reform

Because of the Senate's filibuster rule, a senator from any state can veto the actions of the entire legislative body. Many times, majorities in the House of Representatives and the Senate have supported Kerner-relevant legislation—only to see the legislation blocked. Examples include critical voting rights legislation, raises to the minimum wage, and commonsense gun reforms. Elimination or modification of the filibuster, then, is one of the most important reforms needed for creating new will.[69]

Automatic Voter Registration

The overall percentage of Americans who vote is lower than in many industrialized democracies. To help increase turnout, 24 states and the District of Columbia have automatic voter registration. There is evidence that automatic voter registration boosts turnout rates. Potentially, automatic registration in all states could work to better support Kerner priorities, and so we support advocacy in this direction. But, as Cornell Brooks advocates in Chapter 24, we need to undertake still more—we need to make voting compulsory, as it is, for example, in Australia.[70]

Gerrymandering Reform

Gerrymandering is the longstanding practice of redrawing the lines of legislative districts to help top elections toward the party in power. In recent years, there has been some progress by nonprofit and other organizations in reversing gerrymandering, but this is a Kerner battleground issue, and much more advocacy is needed.[71]

Campaign Finance Reform

The 2010 Supreme Court ruling in *Citizens United v Federal Election Commission* allowed independent political action committees—super PACs—to spend unlimited amounts of money to support or oppose a candidate. *Citizens United* also paved the way for creation of "dark money" organizations which can function like super PACs as long, ostensibly, as election activity is not their primary focus. This financial exploitation has deeply corrupted elections and deeply threatened democracy. The Freedom to Vote Act seeks campaign finance reform.[72]

The Freedom to Vote Act

The Freedom to Vote Act would establish new rules for congressional and presidential elections. States would have to allow no-excuse mail voting, provide at least 2 weeks of early voting, expand the types of identification accepted under voter ID laws, establish automatic voter registration programs, allow people to register to vote at the polls, limit purges from voter rolls, and make sure voters don't have to wait more than 30 minutes in line to cast their ballots. The Act would require super PACs to disclose their major donors and put in place new rules meant to ensure they do not coordinate with candidates. It would also provide more public funding for congressional candidates who focus their fundraising on small donors.[73]

Supreme Court Reform

In recent years, the Supreme Court majority has issued many Kerner-relevant rulings sharply at odds with public opinion. Some of the most controversial decisions have included taking away a woman's right to choose an abortion, gutting civil rights and voting legislation, and giving a president immunity from prosecution. As a result, national polling shows diminution of public support for the Supreme Court. A recent commission has recommended limiting the terms of justices to 18 years. That would create regular turnover on the court and assure that every president would have an equal imprint on the court during a four-year term.[74] A code of ethics also is needed for the Supreme Court.

Establish a Federal Department of Democracy

The nation needs a permanent counter to the threats imperiling the democratic principles upon which America was founded. And we need a laboratory to further develop democracy and democratic methods of decision-making. The Department of Homeland Security demonstrated the effectiveness of a coordinated response to diverse and evolving threats. Likewise, as LaTosha Brown persuasively advocates in Chapter 26, a Department of Democracy would serve as the center for coordinating efforts across various agencies and departments to address the challenges posed by forces seeking to undermine democratic principles.[75]

The mission of the new department would be to strengthen the right to vote in an ongoing way; collaborate with states to fortify election systems against interference; promote civic education on voting and democracy; advance methods of bridge building and conflict resolution; provide guidelines on what is misinformation and disinformation; help advance evidence-based policy across federal, state, and local government; and work to preserve the delicate balance needed in our democracy between individual rights and the common good.[76] The Department of Democracy also would do well to engage with Janet Murguia's ideas in Chapter 19, where she movingly illustrates the power of stories in creating new will.[77]

Create a Third Wave of Moral Fusion and Coalition Building

The movement for new will across most classes and all races needs to be framed in the language of public morality. Moral framing has a long history in America. Morally grounded coalitions among Blacks and whites were successful during Reconstruction. White supremacists then instituted Jim Crow laws in opposition. Moral fusion coalitions among Blacks and whites reemerged in the 1950s and 1960s. These partnerships led to the Civil Rights Act of 1964, the Voting Rights Act of 1965, the Fair Housing Act of 1968, and complementary Great Society programs. Opposing this progress, white supremacists carried out their law and order "Southern Strategy" of "positive polarization"—a racially coded message to the (white) "silent majority" that led to many of the race and class divisions we see in American society today.[78]

As William Barber guides us in Chapter 23, we now need a third wave of moral fusion. A shared and self-reinforcing multileader, multiorganization, multicultural movement needs to be focused on changing the rigged system. Moral fusion requires commitments to build coalitions and community nonprofit networks with the kind of evidence-based programming we have set out in *Creating Justice*.[79]

New moral fusion coalitions need to recognize the role of nonviolent action and civil disobedience, as advocated by Dr. King. The third wave of moral fusion needs to incorporate the passion of the moral partnerships of the 1960s. As Barber urges, we need to speak with Birmingham jail–like outrage, reaffirm our humanity with intensity, become more forceful in making the privileged uncomfortable, and draw power from suffering.[80]

Some of the most powerful examples of the need to speak with moral outrage embrace money and budget decisions. Every budget is a moral budget. For example, as Barber points out, it was immoral for Congress to pass legislation during the pandemic that cut the rate of poverty in half—but then to allow the legislation to lapse, so that the poverty rate now has returned to roughly prepandemic levels.[81]

Barber's Center for Public Theology & Public Policy at Yale University has been designed as a training ground for future moral fusion leaders. The programming of Cornell Brooks at the Harvard Kennedy School does the same. These are models that need to be scaled up.

Expose Exploitation and Denial With More Intensity

The moral fusion of William Barber and Cornell Brooks encourages Anat Shenker-Osorio's principle of identifying who is responsible for the problem. In America today, much of the problem has been created by those who exploit the rest of us and who deny solutions. We now need to better expose exploitation and denial—and to use Shenker-Osorio's call-out as a way of generating new will.

Exploitation

Loretta Ross reminds us in Chapter 27 that:[82]

> The people who profit from the dysfunction of democracy do not seek evidence-based solutions because social cooperation does not serve their electoral or financial interests. Yet they have the biggest microphones provided by a complaint, profit-seeking media ecosystem, more dedicated to staying in business than in journalism. No wonder people are fed up and feel overwhelmed.

With a similar perspective, as Matthew Desmond explains in *Poverty, By America* how in recent years corporations and their stockholders have not fairly shared record profits and have fought unions. In the 1980s, corporate America learned it could crush unions with minimal repercussions. As union membership has fallen, corporations have chipped away at the notion of living wages with associated benefits. The United States now has some of the lowest wages among all industrialized democracies. There has not been an increase in the federal minimum wage for 15 years. In response to labor shortages, companies in some states have lobbied to ease child labor laws and so increase exploitation.[83]

Exploitation cuts across all of the policy areas covered in *Creating Justice*—not just economic policy. In education, exploitive segregation of schools and neighborhoods has been undertaken to help support the advancement of more affluent students and uphold the value of their parents' homes. In criminal justice, the prison-industrial complex has financially benefitted from disproportionate and exploitive incarceration of people of color. In housing, often the only choice for the poor and other low-income people is to rent from exploitive landlords. In public health, the lack of universal insurance exploits the poor who are not treated.

Advocacy for new will, then, needs to better communicate and reverse how affluent, privileged, political elites and market myth–driven financial institutions benefit from policies, laws, other rules and subsidies that enrich them—while they impoverish others, cause humiliation and pain, exploit Kerner constituencies, and constrain choices for the rest of us.[84]

Denial

Exploiters often are deniers—and deniers often are exploiters. Deniers tend to be masters of the Illusory Truth Effect, which, as Nancy Gibbs reminds, holds that people are more likely to believe something, true or not, if they hear it over and over again.[85] A classic example of denial was when, on January 22, 2020, the nation was told about the pandemic: "We have it totally under control. It's one person coming in from China, and we have it under control. It's going to be just fine."[86]

The Supreme Court has denied women's reproductive rights (in *Dobbs v. Jackson Women's Health Organization*), denied affirmative action (in *Students for Fair Admissions, Inc. v. President and Fellows of Harvard College*), denied much of the Voting Rights Act (in *Shelby County v. Holder*), denied reform of gerrymandering (in *Alexander v. the South Carolina State Conference of the NAACP*), denied the need to control campaign finance (in *Citizens United v. Federal Election Commission*), denied the principle that no one is above the law (in *Trump v the United States*), and denied citizens the right to safety against guns in a host of rulings.

Many in America want to ban books, still claim systemic racism ended with Jim Crow, deny the legacy of the Kerner Commission, deny that we know what works, and deny that we can create new will to scale it up.

Building on the moral fusion advocacy of Barber and Brooks and remembering Shenker-Osorio's electoral strategies, we must call out deniers and exploiters—and remind the country that most citizens are impacted, not just Kerner constituencies. Here is where, with Birmingham jail–like outrage, Barber's advice on becoming more forceful in making the privileged uncomfortable comes into full play.

Reinforce the Movement for Evidence-Based Policy

Throughout *Creating Justice*, we have based policy recommendations on evidence and science, as Naomi Oreskes and Erik Conway advocate in Chapter 3.[87] The more evidence that can be assembled, the greater the opportunity to convince people that solutions are possible and replicable. This can generate optimism and new will. But we need to significantly advance the movement to base policy on evidence. Public policy and campaign rhetoric still are framed far too much by ideology and supposition, rather than by evidence and facts. As a result, too few Americans, especially Kerner constituencies, are benefiting from evidence. We have yet to create a culture in which legislators, executive branch executives, and court officials actually utilize solid empirical evidence in their day-to-day decision-making.[88] Too many elected and appointed officials ignore evidence in favor of policies with poll-tested slogans and sound bites.

In Chapter 31, Justin Milner describes how the bipartisan federal Evidence-Based Policymaking Act of 2018 did help advance the evidence movement—but full implementation of the legislation has not taken place, we have not yet addressed the process of scaling up and adequate funding is needed.[89] In addition, not all philanthropies base their funding decisions on evidence.

Institutions like Arnold Ventures and the Coalition for Evidence-Based Policy are crucial for moving the public and private sectors forward to strengthen American democracy based on evidence. In this spirit, Arnold Ventures and the Coalition are now match funding with the governor of Maryland to replicate workforce, K–12, higher education, and crime prevention programs that have proven to be effective and to institutionalize ongoing government funding priority for what works.[90] Maryland is a national model.

Combat Disinformation and Significantly Expand Nonprofit Media

The Kerner Commission was highly critical of media coverage of the 1960s protests: "There is a significant imbalance between what actually happened in our cities and what the newspaper, radio, and television coverage of the riots told us happened."[91] The Commissioners saw the media as failing to report adequately on the causes of civil disorders. The problem, says Julian Zelizer in Chapter 29, was that[92]

> [W]hite reporters, regardless of their talent, didn't have much sense of what the experience of being a Black American in the city was like. Most of them had not been continually harassed by police authorities. Most had not lived in communities where the persons who were supposed to provide protection acted as threats.

Over the decades since Kerner, there has not been sufficient progress in the way people of color have been covered in the news. In a national Pew Research Center survey of Blacks in 2023, just 14% said they were confident that Blacks would be treated fairly by the media in their lifetimes.[93]

One partial exception to media and public inattention to Kerner issues, says Zelizer, has been criminal injustice. Since Kerner, technology has created a breakthrough in coverage of institutional racism in policing. From camcorders to cable television news to smartphones to the advent of social media, platforms have been created that communicate police violence. A young woman in Minneapolis recorded the murder of George Floyd on her smartphone. Protests followed across the nation.[94] The recent police killing of Sonya Massey in Springfield, Illinois, was particularly brutal, as recorded on a police bodycam.[95] And so there has been more widespread media attention given to the carceral state and to the criminal justice system—even though there has been little fundamental reform of police.

Introduction

The broader lack of adequate Kerner-relevant media coverage today reflects the for-profit priorities of major commercial media companies and the difficulty the companies have in sustaining viewer and reader interest in Kerner-like issues. Media culture seeks snapshot sensationalism and reports less on the long term realities that impact people's lives, as Ray Suarez observes in Chapter 28. In addition, a growing number of Americans are unwilling or unable to pay for traditional journalism. Waves of local newspapers and other traditional media sources are shutting down.[96]

The modern challenge, says Suarez, is that the complex world today demands better informed citizens—yet the social media "information tsunami does not make us smarter."[97] We are besieged by public relations influencers and give less attention to professionals who practice the rules of journalism. In Chapter 30, Robert Faris warns against[98]

> the scourge of disinformation and hate on social media and the perils to our democracy and governance systems as more people turn to untrustworthy sources of information to understand the world. This is a legitimate concern that appears to be only getting worse.

Faris, Suarez, and Zelizer are not sanguine about reform over this media landscape in ways that can create new will for Kerner priorities. But two obvious strategies are to combat disinformation/misinformation and expand Kerner-sensitive nonprofit media:

Combat Disinformation and Misinformation

Research by Stanford University to develop curricula for college students on how to handle trust and safety issues on social media platforms has been blocked by naysayers in Congress, just as research on gun control has been blocked.[99] But there are models from Europe that have been successful, and advocacy is needed to scale them up in America. In particular, since 2016 Finland has tested and implemented a national K–12 curriculum to resist fake news. Teachers ask students:[100]

> [W]ho produced this information and why? Where was it published? What does it *really* say? Who is it aimed at? What is it based on? Is there evidence for it, or is this just someone's opinion? Is it verifiable elsewhere?

Observed one Finnish education official,[101]

> Thinking critically, factchecking, interpreting and evaluating all the information you receive, wherever it appears, is crucial. We've made it a core part of what we teach, across all subjects.

In 2023, Finland ranked first among 41 European countries evaluated on resilience against misinformation.[102]

America needs to scale up the model of Finland. In support, schools need to ban smartphones, as we discuss in the online introduction.[103]

Expand Nonprofit Journalism

Given the failures today of commercial for-profit media, including billionaire-owned media, our authors as well as other observers, like Victor Pickard, advocate for development of a new nonprofit model based on funding by foundations, other donors, and the public sector.[104]

In recent years, some nonprofit media organizations have become the most exciting component of modern journalism. Two of the best examples include The Marshall Project and ProPublica. If a viable nonprofit framework can be made to work financially, it hopefully would provide more opportunity for coverage of Kerner priorities and more reporting by people of color. We also need to consider more public media, modeled after the BBC in the United Kingdom.

We discuss nonprofit media and disinformation/misinformation in detail in the online introduction. As we seek reform, Zelizer reminds us of the present limits to what the media can do: "[W]e remain and will remain a nation that is 'separate and unequal' as a result of white racism until our citizens make institutional reform a top priority."[105]

Mobilize Universities to Better Ask What They Can Do for Their Country

After the 2023 Supreme Court ruling against affirmative action, deniers of Kerner priorities have attacked diversity, equity, and inclusion (DEI) programs at universities. But the criticism of DEI has really been about privileged deniers attacking higher education, expertise, and evidence. The antonyms for DEI are uniformity, inequality, and exclusion. These words are in opposition to the recommendations of the Kerner Commission. This opposition to Kerner is a strong argument for continuing DEI programs at universities, even as we refine those programs. Attacks on DEI by billionaire donors to universities further underscore the need for creative DEI programs that can help repair the damage of the Supreme Court ruling against the Kerner principle of affirmative action.

Universities also need to better reinforce President John Kennedy's vision of public service. Kennedy's asking what more we can do for our country should be merged with the vision of the Kerner Commission. New undergraduate and especially master's degree Kerner-relevant public policy programs are needed that better convert knowledge into action by government at the federal, state, and local levels and by nonprofit organizations. In America today, if you want to make money, you can go to business school. If you want to learn the rules, you can attend law school. If you want to heal the human body, you can apply to medical school. But if you want to heal our divided society and create justice, there are relatively few comprehensive and holistic public policy options at America universities. There is a lack of university creativity.

New public policy degree programs need to better link academic knowledge to community practice and lived experience. Students need to know what economic, education, criminal justice, housing, public health and other policies work and what policies don't work. They need to learn the rules of evidence. They need to become proficient in how to evaluate, how to communicate, and how to community organize. They need to practice how to advocate effectively. And they need their universities to create enriched and more efficient pipelines that lead them from higher learning to nonprofit and government positions that make a difference. We must hold universities accountable for doing more, including the establishment of new schools of journalism. Universities need to become more relevant to Kerner. Even though, as Robert Reich has reminded us, it is not the educated class that is holding back America—it is the monied class.[106]

Enhance How the Visual and Performing Arts Can Better Support Kerner-Aligned Action

Over the last 10 years there has been a flourishing of counternarratives, creative interventions, artist-driven activism, and other forms of artistic reckoning in response to the exploitation and anti-democratic assault on rights and diversity that America now is experiencing. In *Creating Justice*, we illustrate this trend with new will–generating examples of nonprofit organizations and public sector institutions that are leading the way—including the Poor People's Campaign, the Kennedy Center's Cartography Project, For Freedoms, the Mellon Foundation's Monuments Project, Bryan Stevenson's Equal Justice Initiative, the Ford Foundation's Arts for Justice program, and the Smithsonian Institution's Reckoning initiative. These examples are discussed in the online introduction.

Consider For Freedoms, the artist run nonprofit organization funded by Hank Willis Thomas that communicates how money, power, art, commerce, education, and the public sector interrelate. Claudia Peña describes in Chapter 33 how For Freedoms has collaborated with over 200 artists in all 50 states to create activist public art billboards and exhibitions on voter rights, campaign finance reform, gun control, racism, gender equality, freedom of expression, and many other Kerner-relevant issues. The billboards are shown out in the open, for example, along highways and roads. But they also have been shown in museums like the Museum of Modern Art in New York. Construction of public art billboards frequently is timed with civic engagement, town meetings, and other community events to discuss public policy issues on the billboards.[107] The For Freedoms model needs to be scaled up.

In Chapter 32, Rocío Aranda-Alvarado, Margaret Morton, and Lena Sze urge government and philanthropy to work together more strategically to partner with artists and visual arts organizations committed to activating public spaces, art spaces, museums, the Internet, and varied forms of popular culture so as to "advance and strengthen truthful civic knowledge."[108] With this advice in mind and consistent with the bridge building values of For Freedoms, we encourage a White House Conference on Arts and New Will. As a means of organizing new partnerships, the White House Conference might consider a significant new online platform that better connects artists and their organizations with local and national advocates who pursue Kerner-grounded evidence-based solutions. In addition, there needs to be dialogue among artists, social scientists, and advocates for Kerner priorities on the extent to which we can empirically measure the cause-and-effect process through which the arts create new will.

Conclusion

Creating Justice is part of a long-term, multicultural movement that builds on evidence and facilitates moral fusion. We set forth a plan for creating new will to scale up Kerner priorities that have proven to work. From our perspective, the roles of government and nonprofit organizations need to be significantly expanded. Sources of finance include eliminating what doesn't work, increasing the resources of philanthropy, and taxing the rich, the privileged, and corporate America. Success will depend in no small part on how the Kerner domestic agenda can be integrated with progress on climate control and wisdom in foreign policy. We seek freedom to revive the heart of democracy.

The full-length online version of this introduction is available as a pdf via the TC Press website. Please visit https://www.tcpress.com/creating-justice-in-a-multiracial-democracy-9780807769942 or scan the QR code:

NOTES

1. *Report of the National Advisory Commission on Civil Disorders* (Washington DC: United States Government Printing Office, 1968).

2. Fred R. Harris and Alan Curtis (Eds), *Healing Our Divided Society: Investing In America Fifty Years After The Kerner Commission*. (Philadelphia, PA: Temple University Press), 2018.

3. Lawrence Mishel, "We Can and Should Address Racial Disparities," *The American Prospect,* June 24, 2024.

4. See note 3.

5. See note 2.

6. See note 2.

7. Valerie Wilson and Adewale Maye, Chapter 4, this volume.

8. See note 2; Linda Darling-Hammond, Chapter 5, this volume; Elliott Currie, Chapter 14, this volume; Richard and Leah Rothstein, Chapter 16, this volume.

9. See note 1.

10. See note 1; Naomi Oreskes and Erik Conway, Chapter 3, this volume; Felicia Wong and Matt Hughes, Chapter 2, this volume.

11. Oreskes and Erik Conway, Chapter 3; Felicia Wong, Chapter 2.

12. Wong and Hughes, Chapter 2

13. Wong and Hughes, Chapter 2.

14. Paul Krugman. *Arguing with Zombies* (W.W. Norton and Company: New York, NY, 2020); Paul Krugman, "Why Zombie Reaganomics Still Rule the G.O.P.," *New York Times,* September 26, 2022.

15. Felicia Wong, Suzanne Kahn, Mike Konczal, and Matt Hughes. *Sea Change* (Roosevelt Institute, November 2023).

16. Dorothy Stoneman, Chapter 9, this volume.

17. See note 15.

18. Sindy Benavides, Chapter 20, this volume.

19. Abha Bhattarai, "Trump Says Immigrants are Taking 'Black Jobs.' Economists Disagree," *Washington* Post, June 28, 2024.

Introduction

20. Graham Ousey and Charles Kubrin, *Immigration and Crime: Taking Stock* (New York, NY, 2023); Glenn Kessler, "The Truth About Illegal Immigration and Crime," *Washington Post,* February 29, 2024; Jasmine Garsd, "Immigrants Are Less Likely to Commit Crimes Than U.S.-Born Americans, Studies Find," National Public Radio, March 8, 2024.

21. Neate Rupert, "Joseph Stiglitz: Tax High Earners at 70% to Tackle Widening Inequality," *The Guardian,* January 23, 2023; see also note 15.

22. Darling-Hammond, Chapter 5, this volume; Weingarten, Chapter 7, this volume.

23. Darling-Hammond, Chapter 5, this volume; Weingarten, Chapter 7, this volume.

24. Darling-Hammond, Chapter 5, this volume; Weingarten, Chapter 7, this volume; Jackson and Ansari, Chapter 6, this volume.

25. Dwayne Kwaysee Wright and Michael Feuer, Chapter 8, this volume.

26. Desmond Drummer and Darrick Hamilton, "Shower Money on HBCUs," *New York Times,* July 5, 2023.

27. Susan Svrluga, "Bloomberg Gives Record $600 Million To HBCU Medical Schools," *Washington Post,* August 2024.

28. See note 2.

29. See Currie, Chapter 14, this volume.

30. Currie, Chapter 14, this volume; Kim Taylor-Thompson, Chapter 12, this volume.

31. Neil Gross, Chapter 10, this volume.

32. See note 2.

33. See note 2; Becca Rothfield, "The Real Origins of America's Gun Culture," *Washington Post,* November 12, 2023; Andrew McKevitt, *Gun Country: Gun Capitalism, Culture, and Control in Cold War America* (Chapel Hill, NC: University of North Carolina Press), 2023; Perry Stein, "Justice Department Finalizes Rules to Close 'Gun Show Loophole,'" *Washington Post,* April 11, 2024; Eugene Robinson, "Kemp is Wrong. This is the Time to Talk Policy," *Washington Post,* September 5, 2024.

34. See note 1.

35. Elizabeth Hinton, *America on Fire: The Untold History of Police Violence and Black Rebellion Since the 1960s*, (Liveright) 2021; see also note 2.

36. Michelle Williams, Chapter 17, this volume.

37. Charles Blow, "The Dawn of a New Era of Oppression," *New York Times,* January 31, 2024.

38. Nazgol Ghandnoosh, Chapter 13, this volume.

39. See note 38; Michelle Alexander, *The New Jim Crow: Mass Incarceration in the Age of Colorblindness* (New York, NY: The New Press), 2010.

40. See note 38.

41. See note 38.

42. See note 38; see Currie in note 8 above; Max Kenner, "Something Wonderful is Happening in American Prisons. Really," *New York Times,* November 17, 2023.

43. See note 2; America's Rental Housing 2024, Joint Center for Housing Studies of Harvard University, 2024, https://www.jchs.harvard.edu/americas-rental-housing-2024; Jason DeParle, "As Need Rises, Housing Aid Hits Lowest level in Nearly 25 Years," *New York Times,* December 19, 2023; National Low Income Housing Coalition, A Shortage of Affordable Homes, March 2024, https://nlihc.org/sites/default/files/gap/2024/Gap-Report_2024.pdf.

44. See note 43.

45. National Low Income Housing Coalition, note 43; DeParle, note 43; Mark Kreidler, "A Whole-Person Approach to Combating Homelessness," *The American Prospect,* April 26, 2024; Lydialyle Gibson, "The Homelessness Public Health Crisis: Addressing a Problem 'Undermining the Very Fabric of our Society,'" *Harvard Magazine,* May–June 2024; Jason DeParle, "Decline in Veterans' Homelessness Spurs Hopes for a Broader Solution," *New York Times,* August 6, 2024.

46. Jason DeParle, note 43.

47. Richard and Leah Rothstein, Chapter 16, this volume; Lisa Rice, Michael Akinwumi, and Nikitra Bailey, Chapter 15, this volume.

48. Rice, Akinwumi, and Bailey, Chapter 15, this volume; National Low Income Housing Coalition, Housing Policy is School Policy: The Case of Montgomery County, MD, October 1, 2018, https://nlihc.org/resource/housing-policy-school-policy-case-montgomery-county-md; Richard and Leah Rothstein,note 47; Simon Kuper, *Impossible City: Paris in the 21st Century* (Public Affairs Press, 2024); note 2.

49. Michelle Williams, Chapter 17, this volume; Herbert Smitherman, Jr. and Anil Aranha, Chapter 18, this volume.

50. Jeneen Interlandi, "Why Doesn't the United States Have Universal Health Care? The Answer Has Everything To Do With Race," *New York Times*, August 14, 2019; Paul Krugman, "Obamacare Is In Grave Danger Again," *New York Times*, March 26, 2024; Williams, note 49; Smitherman and Aranha, note 59; William Barber II, Chapter 23, this volume; Bernie Sanders, "America is Facing A Mental Health Crisis," *The Guardian*, June 13, 2023; Liran Einav and Amy Finkelstein, "We're Already Paying for Universal Health Care. Why Don't We Have It," *New York Times*, July 18, 2023.

51. Williams in note 49; Herbert Smitherman and Aranha, note 49; Interlandi, note 50; Einav and Finkelstein, note 50.

52. See Williams, note 49; Smitherman and Aranha, note 49; Megan Brenan, "Majority in U.S. Still Say Government Should Ensure Healthcare," Gallup, January 23, 2023, https://news.gallup.com/poll/468401/majority-say-gov-ensure-healthcare.aspx; Lauren Weber, "How Ohio's G.O.P. Governor Sells Public Health: Don't Call It That," *Washington Post*, April 10, 2024.

53. Brennan Center for Justice, Voting Laws Roundup: 2023 in Review, January 18, 2024, https://www.brennancenter.org/our-work/research-reports/voting-laws-roundup-2023-review; Katherine Hapgood, "See Which States Are Expanding—Or Restricting—Voting Rights," The Center for Public Integrity, October 27, 2023, https://publicintegrity.org/politics/elections/who-counts/see-which-states-are-expanding-or-restricting-voting-rights/; Elize Viebeck, "Here's When Gop Lawmakers Have Passed New Voting Restrictions Around the Country," *Washington Post*, July 14, 2021; Jim Rutenberg and Nick Corasaniti, "Unbowed by Jan. 6 Charges, Republicans Pursue Plans to Contest a Trump Defeat," *New York Times*, July 14, 2024; Patrick Marley, "New Voting Laws in Swing States Could Shape 2024 Election," *Washington Post*, April 8, 2024; Matthew Brown, "Ahead of 2024 Election, Several States Overhaul Voting Laws," *Washington Post*, May 15, 2023.

54. See note 53; Robert Kuttner, "Defending a Free and Fair Election," *The American Prospect*, September 3, 2024.

55. Anat Shenker-Osorio, Chapter 25, this volume.

56. See note 55.

57. See note 55.

58. William Barber II, Chapter 23, this volume.

59. J. Baxter Oliphant, "Top Tax Frustrations for Americans: The Feeling That Some Corporations, Wealthy People Don't Pay Fair Share," Pew Research Center, April 7, 2023, https://coilink.org/20.500.12592/m4k8dt; Progressive Policy Institute, "Winning Back Working America: A PPI/YouGov Survey of Working-Class Attitudes," November 2023, https://www.progressivepolicy.org/publication/winning-back-working-america-a-ppi-yougov-survey-of-working-class-attitudes/; Harold Meyerson, "Is Reversing Biden's Working-Class Slump Even Possible," *The American Prospect*, May 20, 2024.

60. Nicholas Kristoff, "Here's Why Democrats Shouldn't Demean Trump Voters," *New York Times*, September 1, 2024.

61. Barber, note 58; William J. Barber II and Jonathan Wilson-Hartgrove, *White Poverty How Exposing Myths About Race and Class Can Reconstruct American Democracy* (New York: Liveright), 2024.

Introduction

62. Jason Willick, "Where Can the G.O.P. Go Without Roe?," *Washington Post*, April 9, 2024; Pew Research Center, Public Opinion on Abortion, May 13, 2024, https://www.pewresearch.org/religion/fact-sheet/public-opinion-on-abortion/; Paul Krugman, "Don't Lose Sight of Project 2025," *New York Times*, July 16, 2024.

63. Charles M. Blow, "Young Voters Aren't Happy with Biden. But Will They Abandon Him?," *New York Times*, May 8, 2024; Charles Homans and Neil Vigdor, "Gaza Isn't Root of Biden's Struggles With Young Voters, Polls Show," *New York Times*, May 6, 2024; Jamelle Bouie, "Millennials and Gen Z Are Tilting Left and Staying There," *New York Times*, October 24, 2023; Loretta Ross, Chapter 27, this volume.

64. Smitherman and Aranha, note 49.

65. David Siders, "Wellstone Legacy 'Goes Dormant' After Family Ousted in Democratic Feud," Politico, May 13, 2018, https://www.politico.com/story/2018/05/13/wellstone-family-legacy-feud-minnesota-democrats-584205

66. Dan Balz, "American Democracy Is Cracking. These Ideas Could Help Repair It," *Washington Post*, December 21, 2023.

67. Nick Coransaniti, "Racial Turnout Gap Has Widened With a Weakened Voting Rights Act, Study Finds," *New York Times*, March 2, 2024.

68. Brennan Center for Justice, How Voter Suppression Laws Target Native Americans, May 23, 2022, https://www.brennancenter.org/our-work/research-reports/how-voter-suppression-laws-target-native-americans; Judith LeBlanc, Chapter 21, this volume.

69. Steny H. Hoyer, "Letting the Filibuster Stand Will Break American Democracy," *Time*, October 27, 2021.

70. Cornell William Brooks, Chapter 24, this volume.

71. Ayesha Rascoe, "Former U.S. Attorney General Eric Holder on His Efforts to Counter Gerrymandering," NPR, January 28, 2024, https://www.npr.org/2024/01/28/1227453706/former-u-s-attorney-general-eric-holder-on-his-efforts-to-counter-gerrymandering

72. Brennan Center for Justice, Breaking Down the Freedom to Vote Act, November 9, 2023, https://www.brennancenter.org/our-work/research-reports/breaking-down-freedom-vote-act

73. Brennan Center for Justice, note 72.

74. Kenneth W. Mack, "A Call for Revolt Against the Supreme Court's Originalism," *Washington Post*, July 14, 2024; Tyler Pager and Michael Scherer, "Biden Set to Announce Support for Major Supreme Court Changes," Washington Post, July 16, 2024.

75. LaTosha Brown, Chapter 26, this volume.

76. Brown, note 75.

77. Janet Murguia, Chapter 19, this volume.

78. Barber, note 58.

79. Barber, note 58.

80. Barber, note 58.

81. Barber, note 58.

82. Ross, note 63.

83. Matthew Desmond, *Poverty By America* (New York, NY: Crown Publishing), 2023.

84. See note 83.

85. Nancy Gibbs, "The Debate Was A Mess. What We Pay Attention to Next Is What Matters," *Time*, June 28, 2024.

86. Katie Rogers, "Trump Now Claims He Always Knew the Coronavirus Would Be A Pandemic," *New York Times*, March 17, 2020.

87. See Oreskes and Conway, note 10.

88. Justin Milner, Chapter 31, this volume.

89. See Milner, note 88.

90. Coalition for Evidence Based Policy, Maryland Governor Moore & Arnold Ventures Launch $40M Partnership for Proven Programs, Facilitated by the Coalition, February 15, 2024, https://www.evidencebasedpolicy.org/latest-progress

91. See note 1.

92. Julian Zelizer, Chapter 29, this volume.

93. Michael Lipka, "8 Facts About Black Americans and the News," Pew Research Center, February 13, 2024, https://www.pewresearch.org/short-reads/2024/02/13/8-facts-about-black-americans-and-the-news/.

94. Zelizer, note 92.

95. Mariana Alfaro and Jonathan Edwards, "Harris Condemns Shooting of Sonya Massey, An Unarmed Black Woman," *Washington Post,* July 23, 2024.

96. Ray Suarez, Chapter 28, this volume.

97. Suarez, note 96.

98. Robert Faris, Chapter 30, this volume.

99. Joseph Menn, "Stanford's Top Disinformation Research Group Collapses Under Pressure," *Washington Post,* June 14, 2024; Cat Zakrzewski and Naomi Nix, "Trump Allies Crush Misinformation Research Despite Supreme Court Loss," Washington Post, July 24, 2024.

100. Jon Henley, "How Finland Starts Its Fight Against Fake News in Primary Schools," *The Guardian,* January 29, 2020; Jenny Gross, "How Finland Is Teaching a Generation to Spot Misinformation," *New York Times,* January 10, 2023.

101. See note 100.

102. See note 100.

103. Washington Post Editorial, "Schools Should Ban Smartphones. Parents Should Help," *Washington Post,* November 26, 2023.

104. Emily Russell, "Q&A: Victor Pickard on the Layoffs at NPR, and How To Better Support Public and Local Media," *Columbia Journalism Review,* March 15, 2023, https://www.cjr.org/the_media_today/victor_pickard_qa.php.

105. Zelizer, note 92.

106. Robert Reich, "America's Problem Is Massive Inequality—Not 'Woke' Educated Elites," *The Guardian,* June 11, 2024.

107. Claudia Pena, Chapter 33, this volume.

108. Margaret Morton, Rocío Aranda-Alvarado and Lena Sze, Chapter 32, this volume.

Part I

WHAT EVIDENCE-BASED POLICY WORKS?

Economic and Employment Policy

CHAPTER 1

Should the Federal Government Play a Role in Racial Equity? Of Course

Jared Bernstein

In his sweeping historical account of the Kerner Commission, historian Steven M. Gillon wrote that the report represented "... the last full-throated declaration that the federal government should play a leading role in solving deeply embedded problems such as racism and poverty."[1]

From where I sit today, as the chair of President Biden's Council of Economic Advisers, as well as a contributor to earlier updates of the commission's findings, I would argue that Gillon's assessment was too pessimistic. To be clear, many of the challenges the commission so vividly documented remain as deep today as they were in 1968. And despite the ambitious policy agenda to promote racial equality introduced by the commission and its subsequent updates, the federal approach has been inconsistent and incomplete.

But "full-throated declarations" regarding the federal government's role in this space have been a staple of our administration's outreach and public statements, and we've worked to put our policy where our throats are. Most importantly, in the spirit of the first Kerner Report, we have consistently believed in and elevated the role of the Federal government in addressing racial inequities. We can and should have a robust debate about the success of the agenda, the strategies we have followed, and so on. To say we have a lot more work to do is a massive understatement. But as a member of this administration for 3 years and counting, I can unequivocally tell you that there is no question as to whether the "federal government should play a leading role in solving deeply embedded problems such as racism and poverty."

That question was answered by the president's work to reduce childhood poverty, particularly for Black children. The landmark expansion of the Child Tax Credit was a key component of 2021's American Rescue Plan Act, an historic economic rescue plan signed into law by President Biden just 2 months after taking office. The expanded credit delivered critical fiscal relief for working families by increasing the maximum Child Tax Credit[2] (CTC) and by making the CTC fully refundable so that even the lowest-income families would be eligible for the full benefit. The expanded CTC reached an additional 23 million[3] children, significantly reducing child poverty.[4] For Black children, between 2020 and 2021, poverty[5] fell by an unprecedented 8.8 percentage points: from 16.9% to 8.1%. Then, when, despite our (ongoing) efforts to expand the credit, it expired in 2022, Black child poverty shot back up to 17.8%. In addition to providing short-run assistance

5

to families, such assistance has been shown to have long-run benefits for kids, helping them achieve higher educational attainment, become healthier, and work and earn more as adults.[6] This experience lays bare a critically important policy insight: The child poverty rate is not some predetermined constant based on immutable human conditions. It is a policy choice, and it is one of the most important choices a society can make.

That question was answered in the strong Biden economy for workers and their families. In one of his earliest speeches[7] after taking office, President Biden stressed the importance of quickly getting back to full employment conditions in the labor market. One reason for that is his understanding, one he shared with Reverend Martin Luther King Jr., of the importance of these conditions for Black workers and Black communities. When the labor market is persistently tight, as it has been over President Biden's term, it becomes considerably more costly for employers to discriminate against the workers they need to avoid leaving profits on the table. In such labor markets, we expect Black unemployment to fall more than the decline in the overall rate, and to fall more quickly than white unemployment.

And that's exactly what happened. In 2023, the Black unemployment rate, at 5.5%, was the lowest annual rate on record, with data dating back to the early 1970s. The Black–white gap—the Black rate minus the white rate—was also the lowest on record in 2023.[8]

Of course, that low relative rate is still too high compared to the annual average for the year of 3.6%. As Dr. King realized, full employment is a powerful force, but it alone cannot overcome decades of racial injustice.

That question was answered in our housing policy. Housing supply has failed to keep up with housing demand over the last several decades, leading to a nationwide shortage and an acute housing affordability crisis, particularly for economically vulnerable communities. On his first day in office, President Biden signed a memorandum[9] directing his administration to address racial discrimination in the housing market. Since then, this administration has established a policy agenda that strives to stamp out discriminatory Federal practices and restrictive land-use policies, to increase access to homeownership, and to attack the crisis of housing affordability that is most acutely felt by low-income families and communities of color.

President Biden's American Rescue Plan helped Americans stay in their homes during the pandemic by providing financial assistance to both renters and homeowners, and 41% of rental aid recipients[10] were Black Americans. More recently, this administration released the Property Appraisal and Valuation Equity Action Plan and the Blueprint for a Renters Bill of Rights,[11] which establish actionable reforms to advance equity in home appraisal and renter markets and to further the principles of fair housing.

That question was answered in efforts to make college affordable. With rising college tuition[12] for all and incomes often constrained for lower-income households, too many Americans—particularly those from less-advantaged backgrounds—must take out large student loans to pay for college. The Biden administration has strived to reduce the burden of student debt and ensure that student loans are not a barrier to opportunity for students and families. Consistent with this commitment, the Administration introduced the Saving on a Valuable Education (SAVE)[13] plan to reduce monthly debt burdens for eligible students, making paying down loans easier than any other student loan payment plan in history. The SAVE plan results in lifetime savings of tens of thousands of dollars for many borrowers and is designed to ease the burden of loan payments most significantly for the lowest-income borrowers—many of whom are first-generation students and from communities of color. Additionally, President Biden has approved more than $153 billion in debt cancellation[14] for nearly 4.3 million Americans through administrative reforms, such as public service loan forgiveness (for those like teachers and health care workers), income-driven repayment adjustments, closed-school discharge, and total and permanent disability. These changes allow those from all walks of life to take advantage of all the benefits a college education can provide.

That question was answered in small business policy. Entrepreneurs and small business owners are the backbone of our local communities. Their success translates into the success of our local economies, fostering prosperity for neighborhoods and families. Since President Biden took office, there has been an unprecedented growth[15] in new businesses, and consistent with shared prosperity, the share of Black households that own a business has doubled.[16] In addition, loans backed by the U.S. Small Business Administration to Black-owned small businesses have doubled under the Biden administration. Further, the Administration is committed[17] to increasing the share of federal contracting dollars awarded to underserved small businesses, including woman-owned and Black-owned businesses. The success of Black entrepreneurs undoubtedly contributes to job creation in Black communities, wealth generation among Black families, and the overall resilience of our broader economy.

That question was answered in the Biden health care policy. Health coverage, including through our public programs like Medicaid, is important for financial security and health,[18] and has wide-ranging[19] and long-term[20] benefits for children. Under the Biden administration, the fraction of Americans with health insurance has never been higher.[21] Overall improvements in health coverage have especially large impacts on Black Americans, who are typically more likely to be uninsured[22] than white or Asian Americans. For example, between 2021Q1 and 2023Q2, the uninsured rate for adult (18–64) non-Hispanic Blacks fell[23] from 14.7% to an historically low 9.9%.

Millions of lower- and middle-income Black families enrolled in the health insurance marketplaces, originally established by the Affordable Care Act, and saw their premiums lowered[24] or completely eliminated in 2021 as a result of the American Rescue Plan. Enrollees in these markets will continue to benefit from lowered monthly premiums thanks to the Inflation Reduction Act of 2022.

For many years, Black maternal mortality has been high relative to other groups of U.S. women. In June 2022, the president released a Blueprint for Addressing the Maternal Health Crisis, and in December 2022, the president signed into law many pieces of that blueprint, including a provision that permanently extended the option for states to extend postpartum Medicaid coverage from 60 days to 12 months. As of December 2023, 41 states plus Washington, DC,[25] have implemented the one-year postpartum coverage extension, and extensions are pending in several other states. Because Medicaid covers over 40% of all U.S. births, and because Medicaid is a particularly important source of coverage[26] for Black women and children, these Medicaid expansions are likely to generate significant benefits for Black communities.

Finally, that question was answered by child care policy, which has been a core pillar of President Biden's economic agenda. The president believes that how we care for children, and how we value the efforts of caregivers, is fundamental to who we are as a nation. According to one analysis, child care workers earn 23% less on average than workers in other occupations with similar composition by age, education, and other demographic characteristics.[27] These large pay disparities are important not only because the child care workforce is disproportionately made up of women of color, but also because competitive pay helps to keep classrooms open by attracting and retaining child care workers.

The American Rescue Plan made an historic investment in the child care industry, and these funds stabilized the child care industry during and in the wake of the pandemic.[28] As a result, the growth in child care costs for families slowed, employment stabilized, and wages increased for child care workers, culminating in historically high levels of maternal labor force participation. Affordable and accessible child care is good for all families, but investment in child care could be particularly beneficial for parents of color, who are more likely to experience child care–related job disruptions that affect families' financial stability.[29] More recently, the president signed an historic Executive Order[30] directing agencies to expand access to affordable, high-quality care and provide increased support for care workers and family caregivers, a workforce that has long employed large shares of non-white workers, and has historically been a pathway to the middle class for people of color. These actions and more from the administration demonstrate a deep and unprecedented commitment to families and child care workers, taking seriously the importance of affordable and accessible care for the financial stability for all families.

I have framed this essay as answering the question as to whether the federal government should play a "leading role" in addressing and reversing racial inequities. The record of the Biden administration could not be clearer: Our answer to that question is a strong, unwavering "Yes!" Moreover, the policies we have legislated or are actively pursuing should not be considered in isolation. Combining interventions like affordable housing, lower child poverty, increased health coverage, and so on, in the context of strong labor markets has synergistic interaction effects. Their whole, in terms of uplifting lifetime opportunity, is greater than the sum of their parts.

But no one should confuse our work to answer the "leading-role" question as any sort of "mission accomplished" or victory lap. Even where we have made great progress, unacceptably large racial gaps still remain. But those gaps will never close unless we continue to aggressively and relentlessly pursue the Biden-Harris racial equity agenda. And that is precisely what we intend to do.

NOTES

1. Steven M. Gillon, *Separate and Unequal* (New York: Basic Books, 2018), xiv.
2. Chris Miller, "The Expanded Child Tax Credit: The CTC's History, Impact and Uncertain Future," Brookings Institution, June 18, 2021.
3. Jacob Goldin and Katherine Michelmore, "Who Benefits from the Child Tax Credit?" *National Tax Journal* 75, no. 1 (March 2022): 123–147.
4. Kalee Burns, Liana Fox, and Danielle Wilson, "Expansions to Child Tax Credit Contributed to 46% Decline in Child Poverty Since 2020," U.S. Census Bureau, September 13, 2022.

5. Kalee Burns and Liana E. Fox. "The Impact of the 2021 Expanded Child Tax Credit on Child Poverty" (Working Paper #SEHSD-WP2022-24), Social, Economic, and Housing Statistics Division, U.S. Census Bureau, November 2022.

6. These effects have been found for polices prioritized and expanded under the Biden administration, including Medicaid and tax credits like the EITC and CTC, and SNAP.

7. Joseph R. Biden, "State of the Economy and the Need for the American Rescue Plan," remarks in the White House State Dining Room, February 5, 2021.

8. The White House, "Q4 GDP Advance Estimate: Context for Today's Strong Report," January 25, 2024.

9. The White House, "Memorandum on Redressing Our Nation's and the Federal Government's History of Discriminatory Housing Practices and Polices," January 26, 2021.

10. The White House, "Fact Sheet: The Biden-Harris Administration Advances Equity and Opportunity for Black Americans and Communities Across the Country," February 27, 2023.

11. Domestic Policy Council and National Economic Council, "The White House Blueprint for a Renters' Bill of Rights," January 2023.

12. National Center for Health Statistics, "Digest of Health Statistics, 2022 Tables and Figures," Table 330.10.

13. The White House, "Fact Sheet: The Biden-Harris Administration Launches the SAVE Plan, the Most Affordable Student Loan Repayment Plan Ever, To Lower Monthly Payments for Millions of Borrowers," August 22, 2023.

14. U.S. Department of Education, "Biden-Harris Administration Announces $4.9 Billion in Approved Student Debt Relief," January 19, 2024.

15. The White House, "New Business Surge: Unveiling the Business Application Boom Through an Analysis of Administrative Data," January 11, 2024.

16. Federal Reserve, "Survey of Consumer Finances, 1989–2022, Business Equity by Race and Ethnicity," November 2, 2023.

17. The White House, "Fact Sheet: Biden-Harris Administration Announces Reforms to Increase Equity and Level the Playing Field for Underserved Small Business Owners," December 2, 2021.

18. Jacob Goldin, Ithai Z. Lurie, and Janet McCubbin, "Health Insurance and Mortality: Experimental Evidence from Taxpayer Outreach," *The Quarterly Journal of Economics* 136, no. 1 (February 2021): 1–49.

19. Samuel Arenberg, Seth Neller, and Sam Stripling, "The Impact of Youth Medicaid Eligibility on Adult Incarceration," *American Economic Journal: Applied Economics* 16, no. 1 (2024): 121–56.

20. David W. Brown, Amanda E. Kowalski, and Ithai Z. Lurie, "Long-Term Impacts of Childhood Medicaid Expansions on Outcomes in Adulthood," *The Review of Economic Studies* 87, no. 2 (March 2020): 792–821.

21. Office of the Assistant Secretary for Planning and Evaluation, "National Uninsured Rate Remained Unchanged in the Second Quarter of 2023" (Issue Brief No. HP-2023-27), U.S. Department of Health and Human Services, November 2023.

22. Caroline Hanson et al., "Health Insurance for People Younger Than Age 65: Expiration of Temporary Policies Projected to Reshuffle Coverage, 2023–33," *Health Affairs* 42, no. 6 (2023): 742–52.

23. Office of the Assistant Secretary for Planning and Evaluation, "National Uninsured Rate Remained Unchanged in the Second Quarter of 2023."

24. The White House, "Fact Sheet: The Biden-Harris Administration Advances Equity and Opportunity for Black Americans and Communities Across the Country."

25. KFF, "Medicaid Postpartum Coverage Extensions: Approved and Pending State Action," January 17, 2024.

26. Caroline Hanson et al., "Health Insurance for People Younger Than Age 65."

27. Elise Gould, "Child Care Workers Aren't Paid Enough to Make Ends Meet" (Issue Brief #405), Economic Policy Institute, November 5, 2015.

28. The White House Council of Economic Advisers, "Did Stabilization Funds Help Mothers Get Back to Work After the COVID-19 Recession?" (working paper), November 7, 2023.

29. Christina Novoa, "How Child Care Disruptions Hurt Parents of Color Most," Center for American Progress, June 29, 2020.

30. The White House, "Executive Order on Increasing Access to High-Quality Care and Supporting Care Givers," April 18, 2023.

CHAPTER 2

The New Economics and the Rebalancing of Power

Felicia Wong and Matt Hughes

Elements of this essay have been adapted from earlier Roosevelt Institute work, including *A New Paradigm for Justice and Democracy: Moving Beyond the Twin Failures of Neoliberalism and Racial Liberalism*,[1] and from Felicia Wong's speech at the Eisenhower Foundation's celebration of the 55th anniversary of the Kerner Commission Report.

THE KERNER COMMISSION: PIVOTAL AND UNHEEDED

In February 1968, the Kerner Commission did what our government had largely failed to until that point: It told the truth about racism. The commission's report held a mirror up and showed us a country unable to confront the lingering legacy of slavery and the enduring harms Black Americans faced then, and still face today.

It showed us a country in which Black Americans were suffering from massive disparities in income, wealth, health, housing, and education. It was clear that racial injustice was not only emotional and attitudinal, but economic and systemic. Justice, the report said, required government action to ensure Black peoples' material well-being.

The report was direct and explicit about the causes of the problem. "Race prejudice has shaped our history decisively; it now threatens to affect our future," the commission said. Its most famous lines, oft-quoted, are these: "What white Americans have never fully understood—but what the Negro can never forget—is that white society is deeply implicated in the ghetto. White institutions created it, white institutions maintain it, and white society condones it."[2]

In many ways, the Kerner Commission was braver than we are today, and braver than we have been since the report's publication. It showed us the path forward: "A commitment to national action—compassionate, massive, and sustained, backed by the resources of the most powerful and the richest nation on this earth. From every American it will require new attitudes, new understanding, and, above all, new will." The report was also practical, naming specific steps on everything from creating jobs and increasing the federal minimum wage to building millions of housing units for low-income families. It echoed the Rev. Martin Luther King Jr.'s Poor People's Campaign[3]—which had been announced just months before, in late 1967, and brought economic demands and racial justice together in sharp relief.

That was more than a half century ago. As we all know well, the nation took a different course than the one recommended by the Kerner Commission—a group composed not of activists or organizers, but instead mainstream politicians, mostly white. And at our pivotal moment in history, not far removed from 2020s racial reckoning and the conservative backlash it sparked, we have much to learn from what unfolded after Kerner. Just after the report's 1968 publication, the commission's calls for direct government action and investment in Black communities faded away as a starkly different ideology rose to prominence. An alliance of conservative politicians, movement leaders, and academics took power in the 1970s and 1980s, held together by the promise of a neoliberal, market-oriented approach to politics that, we can see in retrospect, was doomed from the start.[4]

HOW WE GOT HERE: THE TWIN FAILURES OF NEOLIBERALISM AND RACIAL LIBERALISM

Today, even as we see major changes in economic thinking generally, and the beginnings of a move away from neoliberalism, the mainstream approach to race and economics is still primarily dominated by market fundamentalist thinking.

Neoliberalism, as it developed in the 1940s and 1950s, held that markets would bring economic and political freedom, and that our economy and politics should therefore privilege individual choice and profit-driven private-sector companies. Racial liberalism[5] emerged within this narrowed framework beginning in the 1970s. Its calls for antidiscrimination, access to better education and better jobs, and greater opportunity within a market-dominated system, became a prevailing view in both major American parties.

Neoliberalism failed empirically,[6] on its own terms. It did not deliver greater growth, more economic stability, or more income mobility for Americans than the New Deal, mixed-economy liberalism that had preceded it. It did produce inequality that replicated itself over generations. And thus, it is not surprising that the racial liberalism that grew up under the neoliberal era also failed to fully deliver.

Racial liberalism's central promise—work hard, invest in your own education, and then gain a fair share of economic and social security within the private sector—proved hollow. Across nearly every indicator—income, wealth, health, criminal justice—the material effects of inequities are often worse for Black Americans than for white Americans,[7] even taking educational attainment into account. Today, on average, a Black family with a college-educated head of household has less wealth than a white family whose head did not graduate from high school.[8]

Neoliberalism and racial liberalism produced ineffective policy solutions to race equity in part because both held an ahistorical understanding of American economic and political institutions. The neoliberal idea that racial segregation in the labor market could be competed away,[9] as Gary Becker argued, and racial liberalism's notion that antidiscrimination and greater opportunity would be sufficient, could never address what the Kerner Commission understood well. To counter centuries of systemic racism—the web of laws, norms, and institutions that render life chances and basic opportunities for Black Americans less than, and unequal to, those of other Americans—would require direct and significant government intervention, both public investment and legislative action.[10]

But neoliberalism's economic insistence on the logic of market competition and its moral insistence on the purity of individual workers earning their keep smothered big ideas advocated by civil rights leaders, like a federal jobs guarantee and full employment mandates. Instead, nominal race neutrality and market-first solutions—from financial literacy; to loans and tax credits; to individualized, privatized higher education—became the default for 5 decades of policymaking across both Republican and Democratic administrations.

RACIAL LIBERALISM: LEFT, RIGHT, AND CENTER

By the 1980s, neoliberalism's focus on individual skill-building and government tax-cutting had a friend in President Ronald Reagan, and affirmative economic arguments that government should focus on greater Black–white material equity had lost credibility. The perfect complement to his explicitly low-tax, antigovernment stance to governance, Reagan's was a dog whistle approach to race. He launched his presidential campaign in Philadelphia, Mississippi, where three civil rights workers were famously murdered.[11] Reagan's demonization of taxation and welfare were lightly coded, heavily racialized, and narratively sticky. His infamous, if factually dubious, "welfare queens" trope remains instantly recognizable in today's American political vernacular.[12]

But such narratives don't only come from the right. Bill Clinton was, of course, a Democrat. And, as historians from Gary Gerstle[13] to Nelson Lichstenstein and Judith Stein[14] have recounted, the Clinton presidency—despite some of its more aspirational, pro–market-shaping ideas in the early years—institutionalized both race neutrality and neoliberal austerity within the Democratic Party.[15] Clinton's symbolic politics—his personal oversight of the execution of Ricky Ray Rector and his criticism of Black writer and activist Sister Souljah—were designed to triangulate and speak to "Reagan Democrats." His race agenda, the One America Initiative, lacked any clear federal goals or outcomes, and instead focused on town hall meetings, nonprofit and municipal promising practices, and racial reconciliation.[16] The policy agenda that followed focused on both "opportunity" and "responsibility"; empowerment zones that, like many similar tax-break–led efforts before and since, failed to deliver; and K–12 educational policy that normalized charter schools and exclusivity under the rubric of "school choice."[17] Clinton signed a host of laws that led to increased Black incarceration nationwide, and remains most criticized for the 1996 welfare reform bill, of which the work requirements, state block grants, and immigrant prohibitions radically reduced the number of aid recipients and pushed low-income women of color, in particular, into long-term poverty.[18]

Barack Obama's rise to political power a decade later was, in Nils Gilman's words,[19] the "apotheosis" of racial liberalism, "exposing the contradictions and limitations of that consensus in ways that became impossible to ignore." The Obama years were both an end and a beginning. His election as the nation's first Black president was a clear, hopeful sign of racial progress—and also set off tremendous racist backlash that has grown and metastasized.

President Obama took office as Lehman Brothers failed, Wall Street panicked, and millions of Americans lost their homes and livelihoods. And, within the constraints of the Obama administration's policy response (which was itself constrained by the neoliberalism of its time), the long-term effects of the crisis and recession were highly racialized.[20] From 2007 to 2010, Black families lost nearly a third of their wealth, and Latino Americans lost more than 40%.[21] Obama's consensus approach focused on the austerity of a "grand bargain" that never materialized.[22]

In comparison to the Clinton years, the brutality of policing and the criminal justice system became more visible to the American mainstream in the 2010s, and catalyzed greater movement outcry. The 2012 killing of Trayvon Martin and the subsequent acquittal of George Zimmerman, as well as the 2014 police killing of Michael Brown in Ferguson, Missouri, sparked the Black Lives Matter (BLM) movement. And while the Obama administration made real progress for DREAMers (children who were brought to the United States while young), it also oversaw the deportation of nearly 3 million immigrants, many of whom had no criminal records.[23]

None of these approaches, from 1980 through 2016, took seriously a central, muscular, federal government approach to creating greater race equity among Americans. And therefore, by the time Donald Trump became a serious candidate for the U.S. presidency, mainstream racial liberalism had settled into a groove, ripe for weaponization. On the one hand, neither political party permitted overt bigotry within their establishment ranks. But on the other hand, the lack of overt bigotry in the political mainstream and the focus on nondiscrimination rather than more affirmative actions did not lead to materially better outcomes for most people of color. Nor did neoliberalism lead to materially better outcomes for most working Americans of any racial background. Economic frustration was a powder keg.

"Race-neutral" politics went off the rails by 2016 in part because it failed, empirically and according to its own markers, to actually curb racism, and instead contributed to rising inequality, especially for Black Americans. The details are familiar: the rise of the Tea Party as an antigovernmental force; and the rise and political power of birtherism, which is both anti-Black and anti-Muslim, nativist as well as racist. The practice of looking the other way and ignoring the dog whistles in fact exacerbated racism and allowed it to gain power. "Owning the libs" was, in this environment, a successful strategy.

Donald Trump was elected president having run a deliberately racialized campaign. Trump's racism—more than any mainstream national political movement in at least the last 100 years—gained adherents because of its shock value. Trumpism thrived by igniting particularly vitriolic strands of America's racist traditions. In particular, he fused racism and nativism straightforwardly and unapologetically, in his public use of racist slurs and in his hiring of policy advisors like Steve Bannon and Stephen Miller, who encouraged and conferred with white supremacists. He tapped into the "law and order" strains of anti-Black sentiment among mostly white voters, attacking Black Lives Matter protests in the wake of police killings and calling pro-BLM memorials "symbols of hate."[24] Trump stoked a range of anti-Latino and anti-Asian fears, from labor competition to the feeling that Asians and Latino people will be forever "foreign." Meanwhile, he exacerbated post–9/11 anti-Muslim hysteria under the guise of national security.[25]

Donald Trump no longer holds office, but his post-liberal racism and nativism are controlling forces in the Republican Party, and threaten to render mainstream liberals helpless, unable to respond effectively.

A SEA CHANGE—WITHER ECONOMICS, WITHER RACIAL EQUITY?

But the news is certainly not all bad. Joe Biden's presidency has marked the beginnings of deep economic change: a progressive post-neoliberalism focused on the assertive government shaping of markets for the middle class, and for the public good. It's a paradigm shift that Biden himself has touted and that his administration has defined as investing in people and places, strengthening worker power, and taming corporations that have distorting and destructive market power.[26] This is a U-turn from the nominally hands-off neoliberal approach (in the words of Brad DeLong, "the market giveth, the market taketh away, blessed be the market"[27]) that led to the market dominance of the most powerful, and most extractive, firms.

This burgeoning new economics instead seeks to rebalance power.[28] Higher taxes on the rich and corporations. Empowering workers through a higher minimum wage, prioritizing full employment, and direct support for labor unions and workers' right to organize and strike. Greater regulation of Wall Street and especially tech companies, including through a fundamental shift in antitrust policy to focus on workers and market structure rather than prices alone. Greater direct government investment in key sectors of the economy, like clean energy, catalyzing manufacturing investment in communities and regions that have long been economically moribund.

Four years in, these changes are working. Perhaps most important is the strong labor market, which has shown remarkable post-pandemic resilience since 2021[29] as a result of federal support. Wage growth, especially for workers at the middle and bottom of the income distribution, has reduced the Black–white wage gap[30] and the Black–white employment gap[31] to the lowest in a generation, and also enabled increased union membership and worker power.

And one other area in which these new economic policies seem to be taking root: investment, with public dollars "crowding in" private funds. In the wake of the CHIPS and Science Act (2022) and the Inflation Reduction Act (2022), manufacturing and other private-sector investments,[32] especially in targeted sectors like semiconductors and clean energy, reached historic highs by the end of 2023. The IRA's investments are helping to create more than 85,000 new jobs in communities of color, a positive sign in the law's early days.[33]

The question is whether these remarkable economic changes will be enough—and whether they will truly address the problems wrought by racial liberalism. Notably, the race-forward pieces of a post-neoliberal economics have remained part of the Biden team's arsenal, but by his fourth year in office and the beginning of a bitter 2024 election campaign, they have become rhetorically subdued in the face of an anti-antiracist backlash. They have also been less frontal in policy terms than other, investment-forward elements of "Bidenomics."

There are reasons to hope that the new progressive post-neoliberalism will extend to race. Certainly, the 2020 uprisings for racial justice have been exemplary, activating millions in a quest for a more antiracist politics and pushing into the mainstream new understandings of our nation—our history, our culture, and our institutions.

As the Roosevelt Institute has argued elsewhere, this new movement of scholars, activists, and political figures has advanced the idea that a post-neoliberal progressive economics and racial equity are fundamentally and inextricably linked.[34] That policy and moral undertaking has three core themes—material equity; repair and redress; and freedom and liberation.

On material equity, today's race and economic politics has moved beyond racial liberalism, beyond equal access and opportunity. Our aspirations are clearly focused on outcomes, on closing gaps—in wealth, income, health, criminal justice, and education—that have persisted for generations, and worsened over the last half century. The key questions asked by new equity thinkers are: "Who gets what? Under what terms and circumstances? As decided by whom?" This is about a distribution of resources and of decision-making power, with an emphasis not only on individual equity, but on equity for communities that have historically and deliberately been excluded from the benefits of America's economic growth.

It is true that many policies since the racial reckoning of 2020 have not dealt fully with these equity demands. And it is also true that the anti-antiracism backlash has had an effect. This is reminiscent of Richard Nixon's anti-Kerner statements, part of a backlash against that more assertive vision of civil rights. Nixon, of course, won the 1968 presidential race. But past need not be prologue. Because we are still living through this historical moment. And the race and economics demands that seemed to be rising in the wake of George Floyd's murder need not fade away simply because some argue that they are not currently popular[35] and should be electorally avoided.

Some genies are hard to put back into bottles. The other two economic themes that came out of 2020—repair and redress, and freedom and liberation—are enduring as political ideas. With neoliberalism on its heels, we are clearly on the brink of some kind of paradigm shift. The question is whether that shift, whose outcome is deeply uncertain, will include core ideas of racial justice.

Repair and redress is one of the themes that movement thinkers brought again to the fore several years ago, with the blockbuster publication of the *New York Times*'s *1619 Project*, and of course with the movement for racial justice in 2020. We need, as Aria Florant says, the full cycle of repair—"reckoning, acknowledgement, apology, and redress"[36]—because an apology without redress is insufficient for justice. That means an honest reckoning with America's legacy of slavery, white supremacy, violence, and exclusion; and reparative policymaking that expressly tries to make up for past harms.

Freedom and liberation, beyond neoliberalism's concept of free markets, is also part of the new paradigm. This vision of freedom is Rooseveltian in its breadth: the ability of all people to live free from fear and from want, with freedom of expression and of worship. It is economic and social, meaning, as Mike Konczal argues,[37] freedom from the vagaries of the market. And it is also about racial justice. Oppressed and underrepresented groups have, time and again throughout America's history, called for freedom and liberation—from the fight to abolish slavery, to the Civil Rights Movement, to the Black Power movement, to women's liberation, to today's Black Lives Matter movement. These movements demand self-determination, and power, in that people and communities must have the power to shape and structure their own lives.

These themes can and should be integral to the new post-neoliberal economics. As the history of the Kerner Commission teaches us, unless race equity is a central goal of our economic governance, we will not meaningfully address problems of racial justice.

The track record over the past 4 years on this score is decidedly mixed. In some important ways, we have seen these themes from justice movements work their way into mainstream politics. The Biden administration has given unprecedented focus to structural exclusion and the "unbearable human costs of systemic racism," as the president puts it. The fact that Joe Biden is a mainstream Democrat makes his explicit language about race and racism all the more remarkable.

And we have seen the Biden administration work toward policies that will genuinely benefit (or in some cases, cease harming) Black Americans and other Americans of color. Some exemplars include policies that streamline or curb[38] the "time tax," meaning the red tape in accessing government programs and public benefits. This tax works especially against low-income Americans,[39] disproportionately people of color. Or the unprecedented move to cancel student debt, especially debt that has benefited extractive lenders at the expense of students who never see a real return on their educational investment. Those debt efforts are incomplete due to the *Biden v. Nebraska Supreme Court* ruling, but the Biden administration continues to cancel[40] billions of dollars for millions of borrowers, and debt cancellation disproportionately benefits[41] Black and Brown borrowers. The Internal Revenue Service has pledged[42] to investigate and correct algorithmic and other practices that have led to the significant over-auditing, even controlling for income, of Black Americans. And, even after a federal judge blocked efforts to specifically provide redress to Black farmers who faced discrimination in loans, the U.S. Department of Agriculture developed avenues[43] to provide them relief.

But the "whole of government" approach to race equity that the Biden team pledged in 2020 and 2021, when the Black Lives Matter movement was at its strongest, has receded distinctly into the rhetorical and policy background. Perhaps this is because the Supreme Court's Harvard affirmative action ruling has had a chilling effect. Perhaps it is because the anti-antiracism backlash—which lionizes violence[44] and weaponizes teaching about America's racial history[45] in our schools—has had a meaningful political effect. Perhaps it is because the work is simply difficult.

RACE EQUITY IS A CHOICE

We sit at a hinge moment in history, just as the Kerner Commission did 56 years ago. Looking back at all that followed, and all that didn't, teaches several clear lessons. First, economic thriving and race equity go hand in hand. Especially as the U.S. population becomes increasingly multiracial: It is simply untenable economically—and also untenable for a nation that is democratic—not to invest in the future of Black, brown, and Indigenous Americans. Second, achieving real results requires direct federal government commitment and action. Public options for housing, care, education, and employment are all necessary. Of course, the policy design details and practices in all of these sectors matter, as does taxing sufficiently such that we have the government revenue to pay for these efforts. But history is clear that voluntary practices, state and local policies, or hopes that the private sector will step up are all fine, but wholly insufficient.

It is tempting to say, as many have, that race equity is not popular, and so therefore one should not build a politics around it—certainly not a national political identity, given the red-blue-purple mix in America today. But this approach, as Heather McGhee[46] notes well, leaves too much on the table. Its view of the median voter whose popularity must be courted is narrow[47]—likely older, whiter, and more male. Imagine a world in which the Biden approach to race equity were as strong in 2023 as it seemed to be in 2021. Young and millennial voters, who have become lukewarm several years into Biden's term, might see him as a more committed champion of their interests and values.

Again, this is not easy. Purely economically, today's "new economics" approach can be win-win. Truly vanquishing neoliberalism and instituting a more middle-out approach will benefit all but the very top 1%, who will have to cease and desist extractive practices, and pay more in taxes. But, as the post-2020 backlash has shown, adding race equity to the mix can make the politics more complicated.

However, complicated does not mean impossible, and complicated does not mean unwise. One important lesson from the Kerner Commission's fate is that mainstream politics alone will not take a stronger long-term stance on equity, and will not drive the policies to make that equity real. No matter how well-meaning the elected officials, insiders always require outsiders. Outside movements push. They have the time to develop bold policy proposals. They imagine new possibilities in ways that day-to-day political life simply does not allow. Making race equity a reality will require an even stronger and savvier racial justice movement that is funded for the long term, so that it can be more strategic and prepared for the long fight.

Race equity is a choice that this country has never made. But a broad coalition—increasingly deep and increasingly strong—can make that choice today. The Kerner report was published more than a half century ago. It remains time, in the commission's words, "to turn with all the purpose at our command to the major unfinished business of this nation." To do otherwise is not only immoral. It is economic folly.

NOTES

1. Kyle Strickland and Felicia Wong, "A New Paradigm for Justice and Democracy: Moving beyond the Twin Failures of Neoliberalism and Racial Liberalism," Roosevelt Institute, November 3, 2021, https://rooseveltinstitute.org/publications/new-paradigm-for-justice-and-democracy-moving-beyond-the-twin-failures-of-neoliberalism-and-racial-liberalism.

2. The National Advisory Commission on Civil Disorders, *Report of the National Advisory Commission on Civil Disorders* (Washington, DC: U.S. Department of Justice, Office of Justice Programs, 1968).

3. Stanford University, "Poor People's Campaign," Martin Luther King, Jr. Research and Education Institute, May 12, 1968, https://kinginstitute.stanford.edu/poor-peoples-campaign.

4. Felicia Wong, "Overview: Post-Neoliberalism at a Crossroads," *Democracy: A Journal of Ideas*, no. 64 (Spring), https://democracyjournal.org/magazine/64/overview-post-neoliberalism-at-a-crossroads.

5. A term used by Charles Mills and others. Neil Roberts, "The Critique of Racial Liberalism: An Interview with Charles W. Mills," *Black Perspectives* (blog). African American Intellectual History Society (AAIHS), April 3, 2017, https://www.aaihs.org/the-critique-of-racial-liberalism-an-interview-with-charles-w-mills.

6. Mike Konczal, Katy Milani, and Ariel Evans, "The Empirical Failures of Neoliberalism," Roosevelt Institute, January 15, 2020, https://rooseveltinstitute.org/publications/the-empirical-failures-of-neoliberalism/.

7. Mabinty Quarshie et al., "12 Charts Show How Racial Disparities Persist Across Wealth, Health, Education and Beyond," *USA Today*, June 18, 2020, https://www.usatoday.com/in-depth/news/2020/06/18/12-charts-racial-disparities-persist-across-wealth-health-and-beyond/3201129001/.

8. William Darity Jr. et al., *What We Get Wrong About Closing the Racial Wealth Gap* (Durham, NC: Samuel DuBois Cook Center on Social Equity, April 2018), https://socialequity.duke.edu/research-duke/what-we-get-wrong-about-closing-the-racial-wealth-gap.

9. Gary S. Becker, *The Economics of Discrimination*, 2nd ed. (Chicago: University of Chicago Press, 1971).

10. Andrea Flynn, Susan Holmberg, Dorian T. Warren, and Felicia Wong, *Rewrite the Racial Rules: Building an Inclusive American Economy* (New York: Roosevelt Institute, 2016), https://rooseveltinstitute.org/wp-content/uploads/2016/06/RI-RRT-Race-201606.pdf.

11. Federal Bureau of Investigation (FBI), "Mississippi Burning," FBI, May 18, 2016, https://www.fbi.gov/history/famous-cases/mississippi-burning.

12. Bryce Covert, "The Myth of the Welfare Queen," *The New Republic*, July 2, 2019, https://newrepublic.com/article/154404/myth-welfare-queen.

13. Gary Gerstle, *Rise and Fall of the Neoliberal Order* (Oxford, UK: Oxford University Press, 2022).

14. Nelson Lichtenstein and Judith Stein, *A Fabulous Failure: The Clinton Presidency and the Transformation of American Capitalism* (Princeton, NJ: Princeton University Press, 2023).

15. Nelson Lichtenstein, "Bill Clinton's Failure," Princeton University Press, September 13, 2023, https://press.princeton.edu/ideas/bill-clintons-failure.

16. Renée M. Smith, "The Public Presidency Hits the Wall: Clinton's Presidential Initiative on Race," *Presidential Studies Quarterly* 28, no. 4 (Fall 1998): 780–85, https://www.jstor.org/stable/27551931.

17. Timothy Weaver, "The False Promise of Opportunity Zones," *Boston Review*, April 13, 2023, https://www.bostonreview.net/articles/the-false-promise-of-opportunity-zones.

18. Linda Burnham, "Welfare Reform, Family Hardship, and Women of Color," *Annals of the American Academy of Political and Social Science* 577 (September 2001): 38–48, https://www.jstor.org/stable/1049821.

19. Nils Gilman, "The Collapse of Racial Liberalism," *American Interest* 13, no. 5 (March 2018), https://www.the-american-interest.com/2018/03/02/collapse-racial-liberalism.

20. National Employment Law Project (NELP), "Four Years into Recovery, Low-Wage Work Dominates," news release, April 28, 2014, https://www.nelp.org/news-releases/four-years-into-recovery-low-wage-work-dominates.

21. Signe-Mary McKernan, Caroline Ratcliffe, Eugene Steuerle, and Sisi Zhang, "Less than Equal: Racial Disparities in Wealth Accumulation," Urban Institute (2013), https://www.urban.org/sites/default/files/publication/23536/412802-less-than-equal-racial-disparities-in-wealth-accumulation.pdf.

22. Jay Newton-Small, "The Inside Story of Obama and Boehner's Second Failed Grand Bargain," *TIME*, July 23, 2011, https://swampland.time.com/2011/07/23/the-inside-story-of-obama-and-boehners-second-failed-grand-bargain.

23. Sarah Gonzalez, "No One Expected Obama Would Deport More People than Any Other U.S. President," *WNYC*, January 19, 2017, https://www.wnyc.org/story/no-one-thought-barack-obama-would-deport-more-people-any-other-us-president.

24. Laura Barrón-López and Alex Thompson, "Facing Bleak November, Republicans Look to Stoke BLM Backlash," *Politico*, August 10, 2020, https://www.politico.com/news/2020/08/10/elections-republicans-black-lives-matterbacklash-389906.

25. Spencer Ackerman, *Reign of Terror: How the 9/11 Era Destabilized America and Produced Trump* (New York: Penguin Random House, 2022).

26. White House, "Remarks by President Biden in Press Conference," transcript of speech delivered at the White House, Washington, DC, March 25, 2021, https://www.whitehouse.gov/briefing-room/speeches-remarks/2021/03/25/remarks-by-president-biden-in-press-conference.

27. Brad DeLong, *Slouching Towards Utopia: An Economic History of the Twentieth Century* (London: John Murray Press, 2022).

28. Felicia Wong et al., *Sea Change: How a New Economics Went Mainstream*, Roosevelt Institute, November 16, 2023, https://rooseveltinstitute.org/publications/sea-change/.

29. Mike Konczal and Emily DiVito, "The Year the American Rescue Plan Made: 2021 in Review," Roosevelt Institute (blog), December 9, 2021, https://rooseveltinstitute.org/2021/12/09/the-year-the-american-rescue-plan-made-2021-in-review.

30. David Leonhardt, "The Racial Wage Gap Is Shrinking," *New York Times*, June 19, 2023, https://www.nytimes.com/2023/06/19/briefing/juneteenth-racial-wage-gap.html.

31. White House, "The Power of Empowering Workers: Reducing Racial Employment and Unemployment Gaps," White House (blog), November 3, 2023, https://www.whitehouse.gov/cea/written-materials/2023/11/03/the-power-of-empowering-workers-reducing-racial-employment-and-unemployment-gaps.

32. White House, "Ten Charts That Explain the U.S. Economy in 2023," White House (blog), December 19, 2023, https://www.whitehouse.gov/cea/written-materials/2023/12/19/ten-charts-that-explain-the-u-s-economy-in-2023.

33. Climate Power, "The Clean Energy Boom in Communities of Color," Climate Power, August 21, 2023, https://climatepower.us/wp-content/uploads/sites/23/2023/05/Clean-Energy-Boom-Communities-of-Color-Report.pdf.

34. Strickland and Wong, "A New Paradigm for Justice and Democracy."

35. Ezra Klein, "David Shor Is Telling Democrats What They Don't Want to Hear," *New York Times*, October 8, 2021, https://www.nytimes.com/2021/10/08/opinion/democrats-david-shor-education-polarization.html.

36. Aria Florent, "A Dream in Our Name," Liberation Ventures, 2023, https://www.liberationventures.org/a-dream-in-our-name/.

37. Mike Konczal, *Freedom from the Market: America's Fight to Liberate Itself from the Grip of the Invisible Hand* (New York: New Press, 2021).

38. Sam Berger, "Reducing Time Taxes and Administrative Burdens," White House (blog), July 10, 2023, https://www.whitehouse.gov/omb/briefing-room/2023/07/10/reducing-time-taxes-and-administrative-burdens.

39. Annie Lowrey, "The Time Tax," *The Atlantic*, July 27, 2021, https://www.theatlantic.com/politics/archive/2021/07/how-government-learned-waste-your-time-tax/619568.

40. Zach Schermele, "Biden Is Forgiving Millions in Student Loans. He Wants All the Credit," *USA Today*, January 8, 2024, https://www.usatoday.com/story/news/education/2024/01/06/biden-is-forgiving-student-loans-by-the-millions-and-he-wants-credit/72107989007.

41. Alí Bustamante, "How Canceling Student Debt Would Bolster the Economic Recovery and Reduce the Racial Wealth Gap," Roosevelt Institute (blog), December 8, 2021, https://rooseveltinstitute.org/2021/12/08/how-canceling-student-debt-would-bolster-the-economic-recovery-and-reduce-the-racial-wealth-gap.

42. Daniel I. Werfel, "Werfel Letter on Audit Selection," Internal Revenue Service, May 15, 2023, https://www.irs.gov/pub/newsroom/werfel-letter-on-audit-selection.pdf.

43. Chandelis Duster, "USDA Begins Accepting Discrimination Relief Applications from Farmers," *CNN*, July 7, 2023, https://www.cnn.com/2023/07/07/politics/usda-discrimination-relief-applications/index.html.

44. Robert Downen, "Kyle Rittenhouse Launches Nonprofit with Far-Right Texans as He Ramps up Political Engagement in the State," *Texas Tribune*, August 17, 2023, https://www.texastribune.org/2023/08/16/kyle-rittenhouse-texas-foundation.

45. Olivia B. Waxman, "Anti-'Critical Race Theory' Laws Are Working. Teachers Are Thinking Twice About How They Talk about Race," *TIME*, June 30, 2022, https://time.com/6192708/critical-race-theory-teachers-racism.

46. Heather McGhee, *The Sum of Us: What Racism Costs Everyone and How We Can Prosper Together* (New York: Penguin Random House, 2022).

47. Ezra Klein and Michael Podhorzer, hosts, "Are Democrats Whistling Past the Graveyard?" *The Ezra Klein Show* (podcast), November 14, 2023, https://www.nytimes.com/2023/11/14/opinion/ezra-klein-podcast-michael-podhorzer.html.

CHAPTER 3

Guidez-Faire
Why Capitalism Needs Effective Governance

Naomi Oreskes and Erik M. Conway[1]

A wise man once said that the trouble with this generation of Americans is that "they haven't read the minutes of the previous meeting."

Adlai Stevenson, 1962[2]

PAST IS PROLOGUE, BUT WE NEGLECT TO READ IT

Americans are a forgetful people. We look forward, not back. Our business leaders valorize "disruption" over integrity. When we face problems, our tendency is not so much to analyze how we got here, but to figure out how to move forward. As the saying goes, we want to "fix the problem, not the blame."[3]

Often that's a good thing. But it sometimes means that we fail to learn the lessons of history, or forget lessons that our predecessors learned the hard way. Sometimes we break things that did not deserve to be broken. Besides lamenting American historical amnesia, Adlai Stevenson reminded his 1962 audience of Rousseau's pupil, Emile. "The best way to teach Emile not to lean out the window," Rousseau observed, "is to let him fall out." The problem, Stevenson replied, was that "the pupil may not survive to profit by his experience."[4]

In the 19th and early 20th centuries, America had undertaken a great experiment with capitalism. Many people got hurt, others did not survive, but collectively we learned that left to its own devices, the "invisible hand of the marketplace" produced a world of visible hurt and conspicuous suffering. A world that included brutal working conditions, starvation wages, and widespread exploitation of child and immigrant labor. A world that included a pandemic of workplace injury and death, and management-sponsored violence against workers who unionized to bargain collectively for better wages and safer working conditions. A world of ruthless business practices that undermined competition, drove out competitors, and empowered pernicious monopolies.

We also learned that the free market was highly asymmetrical: it protected the "freedom" of industrialists to amass gargantuan fortunes and use those fortunes to solidify their gilded social influence and political power, but it did not include the civil rights of female citizens, of native Americans, or, most obviously, of Black Americans enslaved in the south. Nor did the invisible hand find a way to prevent the Great Depression.

These lessons were channeled into action, often by mobilizing the visible hand of governance. In the late 19th century, the Sherman Anti-Trust Act rendered illegal the anticompetitive practices that had undermined both economic and political competition. In the early 20th century, a panoply of reforms—including the Federal Income Tax (1913) and the institution of the 8-hour working day (circa 1919)—helped to protect the rights of workers and level the economic playing field.[5] In the face of the Great Depression, President Franklin Roosevelt implemented his famous "alphabet soup" of new statutes and agencies to address a variety of ills wrought by inadequately regulated capitalism and inequitable concentrations of power and wealth.

These lessons were so broadly accepted that when Dwight Eisenhower was elected President in 1952—the first Republican since Herbert Hoover—he not only supported Social Security, but expanded it. Eisenhower famously wrote to his brother Edgar Newton Eisenhower that "should any political party attempt to abolish social security, unemployment insurance, and eliminate labor laws and farm programs, you would not hear of that party again . . . . There is a tiny splinter group, of course, that believes you can do these things," but "their number is negligible and they are stupid."[6]

In the late 20th century, we forgot what we had learned about capitalism. Perhaps "forgot" is the wrong verb. Persuaded is more apt, because for decades, across the midcentury, business leaders (and academics they supported) evangelized the American people into market fundamentalism. We were told that the lessons we had drawn from history were wrong or no longer applied, that we could trust "the free market" to solve our problems and meet our needs. Government was the problem, they insisted, not the solution. The solution was for government to "get out of the way," and "let the market do its magic."

We were told this so many times that many of us—on both the right and the left, or at least the center left—forgot what we had learned earlier in the century about the social costs of capitalism. We supported politicians—again on both right and left—who weakened many of the laws and dismantled many of the programs that had been developed to address the problems that inadequately regulated markets had created. The result was not only an explosion of preventable suffering, but a threat to the foundations of our democracy.

THE BIG MYTH

The question of the appropriate role of government oversight versus the freedom of "the market" had arisen in early 20th-century debates over child labor and workplace accidents that maimed and killed large numbers of workers every year. Business leaders generally opposed laws to restrict child labor or implement workmen's compensation on the grounds that this was an inappropriate infringement of the freedom of businessmen to run their businesses as they saw fit, or, in the case of child labor, of the freedom of parents to decide what was right for their children. Despite business opposition, many states passed laws to limit child labor, and between 1908 and 1916 the federal government established a program of workmen's compensation.[7] But in the 1920s a new problem arose that struck at the heart of American capitalism itself: the failure of the private sector electricity market to supply electricity to rural customers.

By the 1920s, cities across America had been electrified, but rural areas had not been.[8] Rural customers wanted electricity as much as their urban counterparts—and many observers argued that they needed it more—but electrical utilities had neglected them. The reason was simple: the profit motive. As General Electric concluded in 1925, "the purchasing power of . . . 1.9 million [farmers] is too low to put them in the potential customer class."[9] Outside the United States, the situation was different. In many countries, electricity was viewed not as a commodity (like soybeans or pork bellies) to be bought and sold at a profit, but as a public good (like water or sewers) that demanded governance to ensure equitable distribution. The contrast in results was stark: By the 1920s, nearly 70% of northern European farmers had electricity, but fewer than 10% of U.S. farmers did.[10]

Gifford Pinchot, the Progressive Republican governor of Pennsylvania, launched an effort to engage government—in his case, the government of his state—in electricity distribution. He proposed a system of "Giant Power" in which the private sector would continue to generate electricity, but the state would oversee its distribution to ensure that all citizens received electric power at equitable prices.

In response, the National Electric Light Association (NELA), a trade group representing large utilities and manufacturers of generating equipment including General Electric and Westinghouse, organized a massive propaganda campaign to counter any suggestion that public management of electricity was desirable (much less necessary), to discredit the idea that the public sector could do anything more fairly or efficiently than the private sector, and to strengthen the American people's conviction that the private sector knew best. Anything other than complete private control of industry, they suggested, was socialistic and un-American.[11] When the Federal Trade Commission (FTC) held hearings on the subject a decade later, they concluded that NELA's effort was the greatest peacetime propaganda "campaign ever conducted by private interests in this country."[12]

NELA organized lecture series aimed at colleges and universities, civic clubs, Boy Scout troops, women's clubs, school assemblies, church congregations, and more. NELA employees and their contractors wrote editorials and letters, met with newspaper editors in cities around the country to persuade them of the industry perspective, and issued press releases and bulletins to provide fodder for articles with pro-industry slants.[13] The historian David Nye concluded that NELA spent up to a million dollars a year for at least several years in efforts to influence politicians, business and civic leaders, newspaper editors, and the public.[14] In current dollars that is about $15 million per year.[15] In the words of one observer, they employed "everything but sky-writing" to promote their message that markets knew best.[16]

Perhaps the most pernicious part of the NELA effort was a wide-ranging effort to influence what was taught in American schools and universities. NELA recruited experts-for-hire to produce competing studies and alternative "facts" about the relative costs of private and public electricity generation. They also recruited academics to rewrite textbooks to support the private electricity industry—including denying corruption charges and promulgating an ethical, trustworthy image—and pressured publishers to modify or withdraw textbooks that NELA found objectionable. Perhaps most important, they offered funding to schools, colleges, and universities—including emerging business schools—to develop courses and curricula designed to extol the benefits of laissez-faire capitalism, in part by arguing that anything else was a threat to individual freedom and the "American way of life." The expert-recruitment initiative was intended to undermine support for municipal electricity programs in the present; the other elements were intended to ensure the private electricity industry's future in the long run.

These NELA studies played a major role in public debate. Americans heard that independent academics had proved that public utilities could not generate electricity at lower cost than the private sector. It would be years before they learned that these studies had been commissioned by the electricity industry and that their authors were not at all independent.

NELA disbanded in the wake of the FTC hearings, but it soon regrouped under a new name: the Edison Electric Institute (which still exists today). More important, it established a template that was used by other trade organizations and business leaders: that you could use public relations and propaganda to convince the American people that markets worked where they had actually failed, that business was trustworthy even when it was corrupt, and that government was the problem, not the solution.

From the 1930s to the 1970s, variations on the NELA strategy were taken up by business groups and individual businessmen to fight the New Deal, to weaken protections for labor, and to argue for lower marginal income tax rates. The groups included powerful trade organizations such as the National Association of Manufacturers (NAM) and powerful Fortune 500 companies such as General Electric (GE) and Dupont. The individuals included Dupont executive Jasper Crane, a funder of the libertarian Foundation for Economic Education that proselytized libertarian ideals in American life. Crane also funded the neo-liberal Mt. Pelerin Society, and the "Free Market Project" at the University of Chicago, unapologetically designed to bolster the intellectual credentials of pro-market, antigovernment thinking.

For the most part, these efforts were not very successful, in part because the American people had seen what happened when the marketplace was left to businessmen to run.[17] But things began to change in the 1970s as memory faded, some regulations became legitimately outdated, and new circumstances challenged the Keynesian economic framework under which the United States (and most Western nations) had emerged from the Great Depression and achieved prosperity in the post-World War II years. These new conditions included something that most economists did not think could happen: stagflation, a stagnant economy characterized by high inflation and high unemployment. Business conservatives, led by the University of Chicago economist Milton Friedman, pointed to "Big Government" as the source of the problem and deregulation as the solution. When Jimmy Carter was elected president in 1976, one of the first things he did was to appoint a "deregulation czar."

While some parts of the American economy may have been overregulated, many of America's economic woes had largely exogenous causes, such as increasing competition from Europe and Asia, inflation caused by abandoning the gold standard, and the effect of rising oil prices from the Middle East. But the idea that "Big Government" was a key source of our problems had taken hold among Democrats and Republicans alike, and business conservatives saw another opportunity to persuade the American people to "trust the magic of the marketplace." When Ronald Reagan was elected president in 1980 on a pro-market, antigovernment platform, he was following the playbook that had been developed by mid-century businessmen. By the time Bill Clinton was elected in 1992, it had been embraced by many Democrats as well.

THE REPEAL OF GLASS–STEAGALL AND TELECOMMUNICATION DEREGULATION

Historical amnesia works in part by the simple process of forgetting: As the past recedes in our memories, its lessons recede as well. But it also occurs when problems are remedied, and people illogically conclude (or disingenuously claim) that the remedies put in place to address them are no longer needed. Such was the case with the repeal of the Banking Act of 1933, also known as Glass–Steagall, during the Clinton administration.

Glass–Steagall was one of the first reforms enacted when Franklin Roosevelt took office, designed to address the banking crisis and restore confidence in the banking system. The law prohibited some of the speculative practices that had contributed to the crash of 1929 by separating commercial banking from investment banking. It also created the Federal Deposit Insurance Corporation (FDIC) to protect depositors when banks failed. The Act was partially repealed by the passage of the 1999 Gramm–Leach–Bliley Act, which ended the restricted affiliations between banks and securities firms and permitted the rise of giant financial companies that combined investment, commercial, consumer, and mortgage banking with insurance of all kinds. Advocates of Gramm–Leach–Bliley argued that the stability of the system since 1933 showed that the restrictions were no longer needed. But the financial crisis of 2008 disproved that claim. With key guardrails removed, it took less than a decade for the system to crash.

As bad as the bank deregulation of the late 1990s was, an arguably worse development was the deregulation of telecommunications. The 1996 Telecommunications Act eliminated ownership limitations on all kinds of media. Just as the repeal of Glass–Steagall permitted the emergence of massive financial conglomerates, telecommunications deregulation permitted the emergence of massive media monopolies, which threatened the foundations of American democracy.

Telecommunication deregulation began in the 1980s under the influence of Ronald Reagan. A key element was the repeal of the Fairness Doctrine, which had been implemented in 1949 to limit bias in electronic media. As enforced by the Federal Communications Commission (FCC) and upheld in 1969 by the U.S. Supreme Court, the doctrine established that a broadcast license was a privilege that carried obligations toward fairness and objectivity. In its 1969 decision, the high court had affirmed that a person who had been attacked on a radio program had the right to an on-air response, and that the First Amendment did not prohibit that claim. But Reagan considered it an inappropriate "encroachment" on business, and under his appointed chair, the FCC repealed the doctrine, asserting that it was antithetical to the public interest and violated the First Amendment. In 1987, Congress attempted to reinstate the doctrine via the Fairness in Broadcasting Act, but Reagan vetoed the bill.[18]

Reagan's veto came on the heels of the Cable Communications Policy Act of 1984, which had deregulated the cable television industry. The bill had been justified on the grounds that cable television would open up new avenues for competition, so the strict regulation of the past was no longer needed. However, within a few years, it was evident that the expected increase in competition had not occurred, while municipalities had lost their ability to regulate now-skyrocketing rates. Still, the idea that regulation was "stifling competition" had taken hold. Within a few years cable was overhauled again—this time, under a Democratic administration.[19]

The 1996 Telecommunications Act was designed to provide a framework for a new technological era that now included not just cable television, but also cell phones and the Internet. The goal was to improve service and lower prices by encouraging competition, "to let any communications business compete in any market against any other." The FCC would play its role by "creating fair rules for this new era of competition."[20] Technological change made it obvious that at least some rethinking of existing frameworks was in order, and the bill was supremely popular: It passed the House 414–6 and the Senate 91–5. (Among the few who opposed it were Senator John McCain and then-Representative Bernie Sanders.)

The new law promised a lot. It would "promote competition and reduce regulation in order to secure lower prices and higher quality services . . . and encourage the rapid deployment of new telecommunications."[21] President Clinton hailed it as not only providing "the key to opening new markets and new opportunities," but also inaugurating the next episode in technological modernity. "It will help connect every classroom in America to the information superhighway by the end of the decade," while still protecting "consumers by regulating the remaining monopolies for a time and by providing a roadmap for deregulation in the future."[22] Many consumer groups and even some economists were skeptical, because the bill offered few provisions to prevent monopolization, but the administration claimed there was no need to fear.[23]

Clinton was wrong about what future technology would bring; the Internet would quickly be duopolized by two companies: Google and Microsoft.[24] The same would prove true of social media, as Facebook—founded in 2004—took over the world it helped to create.[25] The tendency toward monopolization had not gone away. On the contrary, by 2020 it had become routine to say that monopoly was in the tech industry's "DNA."[26] As for the promised Internet superhighway, come the 21st century the United States had some of the highest-priced broadband and the slowest speeds of any wealthy nation.[27] Like electricity a century before, high-speed Internet stalled before reaching rural America, because the profit potential in rural markets was too meager.[28] While the goals of expanding service and decreasing cost were good ones, the costs in terms of media consolidation and polarization were enormous. They were not just financial. They were cultural and political, too.

In the early days of cable television, broadcast networks were not permitted to own cable channels. In 1992, the FCC relaxed the restrictions.[29] This decision, elevated into statute in the 1996 Telecommunications Act, effectively consolidated broadcast, film, and cable channels into a single visual-media content market.[30] It also enabled the creation of multimedia empires, such as Time Warner and Fox News, which would soon control huge segments of the media market.[31] Before telecom deregulation, such megamedia conglomerates would have been illegal.

Similar consolidation occurred in radio. According to an analysis published in 2003, between 1996 and 1998, 4,000 of the nation's 11,000 radio stations changed hands. In that year, the newly consolidated Clear Channel—a merger of Clear Channel Communications and Jacor Communications—was operating 1,225 stations; before the Act, it had 36.[32]

Since the 1990s, media deregulation has permitted the growth of overtly partisan, propagandistic news networks that have helped to create, sustain, and aggravate societal divisions.[33] The most obvious example is Fox News, which repeatedly advanced the false claim that Joe Biden did not win the 2020 presidential election, and paid a settlement of nearly $800 million after the Dominion Corporation sued Fox News for repeated on-air claims that the company had "rigged" its voting machines against Donald Trump.[34]

A less well-known but perhaps even more consequential conglomerate is the Sinclair Broadcast Group, which by 2020 owned 200 television stations.[35] Sinclair describes itself as "one of the largest and most diversified television broadcasting companies in the country," but from a political standpoint it is anything but diverse. *The New York Times* has described it as a "conservative TV giant" that uses its network "to advance a mostly right-leaning agenda."[36] In 2017, *Politico* reported that Donald Trump's son-in-law Jared Kushner boasted "that the campaign had struck a deal with Sinclair to secure better coverage in the states where they needed spots most."[37] Michael Copps, a former FCC chairman appointed by George W. Bush, has described Sinclair as "the most dangerous company most people have never heard of."[38]

Conservatives may point to the counter-partisanship of MSNBC or other outlets, but that is hardly a defense, as partisanship on either side contributes to information polarization that can reinforce political and social division.[39] Even if liberals owned as many radio and television stations as conservatives did, that would not be a good situation. But liberals do not own as many stations. Right- and Left-wing media may be opposite in their political direction, but they are anything but equal in magnitude and reach; overtly Right-wing radio and television stations far outnumber overtly Left-wing ones.

Why did an act intended to increase competition, and with it consumer choice, end up decreasing both? This is not a matter of drift: Consolidation, particularly in radio, began as soon as the ink on the bill was dry. The obvious answer is that the act contained no provision to stop consolidation.[40] A cynic might conclude this was the intent, but the historical context suggests something a bit less cynical but more unnerving: That even liberal and moderate Democrats had been persuaded that all that the government needed to do was stand back and let markets do their magic.

THE HIGH COST OF THE FREE MARKET

Media consolidation is not the only adverse consequence of the weakening of public support for democratic responses to market failure. Across America, we face a variety of problems–from a lack of affordable housing in major American cities to the opioid crisis— that arise at least in part from an excessive faith in self-interest and in markets as an expression of that self-interest, coupled with an excessive skepticism of government. The most obvious one is climate change, which Nicholas Stern, the former chief economist of the World Bank, has called the "greatest and most wide-ranging market failure" ever seen.[41]

Climate change is a market failure, because markets have created a problem that they have proved unable to solve. A perfectly legal everyday commercial activity—burning fossil fuels—is imposing enormous costs: in coastal flooding, hurricanes, cyclones, and wildfires that are more damaging than they would otherwise be; in public health; in biodiversity loss; and in threatening to dislocate tens or even hundreds of millions of people around the globe. As one economist has written, carbon pollution is "free to emit but has costly consequences."[42] Climate change is also textbook environmental injustice, as poor people are disproportionately bearing the brunt of a problem created primarily by the rich.

COVID-19 pandemic mortality can also be partly understood as a consequence of the story told here. America was underprepared for a major pandemic, in part because of decreased commitments over the past decades to public health,[43] and because the steps necessary to avoid the worst effects of an emergent disease—stockpiling supplies, educating people about hand washing and social distancing, developing accurate tests and implementing them equitably, and sustaining the research infrastructure that can kick in to develop a vaccine—are not readily undertaken by the private sector. There's not much of a business case for stockpiling a billion face masks.[44] Nor can we rely on the private sector to step up when a new virus emerges, because by then it is too late. The "just-in-time" supply model that dominates in business is efficient for many purposes, but it does not work in the face of a pandemic.[45]

The United States was also slower than we should have been to respond. As the scope and scale of the COVID-19 crisis became clear, other countries did a better job of implementing public health precautions that were difficult to implement here because of resistance to "Big Government." And when a safe and effective vaccine became available—through an effective public-private partnership—millions of Americans refused it because they distrusted "The Government." These Americans were not randomly distributed across the political landscape; the lion's share were political conservatives.

Arguably all the serious crises facing America today—climate, housing, opioids, health care affordability, income inequality—involve market failure and inadequate governance. Some of them—for example the opioid and climate crises—were created by inadequately regulated markets. Others involve a more complex mix of poorly functioning markets and regulations that serve too narrow interests (e.g. housing, health care). All cry out for better, stronger, clearer governance to solve problems that markets have demonstrated themselves unable to solve. Perhaps what we need is "guidez-faire": A form of capitalism in which government more actively combats corruption, remedies market failure, and redresses the social inequities that history has proven capitalism inevitably creates.[46]

THE CASE FOR THE VISIBLE HAND OF GOVERNANCE

As Americans rallied around Franklin Roosevelt—electing him to the presidency four times—business leaders sought to undermine support for the New Deal by shifting attention away from the business failures that had inspired it, and encouraging Americans to focus their anxieties on the allegedly impending threats of "Big Government." That was a neat rhetorical trick, for it enabled them to displace crucial political, economic, and moral questions into a fight over the size of government. That trick exacerbated our differences, as the American political conversation shifted from what we wanted government to do for us to whether government should even be involved, and it has contributed to our current crisis of governance, where one of our two major political parties threatens to shut down the federal government simply on the grounds that it is too big. The urgent question today is not the size of our government. Rather, it is the same question that preoccupied our nation's founders: What is the purpose of government and how best does it represent the will and needs of the governed?

American government is not, in fact, particularly big. One way to measure the size of a government is by its spending as a proportion of GDP. In recent decades, total U.S. federal government spending, excluding the national debt, has hovered around 20 to 25% of GDP. In contrast, the European Union nations have on average spent 35 to 40% of GDP.[47] As a share of national GDP, U.S. government spending in the past decades has looked more like that of a poor or developing nation than the wealthy, long-industrialized one that we are.

Moreover, there's little evidence that "small government" yields better economic outcomes. As policy analyst Jeff Madrick concluded in his 2008 book *The Case for Big Government*, "History offers no lesson about the values of minimal government . . . To the contrary, the evidence shows that government typically contributed vitally to growth."[48] That was true in the past and remains true today. Veteran journalist E. J. Dionne concludes that history has demonstrated both the need for "regular fine-tuning to a market system . . . and adjustments to spread the riches it produces more fairly."[49] But it's more than fine-tuning. The histories of the Internet, the interstate highway system, and rural electrification are histories of government taking a leading role where the market did not.

Smaller government does not produce better social outcomes, either. It may not be the job of government to make us happy, but it is the job of government to facilitate the conditions that help us to pursue happiness, and Americans are a lot less happy than people in other wealthy countries. Despite our exceptional wealth, the United States consistently falls outside the top 10 of the world's happiest nations, typically ranking between fifteenth and twentieth.[50] Nor are we particularly healthy: The United States ranks forty-third in the world in male life expectancy, trailing not only other wealthy countries, but even relatively poorer nations including Albania, Thailand, and China.[51]

A key part of the market fundamentalist claim is that small government enhances democracy. But does it? Business leaders and conservative thinkers in the 20th century persuaded us to worry about "Big Government" by posing it as a threat to individual freedom, but if we look again at the European Union nations—where government is by most measures bigger than in the United States—they are all at least as democratic as the United States, if not more so. The *Economist*'s Democracy Index 2022 placed the United States at 26, behind all the European social democracies, as well as Japan, South Korea, Uruguay, Costa Rica, and post-Pinochet Chile.[52]

Some conservative economists have conceded this point. Historian Nancy MacLean highlights the work of Professor Tyler Cowen, Holbert L. Harris Chair of Economics at George Mason University and recipient of extensive funding from Charles Koch. In 2000, Cowen surveyed the relationship between economic freedom and democracy and concluded "that 'the freest countries [defining freedom as economic liberty] have not generally been democratic,' with Chile under General Pinochet as 'the most successful' case in point."[53] At least by the end of the 20th century, if not before, leading advocates of market fundamentalism knew that their core argument—that economic freedom protected political freedom—was simply not true.

In recent years, the Right-wing attack on government has not been limited to the federal government: It has extended to attacking corporate investing principles that take social and environmental concerns into account, to states that instituted mask mandates during the COVID-19 pandemics, and to cities and towns that have sought to ban single-use plastics. These attacks underscore the power of governance—on multitudes of levels—as the expression of the will of the people, whether those people are shareholders in a corporation, consumers of particular products, or all the citizens of the United States.

NOTES

1. This chapter is adapted from Naomi Oreskes and Erik M. Conway, *The Big Myth: How American Business Taught Us to Loathe Government and Love the Free Market* (New York: Bloomsbury, 2023).

2. Adlai E. Stevenson, "The American Tradition and Its Implications for Law," *Fordham Law Review* 30, no. 3 (1962): 427, https://ir.lawnet.fordham.edu/cgi/viewcontent.cgi?article =1717&context=flr. The speech is mostly about the United Nations, and Stevenson was suggesting that in the few short years since its founding, the United States had already forgotten its commitment to it, and to the International Court of Justice.

3. See for example, evangelical leader Rick Warren: Rick Warren, "Fix the Problem, Not the Blame," *Rick's Daily Hope* (blog), 2016, https://www.idisciple.org/post/fix-the-problem-not-the-blame.

4. Stevenson, "The American Tradition and Its Implications for Law," 427.

5. On the fight for an 8-hour work day, see Robert Whaples, "Winning the Eight-Hour Day, 1909–1919," *The Journal of Economic History* 50, no. 2 (June 1990): 393–406, https://doi.org/10.1017/S0022050700036512.

6. Dwight D. Eisenhower, "Letter from Dwight D. Eisenhower to Edgar Newton Eisenhower," November 8, 1954, Teaching American History, https://teachingamericanhistory.org/document/letter-to-edgar-newton-eisenhower. See also discussions in Blanche Wiesen Cook, "The Reds and the Blacks," *Washington Post*, May 23, 1993, https://www.washingtonpost.com/archive/entertainment/books/1993/05/23/the-reds-and-the-blacks/d656c6f9-08f0-4ea0-8149-d515260d4aed and Timothy Rives, "Eisenhower, the Frontier, and the New Deal: Ike Considers America's Frontier Gone, Embraces, Adds to FDR's Legacy," *Prologue* (2015): 8–15, https://www.archives.gov/files/publications/prologue/2015/fall/ike-frontier.pdf.

7. "Annual Statistical Supplement, 2013—Workers' Compensation Program Description and Legislative History," Social Security Administration Research, Statistics, and Policy Analysis, n.d., https://www.ssa.gov/policy/docs/statcomps/supplement/2013/workerscomp.html.

8. Ruth Schwartz Cowan argues that many of these appliances did not save labor, but just changed its character. Ruth Schwartz Cowan, *More Work for Mother: The Ironies of Household Technology from the Open Hearth to the Microwave* (New York: Basic Books, 1985).

9. David E. Nye, *Electrifying America: Social Meanings of a New Technology, 1880–1940* (Cambridge, MA: MIT University Press, 1990), 297.

10. Nye, *Electrifying America*. The British model remained decentralized and unstandardized, in part because of tension between the Labor and Conservative parties over centralization. On views of electricity in countries other than the United States at that time, see Harold Evans, "The World's Experience with Electrification," *Annals of the American Academy of Political and Social Science* 118 (1925): 30–42. On the percentage of farmers with electricity, see also Sarah Phillips, *This Land, This Nation: Conservation, Rural America, and the New Deal* (Cambridge: Cambridge University Press, 2007), 26.

11. Ernest Gruening, *The Public Pays: A Study of Power Propaganda* (New York: Vanguard Press, 1931); Nye, *Electrifying America*.

12. Gruening, *The Public Pays*, xi.

13. Gruening, *The Public Pays*, 180.

14. Nye, *Electrifying America*, 340.

15. CPI Inflation Calculator, https://www.in2013dollars.com/us/inflation/1945?amount =1000000.

16. Gruening, *The Public Pays*, 211. See also Judson King, *The Challenge of the Power Investigation to American Educators: Address to the American Political Science Association Convention* (National Popular Government League, 1929). Gruening was the governor of the Alaska Territory from 1939 until 1953 and a U.S. senator from Alaska from 1959 (after Alaska became a state) until 1969.

17. A notable exception was the passage of the Taft–Hartley Act (1947), designed to weaken protections for organized labor, for which the National Association of Manufacturers and other business groups lobbied hard.

18. Victor Pickard, "The Strange Life and Death of the Fairness Doctrine: Tracing the Decline of Positive Freedoms in American Policy Discourse," *International Journal of Communication*, 12 (2018): 3434–53.

19. Jennifer Holt, *Empires of Entertainment: Media Industries and the Politics of Deregulation, 1980–1996* (New Brunswick, NJ: Rutgers University Press, 2011), 66; and John M. Myers and Daniel P. Schuering, "Cable Television Franchise Renewals: A Primer," *Illinois Municipal Review*, January 1991, 21–22 https://www.lib.niu.edu/1991/im910121.html.

20. "Telecommunications Act of 1996," Federal Communications Commission, June 20, 2013, https://www.fcc.gov/general/telecommunications-act-1996.

21. Telecommunications Act of 1996, Pub. LA. No. 104–104, 110 Stat. 56 (1996).

22. David McCabe, "Bill Clinton's Telecom Law: Twenty Years Later," *The Hill*, February 7, 2016, https://thehill.com/policy/technology/268459-bill-clintons-telecom-law-twenty-years-later.

23. Manfred B. Steger and Ravi K. Roy, *Neoliberalism: A Very Short Introduction* (Oxford: Oxford University Press, 2010), 62–63.

24. Robert W. McChesney, *Digital Disconnect: How Capitalism Is Turning the Internet Against Democracy*, Illustrated edition (New York: The New Press, 2013).

25. Fortune 500, "Facebook Company Profile," *Fortune*, December 30, 2020, https://fortune.com/company/facebook/fortune500.

26. For example, A. O. Scott, "The Oscars Are a Mess. Let's Make Them Messier," *New York Times*, January 27, 2021, https://www.nytimes.com/2021/01/27/movies/oscars-2021-changes.html.

27. Robert B. Reich, *Saving Capitalism: For the Many, Not the Few* (New York: Knopf, 2015), 31.

28. Natalie Campisi, "Millions of Americans Are Still Missing Out on Broadband Access and Leaving Money on the Table—Here's Why," *Forbes*, May 26, 2023, https://www.forbes.com/advisor/personal-finance/millions-lack-broadband-access.

29. Holt, *Empires of Entertainment*, 136.

30. Holt, *Empires of Entertainment*, chapter 6.

31. Talia Lakritz, "14 Companies You Didn't Realize Disney Owns," *Insider*, January 28, 2020. https://www.insider.com/companies-disney-owns. See also "Disney End the Historic 20th Century Fox Brand," *BBC News*, Aug 12, 2020, https://www.bbc.com/news/business-53747270; Michael Zhang, "Disney to Buy National Geographic in $52 Billion Deal for Fox," *PetaPixel*, December 15, 2017, https://petapixel.com/2017/12/15/disney-buy-national-geographic-part-52-billion-deal-fox.

32. Gregory M. Prindle, "No Competition: How Radio Consolidation Has Diminished Diversity and Sacrificed Localism," *Fordham Intellectual Property, Media, and Entertainment Law Journal* 14, no. 1 (2003): 49; Andrew Chadwick, *The Hybrid Media System: Politics and Power* (Oxford: Oxford University Press, 2013); Robert Britt Horwitz, *The Irony of Regulatory Reform: The Deregulation of American Telecommunications* (Oxford: Oxford University Press, 1991); and McChesney, *Digital Disconnect*.

33. For one discussion, see William M. Kunz, *Cultural Conglomerates: Consolidation in the Motion Picture and Television Industries* (Oxford: Rowman and Littlefield, 2007). On evidence that polarized media leads to polarized points of view, see Jonathan S. Morris, "The Fox News Factor," *Harvard International Journal of Press/Politics* 10, no. 3 (July 2005): 56–79; Gregory J. Martin and Ali Yurukoglu, "Bias in Cable News: Persuasion and Polarization," *American Economic Review* 107, no. 9 (September 2017): 2565–99.

34. Jane C. Timm, "Fox News and Dominion reach $787.5 million settlement in defamation lawsuit," NBC News, April 18, 2023, https://www.nbcnews.com/media/fox-news-settles-dominion-defamation-lawsuit-rcna80285.

35. Edmund Lee and Amie Tsang, "Tribune Ends Deal With Sinclair, Dashing Plan for Conservative TV Behemoth," *New York Times*, August 9, 2018, https://www.nytimes.com/2018/08/09/business/dealbook/sinclair-tribune-media.html; Gregory J. Martin and Josh McCrain, "Yes, Sinclair Broadcast Group Does Cut Local News, Increase National News and Tilt Its Stations Rightward," *Washington Post*, April 10, 2019, https://www.washingtonpost.com/news/monkey-cage/wp/2018/04/10/yes-sinclair-broadcast-group-does-cut-local-news-increase-national-news-and-tilt-its-stations-rightward; Gregory J. Martin and Joshua McCrain, "Local News and National Politics," *American Political Science Review* 113, no. 2 (May 2019): 372–84.

36. "Sinclair Broadcast Group—The Largest and Most Diversified Television Broadcasting Company in the Country Today," Sinclair Broadcast Group, accessed April 22, 2021, https://sbgi.net. On Sinclair's right-wing orientation: Cecilia Kang, Eric Lipton, and Sydney Ember, "How a Conservative TV Giant Is Ridding Itself of Regulation," *New York Times*, August 14, 2017, https://www.nytimes.com/2017/08/14/us/politics/how-a-conservative-tv-giant-is-ridding-itself-of-regulation.html; Sydney Ember, "Sinclair Requires TV Stations to Air Segments That Tilt to the Right," *New York Times*, May 13, 2017, https://www.nytimes.com/2017/05/12/business/media/sinclair-broadcast-komo-conservative-media.html.

37. Lucia Graves, "This is Sinclair, 'the Most Dangerous US Company You've Never Heard of,'" *Guardian*, August 17, 2017, http://www.theguardian.com/media/2017/aug/17/sinclair-news-media-fox-trump-white-house-circa-breitbart-news.

38. Graves, "This is Sinclair"; For Copps's full critique, see "Fmr. FCC Head: Sinclair Most Dangerous Media in US," *CNN*, https://www.cnn.com/videos/cnnmoney/2018/04/03/michael-copps-sinclair-broadcasting-dangerous-sot-ctn.cnn.

39. Alex Shephard, "The Problem With MSNBC Isn't That It's Too Liberal," *New Republic*, August 6, 2020, https://newrepublic.com/article/158824/problem-msnbc-isnt-its-liberal; Fox has far more viewers than MSNBC: Amy Watson, "Top Cable News Networks U.S. 2020, by Number of Viewers," *Statista*, Feb 5, 2021, https://www.statista.com/statistics/373814/cable-news-network-viewership-usa; see also Anne Nelson, *Shadow Network: Media, Money, and the Secret Hub of the Radical Right* (New York: Bloomsbury Publishing, 2019), 46; Adam Piore, "A Higher Frequency," *Mother Jones*, December 2005, https://www.motherjones.com/politics/2005/12/higher-frequency.

40. The 1996 act attempted to both regulate and deregulate content. It included the Communications Decency Act, which would have restricted obscene content like pornography, but it was struck down by the Supreme Court on First Amendment grounds, but it also included Section 230 (which has become a hot-button issue in recent years), which says Internet Service Providers (ISPs) and other platforms are not responsible for the content their users publish. Sara L. Zeigler, "Communications Decency Act and Section 2030 (1996)," First Amendment Encyclopedia, https://www.mtsu.edu/first-amendment/article/1070/communications-decency-act-of-1996.

41. Nicholas Stern, *The Economics of Climate Change: The Stern Review* (Cambridge: Cambridge University Press, 2006).

42. Conny Olovsson, "The CO2 Market Failure: It's Free to Emit but Has Costly Consequences," *LSE Business Review* (blog), October 15, 2020, https://blogs.lse.ac.uk/businessreview/2020/10/15/the-co2-market-failure-its-free-to-emit-but-has-costly-consequences.

43. Y. Natalia Alfonso et al., "US Public Health Neglected: Flat or Declining Spending Left States Ill Equipped to Respond to COVID-19" *Health Affairs* 40, no. 4 (March 25, 2021). https://www.healthaffairs.org/doi/abs/10.1377/hlthaff.2020.01084.

44. Naomi Oreskes and Erik M. Conway, "The True Cost of the 'Free' Market," *TIME*, February 28, 2023, https://time.com/6258540/true-cost-of-the-free-market. See also Yuki Noguchi, "Not Enough Face Masks Are Made in America to Deal With Coronavirus," *NPR,* March 5, 2020, https://www.npr.org/sections/health-shots/2020/03/05/811387424/face-masks-not-enough-are-made-in-america-to-deal-with-coronavirus.

45. Nicholas Kulish, Sarah Kliff, and Jessica Silver-Greenberg, "The U.S. Tried to Build a New Fleet of Ventilators. The Mission Failed," *New York Times*, March 29, 2020, https://www.nytimes.com/2020/03/29/business/coronavirus-us-ventilator-shortage.html.

46. Thomas Piketty, *Capital in the Twenty-first Century* (Cambridge: Belknap/Harvard University Press, 2017).

47. Santiago Herrera and Gaobo Pang, *Efficiency of Public Spending in Developing Countries: An Efficiency Frontier Approach Vol. 1, 2 & 3*, Policy Research Working Papers, The World Bank, 2005, https://doi.org/10.1596/1813-9450-3645; "Central government expenditure as share of GDP, 1972 to 2022," Our World in Data, n.d., https://ourworldindata.org/grapher/total-gov-expenditure-gdp-wdi?tab=chart&country=USA~PAN~PER~BTN~CAN~DNK~European +Union~DEU~FRA. Of the "big three" countries that first industrialized—the United Kingdom, Germany, and the United States—the United States spends the least. Public spending in all three countries saw a huge spike during World War II, dropped back when the war ended, and then began a steady climb. Spending in the UK dropped dramatically during the years when Margaret Thatcher was prime minister, in part as a result of the influence of conservative economists, who blamed stagflation on this rise in public spending. Public spending may have been too high, but it was probably not a major factor in stagflation; a more likely explanation is that the economies were in their down cycle, and then inflation was triggered by the exogenous shock of dramatically increased oil prices. See Jeff Madrick, *The Case for Big Government* (Princeton, NJ: Princeton University Press, 2008), 6.

48. Madrick, *The Case for Big Government*, xv.

49. E. J. Dionne Jr., *Why the Right Went Wrong: Conservatism—from Goldwater to Trump and Beyond* (New York: Simon & Schuster, 2016), 444. Dionne's comment confirms an observation by political scientist Jonathan Schlefer, cited by Binyamin Appelbaum, "Cambridge, England, saw capitalism as inherently troubled; Cambridge, Massachusetts, came to see capitalism as merely in need of fine-tuning." *The Economists' Hour: False Prophets, Free Markets, and the Fracture of Society*, (New York: Little, Brown and Company), 17 2019.

50. Laura Begley Bloom, "The 20 Happiest Countries in the World in 2021 (Guess Where the U.S. Is Ranked?)," *Forbes*, March 19, 2021, https://www.forbes.com/sites/laurabegleybloom/2021/03/19/the-20-happiest-countries-in-the-world-in-2021/?sh=308a85c970a0.

51. "Average Life Expectancy by Country," Worlddata.Info, n.d., https://www.worlddata.info/life-expectancy.php.

52. "Global Democracy Has Another Bad Year," *The Economist*, January 22, 2020, https://www.economist.com/graphic-detail/2020/01/22/global-democracy-has-another-bad-year. For 2022 see Martin Armstrong, "The Democracy Index," Armstrong Economics, February 17, 2022, https://www.armstrongeconomics.com/international-news/politics/the-democracy-index.

53. Nancy MacLean, "Since we are greatly outnumbered," in *The Disinformation Age: Politics, Technology, and Disruptive Communication in the United States,* eds. W. Lance Bennett and Steven Livingston (Cambridge: Cambridge University Press, 2020), 120, https://doi.org/10.1017/9781108914628.

CHAPTER 4

Worker-Centered and Race-Conscious Policies Are Essential for Equity and Economic Justice

Valerie Wilson and Adewale Maye

The Kerner Commission outlined significant frustrations and economic threats confronting Black Americans. These revelations aligned with entrenched systemic discrimination in the labor market affecting unemployment, wages, equal opportunity, and bargaining power of Black workers. Despite explicit recommendations to promote racial equity in these areas, the nation has failed to consistently meet the conditions necessary to fully achieve economic justice for Black Americans. Consequently, Black workers' wages remain behind white workers', Black unemployment remains twice as high as white unemployment, and critical efforts to fight discrimination have been underfunded or rolled back by the courts. This chapter explores trends related to four specific worker-centered recommendations of the commission:

1. increasing the minimum wage and widening its coverage,
2. creating 1 million jobs in both the public and private sectors within 3 years,
3. strengthening federal, state, and local efforts to ensure equal opportunity, and
4. intensifying efforts on behalf of the Department of Labor to secure commitments from unions to encourage [Black] membership.

TRENDS

Minimum Wage

Minimum wage policy has long influenced the Black–white wage gap. Historically, the lack of coverage for occupations that were disproportionately held by Black men and women unjustly suppressed the wages of Black workers. More recently, the impact has come through a failure to increase the federal minimum wage over time.[1]

The Fair Labor Standards Act (FLSA) of 1938, the legislative framework governing minimum wage policies, was initially crafted to broaden overtime coverage and establish a baseline wage for workers. The FLSA played a pivotal role in shaping labor standards; however, it exempted certain industries from the minimum wage requirement—many of which employed a large share of Black workers.[2] The exclusion of those sectors from minimum wage regulations had a direct impact on the economic well-being of Black workers, leaving them exposed to the risk of having their wages unjustly withheld and enduring extended work hours without proper overtime compensation.[3]

When the FLSA was amended in 1966 and 1974, coverage of the labor force was expanded to include agriculture, schools, nursing homes, and restaurants. Black workers disproportionately employed in these sectors benefited from these expansions.[4] However, the introduction of a tipped minimum wage and the failure to adjust the minimum wage adequately to keep pace with inflation have contributed to wage stagnation and deepening racial wage disparities.

The most recent increase in the federal minimum wage was nearly 15 years ago, on July 24, 2009, when it was set at $7.25 an hour. As shown in Figure 4.1, after adjusting for inflation (in 2023 dollars), the real value of the federal minimum wage ($10.05) is now 39% less than its highest value ($11.82) in 1968.

Since Black workers are overrepresented in low-wage occupations, they remain disproportionately affected by the failure of federal policymakers to pass new minimum wage legislation. In fact, a larger share of Black workers than white workers earn well below the most recently proposed minimum wage threshold of $17 an hour, as illustrated in Figure 4.2. The notable decline in the share of Black workers earning less than $17 an hour between 2015 and 2019 can likely be attributed to a combination of the tightening labor market and progressive state and local policies that have raised their respective minimum wages. While these factors contributed to an overall improvement in the earnings of Black workers, without a higher federal minimum wage, many Black workers living in jurisdictions with less progressive state or local minimum wage policies—particularly in Southern states where a large share of the Black population resides—are left behind.

In the absence of an increase in the federal minimum wage since 2009, a tighter labor market contributed to faster hourly wage growth among workers at the lower end of the wage distribution between 2019 and 2022. For example, as shown in Figure 4.3, the 10th-percentile real hourly wage demonstrated a notable increase of 9.0% over the 3-year span. The rapid rate of economic recovery that contributed to falling rates of unemployment and rising wages during 2021 and 2022 was the result of a robust economic policy response to the COVID-19 pandemic recession. This included broadening unemployment insurance, expanding child tax credits, disbursal of economic impact payments, and funding for states and localities.[5]

This example underscores the critical relationship among policy, a strong labor market, and improved outcomes for lower-wage workers. The observed growth not only reflects the increased leverage of workers but also highlights the potential for reducing wage inequality and increasing economic security among marginalized workers. In the next section, we examine the impact of macroeconomic conditions, particularly job growth, on the employment outcomes of Black workers.

Figure 4.1. Inflation-Adjusted Value of the Federal Minimum Wage Each Time It Has Been Increased

Year Effective	Minimum Wage (nominal)	Inflation-Adjusted Value of Minimum Wage (2023$)
1967	$1.40	$10.64
1968	$1.60	$11.82
1974	$2.00	$10.68
1975	$2.10	$10.51
1976	$2.30	$10.82
1978	$2.65	$11.15
1979	$2.90	$11.28
1980	$3.10	$10.85
1981	$3.35	$10.61
1990	$3.80	$8.25
1991	$4.25	$8.86
1996	$4.75	$8.65
1997	$5.15	$9.21
2007	$5.85	$8.38
2008	$6.55	$8.90
2009	$7.25	$10.05

Source: All values in September 2023 dollars, adjusted using the CPI-U in 2023 chained to the CPI-U-RS (1978–2022) and CPI-U-X1 (1967–1977) and CPI-U (1966 and before). Calculations by Ben Zipperer, Economic Policy Institute.

Figure 4.2. Share of Workers Earning Less Than $17/hour by Race and Ethnicity, Inflation-Adjusted

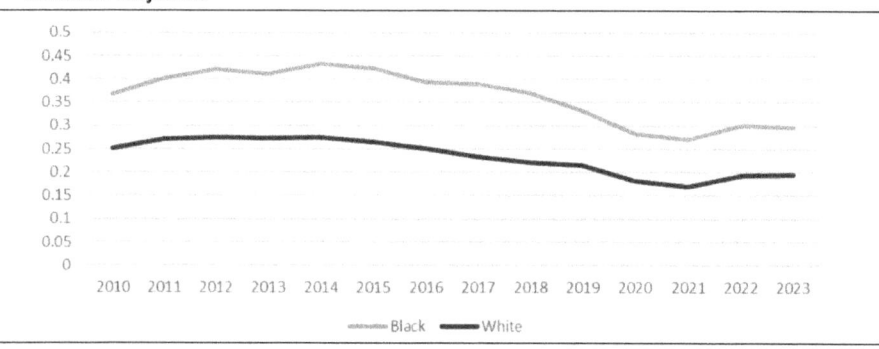

Note: Race and ethnicity categories are mutually exclusive (i.e., white non-Hispanic, Black non-Hispanic, and Hispanic any race).

Source: EPI analysis of the Current Population Survey Outgoing Rotation Group microdata, EPI Current Population Survey Extracts, Version 1.0.37 (2023), https://microdata.epi.org.

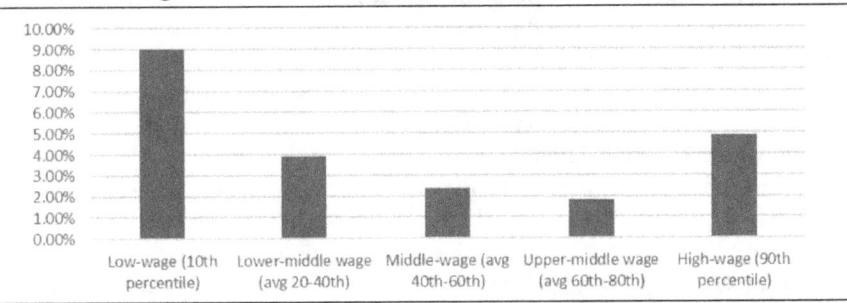

Figure 4.3. Real Wage Growth Across the Wage Distribution, 2019–2022

Low-wage (10th percentile)	Lower-middle wage (avg 20-40th)	Middle-wage (avg 40th-60th)	Upper-middle wage (avg 60th-80th)	High-wage (90th percentile)
~9.00%	~4.00%	~2.50%	~2.00%	~5.00%

Notes: Low-wage is represented by the 10th percentile and high-wage is represented by the 90th percentile. The lower-middle, middle, and upper-middle-wages are the averages of the 20th–40th percentiles, the 40th–60th percentiles, and the 60th–80th percentiles, respectively.

Source: EPI analysis of the Current Population Survey Outgoing Rotation Group microdata, EPI Current Population Survey Extracts, Version 1.0.37 (2023), https://microdata.epi.org.

Job Creation and Unemployment

The Kerner Commission's recommendation to create 1 million jobs in both the public and private sectors within 3 full years was an acknowledgement of the fact that solving the problem of chronically high unemployment in predominantly Black urban communities requires robust job creation to support genuinely tight labor markets and full employment. This recommendation was likely influenced by the fact that the unemployment rate for Black and other workers of color had exceeded 10% for 6 consecutive years between 1958 and 1963.[6] The average white unemployment rate over these years was 5.3%.[7]

During the 10-month recession that lasted from April 1960 to February 1961, the economy lost 1.26 million jobs and the unemployment rate rose from 5.2% in April 1960 to 6.9% in February 1961.[8] Comparatively, the average annual unemployment rate for Black and other non-white workers rose from 10.2% in 1960 to 12.4% in 1961, reflecting the fact that Black workers are often more likely to lose their jobs during an economic downturn than white workers.[9]

The economic expansion that followed continued through the end of the decade. Between February 1961 and December 1969, payroll employment grew by 33%, increasing at a rate of about 2 million jobs per year and resulting in an unemployment rate of 3.5% by December 1969.[10] During that period of economic expansion, public sector employment increased by 45.3% (440,000 jobs per year), faster than the 30.7% rate of job growth in the private sector (1.56 million jobs per year).[11] However, the Black (and other) unemployment rate remained much higher than the white unemployment rate throughout the decade. By 1969, the average unemployment rate among Black and other workers of color was 5.3%, compared to 3.1% for white workers.[12]

In the decades since the Kerner Commission issued its report (1970 to 2022), the labor market has grown at an average rate of 1.57 million jobs per year.[13] However, this rate of average job growth is slower than it would have been in the absence of economic downturns that were longer and more severe than the one experienced in the 1960s. While there has been at least one recession in each of the decades since the 1960s, during three of those decades—the 1970s (16 months), the 1980s (a "double-dip" recession lasting a total of 22 months), and the late 2000s Great Recession (18 months)—the economic downturn officially lasted more than a year.[14]

Such insufficient rates of job creation have resulted in higher average rates of unemployment as job growth has fallen behind the growth of the labor force. Between 1970 and 2022, the national unemployment rate averaged 6.2%—1.6 percentage points higher than the 4.6% average between 1947 and 1969.[15] Given the persistence of the 2-to-1 ratio between Black and white unemployment rates throughout history, higher rates of overall unemployment mean that Black unemployment rates have been at recessionary levels throughout most of the decades since the 1960s. In fact, the Black unemployment rate averaged 11.5% between 1970 and 2022, peaking at an annual high of 19.5% in 1983.[16] On a monthly basis, between 1972 and 2019, the Black unemployment rate had never fallen below 6% until a brief 6 months in 2019.[17] More recently, during the robust recovery from the COVID-19–triggered recession, the Black unemployment rate dipped below 6% again in April 2022, and has averaged 5.7% between April 2022 and November 2023.[18] These record low rates of Black unemployment in 2023 have been accompanied by a historically low percentage point difference between Black and white unemployment rates.

EEOC Budget and Staffing

The Kerner Commission was convened just a few short years after the passage of Title VII of the Civil Rights Act of 1964—legislation that prohibits discriminatory employment and pay practices based on race, color, sex, religion, or national origin. In addition to prohibiting discrimination, Title VII also established the Equal Employment Opportunity Commission (EEOC), the primary federal agency charged with enforcement of antidiscrimination laws. Even then, members of the Kerner Commission recognized that undoing centuries of racist, exploitive, and discriminatory employment practices would require more than just changing the law. Rather, eliminating the large and persistent racial disparities in employment and pay put in place and sustained through systemic discrimination would require vigilant and consistent enforcement of antidiscrimination laws. Thus, at a minimum, the federal, state, and local agencies charged with ensuring equal opportunity would need sufficient funding and staffing capacity to accomplish that goal.

Research on the racial wage gap reveals that the most notable period of narrowing of the Black–white wage gap occurred from the late 1960s through the 1970s and can be traced in part to the passage of important civil rights legislation,[19] combined with the 1960s economic expansion and active enforcement of antidiscrimination and affirmative action policy.[20] However, time has proven that continued progress toward eliminating racial disparities in pay and employment are not guaranteed without focused and intentional efforts to do so.

Worker-Centered and Race-Conscious Policies 41

Retrenchment on antidiscrimination policy over the following decade contributed to a marked widening of the Black–white wage gap during the 1980s.[21] As shown in Figure 4.4, the Black–white wage gap was larger in 2022 than it had been in 1979 despite considerable gains in educational attainment among Black workers over those years.[22] In 2022, the average hourly wage of Black workers was 25.7% less than that of white workers, compared to a gap of 17.3% in 1979. However, at either point in time, less than half of that difference could be explained by factors reasonably presumed to affect a worker's productivity or pay, including education, experience, or regional differences in the cost of living. After controlling for those factors, a gap of 13.2% remained in 2022. Further, one of the most troubling aspects of growing Black–white and Hispanic–white wage gaps over that period of time is the fact that they grew most among college-educated workers.[23]

With respect to employment, for almost 7 decades, national statistics have documented the fact that the average Black worker is roughly twice as likely to be unemployed as the average white worker. However, as recently as 2023, Black workers were not only more likely to be unemployed as similarly educated white workers but were often more likely to be unemployed than less-educated white workers (Figure 4.5). These statistics are consistent with field experiments revealing a pattern of discrimination experienced by Black job applicants that has remained constant over time.[24]

According to publicly reported data, although the number of charges filed with the EEOC has fluctuated over time—including a low of 61,331 in 2021 and a high of 99,992 in 2010—since 1992 (earliest year reported), the EEOC has received an average of over 83,000 charges a year.[25] While racial discrimination is not the sole basis for all those charges, at least a third of charges filed since 1992 included a claim of racial discrimination.[26] As shown in Figures 4.6 and 4.7, the EEOC's budget and staffing levels have been inconsistent over time. In only 13 of the last 43 years has the requested budget amount been provided as staffing levels have consistently declined. In 2022, the EEOC had 40% fewer staff than in 1980 (earliest year reported). Failure to adequately

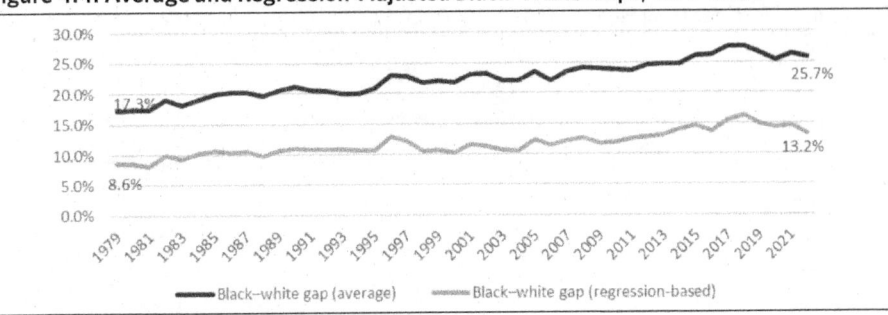

Figure 4.4. Average and Regression-Adjusted Black-White Gaps, 1979–2022

Note: Race and ethnicity categories are mutually exclusive (i.e., white non-Hispanic and Black non-Hispanic).

Source: Economic Policy Institute, State of Working America Data Library, [Black–white wage gap], 2023.

Figure 4.5. Unemployment Rates by Race and Education, 2023

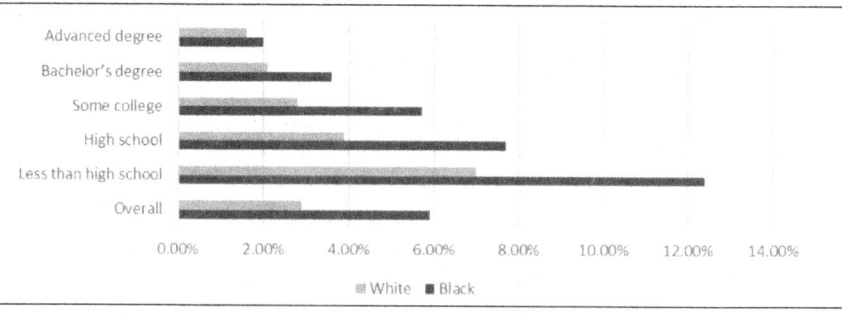

Note: Race and ethnicity categories are mutually exclusive (i.e., white non-Hispanic, Black non-Hispanic, and Hispanic any race). Educational categories are mutually exclusive and represent the highest education level attained for all individuals ages 16 and older.

Source: Economic Policy Institute, State of Working America Data Library, [Unemployment by race and education], 2023.

Figure 4.6. EEOC Budget History, 1980-2022

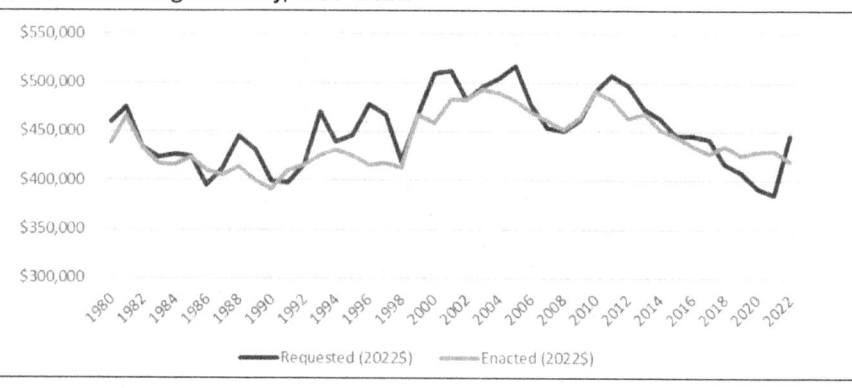

Source: "EEOC Budget and Staffing History, 1980 to Present," Equal Employment Opportunity Commission, https://www.eeoc.gov/eeoc-budget-and-staffing-history-1980-present.

Figure 4.7. EEOC Staffing History (FTE), 1980-2022

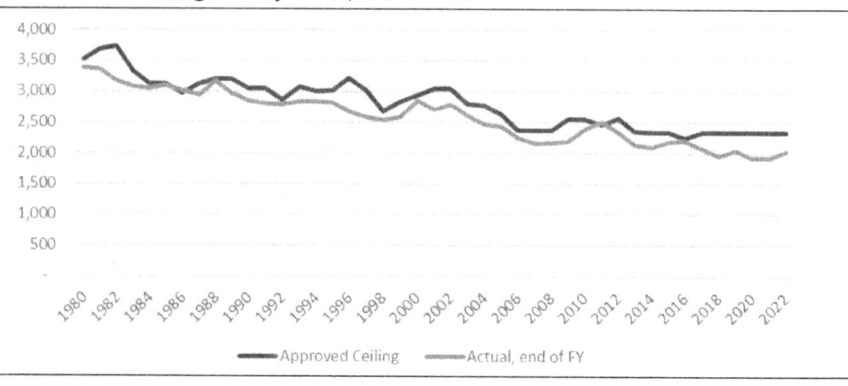

Source: "EEOC Budget and Staffing History, 1980 to Present," Equal Employment Opportunity Commission, https://www.eeoc.gov/eeoc-budget-and-staffing-history-1980-present.

fund and staff the EEOC means larger caseloads for investigators while limiting the agency's capacity to pursue valid charges or proactively challenge systemic discrimination.[27] This forces the agency to make difficult decisions about how to best utilize limited investigatory resources and can also significantly delay investigation and resolution of charges.[28]

The fact that labor market discrimination has persisted well beyond the passage of Title VII of the Civil Rights Act of 1964 and the establishment of the EEOC cannot be overlooked. A web of consciously and unconsciously biased practices in recruitment, salary structures, and promotional pathways continue to generate inequities and hinder the upward mobility and fair representation of Black workers in more lucrative and influential roles. Current enforcement mechanisms presume that employers will voluntarily comply with the law. But, when they don't, individual employees face the unfair burden of bearing most of the responsibility and risk associated with proving discrimination after the fact.

The Kerner Commission also prioritized equitable access to union membership as an additional means of providing Black workers a proactive countermeasure against employment and pay discrimination through collective bargaining and labor contracts. In the next section, we explore trends in union membership and representation.

Union Membership and Representation

The rise of income inequality in recent decades has been significantly influenced by the diminishing membership of labor unions. Unions, which play a crucial role in elevating wages, addressing income inequality, and minimizing racial economic disparities, have faced a decline in both membership and coverage since the 1980s.[29]

Historically, starting in the mid-1940s, there was a notable pattern where Black workers were more likely to be part of unions compared to their white counterparts. However, with declining rates of union coverage and membership, Black workers have seen reduced access to the benefits of unions, such as the union pay premium and enhanced job protections, that help to raise the wages of Black workers closer to those of their white counterparts.[30] The sharp decline in union coverage over the last several decades has greatly narrowed the union membership advantage once held by Black workers. Overall, this decline has eroded workers' collective bargaining power and suppressed wages.

Figure 4.8 shows the percentage of the workforce who are members of unions and/or covered by a collective bargaining agreement. In 2021, Black workers still led all other workers in union coverage at 12.6%. However, compared to earlier estimates, Black workers have seen a significant drop in union coverage, which hovered above 30% in the late 1970s and early 1980s. Throughout the 1980s, a period marked by the most pronounced decrease in union membership, antiunion rhetoric and actions were prominently on the rise.[31] That decade witnessed a significant shift in the political landscape, with government policies contributing to the substantial decline in union density, a trend that has had enduring repercussions on the entire working class, including the notable narrowing of the Black–white wage gap.

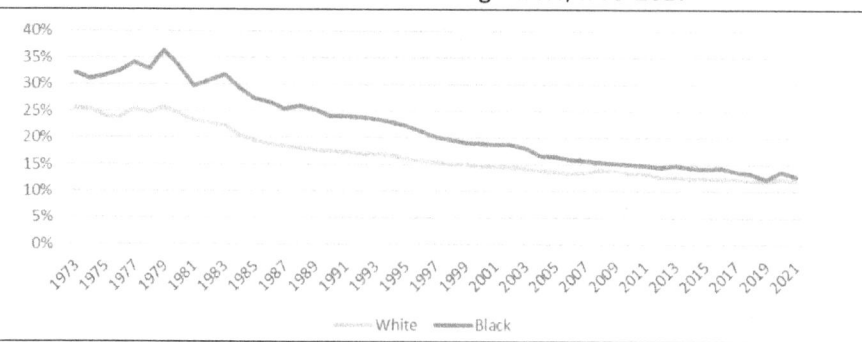

Figure 4.8. Black and White Workers' Union Coverage Rates, 1973-2021

Note: The union coverage rate shows the percentage of the workforce who are members of unions and/or covered by a collective bargaining agreement. Race and ethnicity categories are mutually exclusive (i.e., white non-Hispanic, Black non-Hispanic, and all others).

Source: Economic Policy Institute, "Union Coverage" (data set), State of Working America Data Library, last updated March 2023.

POLICY REMEDIES MOVING FORWARD

Since the release of the Kerner Commission report, substantive lasting change in the economic outcomes described in this chapter has been fleeting. These trends underscore the urgent need to employ the Commission's recommendations as a strategic playbook for advancing race-conscious policies and addressing persistent inequalities. Race-neutral policies have marginally mitigated the harm but have not redressed the systemic failures present within our economy. The following policy remedies lay a crucial foundation for making substantial investments in eliminating racial inequalities, achieving racial equity, and ensuring that our economy is one where all can thrive.

Raise the Minimum Wage

Raising the minimum wage to a fair and adequate wage level is crucial in elevating living standards and advancing economic justice for Black workers who have been disproportionately concentrated in low-wage occupations for generations. The latest policy aiming to raise the federal minimum wage is the Raise the Wage Act of 2023. This proposed legislation outlines a gradual increase in the federal minimum wage, reaching $17 per hour by the year 2028. Furthermore, the bill advocates for a phased approach to augment and eventually eliminate subminimum wages for categories such as tipped workers, employees with disabilities, and youth workers. This policy initiative aims to establish stronger wage parity among all individuals covered by the Fair Labor Standards Act, fostering a more equitable compensation framework. According to recent estimates, raising the federal minimum wage to $17 by the year 2028 would benefit approximately 30% of Black workers.[32]

Expand Funding and Staffing for the EEOC

The EEOC plays a central role in enforcing federal laws that prohibit discriminatory practices in hiring, pay, and promotional opportunities through its responsibilities to investigate, litigate, and remedy instances of workplace bias. The economic security of Black workers is closely tied to their ability to work in environments free from discrimination. An adequately funded and staffed EEOC can contribute significantly to creating a fair and inclusive labor market where all workers are protected from discriminatory practices. By expanding the EEOC's capacity to respond to the tens of thousands of discrimination, harassment, and retaliation charges they receive each year, we not only promote justice on an individual level but also create workplaces that are more equitable and supportive of diverse talent.

A stronger EEOC is instrumental in signaling the government's commitment to combating all forms of discrimination, advancing racial and gender equity, and promoting equal opportunities for all workers. It sends a powerful message that discriminatory practices will not be tolerated, and that the government is actively working to dismantle barriers that hinder economic justice for Black Americans and other marginalized groups.

Defend Affirmative Action

Policymakers must ensure that the spirit and intent of affirmative action is protected. In June 2023, the U.S. Supreme Court ruled against using race-based affirmative action in college admissions. This ruling sets a dangerous precedent for colleges that have used affirmative action as a tool for over 40 years to enhance racial diversity on their campuses and compensate for decades of both explicit and implicit race-based exclusion. Relying on other metrics in replacement of race-conscious admissions policies will leave colleges poorly equipped to achieve meaningful racial diversity on college campuses.[33]

While the recent Supreme Court decision specifically addresses race-based admissions in college, the relevance of affirmative action extends into the workplace where it has proven to be a valuable instrument in promoting diversity and extending opportunities to talented women and men of color. Moreover, when coupled with an adequately funded and staffed EEOC, the two enhance the nation's continued responsibility for addressing systemic inequalities and creating opportunities for historically marginalized and underrepresented groups within the economy.

Pass Legislation to Strengthen Workers' Rights to Join a Union

Black workers have long recognized that joining a union gives them a stronger, collective voice to advocate for better pay and benefits, training and promotional opportunities, and protections against discrimination and harassment. In a unionized workforce, labor contracts help create greater transparency and consistency through clearly defined policies and pay structures and provide workers with critical protections and recourse against exploitation or mistreatment. Thus, unions play a pivotal role in mitigating racial wage and wealth disparities.[34]

The proposed Protecting the Right to Organize (PRO) Act is instrumental in reinstating this fundamental right for workers. By facilitating a more streamlined process for union formation, ensuring the success of unions in negotiating initial contracts, and holding employers accountable for labor law violations, the PRO Act stands as a comprehensive solution. This legislation aims to empower workers, foster equitable economic conditions, and reinforce the significance of collective bargaining in shaping a fair and just workplace.

Pass Policies Geared Toward Maximizing Employment

Recent improvements in the labor market experiences of Black workers—both in absolute and relative terms—point to several things that work. First, given the unique circumstances behind the pandemic recession, the fact remains that the magnitude of job losses far exceeded those even of the Great Recession. The difference this time was that the policy response was at the scale of the problem, resulting in a much faster recovery for all demographic groups. Monetary policy has also proven to be a significant factor in limiting the duration of recessions and the economic harm suffered in marginalized communities. Moreover, a growing body of research shows that tight or high-pressure labor markets are critical to narrowing racial disparities in unemployment and wages.

Implementing policies aimed at maximizing employment and mitigating the adverse effects of economic downturns for Black workers is crucial in ensuring Black workers aren't disproportionately burdened by fluctuations within the economy. Job creation initiatives can create stable employment opportunities that not only contribute to economic growth but also insulate Black workers from the disproportionate impact of recessions. For example, a targeted federal program dedicated to subsidized employment holds significant potential for generating jobs and fostering economic growth in communities that have long experienced neglect. Such a program could play a pivotal role in addressing persistently high rates of unemployment in these marginalized areas.

This proposed federal initiative has the potential to break the cycle of joblessness and stimulate local economies by injecting much-needed resources into areas that have historically been overlooked. By focusing on communities facing chronic unemployment, the program would prioritize inclusivity and equity, striving to bridge the economic gaps that disproportionately affect Black workers. Additionally, subsidized employment initiatives have the dual benefit of not only putting people to work but also enhancing the skill sets of workers, contributing to long-term economic resilience.

By strategically directing resources to communities in need, policymakers can contribute to a more inclusive national economy, where the benefits of growth are shared by all, and systemic inequalities are addressed.

NOTES

1. Jasmine Payne-Patterson and Adewale Maye, "A History of the Federal Minimum Wage. 85 Years Later, the Minimum Wage is Far from Equitable," *Working Economics Blog* (Economic Policy Institute), August 31, 2023.

2. Payne-Patterson and Maye, "A History of the Federal Minimum Wage."

3. Payne-Patterson and Maye, "A History of the Federal Minimum Wage."

4. Ellora Derenoncourt, Claire Montialoux, and Kate Bahn, "Why Minimum Wages Are a Critical Tool for Achieving Racial Justice in the U.S. Labor Market," Washington Center for Equitable Growth, October 29, 2020.

5. Elise Gould and Katherine deCourcy, "State of Working America Wages 2022: Low-Wage Workers Have Seen Historically Fast Real Wage Growth in the Pandemic Business Cycle," Economic Policy Institute, March 23, 2023.

6. Current Population Survey (CPS), Bureau of Labor Statistics (BLS), discontinued unemployment rate series (LFU21000020), 1954–2002. While the BLS did not officially report an unemployment rate for Black workers alone until 1972, prior to that year, the race categories used were white and "non-white" or "Black and other." About 95% of the "Black and other" population in the years prior to 1972 identified as Black, making this the best approximation for the time.

7. CPS, Bureau of Labor Statistics.

8. Dates of recessions based on "US Business Cycle Expansions and Contractions," National Bureau of Economic Research, accessed December 11, 2023, https://www.nber.org/research/data/us-business-cycle-expansions-and-contractions. Job loss statistics based on author's analysis of Bureau of Labor Statistics' Current Employment Statistics public data series. Unemployment rates cited from Bureau of Labor Statistics' Current Population Survey public data.

9. CPS, Bureau of Labor Statistics.

10. National Bureau of Economic Research.

11. National Bureau of Economic Research.

12. CPS, Bureau of Labor Statistics.

13. Based on author's analysis of Bureau of Labor Statistics' Current Employment Statistics public data series.

14. "US Business Cycle Expansions and Contractions."

15. Based on author's analysis of Bureau of Labor Statistics' Current Population Survey public data. The earliest year available in this data series is 1947.

16. Based on author's analysis of Bureau of Labor Statistics' Current Population Survey public data. This average rate of Black unemployment is based on the "Black and other" data series for 1970 and 1971 (see note 6), and the Black alone estimates from 1972 onward.

17. Valerie Wilson and William Darity, Jr., "Understanding Black-white Disparities in Labor Market Outcomes Requires Models that Account for Persistent Discrimination and Unequal Bargaining Power," Economic Policy Institute, March 25, 2022.

18. Valerie Wilson, "Tight Labor Markets Are Essential to Reducing Racial Disparities in the Labor Market and Within the Purview of the Fed's Dual Mandate," *Journal of Policy Analysis and Management* 43, no. 1 (Winter 2024), https://doi.org/10.1002/pam.22545.

19. John Donohue and James Heckman, "Continuous vs. Episodic Change: The Impact of Civil Rights Policy on the Economic Status of Blacks," *Journal of Economic Literature* 29 (December 1991): 1603–43.

20. Charles L. Betsey, "Litigation of Employment Discrimination Under Title VII: The Case of African American Women," *American Economic Review* 84, no. 2 (1994): 98–102; Augustin K. Fosu, "Occupational Mobility of Black Women, 1958–1981: The Impact of Post-1964 Antidiscrimination Measures," *Industrial & Labor Relations Review* 45, no. 2 (1992): 281–94; James J. Heckman and Brook Payner, "Determining the Impact of Federal Antidiscrimination Policy on the Economic Status of Blacks: A Study of South Carolina," National Bureau of Economic Research Working Paper No. 2854 (1989).

21. Jonathan S. Leonard, "The Impact of Affirmative Action Regulation and Equal Employment Law on Black Employment," *Journal of Economic Perspectives* 4, no. 4 (1990): 47–63.

22. Leonard, "The Impact of Affirmative Action Regulation and Equal Employment Law of Black Employment," 17.

23. Valerie Wilson and William M. Rodgers III, "Black-White Wage Gaps Expand with Rising Wage Inequality," Economic Policy Institute (2016).

24. Lincoln Quillian et al., "Meta-Analysis of Field Experiments Shows No Change in Racial Discrimination in Hiring over Time," *PNAS Early Edition* (2017).

25. "Charge Statistics FY 1992 Through FY 1996," Equal Employment Opportunity Commission, https://www.eeoc.gov/data/charge-statistics-fy-1992-through-fy-1996; "Charge Statistics (Charges filed with EEOC) FY 1997 Through FY 2022," Equal Employment Opportunity Commission, https://www.eeoc.gov/data/charge-statistics-charges-filed-eeoc-fy-1997-through-fy-2022.

26. "Charge Statistics FY 1992 Through FY 1996" and "Charge Statistics (Charges filed with EEOC) FY 1997 Through FY 2022."

27. Jenny R. Yang and Jane Liu, "Strengthening Accountability for Discrimination: Confronting Fundamental Power Imbalances in the Employment Relationship," Economic Policy Institute (2021).

28. Yang and Liu, "Strengthening Accountability for Discrimination."

29. Josh Bivens et al. "Unions Promote Equity," Economic Policy Institute, July 31, 2023.

30. Adewale Maye, "Chasing the Dream: How policy has shaped racial economic disparities," Economic Policy Institute, August 1, 2023.

31. Maye, "Chasing the Dream."

32. "Why the U.S. Needs at Least a $17 minimum wage," Economic Policy Institute, July 31, 2023.

33. Adewale Maye, "The Supreme Court's ban on affirmative action means colleges will struggle to meet goals of diversity and equal opportunity," *Working Economics Blog*, Economic Policy Institute, June 29, 2023.

34. Maye, "The Supreme Court's ban on affirmative action means colleges will struggle to meet goals of diversity and equal opportunity," 29.

Education and Youth Development Policy

CHAPTER 5

The Long Quest for Equitable Educational Opportunity

Linda Darling-Hammond

> "Like a gardener trying to increase her fruits' growth merely by weighing them anew each day, we have measured and documented multiple test-score gaps, but we have never mounted a sustained effort to attend to the gaps in sustenance—in opportunities—that must be addressed before we can expect to see meaningful progress."—Carter and Welner, *Closing the Opportunity Gap*[1]

In 1967, in response to widespread civil unrest, President Lyndon Johnson appointed the National Advisory Commission on Civil Disorders (also known as the Kerner Commission) to examine racial division and disparities in the United States. In 1968, the Kerner Commission issued a report concluding that the nation was "moving toward two societies, one black, one white—separate and unequal." Today, more than 55 years after the report was issued, that prediction has not yet been disproved, as ongoing segregation coupled with concentrated poverty are still too often reinforced by disparities in school funding to reinforce educational inequality, locking millions of low-income students of color out of today's knowledge-based economy.

HOW PROGRESS CAN BE MADE

These conditions are not inevitable. The Kerner Report, along with massive civil rights activity during the 1960s, served as a call to action, and in fact, there was a noticeable reduction in educational inequality in the decade after its release, due to desegregation and school finance reform efforts, along with increased investments in urban and poor rural schools through the Great Society's War on Poverty. Childhood poverty was reduced by nearly half during the 1960s, from 27% to 14%. The Elementary and Secondary Education Act of 1965 targeted resources to communities with the most need, recognizing that where a child grows up should not determine where they end up. Employment and welfare supports reduced childhood poverty to levels about 60% of what they are today and greatly improved children's access to health care. Congress enacted the Emergency School Aid Act in 1972, which supported desegregation, the development of magnet schools, and other strategies to improve urban and poor rural schools. These efforts to level the playing field for children were supported by intensive investments in bringing and keeping talented individuals in teaching, improving teacher education, and investing in research and development.[2]

These investments paid off in measurable ways. By the mid-1970s, urban schools spent as much as suburban schools and paid their teachers as well, perennial teacher shortages had nearly ended, and gaps in educational attainment had closed substantially. Federally funded curriculum investments transformed teaching in many schools. Innovative schools flourished in many cities and achievement gaps in reading and mathematics shrank considerably. Financial aid for higher education was sharply increased, especially for need-based scholarships and loans. For a brief period in the mid-1970s, Black and Latino high school graduates attended college at the same rate as Whites—the only time this has ever occurred before or since.

The effects of equity-oriented policies were substantial for a generation of students. For example, in a study on students born between 1945 and 1970, Rucker Johnson found that graduation rates climbed by 2 percentage points for every year a Black student attended an integrated school.[3] A Black student exposed to court-ordered desegregation for 5 years experienced a 15% increase in wages and an 11 percentage point decline in annual poverty rates. The differences are related to the fact that schools under court supervision benefited from higher per-pupil spending and smaller student–teacher ratios, among other resources.

Figure 5.1. Trends in Reading Achievement by Race, 1971–2023

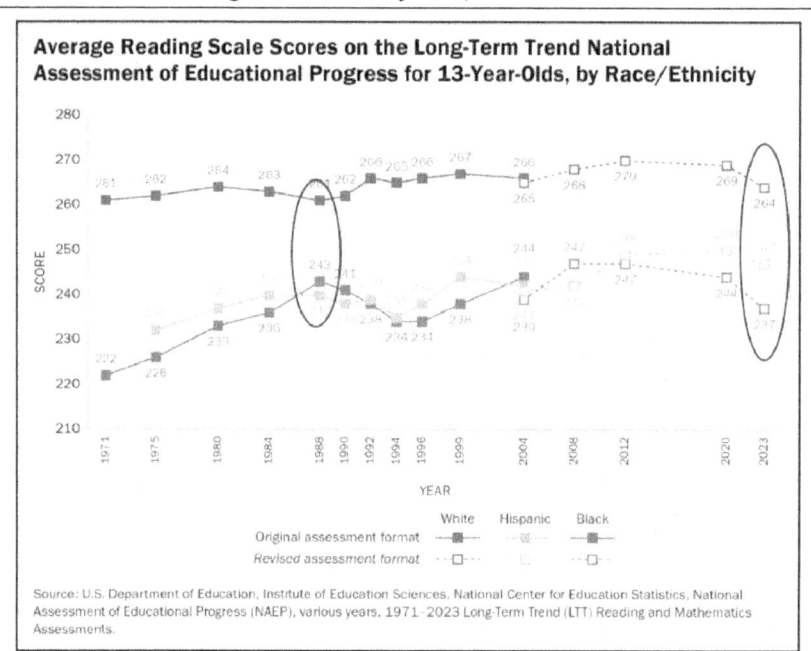

Source: U.S. Department of Education, Institute of Education Sciences, National Center for Education Statistics, National Assessment of Educational Progress (NAEP), various years, 1971–2023 Long-Term Trend (LTT) Reading and Mathematics Assessments.

Another study of school finance reforms experienced by children born between 1955 and 1985 found that, in places where new formulas enabled 20% more funding for schools serving low-income students, thus improving staffing and programs and reducing class sizes, graduation rates were more than 20 percentage points higher, educational attainment increased, along with employment and adult wages, and the poverty gap for adults was eliminated, all of which are associated with large social benefits.[4]

Overall, the Black–White achievement gap was cut by more than half during the 1970s and early 1980s, as Figure 5.1 also shows. Had this progress been continued, the achievement gap would have been fully closed by the beginning of the 21st century.

THE EFFECTS OF PUSHBACKS ON EQUITY

However, the gains from the Great Society programs were pushed back during the 1980s, when most targeted federal programs supporting investments in college access and K–12 schools in urban and poor rural areas were reduced or eliminated, and federal aid to schools was cut from 12% to 6% of a shrinking total. Meanwhile, childhood poverty rates, homelessness, and lack of access to health care grew with cuts in other federal programs supporting housing subsidies, health care, and child welfare.

By 1988, the achievement gap began to grow again, and stark differences reemerged between segregated urban schools and their suburban counterparts, which often spent twice as much on education. Achievement gaps between Black and White students in reading and mathematics are 50% larger now than they were 35 years ago. Educational shortcomings, plus lack of family resources and cuts in federal funding for financial aid, extend these disparities into higher education.

Investments in the education of students of color that characterized the school desegregation and finance reforms of the 1960s and 1970s have never been fully reestablished in the years since. Today, more than half of children attending U.S. public schools qualify for free or reduced-price lunch—the highest percentage since the National Center for Education Statistics began tracking this figure decades ago. Furthermore, U.S. children living in poverty have a much weaker safety net than their peers in other industrialized countries, where universal health care, housing subsidies, and high-quality, universally available child care are the norm.

Under our current educational system, so-called "achievement gaps" for disadvantaged children begin early—even before they enter school—and widen over time.[5] This is a function of significant opportunity gaps in multiple areas of these children's lives.[6] Citing the U.S. General Accountability Office, the Centers for Disease Control and Prevention (CDC), and numerous scholars, Richard Rothstein's *The Color of Law* evaluates a long list of factors contributing to low achievement for students of color, ranging from lack of access to eyeglasses; disproportionate instances of lead poisoning, iron-deficiency anemia, and asthma, and substandard pediatric care; housing instability; food insufficiency; and neighborhood dangers—all amplified by the aftereffects of redlining.[7]

Manuel Pastor and colleagues further document environmental inequalities, such as the siting of toxic facilities in low-income communities of color, and estimate that the side effects of these hazards account for as much as half of the performance differential between students living in Los Angeles neighborhoods with the lowest and highest risk levels, even after controlling for poverty and other demographic factors.[8]

Low-income children also have less access to preschool, although its value in boosting learning and closing gaps is well-established.[9] In 2019, just over half (53%) of 4-year-old children living in poverty were enrolled in preschool compared with more than three-fourths (76%) of their counterparts in families earning $125,000 a year.[10] While affluent families can afford the hefty expense of private preschool, children from low-income families have to compete for limited slots in public preschool programs. The federal Head Start program and most state public preschool programs have never been funded to reach all eligible children.

Furthermore, a growing share of children from low-income families attend school in districts where poverty is concentrated, creating huge educational challenges. In most major U.S. cities, for example, a majority of African American and Latinx students attend public schools where at least 75% of students are from low-income families. Increasingly, these schools are segregated by both race and class. For example, in Chicago and New York City, more than 95% of both Black and Latinx students attend majority-poverty schools, most of which are also majority-minority.

A number of studies have found strong relationships between racial segregation and racial achievement gaps; indeed, the racial composition of a school has educational impacts for students even after accounting for socioeconomic status, particularly due to resource inequities characterizing racially isolated schools.[11] In a case that challenged school desegregation efforts in Jefferson County, Kentucky, and Seattle, Washington, more than 550 scholars signed on to a social science report filed as an amicus brief, which summarized extensive research showing the persisting inequalities of segregated minority schools. The scholars concluded that

> More often than not, segregated minority schools offer profoundly unequal educational opportunities. This inequality is manifested in many ways, including fewer qualified, experienced teachers, greater instability caused by rapid turnover of faculty, fewer educational resources, and limited exposure to peers who can positively influence academic learning. No doubt as a result of these disparities, measures of educational outcomes, such as scores on standardized achievement tests and high school graduation rates, are lower in schools with high percentages of nonwhite students.[12]

Continued inequities deriving from our school funding systems mean that the best-supported students in our highest spending states and districts experience school spending many times greater than our most poorly supported students. While some experience a rich array of curriculum offerings taught by highly experienced teachers in small classes supported by extensive resources, others attend school where buildings are crumbling, classes are overcrowded, instructional materials are inadequate, and staff are often transient and underprepared.

In 2018, only 12 states spent at least 5% more in the districts serving the greatest proportion of underserved students of color than those serving the fewest (see Figure 5.2). Meanwhile, 20 states spent less on those districts, despite the greater needs

The Long Quest for Equitable Educational Opportunity

Figure 5.2. School Funding by Race (Per Pupil Funding Differences between Districts in the Top and Bottom Quartiles of Students of Color, by State)

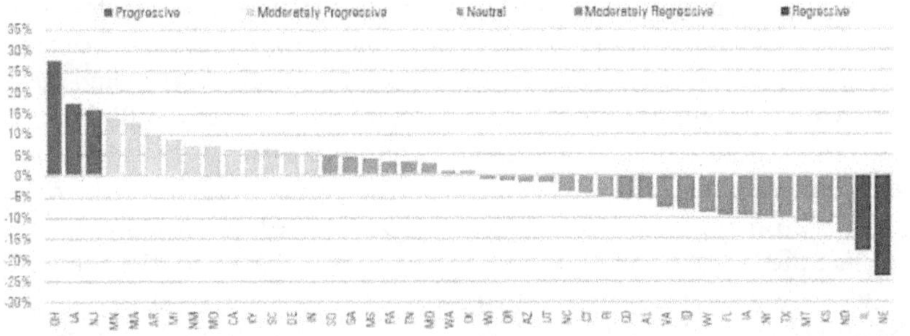

Source: "Funding Gaps 2018," Education Trust (2018), https://edtrust.org/resource/funding-gaps-2018/.

of their students. On average, districts serving the largest populations of Black, Latinx, or American Indian students (in the top quartile) received about $1,800 (13%) less per student in state and local funding than those serving the fewest (in the bottom quartile).

The disparities in funding have serious consequences for student academic outcomes, as research shows that money matters for resources that have significant impact on student outcomes, such as class sizes, curriculum, and access to qualified teachers. Civil rights data show that the odds of high-minority schools having uncertified and inexperienced teachers are four times those of predominantly White schools, and these differences translate into differences in access to quality curriculum and teaching, and ultimately achievement.[13]

They also derive from and further exacerbate racial discrimination that leads to school exclusion and dropping out. High rates of exclusionary discipline, such as suspension and expulsion—which are significantly higher for Black students and students with disabilities—are associated with inexperienced and underprepared educators who often lack strategies for building an engaging curriculum and managing student behavior in positive ways.[14] From 1980, starting in the Reagan years, through 2010, in the Obama administration, there was a rise as well in zero-tolerance policies that use such approaches even for the most minor offenses, including nonviolent "misbehavior," such as tardiness, talking, texting, sleeping in class, or failing to follow instructions, with little consideration of the context or consequences. High rates of suspension have been found to lead to higher rates of dropout, academic losses, and a growing school-to-prison pipeline.[15]

All of these disparities, which have come to appear inevitable in the United States, are not the norm in developed nations around the world, which typically fund their education systems centrally and equally, with additional resources often going to the schools where students' needs are greater. These more equitable investments made by high-achieving nations are also steadier and more focused on critical elements of the system: access to high-quality early learning, a universally high quality of teachers and teaching, the development of curriculum and assessments that encourage ambitious learning by both students and teachers, and the design of schools as learning organizations that support continuous reflection and improvement. With the exception of a few states with enlightened long-term leadership, the United States has failed to maintain focused investments on these essential elements.

Among the exceptions are Massachusetts and New Jersey. As a result of school finance litigation that resulted in progressive funding reforms, these states catapulted to the two top-ranked states in the nation in terms of student achievement and graduation rates. The reforms reallocated money on the basis of student needs, with more going to high-need students in low-income districts, while also establishing quality preschool for those students along with investments in stronger teaching from pre-K through grade 12.[16] The two states have largely maintained these efforts, steadily reducing disparities, since the 1990s as they have sustained their commitment to quality of education for all students. Still, litigators in both states are concerned about slippages that may take them back to court, and in both cases, ongoing segregation combined with poverty is at the root of the concerns.

While some states have seen improvements, over the last 15 years, average achievement for 13-year-old Black students in reading has declined steeply on NAEP (see Figure 5.1). These drops began during the era introduced by the No Child Left Behind Act (enacted in 2002 and in effect until 2015), which focused the nation on closing test score gaps by applying punitive sanctions to schools with scores not moving fast enough to show "100% proficiency." Although the law was launched with a temporary increase in funds for high-poverty schools, the promised increases did not continue, and many states focused on testing without investing in the resources needed to achieve higher standards. During the Great Recession (2008–2012) many states slashed education budgets, and most states were spending less on education in 2017 than they had been in 2007.[17]

Ironically, the most underresourced schools serving students of color—especially Black students—in high-need communities were those that, in the name of equity, were most often closed or "reconstituted,"[18] their teachers and leaders fired or reassigned on the assumption that they were the problem. Large numbers of Black teachers—now known to be critical to the achievement of Black students[19]—were lost to the profession during this time. Research found that these educators were typically replaced by a less-qualified group of teachers and that achievement declined further.[20] Many of these communities had just barely begun to recover when the recent pandemic set in.

THE EFFECTS OF THE PANDEMIC

The effects of the COVID-19 pandemic have only exacerbated the challenges faced by children and families of color, as they experienced the results of greater infection and mortality rates, unemployment, housing and food instability, and the digital divide—which prevented many children from engaging in education and their parents from engaging in telehealth, job searches, access to benefits, or deliveries of groceries and medicine.

The share of families of color living in poverty increased immediately. Despite a gradual decline in rates prior to the pandemic, these numbers shifted for the worse between 2019 and 2020, with a reversal of progress, and a widening of the gap by race/ethnicity and family structure. As Child Trends reported in 2021,

Poverty rates among Latino children rose by 4.2 percentage points, from 23.0 percent to 27.3 percent, and by 2.8 percentage points among Black children, from 26.4 percent to 29.2 percent. . . . In contrast, the rates of white and Asian children in poverty remained relatively stable. In addition, children in female-headed families also saw a large increase in the poverty rate, by 4.1 percentage points, from 33.4 percent to 37.4 percent.[21]

Although President Biden's American Rescue Plan Act (2021) sought to address this growing poverty with income tax credits for low-income families that once again cut child poverty in half for 1 year, plus food and housing security initiatives that prevented evictions and ensured sustenance, these initiatives were not continued by the Congress after they expired.

Throughout the country, profound and long-standing inequalities were highlighted the moment schooling became remote: It became apparent that students from low-income families often had little access to computers and connectivity to use for distance learning, and their schools were often the least well-staffed and resourced to provide the tools and supports needed. Since school doors have reopened, educators have struggled to address student trauma and learning lags, as well as shortages of educators that emerged with COVID-19 surges and quarantines and have continued with mass retirements and resignations, especially from the highest need schools.

The effects of these challenges were made clear when the 2022 National Assessment of Educational Progress (NAEP) results were released for the first time since 2019. Drops in scores for all students were most severe for low-income students and students of color. Dr. Peggy Carr, commissioner of the National Center for Education Statistics (NCES), which issued the report, described the results as "almost 2 decades of educational progress washed away."

An additional analysis by researchers at Stanford and Harvard linked these data to state testing data in every district across the country, finding that test scores generally declined more in school districts serving students from lower-income families than in those serving more affluent families—districts that disproportionately serve students of color.

Indeed, as Figure 5.1 illustrates, by 2023, reading scores for Black 13-year-olds had fallen to their lowest level in the last quarter century, having decreased steadily for the last 15 years. The achievement gap between White and Black students also grew wider than it had been since 1999.

WHAT MUST BE DONE

As a country, we must enter a new era. No society can thrive in a technological, knowledge-based economy by starving large segments of its population of learning. Instead, we must provide all of our children what should be an unquestioned entitlement—an inalienable right to learn.

As noted in *The Civil Rights Road to Deeper Learning*,[22] there is still a long road to travel to access quality learning opportunities for all students, and reaching the destination includes civil rights enforcement and equity policies to ensure access to healthy environments, supportive learning conditions and opportunities, well-resourced and inclusive schools, skillful teaching, and high-quality curriculum. To make good on our national obligation to provide equitable access to high-quality education, policymakers at the federal, state, and local levels need to cultivate universally available high-quality curricular opportunities within well-resourced schools, investments that ensure an adequate and equitably distributed supply of well-prepared educators, and supportive wraparound services (e.g., counseling, health care, social services, and academic supports) to counteract the adverse conditions that many students experience.

First, policymakers will need to rebuild the tattered safety net for children and families, as the American Rescue Plan Act began to do, with investments in nutrition, child care, health care, and child tax credits that reduced child poverty by half in 2021—and could accomplish that permanently if continued in federal law.[23] They will also need to reduce toxins in the environment, as the Infrastructure Investment and Jobs Act of 2021 seeks to do with a $3.5 billion Superfund to clean up toxic waste, mostly in communities of color.[24] And policymakers will need to invest in rebuilding communities that have been cordoned off from investment and opportunity through decades of redlining, so that families in these communities can thrive.

To support optimal conditions for development and learning, the schools that children attend in these communities must be well-supported by adequate and equitable resources that address the intense needs that our social system creates for many children and families. This will require a number of efforts to end the legacy of underresourced and segregated schools, such as:

- ongoing school finance reform litigation and legislation to achieve policies that provide funding based on pupil needs—such as poverty, homelessness, English learner status, and special education status—rather than as a function of property tax wealth in local communities;
- high-quality preschool education that offers key learning resources to close opportunity and achievement gaps before school begins, offering a deeper learning curriculum from the start, when children are developing their initial brain architecture as they explore, inquire, communicate, and play; and
- reengagement of federal support for desegregation through investments in such programs as the Magnet Schools Assistance Program and the Diversity Act to support not only individual schools and districts but also to enable states to pursue inter-district solutions to segregation.[25]

Developing safe and inclusive schools will require ongoing civil rights enforcement that has been essential to pave a path toward nonexclusionary school discipline practices for students of color and students with disabilities. The Office of Civil Rights's ability to monitor suspension and expulsion rates using the Civil Rights Data Collection has been critical, as has its guidance supporting restorative practices that create strong communities, teach conflict resolution, and support positive discipline as an alternative. Though repealed by the Trump administration, the OCR guidance should be reissued to help districts support productive policies. Also important will be expansions of currently modest investments under Titles I and IV of the Every Student Succeeds Act for programs that support restorative practices and community schools that organize whole child supports promoting students' physical and mental health, social welfare, and academic success.[26]

All of these strategies ultimately require a diverse, well-prepared, culturally responsive, and stable teaching force in all schools. To achieve this goal a robust national teacher policy would:

- fully cover preparation costs for recruits who teach in high-need fields or locations;
- support improved preparation that prepares teachers to support culturally responsive, equity-focused learning centered on 21st-century skills for all students;
- provide high-quality mentoring for all beginning teachers, which would reduce churn, enhance teaching quality, and heighten student achievement; and
- design recruitment incentives to attract and retain expert, experienced teachers who can teach and coach others in high-need schools, such as those certified by the National Board for Professional Teaching Standards, skilled in teaching for deeper learning and found to be highly effective as teachers and mentors.[27]

Finally, policymakers can design and encourage supportive accountability and continuous improvement systems that focus on students' opportunities to learn as well as multiple measures of meaningful learning and attainment, rather than on sanctions for schools with low scores. Such systems should emphasize indicators of students' access to educational resources: well-qualified educators, a rich curriculum, high-quality teaching, instructional materials (including digital access at home and school), a positive school climate, social–emotional and academic supports, and expert, culturally responsive instruction.

In the interdependent world we currently inhabit, threatened by conflict and climate change and driven by rapidly changing knowledge and technologies, a highly educated, communally committed populace is necessary for the survival and success of societies as well as individuals. The path to our mutual well-being is built on equitable educational opportunity. The evidence shows that this is possible. But making equitable, high-quality learning commonplace requires creating healthy communities and safe, inclusive, and well-resourced schools for all. We must move beyond litigation and partial solutions to create a system structured to benefit (and benefit from) all its citizens by supporting each and every child.

NOTES

1. Prudence L. Carter and Kevin G. Welner, eds., *Closing the Opportunity Gap: What America Must Do to Give Every Child an Even Chance* (New York: Oxford University Press, 2013), 1.

2. Linda Darling-Hammond, "Education and the Path to One Nation, Indivisible" (research brief), Learning Policy Institute, 2018.

3. Rucker C. Johnson with Alexander Nazaryan, *Children of the Dream: Why School Integration Works* (New York: Basic Books, 2019).

4. C. Kirabo Jackson, Rucker C. Johnson, and Claudia Persico, "The Effect of School Spending on Educational and Economic Outcomes: Evidence from School Finance Reforms," *Quarterly Journal of Economics, 13*(3) (February 2016): 157218, https://doi.org/10.1093/qje/qjv036.

5. Thomas M. Shapiro, *Toxic Inequality: How America's Wealth Gap Destroys Mobility, Deepens the Racial Divide, and Threatens Our Future* (London: Hachette UK, 2017). See also, for example, Richard Rothstein, *Class and Schools: Using Social, Economic, and Educational Reform to Close the Black-white Achievement Gap* (New York: Teachers College Press, 2004).

6. Carter and Welner, *Closing the Opportunity Gap*.

7. Richard Rothstein, *The Color of Law: A Forgotten History of How Our Government Segregated America* (New York: Liveright Publishing, 2017).

8. Manuel Pastor, James Sadd, and Rachel Morello-Frosch, "Reading, Writing, and Toxics: Children's Health, Academic Performance, and Environmental Justice in Los Angeles," *Environment and Planning. C, Government and Policy* 22, no. 2 (April 1, 2004): 271–290, https://doi.org/10.1068/c009r.

9. J. J. Heckman and D. V. Masterov, "The productivity argument for investing in young children," *Review of Agricultural Economics*, 29, no. 3 (Autumn 2007), 446–493; Arthur A. Reynolds et al., "School-based early childhood education and age-28 well-being: Effects by timing, dosage, and subgroups," *Science*, 333, no. 6040 (June 2011): 360–364, https://doi.org/10.1126/science.1203618.

10. Lynn Karoly and Jill Cannon, "Making Preschool Investments Count Through the American Families Plan," RAND, June 3, 2021, https://www.rand.org/pubs/commentary/2021/06/making-preschool-investments-count-through-the-american.html.

11. Jennifer Ayscue, Erica Frankenberg, and Genevieve Siegel-Hawley, *The complementary benefits of racial and socioeconomic diversity in schools*, Research brief no. 10, National Coalition on School Diversity, 2017.

12. American Educational Research Association, brief amicus curiae filed in *Parents Involved in Community Schools v. Seattle School District No. 1*, 551 U.S. 701 (2007).

13. Linda Darling-Hammond, *The Flat World and Education: How America's Commitment to Equity Will Determine our Future* (New York: Teachers College Press, 2010).

14. Melanie Leung-Gagné et al., "Pushed Out: Trends and Disparities in Out-of-School Suspension," Learning Policy Institute, September 30, 2022, https://learningpolicyinstitute.org/product/crdc-school-suspension-report.

15. Edward W. Morris and Brea L. Perry, "The Punishment Gap: School Suspension and Racial Disparities in Achievement," *Social Problems* 63, no. 1 (January 8, 2016): 68–86, https://doi.org/10.1093/socpro/spv026; Tony Fabelo et al., "Breaking Schools' Rules: A Statewide Study of How School Discipline Relates to Students' Success and Juvenile Justice Involvement," Council of State Governments Justice Center & Public Policy Research Institute, July 2011; Daniel J. Losen and Jonathan Gillespie, "Opportunities suspended: The disparate impact of disciplinary exclusion from school," UCLA Civil Rights Project, August 7, 2012.

16. Linda Darling-Hammond, "Investing for Student Success: Lessons From State School Finance Reforms," Learning Policy Institute, April 9, 2019, https://learningpolicyinstitute.org/product/investing-student-success-school-finance-reforms-report.

17. Danielle Farrie and David G. Sciarra, "$600 billion lost: State funding on public education following the Great Recession," Education Law Center, 2020, https://edlawcenter.org/research/600-Billion-Lost.

18. Francis A. Pearman II, Camille Luong, and Danielle M. Green, "Examining racial (in)equity in school-closure patterns in California" [Working paper], Policy Analysis for California Education, 2023, edpolicyinca.org/publications/examining-racial-inequity-school-closure-patterns-california.

19. Desiree Carver-Thomas, Diversifying the teaching profession: How to recruit and retain teachers of color, Learning Policy Institute, https://doi.org/10.54300/559.310.

20. Betty Malen et al., "Reconstituting Schools: Testing the 'Theory of Action,'" *Educational Evaluation and Policy Analysis*, 24. 2: 113–132. https://doi.org/10.3102/01623737024002113

21. Yiyu Chen and Dana Thomson, "Child Poverty Increased Nationally During COVID, Especially Among Latino and Black Children," *Child Trends*, June 3, 2021, https://www.childtrends.org/publications/child-poverty-increased-nationally-during-covid-especially-among-latino-and-black-children.

22. Kia Darling-Hammond and Linda Darling-Hammond, *The Civil Rights Road to Deeper Learning: Five Essentials for Equity* (New York: Teachers College Press, 2023).

23. Zachary Parolin et al., "The potential poverty reduction effect of the American Rescue Plan" (Fact sheet), Center for Poverty and Social Policy, Columbia University, March 11, 2021, https://www.povertycenter.columbia.edu/news-internal/2021/presidential-policy/biden-economic-relief-proposal-poverty-impact.

24. United States of America, "H. R. 3684," legislation, One Hundred Seventeenth Congress of the United States of America, January 3, 2021, https://www.congress.gov/117/bills/hr3684/BILLS-117hr3684enr.pdf.

25. John Brittain, Larkin Willis, and Peter W. Cookson, Jr., "Sharing the Wealth: How Regional Finance and Desegregation Plans Can Enhance Educational Equity," Learning Policy Institute, February 28, 2019, https://learningpolicyinstitute.org/product/sharing-wealth-regional-finance-desegregation-plans-report.

26. Anna Maier et al., "Community Schools as an Effective School Improvement Strategy: A Review of the Evidence," Learning Policy Institute, December 14, 2017, https://learningpolicyinstitute.org/product/community-schools-effective-school-improvement-report.

27. Milton D. Hakel, Judith Anderson Koenig, and Stuart W. Elliot, *Assessing Accomplished Teaching: Advanced-Level Certification Programs* (Washington, DC: The National Academies Press, 2008), https://doi.org/10.17226/12224; Bo Zhu et al., "Effects of National Board Certified Instructional Leaders on Classroom Practice and Student Achievement of Novice Teachers," American Institutes of Research, May 2019, https://files.eric.ed.gov/fulltext/ED607261.pdf.

CHAPTER 6

Building Loving Systems to Create One America for All Children

John H. Jackson and Zakiyah Ansari

What could have been a series of chapters on America's redemptive history has unfortunately become a dissertation on national indifference. As was the case in 1967, the scourge of racism in America continues to stalk Black children and families. The 1968 Kerner Commission[1] report noted unreconciled grievances and areas of gross neglect spanning every facet of Black American life of which educational opportunity was front and center.

As the recent dual COVID-19 and racial justice pandemic elevated, America's persistence of inequitable systemic supports for Black children and families interwoven with the pervasiveness of highly punitive social climates creates a counterproductive living and learning environment for Black children. This dynamic creates a landscape where, more often than not, Black student success is the result of them learning how to move forward carrying the weights of systemic neglect and institutional racism while climbing the proverbial "rough side of the mountain." The fact that a significant percentage of Black students in America succeed remains less about a nation that has delivered on a promise and more about the significance of Black-led anchor institutions (e.g. education justice and civil rights advocacy organizations, Historically Black Colleges and Universities, the Black church, etc.). Over the past several decades, these institutions have increased their ability to cover the multitude of systemic pitfalls that would otherwise impede the success of scores of capable, intelligent, and motivated Black students.

We know, and research supports, that when healthy living support systems are not in place to provide students, educators, and families with the ecosystem necessary to provide a healthy learning environment, students' educational outcomes and wellness are negatively impacted.

As reported in the Schott Foundation's 2024 report on Black males in education, in 2019–2020, 4-year graduation rates were the highest on record since 2010 (when the United States began tracking this rate; Figure 6.1). Prior to the pandemic, between 2012–2020, U.S. graduation rates improved for every group, and racial gaps narrowed, particularly for Black students. Black students' 4-year graduation rates improved sharply by 14% over this 8-year period (compared to a more modest 4% improvement in the 4-year graduation rates of white students, for example). These were the steepest gains seen over the 8-year period.

Building Loving Systems to Create One America for All Children 63

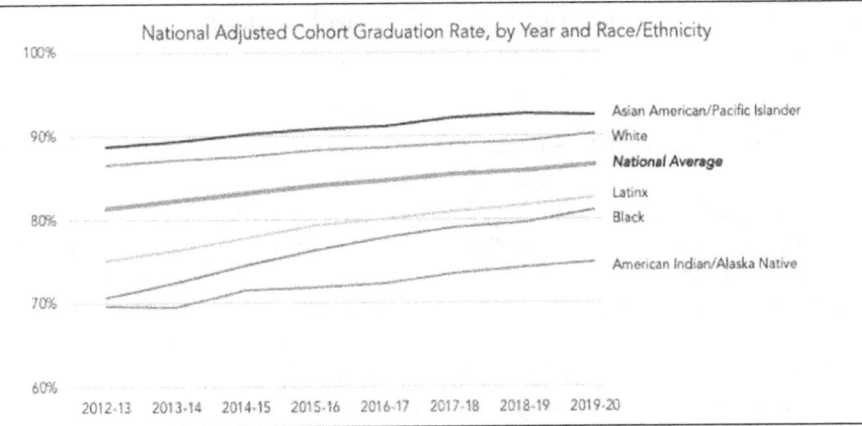

Figure 6.1. U.S. Adjusted Cohort 4-Year Graduation Rates

National Adjusted Cohort Graduation Rate, by Year and Race/Ethnicity

[Line graph showing graduation rates from 2012-13 to 2019-20 for Asian American/Pacific Islander, White, National Average, Latinx, Black, and American Indian/Alaska Native groups, ranging from approximately 60% to 95%]

Note: The ACGR is the percentage of 9th graders who graduate within 4 years of starting 9th grade with a regular diploma. The years presented indicate the year the cohort graduated high school. The most recent year available at the time of publication of this report is 2019–2020. Students entering 9th grade for the first time form the cohort for the graduating class. This cohort is "adjusted" by adding any students who subsequently transfer into the cohort and subtracting any students who subsequently transfer out, emigrate to another country, or die.

Source: U.S. Department of Education, NCES, Common Core of Data, 2021, Table 1. Public high school 4-year adjusted cohort graduation rate (ACGR), by race/ethnicity and selected demographic characteristics for the United States, the 50 states, the District of Columbia, and Puerto Rico, UCLA Center for the Transformation of Schools.(https://nces.ed.gov/ccd/tables/ACGR_RE_and _characteristics_2019-20.asp)

While access to national post-pandemic calculations of 4-year graduation rates are currently unavailable, analysis of California's post-pandemic graduation data reviewed by the Center for the Transformation of Schools at UCLA suggests major setbacks for Black students. The broader social inequities related to the pandemic had a particularly harmful impact on Black male students from the class of 2020–2022, for whom the 4-year graduation rate declined by 7%. Without a high school diploma or GED equivalent, these students are more likely to have lower incomes as well as lower health and wellness outcomes. Ultimately, these factors correlate to shorter life expectancies for Black children.

If we start with the fact that most students, regardless of race, ethnicity, or gender, are born into the world with the cognitive ability to excel in any educational pursuit, the fact that we can gather from U.S. educational outcome data a consistent pattern of "winners" and "losers" identifiable by race and ethnicity speaks to systemic, rather than individual, failures. Far too many federal, state, and local policymakers have failed to institutionalize a policy framework strong enough to provide the healthy living and learning environment necessary for all students to cultivate their cognitive abilities and achieve their full potential.

While there was considerable variation in graduation rates between states, even before the pandemic, states with the highest Black graduation rates performed well for all students. By contrast, states with the lowest Black graduation rates are characterized by substantial inequality, with large gaps in the graduation rates of students by race. Simply stated, the more we begin to provide standard systems of supports, the more we truly see and activate the opportunities that exist within each student.

INEQUITABLE SYSTEMIC SUPPORTS FOR BLACK STUDENTS

One of the main conclusions that the Kerner Commission highlighted in 1968 was that America was divided into two societies. As such, it is virtually impossible to systemically provide any student an opportunity to learn in America without assessing and addressing the degree to which the students and their families have access to the society that provides them with healthy living and learning supports—safe and affordable housing, health care, livable wages, and healthy food, to name a few.

At the time President Johnson called for the Kerner Commission in 1967, inclusive and affordable housing was elusive for many Black families. Black families were battered by redlining, housing codes, and racist policies that limited upward mobility as well as the accumulation of wealth. As NPR summarized, and scholars have long contended, "Most middle-class families in this country gained their wealth from the equity they have in their homes."[2] The federal government's discriminatory practices in housing and housing policy had a direct and outsized impact on Black people, including their ability to accumulate wealth.

As a June 2020 *Washington Post* report indicated, "in 1968, a typical middle-class Black household had $6,674 in wealth compared with $70,786 for the typical middle-class white household."[3] In a stark illustration of how little progress has been made, the same *Post* article cited data from the Historical Survey of Consumer Finances indicating that nearly 5 decades later in 2016, the typical middle-class Black family had $13,024 in wealth compared with white families who had $149,703. In 2019, the Federal Reserve found "Black families' median and mean wealth is less than 15 percent that of White families, at $24,100 and $142,500, respectively." Since the pandemic, Black families' wealth has grown more than any other group, but "Black Americans' net worth remains 70% below that of non-Black households."[4]

This is particularly apparent in the research conducted by Stanford University professor Sean Reardon, which indicates that:

> the income achievement gap (defined here as the average educational achievement difference between a child from a family at the 90th percentile of the family income distribution and a child from a family at the 10th percentile) is now nearly twice as large as the Black-white achievement gap. Fifty years ago, in contrast, the Black-white gap was one and a half to two times as large as the income achievement gap. . . . The relationship between parental education and children's achievement has remained relatively stable during the last fifty years, whereas the relationship between income and achievement has grown sharply.[5]

Family income is now nearly as strong as parental education in predicting children's achievement. As the 4-year graduation data highlights, when Black students do well, most students do well. It is in our collective best interest to see and respond to the needs of all students.

HIGHLY PUNITIVE-ORIENTED CLIMATES FOR BLACK STUDENTS AND FAMILIES

The inequitable systemic supports for Black students say nothing of the trauma many Black students experience in living and learning environments that are hyper punitive-oriented. From unwanted contact with law enforcement, to unreasonable searches and seizures of property, to excessive referrals to law enforcement, exclusionary discipline, and nonstop surveillance, many living and learning environments for Black students remain oppressive and degrading.

Overall, 5 decades after the Kerner Commission report, Black children and youth face an uphill battle. Black girls are often seen as less deserving of protection than others, and Black boys are criminalized and pathologized. Communities of color in general see their children treated less as vessels to be filled and more as threats to be managed.

Black children are too often first criminalized in schools within their community. Corporal punishment remains legal in 19 states, many of which are in the southern United States, where the largest percentage of Black students are located. Police presence is heavier in schools with a predominantly Black student population and in neighborhoods that are primarily Black. Given the historical and present-day trauma that law enforcement has wrought, even the presence of police in schools or communities can be triggering for Black and Brown young people and their parents. The opportunity to drive, walk the streets, and play while Black seems very constrained. Even as we look into the future of education and the opportunities that the integration of artificial intelligence (AI) tools may bring, many of the creators of the tools have failed to address critical racial biases (e.g., face recognition, data privacy, etc.) in the tools, thereby setting the stage for the birth of a new "Jim Code" era of student policing and inequities. We must be diligent in advocating for an AI Bill of Rights that has a racial equity lens.

A Hechinger Report study found that "One in every 11 young black men is incarcerated—a path that too often starts in schools, where black students are three times more likely to be suspended or expelled than white students."[6] From years of research, we know that early contact with law enforcement increases a child's likelihood of being involved in the criminal justice system later in life.

In 2022, two racial and education justice organizations, the Advancement Project and the Alliance for Educational Justice, released the #AssaultAtSpringValley report that documented 285 instances of police assaults in schools from 2011 to 2021. The vast majority of the persons victimized were Black and Latinx students. The report demonstrated "how school policing places students, especially Black students, at a significant risk of criminalization and assault, as evidenced by the heartbreaking, far-too frequent videos of school police officers using physical force on children."[7] These children weren't assaulted because they were inherently bad or behaving any worse than other students. As was the case in 1967 and remains the case today, the lens of white supremacy has one filter for Black bodies: They are a threat to be subjugated. Even with Black students from wealthy families, their race makes them vulnerable in a system that continues to criminalize "Blackness"—and especially Black males.

These punitive outcomes are not by happenstance, but a part of a troubling national policy landscape which created them. As noted in Nikole Hannah-Jones' *1619 Project*,[8] in the early 1970s, U.S. prisons and jails held fewer than 350,000 people; since then, the number has increased to about 2.3 million, with 4.5 million more on probation or parole. In 1980, there were roughly 40,000 people incarcerated for drug-related offenses; today that number is about 450,000. Needless to say, the United States has the highest rate of incarceration of any nation on earth—a country with 4% of the planet's population has 20% of the planet's prisoners, with a disproportionate number of them being Black.

The persistence of inequitable resources and punitive climates for Black children and families in America are both concerning and discouraging, yet they are also instructive. If policymakers were able to construct a policy system that created these outcomes, we have the ability to deconstruct and reconstruct a policy landscape to reverse them. If these systems were built, they can be rebuilt and reconstructed in such a way that they do not create negative outcomes. If we acknowledge the existence of two societies in American states and communities largely divided by race and ethnicity, we can collectively move forward with the common goal of building one America and the best multiracial democracy in the world.

KEY LESSON FOR MOVING FORWARD

As we move forward, what policymakers decide to no longer do is as important as any new efforts. The past 55 years of mercurial educational progress in states and communities across the country has taught us some very significant lessons.

- An educational equity agenda that is primarily built on a pillar of standards-based reforms (test scores, punitive measures, etc.) is neither strong enough nor relational enough to create or sustain the momentum necessary to address systemic equitable educational outcomes.
- The persistent systemic education disparities that exist today are not primarily due to failures in students, families, or educators, but larger community systems.
- Our "North Star" and primary goal for education must go beyond an individualistic goal of preparing students for work toward a collective goal of bridging "two societies."

Mounds of data informed specifically by the students and parents closest to the challenges and solutions (or what is better referred to as "democratized evidence") have proven that moving forward requires the adoption of a new policy framework.

Deconstructing historical policies that were undergirded by elements of hate and racism requires resurrecting a new policy agenda that works at both systems and humanity levels. Hate and racism operationalized at a systems or policy level concretizes institutionalized lovelessness toward the disparately impacted group. Within a policy framework "institutionalized lovelessness" becomes the expressed collective humanity

Building Loving Systems to Create One America for All Children   67

of that city, state, or nation and the lived experience of the disparately impacted group—in this case Black students and families. Over time, this dynamic has set the stage for the persistent systemic disparities that negatively impact the outcomes of Black students, and begs the question that has more recently been a core part of our national discourse—Do Black lives matter?

As such, moving forward, our new national education policy framework must, at minimum, tackle three core realities:

1. Policymakers must replace their "standards-based" reform policy agenda with a "supports-based" agenda focused on identifying and delivering the critical supports needed for all students to have a fair and substantive opportunity to learn.
2. Equity within the education and school settings is essential, but addressing equity in the learning space alone (e.g., education sector, schools, educators, etc.) is not sufficient to overcome the myriad of racial disparities that impact Black student living experiences, thereby contributing to poor learning outcomes.
3. Education as a public good should intellectually, emotionally, and creatively prepare students to be productive contributors to the wellness of our collective democracy, economy, and humanity.

These three realities lay the foundation for community leaders and policymakers to develop the systems to provide Black students equitable access to the holistic supports that are indicative of a loving community, state, or nation. Consistent with Maslow's Hierarchy of Needs (Figure 6.2), each of these supports when accessed provides an essential building block in creating the "learning" social infrastructure for all students to have a fair and substantive opportunity to learn.

Any policy or systems change framework that is not rooted in equity and love will fail to adequately repair years of harm or catalyze the consistent long-term success of students historically disadvantaged. At a systems level, only a consistent diet of equitable

Figure 6.2. Maslow's Hierarchy of Needs

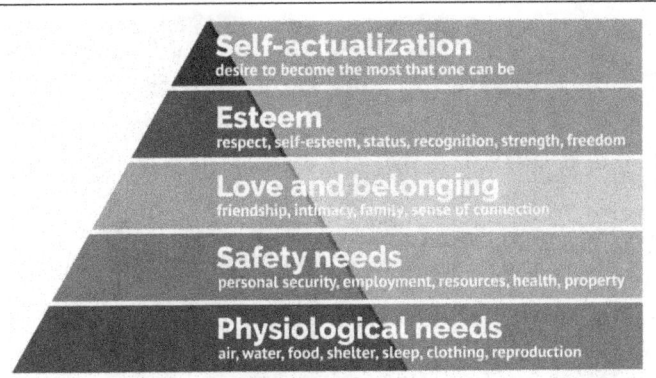

Self-actualization
desire to become the most that one can be

Esteem
respect, self-esteem, status, recognition, strength, freedom

Love and belonging
friendship, intimacy, family, sense of connection

Safety needs
personal security, employment, resources, health, property

Physiological needs
air, water, food, shelter, sleep, clothing, reproduction

Maslow's hierarchy of needs

supports (or "needs" meeting) can repair the impact of persistent systemic disparities. At a human level, only persistent love can defeat forces of hate. Simply stated, all Black children and families in America should have access to loving systems.

IMPLEMENTING A LOVING SYSTEMS FRAMEWORK AT A COMMUNITY LEVEL

Beyond a theoretical framework, what does providing all children access to loving systems look like at a community level? In short, it means giving them access to the core supports that you would provide the children you love. You provide healthy food to those you love. You provide shelter for those you love. You support the health and mental wellness of those you love. And when they make mistakes or fail, you provide them with restorative opportunities.

In 2018, the Schott Foundation developed the Loving Cities Index[9] as a tool for local policymakers to assess the degree to which all students have equitable access to 24 living and learning supports in four areas of need (Figure 6.3) consistent with Maslow's hierarchy of needs:

1. CARE: Health resources and physical environment that foster physical and mental development
2. STABILITY: Community infrastructure supports and policies that foster physical and financial security and civic participation
3. COMMITMENT: School policies and practices that foster the unique potential of each student
4. CAPACITY: Financial policies and practices that foster expertise and resources to meet the needs of all children

Figure 6.3. Loving Cities Index Core Components

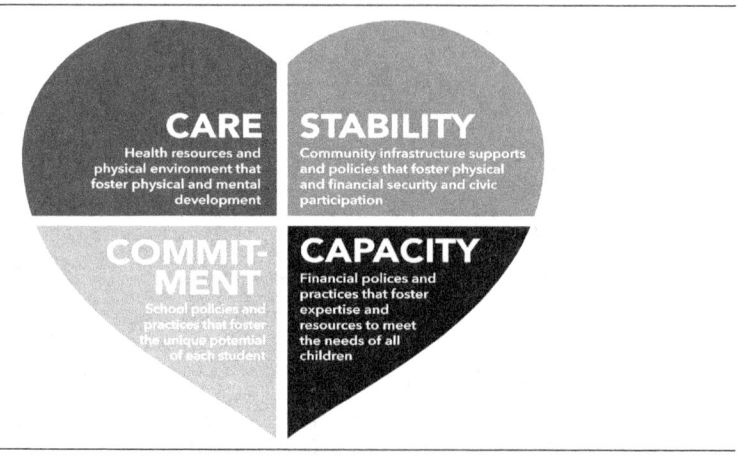

If a community scores 100% on the Loving Cities Index, it means that all children in the community, regardless of race or ethnicity, have access to the 24 loving systems supports. To date, Schott has developed Loving City Index profiles for over 25 cities and no city has scored higher than 52%. That means that at best, of the communities assessed, the children only have access to a little more than half of the supports needed to have an opportunity to learn and thrive. Many of the cities assessed only offered about a third of the level of supports needed. This local systems assessment explains our nation's educational outcomes as well as why parental income remains one of the most influential factors in student educational outcomes.

We can't expect to see high school graduation and college attainment rates go up if local policymakers fail to provide children and families in their communities with the core supports that we know are needed for students to succeed. Local city and county leaders must assess their supports infrastructure for children and families and create the loving systems capable of proving an opportunity to learn for all students. It requires intentionality, transparency, commitment, and, most importantly, action.

STATE ACTIONS TO CATALYZE LOVING SYSTEMS IN COMMUNITIES

States can also play a significant role in catalyzing and supporting local loving systems in communities. After more than 2 decades of fighting against the inequitable resourcing of schools across the state of New York, in 2020, organized parents, educators, and student advocates, led by the Alliance for Quality Education (AQE), pushed the New York State legislature to fully invest in its funding formula. A state's funding formula, or Foundation Aid, is intended to provide equitable supports to underresourced students (in this case Black, Brown, and poor) in districts across the state. Today, the New York State legislature's allocation provides an additional $4 billion to support students and educators in their quest to provide all students an opportunity to learn by ensuring they exist with healthy living and learning environments.

AQE's fight to hold the state to its obligation to fund public education has always been deeply steeped in racial justice and love for all children across New York. The majority of Foundation Aid was owed to school districts with 40% or more Black and Latinx students. The full funding of Foundation Aid represents a major step toward racial and economic equity in education and provides a state model for catalyzing loving systems within communities across a state.

There are other powerful examples, like in Massachusetts. After nearly a decade of advocacy, local advocates and voters passed a Fair Share amendment that increases taxes annually on those making $1 million or more, providing more than $2 billion annually to increase the education and transportation supports to students and families across the state.

These efforts in New York and Massachusetts begin to quilt together the resources to build the type of loving systems necessary to provide an opportunity to learn and produce the outcomes that the Kerner Commission imagined.

FEDERAL ACTION TO CATALYZE LOVING SYSTEMS IN COMMUNITIES

While state and local efforts are significant in ensuring Black students and families have access to loving systems, the federal government has the greatest capacity to establish this as a national norm. Federally, throughout history, we have seen truncated efforts to prioritize providing targeted supports to specific populations of people. Policymakers created the GI Bill (1944) to serve young people returning from war. Minimum wage laws were designed to ensure families could properly care for themselves. The Federal Housing Administration (FHA) subsidized entire neighborhoods for families to boost home ownership and help families recover from the Great Depression. The problem with each of these efforts is they were primarily designed to impact, and in some cases restricted to, white families.

The federal government has and can serve as an equity anchor, crafting policies and funding streams that help large portions of communities to gain access to loving supports. Today, if we are to guarantee all children an opportunity to learn, the federal government must remain an equity anchor and catalyst for all children and families accessing loving systems and supports in their communities. We cannot ignore that there is a small, but loud, contingent within the United States who view Black access to democracy and loving systems as a threat to white superiority. So they seek to limit or destroy the practice of democracy. Even more, seeing that the public education system is the only mandatory public institution for children and families in the United States and offers an anchor within our growing multiracial democracy, they seek to destroy it as well as the values that come with a multiracial democracy—equity, inclusion, and diversity.

While national and local education justice and civil rights organizations are a significant part of the infrastructure that ensures our democracy and public education systems work in spite of these attacks, the weight of federal policy and resources are critical to stabilizing and sustaining our democracy and public education across our United States.

Governments invest resources in what they value, and budgets are moral documents that illuminate those values. As such, we outline here that if federal leaders are truly committed to fulfilling the recommendations of the Kerner Report, they should consider passage of a multiyear, $10–12 trillion federal Loving Communities (Racial Equity) Stimulus Package. The Loving Communities (Racial Equity) Stimulus Package would make significant investments in our states, urban, rural, and tribal communities, and most importantly in historically undersupported American children and families. The stimulus package should be designed to kickstart progress where disparities have been most pronounced. Specifically, policymakers should start in several key areas:

- Stimulate and Liberate Learning for All through significant investments from birth and throughout the public pre-K–12 education system, as well as free community college and significant investments in HBCUs and other minority-serving institutions;

- Stimulate the Closure of Wealth Gaps through increasing home ownership, small business investments, and capital in Black banks and other financial institutions that more often invest in communities and people of color;
- Stimulate the Reduction of Criminal Justice Disparities with significant state and local community infrastructure investments in job training and placement, judicial system reforms, and community infrastructure projects including investments in community organizing institutions; and
- Stimulate the Well-Being of America's Families and People by guaranteeing access to health care, eliminating education debt, and investing in family leave.

The United States has relied on similar fiscal packages for everything except the existential crisis resulting from centuries of systemic racism. This is the right time to take this step.

The Brookings Institution estimates the total racial wealth gap in the United States is $10.14 trillion,[10] so that number can provide a starting point for what is needed. A multiyear, $10–12 trillion Loving Communities (Racial Equity) Stimulus Package would give states, cities, and rural and tribal communities the resources to change the lives of historically undersupported American children and families.

Meeting the tenets of the Kerner Report is not an abstract ideology. It is very much doable and we have all that we need in the United States to accomplish the goal if we truly have the will.

CONCLUSION

If history has taught us anything, it is that despite the platitude suggesting otherwise, time does not heal all wounds. Intentional and deliberate action does. The prerequisite for change is public will and collective determination. Make no mistake about it: Shifting public will does not occur by happenstance. Policymakers, academics, community leaders, grassroots activists, and pop culture have the power to influence public will.

To the extent that the tenets of the Kerner Commission report have not materialized, there has been little to no sustained momentum to achieve the desired outcomes. Instead of viewing the Kerner Commission report as an invitation to act, far too many political leaders were indifferent and disinterested. In times of crisis, people rise up and some say all the right things, but quickly return to their respective silos. Too many policymakers determine how an issue impacts them before they decide to act.

The same is true today. Too many policymakers see the learning gaps as just an "education," "student," or "Black" issue. In actuality, research clearly indicates disparate student outcomes identifiable by race and ethnicity are the symptoms of larger local, state, and federal systems failures. Rather than the Kerner Report anniversary being a joyous moment of reflection, annually it reminds us of the cost of passive inaction.

It is time for change. As a country, every child deserves to access the type of public loving systems and supports that children in our most affluent zip codes can publicly access. If America is to remain a first-class nation, there can be no second-class children.

No two societies. Rather than allowing racism and hate to be the reason why we continue to fail Black children, let's start a new chapter in the history of our communities, states, and country that tells a story of how the power of love bridged "two societies" and created one America.

NOTES

1. The National Advisory Commission on Civil Disorders, *Report of the National Advisory Commission on Civil Disorders* (Washington, DC: U.S. Department of Justice, Office of Justice Programs, 1968).

2. Terry Gross, "A 'Forgotten History' of How the U.S. Government Segregated America," *NPR*, May 3, 2017, https://www.npr.org/2017/05/03/526655831/a-forgotten-history-of-how-the-u-s-government-segregated-america.

3. Heather Long and Andrew Van Dam, "The Black-White Economic Divide Is as Wide as It Was in 1968," *Washington Post*, June 5, 2020, https://www.washingtonpost.com/business/2020/06/04/economic-divide-black-households/.

4. Neil Bhutta et al., "Disparities in Wealth by Race and Ethnicity in the 2019 Survey of Consumer Finances," Federal Reserve, September 28, 2020, https://www.federalreserve.gov/econres/notes/feds-notes/disparities-in-wealth-by-race-and-ethnicity-in-the-2019-survey-of-consumer-finances-20200928.html.

5. Sean F. Reardon, "The Widening Academic Achievement Gap Between the Rich and the Poor: New Evidence and Possible Explanations," Stanford University, July 2011, https://cepa.stanford.edu/sites/default/files/reardon%20whither%20opportunity%20-%20chapter%205.pdf.

6. Christopher Evans, "TEACHER VOICE: Breaking the School-to-prison Pipeline With 'Windows and Mirrors' for Black Boys," The Hechinger Report, December 7, 2021, https://hechingerreport.org/teacher-voice-mentoring-black-boys/.

7. Tyler Whittenberg et al., "#AssaultAtSpringValley: An Analysis of Police Violence Against Black and Latine Students in Public Schools," Advancement Project and Alliance for Educational Justice, 2021, https://advancementproject.org/wp-content/uploads/2022/12/AP-AssaultAt-Report-V3-120922.pdf.

8. Nikole Hannah-Jones (ed.), "The 1619 Project," *The New York Times*, November 9, 2021, https://www.nytimes.com/interactive/2019/08/14/magazine/1619-america-slavery.html.

9. John H. Jackson et al., "Loving Cities Index: Creating Loving Systems Across Communities to Provide All Students an Opportunity to Thrive," Schott Foundation, 2020, https://lovingcities.schottfoundation.org/wp-content/uploads/2022/09/loving-cities-2020.pdf.

10. Vanessa Williamson, "Closing the Racial Wealth Gap Requires Heavy, Progressive Taxation of Wealth," Brookings, December 9, 2020, https://www.brookings.edu/articles/closing-the-racial-wealth-gap-requires-heavy-progressive-taxation-of-wealth/.

CHAPTER 7

A New Great Society

Randi Weingarten

The Kerner Commission made a tremendous contribution to the unfinished quest to make the United States a more perfect union. The commission warned that "our Nation is moving toward two societies, one black, one white—separate and unequal."[1]

Of course, American society was already separate and unequal. And America's system of education, which should have become the great equalizer in the aftermath of the 1954 *Brown v. Board of Education* decision, was wholly inadequate for most children of color and low-income children. Concerning the education of what they described as the "central-city Negro population," the commission presented three choices:

> Providing Negro children with quality education in integrated schools; providing them with quality education by enriching ghetto schools; or continuing to provide many Negro children with inferior education in racially segregated school systems, severely limiting their lifetime opportunities. Consciously or not, it is the third choice that the Nation is now making, and this choice the Commission rejects totally.[2]

The first two choices required dramatically shifting intentions and actions—choices that were not made. Tragically, the consequences of that indefensible third choice—providing millions of children inferior education in racially (and economically) segregated school systems—reverberate throughout the United States to this day.

Just as the commission rejected that unjustifiable choice and called for a "new will" for national action to right these wrongs, today we must reject the legacies of national inaction to do so. Seventy years after the *Brown* decision, and 56 years after the Kerner Commission report, we must make new choices, with new will, to provide all young people in the United States with a free, high-quality, well-rounded public education in safe and welcoming schools that prepare them to realize their full potential as members of our diverse democracy. The promise of public education is as important today as it was when the Kerner Commission report was issued. That promise must be realized. We must look critically at what works to improve education opportunity and equity—and what does not—and focus on real solutions that can help us achieve this goal.

PROMISING PROGRESS, REGRETTABLE RETREAT

In fact, there was real progress toward narrowing the educational divide in the decades after the *Brown v. Board of Education* decision deemed "separate but equal" schooling unconstitutional. The Elementary and Secondary Education Act (ESEA),[3] signed by President Lyndon B. Johnson in 1965 as part of the "War on Poverty," for the first time provided federal funding for education below the college level and mobilized the federal government as a force for educational equity. That same year, Project Head Start was established to offset disadvantages, particularly poverty, and to intervene at an early age to prevent students from falling behind later. As a result of court decisions demanding the implementation of *Brown* and legislation that made ESEA funds contingent upon school desegregation, significant progress was made toward school desegregation and toward education equity in the late 1960s and 1970s. The aim of these programs was to help students overcome obstacles to learning and thus overcome poverty—and they had significant success.

The educator and researcher Linda Darling-Hammond notes that

> [d]uring the 1960s and '70s, many communities took on efforts like these. As a result, there was a noticeable reduction in educational inequality in the decade after the original Kerner report, when desegregation and school finance reform efforts were launched, and when the Great Society's War on Poverty increased investments in urban and poor rural schools. At that time, substantial gains were made in equalizing both educational inputs and outcomes. The Elementary and Secondary Education Act of 1965 targeted resources to communities with the most need, recognizing that where a child grows up should not determine where he or she ends up. Employment and welfare supports reduced childhood poverty to levels about 60 percent of what they are today and greatly improved children's access to health care.[4]

Research by Rucker Johnson, a labor economist who specializes in the economics of education at the University of California–Berkeley, shows that the enactment of desegregation orders in the 1960s and 1970s led to an immediate average increase in per-pupil education spending of 22.5% for Black children.[5]

Johnson's research also shows that, compared to Black children who did not attend integrated schools, Black children who did so throughout their K–12 years had significantly higher educational attainment, including greater college attendance and completion rates. The average effects of a 5-year exposure to court-ordered school desegregation led to a decline of 11 percentage points in the annual incidence of poverty in adulthood and about a 25% increase in annual family income. Exposure to desegregation beginning in the elementary school years led to a reduction of 3 percentage points in the annual incidence of incarceration and a decline of 22 percentage points in the probability of adult incarceration for African Americans. And it improved adult health status outcomes, as well.

But there has been a retreat from the values of integration and inclusion, and a movement toward top-down accountability versus top-down responsibility. Both have hurt the realization of the promise of a great public education for all. The "two societies"—and the unequal educational systems the commission warned about—are evident today.

The retreat started with Johnson's immediate successor. President Richard M. Nixon sought, with mixed success, to dismantle many of the Great Society programs Johnson championed. But the Reagan administration made it a priority to thrust federal education policy into reverse, favoring tuition tax credits and private school vouchers over strengthening public schools and making education more equitable.[6]

We see the results of this retreat today. "Segregation has been increasing steadily," Darling-Hammond writes, "creating a growing number of apartheid schools that serve almost exclusively students of color from low-income families. These schools are often severely under-resourced, and they struggle to close academic gaps while underwriting the additional costs of addressing the effects of poverty—hunger, homelessness, and other traumas experienced by children and families in low-income communities."[7]

From Reagan to today's tuition vouchers and tax credits, and private, for-profit charter schools, we know that these programs actively destabilize our public schools. Private schools are exempt from federal accountability for students. They can—and many do—discriminate,[8] especially against LGBTQ+ students and students with special needs, because private schools are not required to follow most federal civil rights laws protecting students. They drain funds from public schools.[9] On average, vouchers negatively affect achievement. In fact, vouchers have caused "some of the largest academic drops ever measured in the research record."[10] After decades of experiments with voucher programs, the research is clear: They fail most of the children they purportedly are intended to benefit, children who are disproportionately Black, Brown, and poor.[11]

Yet, today, voucher programs are proliferating. Proponents of vouchers used to argue that they were a way for low-income and minority families to transfer out of low-performing schools. No longer. Today most vouchers go to families who already send their kids to private schools.[12]

With this record, how do proponents of school privatization sell it as a better choice than a neighborhood public school? They go negative. They smear the competition—American public education.

Attacks on public education are not new. The difference today is that the attacks are intended to destroy it. In a 2022 speech, culture war operative and Governor Ron DeSantis's appointee Christopher Rufo put it bluntly, "To get to universal school choice, you really need to operate from a premise of universal public school distrust." To this end, he says, his side has "to be ruthless and brutal."[13]

And, I would add, well-funded, which it is. The DeVos, Bradley, Koch, Uihlein and Walton family foundations and others have poured many millions of dollars into anti-public education, pro-privatization groups like the American Federation for Children and EdChoice.

The Betsy DeVos wing of the school privatization movement is methodically working its plan: Starve public schools of the funds they need to succeed. Criticize them for their shortcomings. Erode trust in public schools by stoking fear and division, including attempting to pit parents against teachers. Replace them with private, religious, online, and home schools. All toward their end goal of destroying public education as we know it, atomizing and balkanizing education in America, bullying the most vulnerable among us, and leaving the students with the greatest needs in public schools with the most meager resources.

It's a scheme to destabilize and undermine public education led by an often-extremist minority of Americans.[14] It's hurting our efforts to do the work we need to do, which is educating the 90% of students—nearly 50 million—who attend America's public schools. And the urgent work of helping kids recover from learning loss, loneliness, and literacy challenges.

These systematic efforts to undermine public education and replace it with private alternatives are not new. Recall the segregation decried by the Kerner Commission. We are in a similar fight, against similar forces that are keeping the same children from getting the public education they need and deserve.

These efforts to undermine public education not only hinder opportunity in America, they erode democracy and pluralism. The growing income inequality and high rates of poverty in the United States pose additional threats to our democracy—and to children's ability to thrive.

The United States has one of the highest child income poverty rates of OECD (the Organization for Economic Cooperation and Development) nations—ranking 31st out of 34.[15] Finland, whose education system is frequently held up as the best in the world, is unsurprisingly at number one.

Greatly reducing the child poverty rate in the United States is within our grasp—Congress passed a measure that did so in 2021. The American Rescue Plan expanded eligibility for the Child Tax Credit and the value of the credit—cutting child poverty in half before the Republican-controlled Congress discontinued it.[16]

Income inequality in the United States is the highest of all the G7 nations,[17] according to data from the Organization for Economic Cooperation and Development.[18] The economist Thomas Piketty calculates that it is "probably higher than in any other society at any time in the past, anywhere in the world."[19] In the mid-1950s, 1 in every 3 American workers belonged to a union; today only 1 in every 10 belongs to a union. As union membership has declined, income inequality has grown.[20]

The Black–white income gap in the United States has persisted since the original Kerner Report. The difference in median household incomes between white and Black Americans has grown from about $23,800 in 1970 to roughly $33,000 in 2018 (as measured in 2018 dollars).[21] And the wealth gap remains stunning, with Black households' median wealth at $24,000 compared with white households' $189,000.[22]

President Johnson declared that "The Great Society ... demands an end to poverty and racial injustice."[23] That Great Society still is far from being realized. A great society adheres to an implicit belief that we all do better when we all do better. We must collectively commit to achieving new Great Society ambitions—health care for all; worker voice through unionization, collective bargaining, and pro-worker legislation; affordable good-quality housing; a robust response to climate change; well-funded public schools and colleges; and affordable higher education.

When we all do better, it reduces the inequality that poses a threat to democracy. It is the opposite of the zero-sum thinking that stokes populism and threatens pluralism.

Just as the labor movement changed the trajectory for workers in the 1930s through the 1970s, and Great Society programs improved well-being in the 1960s and 1970s, we can use the levers of public education and the labor movement to change the country's trajectory again.

This new Great Society is a vital long-term vision, but there are steps we can take today to support students' well-being and educational success—real solutions for kids and communities.

REAL SOLUTIONS FOR KIDS AND COMMUNITY

Poll[24] after poll[25] shows that parents support public schools and trust public school teachers. And when public schools need help, parents and the public want schools strengthened,[26] not abandoned. Polling from the Hunt Institute shows that voters' top education priorities are grounded in common sense: teaching students real-world skills and ensuring children read at grade level in schools that are free of guns, violence and bullying.[27] These are the heart of AFT's Real Solutions for Kids and Communities[28] campaign we embarked on in 2023.

I visit schools across the country every chance I get. What I have witnessed, what educators have shown me, what research has proven—all form a set of strategies and solutions that help young people and strengthen public education.

This set of strategies can help not just to overcome the learning loss resulting from the COVID-19 pandemic, but to prepare all children with the knowledge and skills they need for their lives, for college, for career, and for citizenship. These strategies can help us create safe and welcoming environments and bring joy back to learning.

These strategies are

- unlocking the power and possibility that come from being a confident reader;
- ensuring that all children have opportunities to learn by doing—engaging in experiential learning, including career and technical education;
- caring for young people's mental health and well-being, including by demanding that social media companies protect, not prey on, children;
- catalyzing a vast expansion of community schools that wrap services around students and families and meaningfully partner with families;
- and, of course, fighting for the investments that fund the teaching and school staff and other supports students need to thrive.

Parents and educators want school environments that are safe and supportive, where kids can get a well-rounded education, and that help students develop skills that prepare them for life, college and career, and civic engagement.

READING

It starts with reading, the foundation for all other academic learning. The ability to read is a fundamental right, and teaching children to read is the most fundamental responsibility of schooling.

The AFT has been advocating for and training educators in an evidence-based approach to reading instruction for decades. The science of reading points to a systemic approach that includes phonics instruction along with giving students plenty of opportunities to read high-quality books, to develop their background knowledge, and to build their vocabulary.

These principles must be included in teacher preparation programs, in curriculums, and in high-quality professional development. And they should be supported by state policy and legislation and district-level implementation. Educators should have opportunities to work peer-to-peer to improve their practice with ongoing professional learning that the AFT and other credible organizations can partner on.

While some continue to ignore the science of reading or think that tutoring alone will boost literacy, new research from the Albert Shanker Institute evaluating state reading reform laws shows more consensus in this evidence-based approach than we have ever seen.[29]

This is good news, but teachers need to be supported in this work. This change won't happen overnight. The AFT is committed to fighting for and providing opportunities for teachers to learn, practice, and be mentored in evidence-based approaches to reading instruction.

The AFT is also investing in a way for more educators to easily access these approaches through Reading Universe,[30] a project led by one of our longtime partners, WETA, along with First Book and the Barksdale Reading Institute, whose work in Mississippi has moved 4th-grade reading achievement from the bottom of the country up to the national average.

Reading Universe will offer educators everywhere access to the strategies and skills that enable them to help kids be confident and joyful readers, regardless of the curriculum their district or school requires. And it's been built from the start with a cadre of skilled teachers and researchers. This powerful tool is free and available online to every educator because all students need and deserve high-quality literacy instruction.

Students need engaging books of their own. The AFT, in partnership with First Book, has given away more than 10 million free books to children, families, and educators over our decade-long partnership. And, through our Reading Opens the World program, we have given away nearly 2 million books in the last year alone. These efforts build community and bring educators and families together around the joy and importance of reading.

EXPERIENTIAL LEARNING—LEARNING BY DOING

We know that many students are disengaged or don't want to go to school at all. Honestly, I get it. There are a lot of school experiences that don't interest or inspire young people.

But not in Raphael Bonhomme's classroom. Raphael teaches 3rd grade at School Within School on Capitol Hill, in Washington, DC, and he is an AFT Civics Design Team member.

Raphael's students learn about local government by role-playing that they are DC council members, addressing real issues affecting their city. At the end of 3rd grade, his students create DC tour companies, researching the city's historical sites. They then role-play how they would attract people to take their tour.

Denise Pfeiffer, a high school chemistry teacher in Cincinnati, creates escape rooms in her classroom. Her students work in pairs, and, to get out, they have to solve puzzles that embed the content they have learned.

These are examples of experiential learning, and I know how engaging it can be. I had students in my Street Law classes at Clara Barton High School role-play housing court mock trials. And in my AP government course, my students acted out mock appellate court arguments.

In this age of artificial intelligence and ChatGPT, this type of learning is essential to being able to analyze information, think critically, apply knowledge, and discern fact from fiction. Experiential learning engages students in deeper learning and provides them with real-world, real-life skills.

Career and technical education (CTE) is project-based experiential learning at its best. CTE prepares students not only for traditional trades programs like welding, plumbing, carpentry, and auto repair, but also for careers in health care, advanced manufacturing and aeronautics, information technology, graphic design, and so much more. And it works. Ninety-four percent of students who concentrate in CTE graduate from high school, and 72% of them go on to college.

In Syracuse, New York, a new plant being built by the semiconductor manufacturer Micron will create tens of thousands of jobs. At the AFT's initiative, and working with the New York State United Teachers and the United Federation of Teachers in New York City, Micron is partnering with 10 school systems and their local teachers unions in New York State to develop a curriculum framework that prepares high school students for engineering and technical careers in the microchip industry.[31]

In rural southeast Ohio, again with the help of our union, schools in New Lexington have expanded CTE to include everything from robotics for 3rd graders to a partnership with the IBEW to train high school students for in-demand electrical jobs. Their graduation rate has shot up to 97%, and 30% of students earn college credits before high school graduation.

By being intentional about this—starting by high school, partnering with employers, creating paid internships and apprenticeships, and offering industry-approved credentials or college credit—we can set young people on a path to a career or higher education, or both, right out of high school.

Educators who have been empowered to engage in experiential learning with their students know its transformational power. And they know that standardized test-based accountability systems can't capture the richness of experiential learning. We need to reimagine our accountability systems to assess what is needed in today's world, not yesterday's, such as the ability to communicate, work cooperatively, think critically, troubleshoot, and be creative. These are the lifelong skills that will enable students to thrive no matter what the future holds—including changes in the labor market and in artificial intelligence.

Educators are figuring out that juggernaut—generative AI—largely without any guidance. The AFT is offering educators tools and guidance to prepare their students for this new world and we are advocating for policies that will help maximize the benefits and limit the perils of AI. We are partnering with the AFL-CIO and Microsoft to ensure that workers have a voice in the development and implementation of new technology.[32]

Students need to be equipped for all of this—to harness the good and prevent the harm of new and future technologies—so we must support their teachers to help them navigate the complexity of their changing world.

Experiential learning prepares students for the opportunities of tomorrow, and community schools help solve the challenges students and families confront today.

COMMUNITY SCHOOLS

Hunger, housing insecurity, trauma, physical health problems—even the lack of clean clothing—all negatively affect children's ability to learn. And now, after the isolation, stress and, for many young people, loss of loved ones during the COVID-19 pandemic, their needs are even greater.

Sustainable community schools can wrap so much around public schools—health care, mental health services, food assistance, child care, enrichment, tutoring, and sports and after-school activities. It all supports what students and families need to learn, live, and thrive. Through meaningful partnerships with families and deep community engagement, they become centers of their communities.

United Community Schools, a network of community schools in New York City that has expanded into Albany, has higher rates of vulnerable students than other public schools. Yet they perform better on measures like college readiness and the progress of English language learners and students with disabilities.

Likewise with San Francisco's Dr. Martin Luther King, Jr. Academic Middle School. Prior to becoming a community school in 2015, MLK struggled with enrollment and academics, and educators were burned out. Now, with support from 40 community partners, there have been significant increases in math and reading scores at MLK, and teachers are choosing to stay.

A recent RAND study of community schools in New York City found positive impacts on both attendance and graduation rates.[33] In New Mexico, community schools in operation for 5 or more years have better-than-average student achievement growth and higher attendance rates, and employed more highly effective teachers. And Robeson High School in Philadelphia went from nearly closing to a 95% graduation rate after implementing the community school model.

I advocated for a broad expansion of community schools in my first speech as AFT president in 2008. Today, I am proud to say that AFT members have helped create more than 700 community schools across the country, and we are part of a movement calling for 25,000 community schools by 2025.

THE HARMFUL IMPACTS OF SOCIAL MEDIA

While community schools can provide a safe and supportive environment for young people, there is a virtual environment that threatens their physical and emotional well-being—social media and the online world.

Even before the pandemic, many experts connected the harmful impacts of social media and the nefarious practices of social media companies to the youth mental health crisis.

Research has shown that teens who spend more than 3 hours per day on social media are at double the risk for experiencing symptoms of depression and anxiety.[34] Social media can increase bullying and diminish people's ability to interact face to face, and it has been tied to eating disorders, suicidal thoughts, and feelings of being less than or left out. Too many children have an addictive relationship with social media that families can't fix on their own.

Schools are also grappling with an increase in dangerous and disruptive behavior linked to social media, such as viral challenges. Challenges to destroy school property, or to slap a teacher, or to "swat"—the challenge that encourages students to report hoax shootings—are dangerous and traumatic for students, staff, and families.

As schools are struggling to hire mental health professionals and to provide training to teachers to better support students with their mental health, we are calling on social media companies to step up.

Social media companies have shirked their responsibility to protect kids. Facebook's own research showed how their algorithms harm users, especially adolescent girls. Did they change their practices to protect kids based on what they knew? No—they hid it.

The AFT is taking action. We are working with ParentsTogether (a platform of 2.5 million parents), Fairplay for Kids, Design It for Us, and the American Psychological Association, to call on social media platforms to make fundamental changes to prioritize safety for children. Our report "Likes vs. Learning: The Real Cost of Social Media for Schools,"[35] calls for the following safeguards: (1) turn on the strongest safety features by default; (2) make changes that deter students from overuse and addictive behavior; (3) protect children's privacy; (4) shield them from risky algorithms; and (5) directly engage and work with schools and families. Social media platforms could implement these today.

We are calling on Congress to step up, too, by passing legislation to protect young people using social media, and to increase their safety and privacy online.

We are also demanding action to confront the leading cause of death of children in the United States—firearms. We support gun safety legislation to expand background checks, require responsible firearm storage, and raise the age to 21 to purchase semiautomatic firearms.

ENSURING WE HAVE THE SCHOOL STAFF AND RESOURCES STUDENTS NEED TO THRIVE

The stresses of the COVID-19 era—plus the culture wars, attacks on teachers, inadequate pay, poor teaching and learning conditions, and the threat of school shootings—have made recent years the toughest in modern times for educators. Despite it all, teachers have thrown themselves into the mission of helping students recover academically, socially, and emotionally. But many are being pushed over the brink.

Even before the pandemic, nearly 300,000 teachers were leaving the profession each year. Now, it's closer to 400,000. And the teacher pipeline has collapsed as college students and career-changers choose not to go into education. All this contributes to a teacher shortage crisis.[36]

Why do we have a teacher shortage? Because we have a shortage of respect for educators. A shortage of the professional working conditions that allow teachers and other staff to do their best for their students. And teacher pay has been falling relative to other college graduates' pay for the last 40 years, creating a shortage of pay for what is arguably the most important job in the world.

The AFT Teacher and School Staff Shortage Task Force released a report in 2022 that details solutions to this crisis: family-sustaining wages; time to plan and prepare for classes, collaborate with colleagues, and participate in meaningful and in-school professional development; and the power to make day-to-day classroom decisions.[37]

AFT affiliates have used the collective bargaining process to negotiate provisions to support and retain educators. United Teachers Los Angeles's contract includes higher pay and smaller class sizes, more funding for community schools, and support for vulnerable students. The Saint Paul Federation of Educators won an agreement for all schools to have mental health support teams. The Cincinnati Federation of Teachers' contract requires an Instructional Leadership Team in every school that puts decisions about school operations and improvement in the hands of those closest to students.

The Kansas City Federation of Teachers used the AFT staffing shortage report as their contract blueprint. Now, every first- and second-year teacher will be mentored by an exemplary teacher, who will be paid for serving as a mentor. The union secured the highest starting teacher salaries in the region and increases to keep teachers in the profession.

The United Educators of San Francisco used collective bargaining to make major strides in retaining and recruiting educators. The agreement made significant improvements to pay for teachers as well as positions that support student learning and growth like paraprofessionals, nurses, psychologists, and social workers. Like Kansas City, the agreement also establishes a paid mentorship program that assigns a mentor to a first-year teacher.

Addressing the high rates of turnover in the early years of teaching, the United Federation of Teachers in New York City agreement cut in half the time it takes a teacher to earn more than $100,000 from 15 years to 8 years. With an eye toward the future, the agreement also expands career and technical education, growing career pathways for students that is backed by robust professional development opportunities for educators to deliver high-quality CTE curricula.

For as long as I can remember, when I and others advocated for higher pay for teachers and adequate and equitable education funding, opponents would fire back with some variation of "money doesn't matter."

Today, there is a far-reaching consensus among researchers that money matters in education: the level of government funding makes a real, vital difference in the quality of education students receive.[38] A comprehensive review of the best research shows that increased funding significantly improves student academic performance and rates of college attendance, and that additional resources have the greatest positive effect for students from economically disadvantaged backgrounds.[39] Even one-time skeptics, such as the conservative researcher Eric Hanushek, now acknowledge that appropriately spent, increases in funding for schools benefit students in important ways.[40]

To finally address the educational and equity issues raised by the Kerner Commission report, funding of public education must be guided by three principles: adequacy, effort, and progressivity. Adequacy is the extent to which government funding is sufficient to allow all students to achieve the outcomes expected of them in national and state educational standards. Effort is the extent to which government entities are dedicating an appropriate share of their resources to public education. And progressivity is the extent to which funds are being apportioned to provide the most support in achieving educational success to students with the greatest academic needs.

Education in the United States is mainly the responsibility of state governments, and the bulk of education funding in the United States comes from state and local governments. That is why changes to strengthen American education and make it more equitable must begin with those governments, and with a substantially greater fiscal effort and greater resources for the students most in need on their part.

But the federal government has an important role to play, one which goes beyond the original purpose of ESEA to ameliorate the most extreme educational inequalities. Federal funds should be more directed to students with the greatest needs, as Title I and IDEA were and are intended. States that are making greater efforts to fund public education and to ensure that their funds are apportioned progressively should be rewarded with additional federal funds, and incentives should be created to encourage more states to improve on their adherence to the guiding principles I outlined. Further, the federal government should require transparent education funding reports from state and local governments, and it should collect and publish those reports.

Public schools are more than physical structures. They are the manifestation of our civic values and ideals: That education is so important for individuals and for society that a free education must be available to all. That all young people should have opportunities to prepare for life, college, career, and citizenship. That, in a pluralistic society such as the United States, mere tolerance of people with different beliefs and backgrounds is insufficient; we must be open to building bonds across race, class, and culture. And that, as the founders believed, an educated citizenry is essential to protect our democracy from demagogues.

When kids go to school together, they become part of a community and their families become part of a community. That community comes together at school concerts, basketball games, and science fairs, and for shelter and comfort, when people are displaced by natural disasters or, far too often, at vigils for victims of gun violence. In good times and bad, public schools are cornerstones of community, of our democracy, of our economy, and of our nation.

The United States has lacked sufficient will to secure and sustain the goals of the Kerner Commission—to greatly reduce racial injustice, economic inequality, and poverty. Strong public schools in every community and a vibrant, just economy can democratize opportunity in America. But this requires summoning the national will to support great educators in well-resourced public schools; to ensure workers have a voice in the workplace and family-sustaining wages through a thriving labor movement; to safeguard citizens' right to voice and vote; and to protect our democracy from clear and present threats.

We can and must commit to achieving these goals and finally create a great society for all Americans. In a great society, all people have access to adequate housing and health care, and the ability to meet their own and their families' economic needs. A great society does not fear pluralism or foster populism. A great society provides a high-quality, free public education for all so we all can realize our full potential and the full benefits and responsibilities of citizenship. This is the society we must, finally, fully commit to creating.

NOTES

1. The National Advisory Commission on Civil Disorders, *Report of the National Advisory Commission on Civil Disorders* [Kerner Report] (Washington, DC: U.S. Department of Justice, Office of Justice Programs, 1968), 1.

2. Kerner Report, 240.

3. Harvey Kantor, "Education, Social Reform, and the State: ESEA and Federal Education Policy in the 1960s," *American Journal of Education* 100, no. 1 (1991): 47–83.

4. Linda Darling-Hammond, *Education and the Path to One Nation, Indivisible* (Palo Alto, CA: Learning Policy Institute, 2018).

5. Rucker C. Johnson and Alexander Nazaryan, *Children of the Dream: Why School Integration Works* (New York: Basic Books, 2019).

6. Anne Bridgeman, "Reagan Pledges Administration Focus on Choice," *Education Week*, March 6, 1985.

7. Darling-Hammond, *Education and the Path to One Nation, Indivisible*, 1.

8. Julia Donheiser, "When Can Private Schools Discriminate Against Students?" *Chalkbeat*, August 10, 2017.

9. Iris Hinh and Whitney Tucker, "State Lawmakers Are Draining Public Revenues with School Vouchers," Center for Budget and Policy Priorities (blog), June 12, 2023, https://www.cbpp.org/blog/state-lawmakers-are-draining-public-revenues-with-school-vouchers.

10. Josh Cowan, "School Vouchers: There Is No Upside," The Albert Shanker Institute (blog), February 21, 2023, https://www.shankerinstitute.org/blog/school-vouchers-there-no-upside.

11. Kevin Carey, "Dismal Voucher Results Surprise Researchers as DeVos Era Begins," *New York Times*, February 23, 2017.

12. Matt Barnum and Alicia A. Caldwell, "Vouchers Helping Families Already in Private School, Early Data Show," *Wall Street Journal*, December 3, 2023.

13. Hillsdale College, "Chris Rufo | Laying Siege to the Institutions | Livestream April 5, 2022," YouTube, April 6, 2022, https://www.youtube.com/watch?v=W8Hh0GqoJcE&t=2087s.

14. Kathryn Joyce, "Republicans Don't Want to Reform Public Education. They Want to End It," *The New Republic*, September 30, 2021.

15. Sophie Collyer et al., "A Step in the Right Direction: The Expanded Child Tax Credit Would Move the United States' High Child Poverty Rate Closer to Peer Nations," Columbia University, Center on Poverty and Social Policy and UNICEF Innocenti, Global Office of Research and Foresight, 2022, https://www.povertycenter.columbia.edu/publication/2022/child-tax-credit-and-relative-poverty.

16. Joe Hughes, "Lapse of Expanded Child Tax Credit Led to Unprecedented Rise in Child Poverty," *Just Taxes Blog*, Institute on Taxation and Economic Policy, September 12, 2023, https://itep.org/lapse-of-expanded-child-tax-credit-led-to-unprecedented-rise-in-child-poverty-2023.

17. CFR.org Editors, "What Does the G7 Do?" Council on Foreign Relations, June 28, 2023, https://www.cfr.org/backgrounder/what-does-g7-do.

18. "America Has the Most Extreme Income Inequality Among G-7 Peers," Brink News, Marsh McLennan, February 27, 2020, https://www.brinknews.com/quick-take/america-has-the-most-extreme-income-inequality-among-g-7-peers/.

19. Thomas Piketty and Arthur Goldhammer, *Capital in the Twenty-First Century* (Cambridge, MA: Belknap Press, 2017).

20. Laura Feiveson, "Labor Unions and the U.S. Economy," U.S. Department of Treasury, August 28, 2023.

21. Katherine Schaeffer, "6 Facts About Economic Iinequality in the U.S.," Pew Research Center, February 7, 2020.

22. Doug Irving, "What Would It Take to Close America's Black-White Wealth Gap?," RAND, May 9, 2023, https://www.rand.org/pubs/articles/2023/what-would-it-take-to-close-americas-black-white-wealth-gap.html.

23. Lyndon B. Johnson, "Remarks at the University of Michigan," The American Presidency Project, May 22, 1964, https://www.lbjlibrary.org/object/text/remarks-university-michigan-05-22-1964.

24. PDK International, "Local Public School Ratings Rise, Even as the Teaching Profession Loses Ground," 2022.

25. Ipsos, "Americans Trust Teachers, but Some Still Want Parents to be the Primary Voices on What's Taught," June 2, 2023.

26. American Federation of Teachers, "New poll: Voters prioritize school basics over culture wars," January 13, 2023.

27. The Hunt Institute, "2023 Across the Aisle Report: 2024 Voters Communicate "Core Values" for Education—Want Real-World Skills, Safe Schools, and Literacy," December 14, 2023.

28. American Federation of Teachers, "Real Solutions for Kids and Communities," n.d., https://www.aft.org/realsolutions.

29. Susan B. Neuman, Esther Quintero, and Kayla Reist, "Reading Reform Across America: A Survey of State Legislation," Albert Shanker Institute, 2023.

30. Reading Universe, accessed April 22, 2024, https://readinguniverse.org

31. American Federation of Teachers, "Unions, Micron and New York State Launch $4 Million Advanced Technology Learning Framework," December 7, 2023.

32. AFL-CIO, "AFL-CIO and Microsoft Announce New Tech-Labor Partnership on AI and the Future of the Workforce," December 11, 2023.

33. William R. Johnston et al., "Illustrating the Promise of Community Schools: An Assessment of the Impact of the New York City Community Schools Initiative," RAND, 2020.

34. U.S. Surgeon General's Advisory, "Social Media Youth Mental Health 2023," U.S. Department of Health and Human Services, 2023, https://www.hhs.gov/surgeongeneral/priorities/youth-mental-health/social-media/index.html.

35. American Federation of Teachers, "Likes vs. Learning: The Real Cost of Social Media for Schools," 2023.

36. Matt Barnum, "The Teacher Profession Is Facing a Post-Pandemic Crisis," *Chalkbeat*, June 27, 2023.

37. American Federation of Teachers, "Here Today, Gone Tomorrow? What America Must Do to Attract and Retain the Educators and School Staff Our Students Need," 2022.

38. Bruce Baker, "Does Money Matter in Education? Second Edition," Albert Shanker Institute, 2019.

39. C. Kirabo Jackson and Claire L. Mackevicius, "What Impacts Can We Expect from School Spending Policy? Evidence from Evaluations in the U.S.," *American Economic Journal: Applied Economics* 16 no. 1 (January 2024): 412–46, doi:10.1257/app.20220279.

40. Matt Barnum, "An Economist Spent Decades Saying Money Wouldn't Help Schools. Now His Research Suggests Otherwise," *Chalkbeat*, May 16, 2023.

CHAPTER 8

Action to Reaffirm
Equity, Racial Justice, and the Future of College Admissions

Dwayne Kwaysee Wright and Michael Feuer

INTRODUCTION

"Our Nation is moving toward two societies, one black, one white—separate and unequal."[1]

These words became infamous when offered by the National Advisory Commission on Civil Disorders, the entity which became known as the Kerner Commission after Illinois Governor Otto Kerner was chosen to chair it.[2] The commission was established in 1967 by President Lyndon Johnson via Executive Order 11365. Its goals were to investigate the "causes of urban riots in the United States during the summer of 1967" and to provide recommendations to the government.[3] President Johnson charged the commission with analyzing not only the sparks of the riots but their deeper, underlying causes as well. Provocatively and ambitiously, the commission was tasked with developing recommendations for improving America's racial climate, and hopefully contributing to a more general improvement in American life. President Johnson hoped that by analyzing the faults in our union, the Kerner Commission could forge a path together to making the nation a better place.

The Kerner Commission's findings certainly would not be shocking today. However, at the time, more than 55 years ago, it was a groundbreaking report that validated the cries of those in the Civil Rights movement protesting racial injustice and opened the eyes of Americans who had not been aware of deep-rooted inequalities.[4] The commission's report attributed the civil disorders principally to lack of economic opportunity for Black Americans, police brutality, individual and institutional racism, and a biased orientation of national media to perspectives of White Americans versus others.[5]

A major determinant of the lack of economic opportunity for Black Americans was the denial of equal educational opportunity, which by 1967 had been a stain on our society for more than 2 centuries and only partially addressed through federal legislation and landmark Supreme Court decisions.[6] Slavery, aptly called America's "original sin," was by definition an institution of inequality and, perhaps obviously, the foundational obstacle that denied Black Americans—and significantly impeded their progeny—opportunities to advance economically.[7]

According to the NCES Digest of Educational Statistics, 8% of White Americans had a bachelor's or higher degree in 1960 compared to 3% of Black Americans.[8] Data from 2022 shows that 42% of White Americans have a bachelor's or higher degree compared to 28% of Black Americans. Clearly, much progress has been made, but racial disparities persist. As reported by Brookings Institution analysts, "Racial and ethnic achievement gaps have been on a gradual, and at times bumpy, decline since the 1970s."[9]

Still, we are far from fulfilling the ideals enshrined in our founding documents. In the hope that historical lessons can inform a reinforced commitment to the promise of economic, educational, and racial justice, we focus in this chapter on the origins and evolution of one key ingredient in the struggle, namely "affirmative action."

More specifically, in envisioning a Kerner 2.0 for 2024, we revisit the history of race-conscious admissions in higher education up through its recent curtailment by the U.S. Supreme Court. Space limits prevent a more complete history, but we hope here to provide an analysis focused on (1) the origins of affirmative action and (2) options for continuing to aspire toward its principal goals even under evolving legal and constitutional constraints.

WHY AFFIRMATIVE ACTION IS AN UNCOMFORTABLE TOPIC IN AMERICA

Affirmative action is one of the most polarizing topics in American culture today. Disagreement and debate rage on, not only between its proponents and opponents but within those groups as well. Affirmative action is such an uncomfortable topic because it sits awkwardly between two American ideals: the right to be judged on one's individual merits and the right to have past wrongs repaired by institutions where they work or study, and society generally, which benefited from those wrongs.

America's Racist History

On Thursday, March 14th, 1968, Dr. Martin Luther King, Jr. spoke at Grosse Pointe High School in Michigan, giving a speech that came to be known as "The Other America."[10] It was nearly a month after the release of the Kerner Commission's report, and the speech might as well have been a mirror into the commission's prognosis and recommendations.[11] In perhaps its most oft-quoted portion, Dr. King opined on the same "urban racial tension" that the Kerner Commission had been tasked with analyzing:

> But it is not enough for me to stand before you tonight and condemn riots. It would be morally irresponsible for me to do that without, at the same time, condemning the contingent, intolerable conditions that exist in our society. These conditions are the things that cause individuals to feel that they have no other alternative than to engage in violent rebellions to get attention. And I must say tonight that a riot is the language of the unheard. And what is it America has failed to hear? It has failed to hear that the plight of the negro poor has worsened over the last twelve or fifteen years. It has failed to hear that the promises of freedom and justice have not been met. And it has failed to hear that large segments

of white society are more concerned about tranquility and the status quo than about justice and humanity.

The Kerner Commission's report had highlighted the lack of economic opportunity for Black Americans as a major cause of racial unrest in America. In fact, President Lyndon Johnson gave the commission its charge while rioting was going on in Detroit.[12] Again, a major cause of economic inequality suffered by Black Americans was the denial of equal educational opportunity. This disadvantage has its origins in chattel slavery that had existed in various forms for over 200 years, from 1619 through the end of the Civil War in 1865.[13] During that time, the majority of Black Americans, treated more like property than people, were considered ineligible for educational resources afforded to other children and, put simply, were denied the right to learn at every stage of life.[14]

However, even after the end of American slavery *de jure*, racial discrimination and segregation continued *de facto* to deny many Black Americans equal educational opportunity compared to many of their White fellow citizens. The set of government-sanctioned policies that reinforced that lived reality for generations of Black Americans was called "Jim Crow," and they gained protection through the Supreme Court's decision in *Plessy v. Ferguson* (1896).[15] It would not be until 1954—roughly 6 decades after *Plessy* and 90 years after the end of the U.S. Civil War—that racial discrimination and segregation were struck down by the U.S. Supreme Court in the landmark *Brown v. Board of Education* case (1954).[16]

Before connecting *Brown* to what became known as affirmative action, it is important to underscore that the end of legalized segregation did not end discrimination.[17] There is ample research evidence documenting that inequalities experienced by Black Americans today have their origins in the historical denial of equal educational access and opportunity.[18] Black Americans had effectively been denied resources for the 335-year period between 1619 and 1954. At first these policies treated Black Americans as second-class citizens and were intentional and government-supported. However, even after *Brown*, the disadvantage perpetuated through such polices proved extremely hard to mitigate. What would be needed was more than the end to formal, government-sponsored, racially imposed disadvantage; to atone meaningfully for America's original sin, what was needed was something a bit more assertive, or, shall we say, affirmative.

It is useful to trace the history of affirmative action through court cases, policy directives, and executive orders that challenged the use of the practice under the Equal Protection Clause of the Fourteenth Amendment to the U.S. Constitution, ratified after the Civil War to ensure equal treatment of the newly freed slaves. That amendment provides, in relevant part, that "[n]o state shall . . . deny to any person within its jurisdiction the equal protection of the laws" (U.S. Constitution, Fourteenth Amendment).

Brown v. Board of Education

As late as 1954, laws and policies in America either required or at least permitted segregation in public schools based on race, the theory being that separate institutions for

Americans would be acceptable if those institutions were "equal."[19] But separate turned out to be very unequal in the classrooms of America that were under the influence of Jim Crow. The families of Black students sued and alleged that the unequal treatment deprived them of equal protection under the Fourteenth Amendment. The U.S. Supreme Court, *in a unanimous decision*, agreed and overruled the "separate but equal" doctrine affirmed in *Plessy*.

Much has been written and said since the *Brown* decision about what it really meant,[20] and a full examination of the debates surrounding the ruling, its implementation, and aftermath are beyond our scope. But it is important to note that by mandating that schools desegregate, the Court clearly sought not just to impose formal equality going forward but to give Black students opportunities that they had been denied.

President Kennedy's Executive Order

Because of the monumental significance of *Brown* in reversing years of legally sanctioned racial injustice, it is often presented as an end point rather than as the starting point it was intended to be.[21] Rather than eliminating the conditions that Dr. King referred to in his "Other America" speech, *Brown* began to allow for the formation of new cultural norms and values that would eventually allow Black Americans to access the educational opportunity that their ancestors had been denied but which had been available to many, but certainly not all, white Americans, for centuries.[22, 23] Through no fault of their own, many Black American families had much catching up to do. One of the largest gaps existed in advanced degree attainment.

On March 6, 1961, 7 years after *Brown*, President John F. Kennedy signed Executive Order 10925, which required government contractors to "take affirmative action to ensure that applicants are employed, and that employees are treated during employment, without regard to their race, creed, color or national origin."[24] This executive order gave federal contracting agencies authority to institute procedures against federal contractors who violated EEO rules.[25] It also created a Committee on Equal Employment Opportunity, which would go on to become the Equal Employment Opportunity Committee.[26]

President Johnson at Howard University

On June 4, 1965, 2 years before assembling the Kerner Commission and 100 years after the end of the Civil War, President Johnson gave a graduation speech at Howard University that has come to represent the most robust defense of the concept of what is now called "affirmative action."[27] In that speech, Johnson stated

> You do not take a man who for years has been hobbled by chains, liberate him, bring him to the starting line of a race, saying, 'You are free to compete with all the others,' and still justly believe you have been completely fair.

It is important to underscore that Johnson introduced the concept of "fairness" when presenting the idea that formal equality alone would not be enough to bring generations of Black Americans hobbled by individual and institutional racism to an even starting line with those Americans who had not had the same historic experience.

President Nixon's Turn

Affirmative action is often presented as a "partisan" issue in which progressives are typecast as supporters and conservatives as opponents. However, it is noteworthy that the man who would later be called the "father of affirmative action" was a lifelong Republican. Arthur Fletcher, Assistant Secretary of Labor for Wage and Labor Standards in the Nixon administration,[28] is credited with leading the design, revision, and defense of the Philadelphia Plan, which required government contractors to hire minority workers, under the authority of Executive Order 11246.[29] The plan worked in Philadelphia and was extended to other cities.[30] Despite running against Lyndon Johnson as "a law-and-order candidate" and repudiating much of the message of the Kerner Commission, President Nixon in some ways proved as (or more) effective as his Democratic counterparts in implementing affirmative action.

Bakke

The first major U.S. Supreme Court case involving affirmative action was *Regents of the University of California v. Bakke* (1978). Allan Bakke had been denied admission to the medical school at the University of California–Davis. At the time, the school's "special admissions program" allowed members of certain minority groups to be considered exclusively for 16 of the 100 places.[31] Bakke had been denied admission to the school under the general admissions program, while applicants with lower entrance examination scores had been admitted under the special program.

Justice Lewis Powell's opinion became the controlling opinion in *Bakke*. For purposes of the Equal Protection Clause, he argued that all racial/ethnic distinctions were inherently "suspect" and thus called for "the most exacting judicial examination" (i.e., "strict scrutiny"), without regard to whether they are intended to help or hurt the intended beneficiaries. Most importantly, he permitted a "diversity rationale," allowing consideration of race as one of several factors in the admissions process to promote the "educational benefits of diversity."

Grutter/Gratz

Twenty-five years after *Bakke* and about 50 years after *Brown*, the U.S. Supreme Court would again rule on the use of race in college admissions in a pair of cases called *Grutter v. Bollinger* (2003) and *Gratz v. Bollinger* (2003). In *Gratz*, the challenge was brought against the University of Michigan's undergraduate admissions policy, which was based on a point system that automatically granted 20 points to applicants from underrepresented minority groups. The Court found that this policy made race a determining factor for minoritized applicants, and struck it down on grounds it was "not narrowly tailored" to achieve the university's asserted "compelling interest" in diversity.

However, when the Court in *Grutter* examined the University of Michigan Law School's admissions program, it found that the plan did not define diversity solely in terms of race and ethnicity but considered them as "plus" factors affecting overall diversity. Thus, in *Grutter*, the Court held that the law school's admissions plan was "narrowly tailored" to further the school's compelling interest of diversity and upheld the practice.

Fisher

In 2004, Abigail Fisher, a white woman, was denied admission to the University of Texas. That year, 42 white applicants and 5 applicants of color with lower academic scores (grade point average and SAT) gained admission.[32] Fisher challenged her rejection in court, arguing that her race had been the determining factor.

In 2013, the Supreme Court held (in what became known as *Fisher I*) that the trial court and court of appeals had deferred too much to the university's judgment that alternatives to the use of race were insufficient. The Court established a presumption for race neutrality that could only be overcome if a university adequately showed that other "race-neutral" means did not produce the level of diversity necessary. Three years later, in *Fisher II* (2016), the Court upheld the University of Texas's use of race when the case came back before them.

SFFA

In November 2014, an organization called Students for Fair Admissions (SFFA) filed lawsuits against Harvard University and University of North Carolina at Chapel Hill (UNC), alleging that their use of race in their admissions processes was unconstitutional. The plaintiffs recruited for this case were white and Asian American students. Affirmative action opponents claimed that the Harvard and UNC practices unfairly favored Black students and harmed white and Asian American students.

In *Students for Fair Admissions v. Harvard* (2023), the Court ruled for the first time that race-based affirmative action programs in college admissions processes were unconstitutional. While avoiding a complete overruling of previous precedent, and allowing for some wiggle room by conceding that prior experiences and hardships as described in applicants' essays could be used, the majority opinion in *SFFA* severely curtailed the ability of both public and private colleges and universities to use race as a factor in admissions. In addition to the already established case law from *Grutter* and *Fisher*, Chief Justice Roberts (writing for the majority) found that colleges and universities must never use race as a stereotype or in a "negative" way and that every affirmative action program must come with a "logical" end point.[33]

The *SFFA* decision, hailed by opponents of affirmative action as a solid victory, was announced in June 2023. Since then, applicants, colleges, and commentators alike have had to rethink their strategies aimed at achieving greater diversity. It is not hyperbole to say that in reimagining nearly 50 years of precedent, the Supreme Court, at a time of heightened political and social tension, dismissed decades of accepted doctrine and ushered in a new era of uncertainty for dealing with what is one of America's most vexing unsolved problems.

TOWARD A 21ST-CENTURY CONCEPT OF FAIRNESS

In liberal democracies that value individual rights, one purpose of public policy is to design governmental strategies to correct unfairness and inefficiency in the allocation of resources and improve the quality of life for all citizens, especially the less fortunate. There is perhaps no more urgent example of the need for good public policy than America's obligation to acknowledge, understand, and repair its history of racial injustice. Indeed, to call centuries of legalized slavery followed by centuries of continued resistance to the ideals of equality as enshrined in our founding documents an example of unfairness and inefficiency would be a dramatic understatement.

Thankfully, though, as noted in this chapter, the United States has made measurable progress—albeit painfully slow—in the elimination of barriers to improved economic and social standing of Black Americans and other victims of racial injustice. Although unacceptable gaps persist, disparities between the white majority and people of color in earnings, employment, housing, education, and health have narrowed, thanks in part to decades of public investment to expand the great bounty of the American capitalist engine. There is a long way to go, but on balance we are better off today than 50 and 100 years ago.

At least since the 1960s, progress has been fueled by the acknowledgement that fairness of opportunity today is unattainable without attention to the unfairness of opportunity yesterday. The goal of "affirmative action," in general and specifically as applied to race-conscious admissions, reflects an intuitively obvious proposition: to paraphrase President Johnson (who borrowed from Dr. King), it is not enough to talk of "leveling the playing field" without acknowledging—and compensating for—fundamental disparities at "the starting line."

In its various forms, then, affirmative action policies and programs were meant to boost the chances of success for individuals and groups who had suffered significant historical injustice, if not as a moral obligation to repair past wrongs then as a way to bring greater fairness to the competition for future economic and social advancement.[34]

But what is intuitive is not always actionable. In the minds of many Americans, and certainly in the minds of most of today's Supreme Court justices, equalizing opportunity for marginalized groups—in this case Black Americans primarily—and creating a more level playing field in our complex pluralist society does not justify violations of individual rights as codified in the Constitution. In the language of cost–benefit analysis, the burden of collective progress cannot rest unfairly on the shoulders of people whose rights might be compromised. From the standpoint of the Court, the perceived social good, whether measured in terms of reduced inequality and greater inclusion of marginalized populations or in terms of fulfilling the national moral responsibility to acknowledge and correct historical injustice, is not sufficient as a basis for infringement of constitutional protections. This tension, between social benefits and individual costs, is at the crux of the national debate over affirmative action.[35]

Although the legal landscape has shifted in the wake of *SFFA*, the fundamental tension is not resolved. The challenge now is to continue to devise policies, programs, and mechanisms to further the cause of racial and economic justice—within constraints imposed by the Supreme Court. Are we up to that challenge? If there is hope, it emanates from the determination of major organizations and, their leaders—colleges and universities, corporations, philanthropies, and, perhaps most significantly, the military—to look for allowable innovations aimed at sustaining and advancing progress toward racial and economic justice.

What might such innovations entail? Focusing on the higher education sector, where the argument about race-based preferences is the most heated (even if it only affects a small group of the most elite colleges and universities), we find reason for hope in these kinds of initiatives:

- intensifying marketing and recruitment of students from areas with high concentrations of minority and disadvantaged youth;
- increasing need-based financial aid to make attendance more affordable, which could have a positive effect both on economic and racial diversity;
- developing new programs (and perhaps majors) that focus on reduction of racial and economic inequality, thereby signaling institutional commitment to core values of diversity and justice;
- acknowledging adversity that applicants have overcome, as a criterion to include along with standardized metrics of academic performance, in evaluating likelihood of future success;
- developing or reinforcing partnerships with historically black colleges and universities (HBCUs) to encourage minority applicants who might otherwise feel vulnerable in majority white institutions;
- cultivating revived or new coalitions among students from diverse racial and ethnic groups, aimed at furthering the ideals of pluralist integration as antidote to resegregation in (and between) colleges and universities; and
- creating, investing in, and sustaining mentorship programs that allow for those who have been impacted by the denial of equal opportunity to have a chance at being exposed to new tools for their own advancement.

As devoted optimists, we offer these suggestions with eyes wide open to the current fraught state of discourse in our country. We understand the fundamental challenges: Implementation is inevitably harder than pontification. We do not wish to appear naïve to the task ahead, nor do we mean to paint an unrealistic picture about possibilities for progress. We understand that some people may see acquiescence to the current legal reality around affirmative action as moral obfuscation about the condition of Black Americans, particularly when it comes to uneven access to education. Others will applaud the end of affirmative action and criticize any move toward the use of race-conscious policy solutions to ending racial disparities as (perhaps) well-intended but misguided and incomplete.

However, to not make perfect the enemy of good, what we offer here is a sense of realism around what it will take to make our nation a better union and move us toward the beloved community we all hope is possible. The arc of the moral universe is long and perhaps too frayed at times to be considered "fair." But we want to believe it bends toward justice. The political will needed to effect and sustain progress toward the common good is always subject to great gusts of partisan wind that blow across the land.

And because the struggle for racial and economic justice is far from over, the need for collective resolve is now more acute than ever.

NOTES

1. Patrick F. Gillham and Gary T. Marx, "Changes in the Policing of Civil Disorders Since the Kerner Report: The Police Response to Ferguson, August 2014, and Some Implications for the Twenty-First Century," *RSF: The Russell Sage Foundation Journal of the Social Sciences* 4, no. 6 (January 1, 2018): 122, https://doi.org/10.7758/rsf.2018.4.6.06.

2. Gillham and Marx, "Changes in the Policing of Civil Disorders Since the Kerner Report."

3. John Charles Boger, "Race and the American City: The Kerner Commission in Retrospect-An Introduction," *North Carolina Law Review* 71, no. 5 (1993), 1289.

4. Gregory N. Price, "The Kerner Commission Report: Did It Incentivize or Cause an Increase in the Production and Hiring of Black PhD Economists in Academia?," *The Review of Black Political Economy* 46, no. 4 (June 27, 2019): 349–61, https://doi.org/10.1177/0034644619857729.

5. Matthew W. Hughey, "Of Riots and Racism: Fifty Years Since the Best Laid Schemes of the Kerner Commission (1968–2018)," *Sociological Forum*, 33, no. 3 (September 2018): 619–42, https://www.jstor.org/stable/26625942.

6. Shaun R. Harper, Lori D. Patton, and Ontario S. Wooden, "Access and Equity for African American Students in Higher Education: A Critical Race Historical Analysis of Policy Efforts," *The Journal of Higher Education* 80, no. 4 (July–August 2009): 389–414, https://www.jstor.org/stable/25511120.

7. James D. Anderson, "The Historical Context for Understanding the Test Score Gap," *National Journal of Urban Education and Practice* 1, no. 1 (January 2007): 1–21.

8. Cristobal de Brey et al., "Digest of Education Statistics 2019 (NCES 2021-009)," National Center for Education Statistics, Institute of Education Sciences, February 2021, https://files.eric.ed.gov/fulltext/ED611019.pdf.

9. Michael Hansen et al., "Have We Made Progress on Achievement Gaps? Looking at Evidence from the New NAEP Results," Brookings, April 17, 2018, https://www.brookings.edu/articles/have-we-made-progress-on-achievement-gaps-looking-at-evidence-from-the-new-naep-results/.

10. Dayna Bowen Matthew, "Lessons from the Other America: Turning a Public Health Lens on Fighting Racism and Poverty," *University of Memphis Law Review* 49 (November 29, 2018): 229.

11. Jared Yates Sexton, "Take No Interest," *Cultural Critique* 103 (2019): 100–105.

12. Steven M. Gillon, *Separate and Unequal: The Kerner Commission and the Unraveling of American Liberalism* (New York: Basic Books, 2018).

13. Betty Wood, "The Origins of Slavery, 1619–1808," in *A Companion to the American South*, ed. John B. Boles (Oxford, UK: Blackwell Publishing, 202), 54–68.

14. Sean Wilentz, *No Property in Man: Slavery and Antislavery at the Nation's Founding* (Cambridge, MA: Harvard University Press, 2019); Heather A. Williams, *Self-Taught: African American Education in Slavery and Freedom* (Chapel Hill, NC: Univ of North Carolina Press, 2009).

15. Dwayne Kwyasee Wright, Raquel Muñiz, and Sarah Keffer, "The Walking Dead: How the Logic of *Plessy v. Ferguson* Is Preserved in Equal Protection Law in the 21st Century," *International Journal of Qualitative Studies in Education* (February 24, 2023): 1–19, https://doi.org/10.1080/09518398.2023.2181431.

16. Charles J. Russo, J. John Harris, and Rosetta F. Sandidge, "Brown v. Board of Education at 40: A Legal History of Equal Educational Opportunities in American Public Education," *The Journal of Negro Education* 63 no. 3 (Summer 1994): 297–309.

17. Rubén Donato and Jarrod Hanson, "Legally White, Socially 'Mexican': The Politics of De Jure and De Facto School Segregation in the American Southwest," *Harvard Educational Review* 82, no. 2 (2012): 202–25.

18. Thomas M. Shapiro, *The Hidden Cost of Being African American: How Wealth Perpetuates Inequality* (New York: Oxford University Press, 2004).

19. Martha Lash and Monica Ratcliffe, "The Journey of an African American Teacher Before and After *Brown v. Board of Education*," *The Journal of Negro Education* 83, no. 3 (January 1, 2014): 327, https://doi.org/10.7709/jnegroeducation.83.3.0327.

20. Joel K. Goldstein, "Not Hearing History: A Critique of Chief Justice Roberts's Reinterpretation of Brown," *Ohio State Law Journal* 69, no. 5 (2014): 791; Gerardo R. López and Rebeca Burciaga, "The Troublesome Legacy of *Brown v. Board of Education*," *Educational Administration Quarterly* 50, no. 5 (2014): 796–811.

21. Gloria J. Ladson-Billings, "Can We at Least Have Plessy—The Struggle for Quality Education," *North Carolina Law Review* 85, no. 5 (2007): 1279.

22. Joe R. Feagin and Bernice Mc Nair Barnett, "Success and Failure: How Systemic Racism Trumped the *Brown v. Board of Education* Decision," *University of Illinois Law Review* (2004): 1099–1130, https://illinoislawreview.org/print/volume-2004-issue-5/success-and-failure-how-systemic-racism-trumped-the-brown-v-board-of-education-decision/.

23. Lani Guinier, "From Racial Liberalism to Racial Literacy: *Brown v. Board of Education* and the Interest-Divergence Dilemma," *The Journal of American History* 91, no. 1 (2004): 92–118.

24. Judson MacLaury, "President Kennedy's EO 10925: Seedbed of Affirmative Action," *Federal History* (2010): 42.

25. Keith Williamson Pedrick and Sandra Arnold Scham, *Inside Affirmative Action: The Executive Order that Transformed America's Workforce* (New York: Routledge, 2018).

26. Melvin I. Urofsky, *The Affirmative Action Puzzle: A Living History from Reconstruction to Today* (New York: Pantheon, 2020).

27. Ira Katznelson, *When Affirmative Action Was White: An Untold History of Racial Inequality in Twentieth-Century America* (New York: W.W. Norton, 2005).

28. David Hamilton Golland, *Constructing Affirmative Action: The Struggle for Equal Employment Opportunity* (Lexington, KY: University Press of Kentucky, 2011).

29. David Hamilton Golland, *A Terrible Thing to Waste: Arthur Fletcher and the Conundrum of the Black Republican* (Lexington, KY: University Press of Kansas, 2019).

30. J. Larry Hood, "The Nixon Administration and the Revised Philadelphia Plan for Affirmative Action: A Study in Expanding Presidential Power and Divided Government," *Presidential Studies Quarterly* 23 no. 1 (1993): 145–67.

31. Dwayne Wright and Liliana M. Garces, "Understanding the Controversy Around Race-Based Affirmative Action in American Higher Education," *Controversies on Campus: Debating the Issues Confronting American Universities in the 21st Century* (January 2018): 3–21.

32. Sheryll Cashin, *Place, Not Race: A New Vision of Opportunity in America* (Boston: Beacon Press, 2014).

33. Jon S. Iftikar and David Hòa Khoa Nguyễn, "*SFFA v. Harvard*: Understanding and Contextualizing the Decision and Its Impact," *Change: The Magazine of Higher Learning* 56, no. 1 (January 2, 2024): 4–11, https://doi.org/10.1080/00091383.2024.2297627.

34. Michael Feuer, "Zionism Is Affirmative Action," *Jewish Frontier*, June/July 1985.

35. Michael Feuer, *Can Schools Save Democracy? Civic Education and the Common Good* (Baltimore: Johns Hopkins University Press, 2023).

CHAPTER 9

Act Now! Invest in America's Youth

Dorothy Stoneman
with Mary Ellen Sprenkel

The Kerner Report stated that "a sure method for motivating the hardcore unemployed has not yet been devised" but that the unemployed 15- to 24-year-olds represent "a great reservoir of under-used human resources which are vital to the Nation."[1] In the last 55 years, we have absolutely learned and demonstrated sure methods of tapping into this great reservoir. A beautiful force for good is waiting to be liberated.

The Kerner Commission recommended the creation of 2 million public and private jobs to empower young people of all races to join the economy as contributing members.[2] This was never done. It should be done immediately. We have the knowledge.

In a caring context, offer low-income young adults everything they are seeking: a visible and important role in the community that brings them respect from their neighbors and families; skills that can lead to a decent-paying job; a fresh start on their education; personal counseling from respected role models supporting deep healing from past and present trauma; consistent respect for their intelligence from caring adults in authority who include them in key decision-making; a positive and supportive peer group with whom they can share and heal from their common pain and admit that they want to change their lives; a set of positive values strong enough to compete with the negative values of the streets; a stipend or wage to live on while they are learning; a respected mentor; a path to college and/or a career; and something to belong to that they can believe in.

There is a broad ecosystem of proven programs doing exactly this across the country. Among them are Service and Conservation Corps (aka The Corps Network), YouthBuild, AmeriCorps, ChalleNGe, Year Up, and many local programs funded through the Workforce Innovation and Opportunities Act (2014). Sadly, none of the programs have resources to operate at full scale.

The only thing we lack is the political will to prioritize ending poverty through investment in the well-being of all our citizens, especially including the low-income youth and young adults who are desperate to find the opportunities they need.

The power of love coupled with opportunity is transformational when offered to young people who have endured poverty. It unleashes their positive energy, unlocks their many talents, and inspires them to build a successful life and help others. No matter what challenges they face, if they find a caring community that respects their intelligence and illuminates the way to build a productive life, their ability to learn and love is awakened.

I have witnessed this process for decades as the founder of YouthBuild. Low-income 16- to 24-year-olds who left high school without a diploma enroll in YouthBuild full time for about 10 months. They spend half their time working toward their high school equivalency in highly supportive classrooms. They spend the other half learning construction skills and playing a positive role in the community by building affordable housing for their neighbors. It is all knit together with deeply caring adults, personal and peer counseling, a stipend for their work, and a major emphasis on leadership development. At graduation, they are ready for college and/or employment. They receive follow-up support for at least 1 year. Since YouthBuild's authorization in federal law in 1992, over 200,000 participants have produced over 35,000 units of affordable housing. In 2012, the U.S. Department of Labor expanded YouthBuild's training options to include health care, technology, building operations, and others. Many YouthBuild graduates have become lifetime community leaders.

Carmen Williams describes her experience: "Being a young woman from the streets of Philadelphia, I never thought I would achieve anything. Drug and alcohol abuse to cope with wasn't anything compared to the sexual, mental, physical, and emotional abuse I also experienced. There were only two options for the life I was living: to be an addict like my mother, or to die like both of my parents. I didn't want to die, but I didn't have a reason to live, either, until I found YouthBuild. There was always something inside me waiting to have the opportunity to become great. YouthBuild gave me that opportunity. It gave me the chance to heal. Here is where I am able to have the family I always wanted. The people here believe in me, even when I did not believe in myself. I aspire to be what YouthBuild has been to me, to another young person. I do not think there are words to express my gratitude. I will continue the march towards change using the core values I have learned from YouthBuild."[3]

It is this passion we can liberate across the nation by expanding funding for all the effective youth programs.

The national network of Service and Conservation Corps led by The Corps Network (TCN) provides similar full-time comprehensive opportunities for youth to advance their education and prepare for the workforce through service projects that address economic and environmental issues in their own communities. TCN represents approximately 150 organizations operating in every state that collectively enroll nearly 25,000 young adults a year. About half are people of color residing in low-income environmental justice communities. TCN succeeds because each corps provides not only education, job training, a stipend or wage, and often an earned AmeriCorps scholarship to college, but also provides participants with profound acceptance, support, and love.

Ryan Shelton shares his experience in the Conservation Corps of Long Beach: "To be around other youth who looked like me, and who were moving in the right direction was something completely new to me. Every day at work I would have conversations with my peers about the upcoming project or training and how we could put it on our resumé and strengthen our job skills. Those conversations fueled the fire in me to dream bigger. In these conversations I slowly began to find myself again. People dream about their future, but sometimes where you are seems so far away from your destination. That is where the power of positive communities like CCLB and AmeriCorps comes into play. It provides the emotional fuel for people to push towards those goals that seem so distant."

With this energy we can build a movement to generate the political will to provide opportunity for all. Young people emerging from poverty can and want to be active in that movement.

YOUNG PEOPLE AS ADVOCATES CAN HELP BUILD THE WILL

In 2012, a multiracial group of young adults raised in poverty who had overcome many barriers with the support of comprehensive youth programs formed the National Council of Young Leaders. They were nominated by 16 organizations: Aspen Institute, Forum for Community Solutions, Be the Change, City Year, College Advising Corps, Gateway to College, Jobs for the Future, Mikva Challenge, National Congress of American Indians, National Guard Youth Foundation, Partners for Education at Berea College, Public Allies, The Corps Network, The Philadelphia Youth Network, Year Up, and YouthBuild USA, Inc.

The Council gathered for 3 days. With skilled facilitation, they developed an impressive document: "Recommendations to Increase Opportunity and Decrease Poverty in America."[4] They updated it in 2020, detailing changes needed in six basic social systems: (1) education, (2) upward mobility, (3) environmental stewardship and climate justice, (4) criminal justice, (5) community development, and (6) family. They also called for immediate expansion of all the pathways out of poverty for young adults who have fallen off track.

The system changes they call for overlap with those recommended by the Kerner Commission. They are also aligned with those proposed in 1982 by teenagers in the East Harlem Youth Agenda for the Eighties.[5] Decades have passed, with conditions the same, with solutions on the table, but with inadequate action by our elected leaders.

We need to mobilize millions of people to persuade our leaders to invest in our people. We need to reach the leaders of all sectors, one by one, to awaken them to the solutions. All the officials who became champions for YouthBuild did so because they were inspired by the students they met in their DC offices or by the local programs they visited. Movements to build the political will to heal our divided society will be much stronger when they include present and former Opportunity Youth as thought partners, decision-makers, and spokespeople.

WHO ARE OPPORTUNITY YOUTH?

The Kerner Commission reported that the majority of the young people who rioted in the 1960s were young Black men who were high school dropouts and unemployed.[6] It is true that most youth who leave high school without a diploma become stuck on the margins, are often incarcerated, and are rarely employed. They are not only Black men, although the impact of racism in America means the pressures on Black men are intense.

There are currently 4.7 million 16- to 34-year-olds who are not employed or in school in the United States.[7] Thirty-one percent (31%) of them live in households below the federal poverty line.[8] The federal poverty level for a family of 4 in 2022 is $27,750 a year.[10] This group includes all races, gender identities, geographic areas, faith traditions, and immigrant groups. This group will birth and raise the next generation in poverty if education, jobs, and a caring community are not available to them.

Since about 2012, the young people who are out of school and out of work, previously called "at-risk" or "disconnected," have been called "Opportunity Youth" (OY) because they are both seeking opportunity for themselves and offering opportunity to our nation if we would invest in them. They are coming of age, making real decisions as young adults about what kind of life they will live. In hard-pressed communities, many of them have not seen any welcoming path they could choose that would lead to productive adulthood. By their own accounts, many of those raised in poverty expect to be dead or in jail before they are 25. But if we embrace them and offer real opportunity at this critical point in their lives, they will deliberately pivot toward hope. As young adults, they have the agency to choose, but that agency is meaningful only if good choices are available. Our nation must provide those choices.

This is a manageable challenge. If we were to address their needs and aspirations, we could end poverty in a generation. We could rejoice in the humanity of our nation.

WHAT SHOULD BE DONE IMMEDIATELY FOR OPPORTUNITY YOUTH?

If the political will could be generated to produce the resources, we could easily implement the following five steps:

Step 1: Expand Existing Federally Funded Programs

Congress should immediately expand all effective federally funded comprehensive programs for Opportunity Youth to full scale—with "full scale" being defined as reaching either the limit of demand from young people or the limit of capacity of local organizations to deliver high-quality programs. Among these federal programs are the Workforce Innovation and Opportunities Act (WIOA) Youth Formula Program, YouthBuild, Reentry Employment Opportunities (REO), Job Corps, AmeriCorps, the National Guard Youth ChalleNGe program, and the American Climate Corps. Additional local programs exist that could be expanded through WIOA. An interesting current study of 78 existing programs is on the www.youth.gov website under "Resource: Reconnecting Youth Project."

A careful map for expansion was laid out in 2016 by Civic Enterprises in "A Bridge to Reconnection."[10] It studied the size, scope, and potential growth of federal programs. It identified existing annual opportunities for 339,712 youth, and then laid out how to grow them to reach 1,000,000 youth with annual federal expenditures of just $6.5 billion.[11] The study showed that $171 billion in net fiscal gains would be produced through decreased crime, welfare, and health expenses and through increased taxes paid by the young people throughout their lives. A return on investment of $171 billion for a proposed expenditure of $6.5 billion should produce action.

Various coalitions have worked toward these goals but achieved only incremental gains. A promising new coalition is emerging: The National Alliance for Youth and Young Adult Advocates (NAYYAA).

Step 2: Build on New Federal Investments

The federal government in 2021–2023 made historic investments related to infrastructure and industrial policy through the Infrastructure Investment and Jobs Act (IIJA), Inflation Reduction Act (IRA), and CHIPS and Science Act. However, while the trillions of dollars in spending authorized through these laws are bound to reshape the nation's infrastructure and economy, they do not contain dedicated funding for job training. Without concerted advocacy, Opportunity Youth (OY) will not benefit from their largesse.

Federal agencies must do everything in their power, through regulations and guidance, to direct funding toward job training and hiring preferences that will benefit OY. States also have a great deal of discretion in how they award formula funds contained in IIJA. State legislatures and/or agencies should enact new set-asides for training, new statewide hiring preferences for OY, and new requirements to partner with community-based organizations to ensure that these IIJA-funded projects maximally benefit their residents.

Step 3: Reestablish Previously Successful Federal Programs

From 1933 to 1942, the Civilian Conservation Corps (CCC) provided direct training and employment to more than 3 million young men who in 10 years built 800 parks and planted over 1 billion trees.[12] The CCC was responsible for over half the public and private reforestation done in the nation's history.

The Corps Network has long advocated for the reestablishment of a modern, more diverse, CCC program. During his first week in office, President Joe Biden introduced an executive order calling for the creation of a new Civilian Climate Corps (CCC) "to mobilize the next generation of conservation and resilience workers and maximize the creation of accessible training opportunities and good jobs."[13] Several months later the Administration put forward the Build Back Better Framework, which included major funding for the CCC. But the Build Back Better Act, which included $20 billion for national service and workforce development, did not make it through Congress. The Inflation Reduction Act (IRA) did pass, but without those targeted funds. Fortunately, the IRA contains billions of dollars for climate resilience and green infrastructure projects, which the administration hopes to tap into for the American Climate Corps, launched by executive action in 2023. However, most of the specific funding needed for corps member training and support is still missing. An active coalition, the Partnership for the Civilian Climate Corps, is advocating for this new initiative to reach 300,000 people over its first 10 years—but this will require dedicated funding from Congress. Once again, the message is clear: we need to build broad political will to get anything done at the scale required.

Step 4: Collaborate With the Private Sector

In October 2023 corporations reported 8.7 million unfilled jobs.[14] It is clearly in the interests of the private sector to prepare low-income young people for employment.

In recent years, leaders in the corporate sector have initiated meaningful employment projects. In 2015, Howard and Sheri Schultz of Starbucks and the Schultz Family Foundation launched the 100,000 Opportunities Initiative. Twelve other corporations joined, planning to provide jobs for 100,000 OY. By 2019, they had expanded to 50 corporate partners and had hired 200,000 OY. They hosted wonderful job fairs, hiring young people on the spot. In 2020, they launched the Hiring Opportunities Coalition (HOC) to expand the work, which merged with SkillUp in 2022 and became the SkillUp Coalition Employer Network.[15] This is still evolving with many nonprofit and corporate partners, driven by both the need for the workers and the expanding commitment of many corporate leaders to improve the future for OY. The energy and vision are hopeful.

The nonprofit sector has also initiated meaningful collaboration. For example, Year Up has built far-reaching partnerships with the corporate sector for whom they have trained over 43,000 students.[16]

Regarding the public sector's role, the National Youth Employment Coalition (NYEC) notes in its report that the federal workforce system encourages a focus on credential attainment and immediate earnings growth, but many of the largest sectors in the U.S. economy emphasize "soft" skills such as communication and teamwork.[17] NYEC's report calls for federal and state laws to encourage local workforce boards and CBOs to work collaboratively with private-sector employers to ensure that program offerings align with industry needs, and that employers have access to useful support as they work with OY.

Of course, expansion of the federal training programs as called for in Step 1 would prepare more youth for all these jobs and strengthen their success rates.

Step 5: Mobilize for Investment at the Local Level

Dynamic coalitions must advocate for public funds at the local level, with young people speaking steadily to the elected officials about why it makes a difference. City, county, and state funds can be won when advocacy is well-organized for demonstrably effective programs. To make this work, private funding for local coalitions is essential. The philanthropic sector has a key role to play in supporting national and local advocacy.

In summary, taking these five steps could fulfill the Kerner Commission's recommendation to create 2 million annual training and job opportunities to solve the violence stemming from racism, poverty, and despair. We could reconnect most low-income OY to productive citizenship.

WHO IS STILL LEFT OUT AND NEEDS ATTENTION?

Young people who are incarcerated are not counted in the OY data because they are not free to be reconnected to work or school. Many young people raised in poverty face a set of conditions that draw them down what seems to be the only lane open to them on a seemingly irreversible road to trouble. Sadly, society stands ready to punish them for the rest of their lives, making it hard for returning citizens to get jobs, housing, or even the right to vote in some states. Yet they are just as eager for the opportunity to lead a better life as those who never committed a crime or joined a gang.

Given the distorted opportunity structure flowing from racism and classism, it also turns out that the leaders of gangs, who have risen skillfully in the street culture, are often highly intelligent, creative, resilient, and resourceful. Their talents, when harnessed for good, informed by newly internalized positive values, are very powerful.

A few examples of YouthBuild graduates can demonstrate the positive potential of court-involved youth. Mike Dean wrote a book about his own journey from drug dealer to pastor and nonprofit leader.[18] As director of YouthBuild Franklin County in Ohio, he now offers youth the same opportunities that helped him leave the streets. Ely Flores, founding director of a nonprofit called LEAD in Los Angeles, testified before the Judiciary Committee of the House of Representatives about his experiences in a gang lifestyle before finding his way out.[19] Antonio Ramirez, once active in a gang, became the founding director of United at Peace, helping young people end violence in Rockford, Illinois. Michael Donnelly, once gang involved, became an advisor to the police department in Bloomington, Illinois, on how to build positive relationships with youth. Antoine Bennett, who served 18 months for a violent crime, later came to chair the homeowners association in Sandtown, Baltimore. I will never forget the moment he said to Newt Gingrich's staff: "I used to be a menace to my community; now I am a minister to it."

Thousands of stories like this are books and films waiting to be written and filmed. Behind them is an enormous force for good waiting to be liberated. Most Americans who influence our public policies are unaware of this untapped talent and goodness. They are equally unaware of the pain and despair in poverty-stricken urban, rural, and tribal communities. Most have never gotten to know a young person who grew up hungry, who was periodically and unpredictably homeless because of their parents' eviction for inability to pay the rent. They have not mentored a teenager whose father was incarcerated and whose stepfather abused them while their mother was at work earning very low wages. They have not talked with teenagers who were invited by adults to carry bags of drugs here and there to get the $50 that would enable them to bring some money and food home for their younger siblings. They do not know young people who moved through 15 different foster care families, being abused in some, and going to 10 different schools during their vulnerable adolescence. We must educate those with influence. If they knew the reality, they would change their attitudes. They need to meet the young people struggling to live good lives against the odds.

BUILDING THE POLITICAL WILL TO INVEST IN OPPORTUNITY FOR ALL

The Kerner Commission named the necessary condition: "to generate new will—the will to tax ourselves to the extent necessary to meet the vital needs of the nation."[20] But how do we generate that will? Regardless of their unlimited commitment and skill, the efforts of several generations of nonprofit leaders to spread their marvelous programs to full scale, to meet the enormous demand and the heart-wrenching needs in their communities, have led, with very few exceptions, only to incremental gains.

Sadly, every year for 25 years I was told repeatedly on the Hill, "This is not a good year to ask for more. You are lucky and should be grateful for level funding." The acceptance of the status quo must change if we are ever to reverse the conditions in America that predictably produce poverty, despair, hate, rage, mental illness, and violence.

We need a massive citizens' movement that not only calls for the elimination of poverty and the creation of opportunity for all, but also reverses the 2010 Supreme Court *Citizens United* decision that gave unlimited freedom to wealthy individuals and corporations to donate, often invisibly, to political campaigns. As long as corporations primarily dedicated to profit for their shareholders are largely controlling the rules governing the economy and the funding allocations in the federal budget through their intensive lobbying and deep political influence, we are unlikely to produce the political will to end poverty.

It is important to know that many dedicated elected officials care deeply about expanding opportunity. When they see something good, they will move to spread it. YouthBuild never would have been authorized in public law and funded every year if elected officials of both parties had not stepped forward as champions and supporters. In the early 1990s, Senator John Kerry (D-MA) and Representative Major Owens (D-NY) visited local programs, talked with students, and then took the lead. They successfully recruited bipartisan support, with Senator Kit Bond (R-MO), Representative Hal Rogers (R-KY), and others as active allies. Senator Kerry was a proactive champion for as long as he served in the Senate. Nothing good happens in government without active champions on the inside. The current champions for YouthBuild are Senators Kirsten Gillibrand (D-NY) and John Cornyn (R-TX), alongside Representatives Nikema Williams (D-GA) and Don Bacon (R-NE). Broad bipartisan support has occurred through six presidential administrations. This was always in response to being inspired by meeting the young people themselves and visiting local programs.

Nonetheless, to achieve full-scale funding, not just incremental gains, we need a breakthrough in public awareness and political will. Let us build on the good intentions that exist in Congress, the strong programmatic foundations that have been built, the federal agency staff who work skillfully behind the scenes, and the philanthropic and corporate support that exists. Let us open the doors to every young person knocking.

WE NEED A MEDIA AWAKENING

Until the heartbreaking stories of pain and the incredibly inspiring stories of resilience and goodness of the young people who transcend these conditions through participation in well-designed programs are widely known, it is unlikely that we can build sufficient political will. To win the hearts and minds of the public, we need daily stories on every channel and throughout social media about people who have emerged from poverty, are succeeding in life, and are dedicated to bettering their communities. Meanwhile, we need to bring every possible elected official to visit impactful programs and bring inspiring young constituents to their offices. We should bring corporate, philanthropic, sports, and media leaders. And we should elect more leaders who are dedicated to ending poverty.

WE NEED A UNITED MULTIRACIAL MOVEMENT

Although poverty is disproportionately experienced by Black, Native American, and Latinx Americans due to long-term structural racism, it is also importantly and surprisingly true that the largest single group of poor people in America is white. The percentage is lower among whites, but the absolute numbers are higher because they are a large segment of the U.S. population. According to Statista Research Department, in 2022, 25% of Native Americans, 17.1% of Black Americans, 16.9% of Latinx, 8.6% of Asian Americans, and 8.6% of white Americans lived in poverty.[21] The total was 37.2 million people.[22] About 16 million were white.[23] They must be mobilized along with all the groups who suffer from disproportionately higher rates of poverty.

The interests of all people living in poverty are similar. This fact must be understood and integrated into our analyses, our solutions, our coalitions, and our politics. United and engaged, supported by allies, the 37.2 million people living below the government's poverty line could build the political will to end poverty. As described by Reverend William Barber, when we add the rest of Americans who are low income and low wealth, above the government poverty level but still struggling, there are 140 million people.[24] United and active, supported by allies in and out of government, 140 million Americans could absolutely change our political reality.

The perpetual neglect of poor people of all races is founded both on a widespread false narrative about their inferiority and on the private interests of a small minority that controls the flow of resources. Those who control the resources also control much of the narrative and many of the laws. We do not yet know how to persuade enough of them that it is truly in their own interests as humans to end poverty. But even if we fail to persuade them, they are a very small minority that should not control this democratic nation.

At the time of his assassination, 2 months after the release of the Kerner Report, Martin Luther King, Jr. was building a multiracial, nonviolent, united mass movement for economic justice called the Poor People's Campaign. Reverend William Barber relaunched that campaign in 2018. He is deliberately working to build racial unity toward ending poverty, racism, militarism, and climate change, through a nonviolent moral movement. Other organizations and thought leaders are also working toward a fair, prosperous, cooperative, and human-centered economy. There is hope that one day they will together mobilize America's more passive citizens.

To succeed, we will need to tap into the infinite love that lies below the surface in our nation, listen to the hearts and minds of young leaders who have suffered from poverty and have a better vision, and build a dynamic movement that is a magnet to the best in all of us. Together we can build a nation that is more wise, loving, respectful, and united and that produces a reasonable distribution of resources so that all people have the opportunities to fulfill their highest potential and their noblest aspirations within caring communities that offer respect and responsibility for all.

NOTES

1. The National Advisory Commission on Civil Disorders, *The Kerner Report* (Princeton, NJ: Princeton University Press, 2016), 416, 392.
2. *The Kerner Report*, 25.
3. Carmen Williams, email to author, May 30, 2014.
4. National Council of Young Leaders, "Recommendations to Increase Opportunity and Decrease Poverty in America," Opportunity Youth United, January 2020, https://oyunited.org/wp-content/uploads/2020/01/NCYLRecommendationsJAN2020FINAL-1.pdf.
5. Elena Maker Castro, "An Evaluation of the Youth Action Program (The Precursor to Youth-Create) and Its Apparent Power to Promote Life-Long Thriving," Youth Action Youth Build, December 1, 2023, https://www.youthaction.nyc/wp-content/uploads/2023/12/An-Evaluation-of-the-Youth-Action-Program-3-1.pdf.
6. *The Kerner Report*, 108.
7. Kristen Lewis, "Ensuring an Equitable Recovery: Addressing COVID-19's Impact on Education," Measure of America, 2023, 15, https://ssrc-static.s3.amazonaws.com/moa/EnsuringAnEquitableRecovery.pdf.
8. HealthCare.gov, "Federal Poverty Level (FPL)," https://www.healthcare.gov/glossary/federal-poverty-level-fpl/.
9. HealthCare.gov, "Federal Poverty Level (FPL)."
10. John M. Bridgeland, Erin S. Ingram, and Matthew Atwell, "A Bridge to Reconnection: A Plan for Reconnecting One Million Opportunity Youth Each Year through Federal Funding Streams," Aspen Institute Forum for Community Solutions, September 2016. https://www.aspencommunitysolutions.org/wp-content/uploads/2017/06/BridgetoReconnection.2016.pdf.
11. Bridgeland et al., "A Bridge to Reconnection," 12.
12. Eric Foner and John Arthur Garraty, *The Reader's Companion to American History* (New York: Houghton Mifflin, 1991).
13. White House, Executive Order on Tackling the Climate Crisis at Home and Abroad, January 27, 2021, Sec. 215, https://www.whitehouse.gov/briefing-room/presidential-actions/2021/01/27/executive-order-on-tackling-the-climate-crisis-at-home-and-abroad/.
14. U.S. Bureau of Labor Statistics, "Job Openings and Labor Turnover Survey," Economic news release, April 2, 2024, https://www.bls.gov/news.release/jolts.nr0.htm.
15. National Philanthropic Trust, "100,000 Opportunities Initiative: Connecting Young People with Jobs," National Philanthropic Trust, May 16, 2019, https://www.nptrust.org/philanthropic-resources/philanthropist/100000-opportunities-initiative-connecting-young-people-with-jobs/.
16. Year Up, https://www.YearUp.org.
17. Emily Ingram et al., "Opportunity Youth and Employer Engagement: Evidence and Next Steps for an Emerging Field," National Youth Employment Coalition, 8, https://nyec.org/wp-content/uploads/2022/10/Employer-Engagement-Report.pdf.
18. Mike Dean, *What If I Had a Father? The Man I Never Knew* (Columbus, OH: DeanBooks, 2015).
19. Ely Flores, "From a Gang Lifestyle to a Life of Community Activism," Written Testimony Submitted to the Subcommittee on Crime, Terrorism and Homeland Security, June 10, 2008, https://judiciary.house.gov/wp-content/uploads/2008/06/Flores080610.pdf.
20. *The Kerner Report*, 23.
21. Statista, "Poverty rate in the United States in 2022, by Race and Ethnicity," n.d., https://www.statista.com/statistics/200476/us-poverty-rate-by-ethnic-group/.

22. Statista, "Poverty rate in the United States in 2022, by Race and Ethnicity."
23. Talk Poverty, "Basic Statistics," 2022, https://talkpoverty.org/basics/index.html.
24. William J. Barber, "Our Urgency of Now: Converging Global Crises in a Time of Political Evolution," in *Democracy in a Hotter Time: Climate Change and Democratic Transformation*, ed. David W. Orr (Cambridge, MA: MIT Press, 2023), 71.

Crime Prevention and Criminal Justice Policy

CHAPTER 10

Police Reform: Where Do We Go From Here?

Neil Gross

For many of those who poured into the streets in the summer of 2020 to protest the murder of George Floyd in Minneapolis and rally for the cause of Black lives, it is disappointing and dispiriting that today police reform has faded from the national agenda. The George Floyd Justice in Policing Act, a broad piece of legislation aimed at increasing police accountability and reducing unnecessary use of force, passed the U.S. House of Representatives in 2020 on a party-line vote that reflected the anger and the energy of that moment. But the bill stalled before it could reach the Republican-controlled Senate, a cycle that repeated 1 year later. Negotiations for smaller police reform bills also failed, save for an amendment to earlier legislation authorizing grants for de-escalation training. The Department of Justice, under the leadership of President Joe Biden's Attorney General Merrick Garland, ramped up so-called "pattern and practice" investigations of police departments suspected of systematic rights violations, entering into several new consent decree agreements to secure reforms. Yet this was a drop in the bucket given the more than 17,000 state and local police agencies in the United States.

With homicides skyrocketing during and after the pandemic—a trend that has only recently abated—Republicans doubled down on law-and-order rhetoric, putting Democrats on the defensive and relegating criminal justice reform to the back burner. Meanwhile, the number of Americans killed by the police annually has remained largely unchanged, with Black people continuing to die at a disproportionately high rate. This may be one of the reasons why, as of this writing, support for President Biden has softened among Black Americans, a voting bloc that will be crucial if he is to win reelection in 2024. In 2020, Biden campaigned on the promise of saving democracy from 4 more years of Donald Trump, but once elected he also pledged to "finish the job on police reform." At the federal level, he has been unable to deliver on that promise.

The story on the ground in America's cities is more complicated, however. Amid all the bad news, we are seeing—here and there—signs of modest progress in policing and public safety that offer reasons for hope. I begin my discussion in this chapter of the current prospects for police reform by briefly outlining some of the major problems with American policing, focusing in particular on racial inequalities. I consider the institutional, organizational, and political factors that have made those problems difficult to solve. But I also highlight important policy innovations with demonstrated potential to yield better outcomes. The key to further progress is for city residents to maintain pressure on their police departments while encouraging them to embrace one or more of these innovative approaches, or others whose development we can help foster.

THE PROBLEMS WITH AMERICAN POLICING

To the extent that Americans have looked back on the widespread urban unrest of the late 1960s that prompted President Lyndon B. Johnson to empanel the National Advisory Commission on Civil Disorders—the Kerner Commission, whose work this volume updates—they have tended to see that unrest as reflecting the social and economic marginalization that many Black city dwellers experienced at the time. That assessment isn't wrong, as the original Kerner Commission report made clear, notwithstanding gains in Black income in the 1960s. But as historians such as Elizabeth Hinton have reminded us, wanton police brutality and racism were the more immediate impetus for many of the uprisings and riots.[1] Kerner Commission researchers noted that "one of the images frequently encountered" in conversations with Black inner-city residents after the summer of 1967 was "that of the police as intruders who too often appear at the wrong time and for the wrong reason," serving as "both agents and symbols of white authority in the ghettoes [sic]."[2] Echoing and amplifying these concerns, Martin Luther King, Jr. was a fierce critic of police brutality not only in the South but throughout the country.[3]

Today, Black Americans remain disproportionately affected by bad policing. Although it is not always top of mind in policy discussions. consider traffic enforcement. Numerous studies demonstrate that Black drivers are stopped for ostensible traffic offenses at higher rates than white drivers, a pattern that diminishes at night when it is harder for police to see a driver's skin color, suggesting racial targeting. When Black drivers are pulled over, police are more likely to search their cars for contraband even though the "hit rate" for such searches—the percentage that turn up illegal drugs or weapons—is lower than for white drivers. Studies analyzing footage from body-worn cameras show that officers tend to speak to Black drivers in a less respectful tone.[4]

Similar tendencies are apparent in pedestrian stops. Partly because crime rates tend to be higher in impoverished Black neighborhoods, police commanders often direct their officers to engage in sweeps, resulting in frequent stops and pat downs of residents. These sweeps generate fear and resentment and have unintended consequences, such as diminished educational performance for teenage boys.[5] Even where sweeps have been curtailed—as in New York City, where the NYPD's "stop, question, and frisk" practices were deemed unconstitutional in 2013—Black Americans as well as Latinos are stopped far more often than non-Latino white people. In 2023, for example, just 5% of the pedestrians stopped in New York were white, where white people make up more than a third of the city's population.[6]

As Black Lives Matter activists have highlighted, racial disparities are also evident in police use of force. Overall more white than Black Americans are killed by the police each year, but research shows that approximately 1 out of every 1,000 Black men can expect to die at the hands of a police officer, a risk two-and-a-half times that for white men.[7] Black and Latino Americans are subject to higher rates of nonlethal force as well, a gap that can't be fully accounted for statistically by situational factors, with the size of the gap varying across police agencies.[8] Although the proportion of all police-citizen encounters involving force is low—around 2%, according to surveys conducted by the Bureau of Justice Statistics—Black Americans are three times more likely than their white counterparts to report experiencing nonlethal force or being threatened with the use of force.[9] Given this racial disproportionality, it is not surprising that Black Americans express not simply less trust and confidence in police, but greater fear of them. One study found that about 50% of Black Americans would prefer to be robbed or burglarized than to have "unprovoked" contact with a police officer.[10]

Consistent with the pattern of Black Americans experiencing worse policing, some of the biggest police corruption scandals—in Baltimore, for example, where journalist Justin Fenton exposed a ring of uniformed thieves—have involved officers assigned to largely Black neighborhoods, where racism may make supervisory oversight lax.[11] More generally, although racism among police is almost certainly less than it was 50 years ago, evidence of racist attitudes in the ranks of law enforcement continues to surface, as in a recent case in Antioch, California, where investigators unearthed a trove of racist text messages sent by officers.

In a different register, police solve rates for homicide and other violent offenses tend to be substantially higher when the victims are white rather than Black.[12] This may reflect reduced cooperation with police in Black communities more than bias on the part of detectives, but one of the jobs of police is to inspire the confidence needed to secure citizen cooperation. In that sense, racial disparities in investigative outcomes represent a double failure: a failure to generate trust resulting in a failure to bring to justice those responsible for violent crimes. Since Black Americans are dramatically overrepresented among victims of violent crime, these are serious failings indeed.

IMPEDIMENTS TO REFORM

Newly available data and analytic techniques have allowed researchers to document these disparities in greater detail than was possible previously. Yet social scientists, along with activists, civil rights attorneys, and everyday Americans, have long known about the racial skew in American policing and called for change. The history of the U.S. police over the last half century is in no small part a history of reform efforts, from "community policing" to consent decrees to civilian oversight. Why haven't these done more to bring about the fair, equitable, and effective policing that communities of color—all communities—deserve?

Four factors have served as major impediments to police reform. First, decentralization. Although policing in nations with greater centralization of law enforcement authority, such as France or Italy, also leaves much to be desired, it is more difficult to change policing policies and practices in a unified direction when there are so many local police departments, each under the control of different police chiefs and elected officials. Decentralization means not simply that newly identified best practices will be slower to diffuse, but also that there are bound to be disagreements on what constitutes a best practice in light of regional and local differences in culture, politics, crime, and so on.

Over time, the United States has developed coordination mechanisms to mitigate this problem. Federal investigations of troubled police agencies and consent decrees serve this purpose, as do civil suits alleging that the failure of departments to adhere to nationally recognized standards causes harm. Police agencies and training academies must meet statewide accreditation requirements and there is considerable talk among states. Smaller agencies will often emulate their larger peers. And professional associations of police executives and officers draw police from diverse departments into common networks, where new ideas can spread. Yet there is no single lever that can be pulled to bring all U.S. police into line simultaneously.

Even in individual departments, however, reform can be exceedingly difficult to achieve. A second impediment helps to explain why: Because of the nature of their job, frontline officers and detectives have a great deal of power as workers, allowing them to hold the line against policy changes they dislike.

Until the advent of cell phone video and body-worn cameras, most police–citizen interactions could never be directly scrutinized by police supervisors, since there are many more officers than supervisors (who can't be everywhere at once). This meant that if a chief mandated a new policy or practice and an officer on the street ignored it, mistreating someone, the officer could simply lie about his behavior, and it would be his word against that of the individual (or any witnesses). Our legal system assumes de facto that police officers sworn to uphold the law are more truthful than other people, and police departments make the same assumption. Coupled with the code of silence that is part of the ethos of policing, the result has too often been that, except in cases of egregious misconduct where the evidence is irrefutable, officers have too often been free to act with relative impunity.

Despite their promise, body-worn cameras haven't yet substantially altered these dynamics, perhaps because supervisors have lacked the capacity to monitor anything more than a small sampling of footage. (This may change soon because of new, AI-based monitoring technology.) Limitations on employee monitoring also mean that police supervisors have had minimal power to detect and punish work slowdowns or stoppages. Reformist mayors, city counselors, and police chiefs, all answerable to city residents, have been afraid to push officers too far, too fast, for fear that they will become alienated and stage a silent collective revolt, compromising public safety. The lurking possibility of such a revolt is also one of the reasons police unions have grown so powerful—and they too typically push back against reform.

But why wouldn't officers leap to embrace new policies and practices that could limit the use of force, reduce racial disparities, and generally produce better outcomes? Police culture is a big part of the answer: the norms, values, and worldview of those in the profession.[13] Social scientists have been studying police culture for decades and have documented remarkable similarities across departments. Among the features of this culture are an "us vs. them" attitude, a sometimes-exaggerated sense of the dangers of the job, suspiciousness, a strong sense of duty, a belief in the need to display toughness on the street, doubts about rights protections for suspects in criminal cases, and trafficking in stereotypes about racial or ethnic minority groups. Of course, not every police officer thinks this way, and researchers have discovered departmental variation around these core tenets as well—for example, they may be held in different degrees, or in different

Police Reform: Where Do We Go From Here?

configurations, in different agencies. But the culture of policing is so widespread that it likely stems from universal job features such as the fact that the police are one of the few public agencies authorized to use violence to enforce the law, the high level of discretion the justice system grants to "street-level bureaucrats," and the role that police are called on to play in enforcing social status hierarchies.[14]

Not only is the culture of policing in the United States responsible for some of the problems discussed earlier, as the norms and values into which officers are socialized lead them toward greater violence and racially disparate treatment of citizens; it also helps to account for much of their hostility and resistance to reform. Police reform efforts aim at transparency and accountability, reduction in the use of force, and expanded rights for citizens in police encounters, while the standard culture of policing favors a more conservative status quo. In departments where that culture prevails, reform-oriented chiefs may be looked at with disdain, officers who champion reform may be stigmatized by their peers, and agencies may quickly snap back to their old ways of doing things when external pressures such as consent decrees cease.

It is also hard to move the needle on police reform because of how polarized the issues of crime and policing have become. Public opinion polls reveal large and growing gaps between Democrats and Republicans in how serious a problem they regard crime to be, how much confidence they have in the police, and what reforms, if any, they think are necessary, with these gaps undergirded by racial differences in the constituencies of the two parties. With crime and policing now firmly part of the culture wars, and divided government in Washington, legislative action at the national level has become all but impossible, limiting the federal government's scope of action in improving policing to presidential executive orders and efforts of the Department of Justice.

After the murder of George Floyd, police reform legislation was introduced in all 50 states. While many of these bills contained important elements like prohibitions on choke holds, others were largely symbolic. Legislation with the potential to bring significant long-term benefit was passed primarily in states where Democrats controlled state houses and governorships, as in New Jersey, which put in place new procedures for officer certification and decertification, making it harder for an officer fired for misconduct by one department to move to another jurisdiction. But the politicization of policing has meant that even these blue-state reforms have become targets of attack by national conservative figures, resulting in intense negative publicity. In progressive cities, whether in blue, red, or purple states, tensions between far-left advocates of abolition or defunding and liberal or center left supporters of incremental reform have further complicated matters.

INNOVATIONS WE CAN BUILD ON

All this sounds pessimistic. But while it rarely makes the news, some cities and police departments have happened upon truly innovative and promising approaches to public safety in recent years. Building on their advances, we could take at least four steps now to improve the situation everywhere.

Continue to Diversify the Police Profession

At the time of the initial Kerner Commission report, many prominent Black Americans called for greater racial diversity in law enforcement. We don't have solid information on the demography of the police profession in the 1960s, but data from the 1970s indicate that these calls were well-placed: only about 6% of officers in large U.S. police departments then were Black.[15] Civil rights leaders argued that this reflected employment discrimination, keeping Black people from a civil service job that had served for other groups as a steppingstone into the lower middle class. Equally important, it was thought that if police officers came from the communities where they worked, they would have a better understanding of those communities and the people in them, wouldn't be as racist, and would be less prone to brutality.

It has taken decades, but the police profession has grown considerably more diverse. In 2020, about 18% of the officers in midsized or large cities were Black, on average. Nineteen percent were Latino and another 6% were Asian-American or part of a different non-white group.[16] Likewise, more than half of police chiefs in large departments are now people of color.

A diverse police force is no guarantee of good policing, but the evidence suggests that policing problems are lessened the more representative a police department is of its city's population.[17] While it's challenging to reliably estimate the causal effect of racial diversity on policing outcomes, the best studies suggest that, all else equal, officers who are Black or Latino are less likely to use force, particularly against citizens of color, and less likely to make arrests for minor offenses—this, despite the fact that Black and Latino officers are susceptible to elements of traditional police culture, and that their sympathies for residents of marginalized communities may be tempered by dynamics of class differentiation and distinction.[18]

Yet there is much more work to be done on the diversification front. America's cities (and suburbs) continue to grow more diverse. Despite aggregate gains in police diversity, many departments are struggling to catch up. Black officers remain in particularly short supply: Mistreatment of Black Americans by the police, both historically and in the present, dissuades many from entering the occupation.

We should be doing everything we can to build upon recent momentum. Cities should conduct systematic reviews of their police recruitment procedures to ensure that there are no artificial barriers to hiring more officers of color, such as overreliance on referrals from current employees (given that social networks are often racially segregated). Departments also need to step up their outreach and recruiting efforts in minority communities. It would be extraordinarily helpful if they had the support of local groups in doing so. Efforts at building trust between the police and minority residents, including community advisory boards, forums for "difficult conversations," and the forging of close relationships between police administrators and community representatives, can generate such support as a side benefit. By employing these and other strategies, departments such as the NYPD, LAPD, and Miami-Dade Police Department have succeeded in becoming more representative of their cities' changing populations, while in the last decade other departments have moved in the opposite direction.[19]

Departments also lag in diversity in the employment of female officers. Only about 13% of police nationwide are female. But research shows that on average female officers use force less in making arrests, and that on several other metrics they tend to perform better than their male counterparts.[20] Policy changes that would help police departments attract more female recruits, such as on-site child care and rigorously enforced rules around sexual harassment, are long overdue and not as likely as other reform-related efforts to generate pushback from police unions.

Emphasize Procedural Justice

Procedural justice, a theory originally developed by psychologist Tom Tyler, holds that people are most prone to obey the law and cooperate with authorities if they perceive that the procedures governing the administration of justice are fair.[21] This means that if police want to do their utmost to fight crime, gain cooperation in investigations, and avoid situations where people violently resist arrest, they should strive not only to make their treatment of citizens fair and equitable, but to communicate that fairness in interactions on the street, explaining their decisions and the rules they followed in making them.

Over the last quarter century, many U.S. police departments, including Minneapolis and Chicago, have experimented with procedural justice. These departments have designed multiday training sessions for officers; some have attempted to make procedural justice the operating philosophy of their entire department. Typically, these experiments haven't gotten far: Officers and police unions have opposed procedural justice reforms, claiming that they interfere with "real" police work. But there is strong social science evidence that after officers are exposed to procedural justice training, they tend to behave in ways that citizens perceive as fairer and more respectful, while also using less force.[22] Consistent with Tyler's theory, in areas where officers act in these ways, crime rates tend to go down. Procedural justice can even chip away at the traditional culture of policing by instilling a worldview in which transparency and respect for citizens are paramount.

Considering this evidence, cities should invest far more in procedural justice, hiring chiefs who are committed to its implementation over the long term despite officer resistance. My own research, with the police department in Stockton, California, demonstrates that officer resistance can be overcome through slow but sustained rollout of a procedural justice approach by a savvy chief.[23] To ensure the equitable treatment of citizens that procedural justice requires, cities and police departments should also commit to real-time auditing of racial patterns in police activity data. Studies in other domains suggest that such monitoring and managerial accountability is more effective than the currently popular implicit bias training at actually changing behavior in organizations.[24]

Enhance Neighborhood Collective Efficacy

Especially since 2020, police abolitionists have sought ways of addressing community violence that don't entail reliance on the police. Some of the programs they have championed, such as "violence interrupter" models that emerged from the public health sector and employ former gang members as street outreach workers to mediate disputes among conflicting criminal groups, have failed to produce consistently positive effects on public safety, as evaluated by social science research.[25] But there is one strategy along these lines for which the evidence is much stronger—a strategy that could end up improving policing as well.

Anyone who works on public safety has heard of "broken windows," a theory advanced by political scientist James Q. Wilson and criminologist George Kelling in a 1982 *Atlantic* article.[26] The theory holds that when would-be criminals assess a neighborhood as a potential venue for committing crime, they take note of visible public disorder, from graffiti to panhandling to public consumption of drugs or alcohol. According to Wilson and Kelling, such disorder signals that neighborhood residents don't care what is happening on the street, which implies that they won't intervene to stop criminal activity, whether by confronting the law breaker or calling the police. To allow visible disorder is thus to invite more serious crime, and Wilson and Kelling recommended that police departments crack down on public disorder offenses. Their theory proved popular among police chiefs in the 1990s and 2000s. In cities like New York, Chicago, and Los Angeles, officers were directed to increase stops of people suspected of committing such offenses and issue citations.

The rollout of "broken windows" policing corresponded with what legal scholar Franklin Zimring has called the "great American crime decline," and chiefs like the NYPD's Bill Bratton were quick to claim a connection between the two.[27] Critics pointed out that evidence of a causal link was slim.

With the benefit of time, a more nuanced understanding is now emerging. Visible public disorder may indeed be associated with serious criminality, including crimes of violence—but the primary reason is that visible disorder and serious crime are both linked with something else, what the sociologist Robert Sampson calls neighborhood "collective efficacy," or the capacity of residents to work together to solve the neighborhood's problems.[28]

The key components of collective efficacy are trust in one's neighbors and "shared expectations about public behavior," and Sampson has shown in research with colleagues that neighborhoods scoring high on measures of these things look more orderly (because residents pitch in for cleanups and shoo disorderly people along) and also have lower crime rates (because residents monitor rowdy teens and report them to their parents, are present on the street to help if their neighbors are threatened, and are more willing to call the police, engaging in "altruistic intervention").[29] Sampson's studies show that neighborhood collective efficacy is largely determined by "the concentration of disadvantage, racial segregation, family disruption, and residential instability"; tends to be relatively stable over time; and has surprisingly large effects on crime.[30] For example, controlling for other factors, homicide rates in Chicago between 1995 and 2002 were more than 50% greater in neighborhoods with low levels of efficacy as compared to neighborhoods with high levels of efficacy.

But if collective efficacy is stable, what can be done to reduce violent crime in low-efficacy neighborhoods? Sampson points to several areas in Chicago that were revitalized in the 1990s through a combination of municipal action (e.g., tearing down dysfunctional public housing) and private investment, suggesting that economic development efforts can sometimes enhance efficacy by shifting its underlying determinants.

The sociologist Patrick Sharkey identifies another promising intervention: building up community nonprofits. For an important 2017 paper, he and his colleagues studied the relationship between nonprofit growth and crime in the 300 largest U.S. cities between 1990 and 2013.[31] Holding other factors constant, they found that as the number of community nonprofits rose, crime fell—and this wasn't because less crime-plagued cities gave rise to a more vibrant nonprofit sector. The authors reported that "10 additional community nonprofits per 100,000 residents are associated with a 6 percent decrease in the murder rate, a 6 percent decrease in the violent crime rate, and a 5 percent decrease in the violent property crime rate."[32]

The explanation was collective efficacy. Community nonprofits, which do everything from run soup kitchens to clean up local parks, help "establish or strengthen ties between residents and connect individuals to other residents, organizations, or community resources, facilitating voluntary associations, improving social cohesion and informal social control, and building interpersonal trust."[33] Even if the underlying conditions of the neighborhood don't change, collective efficacy can still be given a boost. Beyond that, some nonprofits focus on changing those structural conditions. Sharkey and his coauthors found that workforce development nonprofits had especially large effects on the crime rate (as did those concerned to combat drug abuse). Finally, nonprofits specifically concerned with crime prevention may impact crime both directly (through the types of services they offer—e.g., midnight basketball programs that keep kids off the street and out of trouble) and indirectly (through their contribution to collective efficacy).

In his book *Uneasy Peace*, Sharkey extended this research, demonstrating that the growth of community nonprofits was at least as important—if not more—than factors like the expansion of incarceration in accounting for the major drop in crime of the last 3 decades.[34] It also entailed far fewer social costs. Sharkey drew out the policy implications, suggesting that we double down on funding community nonprofits, from both public and private funding sources, to push crime rates even lower. He envisioned a rich tapestry of nonprofits stretched out across urban America—an even richer tapestry than we have now—empowering residents of disadvantaged neighborhoods to improve their communities.

Could community redevelopment and an expansion of the nonprofit sector also go some way toward making policing better, beyond reducing the need for police presence in neighborhoods and thus limiting potentially dangerous contact between residents and officers? There is reason to think it could: Neighborhoods high in collective efficacy are well positioned to exert political power and increase pressure on City Hall to deliver high-quality police services. Such nonprofits are also good sites for dialogue with the police that can reduce community tensions and soften "us vs. them" attitudes among officers. For example, a promising model is that of nonprofit-funded "safe havens" where youths can gather to do homework, socialize with one another, and build trusting relationships with police.[35]

Ramp Up Focused Deterrence

Finally, cities should embrace focused deterrence, an approach used to address gang or other group-related gun violence. Focused deterrence responds to deficiencies in conventional strategies of police deployment. Although the number of police officers employed per capita by cities is negatively associated with rates of both violent and property crime, suggesting that the presence of police on the street may deter some potential offenders, one of the earliest experiments in American policing research showed that having officers randomly patrol neighborhoods wasn't very effective: The chances are low that an officer will be in the exact same place where a crime is about to occur.[36] Saturating crime-prone neighborhoods with officers and having them conduct a large number of vehicle and pedestrian stops in search of weapons or other contraband can be more effective than random patrolling, but has disastrous consequences for neighborhood residents, as noted earlier. (So-called "place-based" predictive policing, which attempts to predict at a block-by-block level where crimes are likely to occur next and then stations officers there, has shown limited promise for a different reason, namely that human behavior is not reliably predictable at that scale.)

Focused deterrence sidesteps these problems by having officers identify the people or groups who seem the most likely to be imminently involved in violence, sometimes using "person-based" predictive algorithms, but typically through old-fashioned intelligence that speaks to which groups are actively feuding with one another. Officers contact these individuals and arrange meetings, often with prosecutors, social workers and community leaders present. The officers communicate that the individuals appear to be at high risk for committing violence or for violent victimization. The police make clear that they will closely monitor the individuals and the groups to which they belong and promise to immediately arrest them if they are discovered to have committed even a minor infraction. Prosecutors vow to seek the maximum charges possible. At the same time, the individuals are offered an array of social services, including job training, counseling, and tattoo removal, if they express a willingness to leave gang life.

This carrot-and-stick approach concentrates the deterrent message where it will have the largest impact, increasing perceptions of both the certainty and severity of punishment while raising the perceived benefits of not committing a crime (job training, respect from community representatives for making a different choice, and so on). Its greater efficiency relative to either random patrolling or blanket stop, question, and frisk preserves community goodwill. Careful research shows significant violence reductions from focused deterrence.[37] It goes hand in hand with procedural justice because the people targeted to receive the deterrent messaging are more likely to be persuaded if they trust the officers involved; and officers committed to procedural justice are seen as more trustworthy.

Focused deterrence is not without its problems. For example, the specialized gang squads and violence suppression units that often administer it may not be supervised closely, increasing the risk of abusive behavior. Focused deterrence approaches also require that police departments keep close tabs on gang-involved individuals, which may mean maintaining error-prone databases that could compromise people's rights. The National Policing Institute, in conjunction with the Department of Justice, has recently issued best-practice guidance for police departments that use such squads or maintain other "specialized units."[38] Although cities must attend to potential dangers, municipalities with significant gang and group violence problems should recalibrate their policing to give focused deterrence a more prominent role. As with police diversification and procedural justice, community cooperation will be required for these efforts to bear fruit.

BETTER POLICING IS POSSIBLE

While representing less than a complete overhaul of law enforcement, the approaches I have outlined have great potential to improve policing and public safety. Federal or state legislative action could help push more police departments toward embracing them—through grant funding or accreditation requirements, for example. But communities do not need to wait for politicians at the federal or state level to act. Through pressure, encouragement, and above all sustained engagement and dialogue, they can nudge their cities and police departments toward organizational models and practices that control crime while better attending to the demands of equity and justice.

ACKNOWLEDGMENT

For research assistance on this chapter, I thank Ivan Knoepflmacher and Neil Mortimer.

NOTES

1. Elizabeth Hinton, *America on Fire: The Untold Story of Police Violence and Black Rebellion Since the 1960s* (New York: Liveright, 2021).

2. Robert Shellow, ed., *The Harvest of American Racism: The Political Meaning of Violence in the Summer of 1967* (Ann Arbor, MI: University of Michigan Press, 2018), 40.

3. Jeanne Theoharis, "Martin Luther King Knew That Fighting Racism Meant Fighting Police Brutality," *The Atlantic*, September 15, 2021, https://www.theatlantic.com/ideas/archive/2021/09/martin-luther-king-police-brutality/619090.

4. For review, see Neil Gross, "It Is Possible to Reform the Police: How to End the Racial Disparity in Vehicle Stops," *New York Times*, September 8, 2020, https://www.nytimes.com/2020/09/08/opinion/police-reform-biden.html.

5. Issa Kohler-Hausmann, *MisdemeanorLand: Criminal Courts and Social Control in an Age of Broken Windows Policing* (Princeton, NJ: Princeton University Press, 2019); Joscha Legewie and Jeffrey Fagan, "Aggressive Policing and the Educational Performance of Minority Youth," *American Sociological Review* 84, no. 2 (2019): 220–247.

6. Bahar Ostadan, "The NYPD Has Stopped Tens of Thousands of People Under Mayor Adams. Just 5% Were White," *Gothamist*, August 25, 2023, https://gothamist.com/news/the-nypd-has-stopped-tens-of-thousands-of-people-under-mayor-adams-just-5-were-white.

7. Frank Edwards, Hedwig Lee, and Michael Esposito, "Risk of Being Killed by Police Use of Force in the United States by Age, Race-Ethnicity, and Sex," *Proceedings of the National Academy of Sciences* 116, no. 34 (2019): 16793–98. Questions remain as to whether overall population distributions are the appropriate benchmark for assessing racial bias here. See Cody T. Ross, Bruce Winterhalder, and Richard McElreath, "Racial Disparities in Police Use of Deadly Force against Unarmed Individuals Persist After Appropriately Benchmarking Shooting Data on Violent Crime

Rates," *Social Psychological and Personality Science* 12, no. 3 (2021): 323–32. Cf. Brandon Tregle, Justin Nix, and Geoffrey P. Alpert, "Disparity Does Not Mean Bias: Making Sense of Observed Racial Disparities in Fatal Officer-involved Shootings with Multiple Benchmarks," in *Contemporary Issues in American Policing*, eds. Richard K. Moule Jr. and Bryanna Fox (London: Routledge, 2021), 18–31.

8. Carl Lieberman, "Variation in Racial Disparities in Police Use of Force," *Journal of Urban Economics* 141 (2023): 103602, https://doi.org/10.1016/j.jue.2023.103602.

9. Susannah Tapp and Elizabeth Davis, "Contacts Between Police and the Public, 2020—Statistical Tables," U.S. Department of Justice, Bureau of Justice Statistics, 2023, https://bjs.ojp.gov/sites/g/files/xyckuh236/files/media/document/cbpp20.pdf.

10. Justin T. Pickett, Amanda Graham, and Francis T. Cullen, "The American Racial Divide in Fear of the Police," *Criminology* 60, no. 2 (2022): 291–320.

11. Justin Fenton, *We Own This City: A True Story of Crime, Cops, and Corruption* (New York: Random House, 2021).

12. Jill Leovy, *Ghettoside: A True Story of Murder in America* (New York: One World, 2015).

13. Neil Gross, *Walk the Walk: How Three Police Chiefs Defied the Odds and Changed Cop Culture* (New York: Metropolitan, 2023).

14. Michael Lipsky, "Street-level Bureaucracy and the Analysis of Urban Reform," *Urban Affairs Quarterly* 6, no. 4 (1971): 391–409.

15. David Alan Slansky, "Not Your Father's Police Department: Making Sense of the New Demographics of Law Enforcement," *Journal of Criminal Law and Criminology* 96, no. 3 (2006): 1209–1243.

16. Sean Goodison, "Local Police Departments Personnel, 2020," U.S. Department of Justice, Bureau of Justice Statistics, 2022, https://bjs.ojp.gov/sites/g/files/xyckuh236/files/media/document/lpdp20.pdf.

17. Bocar A. Ba et al., "Who are the Police? Descriptive Representation in the Coercive Arm of Government," Working Paper, 2022, https://jmummolo.scholar.princeton.edu/sites/g/files/toruqf3341/files/ba_et_al_2022.pdf. Cf. Aki Roberts and Hannah R. Smith, "Police Diversity and Crime Clearance for Black and Hispanic Victims," *Criminology & Public Policy* 22, no. 2 (2023): 199–232.

18. Bocar A. Ba et al., "The Role of Officer Race and Gender in Police-Civilian Interactions in Chicago," *Science* 371, no. 6530 (2021): 696–702. On Black police officers, see the discussion in James Forman Jr., *Locking Up Our Own: Crime and Punishment in Black America* (New York: Farrar, Straus and Giroux, 2017), chapter 3.

19. Lauren Leatherby and Richard A. Oppel, "Which Police Departments Are as Diverse as Their Communities?" *New York Times*, September 23, 2020, https://www.nytimes.com/interactive/2020/09/23/us/bureau-justice-statistics-race.html.

20. Rosa Brooks, "One Reason for Police Violence? Too Many Men with Badges," *Washington Post*, June 18, 2020, https://www.washingtonpost.com/outlook/2020/06/18/women-police-officers-violence.

21. Tom R. Tyler, *Why People Obey the Law* (Princeton, NJ: Princeton University Press, 2006); Tom R. Tyler and Tracey L. Meares, "Procedural Justice in Policing," in *Police Innovation: Contrasting Perspectives* (2nd ed.), eds. David Weisburd and Anthony A. Braga (Cambridge, UK: Cambridge University Press, 2019), 71–94.

22. David Weisburd et al., "Reforming the Police Through Procedural Justice Training: A Multicity Randomized Trial at Crime Hot Spots," *Proceedings of the National Academy of Sciences* 119, no. 14 (2022): e2118780119.

23. Gross, *Walk the Walk*.

24. Emilio J. Castilla, "Accounting for the Gap: A Firm Study Manipulating Organizational Accountability and Transparency in Pay Decisions," *Organization Science* 26, no. 2 (2015): 311–333; Frank Dobbin and Alexandra Kalev, *Getting to Diversity: What Works and What Doesn't* (Cambridge, MA: Harvard University Press, 2022).

25. Shani A. Buggs, Daniel W. Webster, and Cassandra K. Crifasi, "Using Synthetic Control Methodology to Estimate Effects of a Cure Violence Intervention in Baltimore, Maryland," *Injury Prevention* 28, no. 1 (2022): 61–67; David M. Hureau et al., "Streetwork at the Crossroads: An Evaluation of a Street Gang Outreach Intervention and Holistic Appraisal of the Research Evidence," *Criminology* 61, no. 4 (2023): 758–794; Marisa C. Ross, Erin M. Ochoa, and Andrew V. Papachristos, "Evaluating the Impact of a Street Outreach Intervention on Participant Involvement in Gun Violence," *Proceedings of the National Academy of Sciences* 120, no. 46 (2023): e2300327120.

26. James Q. Wilson and George L. Kelling, "Broken Windows," *Atlantic Monthly* 249, no. 3 (1982): 29–38.

27. Franklin E. Zimring, *The Great American Crime Decline* (New York: Oxford University Press, 2006).

28. Robert J. Sampson, *Great American City: Chicago and the Enduring Neighborhood Effect* (Chicago: University of Chicago Press, 2012).

29. Robert J. Sampson and Stephen W. Raudenbush, "Seeing Disorder: Neighborhood Stigma and the Social Construction of 'Broken Windows,'" *Social Psychology Quarterly* 67, no. 4 (2004): 319–342.

30. Sampson, *Great American City*, 157.

31. Patrick Sharkey, Gerard Torrats-Espinosa, and Delaram Takyar, "Community and the Crime Decline: The Causal Effect of Local Nonprofits on Violent Crime," *American Sociological Review* 82, no. 6 (2017): 1214–1240.

32. Sharkey et al., "Community and the Crime Decline," 1227.

33. Sharkey et al., "Community and the Crime Decline," 1218.

34. Patrick Sharkey, *Uneasy Peace: The Great Crime Decline, the Renewal of City Life, and the Next War on Violence* (New York: W. W. Norton & Company, 2018).

35. The Eisenhower Foundation, *Youth Investment and Police Mentoring: The Third Generation* (Washington, DC: Eisenhower Foundation, 2011) https://www.eisenhowerfoundation.org/docs/Bluebook,%20Gen3.pdf.

36. George L. Kelling et al., *The Kansas City Preventive Patrol Experiment: A Technical Report* (Washington, DC: Police Foundation, 1974).

37. Anthony A. Braga, David Weisburd, and Brandon Turchan, "Focused Deterrence Strategies and Crime Control: An Updated Systematic Review and Meta-analysis of the Empirical Evidence," *Criminology & Public Policy* 17, no. 1 (2018): 205–250.

38. National Policing Institute, *Considerations for Specialized Units: A Guide for State and Local Law Enforcement Agencies to Ensure Appropriateness, Effectiveness, and Accountability* (Washington, DC: Office of Community Oriented Policing Services, 2024), https://portal.cops.usdoj.gov/resourcecenter/content.ashx/cops-r1140-pub.pdf.

CHAPTER 11

Race, Transparency, and Policing
Practical Advice From One Pracademic's Point of View

Branville Bard Jr.

Your author is a noted "pracademic," a practitioner with more than 30 years of policing experience in urban population centers, including Philadelphia, Metro Boston, and Baltimore, and has served as the head of three police departments. I am an academic with advanced degrees of studies in criminal justice and public safety management, and a terminal degree in the administration of government. I have practiced and studied the profession of policing in "normal times" and through many scandals, from the beating of Rodney King to the murder of George Floyd, as well as the ensuing community tensions, unrest, and degradation of trust. As an admitted pragmatist, I often find myself holding the position of staunch critic of policing, particularly of our unwillingness to meaningfully submit to checks on our authority. However, it's the same pragmatic lens that results in me defending the profession against the unrealistic and impractical positions held by a cacophonous minority.

A deep understanding of the prevailing power structure and system of governance confirms my conviction that policing will always be a necessary part of public safety. It is my many experiences working with the community that leaves me resolved in the belief that people of all communities, even communities that have been historically marginalized, both want and know they need good policing. What people do not want is for the police to cause them harm or otherwise make them feel unsafe. I also know that when a community believes policing leadership creates an atmosphere or a culture that does not tolerate the mistreatment or abuse of them, then the kind of trust that is necessary to work meaningfully together on tough issues comes much more easily. In my opinion two of the biggest impediments to attaining consistent trust between the community and police are race and lack of transparency, with race definitively holding the number one slot.

Both the beating of Rodney King and the murder of George Floyd involved minority victims and police officers who were nonminority; both resulted in the widespread erosion of trust in policing and major civil unrest. I would argue, policing as a profession did (or has done) little to meaningfully address the issue of race during the nearly 3 decades between these events; although as a profession we have known of our responsibility to do so, especially if we seek the community's trust, as we so often profess to. Policing's inability to meaningfully address the issue of race is well documented throughout history; however, we need look back no further than the late 1960s. In July 1967, President Lyndon Baines Johnson, through Executive Order 11365, established a National Advisory Commission on Civil Disorders, also known as the Kerner Commission after its chairperson, Illinois governor Otto Kerner. The commission's charge was, among other things, to investigate and make recommendations as to the basic causes and major factors contributing to recent civil disorders in several American cities as well as to determine methods for averting and/or controlling such disorders in the future. The commission submitted its final report, "Report of the National Advisory Commission on Civil Disorders" (Kerner Report), on March 1, 1968. Among the myriad of societal problems noted in the Kerner Report[1] was ". . . [the] abrasive relationships between police and Negroes and other minority groups . . . as a major source of grievance, tension, and ultimately, disorder . . ."[2] Almost 50 years later, in 2014, President Barack Obama, through Executive Order 13684, established the President's Task Force on 21st Century Policing.[3] Like the Kerner Commission, the Task Force on 21st Century Policing was established after civil unrest in several American cities sparked by violent interactions between police and minority citizens.[4] While admittedly taking the short road here, I would argue that the fact that two presidential commissions were established for the same reason(s) nearly 50 years apart can be viewed as strong evidence that the profession has not done enough to meaningfully address the issue(s) of race.

It's beyond time that law enforcement as a profession addresses the issue of race in a manner that is meaningful. To accomplish this task, my recommendation to law enforcement practitioners is threefold: (1) we should establish more meaningful metrics that examine data in a manner that asks and answers the question, "What if any differences exist between how minorities are treated versus how nonminorities are treated when encountered by law enforcement?", (2) we should establish a watchdog-like entities responsible for tracking police–citizen interactions for potential racial disparities, and (3) let's publish data in near real time.

Now, before engaging in the substantive discussion, let's engage in the obligatory digression for my law enforcement practitioner friends, many of whom will insist that as a profession we already collect and analyze data meaningfully—and that we do so ad nauseum. However, the problems associated with the ways we typically analyze data associated with police–citizen interactions (police stop data) are well documented. Two of the most commonly discussed concerns are, first, what to compare—or in academic terms, what to use as a benchmark. And there is what the appropriate level of analysis is—many studies and agency reports focus on the whole and utilize aggregate data. The model I will suggest seeks to sidestep the well-published benchmarking and aggregate problems that plague researchers and others who examine police stop data; although it too will admittedly have limitations.

According to David Harris, the use of appropriate benchmarks "may be the single most important issue in the design of any data collection effort—and probably also the one most often ignored."[5] Brian Withrow argued that ". . . stop data information relating to the racial and ethnic proportional representation of individuals stopped by the police are all but meaningless unless compared against an acceptable benchmark that accurately measures the proportional racial and ethnic representation of individuals available to be stopped...."[6] To get an answer to the question of whether a given police department stops a disproportionate number of minorities, the data collection effort must result in the calculation of two different numbers: (1) how many drivers of each racial or ethnic group (or pedestrians, if conducting an inquiry of stop-and-frisk activity) police stopped during some particular period of time, and (2) the first number must be compared to something in order to know whether the number of stops of each group is out of line with what we should expect.[7]

The overwhelming majority of police department stop data reports utilize a methodology known as "population benchmarking," even though we know, or should know, that this method is at best limited and often does not provide the information the layperson thinks it does. Population benchmarking compares the number or percentage of drivers stopped of a particular race to the percentage of that race in the jurisdiction's population based on census data. Typically, only the population of driving age (≥ 16 years) is utilized as a baseline. Sometimes that comparison is made against the makeup of that particular race within the population of licensed drivers within the jurisdiction or the overall population of licensed drivers in the county, state, or country. Essentially, this method informs us of the proportion of drivers of a certain race who are stopped and/or searched as compared to the proportion of that particular race in some mostly indiscriminate population, and therefore statistical generalizations are mostly inappropriate.[8]

It is well known that the general population cannot serve as a valid baseline since it does not reflect the racial composition of drivers at risk of being stopped.[9] Additionally, there are several limitations in drawing statistical inferences from population comparisons:[10] (1) it is difficult or near impossible to control for transient drivers; (2) differences in traffic law violations by race cannot be ruled out (in fact, using unadjusted residential population or census figures as a benchmark is a mistake because the racial mix of the population that lives in an area is frequently different from the population of people who drive through it); [11] and (3) census data may prove less than accurate. In fact, the problems associated with population data may be too numerous. According to some, these types of analyses are done by those who do not understand the limitations of this benchmark."[12]

Another well-documented problem with the way we handle data analyzation as a profession is that we typically analyze (and report out) in the aggregate. Researchers readily recognize the problems of generalizing and interpreting the results of examinations of aggregate data. In my opinion, the most worrisome problem associated with looking at data in the aggregate is that as officers who do engage in racially disparate practices have their data increasingly mixed with officers who do not engage in racially disparate practices, the effects will appear minimized and/or diluted. Eventually it will appear as if racial profiling or other racially disparate behavior is not occurring as the level of analysis becomes more aggregated. Employing the "bad apple" analogy, as the bad apples (individual officers who engage in racial profiling) become mixed with increasingly larger numbers of good apples, the bad apples become harder and harder to detect, and eventually it will appear as if these bad apples do not exist.[13] Aggregate data is not devoid of purpose; when the focus is on reform rather than individual misconduct, the value of aggregate statistical evidence is more apparent. Gross and Barnes ask, "How else can one describe how an entire agency is behaving?"[14] Walker argues, "It is appropriate for police departments to publish aggregate data, indicating, first, that a review of traffic enforcement activities is regularly conducted, and second, that a certain percentage of officers have been identified for counseling or training."[15]

That we, as a profession, have not taken more direct action toward addressing the many issues associated with race and policing by examining stop data more critically is the best evidence that we will not do so—at least not organically, not on our own—and not in the near future. In fact, many of us will find it easier to craft what amounts to largely unconvincing arguments as to the potential pitfalls of doing so and expend little to no energy considering the many potential benefits of openly examining how race impacts outcomes in our interactions with the public. There is a line in *Pulp Fiction*, the 1994 film by Quentin Tarantino, where Samuel L. Jackson's character (Jules Winnfield) says to John Travolta's character (Vincent Vega), "If my answers frighten you, Vincent, then you should cease asking scary questions."[16] I firmly believe we do not ask scary questions because we do not want to be frightened by answers.

I have long argued there is a need for a simpler, easier-to-understand model to assist in the detection of racial profiling and/or racially biased policing. I suggest that as a profession we take a lesson from professional sports, namely Major League Baseball (MLB). You see, when I think of some of my all-time favorite players like Hank Aaron, Mike Schmidt, and Ken Griffey, Jr., I don't have to guess how they did in their careers because MLB keeps exhaustive stats. I can click a few buttons and find out how any one of them, and particularly any current-day player, hits. And not just how they hit in their career overall, I can drill down into the minutiae and find out, how they hit in day games, how they hit in night games, how they hit with two strikes, how they hit against the curveball, against the fast ball and how they hit with two outs—you name it, you can get the statistic on it in MLB. You cannot tell me Hank Aaron was a bad hitter because I can go right to the stats! And I will not have to review all 12,000+ of Aaron's career at-bats because MLB keeps a statistic that tells me how he typically did at the plate—it's called a batting average (AVG).[17] If you look at it from an advocate's point of view, it makes little sense that we can get such detailed information about our favorite MLB player or MLB team, who at worst can only disappoint or upset us, but not nearly as much detailed information about our police department, which is capable of doing actual harm in the community—whether we as a profession care to admit this capability or not.

It should become commonplace for law enforcement to produce statistics that accurately reflect the difference in how an officer or unit or department typically treats individuals of different races during encounters. We likely (particularly in many larger departments) already collect data sufficient for this type of analysis; the problem is we have simply lacked the will to do this type of analysis. I argue that we should focus on the three main components of a police–citizen encounter: the Reason for the interaction, the Result of the interaction, and the Duration of the interaction (the RRD Model)—the goal of the RRD Model is to quantify or score each category.[18] The model suggested here would allow for weighted comparisons to be made using the amount of discretion an officer has in taking an action versus a compelling governmental (or societal) interest in the officer taking that action. I have previously developed a methodology to examine vehicular stop data, so examples given will focus on examining vehicle stop data;

however, it is my belief that this type of examination should extend to all police–citizen encounters (vehicular stops, pedestrian stops, etc.).

Here is an example related to the examining of police vehicle stop data: even the most ardent critic of law enforcement would agree that there was a compelling governmental (or societal) interest for law enforcement to stop an individual driving through the city streets in excess of 30 mph over the posted speed limit; conversely, no similar urgency or need exists when an individual is driving 3 mph over the posted speed limit. However, the officer has the same amount of discretion to stop (or not to stop) the speeder in each instance. The RRD Model would more heavily weight discretionary actions of law enforcement officers where no compelling governmental (or societal) interests exist.

Each component (Reason, Result, and Duration) will have subcomponents that are weighted based on severity—the inference being that increased severity advances society's interest in the officer taking action to interrupt—and where we expect or direct an officer to take an action, we lower the officer's discretion to not take the action. The first component (variable), Reason, is weighted based on the severity of the infraction, with subcomponents consisting of related factors that will also be weighted ($Reason_{(1)}$ = Severity of Infraction, $Reason_{(2)}$ = Legal Sufficiency for encounter/stop, and $Reason_{(3)}$, etc.). The second component (variable), Result, is weighted by most serious enforcement action, with subcomponents taking into account whether searches were conducted or consent requested. The third component (variable), Duration, is a straightforward weighting of the amount of time spent with enforcement actions, with subcomponents considering whether the encounter was prolonged for searches or awaiting equipment.[19]

Once quantifications are made for each component (and subcomponent), many comparisons can be made. In its simplest application, the RRD model would make comparisons of stops that an officer makes with one group and compare them to the results obtained when that same officer stops other groups. Making comparisons in this manner, helps us to avoid the aggregate and benchmark problems discussed earlier—and it is fair to officers because it does not run the risk of misidentifying their behaviors.[20] Sticking with the MLB analogy, just as Tony Gwynn's and Stan Musial's recorded batting averages are an accurate depiction of their behavior at the plate, the RRD Model would provide an accurate depiction of an officer's behavior in the field.

The RRD Model could certainly provide much needed insight into, and more credibly answer, "scary questions" like "What, if any, differences exist in how we treat minorities versus nonminorities when we stop or otherwise encounter them?" Obviously, such a model lends itself to more detailed comparison. Additionally, by using a weighted analysis, each jurisdiction can decide what actions it values as a community, although there is widespread value in uniformity where this type of analysis is concerned. The statistics should have the same meaning no matter if compiled in Cambridge, Minnesota, Cambridge, Maryland, or Cambridge, Massachusetts.

It has been my experience in my chosen profession that many of us in leadership positions get indignant in situations where we would be better served by introspection. In my experience, this often occurs when our authority, methods, or motives are challenged by advocates. I have spent many years in leadership positions, as I was promoted to the rank of captain in the fourth largest police department in the United States more than 20 years ago now; during this time, I have become firmly resolved in the belief that we as law enforcement practitioners should not treat advocates as adversaries. In fact, I have found the mutual desire to be protective and to have more positive outcomes leads to consensus. However, we cannot (or should not) ask advocates to rely on some ideal, the absence of disparate treatment of minorities in law enforcement and policing, when it does not jibe with any sentiment expressed or more importantly with actions taken, which they have ever seen—this very thought reminds me of a gripe powerfully stated by James Baldwin when discussing American institutions on an old episode of *The Dick Cavett Show*.[21] It is not always an easy experience, as many of these conversations start from emotionally charged places. To the advocate, we personify the oppressive, harmful arm of the power structure; and to law enforcement practitioners, advocates can represent a challenge to our authority, a dilution of the power we wield and a change to our very comfortable existence. But this is before we have the opportunity to humanize each other and come to the realization of the existence of a mutual desire to be protective. The development of this mutual understanding is a phenomenon I have experienced many times during my career.

I'll briefly share one of the more recent experiences relating with advocates. I served as the police commissioner for Cambridge, Massachusetts, for 4 years (2017–2021). During that time, a well-known local business leader and community figure suggested I meet with a local activist/advocate; I had become familiar with this advocate because of their social media presence—quite frankly, for frequently excoriating law enforcement, including my department. I remember the business leader, upon suggesting we meet, saying, "I know both of you and believe me, you two are more alike than you are different; there are way more similarities! . . . a real opportunity for synergy." The advocate was a U.S. combat veteran who had been seriously injured while commanding troops overseas. While we talked, he relayed some personal experiences during his time abroad and some atrocities he saw soldiers attempting to commit (he may have even used the term "committing"—meaning successful attempts). He then paused and said, "Commissioner, you have my guys!" For me, that statement was more than powerful—and not just because I am an admitted misanthrope, but because of the undeniable truth of it. The civil service system recruits and heavily incentivizes employment for veterans of the armed forces. So the undeniable truth is his "guys" are likely policing and enforcing laws in many places—and people capable of committing atrocities abroad are capable of committing atrocities anywhere. I sensed the advocate was armed with facts and figures to support the argument, but may have been taken by surprise when I agreed and shared that I have encountered officers whom I would not trust alone in an alley with my brother or son.

Like many times before with advocates, the mutual desire to be protective brought with it a shared understanding. This was not the time to respond with, "Well, not all . . ." It was the time to validate truths, without qualification. Not treating advocates as adversaries encourages cooperation with law enforcement practitioners and results in practices that reduce opportunities for certain injustices to occur and can imbue trust through the wider community.

In the spirit of approximating "protective asks" and with the historical understanding that power concedes nothing without a demand, it is beyond time the "asks" and "demands" start to come from within; however, it is most important the asks and demands be given proper consideration wherever they originate from. More than a decade ago, while researching ways to combat racial profiling, I came across the work of Howard University law professor Andrew Taslitz. In his 2003 article, "Racial Auditors and the Fourth Amendment: Data With the Power to Inspire Political Action," Taslitz explores the use of "racial auditing" as a method of police regulation. Taslitz argues this type of monitoring "can provide a particularly effective strategy for monitoring and deterring police misconduct . . ."[22] One of the many practical and protective measures elevated in Taslitz's work was posed by Professor Christopher Edley, while serving as a member of the U.S. commission concerning minimizing the encroachment of antiterrorism efforts onto civil liberties. Edley, concerned with the "narrowing of individual rights during war time [in the name of anti-terrorism]," suggested Congress create an independent Office of Rights and Liberties (ORL) within the then-new Department of Homeland Security. Edley proposed that the ORL would ". . . be solely focused on monitoring compliance with civil liberties and civil rights norms . . ."[23] Taslitz suggests, and this pracademic easily agrees, that Edley's proposal could be a model for the establishment of ORL in municipal police departments, thereby ensuring constant monitoring and presumably more compliance where profiling and other racial injustices start, on the local level.

The ORL-like office can come into existence in a number of manners. The office can be mandated through legislation at the local level or created by a police chief at the agency level. The unit can also be created and controlled at the supra-agency level. What is most important is that the head of the office serve as Edley suggested, in the role of "super inspector general," but one who is focused solely on monitoring compliance with civil liberties and civil rights norms.[24]

I was moved by what I felt was a very practical and protective suggestion; therefore, while serving as police commissioner for the city of Cambridge, I took the opportunity to adopt this and many other protective measures by creating the Office of Procedural Justice at the agency level and assigning a newly approved deputy superintendent to run the unit. The Office of Procedural Justice's primary focus was to proactively monitor data relating to police–citizen interactions for indications of possible racial profiling and racially biased policing (including use of force incidents), as well as assessing the department's compliance with statutes, ordinances, and regulations aimed at mandating accountability.[25] I opted to call the unit the Office of Procedural Justice instead of Edley's Office of Rights and Liberties, most prominently because the profession (and the Cambridge Police Department) had already been familiar with, and found palatable, "Procedural Justice"; whereas "Rights and Liberties" carried with it a pronounced watchdog connotation. In my opinion, the path of least resistance was to use the already accepted terminology and assign it the watchdog responsibility rather than deal with the resistance to the name and the function.

In addition to monitoring data and assessing for the possibility of racial profiling and other racial injustices, another function of the Office of Procedural Justice was to provide the answer to the question "What, if any, differences exist in how we treat minorities versus nonminorities when we stop or otherwise encounter them?" using the RRD Model (to assess vehicular stop data only). This data would be published in near real time as evidence of our commitment to increasing transparency, accountability, and introspection. Ultimately, the contracted vendor was unable to satisfy the near real-time publishing of data; in its current iteration the Procedural Justice dashboard is updated quarterly. It is my intention to create the same Procedural Justice–type dashboard within the Johns Hopkins Police Department, which is being stood up as a new law enforcement agency at Johns Hopkins University in Baltimore.[26]

Law enforcement practitioners are not the only group in need of sound advice, though they are the narrow focus of this writing. During my lengthy career, I have seen advocates continually engage in practices that may not align with their grand aim or advance their stated goals. Two of the more common errors in recent times are: (1) allowing a "majority"[27] to advocate for impractical or unrealistic causes, and (2) adopting "protective" stances improperly. As it is not the focus of this writing, the brief discussion to follow is meant to be pragmatic and practical in nature; expanding the discussion in the realm of academia is a likely future undertaking. It is not intended to offend; therefore, other than examples involving the author, it will avoid pointing to specific groups or individuals.

"End Policing," "Police should never use force," "Defund the Police,"[28] "Emmitt was a better runner than Barry": What do all of these statements have in common? They fail to hold up under logical scrutiny; they are impractical and they do not represent the majority sentiment. More and more, small but loud groups, *mijorities*, have become more and more boisterous about championing the impractical, thereby weakening practical demands that seem somewhat adjacent or related. This chapter started off on the premise that the Kerner Commission made sound recommendations for society and policing to address how we deal with the issue of race, yet more than a half century later, organizations like the Milton Eisenhower Foundation exist to advance the recommendations of the Kerner Commission because they have largely failed to be adopted. My point here being if (the power structure of) society and (the profession of) policing can ignore sound, practical recommendations, the likelihood of advancing these impractical suggestions is exceedingly low. I certainly won't attempt to tackle these ill-formed arguments in the limited time and space I have here, particularly the dissertation I would need to address the Barry vs. Emmitt argument; however, I will quickly comment on the issue of "use of force." In recent times, and particularly in the era following the murder of George Floyd, I have been in many settings where individuals have argued that police should never be allowed to use force. The fact of the matter is we have to get away from treating the reasonable use of force by law enforcement officers as a policy failure. The very reason we have "use of force" policies is because of a well-documented understanding of the need for law enforcement officers to use force in limited circumstances. Many years ago when I was a young captain, a well-known community activist, who was also the matriarch of the community, told me, ". . . since you been here, your folks only fight the people we knew y'all was gonna have to f**k up—we know you don't play around when it comes letting us get hurt—and we know you care about us—and your cops know it too! . . . We can support that—hell, that's what we been asking for. . . ." The language was crass, but the sentiment was clear and left me resolved with the understanding that when you create an atmosphere where citizens know you won't tolerate their mistreatment or abuse, the community will have your back and you will have their trust. There's a wide chasm between "police should never use force" and the sentiment expressed by the matriarch—in my experience, the matriarch is more representative of community and society.

Lastly, and quickly, when it comes to adopting protective stances improperly, I will turn to a relatively new advocate, "the progressive prosecutor." In theory, I default to being supportive of individuals who make adopting protective strategies a priority; the criminal justice system is fertile territory when it comes to the need for them. We operate in a system that purports to prefer 10 guilty men go free than one innocent man lose his liberty; this ideal has not been the reality for many minority and poor people. There is a compelling societal interest in undoing wrongs involving the imprisonment of innocents; there is a compelling societal interest in more heavily scrutinizing serious charges, particularly those charges where officers have unchecked discretion and are the witness and victim, such as resisting arrest. Because of the existence of a compelling societal interest in these matters, there will be widespread and enduring support for efforts aimed at undoing and minimizing opportunities for harm in these areas. Go ahead, ramp up your Conviction Integrity Units; go ahead, default to "No" on a very limited number of serious and some minor "victimless crimes."[29] However, excluding victimless crimes, a default to "No" cannot equate to the barring of these charges. If the evidence shows indicia of guilt, charge it! If the evidence shows a "mischarging"[30] but not "misconduct" (falsification of charges), introduce the appropriate charge, and charge it!

In my experience, there is not widespread support in defaulting to "No" or not charging crimes that do not fit into these very limited categories, which does not include crimes such as shoplifting, trespassing, or burglarizing vacant properties and destruction of property. Let us not conflate the fact that society does not support people being locked away for long sentences for these minor offenses to mean that society does not want individuals held accountable for these offenses. We are already beginning to see the deleterious effect these policies have when it comes to failing to charge for the crime of shoplifting, as retailers are being forced to close locations and flee business districts where low-level looting is becoming sport. This type of activity carries with it the type of economic harm that has cascading negative effects throughout the impacted region. Also, it should be understood that as a profession, we in law enforcement will not let an opportunity to fearmonger pass us by. Wisdom tells us "he who would sacrifice liberty for safety deserves neither"; however, history has shown us, when faced with the untenable choice (whether real or manufactured), particularly where the safety of our loved ones is concerned, safety will win out almost every time. Do not provide fearmongers ammunition unnecessarily.

This chapter is intended not as an exercise in finger wagging, but as a narrowly focused, pragmatic advisory to fellow law enforcement executives. As practitioners, we have to become comfortable asking scary questions and dealing with answers that may frighten us. We must be more transparent with how we handle these issues. Let's drop the indignation that results in hasty proclamations such as "race doesn't matter" in favor of the introspection needed to begin to address our well-known shortcomings in how we handle the issue.

If race doesn't matter, why is it that while writing this piece suggesting ways to improve how our profession deals with the issue of race, I experienced much trepidation as to whether or not to attribute statements to James Baldwin and Frederick Douglass because I was worried the mere invoking of their names might cause some of my fellow practitioners to stop reading? Why did I feel no such trepidation with the thought of making a similar attribution to Ben Franklin?[31] Why? Because race will *never not matter*—race will always matter. As long as the construct exists, it will matter. That's why!

As a profession, we are far better served by listening to the advocates and others who seek to be protective of the populations we are sworn to serve. Remember, we profess to "protect" them also. Unbridled hubris and the inability to be introspective results in our failure to admit to, or to properly understand, the harm we are capable of inflicting; although the research continues to be unambiguous when informing us that minorities are disparately impacted at every key decision-making point throughout the entire criminal justice system.

Find protective strategies like the RRD Model and adopt them. Get your local universities to partner and support these efforts. I have asked some brilliant minds in the schools of Johns Hopkins University to assist in the further development the RRD Model, what could be known as "JHU Test of Discretional Variance." There is room for "The Carnegie Mellon Test of Combined Variance," the Berkeley Factor, etc. What naturally follows when the data analysis inevitably shows what we suspect they will is (1) increased regulatory and legislative protections, (2) better law enforcement, and (3) improved relationships between police and citizens in all communities, along with a myriad of other benefits. As a profession we must make some uncomfortable changes; there are far too many illustrations of what happens when a species is incapable of adapting. Let's not become one of them.

NOTES

1. It can be accepted as fact that the Kerner Commission was premised on race; in support of this position, it can be noted the terms race, racial, an actual race (Negro, White, etc.) or a proxy for race (minority") appears in the 400+ pages of the report (in text or reference), more than 3,500 times.

2. "National Advisory Commission on Civil Disorders, Report," Office of Justice Programs, 1968, https://www.ojp.gov/ncjrs/virtual-library/abstracts/national-advisory-commission-civil-disorders-report.

3. President's Task Force on 21st Century Policing, "Final Report of the President's Task Force on 21st Century Policing," 2015, https://cops.usdoj.gov/pdf/taskforce/taskforce_finalreport.pdf.

4. President's Task Force on 21st Century Policing, "Final Report of the President's Task Force on 21st Century Policing."

5. David A. Harris, "The Reality of Racial Disparity in Criminal Justice: The Significance of Data Collection," *Law and Contemporary Problems* 66, no. 3 (2003), 71–98, https://www.jstor.org/stable/20059189.

6. Brian L. Withrow, *Racial Profiling: From Rhetoric to Reason* (Upper Saddle River, NJ: Pearson, 2006).

7. Withrow, *Racial Profiling*; Branville G. Bard Jr., "Racial Profiling: Towards Simplicity and Eradication" (PhD diss., Valdosta State University, 2014).

8. Withrow, *Racial Profiling*; Bard, "Racial Profiling."

9. Samuel Walker, "Searching for the Denominator: Problems with Police Traffic Stop Data and an Early Warning System Solution," *Justice Research and Policy* 3, no. 1 (2001), 63–95.

10. Melissa Whitney, "The Statistical Evidence of Racial Profiling in Traffic Stops and Searches: Rethinking the Use of Statistics to Prove Discriminatory Intent," *Boston College Law Review* 49, no. 1 (2008), 263–98.

11. David A. Harris, *Profiles in Injustice: Why Racial Profiling Cannot Work* (New York: The New Press, 2003).

12. Amy M. Farrell, Jana Rumminger, and Jack McDevitt, "New Challenges in Confronting Racial Profiling in the 21st Century: Learning from Research and Practice," Institute on Race and Justice, Northeastern University, 2003.

13. Whitney, "The Statistical Evidence of Racial Profiling in Traffic Stops and Searches," 279.

14. Samuel R. Gross and Katherine Y. Barnes, "Road Work: Racial Profiling and Drug Interdiction on the Highway," *Michigan Law Review* 101, no. 3 (2002), 651–754.

15. Walker, "Searching for the Denominator," 89–90.

16. *Pulp Fiction*, written and directed by Quentin Tarantino, Miramax, 1994.

17. "Stats," Major League Baseball, https://www.mlb.com/stats/.

18. I explore the concept in more detail, see Bard, "Racial Profiling."

19. Bard, "Racial Profiling."

20. The method addresses how to handle analysis in communities where populations are heavily skewed with or contain only one race.

21. James Baldwin, "Discrimination in America," *The Dick Cavett Show*, May 16, 1969. https://www.youtube.com/watch?v=hzH5IDnLaBA&ab.

22. Andrew E. Taslitz, "Racial Auditors and the Fourth Amendment: Data with the Power to Inspire Political Action." *Law and Contemporary Problems* 66, no. 3 (2003), 221–298.

23. Taslitz, "Racial Auditors and the Fourth Amendment," 296.

24. Christopher Edley, Jr., "A U.S. Watchdog for Civil Liberties," *The Washington Post Outlook Sunday*, July 14, 2002 p. B07.

25. See Cambridge Police, "Office of Procedural Justice," City of Cambridge, n.d., https://www.cambridgema.gov/Departments/cambridgepolice/policeunits/officeofproceduraljustice.

26. For more information and justification for creating this type of entity, see Edley, "A U.S. Watchdog for Civil Liberties," Bard, "Racial Profiling," and Taslitz, "Racial Auditors and the Fourth Amendment."

27. The term "majority" references a small group who are often so loud, or receive so much attention, that they are mistakenly thought to represent the majority opinion.

28. "Defund" here is meant in the context of eliminating, in whole or in part, the police budget and not in the context of rightly assigning some tasks (and perhaps corresponding portions of funds) we have come to rely on policing for when other professionals might be better suited to handle them.

29. A victimless crime is an act that is against the law but that only harms the individuals who consented to engage in the act (prostitution is a commonly cited example).

30. Such as an officer who charges "resisting arrest," when in the prosecutor's view it was not resisting arrest but a simple assault on a peace officer.

31. "Power concedes nothing without a demand" is attributed to Frederick Douglass; "He who would sacrifice liberty for safety deserves neither" is attributed to Ben Franklin.

CHAPTER 12

Two Justice Systems—Separate and Unequal

Kim Taylor-Thompson

"Our Nation is moving toward two societies, one black, one white—separate and unequal."[1] Almost 60 years ago, the Kerner Commission issued its dire warning that racism threatened to polarize this country and to destroy the basic freedoms that America claimed to embrace. The report exposed the myriad ways that systemic racism created and ruthlessly patrolled racial borders. Quite literally, Black and Brown communities were penned in the congested cores of cities, while white Americans flocked to the edges. As the Kerner Commission report made plain, "[w]hat white Americans have never fully understood—but what the Negro can never forget—is that white society is deeply implicated in the ghetto. White institutions created it, white institutions maintained it and white society condones it."[2] Racial subordination and control served as the twin engines that powered inequity and protected white spaces and privilege.[3] Even today, the accuracy of the commission's predictions is remarkable. But for all its prescience, the report still underestimated the pernicious reach of the systemic racism it was describing. The commission simply did not foresee the extent to which racism would infest the country's legal system, lurching our criminal justice system toward two systems: one Black and one white—separate and unequal.

Few have suffered more under this racialized criminal legal system than young Black and Brown kids. Many of this country's justice policy choices trace back to the deeply unsettling impact of crime that the Kerner Commission noted.[4] Americans' generalized anxiety about crime would ultimately narrow to a particularized fear fueled by racism. By the late 1960s, cultural stereotypes linking the Black race with criminality had firmly taken root in the American psyche. In the next 30 years, that racist trope would mutate: The young Black male would emerge as the face of crime. The public would no longer see the young Black or Brown adolescent as one might perceive a white child. Instead, he would morph into something more predatory, more dangerous, and less childlike. Once the American public embraced the idea of a dangerous young offender, it became easier to implement policies and practices that ignored a youthful accused's age, immaturity, and developmental potential. Today, every state prosecutes middle schoolers as adults, exposing them to adult prosecution and punishment. Children as young as 9 have been prosecuted as adults.[5] Black youth—particularly young Black men—are disproportionately charged, disproportionately prosecuted in adult court, and disproportionately sentenced either to lengthy prison terms or death,[6] even though white children commit the same crimes.[7] The "justification" is that these practices somehow make us safer.

They do not.[8] Crime rates have not decreased in the wake of mass incarceration. Instead, marginalized communities have hollowed out from within as young people of color have suffered the irreparable damage of lost childhoods and derailed life trajectories. As a country so often governed by fear, we tend to ration empathy and mercy. Race determines to whom they are dispensed. On a daily basis, we deny Black and Brown kids the care and attention we reflexively—and routinely—afford white kids. Race has become the indelible dividing line that cleaves the nation into two competing visions of who is dangerous and who is not; who counts as a child and who does not; who is valuable and who is not. Disparities in treatment affect all people of color in the justice system, but the stark divide between Black and white adolescents best illustrates the depth of the problem in youth justice.

THE RACISM BACKDROP

Choosing who counts as a child continues to be steeped in this country's racism. When a white 17-year-old, Kyle Rittenhouse, fired on and killed two protesters in Kenosha, Wisconsin, in August 2020, pundits and political operatives moved quickly to describe him as a "little boy out there trying to protect his community."[9] Even when he walked past police toting a semiautomatic rifle, police did not stop or question him. His skin privilege cloaked him in a presumption of innocence. But Black teens do not share the same protective cover. They are presumed dangerous and guilty. A Black 17-year-old armed with a semiautomatic would not have survived to tell the story. Instead, Black kids learn early the impact of being suspected of wrongdoing based on appearance. The public fears children of color more than any other adolescents, regardless of economic background.[10] Black children are victimized at a greater rate and policed more aggressively.[11]

The chronic mistreatment of kids of color traces, at least in part, to a shift in the public narrative about youthful offending. In the mid-1990s, Professor John DiIulio advanced a "superpredator" theory that depicted Black children as "wolf packs" of remorseless animals who would prey on victims. DiIulio insisted that this new, hardened breed of criminal would soon target "upscale central-city districts, inner-ring suburbs, and even the rural heartland." His warning was blunt: white America was in danger. The media immediately seized on his claims and stoked the public's fear. Politicians across both parties responded to public outcry by passing draconian crime bills. And the American public eagerly consumed the story. The superpredator lie went viral, infecting every institution that touches children—courts, schools, law enforcement. In the end, it stripped Black children of the protections of childhood.

But the juvenile crime wave that DiIulio foretold never materialized. Juvenile crime rates actually dropped between 1994 and 2000. Those inconsistent facts did not deter politicians who conveniently ignored that data and urged "adult time for adult crime." The phrase soon became both a rallying cry and a directional imperative. The simplicity of that popular slogan squeezed the inherent complexity out of the problem of youthful offending; however, it appeased a fearful public anxious for any solution. The grim and brutal reality is that when John DiIulio actually admitted being wrong about his predictions, even his retraction could not dislodge this country's already formed assumptions that young Black males were cold-blooded and dangerous.

What made this superpredator story so easy to embrace and so stubbornly intractable? The answer is tragic and damning. The superpredator myth glommed onto a deeper lie embedded in American soil and in the American psyche: A lie that contends that Black children do not merit the care we automatically offer white children. This lie is an American phenomenon with intergenerational effects. During slavery, white slavers separated children from their mothers because a child could garner a greater profit. This was not merely profiteering. This was a conscious designation of Black children as chattel. During Jim Crow, white mobs lynched Black children if they dared cross a racial margin that white society invented and lethally enforced. The United States cultivated a fear of Black people and an appetite for violent punishment.

By the time the superpredator mythology claimed that Black children were predators, the false stories were so culturally embedded that the public easily accepted this newest lie. The nation was primed to accept the disparate treatment of Black children as somehow appropriate or deserved. Dehumanizing Black children allowed Americans to withstand any tug of moral constraint as we pretended that even our youngest and most vulnerable children could only be "controlled" through adult prosecution in the criminal justice system.

RACISM TRUMPS SCIENCE

On a daily basis, we prosecute Black children as adults, ignoring the child in the offender. Studies by the U.S. Department of Justice and the Centers for Disease Control and Prevention have raised serious questions about that policy choice, finding it to be counterproductive as a strategy for preventing or reducing violence.[12] As importantly, brain and behavioral research have exploded the myth that adolescents are miniature adults. Neuroscience research reveals that the regions of an adolescent's brain that govern impulse control and risk avoidance are still developing into the mid- to late-twenties. Without those controls in full operation, young people will more likely yield to impulse and will find it more difficult to resist external influences, such as from peers or unstable environments. Even when adolescents engage in violent conduct that might make the public perceive them as somehow more mature, their judgment is simply not the same as that of a mature adult.

Reckless conduct is so common among adolescents that refraining from criminal conduct as an adolescent is a statistical aberration.[13] The encouraging news is that young people will typically desist from offending as the executive functions in their brains develop. This "age-crime desistance curve" reveals that both violent and less serious crimes peak sharply in adolescence and then drop markedly in young adulthood.[14] By the time young people reach their mid-twenties, most will stop engaging in criminal conduct. The U.S. Supreme Court has recognized this and has urged lower courts to adopt a developmental approach to youthful offending.

The Court issued rulings expecting science to guide the justice system's perception of—and approach to—adolescents who engage in even the most serious crimes. In a trio of decisions over a 7-year period, the Court mapped the reasons for this shift. The Court held unconstitutional the imposition of the death penalty for all youthful offenders under the age of 18.[15] Even in a case in which a 17-year-old, in the company of friends, broke into a woman's home, kidnapped her, and murdered her by throwing her into a river,[16] the Court found the death penalty inappropriate.[17] Despite the heinous crime, the Court concluded that "juvenile offenders cannot with reliability be classified among the worst offenders."[18] The Court further held unconstitutional the imposition of life without parole sentences for juvenile offenders convicted of non-homicide offenses,[19] and the mandatory imposition of life without parole terms for juvenile offenders in homicide cases.[20] In so ruling, the Court emphasized that recklessness and impulsivity are "signature qualities" of youth but noted that these traits are transient.

The Court's decisions centered on the growing body of neuroscience and behavioral science that offers a clearer understanding of a young person's culpability and capacity for change. What that scientific evidence explains—and the Supreme Court recognized—is that teenagers do not have fully developed personalities;[21] their behavior is driven by impulse, context, and opportunity;[22] they are less able than adults to consider and weigh alternative courses of action in order to avoid unduly risky behavior;[23] they are more susceptible to the influences of peers;[24] and they lack the self-control that virtually every one of them will gain later in life.[25] The Court has advised that in assessing a young person's culpability and punishment, decision-makers should consider the immaturity and vulnerabilities that youth characteristically exhibit. The Court presumed that a better understanding of the behavioral and neurological science explaining youthful offending would divert decision-makers from the most severe sentences and lead them instead toward a youth benefit. Unfortunately, the Court's assumption has proved overly optimistic, at best.

The Court simply underestimated the power of racism to misshape justice. The youth benefit that the Court recommends tends to be experienced by only some young people in the justice system, not all. In decisions about whom to prosecute and how severely, we see a disturbing form of racial exceptionalism in play. Rather than being recognized as a still-developing child, the young Black person is more often seen as adultlike. Or equally problematic, the public perceives the Black adolescent as an animal or predator. When the Black teenager exhibits signature adolescent tendencies, he is not considered childlike but mature. He is not impulsive; he is unpredictably volatile. He does not fail to appreciate risks and consequences; he is thoughtless. Once race enters the equation, it changes the calculation. The factors the Court outlines as mitigating are instead misperceived as indicators of dangerousness. The idea of the "senselessly violent" teenager then operates as cover to the choice to withhold the protective impulses that would otherwise define and shape justice options and responses to the criminal conduct of a teenager. Race thwarts the impulse to be merciful. Black kids are then more easily denied rehabilitative care or diversionary treatment even when they have engaged in the exact same criminal behavior as white kids.

The U.S. Supreme Court proclaimed that we have arrived at a "settled understanding that the differentiating characteristics of youth are universal."[26] But the experience of children of color in the criminal justice system belies that overconfident claim. Their overrepresentation in adult prosecutions and punishment reveals that racial bias can and does warp even that which we take to be self-evident.

THE TRIPLE THREAT

Racial bias pervades the criminal justice system.[27] At every discretionary stage in the process of a criminal case, criminal justice actors make decisions that will affect both the path of the case and the life of the person charged. Personal perceptions, beliefs, and biases influence those choices. So it is not surprising that racial disparities emerge at each point of discretion. In this country, the stereotype that young Black men are dangerous has become so ingrained "in the collective American unconscious that Black men now capture attention, much like evolved threats such as spiders and snakes."[28] Age does not immunize the young Black person from that perception. Instead that perception combines with three other misconceptions to pose a triple threat for kids of color: dehumanization, exaggerated perceptions of dangerousness, and adultification.

Let's examine each in turn. Dehumanization is where we suggest that young people of color are not human. They are animals—vicious and predatory. Dehumanization is a process that permits us to believe that certain individuals and groups fall "outside the boundary where moral values and rules of fairness apply."[29] Once we make that designation, we can then take action against that group without moral reservation. Media accounts of crime often deploy animal imagery to describe conduct of young people of color. News stories explicitly label young people of color "animals" or, more subtly, brand them as "predators" who engage in "wilding" behavior in an effort to underscore their supposed primitive natures.[30] Once the person is deemed a vicious animal, we feel no compunction removing that person from society. If that offender is seen as vermin, we can exterminate and not think twice.

The second threat to Black children is an exaggerated perception of their physical size and dangerousness. Empirical studies have shown that people misjudge the size and strength, particularly of young Black men, perceiving them as larger and as more fearsome than young white men of comparable size and build.[31] In a series of studies, researchers showed participants images of 45 white faces and 45 Black faces taken from a college football recruiting website. Participants overestimated the heights and weights of the Black players even though the white players were actually taller and heavier. Perhaps more telling was when researchers asked participants to imagine each face, white and Black, as belonging to an unarmed man who was behaving aggressively in an encounter with the police. Participants had to assess whether it was appropriate for the police to use force to subdue the unarmed man. The participants judged the use of force as more appropriate when the suspect was Black. Race cued participants' acceptance of a more violent reaction and form of restraint against the Black suspects given the perceived dangerousness.

Finally, the third threat is adultification. Young Black boys and girls are routinely perceived as older than their actual chronological age. In a groundbreaking series of empirical studies, Professor Philip Goff and colleagues tested whether Black boys experience fewer protections because they seem less distinct from adults. Participants perceived Black children aged 10–13 as similar to white children aged 14–17. The researchers then set out to examine that gap in criminal justice contexts. Participants overestimated the age of Black children suspected of felonies, seeing them as 4.53 years older than they actually were. As importantly, the older the participant rated the child, the more culpable the child seemed.[32] Similar studies looking at the adultification of Black girls find that we also overestimate their age at almost all stages of development.[33] As early as 5 years old, Black girls were seen as behaving older than their actual age. Data further showed that respondents perceived Black girls as needing less nurturing and protection than their white peers.

The bottom line is that these three threats withdraw from Black children the protections of childhood, which can have dangerous ramifications for them in their experience of justice.

BUILDING "THE INSTEAD"

So, what does it take to forge a new path? In 1967, the Kerner Commission recognized that the American people needed "new will" to divert us from a racially divisive and destructive path. Changing course also requires the courage to imagine what we have not yet seen. Unless we begin to imagine and build "the instead," we will revert to failed carceral strategies that devour our children, disable our communities, and do little to keep us safe. Building and investing in "the instead" involves at least four key steps.

Changing the Racialized Public Narrative About Youthful Offending

The prevailing public narrative about youthful offending has both a villain and a moral. The villain is the young Black man. The moral informs us that public safety turns on our ability to control and remove the villain. That narrative is not only false and misleading, but it has been so widely disseminated that it has become exceedingly difficult to displace. Throughout our history, we have allowed inaccurate narratives to increase fear and to deepen the racial divide. Those narratives drive and shape public policy, too often to the country's detriment. With respect to youthful offending, we witness racist depictions of Black children increasing fear and urging us to view Black kids as dangerously different based on their nature and their race. But science makes clear that young Black children are no more likely to engage in crime and are, indeed, as likely as white children to desist from crime as their brains—and their judgment—mature. Until those narratives are exposed and debunked, our policies will resist change and we will remain tethered in place. We need an era of truth telling, uncovering and uprooting the narrative of racial difference and racial threat, and then substituting one that emphasizes science and fact. In 1967, the Kerner Commission recognized the need to hold media accountable for advancing the sort of narratives that deepen the racial divide. Its admonitions were right, then and now.

Ending the Adult Prosecution of Any Child Under 21

Decades of transferring kids into the adult criminal legal system have not resulted in reduced crimes or safer communities. Adult prosecution has instead led to traumatized and abused young people. Yet the system continues to mislabel Black children as adults, carelessly discarding young Black offenders in a structure never designed for children. There, these young people lose much more than their freedom. They lose the opportunity to develop in a healthier environment. They can expect lifelong challenges associated with less education, increased mental health problems, higher rates of suicide, and greater financial instability. Retaining the discretion to charge a young offender in adult court in the criminal justice system leads to an untenable form of racial exceptionalism where we misperceive Black children's wrongful conduct as willful rather than the product of immaturity. To interrupt this racialized and persistent pattern of mistreatment, we need to adopt a bright line rule prohibiting the prosecution of anyone under 21 in the adult criminal justice system.

Building Public Health Responses to Trauma

Trauma disrupts the lives of far too many Black adolescents, but society rarely makes the connection between trauma and misconduct. The general public certainly recognizes that trauma and victimization affect public health. But victimization of Black adolescents seldom provokes moral outrage or triggers public health action despite the fact that their victimization rates dwarf those for white children. Homicide represents the fifth leading cause of death among white adolescents ages 15 to 19, but it ranks first among Black adolescents.[34] One out of 10 children under the age of 6, living in a major U.S. city, reports witnessing a shooting or stabbing.[35] Eighty-three percent of youth living in urban centers report undergoing one or more traumatic events.[36] The problem is that decision-makers rarely see misbehavior by kids of color as a reaction to trauma. When adults perceive kids of color as choosing to misbehave, they look for ways to punish that choice. They then bypass therapeutic interventions that might better resolve the behavioral issues and instead create a trauma-to-prison pipeline. School-based mental health services have proven effective in addressing the trauma and manifestations of trauma in adolescents. But in rushing to rid schools of children perceived as troublemakers, we miss—and misdiagnose—matters that schools could handle better than prisons.

Investing in Community-Based Violence Interruption Efforts

In 1967, the Kerner Commission urged the engagement of community-based organizations, recognizing that the communities most harmed might hold workable solutions to our nation's failed approaches to justice. Fear of violent crime motivates much of our justice policy. But the conventional approaches to curb violence have had little success. More than 2 decades of data indicates that for every 10 nonprofits focused on reducing violence and building stronger communities, there has been a 9% drop in the homicide rate, a 6% reduction in violent crime, and a 4% reduction in property crime per 100,000 residents.[37] On the back end, there is growing evidence that connecting kids returning from custody with "credible messenger" mentors reduces recidivism.[38] If public safety is our goal, then resourcing communities hardest hit by violence and crime is the response that makes sense because it has succeeded. Those who are proximate to the issues can seed the change we seek.

CONCLUSION

Even as the Kerner Commission delivered its ominous warnings, it struck a hopeful note: "Choice is still possible."[39] Today, our justice system is characterized by intolerable racial disparities in its treatment of Black and Brown youth that we shrug off as a necessary evil. But it is not. Meaningful reform will occur only when we stop seeking refuge in easy answers and myths and, instead, act decisively. We must end the practice of denying kids of color the privilege of innocence that their age would otherwise afford.

NOTES

1. *Report of the National Advisory Committee on Civil Disorders* [Kerner Report] (New York: Bantam Books, 1968), 1.
2. Kerner Report, 1.
3. See Deborah Archer, "'White Men's Roads Through Black Men's Homes': Advancing Racial Equity Through Highway Reconstruction," *Vanderbilt Law Review* 73 (2020), 1259.
4. See, e.g., Kerner Report, 267, noting that "[n]othing is more fundamental to the quality of life in any area than the sense of personal security of its residents and nothing affects this more than crime."
5. See Kim Taylor-Thompson, "There Are Children Here: Reconceiving Justice for Adolescent Offenders" in *Progressive Prosecution: Race and Reform in Criminal Justice*, eds. Kim Taylor-Thompson and Anthony C. Thompson (New York: New York University Press, 2022), 167–212.
6. See National Council on Crime and Delinquency, "And Justice for Some: Differential treatment of Youth of Color in the Justice System," NJC #217050, January 2007.
7. See, e.g., Sarah Gonzalez, "Nearly 90% of New Jersey Children Tried as Adults Since 2011 Were Black or Latino," *The Guardian*, October 11, 2016, https://www.theguardian.com/us-news/2016/oct/11/new-jersey-juvenile-detention-minority-tried-adults.
8. See, e.g., Richard Mendel, "Why Youth Incarceration Fails: An Updated Review of the Evidence," The Sentencing Project, December 2022, https://www.sentencingproject.org/app/uploads/2023/03/Why-Youth-Incarceration-Fails.pdf.
9. Ledyard King, "Trump Ally Pam Bondi Calls Kenosha Shooter Kyle Rittenhouse, 17, 'a Little Boy' Trying to Protect Community," *USA Today*, September 23, 2020, https://www.usatoday.com/story/news/politics/2020/09/23/pam-bondi-calls-kyle-rittenhouse-little-boy-trying-protect/3503699001/.
10. See Stacey Patton, "In America, Black Children Don't Get to Be Children," *Washington Post*, November 26, 2014.
11. See Philip Bump, "Study: Cops Tend to See Black Kids as Less Innocent Than White Kids," *The Atlantic*, March 10, 2014, https://www.theatlantic.com/national/archive/2014/03/cops-tend-to-see-black-kids-as-less-innocent-than-white-kids/383247/.

12. Robert Hahn et al., "Effects on Violence of Laws and Policies Facilitating the Transfer of Youth from the Juvenile to the Adult Justice System," Centers for Disease Control and Prevention, 2007, https://www.cdc.gov/mmwr/preview/mmwrhtml/rr5609a1.htm.

13. Brief for the American Psychological Association, American Psychiatric Association, and National Association of Social Workers as Amici Curiae in Support of Petitioners, 7, *Miller v. Alabama*, 567 U.S. 460 (2012) (Nos. 10–9646, 10–9647), 2012 WL 174239 ("Juveniles' risky behavior frequently includes criminal activity; in fact, 'numerous rigorous self-report studies have . . . documented that it is statistically aberrant to refrain from crime during adolescence.'") Quoting Terrie Moffitt, "Adolescent-Limited and Life-Course-Persistent Antisocial Behavior: A Developmental Taxonomy," *Psychological Review* 100, no. 4 (1993), 674, 685–686.

14. Brief for the American Psychological Association, American Psychiatric Association, and National Association of Social Workers as Amici Curiae in Support of Petitioners, 7–8; *see Roper v. Simmons*, 543 U.S. 551, 570 (2005) ("Only a relatively small proportion of adolescents who experiment in risky or illegal activities develop entrenched patterns of problem behavior that persist into adulthood.")

15. *Roper v. Simmons*, 578.

16. *Roper v. Simmons*, 556–57.

17. *Roper v. Simmons*, 568.

18. *Roper v. Simmons*, 569.

19. *Graham v. Florida*, 560 U.S. 48, 81 (2010)

20. *Miller v. Alabama*, 132 S. Ct. 2455, 2475 (2012)

21. See Elizabeth S. Scott and Laurence Steinberg, *Rethinking Juvenile Justice* (Cambridge, MA: Harvard University Press, 2008), 52. (Noting the "coherent integration of [identity] does not occur until late adolescence or early adulthood.")

22. See Laurence Steinberg, "Adolescent Development and Juvenile Justice", *Annual Review of Clinical Psychology* 5 (2007), 1531, 1538.

23. See Elizabeth Cauffman and Laurence Steinberg, "(Im)maturity of Judgment in Adolescence: Why Adolescents May Be Less Culpable Than Adults," *Behavioral Science & the Law* 18, no. 6 (2000), 741, 756–57. (Observing that "maturity of judgment" is correlated to "antisocial decision-making," but that responsibility, perspective and temperance are more predictive than age alone.)

24. See Dustin Albert, Jason Chein, Laurence Steinberg, "The Teenage Brain: Peer Influences on Adolescent Decision-Making," *Current Directions in Psychological Science* 22, no. 2 (2013), 114–20.

25. See Laurence Steinberg et al., "Age Differences in Sensation Seeking and Impulsivity as Indexed by Behavior and Self-Report: Evidence for a Dual Systems Model, *Developmental Psychology* 44, no. 6 (2008), 1764, 1774–76.

26. *J.D.B. v. North Carolina*, 131 S. Ct. 2394, 2403–04 (2011).

27. Besiki Kutateladze, Whitney Tymas, and Mary Crowley, "Race and Prosecution in Manhattan," Vera Institute of Justice, July 2014, https://www.vera.org/publications/race-and-prosecution-in-manhattan (one of the first studies to document differences among Black, white, Latinx, and Asian people in the justice system).

28. Sophie Trawalter et al., "Attending to Threat: Race-Based Patterns of Selective Attention," *Journal of Experimental Social Psychology* 44, no. 5 (2008), 1322.

29. Susan Opotow, "Moral Exclusion and Injustice: An Introduction," *Journal of Social Issues* 46, no. 1 (1990), 3.

30. David Livingstone Smith, *Less Than Human: Why We Demean, Enslave, and Exterminate Others* (New York: St. Martin's Press, 2011).

31. Forward Thinking, "Racial Bias in Perception," Montclair State University, n.d., https://www.montclair.edu/forward-thinking/spring-2017/racial-bias-in-perception/.

32. Phillip Atiba Goff et al., "The Essence of Innocence: Consequences of Dehumanizing Black Children," *Journal of Personality and Social Psychology* 106, no. 4 (2014), 526.

33. Rebecca Epstein, Jamilia J. Blake, and Thalia González, "Girlhood Interrupted: The Erasure of Black Girls' Childhood," Georgetown Law Center on Gender Justice and Opportunity, 2017, https://genderjusticeandopportunity.georgetown.edu/wp-content/uploads/2020/06/girlhood-interrupted.pdf.

34. Arialdi M. Minino, "Mortality Among Teenagers Aged 12–19, United States, 1999–2006," NCHS Data Brief, May 2010; Five Leading Causes of Death by Race/Ethnicity, New York State Department of Health, www.nyskwic.org. https://www.nyskwic.org/get_data/indicator_profile_lcd_race.cfm?subIndicatorID=127

35. David Finkelhor et al., "Children's Exposure to Violence: A Comprehensive National Study," Department of Justice, Office of Juvenile Justice and Delinquency Prevention, October 2019.

36. Tony Favro, "Urban America Challenged by On-Going Trauma Among the Poor," City Mayors, September 2019, http://www.citymayors.com/society/usa-cities-trauma.html.

37. Patrick Sharkey, *Uneasy Peace: The Great Crime Decline, the Renewal of City Life, and the Next War on Violence* (New York: W. W. Norton and Company, 2018), 53.

38. See Candice Jones, "Let's Invest in Communities, Not Prisons," *Richmond-Times Dispatch*, July 10, 2019, https://richmond.com/opinion/column/candice-jones-column-let-s-invest-in-communities-not-prisons/article_f0942489-38a7-5b7a-8b7f-a227729151a1.html.

39. Kerner Report, 3 [note 1].

CHAPTER 13

One in Five
Progress and Pushback in Lowering the Lifetime Likelihood of Imprisonment of Young Black Men

Nazgol Ghandnoosh

The Kerner Commission's examination of the country's deep racial fissures predated the onset of mass incarceration, which has become one of the most pressing civil rights issues of our time. Until the 1970s, the United States had a higher incarceration rate than other industrialized nations, but it had remained consistent for decades. This inspired scholars to advance "a theory of the stability of punishment."[1] Unfortunately, a dramatic uptick in crime and backlash to the Civil Rights Movement, among other factors, quickly falsified this theory.

In the early 1970s, the United States began what the National Research Council has described as a "historically unprecedented and internationally unique" growth in incarceration, which has disproportionately impacted Black Americans.[2] Between 1972 and 2009, the prison population increased nearly 700%.[3] This dramatic growth occurred both while crime rates were increasing, until the 1990s, and for years afterwards amidst the historic crime drop. A key part of mass incarceration has been the rise of lengthy and extreme sentences. Currently, more Americans are serving life sentences than there were people serving any U.S. prison sentence in 1970.[4]

Fortunately, we have witnessed positive change in the last 2 decades. Levels of incarceration as well as racial disparities—the focus of this chapter—have begun to decline. Reforms to drug law enforcement and to sentencing for drug and property offenses, particularly those impacting urban areas that are disproportionately home to communities of color, have fueled these trends.[5] These changes have led scholars to declare a "generational shift" in the lifetime likelihood of imprisonment for Black men.[6] This risk has fallen from a staggering one in three for those born in 1981 to a still troubling one in five for Black men born in 2001.[7] Black women have experienced the sharpest decline in their imprisonment rate, falling by 70% between 2000 and 2021.[8]

While these changes are still too modest in the face of the dramatic buildup that must be undone, they have inspired this author to predict that we may be at "the beginning of the end of mass incarceration."[9] Time will tell if the efforts of scholars, advocates, and policymakers will make this a reality.

Ten years after national protests catapulted the Black Lives Matter movement following the police killing of Michael Brown in Ferguson, Missouri, and 4 years after a national racial reckoning triggered by Minneapolis police officers killing George Floyd, progress in ending racial inequity in the criminal legal system is at risk of stalling or being reversed.

This chapter will examine both the narrowing and the persistence of racial injustice in the criminal legal system, and highlight promising reforms.[10] This inquiry begins with a discussion of racial differences in rates of serious violent crime, and the absence of such differences for drug crimes. The chapter will then examine four drivers of disparity within the criminal legal system as well as reforms working to tackle them: 1) laws and policies with disparate racial impact; 2) racial bias in criminal legal practitioners' use of discretion; 3) a financially burdensome and underresourced criminal legal system; and 4) laws and policies that exacerbate socioeconomic inequalities for people with criminal legal contact. The chapter will conclude with examples of backlash and backsliding in the face of this progress.

CONTEXTUALIZING RECENT TRENDS

Following a massive, 4-decade-long buildup of incarceration disproportionately impacting people of color, a growing reform movement has made important inroads. The 21st century has witnessed progress in reducing both the U.S. prison population and its racial and ethnic disparities. Despite this progress, imprisonment levels remain too high nationwide, particularly for Black Americans.

The United States experienced a 24% decline in its prison population between 2009, its peak year, and 2022.[11] While notable, this pace of prison downsizing is insufficient in the face of the nearly 700% buildup in imprisonment since 1972.[12] The prison and jail incarceration rate in the United States remains between five and eight times that of France, Canada, and Germany, and imprisonment rates in Mississippi, Louisiana, Arkansas, and Oklahoma are nearly 50% above the national average.[13] At the recent pace of decarceration nationwide, it would take 74 years—until 2098—to return to the size of 1972's prison population (see Figure 13.1).[14]

While all major racial and ethnic groups experienced decarceration, the Black prison population has downsized the most.[15]

Still, as reflected in Figure 13.2, Black Americans were imprisoned at 5.0 times the rate of whites in 2021, while American Indians and Latinx people were imprisoned at 4.2 times and 2.4 times the white rate, respectively.[16] These disparities are even more stark in seven states that imprison their Black residents at over nine times the rate of their white residents: California, Connecticut, Iowa, Minnesota, New Jersey, Maine, and Wisconsin.[17]

While recent promising trends demonstrate the effectiveness of reforms to narrow racial and ethnic disparities in incarceration, far more work is needed to achieve equity.

DISPARITIES IN CRIMINAL OFFENDING VERSUS ENFORCEMENT

To fully eliminate racial disparities in imprisonment, it is critical to understand how much of this disparity stems from factors preceding criminal legal contact, notably

One in Five   145

Figure 13.1. Historical and Projected U.S. State and Federal Prison Population Based on 2009-2021 Rate of Decline

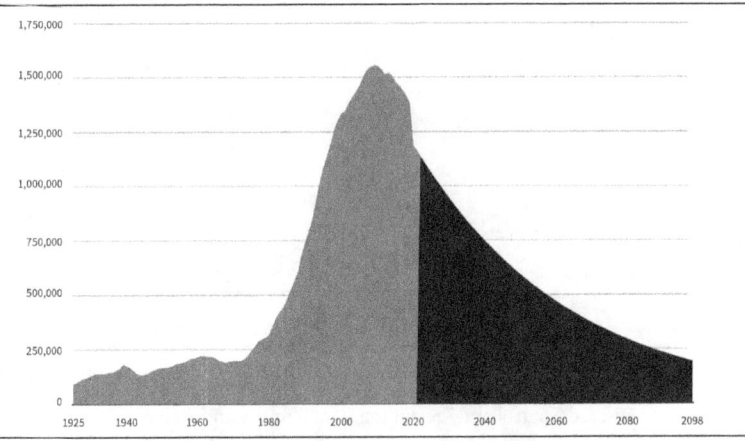

Source of historical figures: Bureau of Justice Statistics, "Prisoners 1925–81," 1982; Bureau of Justice Statistics, "Corrections Statistical Analysis Tool"; E. Ann Carson, "Prisoners in 2021—Statistical Tables," Bureau of Justice Statistics, December 2022.

Figure 13.2. Imprisonment Rates by Race and Ethnicity, 2021

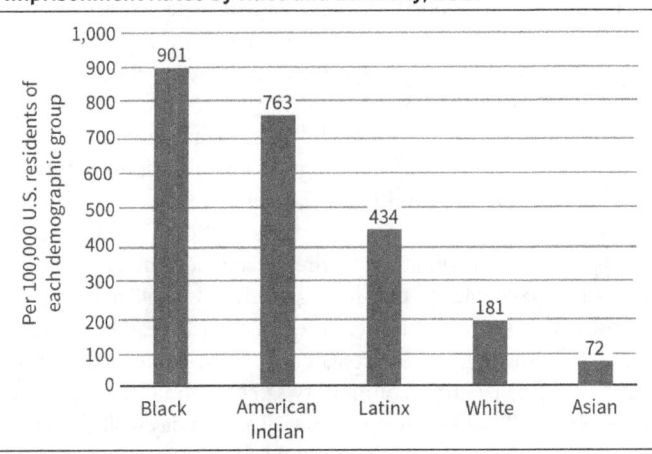

Group	Per 100,000 U.S. residents of each demographic group
Black	901
American Indian	763
Latinx	434
White	181
Asian	72

Source: E. Ann Carson, "Prisoners in 2021—Statistical Tables," Bureau of Justice Statistics, December 2022.

differences in criminal offending. This inquiry leads to starkly different findings for violent versus drug crimes.

Homicides

Black, Latinx, and American Indian communities are more likely than their white counterparts to experience spatially concentrated poverty, the result of longstanding and ongoing segregation, discrimination, and disinvestment. These conditions erode

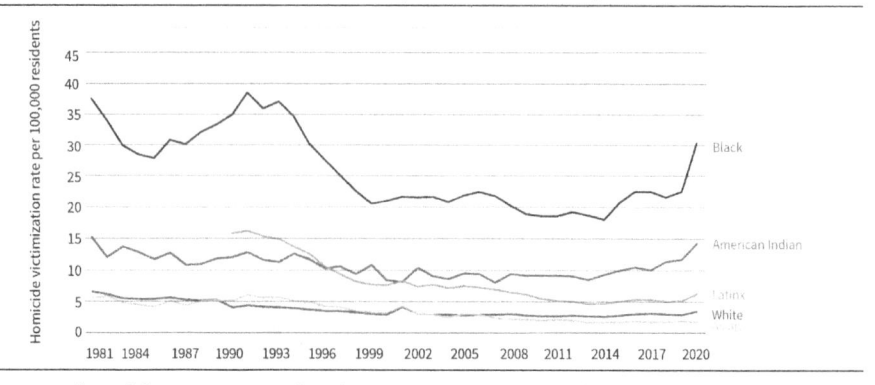

Figure 13.3. Homicide Victimization Rates by Race and Ethnicity

Note: Age-adjusted figures; pre-1990 data do not separate Latinx rates from other racial categories.

Source: Centers for Disease Control and Prevention, "Fatal injury and violence data."

economic and social buffers against crime and contribute to higher rates of certain violent and property crimes among certain communities of color. These facts, noted by the Kerner Commission report nearly 60 years ago, remain tragically true today.[18]

Black, American Indian, and Latinx people are more likely than whites to be victims of property and serious violent crimes.[19] This is especially clear with homicides: Black Americans were 9.3 times as likely as whites to be homicide victims in 2020, American Indians were 4.3 times as likely, and Latinxs were 1.9 times as likely, based on age-adjusted figures (see Figure 13.3).[20]

Since homicide is largely an intraracial crime, meaning that people generally kill others of the same race or ethnicity,[21] these figures correspond to higher rates of homicide offending among these communities of color.

Tackling this source of disparity requires, as the National Academies of Sciences has explained, echoing the recommendations of the Kerner Commission report, making "durable investments in disadvantaged urban neighborhoods that match the persistent and longstanding nature of institutional disinvestment that such neighborhoods have endured over many years."[22] A growing body of research can also guide policymakers to identify near-term interventions to promote community safety without the harms of policing and prisons. For example, the Brookings Institute as well as John Jay College of Criminal Justice have created syntheses of research evidence on public health approaches to crime as guides for funding organizations, community leaders, and lawmakers.[23] Two reports from The Sentencing Project also highlight noncarceral social interventions for youth and adults to promote community safety.[24] These policies include providing universal access to effective drug treatment, investing in community-based violence prevention programs, reimagining crisis response, and expanding mentorship and therapeutic support for youth.

Drugs

In contrast to rates of serious violent offending, surveys by federal agencies show that both recently and historically, whites, Blacks, and Latinx have used illicit drugs at

Figure 13.4. Racial Disparities in Marijuana Use in Past Month and Marijuana Possession Arrest Rates, 2018

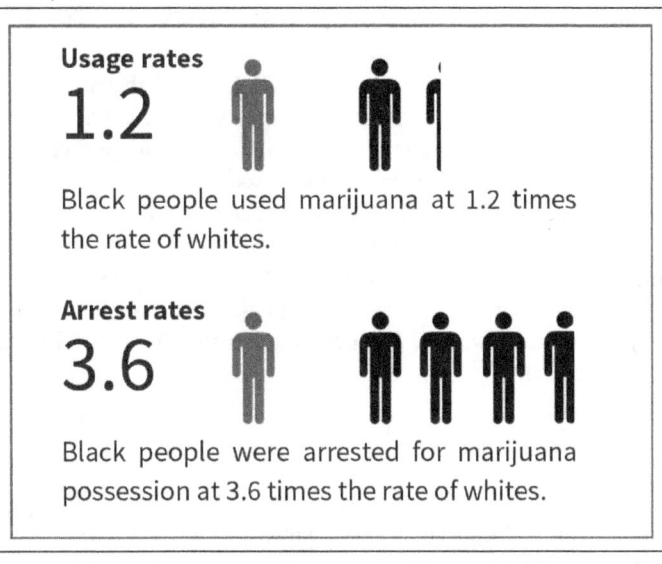

Usage rates
1.2
Black people used marijuana at 1.2 times the rate of whites.

Arrest rates
3.6
Black people were arrested for marijuana possession at 3.6 times the rate of whites.

Source: Substance Abuse and Mental Health Service Administration [SAMHSA], "Results from the 2018 National Survey on Drug Use and Health: Detailed tables," 2019; Ezekiel Edwards, Brooke Madubuonwu, and Emily Greytak, "A Tale of Two Countries: Racially Targeted Arrests in the Era of Marijuana Reform," American Civil Liberties Union, 2020.

roughly similar rates, though American Indians have done so at comparatively higher rates.[25] Many studies also suggest that people who use drugs generally purchase drugs from people of their own race or ethnicity.[26]

Racially disparate policies and bias largely drive racial and ethnic disparities in drug arrests and incarceration. For example, looking specifically at marijuana possession arrests, the ACLU found that Black Americans were 3.6 times as likely as whites to be arrested (Figure 13.4) for this offense in 2018, even though Black Americans used marijuana at 1.2 times the rate of whites.[27]

These disparities widen at later stages of the criminal legal system such that 62% of people in state prisons for drug offenses are people of color, even though people of color comprise 41% of the U.S. population.[28] The remainder of this chapter examines sources of disparity from within the criminal legal system that produce results like this, as well as reforms that are mitigating their impact.

KEY DRIVERS OF RACIAL DISPARITY WITHIN THE CRIMINAL LEGAL SYSTEM

Four key factors drive racial inequality from within the criminal legal system. While the consequences of these policies and issues continue to perpetuate racial and ethnic disparities, jurisdictions around the country have initiated promising reforms to lessen their impact.

Laws and Policies That Appear Race-Neutral Have a Disparate Racial Impact

Extreme Sentences for Violent Crimes and the War on Drugs

While racial disparities can be found at every sentencing level, they are most pronounced in lengthy and extreme sentences. As Figure 13.5 shows, in 2019, Black Americans represented 14% of the total U.S. population, 33% of the total prison population, and 46% of the prison population who had already served at least 10 years.[29]

Extreme sentences for violent crimes and reliance on criminal histories as a basis for determining prison sentences are drivers of racial disparities in imprisonment. In addition, the punitive nature of the War on Drugs and the associated sentencing laws that it sprouted, including mandatory minimum sentences, crack cocaine sentencing disparities, drug-free school zone laws, and felonization of drug possession, disproportionately impact Black Americans.

Revising Laws With Disparate Racial Impact

Various jurisdictions have reformed laws with disparate racial impact. To scale back extreme sentences imposed on past violent crimes, Washington, DC allows many incarcerated people who have already served 15 years to petition the courts

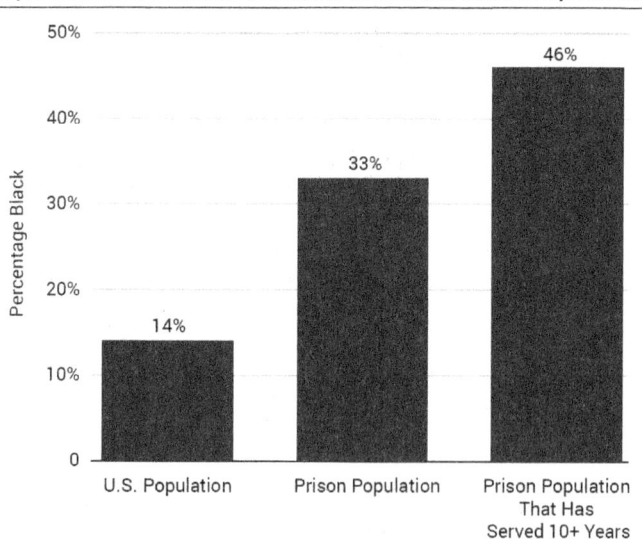

Figure 13.5. Representation of Black Americans in U.S. and Prison Populations, 2019

Sources: U.S. Census Bureau, "American Community Survey 1-Year Estimates, 2019"; E. Ann Carson, "Prisoners in 2019," Bureau of Justice Statistics, 2020; Bureau of Justice Statistics, "National Corrections Reporting," U.S. Department of Justice.

for resentencing.[30] To mitigate the inequities of the War on Drugs, Congress passed the First Step Act in 2018, which included the retroactive application of the Fair Sentencing Act of 2010s, reduction of the crack and powder cocaine sentencing disparity from 100:1 to 18:1. In 2022, the Department of Justice enacted a charging policy designed to prospectively eliminate this disparity during the Biden administration, to the extent possible absent a statutory change.[31] In addition, over half of states have also decriminalized possession of small amounts of marijuana, helping to reduce the number of people arrested for marijuana possession from a peak level of 585,000 in 2009 to 377,000 in 2019. Still, 29% of drug arrests in the United States in 2019 were for marijuana possession, reflecting the need for greater adoption of legalization and decriminalization laws.[32]

Racial Bias Influences Criminal Legal Practitioners' Use of Discretion

Bias Permeates Criminal Legal Decision-Making

Communities of color are over-policed through biased traffic stops, pedestrian searches, and drug arrests.[33] For example, police officers' reliance on millions of minor traffic stops annually as a pretext to investigate drivers for criminal activity disproportionately impacts Black and Latinx drivers. Among those they pull over, police are more likely to search Black (6.2%) and Latinx drivers (9.2%) than whites (3.6%).[34] But police are often less likely to find drugs or weapons among the Black and Latinx drivers that they search, compared to whites.[35]

In addition, prosecutors and judges often treat Black and Latinx people more harshly in their charging and sentencing decisions. Federal prosecutors, for example, have been twice as likely to charge African Americans with offenses that carry mandatory minimum sentences than whites with similar offenses and criminal histories.[36] Bias also affects the work of juries, correctional officers, and parole boards.[37] Lastly, police and prosecutors, via their unions and professional associations, often lobby, litigate, and engage in public advocacy against reforms.[38]

Curbing the Impact of Biased Decision-Making

State and city lawmakers as well as local prosecutors are reducing police enforcement of minor traffic violations, which are often used as a pretext for criminal investigation and can become fatal for drivers. In 2021, Philadelphia passed the Driving Equality Act and became the first major city to prohibit police from making non-public safety traffic stops—such as for driving with a broken taillight or with a registration plate that is not clearly displayed.[39]

Several jurisdictions have also taken steps to mitigate the impact of bias in discretion at later stages of the criminal legal process. For example, Arizona is the first state to eliminate peremptory challenges in jury selection, so that prospective jurors cannot be rejected without an explanation.[40] In a growing movement of reform-oriented prosecutors, organizations such as Fair and Just Prosecution, For the People, Prosecutors

Alliance of California, and Vera's Motion for Justice are uniting prosecutors who support scaling back excessively punitive sentences.

A Financially Burdensome and Underresourced Criminal Legal System

Key segments of the criminal legal system are underfunded or are biased against people who are poor. With Black Americans earning half as much as white Americans annually and having one-seventh their average net worth,[41] criminal justice laws, policies, and practices that disadvantage people with limited income and assets disproportionately harm Black Americans and other communities of color. This impact can be seen in bail requirements for pretrial release and access to drug treatment, as discussed below, as well as in underfunded indigent defense and re-entry programs.

The Movement to Reduce Pretrial Detention

Pretrial detention largely affects people with limited financial resources. Of the 636,000 individuals confined in jails at year-end 2021, nearly three-quarters were unconvicted, having been detained prior to the resolution of their case.[42] With over a third of jailed individuals earning less than $10,000 in the year before arrest, cash bail requirements are often onerous.[43] People who remain in jail while grappling with a criminal charge are more likely to accept less favorable plea deals, to be sentenced to prison, and to receive longer sentences.[44]

In 2023, Illinois became the first state to end cash bail.[45] New Jersey's Criminal Justice Reform program, launched in 2017, reduced monetary bail requirements and pretrial incarceration using updated risk assessment tools.[46] These reforms cut the state's pretrial jail population by nearly half from 2015 to 2018.[47] Yet, unfortunately, first quarter 2023 data shows a loss of momentum, with pretrial incarceration rates now at just 27% below 2015 levels.[48]

Increasing Access to Drug Treatment

Nearly half of people in U.S. prisons had a substance use disorder in the year prior to their admissions, and many people—especially people of color—struggle to access drug treatment programs in communities and in prisons.[49] Some states and the federal government have begun to improve access to mental health care and drug treatment, both during and following incarceration. The White House Office of National Drug Control Policy has begun encouraging states to use Medicaid funds to provide mental health and drug treatment in jails and prisons.[50] A 2018 federal law allowed states to reconnect incarcerated people with Medicaid benefits, and California is the first to adopt the change, by providing certain Medicaid benefits to incarcerated individuals 90 days prior to their release.[51] The First Step Act of 2018 requires the federal Bureau of Prisons to expand access to medication for opioid use disorder (MOUD). However, the agency has struggled with implementation.[52] Rhode Island has led the nation in providing MOUD to its incarcerated population.[53]

Laws and Policies That Exacerbate Socioeconomic Inequalities

The fourth driver of disparity in imprisonment relates to the damaging consequences of criminal legal contact—contact that is disproportionately experienced by communities of color. For example, a criminal conviction creates lifelong barriers to securing steady employment and housing, and many states disqualify people with felony drug convictions from cash assistance and food stamps. Nearly all states also restrict voting rights for people with criminal convictions.[54] Yet research has shown that post-incarceration employment, access to food stamps, and voting are associated with lower recidivism rates.[55]

Fortunately, jurisdictions around the country have initiated promising reforms to reduce the harms of criminal convictions and ease re-entry. For example, to reduce labor market discrimination resulting from a criminal record, a majority of states and many cities "Ban the Box"—removing the question about conviction history from initial job applications and delaying a background check until later in the hiring process.[56] In addition, a majority of states no longer impose bans on food stamps or cash assistance for people with a felony drug conviction.[57] Finally, Washington, DC has joined Maine, Vermont, and Puerto Rico in fully untangling voting rights from criminal legal involvement by permitting its prison population to vote.[58]

Policymakers are also beginning to undo some of the penal austerity measures of the 1990s, most notably regarding college access. The Second Chance Pell pilot program created in 2015 allowed colleges and universities to offer incarcerated students Pell Grant–funded postsecondary education. In 2020, Congress restored Pell eligibility to people in prison, with broad eligibility having begun in summer 2023.[59] This reform broadens the population that can benefit from the success of programs such as the Bard Prison Initiative.

BACKLASH AND RESISTANCE TO PROGRESS

The momentum for continued progress is precarious. Following a dramatic crime drop since the 1990s, the recent uptick in some crime categories—particularly homicides—during the COVID-19 pandemic, as well as the opioid overdose crisis, have led many lawmakers to retreat to the failed punitive policies of the past. A bipartisan backlash to criminal justice reform includes a Congressional proposal to expand mandatory minimum sentences for federal drug offenses[60] and a Congressional resolution overturning Washington, DC's criminal code overhaul—both without objection from the Democratic president who campaigned on cutting incarceration levels by half.[61] This backlash also includes New York's narrowing of bail reform[62] and Florida's re-disenfranchisement of people with felony convictions.[63] These efforts impose a double harm on communities of color that are most likely to experience the harms of incarceration and of serious violent crime victimization, which mass incarceration fails to address.

CONCLUSION

While recent reforms have reduced overall levels of criminal-legal system contact and its racial and ethnic disparities, we remain fully within the era of mass incarceration. Excessive levels of control and punishment, particularly for people of color, are not advancing community safety goals and are damaging families and communities.[64] Consequently, although people of color experience more crime than whites, they are less supportive than whites of punitive crime control policies.[65] For the criminal legal system to uphold the principle of justice and promote public safety, policymakers and practitioners will need to protect and expand reforms like those noted in this chapter.

NOTES

1. Alfred Blumstein and Jacqueline Cohen, "A Theory of the Stability of Punishment," *Journal of Criminal Law & Criminology* 64, no. 2 (1973): 198–207, https://doi.org/10.2307/1142990.

2. Jeremy Travis, Bruce Western, and F. Stevens Redburn, *The Growth of Incarceration in the United States*, National Academies Press eBooks, 2014, 2, https://doi.org/10.17226/18613.

3. E. Ann Carson, "Prisoners in 2021—Statistical tables," Bureau of Justice Statistics, December 2022; Chet Bowie, "Prisoners 1925–81," Bureau of Justice Statistics, December 1982.

4. Ashley Nellis, "No End in Sight: America's Enduring Reliance on Life Sentences," The Sentencing Project, December 16, 2022.

5. William J. Sabol and Thaddeus L. Johnson, "Justice System Disparities: Black-White National Imprisonment Trends, 2000 to 2020," Council on Criminal Justice; Bruce Western et al., eds., *Reducing Racial Inequality in Crime and Justice: Science, Practice, and Policy* (Washington, DC: National Academies of Sciences, Engineering, and Medicine, 2002); Eli Hager, "A Mass Incarceration Mystery," *Washington Post*, November 24, 2021.

6. Jason P. Robey, Michael Massoglia, and Michael T. Light, "A Generational Shift: Race and the Declining Lifetime Risk of Imprisonment," *Demography* 60, no. 4 (2023): 977, https://doi.org/10.1215/00703370-10863378; see also Alexander F. Roehrkasse and Christopher Wildeman, "Lifetime Risk of Imprisonment in the United States Remains High and Starkly Unequal," *Science Advances* 8, no. 48 (December 2, 2022), https://doi.org/10.1126/sciadv.abo3395.

7. Robey, Massoglia, and Light, "A Generational Shift," 977.

8. Carson, "Prisoners in 2021"; Allen J. Beck and Paige M. Harrison, "Prisoners in 2000," Bureau of Justice Statistics, August 2001.

9. Nazgol Ghandnoosh, "A Second Look at Unjust Prison Terms," *San Gabriel Valley Tribune*, January 12, 2021, https://www.sgvtribune.com/2021/01/12/a-second-look-at-unjust-prison-terms.

10. This chapter draws heavily on The Sentencing Project's four-part series of reports on this theme; https://www.sentencingproject.org/one-in-five/

11. The prison population increased for the first time in almost a decade between 2021 and 2022. E. Ann Carson and Rich Kluckow, "Prisoners in 2022—Statistical Tables," Bureau of Justice Statistics, November 2023.; E. Ann Carson and William J. Sabol, "Prisoners in 2011," Bureau of Justice Statistics, December 2012.

12. Carson, "Prisoners in 2021"; Bowie, "Prisoners 1925–81."

13. Carson, "Prisoners in 2021"; E. Ann Carson, "Correctional Populations in the United States, 2021—Statistical Tables," Bureau of Justice Statistics, February 2023; World Prison Brief,

"Highest to Lowest—Prison Population Total," n.d., https://www.prisonstudies.org/highest-to-lowest/prison-population-total.

14. Nazgol Ghandnoosh, "Ending 50 Years of Mass Incarceration: Urgent Reform Needed to Protect Future Generations," The Sentencing Project, February 8, 2023.

15. This report uses the terms Black and African American interchangeably. The number of imprisoned Black Americans decreased 38% between peak year 2002 and 2022. Carson and Kluckow, "Prisoners in 2022"; William J. Sabol, Heather C. West, and Matthew Cooper, "Prisoners in 2008," Bureau of Justice Statistics, December 2009.

16. Carson, "Prisoners in 2021."

17. Ashley Nellis, "The Color of Justice: Racial and Ethnic Disparity in State Prisons," The Sentencing Project, December 16, 2022.

18. National Advisory Commission on Civil Disorders, *Report of the National Commission on Civil Disorders* (New York: Bantam Books, 1968).

19. Western et al., *Reducing Racial Inequality in Crime and Justice*.

20. Asian/Pacific Islander people experience lower rates of victimization than whites. Centers for Disease Control and Prevention, "Fatal Injury and Violence Data," n.d.

21. Alexia Cooper and Erica L. Smith, "Homicide Trends in the United States, 1980-2008," Bureau of Justice Statistics, November 2011.

22. Western et al., *Reducing Racial Inequality in Crime and Justice*.

23. John Jay College Research Advisory Group on Preventing and Reducing Community Violence, "Reducing Violence Without Police: A Review of Research Evidence," 2020; Thea Sebastian et al., "A New Community Safety Blueprint: How the Federal Government Can Address Violence and Harm Through a Public Health Approach," Brookings, September 21, 2022.

24. Nicole D. Porter, "Ending Mass Incarceration: Social Interventions That Work," The Sentencing Project, October 17, 2022; Richard Mendel, "Effective Alternatives to Youth Incarceration," The Sentencing Project, June 28, 2023.

25. Substance Abuse and Mental Health Services Administration (SAMHSA), "Key Substance Use and Mental Health Indicators in the United States: Results from the 2021 National Survey on Drug Use and Health," December 2022; SAMHSA, "Results from the 2018 National Survey on Drug Use and Health: Detailed Tables," 2020; see also Ojmarrh Mitchell, "Is the War on Drugs Racially Biased?," *Journal of Crime and Justice* 32, no. 2 (2009): 49–75, https://doi.org/10.1080/0735648x.2009.9721270.

26. Katherine Beckett, Kris Nyrop, and Lori Pfingst, "Race, Drugs, and Policing: Understanding Disparities in Drug Delivery Arrests," *Criminology* 44, no. 1 (2006): 105–37, https://doi.org/10.1111/j.1745-9125.2006.00044.x.; K. Jack Riley, "Crack, Powder Cocaine, and Heroin: Drug Purchase and Use Patterns in Six U.S. Cities," National Institute of Justice, December 1997.

27. Ezekiel Edwards, Brooke Madubuonwu, and Emily Greytak, "A Tale of Two Countries: Racially Targeted Arrests in the Era of Marijuana Reform," American Civil Liberties Union, 2020, https://assets.aclu.org/live/uploads/publications/marijuanareport_03232021.pdf; SAMHSA, "Key Substance Use and Mental Health Indicators in the United States: Results from the 2019 National Survey on Drug Use and Health," September 2020.

28. Carson, "Prisoners in 2021"; SAMHSA, "Racial/Ethnic Differences in Substance Use, Substance Use Disorders, and Substance Use Treatment Utilization Among People Aged 12 or Older (2015–2019)," 2021.

29. Nazgol Ghandnoosh and Ashley Nellis, "How Many People Are Spending Over a Decade in Prison?," The Sentencing Project, September 8, 2022.

30. Nazgol Ghandnoosh, "A Second Look at Injustice," The Sentencing Project, May 12, 2021.

31. Office of the Attorney General, "Memorandum for All Federal Prosecutors: Additional Department Policies Regarding Charging, Pleas, and Sentencing in Drug Cases," U.S. Department of Justice, December 16, 2022.

32. Federal Bureau of Investigation, "Crime Data Explorer," n.d. Note: Arrest data from 2019 were used since they occurred before the pandemic, when marijuana arrest rates became anomalously low, and because law enforcement participation in the FBI's crime data collection system decreased after 2019. Drug arrests comprised 15% of all nontraffic arrests in 2019. See Priya Krishnakumar, "The FBI Released Its Crime Report for 2021–but It Tells Us Less About the Overall State of Crime in the US Than Ever," *CNN*, October 5, 2022.

33. Nazgol Ghandnoosh and Celeste Barry, "One in Five: Disparities in Crime and Policing," The Sentencing Project, November 2, 2023.

34. These numbers are based on data from 2018, rather than 2020, to bypass the anomalies created by COVID-19. Susannah N. Tapp and Elizabeth Davis, "Contacts Between Police and the Public, 2020," Bureau of Justice Statistics, November 2022.

35. Samantha Melamed, "As Philadelphia Aims to Curb Racial Disparities, Why Are Police Stops of Black Drivers Skyrocketing?," *The Philadelphia Inquirer*, October 14, 2019; Magnus Lofstrom et al, "Racial Disparities in Law Enforcement Stops," Public Policy Institute of California, 2021.

36. Sonja B. Starr and M. Marit Rehavi, "Mandatory Sentencing and Racial Disparity: Assessing the Role of Prosecutors and the Effects of *Booker*," *The Yale Law Journal* 123, no. 1 (2013): 2–80; M. Marit Rehavi and Sonja B. Starr, "Racial Disparity in Federal Criminal Sentences," *Journal of Political Economy* 122, no. 6 (2014): 1320–54, https://doi.org/10.1086/677255.

37. Kristen Bell, "A Stone of Hope: Legal and Empirical Analysis of California Juvenile Lifer Parole Decisions," *Harvard Civil Rights-Civil Liberties Law Review* 54: 455–548. See also Legislative Analyst's Office, The California Legislature's Nonpartisan Fiscal and Policy Advisor, "Promoting Equity in the Parole Hearing Process," March 27, 2023; Shamena Anwar, Patrick Bayer, and Randi Hjalmarsson, "The Impact of Jury Race in Criminal Trials," *The Quarterly Journal of Economics* 127, no. 2 (2012): 1017–55, https://doi.org/10.1093/qje/qjs014; Lucy Lang, "Racial Disparities in the Administration of Discipline in New York State Prisons," State of New York Offices of the Inspector General, November 2022.

38. Angela J. Davis, "The Carceral Force of Prosecutor Associations, Explained," *The Appeal*, February 26, 2021.

39. Jonaki Mehta, "Why Philadelphia Has Banned Low-level Traffic Stops," *NPR*, November 8, 2021.

40. Paul Davenport, "Arizona to End Peremptory Challenges to Potential Jurors," AP News, August 29, 2021.

41. Average income for Latinxs is comparable to that of Black Americans. Latinx net worth, on average, is one-sixth that of whites. Aditya Aladangady et al., "Changes in U.S. Family Finances from 2016 to 2019: Evidence from the Survey of Consumer Finances," Board of Governors of the Federal Reserve System, October 2023.

42. Zhen Zeng, "Jail Inmates in 2021—Statistical Tables," Bureau of Justice Statistics, December 2922.

43. Alexi Jones and Wendy Sawyer, "Arrest, Release, Repeat: How Police and Jails Are Misused to Respond to Social Problems," Prison Policy Initiative, August 2019.

44. Cynthis E. Jones, "'Give Us Free': Addressing Racial Disparities in Bail Determinations," *New York University Journal of Legislation and Public Policy* 16, no. 4 (2013): 919–62; Ellen A. Donnelly and John M. MacDonald, "The Downstream Effects of Bail and Pretrial Detention on Racial Disparities in Incarceration," *The Journal of Law and Criminology* 108, no. 4 (2018): 775–813.

45. Harm Venhuizen, "Republican Bills Push Cash Bail, Subvert Democratic Changes," *Los Angeles Times,* March 19, 2023.

46. Chloe Anderson et al., "Evaluation of Pretrial Justice System Reforms That Use the Public Safety Assessment: Effects of New Jersey's Criminal Justice Reform," Pretrial Justice Reform Study, MDRC Center for Criminal Justice Research, November 2019.

47. Glenn A. Grant, "Criminal Justice Reform: 2018 Report to the Governor and the Legislature," New Jersey Courts, April *2019.*

48. "Criminal justice reform statistics: Jan 1, 2023 - Jun 30, 2023," New Jersey Courts, https://www.njcourts.gov/sites/default/files/courts/criminal/criminal-justice-reform/cjrreport2023.pdf

49. Jennifer Bronson and Marcus Berzofsky, "Indicators of Mental Health Problems Reported by Prisoners and Jail Inmates, 2011–12," Bureau of Justice Statistics, June 2017; See also: Laura M. Maruschak, Jennifer Bronson, and Mariel Alper, "Survey of Prison Inmates, 2016: Alcohol and Drug Use and Treatment Reported by Prisoners," Bureau of Justice Statistics, July 2021; Jennifer Bronson et al., "Drug Use, Dependence, and Abuse Among State Prisoners and Jail Inmates, 2007-2009," Bureau of Justice Statistics, June 2017; Martha Bebinger, "Opioid Addiction Drug Going Mostly to Whites, Even as Black Death Rate Rises," *NPR,* May 8, 2019.

50. Geoff Mulvihill, "US Plans to Allow Medicaid for Drug Treatment in Prisons," *AP News,* February 21, 2023.

51. Lila Seidman, "Leaving Prison for Many Means Homelessness and Overdose. California Hopes to Change That," *Los Angeles Times,* February 13, 2023; Sweta Haldar and Madeline Guth, "Section 1115 Waiver Watch: How California Will Expand Medicaid Pre-Release Services for Incarcerated Populations," KFF, February 7, 2023.

52. Beth Schwartzapfel and Keri Blakinger, "Federal Prisons Were Told to Provide Addiction Medications. Instead, They Punish People Who Use Them," The Marshall Project, December 12, 2022.

53. Christine Vestal, "This State Has Figured Out How to Treat Drug-Addicted Inmates," *Stateline,* February 28, 2020; Shelly R. Weizman et al., "To Save Lives, Prioritize Treatment for Opioid Use Disorder in Correctional Facilities," *Health Affairs,* June 22, 2022.

54. Christopher Uggen et al., "Locked Out 2022: Estimates of People Denied Voting Rights," The Sentencing Project, October 25, 2022.

55. Ghandnoosh and Barry, "One in Five."

56. Beth Avery and Han Lu, "Ban the Box: U.S. Cities, Counties, and States Adopt Fair Hiring Policies," National Employment Law Project, October 1, 2021.

57. CCRC Staff, "Accessing SNAP and TANF Benefits after a Drug Conviction: A Survey of State Laws," Collateral Consequences Resource Center, December 6, 2023.

58. Kevin Muhitch and Nazgol Ghandnoosh, "Expanding Voting Rights to All Citizens," The Sentencing Project, March 2, 2021.

59. Aaron Morrison, "Student Loan Relief Limited for Many by US Drug War's Legacy," *AP News,* August 30, 2022; Nicholas Turner, "More Than Half a Million People in Prison May Soon Be Able to Afford College," Vera Institute of Justice, August 23, 2022.

60. H.R. 467 - HALT Fentanyl Act, 118th Congress (2023); Human Rights Watch, "More Than 150 Groups Urge Congress to Vote No on HALT Fentanyl Act," May 23, 2023, https://www.hrw.org/news/2023/05/23/more-150-groups-urge-congress-vote-no-halt-fentanyl-act.

61. Nazgol Ghandnoosh and Bill Underwood, "Joe Biden Hasn't Kept His Promise to Reduce the Prison Population," *The Daily Beast,* January 31, 2023.

62. Jesse McKinley, Grace Ashford, and Hurubie Meko, "New York Will Toughen Contentious Bail Law to Give Judges More Discretion," *New York Times,* April 28, 2023, https://www.nytimes.com/2023/04/28/nyregion/bail-reform-ny.html.

63. Nicole D. Porter and Morgan McLeod, "Expanding the Vote: State Felony Disenfranchisement Reform, 1997–2023," The Sentencing Project, October 18, 2023.

64. Sara Wakefield and Christopher Wildeman, "Mass Imprisonment and Racial Disparities in Childhood Behavioral Problems," *Criminology & Public Policy* 10, no. 3 (2011): 791–92.

65. Nazgol Ghandnoosh, "Race and Punishment: Racial Perceptions of Crime and Support for Punitive Policies," The Sentencing Project, September 3, 2014; John F. Pfaff, "The Poor Reform Prosecutor: So Far from the State Capital, So Close to the Suburbs," *Fordham Urban Law Journal* 50, no. 5 (2023): 1013–66. See also James Forman, Jr., *Locking Up Our Own: Crime and Punishment in Black America* (New York: Farrar, Straus and Giroux, 2017).

CHAPTER 14

Violence in Post-Pandemic America
Hard Truths and Enduring Lessons

Elliott Currie

In tandem with the arrival of the COVID-19 pandemic in the United States in early 2020, the nation suffered unprecedented rises in interpersonal violence. At this writing, those increases have eased off in many places. No one knows whether that trend will last, or for how long. But what's clear is that the stunning surge in violence confirms some hard truths about violence in America that are too often forgotten and too easily ignored. And it offers a resounding confirmation of the core analysis of the Kerner and Violence Commissions of the 1960s—a striking reminder of the costs of allowing unjust and unsustainable social conditions to fester, and of the tragic and lasting consequences of social abandonment.

In what follows, I want to explore the nature and implications of the pandemic era surge in violence, looking both at the raw figures we have so far on recent trends, especially in homicide, and at an emerging body of careful research on the social context of those trends.

Let's look first at what the numbers tell us about where we are now. It is crucial to understand that even prior to the rises in violence during the pandemic, and despite a popular narrative about steadily declining crime in America, serious violence in the United States was both startlingly high by rich country standards and shockingly stratified by race. But the emergence of COVID-19 in 2020, and of public health measures to try to contain its spread, was accompanied by sharp flares in homicide and in firearm violence generally across the country that were concentrated among the people and places where the risk of serious violence had always been concentrated. By the end of 2021, a number of American cities had reached homicide death rates that matched or surpassed any in their history. Some preliminary evidence from 2022[1] suggests that homicide decreased in many—but not all—of these places, a decline that may have continued into 2023. But despite what may be a welcome easing of the worst levels of violence in some places, at this writing the risk of dying by violence in America remains much higher than it was before the pandemic. Thus, an already dire, and in some places already worsening, situation proved to be remarkably vulnerable to adverse external impacts.

Public health data on homicide, gathered by the Centers for Disease Control and Prevention, give us the most reliable picture of this trajectory.[2] What these figures tell us is a story of both generally rising violence and widening racial disparity in the chances of violent death. In brief, between 2019 and 2021, America became both a deadlier and a more unequal place.

Nationally, the homicide death rate rose by roughly 36%—again, a startling, unprecedented increase. Roughly 6,900 more Americans died by violence in 2021 than in 2019; 95% of those "excess" deaths were firearm related. Of the 6,890 homicides, indeed only 346 were not committed with a firearm. And the sudden sharp rise in violent deaths was not an equal opportunity event. The homicide death rate rose by 43% for Black Americans, by 38% for Hispanics, and by 21% for non-Hispanic whites. A 21% rise in violent deaths is a startling enough pace in itself. But it was less than half the Black pace of increase in those years. Blacks, roughly 13% of the general population, were an already astonishing 53% of homicide victims in the United States in 2019: by 2021, they were 56%. Put in another way, that 13% of the American population accounted for 65% of the overall increase in violent deaths in America in those years.

This unequal pace of increase in violent deaths meant that the already staggering Black–white disparity in homicide grew even wider in the pandemic years. Blacks were a little more than eight times as likely to die by violence in 2019 as non-Hispanic whites. By 2021, the ratio was 9.7 to 1. And these racial differences in the likelihood of death by violence, as always, were often exacerbated by other factors—most notably, gender and age. The special risk for Black men, and especially young Black men, always a feature of Black life in America, became even more pronounced in the last few years. Black men as a group, of all ages, were already 10.7 times as likely to be killed as white men in 2019: by 2021, more than 12 times. That's not because white men's level of risk was declining—quite the contrary. Across the United States, white men's chances of death by violence climbed by 25%—again, a startling leap in a very short time. But the risk for Black men rose even faster—by more than 40%.

It's important to keep that white increase in mind, because it reminds us of another hard truth about American violence: While race powerfully, even grotesquely, shapes it, violence on the level we experience it in the United States cuts across racial boundaries and leaves even less vulnerable groups with a risk of violent death that is found nowhere else in the advanced industrial world. The homicide death rate for non-Hispanic white men in the United States in 2021, at 4.6 per 100,000 population, towers over that of every one of America's peers in the world of high-income countries.

And what's true for Black men in general is even more true for young Black men, who continue to be the group at highest risk for violent death in the United States. Both the sheer level of death by violence among young Black man in America, and the gap between them and their white counterparts, grew sharply in the years from 2019 through 2021. In the process, young Black man in America further cemented their status as among the most endangered groups for violent death anywhere on the planet.

In 2021, Black men aged 15 to 29 died by homicide at a rate of 121 per 100,000 population, up from 84 per 100,000 in 2019. Again, it is important to bear in mind that the earlier number vastly exceeds anything outside of some of the most volatile societies of the Global South. Their rate of violent death rose from roughly 19 times the rate for young white men in 2019 to fully 22 times in 2021. Despite the far greater numbers of white youth than Black youth in the United States, for every young white man who died by violence in 2021, six young Black men did.

We can get an even deeper, if still painfully technical, sense of the magnitude of this increasing devastation by using another common public health measure—years of potential life lost, or YPLL. This measures not just the sheer incidence of a particular cause of death, but its cumulative effect on life expectancy—thus giving us an even more compelling measure of the long-term impact on individuals, families, and communities.

YPLL is affected very disproportionately by different causes of death. People of all races die, on average, much later from heart disease, stroke, or lung cancer than they do from accidental injuries or violence. YPLL is often calculated with age 65 as an endpoint, meaning that someone who dies at age 20 from a gun assault has lost 45 years of potential life, while someone who dies at age 60 of a stroke has lost only five potential years. YPLL, then, can give us a powerful snapshot of the enormous human devastation that widespread fatal violence can cause, and how much that devastation varies by what kind of community you live in—or die in.

In 2021, Blacks in the United States lost nearly half a million years of potential life to violence, up from about 340,000 years in 2019—again, about a 44% increase, versus a 21% rise for whites. In 2021, the Black population as a whole was less than one-fourth the size of the white, non-Hispanic population, but actually lost more than three times as many years of potential life in that year to violence.

And as bad as these national numbers are, it gets worse in many American places that have been especially hard hit by the upsurge in violent deaths in recent years. In Louisiana and Missouri, the homicide death rate for young Black men rose to 213 and 214 per 100,000, respectively, in 2021: in Illinois, to 241—twice the already astounding national rate. This produces a racial violence divide that is nothing short of stratospheric. According to the CDC figures, over 500 young Black men died by violence in Illinois in 2021: so did 29 of their young white counterparts. Given the far larger white youth population in the state, this translates into a risk of violent death among 15- to 29-year-old Black men that is 57 times that of white youth. In the District of Columbia, 83 Black men aged 15 to 29 lost their lives to violence in 2021, giving them a stunning homicide death rate of 273 deaths per 100,000 of the young Black male population. Though the population of white males that age was similar overall, none of them died by homicide in 2021, making the racial disparity in homicide death rates in the nation's capital literally incalculable.

During this period, homicide death rates rose even faster among Black women than they did for Black men, and the risks of violent death for Black women continued to be far higher than for white men, scrambling the typical effects of gender on homicide. Nationally, Black women's overall homicide death rate in 2021 outstripped that of white men by about two to one: at age 15–29, by 3 to 1.

At this writing, some early CDC data on fatal gun violence in 2022 offer some hope that these extraordinary levels of violent death may be receding a bit, at least for now. Overall, the declines are not large. The CDC calculates that America lost 19,637 people to gun violence in 2022—down from 20,958 the year before, which was the highest number in years. The drop was highest among Blacks, whose rates of death from gun homicide fell from a high of 30.4% in 2021 to 27.5% in 2022. But though that is certainly good news and much better than nothing, it leaves us, at last count, with a rate of homicide death among Black Americans that was still more than a third higher than it was in 2019.[3]

There is some preliminary evidence that these unprecedented numbers may have fallen more during 2023. That's great, if true. And some commentators have seized on this to claim that concern about violence in American cities are overblown. But that must be considered as more an ideological position than it is an accurate reflection of the reality of American violence. The recent COVID-era rises—again, unprecedented in recent history—reveal several facts about American violence about which no one should be complacent: It is stunningly high even in "normal" times, brutally concentrated among the most vulnerable parts of the population, and subject to unpredictable rises that result from adverse forces that impact some communities much more than others.

And beyond the bare figures, recent research undertaken since the onset of the COVID-19 pandemic, examining both fatal and nonfatal violence, allows us a closer look at the social context and human impact of these trends.

Nationally, according to one recent analysis, over 9,000 more Americans died from firearm homicide in the first months of the pandemic era from April 2020 through December 2021 than would have been predicted based on the trends in gun killings in the months immediately before the pandemic began.[4] And research consistently shows that those excess deaths were concentrated overwhelmingly in places that were entirely predictable. Much of this research focuses on the impact of COVID-19 on a variety of cities across the country, and though the experience of those cities differed in some respects, the underlying similarities are striking and revealing.

Perhaps the most consistent of those similarities is the strong relationship between increases in violence and the level of economic and racial inequality in America's cities. Julia P. Schleimer and others at the University of California–Davis, for example, studied the experience of violence in 13 American cities just before and just after the onset of the pandemic.[5] As in the nation as a whole, the pandemic era saw sharp rises in homicide and in nonfatal firearm violence (though not in robbery or rape) in these cities. Both the ongoing level of violence and its rise during the pandemic were most pronounced in the specific zip codes within those cities that were the least "privileged"—areas characterized by extremes of economic or racial disadvantage, or a combination of both, as well as histories of housing instability and limited access to social support services.

These connections also appear again and again in studies focusing on the experience of individual cities during the pandemic. In Boston, for example, Elizabeth Piño and her colleagues studied patients suffering from "violent penetrating injuries" who were admitted to what was described as the "largest safety net hospital and busiest trauma center in New England," which treated from 50 to 70% of all such injuries in the city. Comparing those seen during the 5 years before the start of the COVID-19 pandemic to those admitted afterward, from early 2020 until February 2021, the researchers found that these patients were overwhelmingly young people of color before the pandemic and became even more so thereafter. Over the entire period of the study, from 2015 to 2021, the patients who had been stabbed or shot were roughly two-thirds Black and one-fifth Hispanic. Whites, on average, were less than 9% of victims. After pandemic containment measures were put in place, the white proportion fell to zero, the number of Hispanics doubled, and Blacks "continued to carry most of the burden" of violent firearm injuries. Adding in the small number of patients classified as being of "other" races, the entire cohort presenting with these violent injuries after the onset of the pandemic consisted of people of color.

Overall, there was a 32% increase in admissions for violent firearm injuries in the first months of the pandemic era compared to the average of the 5 years before COVID-19. In addition to the deep racial and ethnic imbalance, the Boston patients, overwhelmingly male before the pandemic (88%), were even more so (93%) after it. And they were drawn heavily from the ranks of the economically marginal. Where nearly half (47%) were unemployed before the pandemic, 57% were afterward. Though the patients seen post-pandemic tended to share the broad demographic characteristics of those who had come before, they were less likely to have been victims of gun violence previously. It appeared, in other words, that during the pandemic the forces that led to higher levels of gun violence in Boston—perhaps especially unemployment, which shot up from less than 3% before the pandemic to more than 16% in 2020—were ensnaring new "recruits," but those recruits were drawn from the traditionally most vulnerable parts of the population.[6]

That same phenomenon—adversities associated with COVID-19 striking on top of long-standing structural conditions of racialized disadvantage to ensnare widening swaths of the most vulnerable populations—can be seen in other cities as well. Researchers in Philadelphia, for example, using a comprehensive registry of shootings kept by the Philadelphia Police Department, found that gun violence in Philadelphia, as in Boston, rose sharply after the pandemic began as compared to the years before. The sheer volume of gun violence in the city was striking even before the impact of the pandemic; Philadelphia logged nearly 7,000 shootings in the 5 years pre-pandemic and close to 2,500 in the period of a little over a year afterward. A stunning racial imbalance was maintained throughout both periods: Blacks were 82% of shooting victims in the period before COVID-19, and 84% after March 2020 when containment policies were instituted in the city. Adding in Latinos and "others" brought the proportion of Philadelphia's shooting victims who were people of color up to 94% in 2020.[7]

But within that generally predictable pattern, there were two noteworthy shifts in violence after the start of the pandemic: The victims became both notably younger and more often female. The proportion of shooting victims who were women rose by 39%, and the proportion who were under 18 by 13%. Both of these increases were overwhelmingly concentrated among Blacks: Black women were already 72% of female victims of Philadelphia shootings before the pandemic, but were 80% afterward. Black children went from an already startling 85% of all children under 18 shot in the city to 92% after the onset of COVID-19 and the city's response to it. There was also what the researchers describe as an increasing "intensification" of the severity of the city's gun violence, with a significantly larger proportion of shootings after the pandemic involving more than four victims at a time.

The researchers conclude that "increasing firearm violence among Black women and children in Philadelphia is one manifestation of the differential impact of the pandemic and its associated containment policies on already disadvantaged Americans living in places with a long history of disinvestment."[8] In the case of children, they suggest that the increase in both the number and proportion of those shot during the pandemic months may have reflected "the combined detrimental effects of socioeconomic deprivation, school closures, and lack of social support and services such as childcare which occurred as a result of unmitigated COVID-19 containment policies." Because schools are such a critical source of social supports for low-income children in particular, their closure "disproportionately affected the most economically and socially vulnerable children in Philadelphia, removing this safety net, deepening structural inequities, and, in turn, increasing the risk for firearm injury."

If the closing off of normal sources of social support may help explain why gun violence rose among already vulnerable children, recent research also suggests that sharply rising unemployment in the early stages of the pandemic may have helped to intensify violence in the hardest hit communities during the COVID-19 era. Julia Schleimer's team of researchers at the University of California–Davis, for example, looked at the association between unemployment and violence in 16 U.S. cities in the period immediately before the pandemic, between January 2018 and March 2020, and the 3 months afterward, through June 2020. On average, the unemployment rate in those cities jumped roughly 8 percentage points over what would have been expected given unemployment trends before COVID-19 and the public response to it. The rise was considerably higher in some cities—more than 11 percentage points, for example, in Chicago. The researchers found that this excess unemployment didn't affect all kinds of crime in these cities—it had little or no impact on the level of what they called "acquisitive crimes." But it did have a significant impact on homicide and on firearm violence specifically. The researchers suggest that the notably different impacts of COVID-19 on firearm violence and homicide versus acquisitive crime may reflect specific characteristics of the social context produced by the pandemic itself and by the measures taken to contain it in these cities. "Stay at home" orders may have decreased some kinds of property crime by increasing "the guardianship people had over their homes and property."[9] On the other hand, the weakening of both formal and informal social control as people were kept away from institutions like work and school may have had an opposite effect, helping to explain the rise in interpersonal violence.

A study of the trajectory of nonfatal gun violence in Indianapolis shows a similar pattern: sharp increases in shootings early in the pandemic era, which were concentrated in parts of the city where violence had long been a fixture of neighborhood life, but which also shifted to strike groups within those communities that had been less hard hit by violence in the past. Overall, according to a team of researchers from Indiana University–Purdue University Indianapolis, nonfatal shootings rose by 15% in the city between the pre-pandemic period of January 2017 to March 2020 and the post-pandemic period through June 2021. Throughout the entire period, Blacks, who are about 28% of the city's population, were fully 77% of its victims of nonfatal shootings. The pandemic and the response to it didn't change the racial balance among victims overall or the concentration of violence in neighborhoods characterized by what these researchers called "structural disadvantage"—measured by a combination of rates of poverty, unemployment, and single female parent families. But it did cause a striking increase in the proportion of women victims, and of shootings of people over 30. Women's rate of victimization by gun violence in particular jumped by more than 50% from before the pandemic; men's by only about 7%. Men, especially Black men, were still far more likely to suffer from nonfatal violence than women. But the pandemic year had sharply increased women's vulnerability within the city's most disadvantaged neighborhoods.[10]

As these examples suggest, American cities were not all completely alike in their experience of violence after the start of the COVID-19 pandemic. They varied both in the severity and pace of increases post–COVID-19 and in how, exactly, those increases were distributed among different groups. But running throughout these variations is an overarching similarity: the concentration of COVID-19–era increases in "disinvested and structurally disadvantaged neighborhoods that had high rates of gun violence to begin with," in the words of a recent Brookings Institution analysis of homicide trends in four cities.[11] In the four cities they analyzed, the post-pandemic increases in homicides ranged from a stunning 53% in Chicago to 36% in Nashville, Tennessee, and 16% in Kansas City, Missouri, to a slight decline of about 3% in Baltimore—a city that, however, began the period with the highest homicide rate of all. But in every case, the researchers concluded, homicide, whether it radically increased or remained roughly the same, was overwhelmingly concentrated in some parts of these cities and not others, and the pandemic-related changes most often intensified, but did not alter, that fundamental existential difference. Like others, the Brookings analysts also concluded that what characterized areas of ongoing excess vulnerability was not high levels of poverty alone, but a more specific combination of economic deprivation, racial segregation, and "systemic disinvestment."[12]

That conclusion squares with what is by now a long history of increasingly sophisticated research stretching back more than 100 years.[13] And it also squares with the Kerner Commission's finding in 1968 that the state of personal security was "startlingly" different in America's most disadvantaged urban neighborhoods than outside of them.[14] There is surely much more research to be done on the impact of COVID-19 on the problem of violence in urban America. But at the end of the day, all of this research so far says basically the same thing. The pandemic era saw unprecedented surges in violence, notably gun-related violence, which was concentrated overwhelmingly in places, and among people, where it had been concentrated for decades and indeed generations. It took place in contexts of sharply rising unemployment, sharply reduced access to critical education, health care, and mental health services and supports, and radically disrupted personal and communal lives. While these adversities affected many people across the social spectrum, they hit most devastatingly at places that were among the most racially and economically deprived and marginalized, exacerbating already existing disparities and both broadening and deepening risk among the country's most vulnerable populations.

The remedy, as always, is implicit in the diagnosis. To reduce violence and related racial disparities, the University of California–Davis researchers conclude, "Immediate and long-term investments in low-income neighborhoods of color are warranted."[15] That sounds remarkably like the Kerner Commission's call, more than 55 years ago, for a "massive, compassionate, and sustained" response. But far too often, what we've seen in response to recent trends in violence is a tired and a counterproductive replay of attitudes we've encountered again and again in the past, and of "solutions" we've heard many times before—ones that seem almost schizophrenically disconnected from what we've learned about the roots of this ongoing American emergency. In the face of the troubling rises in violence in the pandemic era, the most common response has been what the Brookings researchers call the "punitive turn"[16]—a renewed call for getting "tough" and rolling back the limited but important reforms in the criminal punishment system we've achieved in recent years. This attitude has shown remarkable staying power despite the fact that we were already increasingly "tough" on serious violent offenders during the years that preceded the recent rises in violence. As a recent report from The Sentencing Project points out, a significant decline in incarceration for less serious offenses has gone along with increased sentences for serious crimes of violence, including life or "virtual" life in prison—a trend that has disproportionately affected Blacks.[17] No credible evidence exists, moreover, that efforts at the reform of cash bail or increased scrutiny of police use of force were in any way responsible for the rises in deadly violence the country endured in the last few years.

Another common response is to call for a range of essentially cosmetic reforms—more interagency cooperation, the addition of more sheer numbers of bodies to urban police forces, exhortations to besieged communities to take more control of their quality of life—that may be well-intended, but for which there is, unsurprisingly, scant evidence, at best, of effectiveness in the face of a deeply entrenched, enduring problem that reflects generations of social and economic abandonment. But probably equally destructive in the long run is a surprisingly tenacious denial that the problem actually exists. Not for the first time in our recent history, one common response to the endemic violence in America is to claim that its seriousness is exaggerated and that focusing overly on urban violence is little more than a pretext for justifying repressive measures against marginalized communities. That view may be well-meaning too. But it also has no answers for those who are genuinely—and rightly—concerned about violence, and as a result, hands this critical social issue to the people who caused it in the first place. And it is troubling to willingly write off the lives of tens of thousands of the most vulnerable people in the United States.

Fortunately, however, this is not the whole story. One of the most encouraging, though inadequately reported, developments in the last few years has been the burst of serious and well-conceived legislation explicitly designed to counter the long legacy of discrimination, neglect, and abandonment that has bred endemic violence in America. In several ways, we are not where we were in the early, tumultuous years at the start of the COVID-19 pandemic. In particular, a variety of economic and social measures put in place from 2020 onward changed the social and economic landscape in ways that are often underappreciated and underdiscussed. The pandemic brought unemployment rates to levels not seen since the Great Depression of the 1930s; by 2022 unemployment rates were, in most places, back roughly to pre-pandemic levels. Unprecedented increases in federal income support and medical benefits for low-income Americans kept millions from what could have been far more dire consequences during and after the pandemic. Perhaps even more far-reaching in their impact, economic interventions in the form of 2021's Infrastructure Investment and Jobs Act and 2022's Inflation Reduction Act began to channel levels of funding not seen in decades into socially and environmentally crucial, job-creating investments targeted at historically underserved communities.

We will need a great deal more research to know for sure whether these investments have helped to mitigate, or even reverse, the devastating rises in violence that the pandemic brought. But it's clear from what we know about the structural roots of violence that measures like these are steps in the right direction. They target the communities that have historically been the most affected by the structural forces that have bred devastatingly high levels of violence through good times and bad, and that render them vulnerable to adverse external shocks.[18] If we want to promote an effective and consequential attack on American violence, we will need to showcase these positive developments much more than we now do.

As so often in the past, America has a choice. We can pretend the problem doesn't exist. We can try to punish our way out of it. We can try to muddle through with vague ideas about community involvement and interagency cooperation. Or we can build on some of the most promising efforts of the past few years to finally bring a greater measure of opportunity and justice to communities we have abandoned for much too long. The alternatives seem particularly stark in today's social and political climate. It's not farfetched to envision a world in which the ongoing failure to address endemic violence in humane and constructive ways ushers in an age of increasingly authoritarian "solutions." Or, alternatively, a world in which we tolerate a continuing state of routine social disintegration—one that requires us to accept as natural a toll of death and suffering that no advanced society should permit. The choice before us, in short, is about exclusion versus justice, cynicism versus hope.

NOTES

1. See Scott R. Kegler, Thomas P. Simon, and Steven A. Sumner, "Firearm Homicide Rates, by Race and Ethnicity—United States, 2019–2022," Centers for Disease Control and Prevention, *Morbidity and Mortality Weekly Report* 92, no. 42 (October 20, 2023): 1149–50.

2. Unless otherwise noted, the following figures are from Centers for Disease Control and Prevention, WISQARS Fatal Injury Reports, accessed November/December 2023, http://www.cdc.gov/injury/wisqars/index.html.

3. Kegler et al., "Firearm Homicide Rates, by Race and Ethnicity," 1150.

4. Eric W. Lundstrom et al., "Excess US Firearm Mortality During the Covid-19 Pandemic Stratified by Intent and Urbanization," *JAMA Network Open* 6, no. 7 (2023): 3.

5. Julia P. Schleimer et al, "Neighborhood Racial and Economic Segregation and Disparities in Violence During the Covid-19 Pandemic," *American Journal of Public Health* 112, no. 1 (2022): 144–53. The persistence of striking racial disparities in community exposure to violence in recent years is also explored in Charles C. Lanfear et al, "Inequalities in Exposure to Firearm Violence by Race, Sex, and Birth Cohort from Childhood to Age 40 Years,1995–2021," *JAMA Network Open* 6, no. 5 (2023).

6. Elizabeth Pino et al., "Trends in Violent Penetrating Injuries During the First Year of the Covid-19 Pandemic," *JAMA Network Open* 5, no. 2 (2022).

7. Iman N. Afif et al., "The Changing Epidemiology of Interpersonal Firearm Violence During the COVID-19 Pandemic in Philadelphia, PA," *Preventive Medicine* 158 (2022): 107020.

8. Afif et al., "The Changing Epidemiology of Interpersonal Firearm Violence During the COVID-19 Pandemic in Philadelphia, PA," 5; Cf. Hatem O. Abdallah et al., "Increased Firearm Injury During the Covid-19 Pandemic: A Hidden Urban Burden," *Journal of the American College of Surgeons* 232, no. 2 (2021): e1–e10; Jessica H. Beard et al., "Changes in Shooting Incidence in Philadelphia, Pennsylvania, Between March and November 2020," *Journal of the American Medical Association* 325, no. 13 (2021): 1327–28.

9. Julia P. Schleimer et al., "Unemployment and Crime in US Cities During the Coronavirus Pandemic," *Journal of Urban Health*, 99 (2022): 82–91.

10. Lauren A. Magee, Bailee Lucas, and James Dennis Fortenberry, "Changing Epidemiology of Firearm Injury: A Cohort Study of Non-fatal Firearm Victimization Before and During the Covid-19 Pandemic, Indianapolis, Indiana," *BMJ Open* (2022): 1–7.

11. D. W. Rowlands and Hannah Love, "Mapping Gun Violence: A Closer Look at the Intersection Between Place and Gun Homicides in Four Cities," Brookings Institution, April 21, 2022, 2.

12. Rowlands and Love, "Mapping Gun Violence," 3.

13. See Elliott Currie, *A Peculiar Indifference: The Neglected Toll of Violence on Black America* (New York: Metropolitan Books, 2020).

14. National Advisory Commission on Civil Disorders, *Report* (New York: Bantam Books, 1968), 267.

15. Schleimer et al., "Neighborhood Racial and Economic Segregation," 144.

16. Rowlands and Love, "Mapping Gun Violence," 2.

17. Ashley Nellis, "No End in Sight: America's Enduring Reliance on Life Imprisonment," The Sentencing Project, December 16, 2022.

18. For a larger discussion of those social forces and their relevance today, see Michael K. Brown et al., *Whitewashing Race: The Myth of a Colorblind Society* (Rev. Ed.) (Berkeley and Los Angeles: University of California Press, 2022).

Housing and Neighborhood
Investment Policy

CHAPTER 15

Scaling Economic and Housing Justice

Lisa Rice, Michael Akinwumi, and Nikitra Bailey

INTRODUCTION

The 1968 Kerner Commission report included recommendations for overcoming injustice in housing and lending markets. Even if those recommendations had been implemented (the lion's share were not), people of color would still experience significant housing injustice. At the federal, state, and local levels, thousands of race-conscious, biased laws were enacted and trillions of dollars were spent to create sweeping inequality. Scaling housing justice calls for strategies and resources that match those expended to create our deeply inequitable society. The commission's report identified significant barriers to housing equality, including residential segregation; the concentration of substandard and overcrowding housing conditions in communities of color; insufficient affordable housing units; unfair code enforcement policies; people of color disproportionately paying higher rents for poorer housing and experiencing housing cost burdens; inadequate access to insurance; and racial discrimination in the rental and sales housing market. However, the report did not sufficiently recognize lending redlining and lending discrimination, appraisal bias, discriminatory zoning policies, and environmental injustice.

Moreover, when the Kerner Commission was convening throughout 1967 and 1968, it was likely not aware of the efforts of a group of scientists and mathematicians who met in 1956 to explore the idea of "artificial intelligence," the notion that machines could be created to simulate human functions and intelligence. Just 2 years later, Fair Isaac would develop the first credit risk scoring system.[1] These systems were hardly in use in 1968, but today they are used by virtually every mainstream lender. The commission considered the impact of technological innovation in its report—there are a few references to the word "technology"—interestingly, some of these relate to using innovative technologies as a means of distressing, disabling, and controlling protestors, thus weaponizing technology against people fighting for better conditions in their communities. However, the commission was not considering technology in terms of its application to the housing and lending markets. Today, technologies control the functioning of these markets. Any update of the commission's recommendations must therefore include consideration of how technology can exacerbate or mitigate housing inequality.

While the commission's recommendations for overcoming bias were important, and if fully implemented would have been quite helpful, a broader set of recommendations designed to fundamentally overhaul our housing and finance markets is in order.[2]

FAILURE TO IMPLEMENT KERNER COMMISSION RECOMMENDATIONS CEMENTED SYSTEMIC BARRIERS

Communities of color continue to experience difficulty advancing in every area of our society because of structural inequality. A failure to implement all of the recommendations included in the Kerner Commission report helped create and further entrench systems that create and perpetuate racial inequality. Centuries of race-conscious policies and actions by public and private actors have created structures like residential segregation, exclusionary zoning, biased technologies, the biased appraisal market (discussed below), and other structures that must be dismantled and replaced with fair systems that provide equitable opportunities for all.

Residential Segregation. Segregation is a bedrock of inequality. Place is inextricably linked to opportunity. Resources are spatially distributed, making housing and where a person lives a key driver of people's access to education, quality foods, health, employment, clean environments, security, technology, responsible credit, wealth, quality housing, social networks, and other resources.[3] In fact, housing is so central to the economy and other elements of our society that it is the number one driver of inflation.[4] Yet our neighborhoods are still highly segregated, with Black people in America being the most racially isolated.[5] Even high-income Blacks are racially isolated. This matters because racial population is deeply tied to the amenities that are available in certain communities.

Because amenities are not evenly disseminated throughout our society, certain areas receive far more resources than others.[6] For example, higher-paying jobs are more likely to be located in majority-White communities. Predominately White neighborhoods have three and two times as many full-service grocery stores as do Latino and Black neighborhoods, respectively. Across the nation, school districts that primarily serve students of color receive $23 billion less each year in funding than do predominately White districts even though non-White districts educate slightly more children. Predominately Native American, Black, and Latino communities have less access to high-speed Internet and receive fewer investments in infrastructure for faster, more reliable broadband services.[7]

Segregation fuels these and other disparities, making living, transportation, health, Internet, and other costs higher for marginalized groups. It is also a major social determinant of health. Studies show deep links between higher levels of segregation and negative health outcomes. This led Melody Goodman, a professor at Washington University, to assess, "Your zip code is a better predictor of your health than your genetic code."[8] People of color are more likely to live in health care and pharmacy deserts. Moreover, communities of color have higher mortality rates than predominately White areas. Ensuring equitable distribution of resources, increasing investments in communities of color while staving off displacement of long-term residents, addressing environmental health issues, redressing technology and algorithmic bias, and removing barriers to fair housing will help reverse the negative impacts of segregation.

Exclusionary and Restrictive Zoning. In the aftermath of slavery, municipalities implemented overtly racist zoning policies restricting where residents could live based on race and national origin. Real estate professionals, architects, city planners, and others opined that developing racially homogenous communities was critical for ensuring public safety and protecting land values. Baltimore passed the first explicit racial zoning ordinance in 1910 but other jurisdictions soon caught on.[9] The U.S. Supreme Court declared that racial zoning was unconstitutional in 1917 but that did not stop the use of these discriminatory policies.[10] Furthermore, jurisdictions soon figured out how to employ other mechanisms to segregate communities via the use of racial covenants, real estate discrimination, intimidation, and exclusionary zoning policies. Cities employed real estate and planning experts to devise ways to achieve racial zoning without explicitly including race in the codes.

Cities adopted "beautification" plans and created planning commissions and advisory councils that worked to assess where people could live based on their race. Municipalities implemented schemes requiring a majority of current residents to decide whether someone could move into a neighborhood. They established "historic districts" to preserve the character and nature of certain communities that resulted in not only increasing housing costs but the removal of Black residents from these areas. White residents were not removed from these historic districts to make way for preservation efforts; however, if city officials wanted Black residents eliminated from an area, they could invoke the city ordinance to have these citizens removed, all in the name of beautification. They sanctioned police departments to use their authority to help maintain land use provisions. Once people of color were relocated to other areas, those neighborhoods were down-zoned from residential to "special," "commercial," or "non-residential" uses, making it difficult for people of color to migrate out of those areas.

These exclusionary practices have been preserved in some form but have also morphed into other strategies that restrict people of color from accessing housing in well-resourced areas. Minimum lot size, single-family zoning, ordinances requiring housing to be stick-built, minimum square footage requirements, building height restrictions, special requirements for properties accepting Housing Choice Vouchers, public hearing/input processes that give way to NIMBYism, floor-to-area ratio requirements that add restrictive density guidelines impeding the development of affordable housing units, and other modern-day impediments all make it difficult for communities to build affordable and accessible housing units in well-resourced communities.

Dual Credit Market. Credit access varies based on where people live. The United States has a bifurcated credit market. On the one hand, there is the mainstream market comprised of banks, credit unions, government-sponsored enterprises (GSEs), and other financial services providers that are highly regulated and offer lower-cost credit to consumers. Mainstream entities issuing credit generally report consumers' positive payment history to the credit repositories, thereby allowing consumers who access credit in the financial mainstream to build up their credit profiles. Alternatively, nontraditional financial services providers such as payday lenders, check cashers, title money lenders, and subprime lenders, offer services and products at higher costs and generally don't report positive payment information to the credit repositories, leaving consumers to be credit invisible.[11] Moreover, banks are concentrated in predominately White communities whereas nontraditional financial entities are concentrated in communities of color.

Banks are closing their branches at higher rates in high-income predominately Black communities than they do in low-income non-Black communities.[12] As a result, people of color disproportionately access credit from nontraditional servicers, and are more likely to be credit invisible or unscoreable and have lower credit scores.

Environmental and Climate Injustice. There is a deep connection between exclusionary and restrictive zoning policies, siting processes, segregation, and housing discrimination that, together, have resulted in people of color disproportionately living in areas with contaminated land, air, and water and that are disproportionately impacted by climate change and natural disasters. People of color, and Blacks in particular, live in areas with higher exposure to dangerous air pollutants as compared to Whites. As a result, Blacks are three times as likely as Whites to die from pollution and Latinos and Asians have a higher risk of premature death from particle pollutants than do Whites.[13]

Bias in Automated Systems. Automated systems in housing and financial services often perpetuate systemic barriers against consumers of color, contravening the ethos of the Kerner Commission's recommendations. These systems, which include automated underwriting, credit scoring, and risk-based pricing models, are imbued with biases rooted in data generated by historical and current discrimination and socioeconomic inequalities. The Kerner Commission highlighted the role of "white society" and governmental policies in fostering residential segregation and inequality. The report emphasized that this segregation was not just a result of societal attitudes but was significantly perpetuated by unconstitutional government policies at various levels, including state agencies and federal regulators.

These unconstitutional policies, which included redlining and the enforcement of racial segregation in public housing, have had lasting impacts on Black communities and left a legacy of digital footprints in the data that power many automated systems and in patterns that inform modern algorithmic solutions. Researchers found that algorithmic systems overcharge Black and Latino borrowers by $765M yearly[14] and Automated Valuation Models[15] perpetuate discrimination against homeowners of color. Even marketing[16] and real estate[17] platforms can perpetuate bias. The automated systems in use today echo and amplify these historical biases present in data, thereby limiting fair access to housing and financial opportunities for people of color.

THE EXPANSION OF HOUSING INEQUALITY SINCE THE KERNER COMMISSION REPORT

Since the release of the Kerner Commission report, inequality has expanded in many ways. The commission did not recognize all forms of discrimination happening in the housing and lending markets in 1968. The commission was not able to recognize many systemic barriers that precluded people from obtaining housing and lending opportunities. Nor could it foresee new forms of discrimination and emerging structures that would exacerbate housing injustice. As a result, disparities in access to housing and lending opportunities persist leading to continuing patterns of residential segregation;

a widening of the racial wealth and homeownership gaps; expansion of the affordable housing crisis; entrenched appraisal bias; and persistent patterns of real estate sales, rental, and lending bias. The failure to implement a comprehensive prescription of solutions to overcome centuries of race-based, discriminatory policies and practices also meant that when the nation experienced macrolevel crises, like the Great Recession and the COVID-19 pandemic, communities of color were disproportionately impacted, further widening inequality.

Racial Wealth Gap Expansion. Discriminatory policies created distinct advantages for white families, leading to massive homeownership, wealth, and credit gaps that persist today. Because home value has been the cornerstone of intergenerational wealth in the United States, historical housing practices have had long-term effects in creating some current wealth inequalities, where white wealth has soared while Black wealth has remained stagnant. In 2019, white family wealth sat at $188,200 (median) and $983,400 (mean).[18] Conversely, Black family wealth during the same period was $24,100 (median) and $142,500 (mean).[19] These wealth disparities, in turn, reflect intergenerational transfer disparities: 29.9% of white families have received an inheritance, compared with only 10.1% of Black families.[20] Without inclusive policies to redress this disparity, it could take 228 years for the average Black family, and 84 years for the average Latino family, to reach the level of wealth white families own today.[21]

Racial Homeownership Gap Expansion. The Black–white homeownership gap today, which is an extension of racial wealth gaps, is at a 29-point difference (44% compared to 73.3%). This gap is wider than it was when the Fair Housing Act was passed in 1968 when the gap stood at a 27-point difference. The Latino–white homeownership gap today, at a 23-point difference (50.6% compared to 73.3%), is almost the same as it was when the Fair Housing Act was passed when the gap stood at a 24-point difference. The White homeownership rate is 67% higher than the Black homeownership rate, 45% higher than the rate for Latinos, and 20% higher than the rate for the Asian community.[22]

Expanded Fair and Affordable Housing Crisis. Failure to build an additional 6.6 million safe, decent, and affordable units over a 6-year period, as recommended by the Kerner Commission, has contributed to long-term housing instability for millions of families threatening their overall economic health. Not only is the rent "too damn high," investors aided and abetted by historic low interest rates[23] have purchased increased portions of the nation's affordable housing stock. These purchases in Black neighborhoods, ravaged by the Great Recession in southern and Midwest cities, ramped up during the COVID-19 health pandemic and left many first-time and owner-occupant homebuyers sidelined. In the first quarter of 2023, investors purchased nearly one-third of all single-family homes and almost one-third of lower-cost homes, exacerbating existing housing unaffordability.[24] Decades of underbuilding resulted in a current affordable housing gap that is estimated to be between 4.5 and 7 million units, making it even harder for people of color to access homeownership opportunities and benefits that come with it.[25] As a result, the racial wealth and homeownership gaps will be impossible to close without significant and justice-based interventions.

Appraisal Discrimination. Laws passed by Congress to govern the appraisal sector have only entrenched the bias first institutionalized by the federal government. The federal government did not create discrimination in the property valuation process, but it did develop a systemized mechanism for infusing race into the appraisal calculation. The Home Owners Loan Corporation (HOLC) and Federal Housing Administration (FHA), both New Deal programs, developed systems for valuing properties that considered the race and ethnicity of people living in the community where the house was located. Still today, race plays a significant role in property appraisals. Researchers estimate appraisal bias is costing homeowners in Black communities $162 billion in lost wealth.[26]

Moreover, research from the Federal Housing Finance Agency found thousands of appraisal reports containing inappropriate race-related language such as "Black race population above state average" and "more Asian influence of late."[27] Freddie Mac researchers analyzed millions of purchase transaction appraisals and found that homes in Black and Latino census tracts disproportionately received values below the contract price versus homes in white census tracts.[28] Researchers from Fannie Mae found racial disparities in appraisals in refinance transactions.[29] Their study showed appraisers were more likely to overvalue White-owned homes in Black neighborhoods and also more likely to undervalue Black-owned homes in White communities.[30] Two researchers analyzing millions of appraisals found that appraisers valued homes in White communities 200% higher than comparable homes in similar communities of color.[31]

Persistent Housing Bias. Housing discrimination is not a relic of the past and continues in housing transactions, including rental, real estate sales, mortgage lending and housing-related insurance, appraisal bias, algorithmic bias, discriminatory advertising, exclusionary zoning policies, discrimination by homeowners and condo associations, biased tax policies, and more. According to the Fair Housing Trends Report, in 2022, housing discrimination complaints reached their highest level since the National Fair Housing Alliance began collecting this annual data more than 25 years ago.[32] The invidious nature and difficulty of documenting harms make it such that many incidents of housing discrimination go unreported. And its victims feel hopeless that accountability is possible for those engaged in these unlawful actions that violate longstanding civil rights. Economists estimate that annually there are over 4 million instances of housing discrimination.[33]

Real Estate Sales Discrimination. Major investigations, such as *Newsday*'s "Long Island Divided," detail the nature and extent of discriminatory real estate sales practices. The 2019 investigation was a culmination of a 3-and-a-half-year scrutiny and entailed 240 hours of secretly recorded meetings with real estate agents and analysis of 5,764 house listings. The investigation showed that agents gave White testers 50% more listings than those given to equally qualified Black testers. It revealed a 19% rate of discrimination against Asian Americans, 39% rate of discrimination against Latino Americans, and 49% rate of discrimination against Black Americans.[34]

Mortgage Lending Discrimination. The Department of Justice's 2023 record settlement totaling more than $100 million in redlining cases in Black and Latino neighborhoods nationwide is a stark reminder that redlining persists and underscores the importance of using all the tools at our disposal to root it out. Moreover, Home Mortgage Disclosure Act data reveals each year that Black and Latino borrowers in particular are denied home mortgages at rates significantly higher than the whole market.[35] These practices harm communities while also threatening the health of the future housing finance system and our nation's economy. Predictions show that 7 out of 10 future homebuyers will be Latino and Black consumers. If these potential homebuyers are unable to equitably access homeownership, the system's safety and soundness is jeopardized and retirement security for older homeowners who plan to sell their homes to achieve successful retirement is threatened.

Disparate Impacts of the Great Recession and COVID-19 Impacts. The Great Recession disproportionately devastated communities of color as Wall Street chased excessive profits. Black and Latino communities lost $1 trillion in wealth after being steered into risky subprime mortgages. Even after many qualified for safer and more affordable loans, they ended up in unnecessary foreclosures.[36] This reckless lending devastated communities and tanked the global economy.

The aftershocks landed unjustly on hardest-hit communities of color during COVID-19, which made it clear that housing and residential segregation are social determinants of health.[37] As a result of disproportionately being impacted by the health pandemic and its downward economic trends, a year into the pandemic, Blacks and Latinos were more than twice as likely to report being unable to meet their monthly housing payments and facing eviction.[38]

Rental Discrimination and Older Housing Stock. Blacks continue to pay more than Whites for the same units, and more in application fees and security deposits. People of color, especially Blacks and Latinos, are more likely to be house-cost burdened (for both rental and homeownership). Less than 10% of Black renters are able to afford the price of a typically priced home.[39] Moreover, Blacks and Latinos live in older housing, which exacerbates inequitable outcomes as these properties are more likely to require major renovations and cost more in upkeep. Further, the properties have suffered from decades of undervaluation, which makes it difficult to secure financing to fund necessary home renovations.

SOLUTIONS FOR ADVANCING HOUSING JUSTICE AND EQUALITY

The Kerner Commission report contained critically important recommendations that, if fully implemented, would have helped advance racial justice. However, the commission could not have foreseen how new innovations would significantly impact the housing and financial services market. Nor did the commission fully grasp how structural barriers created deeply engrained, self-perpetuating systems that dramatically drive disproportionate discriminatory outcomes. This means that programs that are neutral on their face will result in discriminatory outcomes. What is needed is comprehensive reforms. We offer detail on certain solutions we believe should be added to the those initially developed by the Kerner Commission, and we round out the section with a chart in the Appendix describing how the Commission's original recommendations might be modernized for greater impact. Finally, it is important to recognize that investments in and commitments to redressing housing injustice must match the resources used to create rampant inequality.

Fully Enforce Fair Housing and Lending Laws. While we have passed civil rights statutes designed to stop discrimination, we have not designed laws to dismantle the systems of inequality that are still producing biased impacts. Laws like the Fair Housing Act of 1968 or the Equal Credit Opportunity Act of 1974 prohibit housing and financial services providers from considering race, national origin, or gender when making a housing-related decision, and can be effective, when enforced. But we have done little to nothing to remedy or rectify the discriminatory structures that were created from centuries of discriminatory laws. For example, although the Fair Housing Act does contain a provision for dismantling systemic inequality—the Affirmatively Furthering Fair Housing (AFFH) mandate—it has never been meaningfully enforced. Enforcement of the Fair Housing Act's AFFH obligation would have significant benefits. Lawmakers must ensure enforcement agencies, like the Department of Housing and Urban Development, Department of Justice, and Consumer Finance Protection Bureau, as well as private, nonprofit fair housing organizations, have ample resources to root out discrimination.

Affirmatively Furthering Fair Housing. The Fair Housing Act's AFFH mandate is an equity framework to address the nation's fair and affordable housing crisis. Entities that receive federal funding for housing or community development–related activities must ensure that none of the funding is used to discriminate and take steps to create inclusive communities where everyone has access to the resources and amenities needed to thrive. While HUD's AFFH responsibilities are clear, and it must quickly release its proposed AFFH rule,[40] this obligation extends to all executive-level federal agencies. It is critical that all federal infrastructure–related initiatives such as the bipartisan Infrastructure Investment and Jobs Act, Inflation Reduction Act, CHIPs and Science Act, and others be implemented in a way that fulfills this obligation. Otherwise, these massive federal investments will further entrench racial inequities.

Equipping Fair Housing Groups to Advance Fair Housing. While local fair housing agencies continue to process the largest number of cases in comparison to HUD, Fair Housing Assistance Program agencies, and the Department of Justice, they remain grossly underfunded to conduct their important work. Currently, these agencies are funded through Congress' annual appropriations process, which is not consistent, and HUD distributes grants through a competitive process. However, reforms to this process are necessary, and HUD should simplify and revamp the funding mechanism for the Fair Housing Initiative Program's Private Enforcement Initiative, including eliminating its competitive process and replacing it with a framework that guarantees consistent, adequate funding for well-performing private, nonprofit fair housing groups.

Implement a Rigorous, Responsible AI Strategy. Algorithmic systems that identify patterns in data, create new patterns, or automate identified patterns are known as automated systems or, in their most popular name, artificial intelligence (AI). To address the biases inherent in housing and finance AI systems, a federal comprehensive responsible AI strategy must be implemented. This strategy should include:

1. Policy and Regulatory Reforms: Introduce regulations that mandate fairness and transparency in AI systems used in housing and finance. This includes regular audits for bias, ensuring diverse data sets, and making AI decision-making processes transparent to consumers.
2. Inclusivity in AI Development: Involve diverse stakeholders, including civil rights advocates, in the development and testing of AI systems. This diversity can help identify potential biases early in the design process.
3. Training and Awareness: Implement training programs for developers and users of AI systems in housing and finance to sensitize them about potential biases and the ethical implications of AI decisions.
4. Public Accountability: Establish mechanisms for public reporting and accountability where AI systems are used in critical sectors like housing and finance. This can include public oversight committees or disclosure requirements about the algorithms used.
5. Legal Frameworks: Strengthen legal frameworks to protect against discrimination in automated decisions. This involves updating existing laws to address the nuances of AI and machine learning.
6. Consumer Education and Advocacy: Enhance consumer education about how AI impacts housing and financial services. This should include information on how to seek redress in cases of suspected discrimination.
7. Research and Development: Encourage and fund research into AI systems that actively counteract historical biases, focusing on creating algorithms that mitigate discrimination and promote equity and inclusion.
8. Collaboration Across Sectors: Foster collaboration between tech companies, policymakers, civil rights groups, and financial institutions to jointly develop standards and best practices for responsible AI in housing and finance.

By implementing these policies, we can work toward mitigating the biases prevalent in automated systems, ensuring fairer and more equitable access to housing and financial services for all, especially consumers of color.

First Generation Homebuyer Programs. Targeting downpayment assistance by first generation is a proven strategy to help make homeownership a reality for families who do not have the benefit of prior generational wealth-building from homeownership. Many Black, Latino, and AAPI consumers have sufficient income to pay a monthly mortgage obligation and are currently paying rental housing payments equal to or exceeding what they might pay on a mortgage. Consumers who are the first generation of would-be homeowners face significant challenges because their families lack the wealth that homeownership can provide and they often cannot rely on guidance, networks, and assistance from family to access homeownership opportunities. Moreover, existing first-time buyer downpayment assistance (DPA) models have failed to close the racial homeownership gaps.

Congress should provide $100 billion in targeted DPA for first-generation homebuyers as outlined in the Downpayment Toward Equity Act sponsored by House Financial Services Committee Ranking Member Maxine Waters and Senate Banking Committee Member Senator Raphael Warnock. Their legislation has the backing of the White House and draws from a policy proposal developed by the National Fair Housing Alliance (NFHA) and the Center for Responsible Lending (CRL) based off the STASH program of the Massachusetts Affordable Housing Alliance.[41]

Urban Institute research reveals there are over 5 million potential first-generation homebuyers. Over 70% would be consumers of color. Roughly 34% of this group are Black and 26% are Latino. This important investment has the potential to create millions of new homeowners among people who would be the first in their family to buy a home, spur massive economic activity and growth, and position people of color to sustain the future housing market as many older Americans sell their homes to downgrade for a stable retirement.

Massachusetts, Minnesota, New Jersey, North Carolina, and Vermont have already operationalized first-generation programs and can serve as models for smaller scale, regional, state, and local programs. For-profit entities, like banks and credit unions, can adopt first-generation programs. Nonprofit organizations, like community development financial institutions, can implement them as well. Finally, philanthropic organizations and the GSEs[42] can mandate that the downpayment assistance programs are targeted to first-generation homebuyers or provide capital to CDFIs to purchase first-generation mortgage loans on the secondary market to increase liquidity for these programs.

Special Purpose Credit Programs (SPCPs). The Equal Credit Opportunity Act and Fair Housing Act allow lenders to design SPCPs in a tailored way to meet consumers' special social needs and benefit economically disadvantaged groups, including groups that share a common characteristic, such as race, national origin, or gender.[43] Properly designed, SPCPs can play a critical role in promoting equity and inclusion, building wealth, and removing persistent barriers that have contributed to financial inequities, housing instability, and residential segregation.

The federal government demanded discrimination in its programs, advanced race-conscious policies for Whites through institutionalized redlining, and systematized the false association between race and risk in housing and finance markets that is still with us today. The federal government was not the only actor; these schemes were supported by banks, real estate firms, housing developers, urban planners, local jurisdictions, and others. This harm was never repaired, which is why the nation's racial wealth and homeownership gaps are persistent and generally as large as they were when the 1968 Civil Rights Act was passed. The nation's attempts at solving income disparities have not solved racial bias. Low-to-moderate income (LMI) programs have not moved the needle. We need programs like SPCPs that provide specific remedies for overcoming barriers faced by communities of color.

APPENDIX

Comparison of Kerner Commission Recommendations Versus Solutions Needed Today

Kerner Commission Recommendations[44]	2024 Update
• Increase Supply of Affordable Housing • 6.6 million low- and moderate-income housing units (over a 6-year period) • Improve ability of low-income households to pay rental obligations	• Optimizing Land Use and Planning: AI can analyze large datasets to identify optimal locations for affordable housing development, taking into account factors like proximity to public transportation, employment centers, and community services. • Streamlining Construction Processes: AI can enhance efficiency in the construction of affordable housing by optimizing design, materials procurement, and project management, leading to reduced costs and faster completion times. • Build 4.3 million to 7 million new affordable housing units over the next 10 years. • Pass federal statute to prohibit discrimination against Housing Choice Voucher holders (HCV). Administratively, no housing unit built using federal funds (including those funded by the GSEs) should be able to deny HCV holders.
• Reduce segregation by opening up housing opportunities for people of color in predominately White, well-resourced areas	• Ensure funding from the bipartisan Infrastructure Investment and Jobs Act, Inflation Reduction Act, disaster relief, and future federal investments are equitably distributed and quickly flow to communities of color. • Via the Affirmatively Furthering Fair Housing provision, ensure people in areas receiving increased investments do not succumb to displacement due to gentrification. • Increase funding for Moving to Opportunity programs. • Leverage responsible AI to enhance the effectiveness of Moving to Opportunity programs and increase entities' compliance with the Fair Housing Act's AFFH provision.
• Expanded and modified below-market interest rate mortgage program for nonprofit and limited-profit corporations for affordable housing development	• Increase National Housing Trust Fund funding. Pass and implement the Neighborhood Homes Investment Act with fair housing principles and other laws to increase affordable housing production. • Expand Low Income Housing Tax Credit program and add fair housing provisions to ensure housing is built in well-resourced communities. • Risk Assessment and Management: Use responsible AI to analyze vast data sets to more accurately assess and manage the risks associated with lending to nonprofit and limited-profit corporations, enabling more tailored and favorable interest rates. • Efficient Allocation of Funds: Use AI to optimize allocation of funds by identifying the most impactful projects and ensuring that resources are directed to areas where they will have the greatest effect on affordable and fair housing development.

(continued)

Kerner Commission Recommendations[44]	2024 Update
• Expanded and modified rental payment supplemental program	• Increase funding for Housing Choice Voucher Programs. • Predictive Analysis for Financial Assistance: Utilize AI to predict which tenants may require rental assistance in the future, allowing for proactive allocation of funds. • Customized Assistance Programs: Implement AI algorithms to tailor assistance programs based on individual tenant needs, ensuring efficient and fair distribution of funds. • Automated Monitoring and Reporting: Use AI for continuous monitoring and reporting on the effectiveness of the rental assistance programs, enabling timely modifications and transparency in fund utilization.
• Expanded and modified rent supplemental program to allow for homeownership opportunities • Senate Banking and Currency Committee introduced bill for homeownership subsidy loan payment program	• Amend current guidelines and protocols to increase the ability of entities to accept HCV payments for homeownership opportunities. • Market Analysis for Subsidy Allocation: Utilize AI for real-time housing market analysis to dynamically adjust subsidy amounts, ensuring they are used to advance inclusive communities and equitable housing. • Legislative Impact Forecasting: Use AI to search for the most impactful alternative model for the potential socioeconomic outcomes of proposed legislation, providing the Senate Banking and Housing Committee with data-driven insights to craft bills that effectively promote homeownership among diverse populations.
• Federal write-down of interest rates on loans to private builders to develop affordable housing	• Develop a Below Market Interest Rate Program for First-Generation Homebuyers • Build incentives into the LIHTC, National Housing Trust Fund, HOME fund, and other federal programs that provide lower interest rates based on the length of years the housing development will be used for LMI/MI populations. • Increase support for Special Purpose Credit Programs across federal agencies and where applicable. • Financing Models: Implement Federal AI-driven predictive models to assess the long-term viability and impact of affordable housing projects, enabling more informed decisions on interest rate reductions for developers and builders. • Real-Time Market Analysis: Federal use of AI for real-time analysis of housing market trends and construction costs, allowing for dynamic adjustment of interest rates in response to market conditions, ensuring the effective use of government resources in promoting affordable housing.

Kerner Commission Recommendations[44]	2024 Update
• Expanded and diversified public housing program (scattered site)	• Demographic and Needs Analysis: Utilize AI to analyze demographic data and housing needs across different regions, ensuring equitable distribution and diversification of public housing resources. • Optimization of Resource Allocation: Implement AI algorithms to optimize the allocation of funding and resources, focusing on areas with the highest demand and potential impact for public housing. • Enhanced Community Engagement: Use AI tools for analyzing community feedback and preferences, facilitating the development of public housing programs that are more responsive to the specific needs and cultural aspects of diverse communities.
• Implement an expanded Model Cities program	• Data-Driven Urban Planning: Leverage AI for comprehensive data analysis on urban development, identifying areas in need of revitalization and planning effective interventions. • Impact Monitoring and Evaluation: Implement AI systems to continuously monitor and evaluate the outcomes of HOME, Inclusive Communities, and other federal housing and community development programs, allowing for real-time adjustments and long-term strategy optimization.
• Implement a reoriented and expanded urban renewal program	• Require the U.S. Treasury Department to ensure compliance with the Fair Housing Act's AFFH mandate in all its housing and community development funding programs, including the CDFI Fund, LIHTC, disaster recovery, and other housing or community development programs.
• Reform obsolete building codes to remove obstacles to affordable housing development and allow use of updated technologies	• Analyzing Current Codes for Obsolescence: Use AI to review existing building codes across various jurisdictions to identify outdated regulations that hinder the use of modern, cost-effective building technologies and promote the development of resilient housing units. • Simulation and Modeling: Utilize AI for simulating and modeling the impacts of new building technologies, providing data-driven insights for updating codes to facilitate affordable housing development. • Stakeholder Input Analysis: Use AI to process and analyze vast amounts of stakeholder input, including from builders, architects, and community groups, to inform more inclusive and practical building code reforms and identify where zoning codes support NIMBYism and other potential activity that could violate fair housing laws.

(continued)

Kerner Commission Recommendations[44]	2024 Update
• Enactment of a national, comprehensive, and enforceable open-occupancy law (Fair Housing Law)	• The Fair Housing Act was passed just months after the release of the report and 7 days after Dr. King's assassination. The act has not been effectively enforced. In particular, there is wide-ranging lack of compliance with the Affirmatively Furthering Fair Housing provision. Significant funds for private fair housing centers, the Department of Housing and Urban Development, and DOJ are needed to increase enforcement and compliance. Moreover, federal regulators, including prudential regulators, must enhance their oversight and enforcement of fair housing and fair lending laws, particularly as it relates to addressing algorithmic bias.
• Reorientation of federal housing programs to place more low- and mod-income housing outside of "ghetto" areas	• Implement the complete, comprehensive "Housing" package initially included in the Build Back Better bill, reintroduced as the Housing Crisis Response Act by House Financial Services Committee Ranking Member Waters. This comprehensive package of housing reforms and support for fair and affordable housing programs will help implement more equitable solutions for closing the racial wealth and homeownership gaps and improve the nation's economy.

NOTES

1. See Form 1-K: Fair, Isaac and Company Incorporated Annual Report, *FICO Investor Relations*, December 1998, https://investors.fico.com/static-files/461a5d42-97be-45d8-a837-38cc25a0c267.

2. The Kerner Commission report references the National Housing Act of 1949 and its lofty promises to support Americans in their quest for housing security. However, when Congress passed the law, which established a national goal of achieving "a decent home and suitable environment for every American family," it did not quite mean the benefits of the law would be applied to everyone. At the time state-sponsored, de jure segregation was the norm. There were no provisions in the law that would strike down the United States' apartheid systems and structures. In fact, the civil rights laws passed prior to and after the commission's report did not include comprehensive mechanisms for significantly upending the policies and practices driving injustice and discrimination related to housing and finance.

3. Alexandre Lee, "Where You Live Matters: Access to Key Amenities is Worse in Communities of Color," *Zillow*, June 23, 2021, https://www.zillow.com/research/nfha-where-you-live-matters-29661.

4. Katy O'Donnell, "The Main Driver of Inflation Isn't What You Think It Is," *Politico*, March 18, 2022, https://www.politico.com/news/2022/03/18/housing-costs-inflation-00015808.

5. Jake Intrator, Johnathan Tannen, and Douglas S. Massey, "Segregation by Race and Income in the United States 1970–2010," *Social Science Research* 60 (2016): 45–60, https://doi.org/10.1016/j.ssresearch.2016.08.003.

6. See National Fair Housing Alliance, "Where You Live Matters," n.d., https://nationalfairhousing.org/issues/where-you-live-matters.

7. Stephen Rodriguez-Elliott and Karl Vachuska, "Measuring the Digital Divide: A Neighborhood-Level Analysis of Racial Inequality in Internet Speed During the COVID-19 Pandemic," *Societies* 13, no. 4 (2023): 92, https://doi.org/10.3390/soc13040092; see also Leon Yin and

Aaron Sankin, "Dollars to Megabits, You May Be Paying 400 Times as Much As Your Neighbor for Internet Service," *The Markup*, October 19, 2022, https://themarkup.org/still-loading/2022/10/19/dollars-to-megabits-you-may-be-paying-400-times-as-much-as-your-neighbor-for-internet-service; see also Shara Tibken, "The Broadband Gap's Dirty Secret: Redlining Still Exists in Digital Form," *CNET*, June 28, 2021, https://www.cnet.com/home/internet/features/the-broadband-gaps-dirty-secret-redlining-still-exists-in-digital-form.

8. Amy Roeder, "Zip Code Better Predictor of Health Than Genetic Code," Harvard T. H. Chan School of Public Health, August 4, 2014, https://www.hsph.harvard.edu/news/features/zip-code-better-predictor-of-health-than-genetic-code.

9. Christopher Silver, "The Racial Origins of Zoning in American Cities," in *Urban Planning and the African American Community: In the Shadows*, June Manning Thomas and Marsha Ritzdorf, eds. (Thousand Oaks, CA: Sage Publications, 1997).

10. As an example, in 1925, well after the *Buchanan v. Warley* decision, Birmingham, Alabama, enacted a race-based planning ordinance that included plans to "restrict the negroes to certain districts." Post *Buchanan*, Birmingham's laws also allowed the city to use its authority to deny building permits to stop "construction of Negro housing contiguous to White neighborhoods."

11. See National Fair Housing Alliance, "Access to Credit," n.d., https://nationalfairhousing.org/issue/access-to-credit.

12. Zach Fox et al., "Bank Branch Closures Take Greatest Toll on Majority-Black Areas," S&P Global, July 25, 2019, https://www.spglobal.com/marketintelligence/en/news-insights/latest-news-headlines/bank-branch-closures-take-greatest-toll-on-majority-black-areas-52872925.

13. Qian Di et al., "Air Pollution and Mortality in the Medicare Population," *The New England Journal of Medicine* 376, no. 26 (2017): 2513–22, doi:10.1056/NEJMoa1702747; see also Bartees Cox, "Environmental Racism Has Left Black Americans Three Times More Likely to Die from Pollution," *Quartz*, March 13, 2018, https://qz.com/1226984/environmental-racism-has-left-black-americans-three-times-more-likely-to-die-from-pollution; Hiroko Tabuchi and Nadja Popovich, "People of Color Breathe More Hazardous Air. The Sources Are Everywhere," *New York Times*, September 7, 2021, https://www.nytimes.com/2021/04/28/climate/air-pollution-minorities.html; American Lung Association, "Disparities in the Impact of Air Pollution," n.d., https://www.lung.org/clean-air/outdoors/who-is-at-risk/disparities.

14. Robert Bartlett et al., "Consumer-Lending Discrimination in the FinTech Era," University of California–Berkeley, November 2019, https://faculty.haas.berkeley.edu/morse/research/papers/discrim.pdf.

15. Linna Zhu, Michael Neal, and Caitlin Young, "Revisiting Automated Valuation Model Disparities in Majority-Black Neighborhoods," Urban Institute, May 19, 2022, https://www.urban.org/research/publication/revisiting-automated-valuation-model-disparities-majority-black-neighborhoods.

16. See National Fair Housing Alliance, "Facebook Settlement," March 14, 2019, https://nationalfairhousing.org/facebook-settlement.

17. Nate Berg, "Redfin to Pay $4 Million to Settle Lawsuit Over Digital Redlining," *Fast Company*, May 2, 2022, https://www.fastcompany.com/90747572/redfin-to-pay-4-million-to-settle-lawsuit-over-digital-redlining.

18. Neil Bhutta et al., "Changes in U.S. Family Finances from 2016 to 2019: Evidence from the Survey of Consumer Finances," *Federal Reserve Bulletin* 106, no. 5 (September 2020), https://www.federalreserve.gov/publications/files/scf20.pdf.

19. Bhutta et al., "Changes in U.S. Family Finances from 2016 to 2019."

20. See Neil Bhutta et al., "Disparities in Wealth by Race and Ethnicity in the 2019 Survey of Consumer Finances," FEDS Notes, Board of Governors of the Federal Reserve System, September 2020, https://doi.org/10.17016/2380-7172.2797.

21. See Dedrick Asante-Muhammad et al., "The Road to Zero Wealth: How the Racial Wealth Divide Is Hollowing out America's Middle Class," Institute for Policy Studies and Prosperity Now, September 2017, 15, https://prosperitynow.org/files/PDFs/road_to_zero_wealth.pdf.

22. Analysis based on latest updates to the U.S. Census American Community Survey data, "2021 ACS 1-Year Estimates," U.S. Census Bureau, n.d., https://www.census.gov/programs-surveys/acs/news/data-releases/2021/release.html#oneyear. Research has shown that homeownership overall is likely to drop in the next 2 decades. This drop will be more pronounced for Black Americans unless actions are taken to ensure that they have equitable access. In other words, future housing demand will be driven by people of color. A robust housing market, both for new homebuyers seeking to purchase homes and for existing homeowners seeking to refinance or sell their homes, cannot exist in the absence of access to homeownership and mortgage credit on fair and equal terms for all creditworthy borrowers.

23. The Federal Reserve's actions to mitigate the economic impacts of COVID-19 exacerbated existing inequality and its research showed the board's interventions of lowering the federal funds rate and monthly $40 billion purchases in mortgage-backed securities did not benefit the whole housing market equally. See Kristopher Gerardi, Lauren Lambie-Hanson, and Paul Willen, "Racial Differences in Mortgage Refinancing, Distress, and Housing Wealth Accumulation during COVID-19," Federal Reserve Banks of Atlanta, Philadelphia, and Boston, June 2021, https://www.bostonfed.org/publications/current-policy-perspectives/2021/racial-differences-in-mortgage-refinancing-distress-and-housing-wealth-accumulation-during-covid-19.aspx.

24. Alexander Hermann, "8 Facts About Investor Activity in the Single-Family Rental Market, Housing Perspectives," Joint Center for Housing Studies of Harvard University, July 18, 2023, https://www.jchs.harvard.edu/blog/8-facts-about-investor-activity-single-family-rental-market.

25. See Zillow, "Affordability crisis: United States needs 4.3 million more homes," June 22, 2023, https://zillow.mediaroom.com/2023-06-22-Affordability-crisis-United-States-needs-4-3-million-more-homes; Mary Louise Kelly, et al., "Housing experts say there just aren't enough homes in the U.S.," NPR: All Things Considered, April 23, 2024, https://www.npr.org/2024/04/23/1246623204/housing-experts-say-there-just-arent-enough-homes-in-the-u-s.

26. Jonathan Rothwell and Andre M. Perry, "How racial bias in appraisals affects the devaluation of homes in majority-Black neighborhoods," Brookings Institution, December 5, 2022, https://www.brookings.edu/articles/how-racial-bias-in-appraisals-affects-the-devaluation-of-homes-in-majority-black-neighborhoods/.

27. See FHFA, "Reducing Valuation Bias by Addressing Appraiser and Property Valuation Commentary," FHFA Insights Blog, Dec. 14, 2021; https://www.fhfa.gov/Media/Blog/Pages/Reducing-Valuation-Bias-by-Addressing-Appraiser-and-PropertyValuation-Commentary.aspx.

28. Melissa Narragon, et al., "Racial and Ethnic Valuation Gaps in Home Purchase Appraisals," Freddie Mac Economic and Housing Research Note, Sept. 2021, http://www.freddiemac.com/fmac-resources/research/pdf/202109-Note-Appraisal-Gap.pdf.

29. Jake Williamson and Mark Palim, "Appraising the Appraisal," Fannie Mae, Feb. 2022, https://www.fanniemae.com/media/42541/display.

30. Maureen Yap et al., "Identifying Bias and Barriers, Promoting Equity: An Analysis of the USPAP Standards and Appraiser Qualifications Criteria, The Appraisal Subcommittee, January 2022.

31. Junia Howell, "2022 Appraised Update," Eruka, May 2023, https://static1.squarespace.com/static/62e84d924d2d8e5dff96ae2f/t/6465321aca101a0b82e45344/1684353568112/Howell+2022+Appraised+Update_05_01_23.pdf.pdf.

32. Lindsay Augustine et al., "2023 Fair Housing Trends Report: Advancing a Blueprint for Equity," National Fair Housing Alliance, August 2023, https://nationalfairhousing.org/wp-content/uploads/2023/08/2023-Trends-Report-Final.pdf.

33. See National Fair Housing Alliance, "The Case for Fair Housing," October 1, 2017, https://nationalfairhousing.org/resource/2017-fair-housing-trends-report.

34. Ann Choi et al., "Long Island Divided," *Newsday*, November 17, 2019, https://projects.newsday.com/long-island/real-estate-agents- investigation/.

35. Jacob Channel, Dan Shepard, and Xiomara Martinez-White, "Black Homebuyers in 50 Largest US Metros 1.6 Times More Likely to Be Denied for Mortgage Than Overall Population," *LendingTree*, July 24, 2023, https://www.lendingtree.com/home/mortgage/lendingtree-study-black-homebuyers-more-likely-to-be-denied-mortgages-than-other-homebuyers.

36. Actions leading to the Great Recession, and the response to it, created a net drain on homeownership. As a result, Black and Latino families lost $1 trillion in wealth from being steered unnecessarily into risky subprime loans. See Debbie Gruenstein Bocian, Peter Smith, and Wei Li, "Collateral Damage: The Spillover Costs of Foreclosures," Center for Responsible Lending, October 24, 2012, 2, https://www.responsiblelending.org/sites/default/files/nodes/files/research-publication/collateral-damage.pdf. Much evidence indicates that many subprime borrowers, including higher-income families of color, qualified for safer loans that were lower cost. See Rick Brooks and Ruth Simon, "Subprime Debacle Traps Even Very Credit-Worthy," *Wall Street Journal*, December 3, 2007, https://www.wsj.com/articles/SB119662974358911035. However, Wall Street's appetite for excessive profits and lax federal regulation drove these outcomes. The Financial Crisis Inquiry Report Commission, "The Financial Crisis Inquiry Report, Final Report of the National Commission on the Causes of the Financial and Economic Crisis in the United States," February 25, 2011, xxvii, https://www.govinfo.gov/content/pkg/GPO-FCIC/pdf/GPO-FCIC.pdf.

37. The Centers for Disease Control and Prevention (CDC) found that residential segregation is linked to a variety of adverse health outcomes and underlying health conditions, which can also increase the likelihood of severe illness or death from COVID-19.

38. Consumer Financial Protection Bureau, "Housing insecurity and the COVID-19 pandemic," March 2021, https://files.consumerfinance.gov/f/documents/cfpb_Housing_insecurity_and_the_COVID-19_pandemic.pdf.

39. National Association of Realtors, "More Americans Own Their Homes, but Black-White Homeownership Rate Gap Is Biggest in a Decade, NAR Report Finds," March 2, 2023, https://www.nar.realtor/newsroom/more-americans-own-their-homes-but-black-white-homeownership-rate-gap-is-biggest-in-a-decade-nar.

40. See Notice of Proposed Rulemaking (NPRM) entitled "Affirmatively Furthering Fair Housing," U.S. Department of Housing and Urban Development, February 9, 2023, https://www.federalregister.gov/documents/2023/02/09/2023-00625/affirmatively-furthering-fairhousing.

41. Nikitra Bailey et al., "First Generation: Criteria for a Targeted Down Payment Assistance Program," National Fair Housing Alliance and Center for Responsible Lending, May 21, 2021, https://nationalfairhousing.org/wp-content/uploads/2021/06/crl-nfha-first-generation-jun21.pdf.

42. Government Sponsored Enterprises are quasi-governmental agencies. They include Freddie Mac, Fannie Mae, the Federal Home Loan Banks, Sallie Mae, Farmer Mac, and the Farm Credit System.

43. Equal Credit Opportunity Act, 15 U.S.C. § 1691(c); Regulation B, 12 CFR § 1002.8; HUD, Guidance on the Fair Housing Act's Treatment of Certain Special Purpose Credit Programs that Are Designed and Implemented in Compliance with the Equal Credit Opportunity Act and Regulation B (Dec. 6, 2021), https://www.hud.gov/sites/dfiles/GC/documents/Special_Purpose_Credit_Program_OGC_guidance_12-6-2021.pdf

44. The National Advisory Commission on Civil Disorders, *Report of the National Advisory Commission on Civil Disorders* [Kerner Report] (Washington, DC: U.S. Department of Justice, Office of Justice Programs, 1968).

CHAPTER 16

What the Kerner Commission Got Wrong and How We Can Get It Right
Remedying Segregation Requires Recognizing Its True Origins

Leah Rothstein and Richard Rothstein

(I)

In 1865, Congress and the states adopted the Thirteenth Amendment. Section 1 banned slavery; Section 2 authorized legislation to enforce the prohibition.

In 1866, using its Section 2 power, Congress passed a Civil Rights Act that outlawed burdens on freed slaves that were not imposed on free whites; it reasoned that racial discrimination, public or private, undermined effective emancipation. Along with other provisions, the act said that all persons should have the same rights as white persons to buy or sell property or otherwise participate in the private market. President Andrew Johnson vetoed the law. Congress overrode his veto.

To clarify the racial equality explicitly protected by the 1866 law, Congress then adopted the Fourteenth Amendment that defined emancipated slaves as full citizens (because they had been born on U.S. soil) and prohibited their unequal treatment. The amendment was ratified in 1868. To avoid any further doubt, Congress reenacted the provisions of the 1866 law in a new Civil Rights Act of 1870, now also claiming the authority of the new amendment. Another civil rights law, adopted in 1875, prohibited private discrimination in public accommodations, such as hotels.

In 1883, the Supreme Court agreed that the Thirteenth Amendment's Section 2 power could indeed be exercised to prohibit continuation of the "badges and incidents" of slavery and recognized that a prohibition on holding property could be understood as such a badge.[1] But the justices went on to say that the Constitution could prohibit only discrimination by government, not by individuals. In 1896, the Justices added that even governmentally imposed racial segregation did not violate that amendment because forced separation of the races was not necessarily unequal. Justice John Marshall Harlan dissented in both cases, showing that the Thirteenth Amendment, the 1866 law, the Fourteenth Amendment, and the 1875 law all were legitimate exercises of federal power to eliminate not only state but private perpetuation of the badges and incidents of slavery, including discrimination in commerce by individuals and corporations. He effectively exposed the racial hypocrisy of the other eight justices, observing that prior to the Civil War, Congress passed laws protecting the right of slaveholders to capture runaway slaves, even when state government was not involved; if Congress had the right to prohibit interference with that private slave-catching activity, Justice Harlan noted, surely it had the same right now to prohibit abridgment by individuals and corporations of black citizens' private sector rights.[2]

If the 1866 law and its successors had been honored, we would not today be a residentially segregated society; the resulting racial inequality would be much diminished. But over the course of the next half century and more, federal, state, and local governments enacted blatantly unconstitutional and unlawful policies that denied entirely to African Americans some benefits that whites enjoyed; provided other benefits to black citizens on dramatically inferior and unequal terms; and blessed private racial discrimination without meaningful restriction. The badges and incidents of slavery flourished.

The result was not only a rigidly segregated society but a black population that was packed into overcrowded "ghettos," denied most employment opportunity except in the most menial and servile jobs, and prohibited from attending well-resourced schools including, in almost all cases, institutions of higher education, except for those explicitly designated for their segregated use (HBCUs).

In the summer of 1967, African Americans rioted to protest their murder and abuse by police in cities nationwide. The precipitating events were little different from those protested in the Black Lives Matter demonstrations of 2020.

In the fall of 1967, President Lyndon B. Johnson appointed a commission to investigate the causes of the summer's uprisings and make recommendations to prevent a recurrence. Headed by Illinois Governor Otto Kerner, it published a report on February 29, 1968.

The panel mentioned a few government programs whose segregation had exacerbated the desperate conditions of black neighborhoods, but its emphasis was on "white society," a phrase that was not otherwise defined. It implied that racial prejudice of white citizens and businesses was the cause of our inequality. In a famous line, the Kerner Commission asserted: "White society is deeply implicated in the ghetto. White institutions created it, white institutions maintain it, and white society condones it." The report concluded that "Our Nation is moving toward two societies, one black, one white—separate and unequal."

The conclusion was conceptually inadequate. It was not "white society" that created our nearly apartheid neighborhood system but a blatantly unconstitutional, unlawful, and racially explicit program at all levels of government to impose residential inequality. Private discrimination was rarely independent of governmental requirements, and racial bigotry could not have found its powerful expression without the blessing of federal, state, and local laws and administrators acting in their official capacities.[3]

State licensing agencies violated their Fourteenth Amendment responsibilities by consistently certifying real estate agents who subscribed to their national association's code of ethics that prohibited giving African Americans access to white neighborhoods. Only a few prominent license denials would have brought an end to the discriminatory system.[4]

Federal and state regulators, flouting their constitutional obligations, protected and sometimes insisted upon practices of national banks and savings and loan associations that redlined African American neighborhoods, denying mortgages to black applicants who lived in low-income urban areas as well as to those who wished to move to newly created suburbs where poverty wasn't concentrated.[5]

For the most part, developers of these new communities were bigots who, if free to discriminate in their purely private capacities, would have refused sales to African Americans. But their racial bias was irrelevant. They required federal subsidies (from the Federal Housing and Veterans Administrations); if agency officials had kept their sworn oaths to uphold the Constitution and required nondiscrimination by the builders, private bigotry would have been inoperative and the new suburbs, affordable at the time to both blacks and whites, would have been open to all.

Federal, state, and local public agencies imposed racial segregation in public housing, sometimes creating greater racial separation than previously existed in the neighborhoods where projects were constructed.[6] *The Color of Law* describes these and other policies at all levels of government, many racially explicit, and others that barely disguised a discriminatory racial motivation.

Terming all this simply "white society" named no perpetrators and so implied no requirement for remediation. Many Americans feel badly about living in a segregated country but with its origins so hidden, it has been difficult to imagine what might be done to fix it. It has been too easy to believe that what happened in so unspecified a way can only be undone in an equally mysterious and accidental fashion.

The Kerner Commission's proposals to attack housing segregation were substantial but, even if implemented (and they mostly weren't), fell far short of the task. Its chief recommendation was a crash 1-year program to construct 600,000 new low- and moderate-income residential units to relieve the overcrowding of segregated black households, with the added goal of a total of 6 million such units by 1973.[7] President Johnson was horrified by the proposal: he needed the funds instead for war in Vietnam, not housing.[8] He needn't have worried—over half a century later, the 6 million goal has barely been reached.[9]

The Kerner Report properly insisted that housing reform should be balanced between improving conditions in low-income segregated neighborhoods and opening white middle-class areas to African American residents. Housing policy advocates typically refer to these as "place-based" and "mobility" efforts, respectively. But in too many cases, federal programs following 1968 reinforced segregation rather than diminished it. The largest of the subsequent efforts has been a tax credit program, adopted 20 years later, for builders of low-income housing. States, with input from the public, adopt regulations to determine which projects receive the subsidy. These allocation plans often include incentives to place the projects in low-income communities; for example, to win the tax credits, developers should demonstrate community support, much less likely to be won in middle-class neighborhoods.[10]

Two months after the Kerner Commission released its report and in the wake of the assassination of the Rev. Dr. Martin Luther King Jr., Congress passed and President Johnson signed the Civil Rights Act of 1968, including the Fair Housing Act that banned public and private racial discrimination in the sale and rental of housing, reiterating what had already been prohibited in the post-Civil War years.

And then in June 1968, a month and a half after passage of the Fair Housing Act, the Supreme Court concluded in the underappreciated case of *Jones v. Mayer* that it had been wrong back in the 19th century.[11] The Civil Rights Act of 1866, the justices now found, had actually been a reasonable implementation of the Thirteenth Amendment's authority for Congress to ban the badges and incidents of slavery, including private as well as public racial discrimination. The justices offered no remedies for the Court's instigation of 102 years of unlawful imposition upon African Americans of second-class citizenship, with its enormous multigenerational consequences. Let bygones be bygones was the result, with the 1883 ruling deemed only an honest mistake of justices who had misinterpreted Section 2.[12]

Jones v. Mayer was announced just 3½ months after the Kerner Report's release. What if the sequence had been reversed and, with *Jones v. Mayer* having transformed its understanding, the commission had reconsidered the Thirteenth Amendment's implications? Might it have recognized that the depredations of "white society," however private they might have been, were nonetheless unlawful as defined by the 1866 Civil Rights Act, and required remedy? Might the Kerner Commission have judged that its forthcoming recommendations, controversial though they already were, were insufficient to rise to the challenge of redressing a century of an unconstitutional and unlawful public–private partnership to impose rigid segregation on American cities?[13]

With their report preceding *Jones v. Mayer*, Kerner commissioners were undoubtedly aware of a well-known (at the time) lower court opinion from 3 years previous. In 1965, John Lewis on behalf of the Student Nonviolent Coordinating Committee, Hosea Williams on behalf of the Southern Christian Leadership Conference, and other civil rights leaders applied for a permit to march from Selma to Montgomery to protest Alabama's nearly universal denial to African Americans of the right to register to vote. The state rejected the permit application, claiming that the burdens of police protection and highway closure were too great to allow the march. The activists sued in the court of federal district judge Frank Johnson, seeking an order to allow the march.

Judge Johnson was one of the few southern jurists who cared about civil rights, although he was not convinced that the movement's First Amendment right to protest outweighed the public inconvenience of closing a highway and risking violence. But his courtroom was a better bet than most for a favorable decision—9 years earlier he had exonerated Rosa Parks and ruled that Montgomery's bus segregation ordinance was unconstitutional.

To evaluate the request for permission to march, Judge Johnson researched the exclusion of African Americans from voting and created a table that listed the counties in Alabama's "black belt," with month-by-month data during the prior half-dozen years, showing the number of blacks and whites who were eligible to vote and those who were permitted to register: zero or nearly so in almost all cases for the black citizens who had attempted to do so.

The judge then not only ordered that marchers be given a permit but included his table as an appendix to an explanation for the ruling. He stated that the remedy for a constitutional violation "should be commensurate with the enormity of the wrongs" that require it.[14] This principle of proportionality was commonplace in American civil cases—remedies for suffering ought to be scaled to the seriousness of an injury—but not in constitutional law, although it made perfect sense that it should be.

The remedies of neighborhood segregation proposed by the Kerner Commission were not commensurate with the enormity of the unconstitutional and unlawful policies and practices that it purported to address. It would have been difficult for the commission to do so if it could get no more specific than to lay responsibility for the harms at the feet of "white society."

(II)

There is yet no public or political will to adopt national remedies that are commensurate with the enormity of the damage segregation has caused. Yet although federal policy played an important role in the imposition of racial segregation, its sustenance is now often maintained and even exacerbated by local programs and practices. The 20 million Americans who participated in racial justice protests and marches in 2020—black, white, and of other ethnicities, from low-income as well as middle-class and affluent neighborhoods—are a potential base for a reinvigorated activist civil rights movement that could begin the redress of segregation in their own communities. After the demonstrations were over, however, too many went home, put Black Lives Matter signs in their windows and on lawns, and did nothing further to make their posters' call a reality. In large part, they did not know what to do, and nobody asked them to do anything.

Our 2023 book *Just Action* describes many local programs and practices that reinforce racial segregation and suggests how community groups could challenge them to win significant victories. We begin by noting that few blacks and whites now have the biracial and multiethnic social relationships that could undergird a reinvigorated activist civil rights movement. Many Americans interact with other races in their workplaces but then return to segregated neighborhoods where their conversations about personal, social, or political issues almost exclusively take place with people of similar racial and ethnic backgrounds. This makes building the relationships needed for an effective movement seem daunting, but it is not impossible.

Just Action introduces Tonika Johnson, an African American photographer from Englewood, a neighborhood on Chicago's mostly black south side where median incomes and homeownership rates are lower and poverty rates are higher than in the mostly white neighborhoods on the north side.

Ms. Johnson took photos of similar homes on each side of the city, equally distant from downtown. She then asked the residents if they'd like to meet their house "twins." Most had never been to the other-race side of Chicago, even if they'd lived in the city all their lives. Many agreed to her request, met at each other's homes, and took their twin on a neighborhood tour.

The twins found they had much in common and developed real friendships. They met regularly, supported each other's businesses, and visited each other's communities. One set created "block twins" to include their neighbors. A white group went to their twins' area to clean and paint abandoned houses and plant flowers. They held regular social events, created a newsletter, and continued to meet over Zoom during the pandemic.

The twins may not become activists. The groups they've formed don't (yet) campaign for policy change to redress the segregated areas they span. But Tonika Johnson's project demonstrates that building relationships and coalitions across segregated neighborhoods is achievable.

To build on such relationships to create committees that can redress segregation, a group might begin by learning how its own city segregated. In several communities we profile in *Just Action*—Charlottesville, Virginia; Modesto, California; Rochester, New York; San Mateo, California—residents researched racially restrictive clauses in their property deeds. These covenants, sometimes required by federal agencies for subsidized suburban developments, specified that a property could only be owned or occupied by whites.

Some states have attempted to simplify removal of this offensive deed language. When successful, advocates may feel that removing or obliterating the clause is a victory because it relieves their discomfort of knowing they live in a once-segregated community. But erasing evidence of past sins can remove a source of motivation to atone. If restrictive covenants had been removed in Charlottesville, Modesto, Rochester, and San Mateo, those communities would likely not have delved into their histories and begun programs of remediation.

Localities can follow the example of Marin County, California, which allows a homeowner to request the county to certify that its deed includes illegal language that is inconsistent with community values. The clerk then staples a denunciation of the clause atop the original. This repudiates the offensive history while preserving opportunities to learn from it.

In many other cities, activists have used racially restrictive covenants to illustrate metropolitan educational campaigns, with lectures at churches, synagogues, service clubs, schools, and neighborhood tours. As residents learned more, opportunities for remedy presented themselves.

The deed clauses are dramatic and visual. But their impact on current efforts to challenge segregation can extend beyond helping a community learn its history: The documents' signature pages frequently name the banks, realtors, developers, and government agencies that imposed the racial restriction. For example, covenants publicized in the four illustrative cities described in *Just Action* identify perpetrators of segregation—the American Trust Company, Bohannon Company, Coldwell Banker, Eastman Kodak, Howard Hanna, Lee Building Company, Virginia National Bank, Wells Fargo, various other realtors and builders, as well as local and federal government agencies. Community groups can organize campaigns to press the firms that created their cities' segregation to take an active role, political and financial, to remedy it. In some cases, the original signatories later merged with larger firms. Successors should be considered to have absorbed not only the financial assets and liabilities of companies they acquired, but the moral liabilities as well. Residents can urge and expect these institutions to contribute to remedies for segregation.

Once groups form to challenge segregation, there are many remedial actions they can pursue. Some committees may choose to focus on improving resources in existing lower-income black neighborhoods, where poverty concentration results from governmentally imposed segregation. These approaches should be coupled with work to resist the displacement of black and Hispanic residents as resources improve and the areas become more desirable and expensive, even gentrifying. Inclusionary zoning, property-tax relief, creation of land trusts to keep housing prices affordable, and protection of renters from eviction are among the possible efforts. *Just Action* describes campaigns of community groups against banks that frequently issued loans to apartment owners whose ability to repay depended on eviction of existing renters so higher-paying tenants could be recruited.[15]

Other committees may begin by pressing for changes that open up exclusive white neighborhoods to diverse residents and stabilize the desegregation of newly diverse areas. Zoning reform, support for mixed-income housing development, removal of barriers that subsidized renters face when attempting to move to higher-cost areas, and homeownership assistance for African Americans are among the potential strategies. The Kerner Commission insisted that both types of reforms—"place-based" and "mobility"—are essential and should be in balance. Which approach any group may initiate will vary, based on its unique interests, opportunities, and challenges. What is important is to start somewhere and allow small victories to build toward larger ones.

(III)

Once federal policies led to the creation of two societies, one black and one white, separate and unequal, race-neutral policies and practices exacerbated the inequality. An example is our property tax system that has a disparate impact on African American households. In almost every city and county nationwide, black homeowners pay property taxes at a higher rate relative to the value of their homes than white homeowners do.[16] There are many reasons for this; one is that most city and county assessors don't physically inspect properties annually. Sometimes they wait decades to reassess, with an annual inflation adjustment as a substitute. Between the actual assessments, homes in white neighborhoods tend to appreciate in value faster. Over time, their assessed values fall farther below real sale prices than assessed values of homes in black neighborhoods. The result is that African Americans usually pay higher taxes than whites pay relative to their properties' market prices.

Renters in lower-income areas also suffer because for similar reasons their landlords' property taxes are also discriminatorily high, with the costs passed on to tenants. Black households, owners and renters, then bear an unfairly greater burden of financing their cities or county's schools, libraries, fire departments, and other public services that local taxes support. The inequality in neighborhoods was created in large part by the federal government but assessment practices that increase that inequality are a purely local problem. The discriminatory system is no mystery. City and county assessors know it but they won't have an incentive to fix it unless forced to do so. That's where a local activist group can engage.

(IV)

Not all ongoing segregation results from the disparate impact of facially race-neutral policy. Openly discriminatory violations of the Fair Housing Act also continue and beg for remedy by local community organizations.

Newsday, a newspaper on Long Island east of New York City, investigated continued unlawful practices of real estate agents in 2019 with a "paired testing" program, sending pretend home buyers, one black, one white, to a real estate agent, a short while apart. The testers came with nearly identical financial records, ability to afford the home, family characteristics, and professional backgrounds. An editor who oversaw the project went so far as to purchase identical purses for the black and white testers. The testers wore hidden cameras to record their interactions with agents. (Most states permit such one-way recording.) *Newsday* reported that black testers received discriminatory treatment in 50% of their realtor interactions. For Hispanics it was 40%, for Asians 20%. They were shown different homes and different areas than equally qualified white pairs. Other-race testers were given different information about the same neighborhood; those of one race told it was a great place, those of the other race that they "wouldn't want to live there."

Reporters also observed refresher courses required of realtors for license renewal. States require that nondiscrimination training be included, but it was given short shrift. In one course, the instructor, a former president of the local realtors' association, explained that nondiscrimination is like highway speed limits: if you are in a rush, "you get to choose whether you break the law."

There is no reason to think that the behavior of realtors on Long Island is much different from that of those in any metropolis nationwide.

Black home seekers who get information from real estate offices have no way to realize they experienced unlawful treatment. They can't know that a white client received different and better information about homes for sale. The only way to identify this unlawful discrimination is with a paired testing program like the newspaper sponsored. Similar testing can uncover discriminatory practices by landlords of rental units.

Fair housing centers in cities across the country conduct paired testing. But with only small federal grants and some additional foundation support, the centers don't have funds to do much of it. Local civil rights groups could recruit volunteer testers, in short supply in most communities, and raise funds to support the work. When fair housing centers uncover discrimination, they can (and do) pursue legal action against an offending realtor or landlord. Activists can go further and campaign to force state licensing agencies to lift the accreditation of agents who discriminate. New York State violated its Fourteenth Amendment obligations when it renewed licenses of agents who took courses with deficient fair housing training, such as those monitored by *Newsday*.

Neighborhood inequality that discriminatory practice exploits may have been created by the federal government, but remedies are in local control. Like reform of tax assessment policy, enforcement of nondiscrimination in the sale and rental of housing is within the capacity of local organizations.

(V)

Most of us want to live in areas with low crime, well-resourced schools, open space, markets that sell fresh and healthy food, access to jobs and the transportation to reach them, and good retail options. These are commonly termed "high opportunity" neighborhoods. But most lower-income families, and especially those who are African American, don't live in such places.

The Kerner Report recommended a voucher program to enable low-income households to escape poorly resourced communities, but the Section 8 program (authorized in 1974) has resulted in only 5% of voucher holders living in high opportunity places, and African American recipients are less likely to do so than whites. The result: Section 8 has reinforced segregation. Program rules have made this nearly inevitable. Administered by local public housing authorities, the voucher was designed to permit households with incomes of up to 80% of their metropolitan area median to spend no more than 30% of that income on rent. (Currently, however, HUD requires that three-fourths of vouchers must go to those earning no more than about one-third of the area median.) Vouchers are to make up the difference between households' 30% of income share and a bit below the mid-point of all the area's rents. The result was that recipients were unable to afford most of the area's units: those in the high-opportunity places to which the vouchers had been intended to give access. The affordable lowest-cost apartments are almost all located in lower-income neighborhoods.

In 2010, the Inclusive Communities Project of Dallas sued its housing authority, claiming that such operation of Section 8 violated the Fair Housing Act by intensifying segregation. A settlement required two housing authorities in the Dallas region to base voucher amounts on median rents of smaller local areas so that the maximum Section 8 contribution would be higher in higher-cost areas and lower where costs were less. HUD then required housing authorities in 23 additional metropolitan areas to adopt this small-area fair market rent standard (SAFMR). Beginning in 2025, housing authorities in another 41 metropolitan areas must also use SAFMR calculations. Other housing authorities are permitted to adopt them without a HUD mandate. Community groups should monitor their public housing authorities to ensure that they faithfully implement SAFMRs, where required, and campaign for others to use them voluntarily. With the added metropolitan areas, almost half of Section 8 households nationwide will have access to higher opportunity communities—if landlords will rent to them.

Building owners in more middle-class areas frequently refuse to accept Section 8 applicants. The federal government allows this, but 20 states and over 100 localities have outlawed such discrimination. Campaigning for the prohibition elsewhere is another opportunity for local activists—as is enforcement where discrimination is banned on the books but still practiced.

Paired testing here too can play a role, even where Section 8 discrimination is permitted but landlords' true bias is racial. Apartment owners who tell white testers with vouchers that units are available but tell black testers that they do not accept Section 8 are using allowable source-of-income discrimination as a pretext for racial exclusion, a violation of the Fair Housing Act.

Some jurisdictions have gone further and adopted comprehensive mobility programs to help voucher holders move to higher-opportunity locales. They provide counselors who help participants look for and apply for units in these neighborhoods, navigate the application process, and settle into neighborhoods with which they may be unfamiliar. Staff educate landlords in higher-cost areas to demolish negative stereotypes about Section 8, and recruit them to rent to voucher households. Mobility support can also include financial aid to help with higher security deposits, rental application fees, and moving expenses. These programs are often run by housing organizations with the cooperation of local public housing authorities and with foundation funding.

(VI)

Local groups can undertake many other policies described in *Just Action* that begin the process of redressing segregation and fulfilling a promise at which the Kerner Commission's report only hinted. But its warning that if we did not take such actions we would become two racially distinct (and frequently mutually hostile) societies has not only become reality but been surpassed. Although progress has been made in some areas of American life, most notably in the growth of a well-educated black middle class that has desegregated many workplaces, we are more segregated residentially than we were in 1968. Civil rights advocates devote too much of their time and effort proposing federal reforms with little chance of enactment. The place to start is local, mobilizing neighbors to act to redress segregation in their own communities.

NOTES

1. Civil Rights Cases, 109 U.S. 3 (1883), 22, https://www.law.cornell.edu/supremecourt/text/109/3.

2. Civil Rights Cases, 28.

3. Richard Rothstein, *The Color of Law: A Forgotten History of How Our Government Segregated America* (New York: Liveright, 2017).

4. Richard Rothstein and Leah Rothstein, *Just Action: How to Challenge Segregation Enacted Under the Color of Law* (New York: Liveright, 2023), 207–09.

5. Federal Reserve Board Chairman William McChesney Martin testified in 1961 that it was unnecessary for the board to include prohibition of racial discrimination in its bank regulatory policy because if a black family was denied a loan because of race, "the forces of competition" would ensure that another bank would come forward to make the loan. Rothstein, *The Color of Law*, 107–09.

6. For illustrations of how public housing policy created segregation in Austin, Texas, Cambridge, Massachusetts and Cleveland, Ohio, see Rothstein, *The Color of Law*, 23–24, 26, and 172–73, respectively.

7. The National Advisory Commission on Civil Disorders, *The Kerner Report* (Princeton, NJ: Princeton University Press, 2016), 471.

8. *The Kerner Report*, "Foreword" by Julian E. Zelizer, xxxii–xxxiii.

9. A total of about 6.2 million low- and moderate-income units have been created by all federal programs and subsidies in the 55 years since 1968. If we subtract from that total the units destroyed by urban renewal and the abandonment of many public housing projects, it seems that we still have not reached the Kerner Commission's 10-year goal of 6 million net new units. We are grateful to Alexander von Hoffman, senior research fellow at the Joint Center for Housing Studies at Harvard University, for his assistance in our development of this estimate.

10. Rothstein and Rothstein, *Just Action*, 183–85. The Low-Income Housing Tax Credit Program was created in 1986.

11. Jones v. Alfred H. Mayer Co, 392 U.S. 409 (1968), http://www.law.cornell.edu/supct/html/historics/USSC_CR_0392_0409_ZS.html.

12. Splitting hairs, the Court in *Jones v. Mayer* claimed it wasn't really overruling its 1883 decision because that opinion only asserted that the 1875 law prohibiting discrimination in public accommodations was unconstitutional and did not address the issue of discrimination in the sale and rental of property. Instead, the Court said it was overruling a 1906 decision that permitted private discrimination in employment. The distinction made no sense because the 1883 majority accepted a definition of the badges and incidents of slavery that specifically included property rights.

13. The 1866 Civil Rights Act did not provide a governmental enforcement mechanism for violations. The only recourse for an individual African American who was denied the civil right of having the same access to property as whites was to initiate a civil suit.

14. Williams v. Wallace, 240 F. Supp. 100 (M.D. Ala. 1965), https://law.justia.com/cases/federal/district-courts/FSupp/240/100/2145163.

15. The two banks were First Republic Bank in California and Signature Bank in New York. Both banks later failed, nearly provoking a panic that, if it were to spread, would have put the entire financial system at risk. One reason for the banks' failures, not the most important one, was that both were overinvested in loans made to owners of large multiunit apartment buildings.

16. Rothstein and Rothstein, *Just Action*, 143–51. Christopher Berry's interactive website provides estimates for many cities and counties of tax regressivity, the extent to which homeowners in lower-income neighborhoods have a higher effective tax rate than those in higher-income neighborhoods. Christopher Berry, *Property Tax Fairness, Interactive Reports*, The Center on Municipal Finance, Harris School of Public Policy, University of Chicago, https://propertytaxproject.uchicago.edu.

Public Health Policy

CHAPTER 17

An Accidental Public Health Manifesto

Michelle A. Williams

The Kerner Commission's membership reflected a commitment to diversity of ideology, geography, and experience, consisting of federal and state officials from both parties as well as representatives from organized labor, industry, the Civil Rights movement, and law enforcement. But the panel's diversity did not extend to race and gender. The 11-member commission included just two people of color (Black men, more specifically), and only one (white) woman. By centering the opinions of white men on the struggles plaguing Black communities, the Kerner Commission was a product of its time. Yet, remarkably, this group was able to produce a report far ahead of its time.

Instead of narrowly focusing on the riots that dominated news coverage, the Kerner Commission dug into the underlying and systemic causes making life disproportionately difficult for Black Americans: economic fragility, police brutality, a struggling educational system, housing insecurity, and more. Famously, the commission concluded that "Our Nation is moving toward two societies, one black, one white—separate and unequal."[1] To their credit, the commissioners also identified the culprit by boldly highlighting white America's complicity in establishing and maintaining the racial hierarchy fueling the unrest.

The Kerner Commission's suggestions were driven by a fundamental understanding that American life was stacked against Black people; members recognized the best way to prevent future riots was to overhaul the system that inflicted disproportionate pain and suffering on Black Americans. By rooting their work in the desire to spur societal change that improved overall well-being, the Kerner Commission was advancing a public health agenda—even if they didn't know what to call it.

AHEAD OF ITS TIME ON PUBLIC HEALTH

The Kerner Commission did not spend much of its time engaging directly with health; throughout the report's hundreds of pages, the concept is only explicitly mentioned a handful of times. There is a particular subsection devoted to health disparities, in which the commission writes: "The residents of the racial ghetto are significantly less healthy than most other Americans. They suffer from higher mortality rates, higher incidence of major diseases, and lower availability and utilization of medical services."[2] This introduction, and the handful of ensuing charts, is the extent of the commission's direct examination of health; even in its final recommendations, the report does not offer suggestions to address the extreme health disparities presented earlier in the volume. The omission is understandable, both due to the panel's assignment to focus on "civil disorders" and the commissioners' lack of medical or public health expertise. However, just because they lacked the vocabulary to talk about public health does not mean they ignored it; in fact, the report is filled with discussions of some of the field's core pillars.

First, a definition: Public health is not limited to the treatment that happens in doctors' offices and hospital rooms. Access to medical care is certainly a key concern for public health—but it is also about making sure that all people can live in safe communities, access sufficient nutrition, attend good schools, and pursue gainful employment, among other critical factors that contribute to our overall health. In short: The field's goal is to holistically improve the well-being of all people.

There isn't a single sector in society where public health does not play a pivotal role—a fact that was painfully obvious during the COVID-19 pandemic. The crisis made it clear that our health is overwhelmingly defined by events and circumstances outside the acute triggers of medical emergency—the jobs we work, the neighborhoods we live in, the quality of health care we receive.

Those factors were key reasons that Black people died from COVID-19 at nearly double the rates of white people.[3] But the COVID-19 pandemic did not create these racial disparities in health. The virus isn't the reason that Black babies are twice as likely as white babies to die before their first birthday, or that Black adults are at significantly higher risk of heart disease or Alzheimer's. The pandemic simply highlighted a painful but longstanding truth: From the moment a baby is born to the moment they draw their last breath, Black Americans are fighting for their lives on an uneven playing field.

The commission argued that we cannot ignore the hardships of the least fortunate, stating, "None of us can escape the consequences of the continuing economic and social decay of the central city and the closely related problem of rural poverty."[4] In other words: When we look the other way instead of acting to correct injustice, the rot spreads. Unfortunately, that is where we find ourselves today. Despite spending 16.6% of our national GDP on health care—80% higher than the averaged developed nation—American health outcomes lag far behind our peers on critical metrics including avoidable deaths, obesity, and infant mortality.[5] Obviously, the problem isn't how much we're spending; if increased investment correlated to better results, America would be the healthiest nation on Earth. Instead, the issue is how we are spending our money. In 2021, only 4.5% of our health care dollars were spent on the preventative measures associated with public health, and that was after the emergence of the COVID-19 pandemic that forced the government to mobilize resources for testing, tracing, and research. That lopsided ratio has contributed to America's worsening life expectancy—not just for people of color, but for all people.[6]

The most important change we can make is to shift our mindset from one of treatment to one of prevention and primary care. That means not only relying on our incredible high-tech interventions to work medical miracles; we must also prioritize high-touch medical care and implement improved safety nets at all levels of society to address troubles before they spiral into emergencies. Fortunately, we don't have to reinvent the wheel in this quest for a better world. The Kerner Commission's unfulfilled vision for a stronger, unified society is a great place to start; by combining its recommendations with more than 50 years' worth of public health expertise, we have an opportunity to bring about significant change.

WEALTH BEGETS HEALTH

If you close your eyes and picture Boston in your mind, you'll likely conjure an image of someplace that looks like the Back Bay neighborhood. The area resembles the quintessential image of Boston that has traveled across the world; cobblestone sidewalks lined with 18th-century brownstones alongside modern centers of business and commerce.

Take the T just a couple of stops south to the geographic heart of the city, and you'll find yourself in Roxbury. You likely won't see this neighborhood on a postcard, but it still vibrates with life and activity; the area is densely populated with homes and businesses, and is home to Franklin Park, the city's largest green space, offering woods, a golf course, and a large zoo.

Despite being just a few miles apart, these neighborhoods have deep differences beyond just the architecture. Recent data from the Boston Planning & Development Agency tells us that

- Back Bay is more than 75% white, while Roxbury is more than 50% Black;
- Back Bay's median income in 2015 was nearly $90,000, while Roxbury's was less than $26,000; and
- 86% of Back Bay's residents over the age of 25 had received a bachelor's degree or higher, while only 2% did not complete a high school degree. In contrast, only 21% of Roxbury residents attained a bachelor's or higher and 25% did not finish high school.[7]

All these statistics contribute to the most shocking and disturbing figure: People in Back Bay have a life expectancy of close to 90 years. Just a few miles away in Roxbury, that life expectancy plummets to closer to 60 years.[8] We are talking about people living in the same city—neighbors!—who, for all intents and purposes, are living worlds apart. Boston isn't unique in this disparity. Across the country, life expectancy drops in areas where a large proportion of the population have not graduated from high school and are low income or unemployed.[9]

The old saying tells us that "health is wealth"—shorthand for the idea that no amount of money can substitute for physical, mental, and spiritual prosperity. That's true, of course, but an inverse formulation is equally important: "wealth begets health." The presence of wealth allows individuals to invest in building blocks of life that define 80 to 90% of our health. They can eat good whole foods, maintain a stable home in a nonpolluted neighborhood, and avoid financial stresses that undermine mental health.

On the other hand, the absence of wealth fuels and exacerbates health obstacles. For example, Black people are nearly 20% more likely to be obese and 60% more likely to be diagnosed with diabetes—both of which are driven in part by lack of access to healthy foods and safe exercise spaces.[10] They are 2.5 times more likely to be hospitalized due to diabetes and associated long-term complications than white people—which is impacted by their higher likelihood of housing insecurity, creating challenges to consistent treatment of chronic conditions.[11] Black children are five times more likely to die from asthma than white children—which is directly connected to the fact that families of color are far likelier to live in communities blanketed in pollution.[12] These are not genetic issues; underlying each of these statistics is the fact that Black Americans are more than twice as likely to live in poverty as white Americans.

Clearly, wealth supports health—which is why the racism inherent in American life continues to hold back Black health. From its very founding, America was built on the exploitation of Black people. Slavery facilitated American prosperity, but neither the enslaved people nor their descendants reaped the fruits of that labor. The Homestead Act, the GI Bill, federal mortgage protections—at every turn in our nation's history, policies have been designed to bolster the white middle class while leaving Black folks on the outside looking in. A white ruling class has erected barriers to prosperity time and again; as a result, Black people have been blocked time and again from accumulating and passing down generational wealth.[13] The data are stark: In 2019, the median white household possessed a wealth of $188,200, while the median Black household held only $24,100. That means we're dealing with a wealth disparity of nearly 800%—talk about compound interest at work.[14]

That increased wealth does not only inform present-day decisions for Black families; thanks to America's education system, it also helps define their future. Higher educational attainment is central to improved health, and the privileges of wealth are prevalent at every step in the educational ladder.[15] The advantages are baked into the mechanisms that determine public school funding. Most school funding comes from local and state taxes, meaning that wealthier communities will benefit from better-resourced schools. In addition, rising higher education costs mean that the average Black young adult, who is less likely to come from family wealth, is more likely to take out student loans and on average borrows more than their white classmates in order to pursue a college degree.[16] In a nation where higher educational attainment is key to financial success and long-term health, Black youth continue to find themselves locked out.

When we review these figures, we are seeing the results of societal priorities. The Kerner Commission spent much of its report tackling these policy choices and urging a new path forward—with specific attention paid to opportunities to close wealth gaps, improve education in Black neighborhoods, and address housing discrimination. The commissioners might not have recognized it, but they were recommending policies to address the social determinants of health.

RACISM IS A PUBLIC HEALTH CRISIS

Of course, not all health inequities plaguing Black Americans are the result of an intersection between race and class. Some are just racism, pure and simple.

We saw a clear example of racism's damage to Black health in June 2020, when, against the backdrop of the COVID-19 pandemic, a familiar public health crisis took center stage. After the nation watched the video footage of George Floyd's murder by a police officer, reaction was swift and fierce as protests spilled into the streets of Minneapolis and other cities. The entire scene—police brutality to a Black body, a subsequent outcry, and ensuing conflicts between protesters and law enforcement—painfully echoed the "civil disorders" that prompted the creation of the Kerner Commission more than a half century earlier.

The painful truth is that in the years since the Kerner Commission, police brutality has continued unabated. Eric Garner in Staten Island. Freddie Gray in Baltimore. Breonna Taylor in Louisville. Michael Brown in Ferguson. Rodney King in Los Angeles. The list goes on and on, stretching across the country and back in time, as Black lives are extinguished by those appointed to "protect and serve" the citizenry. Black people are nearly three times as likely to die at the hands of the police than their white counterparts.[17]

The Kerner Commission listed police practices as the single most deeply held grievance by Black communities, and extensively explored opportunities to rebuild trust between the police and the communities they are meant to protect.[18] The commission proposed several solutions to mend the relationship. Some, like efforts to review procedures to ensure proper conduct and "establish fair and effective mechanisms for the redress of grievances," have been stymied by public policies such as qualified immunity and outright opposition from police unions, who are more likely to close ranks around an officer accused of misconduct than support accountability measures.[19] Other suggestions, like recruiting more Black police officers, have been accomplished without significant impact; in 2023, we saw the beating and killing of Tyre Nichols in Memphis committed by five Black officers. Simply because a police officer is Black does not mean they are incapable of possessing implicit biases or perpetuating a racist system.

The damage inflicted on Black health by police brutality does not end with physical violence. Research from my Harvard colleague David R. Williams found that after an unarmed Black person is killed by police, Black people in the state where the violence took place reported poorer mental health in the following weeks.[20] The study found that white people's mental health was unaffected. The damage may be even more widespread, as the proliferation of videos of this brutality—which can now be quickly and widely spread on social media, without the news media's participation—means more Black people are forced to bear witness to the trauma. It seems that every few months, a new hashtag arrives to remind us that even the most mundane of activities is unsafe if performed by those with Black skin.

Law enforcement drew significant attention from the Kerner Commission, but it is not the only profession eyed with distrust from many Black Americans. A wide body of research shows that many Black people harbor significant distrust in medical professionals, informed by both personal experiences and from the dark legacy of Black Americans being used in unethical studies like the Tuskegee Syphilis Experiment.[21] This wariness is not misplaced; research tells us that Black patients' pain is taken less seriously due to racial bias and that Black people in every age group are less likely to receive quality health care than white people.[22] Both this trust deficit and the subpar care are influenced by the underrepresentation of Black people in medicine—only 5.7% of American doctors are Black, compared to roughly 12% of the overall population.[23]

Nowhere is the gap in care for Black and white patients more egregious than in maternal mortality. America's overall record on maternal mortality is abysmal compared to peer nations; in 2020, the maternal mortality rate for white women is 19.1 deaths per 100,000 live births, nearly double the average for the industrialized democracies in the Organization for Economic Co-operation and Development.[24] That is an awful statistic—but it pales in comparison to the danger for Black women, who face a maternal mortality rate of 55.3 deaths per 100,000 live births. These numbers point to two undeniable facts: The richest country on Earth is failing the health of all mothers and children, and Black women are bearing by far the heaviest burden.

These gaps persist even when researchers control for wealth, telling us that no Black woman—no matter how rich—is safe from this crisis. We received a glaring example of this in 2022, when Serena Williams, one of the greatest tennis players of all time, shared her challenging birth experience in an essay for *Elle* magazine.[25] In the piece, Williams detailed how she needed to continually urge her care team to consider her history of blood clots during a wave of post-birth complications and surgeries. She eventually told her nurse the specific test she needed; the doctor granted her request, and the test found clots in her lungs. Take a step back and look at the circumstances of the story: Williams is a world-class athlete who knows her body well, has a strong family support, and is able to afford the best care money can buy—and even still, her birth experience nearly ended in catastrophe. If these are the obstacles facing Serena Williams, what hope does an average Black woman have?

Unfortunately, the Supreme Court's decision to overturn *Roe v. Wade*'s abortion protections means that America's horrific record on maternal mortality is likely to get worse before it gets better. The Court's decision to rip away long-established reproductive rights and the ensuing state legislation enacting strict abortion bans will force some women to carry unwanted pregnancies to term, a uniquely dangerous prospect for Black women.[26] These laws have also raised questions about whether obstetricians can legally perform life-saving procedures in crisis situations, causing some specialists to move their practices, leaving maternity deserts in their wake.[27] Sadly, poor policy choices are going to cost even more lives in the years ahead.

These biases—from law enforcement, the medical establishment, and countless other sources throughout American life—wear on Black people both mentally and physically. The psychological strain of ever-present discrimination contributes to a life of heightened stress. Studies conducted by Arline Geronimus, among others, have found evidence that exposure to racism accelerates aging, creating a phenomenon known as "weathering."[28] Through both individual acts and systemic forces, racism leaves a mark on Black lives; the Kerner Commission's minimal focus on health outcomes means that the report could not recognize just how deep the damage ran.

RACISM SPURS UNDERINVESTMENT IN PUBLIC HEALTH—AND HARMS ALL

Though the Kerner Commission's attention to health was limited, they did recognize that the stakes of American inequities expanded beyond the impact on Black people. "Much of our report is directed to the condition of those Americans who are also Negroes and to the social and economic environments in which they live—many in the black ghettos of our cities," the commission wrote in their report. "But our nation is confronted with the issue of justice for all its people—white as well as black, rural as well as urban." In the immortal (and pithier) words of Martin Luther King, Jr.: "Injustice anywhere is a threat to justice everywhere."[29]

The idea that racism harms white people as well was explored in depth in *The Sum of Us*, an excellent public health book from Heather McGhee. Reaching across disciplines and back through history, McGhee details again and again how racial animus against Blacks has prevented whites from acting in their own self-interest. The book provides real-life examples of how racial resentment leads to worse outcomes for all, from communities draining swimming pools to avoid integration to racial squabbles derailing unionization efforts and harming workers.[30] McGhee chalks it up to the zero-sum mindset; "I may not have much," low-income whites think, "but at least I have more than them."[31] The zero-sum philosophy is misguided, of course; America is the wealthiest country in the world, and we have the capability to take care of each of our citizens with the proper political will. We can make investments and commitments that improve quality of life for not only Black people, but also white people and Asian people and Hispanic people and Native people. But unfortunately, racism is holding us back—and our broken health care system is an important example of how that is happening.

America stands alone as the world's sole industrialized nation without universal health insurance—a distinction that contributes to poorer health outcomes and inefficiency in how our health care dollars are spent.[32] According to the U.S. Census Bureau, 8.6% of Americans went without health insurance in 2021—making them less likely to seek out care to address their medical needs, and putting them just one severe injury or illness away from financial ruin. Looking at a demographic breakdown does not bring any surprises; 9.6% of Black Americans were uninsured, compared to only 5.4% of white people. This racial disparity was not an unexpected side effect; in fact, racism has been a central part of campaigns against more expansive public insurance dating back to pre-Kerner.[33] The racialization of health care reform, however, hit a fever pitch following President Barack Obama's election. Studies have found that white people who displayed higher levels of racial resentment were significantly more opposed to a health care reform if they thought it was proposed by President Obama.[34] This race-based opposition is part of the reason why 10 states have still refused to expand Medicaid under the Affordable Care Act—even though the expansion would significantly ease burdens for both patients and health care providers.[35]

Texas is among the 10 states standing strong against additional Medicaid dollars, despite being in desperate need of the help. Adopting the ACA's expansion would extend new coverage to about 1.5 million uninsured Texans, and the benefits wouldn't just help people of color. One of the state's biggest beneficiaries would be rural hospitals, which are facing an existential crisis. These hospitals are the lifeblood of rural, largely white communities, creating jobs and providing the basic medical infrastructure needed to support health. When these hospitals close or limit services—as 21 Texas hospitals have over the last decade—the whole community suffers.[36] However, that suffering is apparently not enough for the predominantly white legislators who control the levers of change, or the predominantly white rural residents who continue to elect them. Similar crises are playing out in the other states refusing Medicaid expansion, as race-fueled opposition threatens to upend rural life.[37] The Kerner Commission famously wrote that "white society is deeply implicated" in the hardships facing Black people; today, it is obvious that white people cannot escape the consequences of structural racism either.[38]

LEARNING FROM THE PAST AND PROTECTING OUR PROGRESS

The challenges that the Kerner Commission studied are heartbreakingly akin to our current circumstances, with shared difficulties including racial strife, gaping inequalities that grow larger by the day, and millions suffering needlessly across the country. If we had heeded the Kerner Commission's recommendations when they were first offered, our country would look very different today. Unfortunately, inaction triumphed. Instead of addressing our national wounds, we allowed them to fester. Despite the Kerner Commission's best warnings, our society has focused on treating the symptoms instead of the root causes of the illness—or in some cases, simply pretending that there are no symptoms. The whole of the nation is poorer and sicker because of that failure.

Today, we have an opportunity and a responsibility to address these failures. We should start where the Kerner Commission left off when it argued, "Only a greatly enlarged commitment to national action—compassionate, massive, and sustained, backed by the will and resources of the most powerful and the richest nation on this earth—can shape a future that is compatible with the historic ideals of American society."[39] The commission's vision for this national action amounted to a radical antipoverty agenda for the federal government: The plan's cornerstones included establishing a large-scale public jobs program, extending early childhood education to disadvantaged children, taking on responsibility for at least 90% of total welfare payments, and establishing an "ownership supplement program" analogous to rent supplements so low-income families could own homes. The boldness of the suggestions is matched by the nerve of the proposed funding mechanism; the Kerner Commission argued that "the major need is to generate new will—the will to tax ourselves to the extent necessary to meet the vital needs of the Nation."[40]

We could have risen to the Kerner Commission's call. We could have put the needs of the poor ahead of the desires of the wealthy. We could have prioritized the worst off amongst us at the expense of those who could bear the burden. Instead, we have slashed taxes for corporations and the ultra-rich, and sought to make up the difference by hacking away vital components of the social safety net.

We can go forward by looking back. Our first step to support not only Black Americans, but all people in need across our country, should be to summon that new will to implement the ideas the Kerner Commission laid out more than half a century ago.

Beyond seeking to implement the Commission's unrealized goals, we must also recognize that there has been progress in recent years, and we must vigorously challenge those who would roll back that progress. Notably, two key government efforts to counteract the racism ingrained in American society have been undermined by the Supreme Court: affirmative action and voting rights. Both are valuable tools to use against discrimination's long shadow: Affirmative action helps create opportunities for Black youth who may not come from the wealthy families that can afford to support expensive extracurricular activities or SAT tutors, and the Voting Rights Act (VRA) protects Black voters who are too often disenfranchised and politically silenced. Both yield large benefits for society as a whole. Affirmative action helps educational institutions create diverse environments that yield better learning results for students of all backgrounds, and the Voting Rights Act enables increased democratic participation in a government meant to be of, by, and for the people. However, recent Supreme Court rulings have wholly undermined affirmative action and left the VRA hanging in peril, with more legal challenges arriving soon. Protecting these advances will not attenuate the many public health problems that have remained harmful over the last half century—but rolling over and accepting their loss will certainly set us back.

BOLD STEPS FOR A HEALTHIER FUTURE

Enacting the Kerner Commission's unrealized vision and protecting the progress we have made are important ways to close the inequities that harm the health and well-being of Black Americans—but they are not enough. We must do more. Fortunately, we have the benefit of more than 55 years of hindsight and a wealth of scholarship to draw on as we look for bold solutions that will make concrete differences in our public health.

First, the United States should grapple with the destructive legacy of slavery and structural racism by paying reparations to Black Americans. The massive wealth gap between Blacks and whites, which stems from slavery and the racist systems left in its wake, has contributed to the immense health disparities that plague Black people at every age. If done properly, reparations could help close the unacceptable health gaps that linger to this day. There are a variety of options to effectively distribute these funds; some reparations could come in the form direct cash transfers, such as baby bonds—accounts created when a child is born that reach maturity when the child comes of age, giving them the capital needed to pursue wealth-building activities such as higher education, entrepreneurship, or home ownership.[41] Other options include significant investments in schools, environmental justice, or other public projects designed to end obvious inequities. Some will say that reparations are too expensive—but in reality, the status quo is too expensive to maintain. Anti-Black racism has cost the U.S. economy $16 trillion over the past 2 decades, and the costs will continue to accumulate for as long as we continue to hold back a broad swath of our population.[42] The state of California, along with more than a dozen cities nationwide, has recently begun exploring opportunities to implement reparations.[43] Other state and local governments across the country, along with the federal government itself, would do well to follow in their footsteps.

America must also grapple with the scourge of police brutality, which precipitated the initial social disorders studied by the Kerner Commission and continues to inflict harm on Black communities today. The commission proposed a variety of solutions, including new regulations on use of force and diversified police departments, but policies and quotas won't be enough to remake a culture built on the ability to operate with impunity. The most compelling suggestion offered by the Kerner Commission was the creation of a "specialized agency . . . to handle, investigate, and to make recommendations on citizen complaints." Too often, however, these oversight agencies are not fully independent from police and prosecutors. That is why any efforts to hold officers accountable must begin with the end of qualified immunity, which has long been used to shield law enforcement officers from consequences, preventing departments from weeding out the "bad apples" that are spoiling the bunch. When citizens watch acts of brutality go unpunished, their faith in the police and in the justice system suffers. Doing away with qualified immunity and ensuring that a badge does not place an officer above the law will go a long way to both prevent bad behavior and rebuild trust with the community.

The end of qualified immunity should be just the start of the overhauls to the criminal justice system. We also must fight to end the War on Drugs—which was explicitly started as an attempt to target Black people, and has more than fulfilled its goal—and fundamentally rethink how our criminal justice system addresses mental health issues.[44] The War on Drugs has disproportionately funneled Black people—largely Black men—into prisons, handing out long sentences that can create or exacerbate serious mental health problems. The federal government creates this problem; it has the responsibility to solve it, too.

Finally, any effort to bolster the public health of Black people—or any people, really—must include an emphasis on the social determinants of health. We cannot throw more money at medicines or surgeries, then send people back out to unsafe homes with insufficient nutrition and hope for the best. We've seen those results, and they are woeful; instead, it is critical that decision-makers at all levels consider how their choices will impact public health. We can see how the Kerner Commission struggled to explicitly address health inequities due to a knowledge shortfall; to fully realize the commission's goals today, we must learn from that oversight and ensure that public health leaders have seats at every table.

One interesting opportunity for action can be found in North Carolina, which has received a federal waiver allowing the state to create the Healthy Opportunities Pilot. The pilot program enables the state to direct Medicaid dollars to address challenges in Medicaid patients' lives that can't be treated by a doctor, including homelessness, food insecurity, and transportation insecurity.[45] The program's focus on prevention instead of treatment is a model for how we can remake our approach to health care. Additionally, a valuable framework for how state and local governments can incorporate "Health in All Policies" has been proposed by a consortium of health-focused organizations, including the American Public Health Association.[46] The proposal was based on the experiences of the California Health in All Policies Task Force, and emphasizes the need for—and benefits of—wide-scale collaboration that incorporates public health expertise while making seemingly unrelated decisions.

While local, state, and federal governments play a vital role in such efforts, the public sector can't do it alone. Donald Berwick, the former administrator of the Centers for Medicare & Medicaid Services and a longtime champion of public health efforts, has proposed that hospitals and health systems should establish and provide resources to Ten Teams aimed at addressing problems that fuel poor health in their community. The Teams would focus on topics such as health coverage, immigrant needs, climate change, and loneliness—with the goal of catching problems before they rise to the level of hospitalization. This may seem like a daunting expansion of a hospital's mission, but, in fact, it would improve health outcomes and reduce costs. Kaiser Permanente has taken up the charge by pledging $400 million to build affordable housing and invest in economic development in communities with poor health outcomes.[47] Other hospitals and health systems are also moving in this direction, and for-profit companies would be smart to do the same to reap the benefits of healthier and happier employees. On both a moral and a fiscal level, investing in the health of the whole person is the right thing to do.

Now, I must acknowledge that none of these proposed solutions will be easy to achieve. Our current world feels even more divided than the Kerner Commission's, and the distances to bridge between rich and poor, white and Black, and red and blue feel like they grow larger by the day. The Internet and social media allow us to spread vitriol more efficiently than ever before, and getting folks to agree on anything at all feels like a Sisyphean task; just when people start to come together, another crisis will come along and knock the boulder back down the hill.

But there is reason to hope that we can effect change, because nothing spurs action like crisis—and we are facing ample crises. American life expectancy is dropping, and dissatisfaction with our health care system is growing. Both problems are likely to be exacerbated by looming challenges including climate change and shortages of health care providers. Faced with an existential threat to our health, we will have two options: We can retreat to our corners and blame "others," or we can come together and build something better. Our instincts will push us toward the former; we must fight to achieve the latter.

The Kerner Commission's prescient calls were not met by national action; now, it is our turn to pick up the baton. We have the knowledge and the resources to create a stronger, more equitable society; now, we simply need that "new will" the commission called for 55 years ago. Now is our moment to address the longstanding and wide-reaching impacts of inequality that have held back not only Black Americans, but all Americans. Now is our moment to build a healthier world—a world where everyone can thrive.

ACKNOWLEDGMENT

With thanks to Jeff Sobotko, senior writer at the Harvard TH Chan School of Public Health, for his contributions to this chapter.

NOTES

1. The National Advisory Commission on Civil Disorders, *Report of the National Advisory Commission on Civil Disorders* [Kerner Report] (Washington, DC: U.S. Department of Justice, Office of Justice Programs, 1968).

2. Kerner Report, 136.

3. Latoya Hill and Samantha Artiga, "COVID-19 Cases and Deaths by Race/Ethnicity: Current Data and Changes over Time," KFF, August 22, 2022, https://www.kff.org/racial-equity-and-health-policy/issue-brief/covid-19-cases-and-deaths-by-race-ethnicity-current-data-and-changes-over-time/.

4. Kerner Report, 229.

5. OECD, "Health at a Glance 2023: OECD Indicators," OECD Publishing, Paris, https://doi.org/10.1787/7a7afb35-en.

6. Selena Simmons-Duffin, "'Live Free and Die'? The Sad State of U.S. Life Expectancy," *NPR*, March 25, 2023, https://www.npr.org/sections/health-shots/2023/03/25/1164819944/live-free-and-die-the-sad-state-of-u-s-life-expectancy.

7. Boston Planning & Development Agency, "Back Bay," July 2017, https://www.bostonplans.org/getattachment/e3ce9e78-3bf0-4ec9-bc5c-96bbb0198c64; Boston Planning & Development Agency, "Roxbury," July 2017, https://www.bostonplans.org/getattachment/e3ce9e78-3bf0-4ec9-bc5c-96bbb0198c64.

8. Emily Zimmerman et al., "Social Capital and Health Outcomes in Boston," Virginia Commonwealth University Center on Human Needs, September 2012, https://societyhealth.vcu.edu/media/society-health/pdf/PMReport_Boston.pdf.

9. Raj Chetty et al., "The Association Between Income and Life Expectancy in the United States, 2001–2014," *Journal of the American Medical Association* 315, no. 16 (2016): 1750–66, https://doi.org/10.1001/jama.2016.4226; Steffie Woolhandler and David U. Himmelstein, "The Relationship of Health Insurance and Mortality: Is Lack of Insurance Deadly?" *Annals of Internal Medicine* 167, no. 6 (2017): 424, https://doi.org/10.7326/m17-1403.

10. Holly Lofton et al., "Obesity Among African American People in the United States: A Review," *Obesity* 31, no. 2 (2023): 306–15, https://doi.org/10.1002/oby.23640; Centers for Disease Control and Prevention, "Adult Obesity Facts," May 17, 2022, https://www.cdc.gov/obesity/data/adult.html; Office of Minority Health, "Diabetes and African Americans," U.S. Department of Health and Human Services, n.d., https://minorityhealth.hhs.gov/diabetes-and-african-americans.

11. Elise Mosley-Johnson et al., "Relationship Between Housing Insecurity, Diabetes Processes of Care, and Self-Care Behaviors," *BMC Health Services Research* 22, no. 1 (2022): 61, https://doi.org/10.1186/s12913-022-07468-7.

12. Christopher W. Tessum et al., "$PM_{2.5}$ Polluters Disproportionately and Systemically Affect People of Color in the United States," *Science Advances* 7, no. 18 (2021), https://doi.org/10.1126/sciadv.abf4491.

13. Heather C McGhee, *The Sum of Us: What Racism Costs Everyone and How We Can Prosper Together* (New York: One World, 2021), 21.

14. Emily Moss et al., "The Black-White Wealth Gap Left Black Households More Vulnerable," Brookings, December 8, 2020, https://www.brookings.edu/articles/the-black-white-wealth-gap-left-black-households-more-vulnerable/.

15. Anna Zajacova and Elizabeth M. Lawrence, "The Relationship Between Education and Health: Reducing Disparities Through a Contextual Approach," *Annual Review of Public Health* 39, no. 1 (2018): 273–89, https://doi.org/10.1146/annurev-publhealth-031816-044628.

16. Marisa Wright, "How Student Loan Forgiveness Can Help Close the Racial Wealth Gap and Advance Economic Justice," Legal Defense Fund, April 17, 2023, https://www.naacpldf.org/student-loans-racial-wealth-gap/.

17. Campaign Zero, "Mapping Police Violence," last updated April 10, 2024, https://mappingpoliceviolence.org/.

18. Kerner Report, 4.

19. Kerner Report, 8.

20. Jacob Bor et al., "Police Killings and Their Spillover Effects on the Mental Health of Black Americans: A Population-Based, Quasi-Experimental Study," *The Lancet* 392, no. 10144 (2018): 302–10, https://doi.org/10.1016/s0140-6736(18)31130-9.

21. Marcella Alsan and Marianne Wanamaker, "Tuskegee and the Health of Black Men," *The Quarterly Journal of Economics* 133, no. 1 (2018): 407–55, https://doi.org/10.1093/qje/qjx029.

22. Kelly M. Hoffman et al., "Racial Bias in Pain Assessment and Treatment Recommendations, and False Beliefs about Biological Differences between Blacks and Whites," *Proceedings of the National Academy of Sciences* 113, no. 16 (2016): 4296–4301, https://doi.org/10.1073/pnas

.1516047113; Martha Hostetter and Sarah Klein, "In Focus: Reducing Racial Disparities in Health Care by Confronting Racism," The Commonwealth Fund, September 27, 2018, https://www.commonwealthfund.org/publications/2018/sep/focus-reducing-racial-disparities-health-care-confronting-racism.

23. Jacqueline Howard, "Only 5.7% of US Doctors Are Black, and Experts Warn the Shortage Harms Public Health," *CNN*, February 21, 2023, https://www.cnn.com/2023/02/21/health/black-doctors-shortage-us/index.html.

24. Donna L. Hoyert, "Maternal Mortality Rates in the United States, 2020," CDC, February 22, 2022, https://www.cdc.gov/nchs/data/hestat/maternal-mortality/2020/maternal-mortality-rates-2020.htm; Munira Gunja, Evan Gumas, and Reginald Williams II, "U.S. Health Care from a Global Perspective, 2022: Accelerating Spending, Worsening Outcomes," The Commonwealth Fund, January 31, 2023, https://www.commonwealthfund.org/publications/issue-briefs/2023/jan/us-health-care-global-perspective-2022.

25. Serena Williams, "How Serena Williams Saved Her Own Life." *ELLE*, April 5, 2022, https://www.elle.com/life-love/a39586444/how-serena-williams-saved-her-own-life/.

26. Zara Abrams, "Abortion Bans Cause Outsized Harm for People of Color." American Psychological Association, April 14, 2023, https://www.apa.org/monitor/2023/06/abortion-bans-harm-people-of-color.

27. Sheryl Gay Stolberg, "As Abortion Laws Drive Obstetricians from Red States, Maternity Care Suffers." *New York Times*, September 6, 2023, https://www.nytimes.com/2023/09/06/us/politics/abortion-obstetricians-maternity-care.html.

28. Arline T. Geronimus et al., "'Weathering' and Age Patterns of Allostatic Load Scores Among Blacks and Whites in the United States," *American Journal of Public Health* 96, no. 5 (2006): 826–33, https://doi.org/10.2105/ajph.2004.060749.

29. Martin Luther King, Jr., "Letter from a Birmingham Jail," April 16, 1963, https://www.africa.upenn.edu/Articles_Gen/Letter_Birmingham.html.

30. McGhee, *The Sum of Us*, 23–28, 104–28.

31. McGhee, *The Sum of Us*, 5–14.

32. Gunja et al., "U.S. Health Care from a Global Perspective, 2022."

33. McGhee, *The Sum of Us*, 50.

34. McGhee, *The Sum of Us*, 52–53.

35. McGhee, *The Sum of Us*, 53–59; Stephen Neukam, "These 10 States Have Not Expanded Medicaid," *The Hill*, March 23, 2023, https://thehill.com/homenews/state-watch/3914916-these-10-states-have-not-expanded-medicaid/.

36. Tom Mueller, "Rural Texas Hospitals Are in Trouble. Why Won't Legislators Help?," *Austin American-Statesman*, April 15, 2023, https://www.statesman.com/story/opinion/columns/your-voice/2023/04/15/opinion-rural-texas-hospitals-are-in-trouble-why-wont-legislators-help/70110716007/.

37. Garrett Hall, "With Impending Funding Crises, Rural Hospitals Need a Medicaid Expansion Lifeboat to Stay Afloat," Families USA, January 9, 2023, https://familiesusa.org/resources/with-impending-funding-crises-rural-hospitals-need-a-medicaid-expansion-lifeboat-to-stay-afloat/.

38. Kerner Report, 1.

39. Kerner Report, 229.

40. Kerner Report, 11.

41. Madeline Brown et al., "The State of Baby Bonds," Urban Institute, February 2, 2023, https://www.urban.org/research/publication/state-baby-bonds.

42. Dana M. Peterson and Catherine L Mann, "Closing the Racial Inequality Gaps: The Economic Cost of Black Inequality in the U.S.," Citi GPS, September 2020, https://www.citigroup.com/global/insights/citigps/closing-the-racial-inequality-gaps-20200922.

43. Taylor Miller Thomas and Lara Korte, "Behind the Math: How California Got to $1.2 Million for Reparation Payouts," *Politico*, August 17, 2023, https://www.politico.com/news/2023/08/17/black-reparations-price-tag-california-00110137.

44. Nkechi Taifa, "Race, Mass Incarceration, and the Disastrous War on Drugs," Brennan Center for Justice, May 10, 2021, https://www.brennancenter.org/our-work/analysis-opinion/race-mass-incarceration-and-disastrous-war-drugs.

45. Nicole Rapfogel and Jill Rosenthal, "How North Carolina Is Using Medicaid to Address Social Determinants of Health," Center for American Progress, February 3, 2022, https://www.americanprogress.org/article/how-north-carolina-is-using-medicaid-to-address-social-determinants-of-health/.

46. Linda Rudolph et al., *Health in All Policies: A Guide for State and Local Governments* (Washington, DC, and Oakland, CA: American Public Health Association and Public Health Institute, 2013).

47. Jeff Lagasse, "Kaiser Permanente Is Spending $400 Million on Affordable Housing Initiatives," *Healthcare Finance News*, April 19, 2022, https://www.healthcarefinancenews.com/news/kaiser-permanente-spending-400-million-affordable-housing-initiatives.

CHAPTER 18

U.S. Health Care Policy, the Evidence, and the Will for Change
What Will It Take to Transform Decades of Evidence Regarding U.S. Race and Income Based Health Disparities to a "Will for Change"?

Herbert C. Smitherman Jr. and Anil N. F. Aranha

Authors' Note: The authors use Black, Black American, and African American interchangeably throughout this chapter. We chose to capitalize Black in order to reflect that we are discussing a group of people and to be consistent with the capitalization of African American. We also use White, White American, and European-American interchangeably in the same way.

> We do not learn from experience. We learn from reflecting on experience.
>
> —John Dewey[1]

In an academic context, reflection is an essential tool for using evidence to drive learning. Reflective learning for that reason enhances developmental insight and leads to a higher level of understanding. Improved insight and understanding inspire "Will" and only then can "Change" occur.[2]

Our chapter is a reflection on the evidence of how far we have come since the Kerner Report of 1968 regarding U.S. racial/ethnic and income-based health disparities and their root causes, and considers the question: What will it take to transform decades of overwhelming evidence and experience—documenting worsening disparities in Black and White health and socioeconomic indicators in the United States—into a "Will for Change."[3] In the course of this chapter, we will look at

- the relationship between health status, income, and poverty, that is, social determinants of health as the major driver of U.S. health status and the likely mechanisms through which poverty and income inequity affect health;

- the documented evidence of the health status comparison of the years 1967 and 2022;
- government policy as a driver of social determinants of health;
- policy levers that might reduce income-related health disparities; and
- what it will take (the "Will") to change U.S. policy direction for the betterment of all.

In an essay I wrote in 2021, "I'm a Black doctor. Here's why we all should take the COVID vaccine," I suggested that the COVID-19 pandemic and its broad disparate racial impact on the United States is an instructive example that laid bare to the world health community the consequences of centuries of harmful U.S. public policy on the African-American community and other communities of color.

> This disparity in COVID-19 infection and death rates among African Americans is not because this population is inherently more susceptible to getting the virus. It is because of the significant disparate poverty levels and its related higher burden of chronic disease. African Americans are more likely to have pre-existing health conditions (diabetes, asthma, hypertension, heart disease, cancer and obesity) that make the coronavirus particularly deadly. Higher poverty rates and higher burdens of disease are the result of 402 years of negative U.S. social, economic, political and health policies resulting from enslavement, Jim Crow, lynching, segregation, disproportionate mass incarceration secondary to an inequitable U.S. justice system destroying the black family, redlining, unfair housing policies, unfair employment practices, job discrimination, discriminatory education polices, economic discrimination, disparate health care policies, etc. COVID-19 has simply exposed how a long history of racial discrimination and institutional race-based policies has uniquely tied African-Americans to the bottom of the U.S. economic and class hierarchy. . . . This illness hit Detroit quick and hard, with African Americans, who make up only 14 percent of Michigan's population, accounting for 33 percent of its reported [COVID-19] infections and 40 percent of its deaths. Detroit [the city with the highest poverty rates in the United States], which is 79 percent African American, has 7 percent of Michigan's population, but represents 26 percent of the state's COVID-19 infections and 25 percent of its deaths. The pace at which African Americans are dying has transformed this national health crisis into an abject lesson on racial and class inequality. African-Americans are more likely to die of COVID-19 than any other ethnic group in the nation. That's why Black Americans—and all Americans—must be vaccinated against COVID.[4]

As we begin this chapter, we must first define what we mean by "health" and other factors that drive and determine health, referred to as *social determinants of health*. We adopt a modified version of the famous World Health Organization (WHO) definition of health, which is, "Health is a state of complete physical, mental and social well-being and not merely the absence of disease or infirmity." Our modified version of the WHO definition of health and the one used in this chapter is "Health is the state of physical, mental, spiritual and socioeconomic well-being of the individual and thus their community, not simply the absence of disease or infirmity." This modified definition of health simply recognizes the role of economic factors and potentially one's spiritual beliefs in shaping one's health, and highlights the holistic influence of community conditions of living on an individual's health status.[5]

SOCIAL DETERMINANTS OF HEALTH

Social determinants of health (SDOH) are defined as the wide range of personal, social, economic, and environmental factors that determine the health of an individual and the entire population. They are the nonmedical factors that influence health outcomes and include the community conditions of living in which people are born, grow, work, live, play, and age. They include the wider set of forces and care systems shaping the broad conditions of daily life.[6] In this chapter, we discuss the implications of SDOH on the U.S. population and provide a current account of the overall health of the nation.

Social determinants of health can be classified into two categories: medical factors and nonmedical factors. Medical factors account for about 20% of health outcomes in the United States and include the quality and type of medical care received, such as access to care, affordability of care, availability of services, appropriateness of care, and effectiveness of care. Nonmedical factors account for about 80% of health outcomes and include socioeconomic factors, health behaviors, and physical environment (Figure 18.1). The nonmedical factors—now commonly referred to as SDOH and discussed throughout this chapter—have a significant bearing on human health. Thus, this

Figure 18.1. Social Determinants of Health.

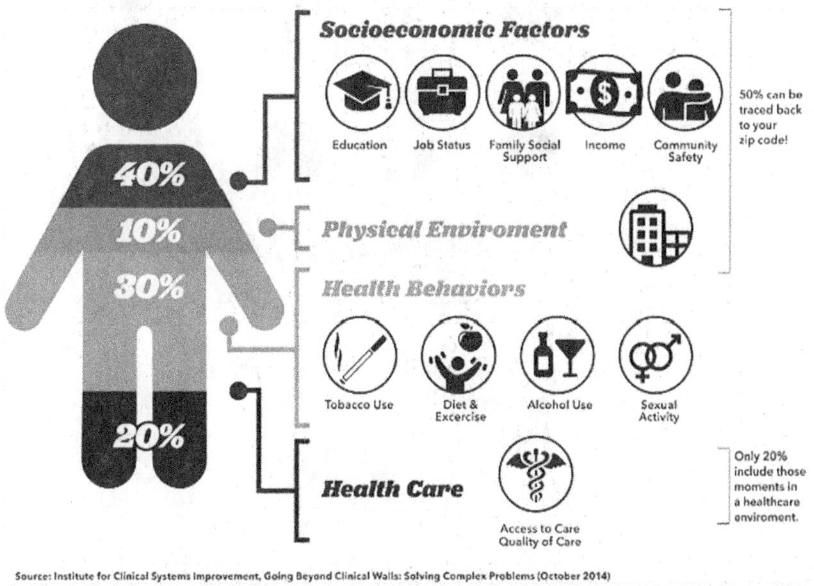

Source: Neighborhood Outreach Access to Health, https://noahhelps.org/sdoh/.

chapter, in a sense, brings to bear information provided about these factors and how they drive health.

Socioeconomic factors make up 40% of nonmedical factors and include individual income, education, employment, and job security. These factors affect people's access to resources, opportunities, and social support that can promote or hinder their health. For example, people with higher income and education levels tend to have better health outcomes than people with lower income and education levels (Figure 18.2). Health behaviors make up 30% of nonmedical factors and include diet, alcohol use, tobacco use, physical activity, and sexual practices. These behaviors are influenced by personal choices as well as by social and environmental factors that constrain behavior.

Figure 18.2. Social Determinants of Health

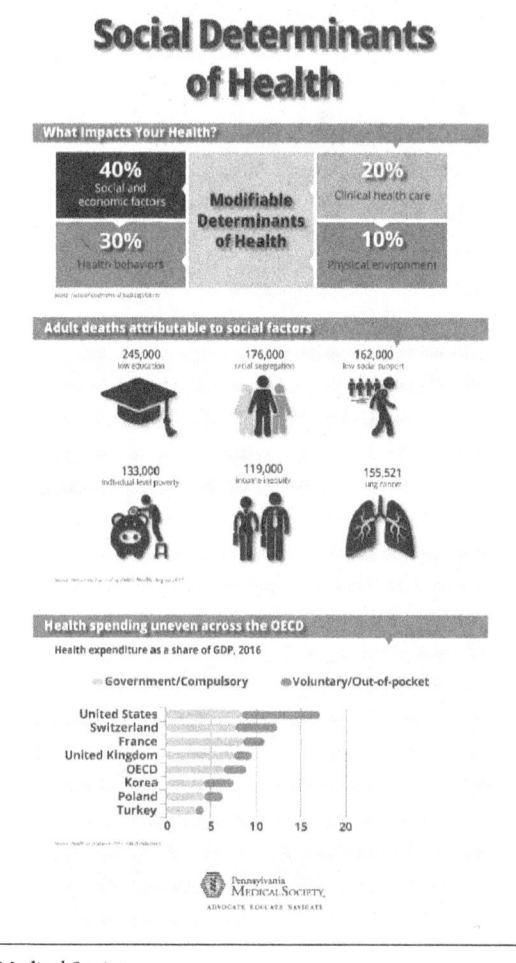

Source: Pennsylvania Medical Society.

U.S. Health Care Policy, the Evidence, and the Will for Change 217

For example, people who live in neighborhoods with limited access to healthy foods and safe places for physical activity may have poorer diets and lower levels of physical activity than people who live in neighborhoods with more resources. Physical environment makes up 10% of nonmedical factors and includes housing, air and water quality, living conditions, and exposure to hazards. These factors affect people's exposure to pathogens, pollutants, allergens, and other harmful substances that can affect their health. For example, people who live in substandard housing or in areas with poor air and water quality may have higher risks of respiratory diseases, infections, and cancers than people who live in better environments. These factors interact with each other and with biological factors to influence health status and well-being.

COMMUNITY HEALTH FRAMEWORK FOR REDUCING HEALTH INEQUITIES

Another concept that is important to understand while reading this chapter is both the community health framework we are using to foster health inequity reduction and how we view reality, equality, equity, and justice. The four-panel graphic in Figure 18.3 pictorially describes the differences between the terms reality, equality, equity, and justice. The first panel of the graphic depicts current American society—reality—where some get more than is needed while others get less. Equality, where everyone receives the same support, is illustrated in the second panel. Equity, where everyone receives the support they need, is represented by the third panel, and finally, justice, where barriers to success are removed, is portrayed by the fourth panel. As an American society, despite

Figure 18.3. Pictorial Description of Reality, Equality, Equity and Justice

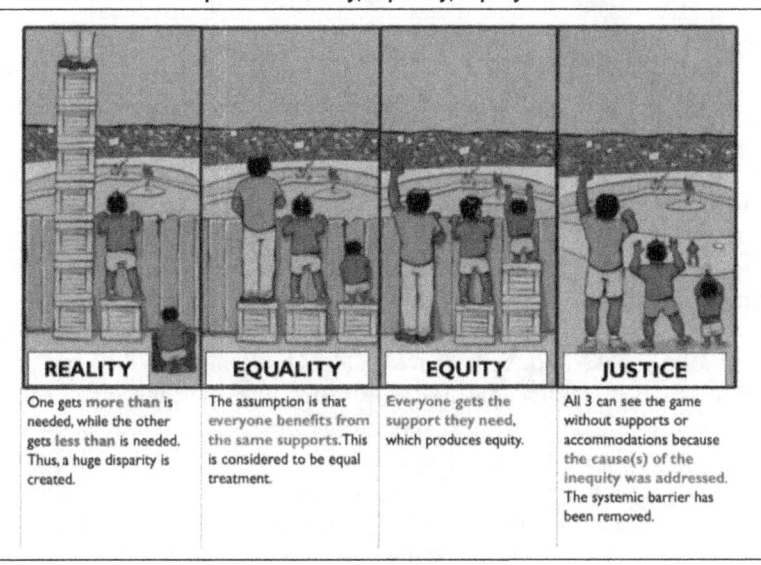

REALITY	EQUALITY	EQUITY	JUSTICE
One gets more than is needed, while the other gets less than is needed. Thus, a huge disparity is created.	The assumption is that everyone benefits from the same supports. This is considered to be equal treatment.	Everyone gets the support they need, which produces equity.	All 3 can see the game without supports or accommodations because the cause(s) of the inequity was addressed. The systemic barrier has been removed.

Source: @restoringracialjustice on Instagram.

numerous historic, economic, and social obstacles, we collectively are trying to move America from our current reality to ultimately justice for all.[7]

One framework for reducing health inequities is proposed by the Bay Area Regional Health Inequities Initiative (BARHII), which is a coalition of public health departments in California. A revision of the BARHII framework diagram is presented in Figure 18.4 and illustrates the links between the inequities.

Institutional Inequities. The policies, practices and norms of institutions that create differential access to opportunities and resources for different groups of people, such as education, employment, housing, health care, criminal justice, and political representation.

Social Inequities. The unequal distribution of power, wealth, income, and status among social groups, such as those defined by race, ethnicity, gender, class, sexuality, and disability.

Living Conditions. The physical and social environments where people live, work, learn, and play, such as neighborhood quality, air quality, water quality, food security, safety, and social cohesion.

Risk Behaviors. The actions or inactions that affect the health of individuals and communities, such as smoking, drinking, diet, exercise, and sexual behavior.

Disease and Injury. The occurrence and severity of health problems that affect the well-being of individuals and communities, such as communicable diseases (e.g., COVID-19, HIV/AIDS), chronic diseases (e.g., diabetes, heart disease), and injuries (e.g., accidents, violence).

Mortality. The death rates and life expectancy of different groups of people.

The BARHII framework suggests that institutional inequities and social inequities are the root causes of health disparities, and that they help shape and drive the living conditions that influence risk behaviors, disease and injury outcomes, and mortality. Therefore, to achieve health equity, it is necessary to address the upstream factors that create and maintain these inequities. Our actions affect our well-being in multiple dimensions, such as physical (body), mental (mind), emotional (heart), psychological (psyche), and spiritual (soul). To improve health at both the individual and population levels, we need to consider not only the downstream causes of health and disease, such as individual behaviors and biological factors, but also the upstream factors, such as social, environmental, and institutional determinants. These upstream factors shape the conditions in which people live, work, learn, and play, and they often create health inequities among different groups of people. Health professionals can help patients make healthy changes in behavior, but it is also necessary to address the upstream factors through policies, laws, and regulations that support health for the entire population. These are preventive interventions that aim to avoid disease and reduce the need for medical intervention.[8]

Figure 18.4. Community Health Framework for Reducing Health Inequities

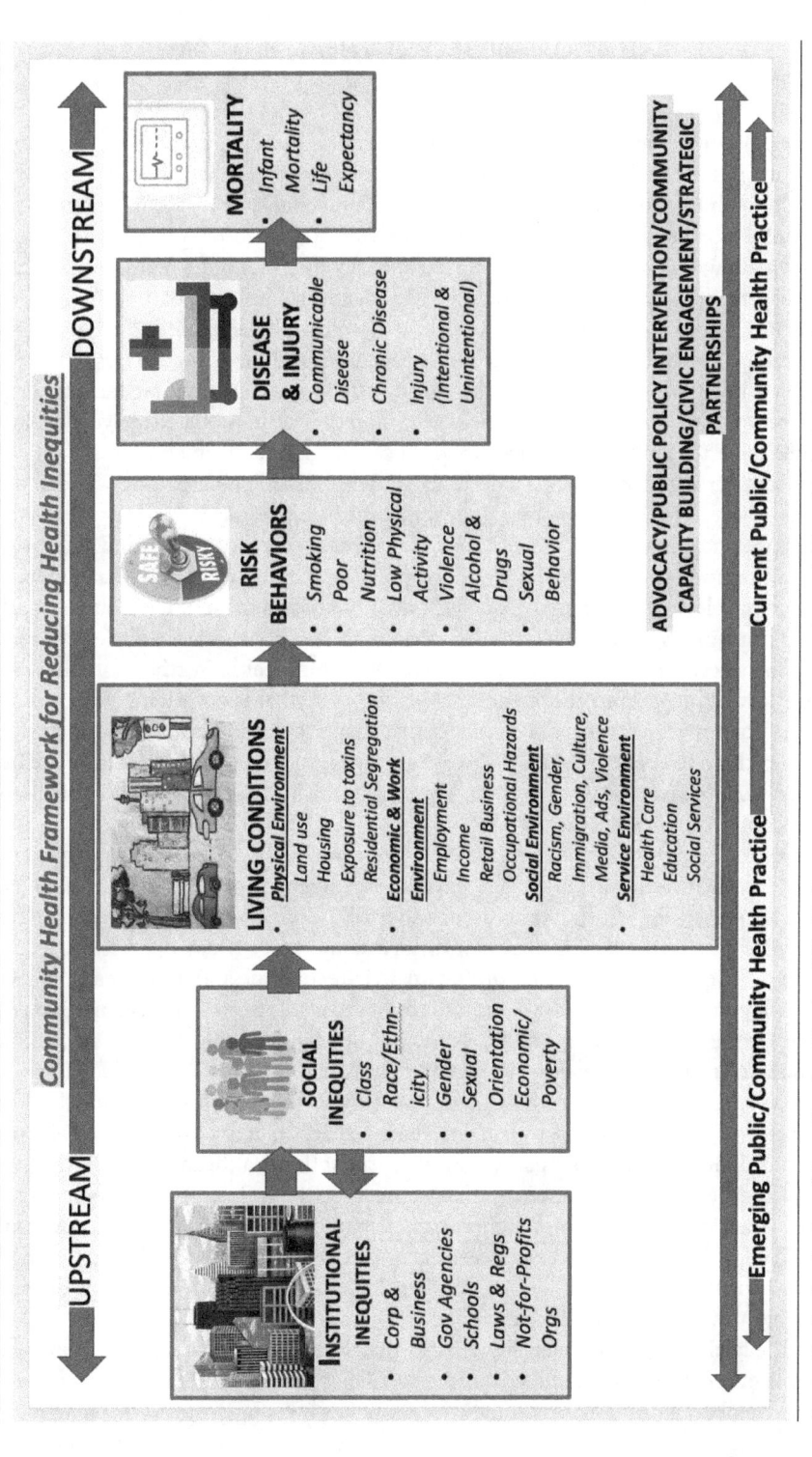

Source: Revised and adapted from Bay Area Regional Health Inequities Initiative Framework. Available at: https://barhii.org/framework.

RELATIONSHIP BETWEEN HEALTH, INCOME, AND POVERTY IN THE UNITED STATES

It is well known that health, income, and poverty are closely intertwined. Families with low incomes are more likely to suffer from disease and premature death compared to families with high incomes. In addition, income inequality in the United States has significantly worsened over the last 55 years driving stagnated or worse health outcomes and widening life expectancy gaps by race and income. Therefore, many entities that are not directly related to medical care, such as education, employment, housing, nutrition, transportation, race, ethnicity, the U.S. legal system, and geography affect health. Gaps in these factors are widening in the United States. Since the United States has the largest health disparity by income in the world, it is important to understand how social determinants of health, including income, influence health. As stated above, people with higher incomes tend to live longer than those with lower incomes, and this difference has been increasing over the past decades. In the 1970s, a high income 60-year-old man could expect to outlive someone with low income by 1.2 years. But by the year 2000, this life expectancy difference jumped to 5.8 years. To improve the health and well-being of low- and middle-income people, we need policies that allow fair and equal opportunities for people to obtain better jobs, fair pay, a quality education, fair housing, and social opportunities, especially when they are young. These structural policies can provide a means to escape poverty and its negative effects on health. Furthermore, low health status leads to lower income, creating a vicious cycle that is occasionally known as the health-poverty trap. Thus, public policies that shape social and economic conditions are also health policies and have a significant impact on health outcomes. To improve health equity, policymakers should consider the long-term health implications of their social and economic policy decisions.[9]

In addition to income, race also affects many other aspects of socioeconomic status. Black Americans on average have lower incomes and shorter lives than White Americans, as race affects many other aspects of their socioeconomic status. This is partly because of the lasting effects of historical and present-day oppression, discrimination, and government policies on the financial/economic and, thus, health outcomes of Black Americans and other communities of color. Black Americans continue to face more barriers to education, credit, economic opportunity, and healthy environments than their White counterparts. The basic fact in America is that wealth inequality is very high and has been rising in the United States over the past 55 years since the Kerner Report, with the richest 10% owning more than three-quarters (76%) of all U.S. wealth, the middle 40% owning less than a quarter (22%) of the wealth, and the bottom 50% just 1% of the wealth. White Americans have a net worth that is over 15 times higher than Black Americans and 13 times higher than Hispanic Americans. The link between race, income, and health is not only between races, but also within races. High-income Black Americans live longer than low-income Black Americans, and both groups die sooner than high-income White Americans.[10]

The health disparities that affect Black Americans have roots in the past and present actions of the government and government policies that have excluded them from various societal domains—such as equal education, fair housing, justice, equal employment opportunities, and health care access. These actions, whether explicit or subtle, have damaged the well-being and the opportunities for minority communities. This is due to health being a precondition for achievement in any society, and, therefore, it cannot be used as a reward for achievement. No real social or economic advancement of a people can occur with inequities in health. Children cannot learn appropriately in school if they are not healthy. One cannot be effective in a job if one is not healthy. One cannot fully and appropriately contribute to society if one is not healthy. Therefore, health is the prerequisite for a person to effectively participate and advance in any society. Also, the distribution of resources for supporting a person's health in a just democracy must accordingly be fair and just.

Over the last 55 years since Detroit's 1967 rebellion, because fair access to the distribution of health and socioeconomic resources has largely not occurred, race-based health metrics such as life expectancy and mortality rates continue to widen. One way to improve health equity is to implement policies that fairly increase income and wealth through U.S. tax policy, for example, and enhancing educational opportunities and investment, expanding housing and housing options, and increasing a whole host of broad opportunities for social mobility, especially for children. These policies can reduce poverty and improve health outcomes not only for Americans with low incomes but also for those in the middle class.[11]

THE EVIDENCE: HEALTH STATUS COMPARISON OF THE YEARS 1967 AND 2022

The following is a summary of health care disparities between Black and White Americans based on the Centers for Disease Control and Prevention for 1967 and 2022, a span of 55 years:

- Life expectancy of Black Americans was 6.5 years lower than that of White Americans in 1967 and is 5.5 years lower in 2022.[12]
- Infant mortality rate of Black infants was 1.9 times higher than that of White infants in 1967 and is 2.4 times higher in 2022.[13]
- Maternal mortality of Black mothers was 3.6 times higher than that of White mothers in 1967 and is 2.6 times higher in 2022.[14]
- Mortality rate from all causes for Black Americans was similar to that of White Americans in 1967 and is 26.7% higher in 2022.[15]
- Chronic diseases including heart disease, cancer, cerebrovascular disease, diabetes, and HIV impact Black Americans at higher rates than White Americans at all ages younger than 65 years.[16]

The three widely accepted measures to assess trends in health status in the United States are All-Cause Mortality (previously known as General Mortality), Infant Mortality, and Life Expectancy. These Leading Health Indicators (LHIs) are a small subset of high-priority health status metrics selected to drive policy toward improving health and well-being. Therefore, to summarize, even after 55 years with significant advancements in medical care and improvements in access to health care for minority communities as compared to 1967, the health disparities by race in the United States have either remained essentially static or have worsened. This is based on some of the LHIs of Healthy People 2030 developed by the U.S. Department of Health and Human Services, Office of Disease Prevention and Health Promotion.[17] It must also be noted that COVID-19 took a toll on the entire American population, but even more so on people of color, and has been responsible for about a 3-year reduction in the life expectancy of an American child at birth (Figure 18.5).

Furthermore, there has been inequitable health improvement throughout the different parts of the American society. Even though the rates of infant mortality, death, and life expectancy have improved compared to 55 years ago, the differences in these health indicators between Blacks and Whites have worsened. In 1967, the life expectancy for Whites was 6.5 years higher than that of non-Whites. The more recent statistics of 2022 essentially tells the same story, that the life expectancy of a non-Hispanic Black American is 71.2 years and that of a non-Hispanic White American is 76.7 years, a difference of 5.5 years. Hence, even the passage of 55 years since the Kerner Report and the great advancement of medical knowledge has not enabled substantial reduction in the disparity of life expectancy among Black Americans compared to Whites.[18]

Infant mortality, defined as the death of a baby before their first birthday, another population health indicator, has also been frequently used as a gauge of the health and well-being of a nation. In 1967, the infant mortality rate was 19.7 deaths per 1,000 live births for White Americans versus 37.5 deaths per 1,000 live births among Black Americans. This disparity in mortality rate has not changed 55 years later; although infant mortality rates were relatively lower by 77.2% for non-Hispanic White (4.5 deaths per 1,000 live births) and 70.9% for non-Hispanic Blacks (10.9 deaths per 1,000 live births), the disparity between the two groups of the population has seen an increase

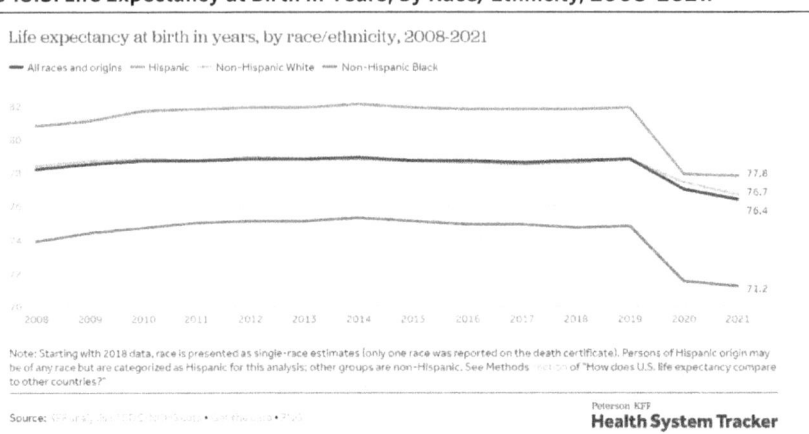

Figure 18.5. Life Expectancy at Birth in Years, by Race/Ethnicity, 2008-2021.

Source: Adapted from: Peterson-KFF Health System Tracker. Available at https://www.healthsystemtracker.org/indicator/health-well-being/life-expectancy.

(Figure 18.6). The infant mortality rate of Black people in 1967 was 47.5% higher than that of White people and the difference has grown to 58.7% in 2022—with an overall U.S. infant mortality rate of 5.6 deaths per 1,000 live births.[19]

Maternal mortality, defined as the death of a woman while pregnant or within 42 days of termination of pregnancy, irrespective of the duration and the site of the pregnancy, from any cause related to or aggravated by the pregnancy or its management, but not from accidental or incidental causes, is a serious public health issue in the United States, where the number of women dying from pregnancy-related complications is significantly higher than in all other developed countries (Figure 18.7). In recent years, the United States has seen a rapid rise in the maternal mortality rates with an increase of 40% from 2020 to 2021, reaching the highest level in over 55 years. The maternal mortality rates for 2021 were 32.9 deaths per 100,000 live births, compared with 23.8 in 2020 and 20.1 in 2019.[20]

There are significant racial and ethnic disparities in maternal mortality in the United States, more so for Black women who face stark racial disparities in maternal outcomes. The maternal mortality rates for non-Hispanic Black women were 69.9 deaths per 100,000 live births in 2021, 2.6 times the rate for non-Hispanic White women, which was 26.6 deaths per 100,000 live births (Figure 18.8). This gap has persisted for decades with the maternal mortality rate ratio difference fluctuating between 2.5 times and 4.1 times higher for Black women. It is of interest and concern to note that the maternal mortality rates continue to remain high, as in the past, for Black women (69.5 deaths per 100,000

Figure 18.6. Infant Mortality Rate, by Race and Hispanic Origin: United States, 2021 Final and 2022 Provisional

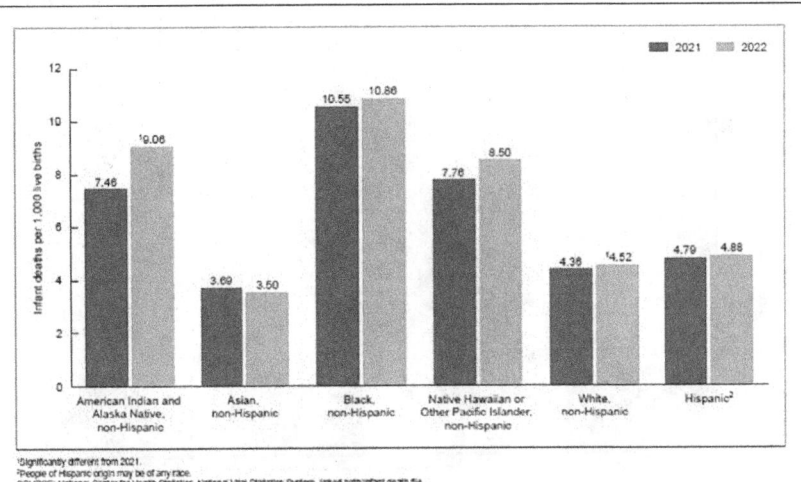

Source: Adapted from Danielle M. Ely and Anne K. Driscoll, "Infant Mortality in the United States: Provisional Data From the 2022 Period Linked Birth/Infant Death File," *Vital Statistics Rapid Release* no 33 (November 2023), https://doi.org/10.15620/cdc:133699.

Figure 18.7. Comparison Between Maternal Mortality Rates of the United States and Other Industrialized Nations

Maternal Mortality in the U.S. Far Outstrips That of Other Industrialized Nations

Country	Deaths per 100,000 live births
U.S.	23.8
France	8.7
Canada	8.6
UK	6.5
Australia	4.8
Switzerland	4.6
Sweden	4.3
Germany	3.2
Netherlands	3
Norway	1.8
New Zealand	1.7

*Deaths per 100,000 live births

Source: https://www.cdc.gov/nchs/data/hestat/maternal-mortality/2020/maternal-mortality-rates-2020.htm

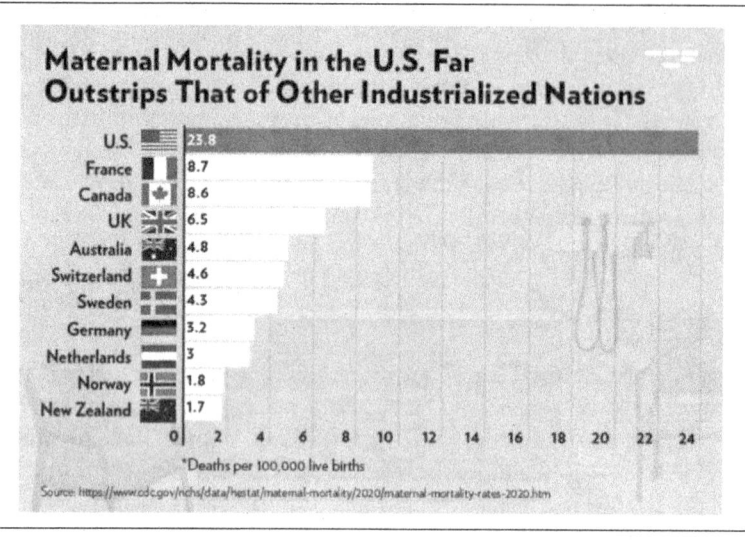

Source: Adapted from Jamila Taylor et al., "The Worsening U.S. Maternal Health Crisis in Three Graphs," The Century Foundation, https://tcf.org/content/commentary/worsening-u-s-maternal-health-crisis-three-graphs.

Figure 18.8. Maternal Mortality Rates, by Race and Hispanic Origin: United States, 2018–2021.

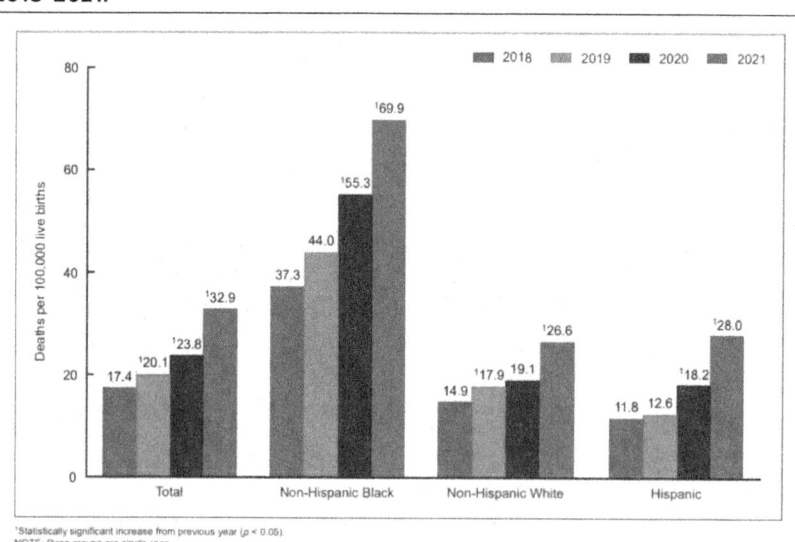

	2018	2019	2020	2021
Total	17.4	20.1	23.8	32.9
Non-Hispanic Black	37.3	44.0	55.3	69.9
Non-Hispanic White	14.9	17.9	19.1	26.6
Hispanic	11.8	12.6	18.2	28.0

¹Statistically significant increase from previous year ($p < 0.05$).
NOTE: Race groups are single race.
SOURCE: National Center for Health Statistics, National Vital Statistics System, Mortality

Source: Adapted from: Donna L. Hoyert, "Maternal Mortality Rates in the United States, 2021," Health E-Stats, March 2023, https://dx.doi.org/10.15620/cdc:124678.

live births), although the disparity between Black and White women (19.5 deaths per 100,000 live births) has slightly reduced from 3.6 times in 1967 to 2.6 times now.[21]

The leading causes of maternal death for Black women have been eclampsia, pre-eclampsia, and postpartum cardiomyopathy, with rates five times those for White women. Other factors that have contributed to the disparity include access to quality prenatal care, chronic health conditions, socioeconomic status, implicit bias, and racism in the health care system.[22]

The mortality rate from all causes in the United States has significantly changed over time and across different racial and ethnic groups. According to the Centers for Disease Control and Prevention (CDC), the age-adjusted death rate for all causes in 2022 was 832.8 per 100,000 population, which is 12.1% or 114.3 per 100,000 population lower than the rate of 947.1 per 100,000 population in 1967. However, the mortality rate in 2022 was 5.3% lower than the death rate of 879.7 per 100,000 population in 2021, indicating a significant impact of the COVID-19 pandemic (61.3 deaths per 100,000) on overall mortality. The death rate for Black Americans has been consistently higher than that for White Americans throughout the period, reflecting persistent racial and ethnic health disparities in the United States. In 2022, non-Hispanic Black Americans had a death rate of 1,032.9 per 100,000 population, a rate higher by 26.7% or 217.9 per 100,000 population in comparison to the death rate of 815.0 per 100,000 population for White Americans. The gap between the death rates for Black and White Americans has narrowed only slightly between the years 1967 and 2022.

A comparison of the causes of death shows that there have been a few changes in the mortality patterns during the 55 years from 1967 to 2022. Among the leading causes of death during the period have been heart disease, cancer, stroke, unintentional injury, and chronic lower respiratory diseases, with some causes of mortality—stroke and respiratory diseases such as chronic bronchitis and emphysema—having decreased in rank or prevalence, whereas other causes of mortality—COVID-19 and unintentional injuries—having emerged or increased in rank or prevalence. COVID-19 emerged as a new cause of death in 2022, ranking as the fourth leading underlying cause of death with 246,166 deaths (peak annual U.S. COVID-19 deaths were 463,267 in 2021, and total U.S. deaths were 1,1437,724 from 2020 to September 9, 2023), thereby earning a spot ahead of stroke (Figure 18.9). The impact of COVID-19 on mortality rates has also varied by race and ethnicity, with Black Americans having a higher COVID-19 death rate than White Americans in 2022.[23] This reflects the persistent racial disparities in the United States mortality from all causes.[24]

The improvement in health outcomes for the whole society has in general not been equally distributed among the diverse racial/ethnic groups. The data show that racial and ethnic minority groups, especially Black Americans, experience higher rates of illness and death across a wide range of health conditions, such as diabetes, hypertension, obesity, asthma, and heart disease, when compared to their White counterparts. These health disparities indicate that while the health of Black Americans has improved, the gaps in health status between Black and White Americans continue to widen.[25] What is the reason? There is extensive research that points to a direct association between income, wealth, and life expectancy, even when comparing a nation to another, a state to another, a local municipality to another, a city suburb to another,

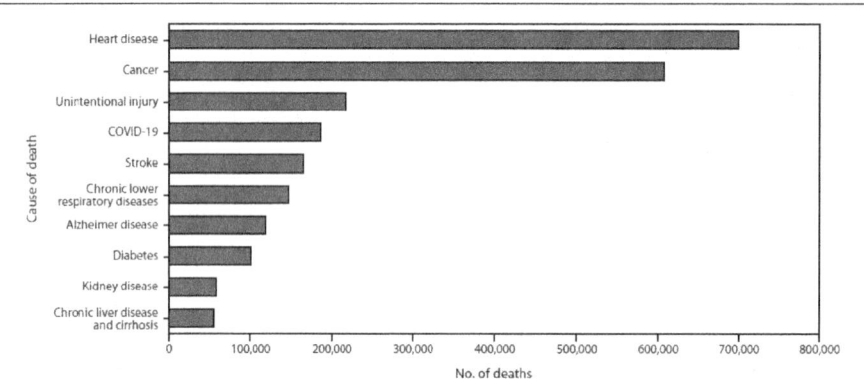

Figure 18.9. Leading Underlying Causes of Death in the United States in the Year 2022.

*Data are provisional; National Vital Statistics System provisional data are incomplete, and data from December are less complete because of reporting lags. Deaths that occurred in the United States among residents of U.S. territories and foreign countries were excluded.
† Deaths are ranked by number of deaths per underlying cause of death.

Source: Adapted from Farida B. Ahmad et al., "Provisional Mortality Data—United States, 2022," 72, no. 18 (May 5, 2023), https://www.cdc.gov/mmwr/volumes/72/wr/pdfs/mm7218a3-H.pdf.

or a community to another. As the income and wealth of a community rises, so does the life expectancy of its entire population (Figure 18.10). Similarly, as the economy of a community or a country improves, so do its Health Status Indicators. More importantly, as the income inequities within a society declines, so does its death rates (Figure 18.11).[26]

The racial wealth gap in the United States has widened over the last quarter century, as recent research indicates. White households had a median wealth of $285,000 in 2022, while Black and Hispanic households had only $44,900 and $61,600, respectively. This means that for every dollar of wealth that White households have, Black and Hispanic households have less than 22 cents.[27] This gap reflects the structural barriers that prevent many people of color from accessing economic opportunities and resources.[28] Without adequate income, education, health care, and social support, many communities of color face chronic poverty and poor health outcomes. These conditions undermine the social fabric and the institutions that sustain society, such as family, economy, education, community, health, politics, and so on. Therefore, lifestyle choices are not the main drivers of health disparities, but rather the social and cultural factors that shape and limit them. The goal should be to address poverty, as opposed to blaming people in poverty. The experience of the United Kingdom shows that having universal health care is not enough to reduce health inequalities based on income differences. The Whitehall Study noted that although British citizens have access to National Health Care, they still face class and income disparities in health outcomes, thus recommending that the social contexts, the nature of work, and the effects of income disparity should receive more consideration in health care decision-making.[29]

Figure 18.10. Life Expectancy Versus Gross Domestic Product Per Capita in 2021.

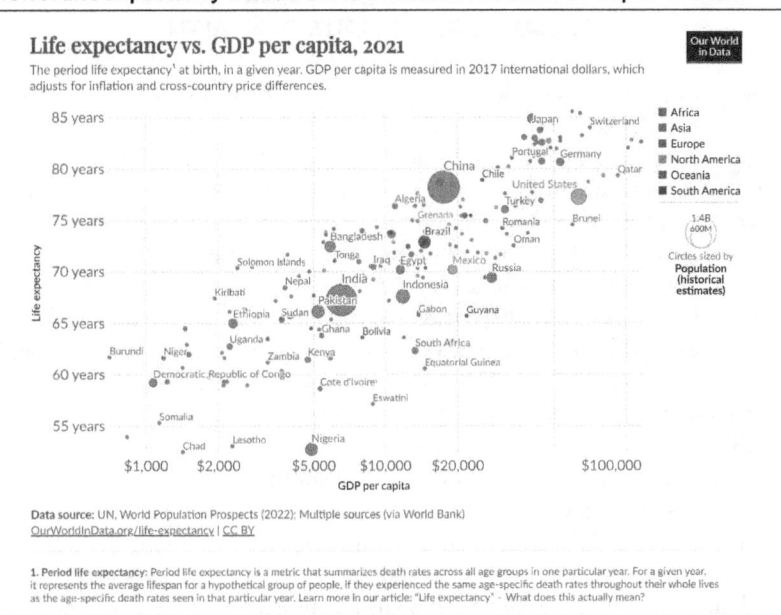

Source: From Our World in Data: https://ourworldindata.org/grapher/life-expectancy-un-vs-gdp-per-capita-wb?time=latest.

Figure 18.11. A Pictorial Depiction of the Association Between Death Rates and Income Inequity.

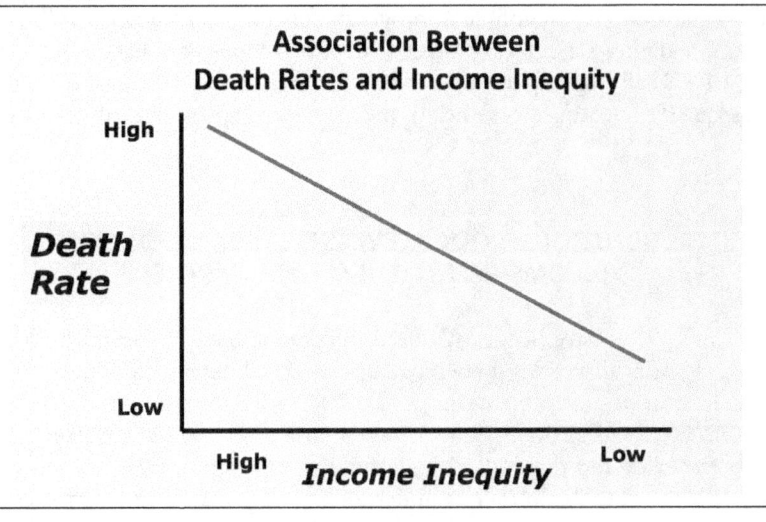

GOVERNMENT POLICY AS A DRIVER OF SOCIAL DETERMINANTS OF HEALTH

A new way of looking at the relationship between income and health is needed, as the U.S. economy is changing and the income and wealth gap between rich and the poor Americans is widening over time. Research shows that health differences are not only between low-income and high-income Americans, but also stepwise between every income level, up and down the income ladder, creating a consistent and persistent income/health gradient. Policies that support more economic fairness in society, therefore, can have a comprehensive impact on health, not only for the poor but also the middle class. Political systems and policies that foster poverty and continually one-sidedly favor the interests of the wealthy create more inequity and unfairness in income, wealth, and health in the society as a whole. Those who have the resources and, therefore, the ability to lobby have considerable disproportionate advantages and influence in U.S. politics and public policy, which usually benefits the wealthy and well-connected. For example, the political right advocates cuts to many government social support programs for Americans with low incomes—including the Supplemental Nutrition Assistance Program (SNAP, formerly known as the food stamp program), which became a permanent program in 1964 and now helps more than 45 million low-income families maintain adequate nutrition; the Head Start program, founded in 1965 as a comprehensive child development program to help communities meet the needs of disadvantaged children; and the Earned Income Tax Credit (EITC) program benefiting working low-income and middle-income households and has become the largest federal aid program targeted to the working poor. Cuts to these programs, as examples, exacerbates poverty and income inequity and, therefore, poor health. In addition, promoting cuts to women's health, subsidies for mass transit, school lunch programs, funding for job training, attempting to repeal the Affordable Care Act, school loan programs for minority students, college aid and Pell Grants, and after-school programs, to support trillions of dollars in tax cuts to the wealthiest 1%, is all working toward eroding the middle class, increasing poverty, and, as a consequence, creating worse health indicators and worse overall health status for the country.[30]

SOLUTIONS: POLICY LEVERS THAT CAN REDUCE INCOME-RELATED HEALTH DISPARITIES

Government policies have historically been the predominant driver for health, wealth, income, and social disparities between Blacks and Whites in the United States and, therefore, it must be government's responsibility to play the leading role in correcting the problem it created. A discussion of the response of the federal government as it relates to both policy and the cyclical underfunding of the programs it started over the past 60 years is critical. Continuous underfunding of programs meant to resolve race and income disparities is why there's been very little change in the health, wealth, and income disparities between Black and White Americans. The U.S. government has never adequately addressed the gross human rights violations perpetrated against Black people as part of chattel slavery or the exploitation, discrimination, segregation, and violence unleashed on Black people that followed their emancipation in 1863. The discrimination against Black people that is a legacy of their enslavement persists today and is perpetuated by economic, health, education, law enforcement, housing, and other policies and practices that fail to adequately address racial disparities. This ongoing institutional and structural racism and racial subjugation prevents many Black Americans from advancing in society. It also persistently enables police violence, housing segregation, and a lack of access to a quality education and fair employment opportunities, among other things.[31]

There are proven policy ideas that can help reduce the health, wealth, and income disparities between Black and White, and rich and poor, Americans, and increase the chances of fair and equitable upward social mobility. Sustained investment (rather than investing in a program in one congressional cycle and cutting those resources in the next cycle) in early childhood education is especially important, as it can improve children's social, emotional, cognitive, and health outcomes. The RAND Corporation estimated that for every dollar spent on such programs, society gains between $2 and $4 in benefits.[32] However, there are other studies that have noted even higher benefits—$8.60 for every dollar spent—such as increased future income for children, less need for special education, and less crime in the community.[33]

Sustained investment in housing relocation and moving to low-poverty areas benefits families, according to research. A study examined the long-term outcomes of the Moving to Opportunity (MTO) program, which randomly gave vouchers to families in high-poverty neighborhoods to relocate to places with less poverty. The study found that the children who moved before they turned 13 earned 31% more in their twenties than those who stayed in high-poverty neighborhoods. Thus, MTO had positive effects on the health and well-being of the parents and their children, reducing obesity and depression rates and increasing optimism and aspirations.[34] Other programs that provide sustained financial and material support to low-income families also work well. As stated earlier, the Supplemental Nutrition Assistance Program (SNAP) is the second-largest program in the United States that helps families with children escape poverty, and evidence shows that it boosts economic activity and improves the well-being of people who face food insecurity. One study estimated that every $1 spent on SNAP created $1.73 in economic activity and concluded that it was one of the most effective programs for stimulating the economy.[35] Another study showed that SNAP users incurred $1,400 less in health care costs per year.[36]

A more direct financial support program for low-income workers, the Earned Income Tax Credit (EITC), has been linked to lower infant mortality rates and low-birthweight rates, as well as better health outcomes for mothers. EITC puts money back in the pockets of working people, reduces food insecurity, frees up money for child care expenses, medical care, and healthy food, and puts more money back into local economies. EITC lifts all races and ethnic groups out of poverty. Expanding the EITC, especially in regions that are economically disadvantaged, can help reduce poverty and, therefore, health disparities that are influenced by geography.[37]

A familiar argument is that health behaviors are simply a matter of personal choice, and that health and social disparities are simply the consequences of the conscious choices an individual makes. However, this argument ignores the data-supported evidence that shows how government policies' effects on the social determinants of health (SDOH) shape and affect the behavioral health of vulnerable segments of the population.[38] Individuals do have responsibilities for themselves; however, a child who is born into and grows up in extreme poverty, attends a low-quality school, faces frequent utility shutoffs, and suffers from housing and food insecurity with poor access to basic health care, will have involuntary effects on their behavior, with limited choices and restricted life options that are real.

The legacy of 4 centuries of governmental, institutional, and societal health inequities, discrimination, and injustice cannot be addressed by federal policies that raise the effective taxes on the middle class and reduce the programs, earlier stated, that have been shown to improve society as a whole. Cuts and chronic underfunding of such programs to provide massive tax breaks amounting to trillions of dollars over time to the richest 1% of the U.S. society—who already pay far less than their fair share—undermines the sustainability of the country. Is there really a sound, fair, and just reason why capital gains are taxed at 0%, 15%, and 20%, whereas working people's income is taxed at 32%, 35%, and 37% in the United States, other than disproportionate lobbying access to policymakers by the wealthy? What is needed in American society is more thoughtful, long-term, durable, and sustained government policies and funding that create more fairness and opportunity in the American society. The higher the sense of unfairness, inequity, and injustice there is in the American society, the higher the risk of a political leader who emerges and seeks support by appealing to and manipulating the desires and prejudices of ordinary people. This leads to increasing ideological uniformity, more partisan antipathy, and less willingness to compromise.

The question thus becomes . . .

As we have shown, there is abundant well-documented evidence regarding the overall worsening disparities in health status and social indicators in the United States since the 1968 Kerner Report, especially driven by race, income, and other SDOH. The real question, therefore, becomes, what are we going to do about it? Is there the "Will" to do something about it? And finally, if not, why not, and how then do we generate that Will for Change?

THE WILL

What will it take (the "Will") to change U.S. policy direction for the betterment of all?

Societal, institutional, and organizational inclusion and diversity in the context of a more fair, just, and equitable societal environment are key strategic drivers for a successful plural America and, given America's leadership role in the world, for a successful plural world. Shifting U.S. demographics requires a greater understanding of a variety of cultures to provide high-quality care across multiple and complex American social and health care environments. Knowing how to work within a culturally diverse society is essential to meeting the needs of the nation, improving health and social outcomes, reducing health and social disparities, and eliminating health and social inequities, especially among underserved populations. The challenge is that the political center and political left within American society have not articulated a clear, cohesive, and collective vision of America's future in the context of this shifting U.S. demographic. They instead have an array of laudable but siloed movements/organizations that target specific domains of U.S. society toward a more just and equitable American society. However, collectively they do not seem coordinated with one another, nor have they been able to form a more united whole. They also at times do not present or articulate to the American people a clear vision of the future of what their pluralistic American democracy looks like. So again, what does the society they are trying to create look like, and can they come together and articulate that vision to the American people?

Movements/organizations such as the voting rights movement, women's rights movement, diversity, equity, inclusion, and belonging movement, workers' rights movement, Black Lives Matter movement, global justice movement, pro-choice movement, LGBTQ+ movement, anti-war movement, climate change movement, the American Civil Liberties Union (ACLU), the young peoples movement, Feeding America (largest domestic hunger-relief organization), faith-based organizations, the student movement, the National Association for the Advancement of Colored People (NAACP), the labor movement, human rights movement, #MeToo movement, The Urban League, the union movement, national health care reform campaigns and movements, farm worker movement, Southern Christian Leadership Conference, reproductive justice movement, March For Our Lives and Moms Demand Action (end gun violence) movements, Global Citizen movement, Fair Immigration Reform Movement, the National Council of La Raza and National Alliance of Latin American and Caribbean Countries, movements to end homelessness and to provide quality and affordable housing, and the Poor People's Campaign, etc., have each independently, and in and of themselves, earned our deepest respect. However, independently, and each to itself, they do not provide a complete picture of the future canvas of America. The political right within our society, particularly and mostly the Make America Great Again (MAGA) right, in contrast, is expressing a very united and singular vision of America. It is a romanticized vision of a version of the American past. An American past that will never return. The political right's objective, though, is to advance and nurture a vision and version of the American societal past that is familiar and appealing to segments of the American public, which consider this past "the good old days." The question is, "good old days" for whom? The political right wants Americans to emotionally embrace this version of America, that of a White Christian Male–dominated American society of the past that for them, not the country as a whole, was "the good old days." This, while the political right also simultaneously and emotionally creates fear of an unknown socially pluralistic American future. Emotion mobilizes and unites people. People understand how they feel about something. Promoting math alone, on the other hand, e.g., the economic metrics of the U.S. economy (Gross Domestic Product growth rate, unemployment rate, inflation, interest rate, stock market growth, business confidence, income tax rate, corporate tax rate, etc.), even with good metrics, does not emotionally unite a society around a vision; does not emotionally unite a society around a future, especially when many (as we have shown in this chapter) are not benefiting and experiencing that economic prosperity equitably. The Biden administration seems confused as to why the U.S. economic indicators are doing so well while the president's favorability metrics are not. And the simple answer is that the majority of the country are not experiencing the economic prosperity uniformly. Real wages have been stagnant for over 30 years. The compensation of U.S. CEOs increased 1,460.2% from 1978 to 2021 (adjusting for inflation) with income inequality in the United States at an all-time high since the Kerner Report. CEO compensation grew roughly 37% faster than stock market growth during this period and far eclipsed the slow 18.1% growth in a typical worker's annual compensation. Automation is replacing workers as companies are downsizing their workforce. The CEO-to-worker compensation ratio reached 399-to-1 in 2021, a new high. This stands in stark contrast to the 20-to-1 CEO-to-worker compensation ratio in 1965.[39] This does not mean that the political center and political left would not implement their usual campaign methods during the 2024 presidential race. That is too much to ask. However, what the political center and left can do is first and foremost come together themselves, and add to their political methodology a formulation and articulation for the American people, of a vision for a more fair, more just, and more equitable version of an American future for all Americans, and what that future would look like. Currently, based on the evidence, America is headed in the direction of widening gaps in income and wealth and, therefore, a health inequitable society; and the American people feel this inequity, this unfairness in their daily lives. Rising income, wealth, and health inequalities isolates and marginalizes segments of the society. This allows some leaders to use this feeling of isolation, marginalization, and unfairness in the society to manipulate and divide the American public and polarize our country's politics based on cultural and ideological issues that are not the major drivers of their everyday well-being. "The reason you are having problems in your life is because of those people over there" language. In contrast, creating public policies that give rise to reasonable fairness, equity, and equal opportunity in a society counteracts this statement's falsehood, and motivates people to do better and work harder because they feel a part of the society. They feel united by the fair and just opportunities and ideals of America. Widening wealth and income inequality, on the other hand, is severely overburdening the middle class and tears at the very fabric of what America is, creating economic stress and social unease. As Robert Reich said, "What defines America? We are not a race. We are not a creed. We are a conviction."[40] Justice Louis D. Brandeis said, "What are the American ideals? They are the development of the individual for his own and the common good; the development of the individual through liberty; and the attainment of the common good through democracy and social justice."[41] Is there the "Will" to bring this country together around a vision and a version of a more equitable and fair future for America, through building partnerships and alliances of common interests, creating common purpose, creating the environment for authentic policy compromises, leadership that manages our differences in the interest of the country, and each of us operating with a willingness to be accountable for the well-being of the country? The answer is yes, and the Biden administration needs to paint a vision of that American future and take that vision directly to the American people.

The way to help understand the challenge of getting to the "Will for Change" is to consider the metaphor that each of the movements above are individual cars, with individual drivers on different highways, many going in different directions, some even crashing into one another. A more cohesive approach would be to have each of these different movements make the decision to get on the same bus together, and go in the same direction on the same highway. The literal force and impact of the combined, coordinated, and collaborative effort of these individual movements working together will far outweigh and amplify any singular efforts they could do alone. The synergy of this combined effort creates a pathway away from the notion of simply "hoping" one's way to something more tangibly positive for the country, to fueling and empowering an authentic unified whole, pointed in a similar direction by leadership, producing the "Will for Change." The political objective of the right is twofold: 1) to suppress an individual's right to vote and, therefore, to suppress a person's most valuable tool in a democracy, their right to freely participate in their democracy, and 2) to divide us using the old but effective "divide and conquer" strategy. The correct response to the political right's objective is to unite. And that also means uniting with those on the political right who do not see compromise as a dirty word. Unity does not mean agreement on every issue. It does, however, mean agreement on the most fundamental tenets of American society. This means being governed by the rule of law, that the United States Constitution is the supreme law of the land and provides standards against which all statutory laws and administrative rules and regulations are to be judged; and a belief in democracy as our system of government in which state power is vested in the people and the only legitimate form of government is one in which public authority derives from the people. Unity (these different movements making the decision to get on the same bus together, going in the same direction, on the same highway, not necessarily agreeing on everything) governed by the above principles, creates a greater movement, with greater political power based on increased fairness and justice and therefore a greater sense of participatory democracy. "This ultimately facilitates and enables the 'Will for Change' in a country where the progress of the American experiment always continues, is ever evolving, but never complete."[42]

NOTES

1. John Dewey, *How We Think: A Restatement of the Relation of Reflective Thinking to the Educative Process* (Boston: D. C. Health, 1933).

2. Herbert C. Smitherman, "The Impact of Affirmative Action on U.S. Medical Education," Wayne State University School of Medicine, September 27, 2017.

3. The National Advisory Commission on Civil Disorders, *Report of the National Advisory Commission on Civil Disorders* (Washington, DC: U.S. Department of Justice, Office of Justice Programs, 1968), 1; History Matters, "'Our Nation Is Moving Toward Two Societies, One Black, One White—Separate and Unequal,'" excerpts from the Kerner Report, available at http://historymatters.gmu.edu/d/6545; Herbert C. Smitherman, Jr., Lamar K. Johnson, and Anil N. F. Aranha, "Fifty Years Since the 1967 Rebellion, Have Health and Health Care Services Improved?," in *Healing Our Divided Society: Investing in America Fifty Years After the Kerner Report*, eds., Fred Harris and Alan Curts (Abilene, KS: Eisenhower Foundation and Philadelphia: Temple University Press, 2018), 178–190.

4. Herbert C. Smitherman, "I'm a Black Doctor. Here's Why We All Should Take the COVID Vaccine," BridgeDetroit, January 18, 2021.

5. World Health Organization, "Constitution," 1946, https://www.who.int/about/governance/constitution; Herbert C. Smitherman Jr., L. Kallenbach and Anil N.F. Aranha, An Urgent Need for Healthcare Collaboration to Decrease Excess Mortality Among the Older Population of the Detroit/Wayne, Wayne County Medical Society of Southeast Michigan—Medical Bulletin, March 2020, http://pageturn.vpdemandcreationservices.com/DMN/1Q20/mobile/index.html#p=20; James

D. Chesney, Herbert C. Smitherman, Cynthia Taueg, Jennifer Mach and Lucille Smith, *Taking Care of the Uninsured* (Detroit, MI: Wayne State University, 2008), 36.

6. Healthy People 2030, "Social Determinants of Health," United States Department of Health and Human Services, Office of Disease Prevention and Health Promotion, n.d., https://health.gov/healthypeople/priority-areas/social-determinants-health. Ibid; World Health Organization, "Social Determinants of Health," n.d., https://www.who.int/health-topics/social-determinants-of-health;World Health Organization, "Closing the Gap in a Generation: Health Equity Through Action on the Social Determinants of Health, https://www.who.int/publications/i/item/WHO-IER-CSDH-08.1; Neighborhood Outreach Access to Health, "Social Determinants of Health," n.d., https://noahhelps.org/sdoh/; Pennsylvania Medical Society, "Social Determinants of Health," n.d.

7. Restoring Racial Justice, Instagram page, n.d., @restoringracialjustice.

8. Bay Area Regional Health Inequities Initiative, "BARHII Framework," n.d., https://barhii.org/framework. Revised and adapted for a presentation by Herbert C. Smitherman, Jr., "Social Determinants of Health," Medical Network One, Manage Care Organizations, April 17, 2019, Rochester, Michigan.

9. Michael Marmot, "Social Determinants of Health Inequalities," *The Lancet* 365, no. 9464 (2005)): 1099–1104, https://doi.org/10.1016/S0140-6736(05)71146-6; Hilary Waldron, "Mortality Differentials by Lifetime Earnings Decile: Implications for Evaluations of Proposed Social Security Law Changes," *Social Security Bulletin* 73, no. 1 (2013): 1–37; Johan P. Mackenbach et al., "Socioeconomic Inequalities in Health in 22 European Countries," *New England Journal of Medicine* 358, no. 23 (2008): 2468–2481, doi:10.1056/NEJMsa0707519; Raj Chetty et al., "The Association Between Income and Life Expectancy in the United States, 2001–2014," *Journal of the American Medical Association* 315, no. 16 (2016): 1750–66, doi:10.1001/jama.2016.4226; Jacob Bor and Sandro Galea, "The Cost of Economic Inequality to the Nation's Physical Health," *Boston Globe*, April 25, 2017, https://www.bostonglobe.com/opinion/2017/04/25/the-cost-economic-inequality-nation-physical-health/JTsEP3XkNx3425ypbw4KRI/story.html; Dhruv Khullar and Dave A. Chokshi, "Health, Income, & Poverty: Where We Are & What Could Help," Health Affairs, October 4, 2018, doi:10.1377/hpb20180817.901935.

10. Centers for Disease Control and Prevention, "Racism and Health," last reviewed September 18, 2023, https://www.cdc.gov/minorityhealth/racism-disparities/index.html; Courtney D. Cogburn, "Culture, Race, and Health: Implications for Racial Inequities and Population Health," *Milbank Q* 97, no. 3 (2019): 736–61, doi:10.1111/1468-0009.12411; David R. Williams, "Miles to Go Before We Sleep: Racial Inequities in Health," *Journal of Health and Social Behavior* 53, no. 3 (2012): 279–95. doi:10.1177/0022146512455804; David R. Williams and Selina A. Mohammed, "Racism and Health I: Pathways and Scientific Evidence," *American Behavioral Scientist* 57, no. 8 (2013): 1152–73, doi:10.1177/0002764213487340; David R. Williams and Selina A. Mohammed, "Racism and Health II: A Needed Research Agenda for Effective Interventions," *American Behavioral Scientist* 57, no. 8 (2013): 1200–26, doi:10.1177/0002764213487341; Ana Hernández Kent, Lowell R. Ricketts, and Ray Boshara, "What Wealth Inequality in America Looks Like: Key Facts & Figures," Federal Reserve Bank of St. Louis, August 14, 2019, https://www.stlouisfed.org/open-vault/2019/august/wealth-inequality-in-america-facts-figures; Ana Hernández Kent and Lowell R. Ricketts, "Has Wealth Inequality in America Changed over Time? Here Are Key Statistics," Federal Reserve Bank of St. Louis, December 2, 2020, https://www.stlouisfed.org/open-vault/2020/december/has-wealth-inequality-changed-over-time-key-statistics.

11. Centers for Disease Control and Prevention, "Impact of Racism on Our Nation's Health," last review August 16, 2023, https://www.cdc.gov/minorityhealth/racism-disparities/impact-of-racism.html; also see Boughaba Charaff Edine and Selkhan Ismail, "The Removal Act and Ethnic Cleansing of the Indigenous" (PhD diss.), Kasdi Merbah Ouargla University, 2022.

12. U.S. Department of Health, Education, and Welfare, *Vital Statistics of the United States, 1967, Volume 2—Mortality* (Washington, DC: U.S. Government Printing Office, 1969). Elizabeth Arias et al., "Provisional Life Expectancy Estimates for 2021," *Vital Statistics Rapid Release* report no. 23, National Center for Health Statistics, August 2022, https://stacks.cdc.gov/view/cdc/118999.

13. Danielle M. Ely and Anne K. Driscoll, "Infant Mortality in the United States: Provisional Data from the 2022 Period Linked Birth/Infant Death File," *Vital Statistics Rapid Release* report no. 33, National Center for Health Statistics, November 2023, https://stacks.cdc.gov/view/cdc/133699; U.S. Department of Health, Education, and Welfare, *Vital Statistics of the United States, 1967*, vol. 2, *Mortality* (Washington, DC: U.S. Government Printing Office, 1969).

14. Donna L. Hoyert, "Maternal Mortality Rates in the United States, 2021," NCHS Health E-Stats, 2023, https://dx.doi.org/10.15620/cdc:124678; The Century Foundation. America's Maternal Mortality Crisis is Worsening. Available at: https://tcf.org/content/facts/americas-maternal-mortality-crisis-is-worsening/; The Century Foundation. The Worsening U.S. Maternal Health Crisis in Three Graphs. Available at: https://tcf.org/content/commentary/worsening-u-s-maternal-health-crisis-three-graphs/.

15. Farida B. Ahmed et al., "Provisional Mortality Data—United States, 2022," *Morbidity and Mortality Weekly Report* 72, no. 18 (2023): 488–2, https://www.cdc.gov/mmwr/volumes/72/wr/pdfs/mm7218a3-H.pdf.

16. Centers for Disease Control and Prevention, "About Chronic Diseases," last reviewed July 21, 2022, https://www.cdc.gov/chronic-disease/about/index.html.

17. Healthy People 2030, "Leading Health Indicators," United States Department of Health and Human Services, Office of Disease Prevention and Health Promotion, n.d., https://health.gov/healthypeople/objectives-and-data/leading-health-indicators.

18. See notes 12 and 13.

19. See notes 12 and 14.

20. The Century Foundation, "America's Maternal Mortality Crisis is Worsening," April 4, 2023, https://tcf.org/content/facts/americas-maternal-mortality-crisis-is-worsening; Jamila Taylor et al., "The Worsening U.S. Maternal Health Crisis in Three Graphs," The Century Foundation, March 2, 2022, https://tcf.org/content/commentary/worsening-u-s-maternal-health-crisis-three-graphs/. Also see note 15.

21. See notes 12 and 15. Centers for Disease Control and Prevention, "Maternal Mortality," last reviewed April 26, 2023, https://www.cdc.gov/maternal-mortality/index.html; Marian F. MacDorman et al., "Racial and Ethnic Disparities in Maternal Mortality in the United States Using Enhanced Vital Records, 2016–2017," *American Journal of Public Health* 111, no. 9 (2021): 1673–81; Elizabeth A. Howell, "Reducing Disparities in Severe Maternal Morbidity and Mortality," *Clinical Obstetrics and Gynecology* 61, no. 2 (2018): 387–99; Juanita J. Chinn, Iman K. Martin, and Nicole Redmond, "Health Equity Among Black Women in the United States," *Journal of Women's Health* 30, no. 2 (2021): 212–19. See also note 16.

22. See notes 12 and 16.

23. Centers for Disease Control and Prevention, "COVID-19 Death and Data Resources," last reviewed June 23, 2023, https://www.cdc.gov/nchs/nvss/covid-19.htm.

24. See notes 12, 16, and 17.

25. See notes 16 and 17.

26. Our World in Data, "Life Expectancy Versus Gross Domestic Product Per Capita in 2021," 2022, https://ourworldindata.org/grapher/life-expectancy-un-vs-gdp-per-capita-wb?time=latest; Stephanie A. Bond Huie et al., "Wealth, Race, and Mortality," *Social Science Quarterly* 84, no. 3 (2003): 667–84.

27. Tami Luhby, "White Americans Have Far More Wealth Than Black Americans. Here's How Big the Gap Is," CNN, October 23, 2023, https://www.cnn.com/2023/10/31/us/us-racial-wealth-gap-reaj/index.html.

28. Ellora Derenoncourt et al., "Wealth of Two Nations: The U.S. Racial Wealth Gap, 1860–2020," National Bureau of Economic Research Working Paper 30101, June 2022, https://www.nber.org/papers/w30101.

29. M. G. Marmot et al., "Employment Grade and Coronary Heart Disease in British Civil Servants," *Journal of Epidemiology and Community Health* 32, no. 4 (1978): 244–49; M. G. Marmot, M. J. Shipley, and Geoffrey Rose, "Inequalities in Death—Specific Explanation of a General Pattern," *The Lancet* 323, no. 8384 (1984): 1003–06, https://www.thelancet.com/journals/lancet/article/PIIS0140-6736(84)92337-7/fulltext; M.G. Marmot et al., "Health Inequalities Among British Civil Servants: The Whitehall II Study," *The Lancet* 337, no. 8754 (1991): 1387–93.

30. Food and Nutrition Service, "Supplemental Nutrition Assistance Program (SNAP)," U.S. Department of Agriculture, n.d., https://www.fns.usda.gov/snap/supplemental-nutrition-assistance-program; National Head Start Association, "Facts and Impacts," n.d., https://nhsa.org/resource/facts-and-impacts; Office of Policy, Performance, and Evaluation, "Earned Income Tax Credit: Interventions Addressing the Social Determinants of Health," Centers for Disease Control and Prevention, last reviewed December 15, 2022, https://www.cdc.gov/policy/hi5/taxcredits/; U.S. Department of Health and Human Services, "About the Affordable Care Act," last reviewed March 17, 2022, https://www.hhs.gov/healthcare/about-the-aca/index.html; U.S. Department of Education, "Federal Pell Grant Program," n.d., https://www2.ed.gov/programs/fpg/index.html; Council on Community Pediatrics, "Poverty and Child Health in the United States," *Pediatrics* 137, no. 4 (2016): e20160339, doi:10.1542/peds.2016-0339.

31. Amelia Costigan, Keshia Garnett, and Emily Troiano, "The Impact of Structural Racism on Black Americans," Catalyst, September 30, 2020, https://www.catalyst.org/research/structural-racism-black-americans.

32. Jill S. Cannon et al., "Decades of Evidence Demonstrate That Early Childhood Programs Can Benefit Children and Provide Economic Returns," RAND Corporation, RB-9993-RWJF, 2017, https://www.rand.org/pubs/research_briefs/RB9993.html.

33. The White House, "The Economics of Early Childhood Investments," December 2014, https://obamawhitehouse.archives.gov/sites/default/files/docs/the_economics_of_early_childhood_investments.pdf.

34. Rebecca Gale, "Housing Mobility Programs and Health Outcomes," *Health Affairs Health Policy Brief*, June 7, 2018, doi:10.1377/hpb20180313.616232.

35. Mark M. Zandi, "Assessing the Macro Economic Impact of Fiscal Stimulus 2008," Moody's, January 2008, https://www.economy.com/mark-zandi/documents/Stimulus-Impact-2008.pdf.

36. Seth A. Berkowitz et al., "Supplemental Nutrition Assistance Program (SNAP) Participation and Health Care Expenditures Among Low-Income Adults," *JAMA Internal Medicine* 177, no. 11 (2017): 1642–49, doi:10.1001/jamainternmed.2017.4841.

37. David Simon, Mark McInerney, and Sarah Goodell, "The Earned Income Tax Credit, Poverty, and Health," *Health Affairs Health Policy Brief*, October 4, 2018, doi:10.1377/hpb20180817.769687; Sara Markowitz et al., "Effects of State-Level Earned Income Tax Credit Laws in the U.S. on Maternal Health Behaviors and Infant Health Outcomes," *Social Science & Medicine* 194 (2017): 67–75; Hilary Hoynes, Doug Miller, and David Simon, "Income, the Earned Income Tax Credit, and Infant Health," *American Economic Journal: Economic Policy* 7, no. 1 (2015): 172–211; Rita Hamad and David H. Rehkopf, "Poverty, Pregnancy, and Birth Outcomes: A Study of the Earned Income Tax Credit," *Paediatric and Perinatal Epidemiology* 29, no. 5 (2015): 444–52. See also Office of Policy, Performance, and Evaluation, "Earned Income Tax Credit: Interventions Addressing the Social Determinants of Health."

38. Domestic Policy Council, Office of Science and Technology Policy, "U.S. Playbook to Address Social Determinants of Health," The White House, November 2023, https://www.whitehouse.gov/wp-content/uploads/2023/11/SDOH-Playbook-3.pdf.

39. Doug Baker, Josh Bivens, and Jessica Schieder, "Reining in CEO Compensation and Curbing the Rise of Inequality," Economic Policy Institute, June 2019, https://www.epi.org/publication/reining-in-ceo-compensation-and-curbing-the-rise-of-inequality; Josh Bivens and Jori Kandra, "CEO Pay Has Skyrocketed 1,460% Since 1978," Economic Policy Institute, October 4, 2022, https://www.epi.org/publication/ceo-pay-in-2021; Economic Policy Institute, "The Productivity–Pay Gap," updated October 2022, https://www.epi.org/productivity-pay-gap.

40. Robert Reich, "Robert Reich: The Meaning of America," *Eurasia Review*, February 20, 2018, https://www.eurasiareview.com/20022018-robert-reich-the-meaning-of-america-oped.

41. Louis D. Brandeis, "True Americanism—Address of Louis D. Brandeis (1915), VCU Social Welfare History Project, July 5, 1915, https://socialwelfare.library.vcu.edu/issues/immigration/true-americanism-address-louis-d-brandeis-1915.

42. Herbert C. Smitherman, "The 1967 Kerner Report: How Far Have We Come?," Wayne State University School of Medicine, October 29, 2023.

Latino, Native American, and Asian American Policy Perspectives

CHAPTER 19

The Power of Stories

Janet Murguía

INTRODUCTION[1]

The typical response for analysts asked to update the prescriptions outlined in *Healing Our Divided Society*[2] would be to outline demographic changes and progress since that landmark 2018 book, list remaining challenges, and conclude with a series of policy proposals. This chapter doesn't do that, for a couple of reasons. First, one is hard-pressed to come up with many startlingly new or innovative policy proposals to address the nation's racial divides either generally, or with respect to Latinos in particular. Indeed, Henry Cisneros' brilliant chapter[3] in *Healing Our Divided Society* manages to be both comprehensive and succinct in outlining key interventions in education, income and wealth, health, housing, and immigration policy required to close socioeconomic gaps between Latinos[4] and other Americans.

Second, I agree with those who observe that what is lacking in today's debate is the political will to enact policy changes to address racial inequalities, not the absence of sound proposals. The question is: Why? One answer might lie in a topic few policy wonks address: arts and culture. And more specifically, ways through which our fellow Americans learn accurate and accessible stories about how today's inequalities arose, and what it takes for society to break down barriers.

So instead of a "traditional" policy piece, this chapter considers how we might deploy the power of stories to build a more favorable political and social environment conducive to progress. These stories include important roles played by the courts, lawmakers, and institutions like civil rights organizations in producing substantive advancements. But mostly they're about the people who catalyzed change, and how we might look to their example for clues about our own next steps.

STILL INVISIBLE AFTER ALL THESE YEARS

Experts in neuroscience and political psychology have long known about the persuasive power of simple, emotionally compelling stories.[5] Despite the fact that the nation's nearly 64 million Hispanics are now our largest ethnic minority constituting nearly one in five Americans,[6] few of us are exposed to many stories about the Latino community. To cite just a few examples, in news media discussions about racial equity, fewer than 6% even mention Latinos, and few of those actually cite people of Hispanic origin.[7] Even the well-informed readers of this volume may not be aware that Hispanics had among the highest rates of COVID-19 infections and mortality,[8] a result that isn't surprising since less than 2% of news coverage of the pandemic even mentioned Latinos.[9]

There is a similar pattern in arts and culture. A study by the Annenberg Inclusion Initiative at the University of Southern California found "an epidemic of invisibility" of Latino characters in film,[10] just the latest in a long line of such reports. This finding is also unsurprising since Latinos are heavily underrepresented in the media industry, according to two Government Accountability Office reports commissioned by Representative Joaquin Castro and the Congressional Hispanic Caucus.[11]

Perhaps underlying both of these phenomena is the near absence of the teaching of Latino subjects in schools. A recent report by UnidosUS and the Johns Hopkins University School of Education found that only 28 of the 222—or 13%—of the "seminal content" items determined by expert historians to be essential in understanding the Latino experience were covered in the widely used high school history textbooks.[12] The situation isn't much better in college. Despite the rapid growth of the Hispanic population in the 5 decades since the Kerner Commission report, the number, size, and resources of Latino Studies centers have not grown commensurately.[13]

Latino roots in our country run deep. We have fought in all its wars, helped build its cities, put food on its tables, competed at the highest levels in business, academia, and government, and broken new ground in science, medicine, and the law. Latinos are woven into the fabric of America as much as any other community. Our beginnings as an American community, however, were framed by conquest. Many of us know quite a bit about aspects of the European conquest of the "New World" because we've been taught about the history of Spanish, English, and Portuguese colonizers' dominance of the indigenous peoples of Latin America. Most of us are aware that the United States seized much of what is now the American Southwest during the Mexican–American War. Some may even recall that the United States acquired Puerto Rico after the Spanish–American War.

However, few of us are aware of the underside of this history or the stories of how courageous people stepped up to catalyze changes in law, policy, arts, and culture that have made this nation more inclusive of all of its people.

PEOPLE WHO MADE A DIFFERENCE

Gonzalo and Felicitas Mendez

Under the Treaty of Guadalupe Hidalgo in 1848, all those in the newly acquired territories of Texas, California, Colorado, New Mexico, Nevada, Utah, and Arizona—including people of Mexican origin—were declared American and guaranteed rights as U.S. citizens. But much like the rights of newly freed slaves after the Civil War, the status of many of these citizens was soon violated by the same tactics used in the South under Jim Crow laws. "Anglos," as the majority-white population called themselves, treated the native "Mexicans"—regardless of their citizenship status—as an inferior race, meant only for manual labor. People of Mexican origin were excluded politically, relegated to segregated housing, segregated entertainment, and segregated schooling. Signs posted in restaurants and swimming pools typically stated, "No dogs or Mexicans allowed."[14]

Even as recently as 1930, an estimated 85% of Latino students in the Southwest attended segregated "Mexican" schools that were vastly inferior to the "White" schools.[15] In 1943, Gonzalo Mendez, a Mexican American, moved his family to the city of Westminster in Orange County, California. A respected business owner, Gonzalo and his wife, Felicitas, a native of Puerto Rico, took their children to enroll in the neighborhood school. But, when they arrived, they were told it was a "White" school and their children were refused admittance. As U.S. citizens, they found this unacceptable. They hired a lawyer and—in partnership with the League of United Latin American Citizens (LULAC)—filed suit against the school district. In 1947, the 9th Circuit Court of Appeals ruled for the first time that school segregation was unconstitutional in the groundbreaking case, *Mendez v. Westminster*.[16]

The historical significance of *Mendez* to the fight for educational equality cannot be overstated. It was the first Supreme Court case to declare the policy of "separate but equal" unconstitutional. It catalyzed the court's reversal of *Plessy v. Ferguson*, the infamous case that enshrined Jim Crow laws requiring racial segregation as constitutional. NAACP attorney Thurgood Marshall recognized the enormous significance of the *Mendez* decision and joined the *Mendez* plaintiffs and assisted in the successful appeal of the case in the California Supreme Court. It helped shape Marshall's and the NAACP's legal strategy to achieve victory in *Brown v. Board of Education* 7 years later. And it all started because two brave parents refused to take no for an answer.

Antonia Pantoja

Another pioneer fought for the rights of Puerto Rican students in New York City. Like Mexican Americans, Puerto Ricans became subject to U.S. jurisdiction via conquest after the Spanish–American War in 1898. Systemic discrimination and disruptions of the island's economy brought about by the United States led to a massive out-migration of Puerto Ricans to the mainland, mainly to New York City.[17] For decades, the school system there insisted that the lack of educational achievement among Puerto Rican students was the fault of their parents and their "culture." But Puerto Rican educators such as Antonia Pantoja knew that it was the school system, itself, that neglected and marginalized these students. In 1961, she founded ASPIRA, a major educational advocacy and leadership development organization. Even today, virtually every major Puerto Rican leader in the United States was once an "Aspirante."[18]

Antonia Pantoja is best known for founding Aspira. But her personal story is extraordinarily compelling. The daughter of poor tobacco and laundry workers on the island, in her early twenties, Pantoja arrived in New York in 1944, during World War II. Although she had a teaching degree from Puerto Rico, she could only find work as a welder, and she promptly helped organize a union at her workplace. She earned a scholarship to Hunter

College, and later to Columbia, where she was awarded a master's degree in social work. I can only imagine what life was like for the young, Afro-Latina, queer Pantoja as she juggled her job, her studies, and her activism to overcome the enormous barriers she faced based on her ethnicity, race, gender, and sexual orientation.[19]

By 1971, the high school dropout rate among Puerto Rican students had grown to an estimated 60–65%. ASPIRA, represented by the Puerto Rican Legal Defense and Education Fund (now LatinoJustice), filed suit against the New York City Board of Education in 1972, arguing that the equal opportunity promised by *Brown* was being denied Puerto Rican students based not only on ethnicity, but also their language. The board fought the lawsuit vigorously until it was preempted by the U.S. Supreme Court decision *Lau v. Nichols*, brought by a group of Chinese parents in California. The *Lau* decision stated for the first time that refusing to provide instruction in a student's native language violated their civil rights. Immediately thereafter, the New York City Board of Education and ASPIRA entered into a consent decree[20] that provided bilingual education to English learner students.[21] *Lau* and the ASPIRA consent decree established the importance of providing equal educational opportunity to English learners, a fight that continues to this day. All because Antonia Pantoja courageously stepped up to demand equity for her community.

Lidia and Jose López

Perhaps even more courageous were the families in the landmark *Plyler v. Doe* case that established the right of a child to attend school regardless of their family's immigration status. In a fit of anti-immigrant sentiment, in 1975, the Texas legislature passed a law that allowed school districts to charge undocumented immigrant families tuition to attend public schools. Based on that law, the Tyler school district just east of Dallas, Texas, informed Lidia and Jose López that their children had been expelled from school and could only return if they paid a tuition of $1,000 each. Despite the fact that most similarly situated families rightly feared that publicly involving themselves in the lawsuit could lead to their deportation, aided by the Mexican American Legal Defense and Educational Fund (MALDEF), they sued the district.

They continued to be plaintiffs even after a judge said he could not guarantee their safety or their ability to remain in the United States. They stuck with it even after the Immigration and Naturalization Service (INS) began a series of raids around Tyler.[22] They remained plaintiffs even though the Texas state government kept appealing, and it took 5 years for the courts to reach a decision. Finally, in 1982, the Supreme Court ruled 5–4 in *Plyler* that denying undocumented children an education was unconstitutional. The majority opinion recognized the grave societal harms of creating a class of children without the right to go to school.[23] Some eminent court watchers thought the decision "a doubtful" precedent," noting the bare majority at a time that the court seemed to be trending conservative.[24] But the decision has withstood the test of time, more than 4 decades later.

This case, along with *Mendez*, the Aspira consent decree, and *Lau*, provided the foundation for equal opportunity in education for millions of Latino and other language-minority children.

THE ROLE OF INSTITUTIONS

Gonzalo and Felicitas Mendez, Antonia Pantoja, and Lidia and Jose López didn't effect change alone. They relied on help from civil rights organizations like LULAC, Aspira, LatinoJustice, and MALDEF to change inequitable systems. UnidosUS, the organization I'm privileged to lead, is perhaps best known for its work on changing policy and practice to advance opportunity for Hispanic Americans. But from its very beginnings it has also recognized the importance of shaping arts and culture to better inform our fellow Americans about the history of the Latino experience in this country.

In the 1970s and 1980s UnidosUS played a pivotal role in bringing critically acclaimed, compelling films like *The Ballad of Gregorio Cortez* and *The Milagro Beanfield War* to the silver screen. *Cortez*, which featured Edward James Olmos in his first starring role, is a true story that draws its dramatic power from Cortez's escape from a massive manhunt. Its substantive lesson is that Cortez's purported offense was a shooting in self-defense, brought about by an Anglo's mistranslation of Spanish in the Texas frontier at the turn of the 20th century.[25] The Robert Redford and Moctezuma Esparza–produced *Milagro Beanfield War* is an apocryphal tale of the displacement of Hispanos in New Mexico. The movie is based on the John Nichols novel that has been compared to John Steinbeck's *Grapes of Wrath* in that both are fictional accounts based on actual events that describe common people fighting injustice.[26] Importantly, both the novel and the movie portray Latinos as protagonists in responding to injustice; the film was known to produce outbursts of "Viva La Raza" at showings in communities with large Latino audiences.[27]

Starting in the mid-1990s, for more than 2 decades, we also sponsored the American Latino Media Arts (ALMA) Awards, a network-broadcast award show to honor Latino-themed achievements in music, film, and other performance arts.[28] In addition to recognizing established stars, the ALMA Awards also introduced millions of Americans to then new-and-emerging talent including such now-global icons as Cristina Aguilera, Jennifer Lopez, and Shakira.[29]

Similarly, we have long decried the near invisibility of our community in the media, arts, and culture.[30] Today, we continue to educate the public about the importance of including Latino stories in all aspects of American life. And because we understand that Americans learn through multiple channels, increasingly we augment our reports, other publications, and mainstream media outreach with social media postings, graphic presentations, and videos.[31] We don't do this work because it's lucrative financially; indeed, most of it is supported through our own discretionary resources. We do this work because we know that it is vitally important for our fellow Americans to understand our community's experiences and contributions to building our country.

Raul Yzaguirre, my predecessor at UnidosUS, helped advance equity for all Americans in many ways. But perhaps his most lasting achievement was, at least at the time, among his least heralded. In 1994, he persuaded the Smithsonian Institution to commission, and then co-chaired with Mari Carmen Aponte a 15-member task force to examine the Smithsonian's responsiveness to the Hispanic community. The task force produced the report "Willful Neglect," criticizing the virtual absence of Latinos in the Smithsonian's exhibits and staff. Among dozens of recommendations, the report called for the Smithsonian to establish "a museum or museums" dedicated to telling the story of the Hispanic experience in the United States.[32] Legislation to establish the museum was introduced in 2003,[33] although it wasn't until 2020 that it was finally passed by Congress. The advocacy effort to establish the museum has been arduous and there is still a long road ahead. But with the Smithsonian now a partner, not an adversary, and aided by key coalitions like the Friends of the Museum of the American Latino,[34] I am absolutely confident it will happen.

THE ROAD AHEAD

As confident as I am, I'm also fully aware that change won't happen without struggle. The Latino Museum's very first exhibit, called ¡Presente!,[35] is in my judgment an excellent first step in bringing vital information about the Latino community to ordinary Americans that has received considerable critical acclaim.[36] The exhibit has also been controversial, attacked by some prominent Hispanics as portraying "Latinos as victims of an oppressive United States."[37] (Full disclosure: UnidosUS is a content partner of the Smithsonian on this and future exhibits.) To put my cards on the table, I believe any fair reading of history demonstrates that "structural" or "systemic" systemic racism has played a significant role in explaining socioeconomic disparities that Latinos experience today, and my organization has produced extensive substantive analyses supporting this point of view.[38] But I also believe that these, like other similar controversies, can and should be addressed by historians, curators, and other experts from diverse perspectives.

Similarly, anyone paying attention to what children are taught in school is aware of the increasingly intense public debate about books that address race, sexual orientation and identity, climate change, and a host of other subjects. One book deemed by some school officials as inappropriate for young students is *Roberto Clemente: Pride of the Pittsburgh Pirates*,[39] the story of the first Latino to be inducted into the Baseball Hall of Fame. The book's apparent fault was its portrayal of the racism that the Afro-Latino, Puerto Rican Clemente faced.[40] Ultimately, the book was approved for use after extensive advocacy by PENAmerica, LatinoJustice, other advocates, and scholars.[41] In this case, once again, after robust public debate, the right outcome was achieved.

Progress never happens without struggle, yet I remain optimistic.

MY STORY

One of the things that gives me optimism is the inspiration of people like Gonzalo and Felicitas Mendez, Antonia Pantoja, and Lidia and Jose López. My own parents' story is equally inspirational. Although my father, Alfredo Murguía, was born in Oklahoma, his family, facing both the Great Depression and the Dust Bowl, returned to Mexico in the 1930s. Other families were forcibly repatriated to Mexico due to a policy historians call the "Decade of Betrayal" that saw millions of Mexican-origin people uprooted, most with no semblance of due process.[42] My dad grew up in Mexico as a young boy with his parents. During World War II, he returned to the United States initially to report for military service, ended up settling in Kansas City, Kansas, with my mom, Amalia, and my oldest sister.

My dad worked at an ice plant and spent 37 years as a steel worker. With seven kids, my mom did not work outside the home, but chipped in with babysitting money. We lived in a very small house with only one bathroom. My siblings and I slept dormitory style in one large bedroom. We had no phone until I was in the 8th grade, no clothes dryer until I went to college—my mom washed clothes in a wringer-washer until then. In Kansas City in the 1950s, when my parents went to the movie theater, they had to sit in a separate section. My father and other people of color were directed to use a bathroom separate from the Whites Only restroom at the steel plant where he worked. My dad saw no good reason why he should have to walk far away to a different bathroom when there was another close by. One day when he was entering this Whites Only bathroom, another worker blocked his path, so my father punched him. My father was a humble man with little education, but he knew right from wrong. My siblings and I learned the importance of being tough but fair, and of standing up for what's right, from him.[43]

My parents instilled in us strong values and the importance of personal responsibility: a strong sense of family, faith, community, hard work, and sacrifice. They often faced hard times, but I never once heard them complain. Thanks to the generosity of scholarships, work-study programs, and financial aid opportunities, six of their seven kids went to college and earned post-secondary education degrees. Martha, the oldest of my siblings, has special needs but she still managed to take three buses to work every day for 30 years. Four of us are lawyers; two became federal judges.

I've been honored to serve as president and CEO of UnidosUS, the nation's largest Latino civil rights organization, and before that as executive vice chancellor of my alma mater, the University of Kansas. But my proudest moment came in the mid-1990s when my parents paid me a visit when I worked in the West Wing of the White House. I'll never forget walking them down the hallway to the Oval Office so they could meet President Clinton. My mom—just outside the door about to enter—had tears streaming down her face and said, "Como llegamos hasta aqui?" (How did we get here?) My father made a beeline for President Clinton, stretching out his hand, and thanked the president for giving me a chance to work there. The president replied, "I hired Janet, and she may have just walked you into this office, but you're the ones who got her here." To me, my story is emblematic of how Latinos and immigrants have contributed to, and strengthened, the United States. And it represents their continued belief in the American Dream.

CONCLUSION

Where we have been invisible, stories make us visible. They reflect the reality of our contributions and help lead to a more accurate narrative of our community.

So when the book commemorating the 100th anniversary of the Kerner Commission report is published, I'm confident it will be filled with the stories of how people of all races, ethnicities, faiths, and gender identities came together to make our country a more equitable place. I'm equally confident that it will include more than one chapter addressing the contributions of Latinos in catalyzing this progress. No doubt famous lawmakers, lawyers and litigators, and civil rights institutions will have played a role in the headline-producing laws, court cases, and other policies that will bend the arc of history toward justice.

But I'll bet that along with pop music, rock, rhythm and blues, bluegrass, hip-hop, country and western, and other genres yet to be invented, the soundtrack to this story will include a few salsas and cumbias. I suspect that the lists of the best movie directors of all time will still include names like Steven Spielberg and Francis Ford Coppola, but many others like Gregory Nava[44] or Alejandro González Iñárritu[45] also will be on the list. Inspired by the example of Lin-Manuel Miranda, whose smash hit *Hamilton* rocked Broadway, a whole new generation of Latino playwrights and performance artists will have produced diverse portrayals of American history for both stage and screen. Television shows like John Leguizamo's MSNBC program *Leguizamo Does America*,[46] which highlights diverse Hispanic cultures across the country, and Eva Longoria's *Searching for Mexico*[47] series on CNN exploring the cultural and social, as well as culinary, aspects of Mexican cuisine, will no longer be unique, but ubiquitous.

High school textbooks will routinely cover the history and contributions of Latinos, LatinX Studies will be de rigueur for any college student with even a passing interest in race relations, and the Museum of the American Latino will be a must-see venue for visitors to the nation's capital.[48] The prevalence of Hispanic-themed artists and topics will, as with many social changes, be both a cause and effect of socioeconomic progress of the Latino community. As more Americans, including the nation's scholars, lawmakers, scientists, journalists, corporate CEOs, and opinion leaders, both Latino and non-Latino, come to understand the contributions of and challenges facing the Hispanic community, barriers that had limited opportunity previously will have fallen.

Instead of verging on "separate and unequal" societies, America will be far closer to fulfilling its promise as the greatest multiracial democracy in the history of the planet. Yes, lawyers and activists, politicians and bureaucrats, academics and advocates, community organizers and social workers will all have played a role in transforming our society. But it will also be the result of ordinary people doing extraordinary things. People like Gonzalo and Felicitas Mendez. José and Lidia López. Antonia Pantoja. Alfredo and Amalia Murguía.

The power of their stories inspires me every day. One day they will inspire all Americans.

NOTES

1. This chapter is based in part on "The Quest for Educational Equity," The John P. Frank Memorial Lecture delivered by the author on April 23, 2019, at Arizona State University: https://www.youtube.com/watch?v=aIfJiQCDHNs. Viviana López Green and Charles Kamasaki, UnidosUS Senior Director, Racial Equity Initiative, and Senior Advisor, respectively, assisted in preparing this chapter for publication. Lisa Navarrete, UnidosUS Advisor to the President, and Joseph Gleason, consultant, helped to develop the original lecture remarks.

2. Fred Harris and Alan Curtis, eds., *Healing Our Divided Society* (Abilene, KS, and Philadelphia: Eisenhower Foundation and Temple University Press, 2018).

3. Henry G. Cisneros, "New Dimensions of Equity," in *Healing Our Divided Society*, eds. Fred Harris and Alan Curtis (Abilene, KS: Eisenhower Foundation and Philadelphia: Temple University Press, 2018), 322–333.

4. The terms "Hispanic" and "Latino" are used interchangeably by the U.S. Census Bureau and throughout this chapter to refer to persons of Mexican, Puerto Rican, Cuban, Central and South American, Dominican, Spanish, and other Hispanic descent. According to the technical definitions used by the Census, Latinos may be of any race. This document uses the sociological construct of "race" whereby, at least historically, most Latinos were treated as a distinct racial group, regardless of ethnicity. Many, including UnidosUS, also refer to this population as "Latinx" to represent the diversity of gender identities and expressions that are present in the community.

5. See, for example, Drew Westen, *The Political Brain: The Role of Emotion in Deciding the Fate of the Nation* (New York: Public Affairs, 2008).

6. U.S. Bureau of the Census, "Hispanic Heritage Month: 2023," August 17, 2023, https://www.census.gov/newsroom/facts-for-features/2023/hispanic-heritage-month.html.

7. Kim Garcia, Sarah Perez-Sanz, and Pamela Meija, "Elevating Latino Experiences and Voices in News About Racial Equity," Berkeley Media Studies Group and UnidosUS, March 15, 2023, https://www.bmsg.org/resources/publications/elevating-latino-experiences-and-voices-in-news-about-racial-equity-findings-and-recommendations-for-more-complete-coverage.

8. Latoya Hill and Samantha Artiga, "COVID-19 Cases and Deaths by Race/Ethnicity: Current Data and Changes Over Time," KFF, August 22, 2022.

9. Julia Weis, "Data: Latinos Make Up Less Than 2% of COVID-19 Media Coverage," Salud America, June 29, 2021, https://salud-america.org/data-latinos-make-up-less-than-2-of-covid-19-media-coverage.

10. Gwen Aviles, "Latinos face 'an epidemic of invisibility' in film: A new report unpacks how Hollywood falls short on diversity," Business Insider, September 26, 2021, https://www.insider.com/hispanics-and-latinos-face-an-epidemic-invisibility-in-hollywood-per-new-report-2021-9.

11. U.S. Government Accountability Office, "Workforce Diversity: Analysis of Federal Data Shows Hispanics Are Underrepresented in the Media Industry," September 21, 2021, https://www.gao.gov/assets/gao-21-105322.pdf; U.S. Government Accountability Office, "Workforce Diversity: Hispanic Workers Are Underrepresented in the Media, and More Data Are Needed for Federal Enforcement Efforts," October 5, 2022, https://www.gao.gov/products/gao-22-104669.

12. Ashley Berner et al., "Analyzing Inclusion of Latino Contributions in U.S. History Curricula for High School," UnidosUS and Johns Hopkins University School of Education, May 2023, https://unidosus.org/wp-content/uploads/2023/05/unidosus_johnshopkins_analyzinginclusionoflatinocontributionsinushistorycurriculaforhighschools.pdf.

13. G. Cristina Mora, Nicholas Vargas, and Dominic Cedillo, "Latino Studies Stagnation," The Latinx Research Center, n.d.

14. There is extensive literature documenting this period. Among many others see David Montejano, *Anglos and Mexicans in the Making of Texas: 1836–1986* (Austin, TX: University of Texas Press, 1987); Edward Telles and Vilma Ortíz, *Generations of Exclusion: Mexican Americans, Assimilation, and Race* (New York: Russell Sage Foundation, 2008); Cynthia E. Orozco, *No Mexicans, Women, or Dogs Allowed* (Austin, TX: University of Texas Press, 2009).

15. Gilbert C. González, *Chicano Education in the Era of Segregation* (Denton, TX: University of North Texas Press, 1990), 12.

16. See the documentary film *Mendez v. Westminster: Desegregating California's Schools*, WBGH Boston, April 8, 2005, trailer at https://www.pbslearningmedia.org/resource/osi04.soc.ush.civil.mendez/mendez-v-westminster-desegregating-californias-schools.

17. For a summary of conditions on the island after U.S. occupation see Claudia Ruíz, "The evolution of the Puerto Rican community in New York City" *UnidosUS Blog*, April 8, 2021, https://unidosus.org/blog/2021/04/08/the-evolution-of-the-puerto-rican-community-in-new-york-city.

18. See Aspira, "What Is Aspira?," https://aspira.org/about-us/what-is-aspira, n.d.

19. Monxo López, "Antonia Pantoja: Organizer and Activist for New York's Puerto Rican Community," Museum of the City of New York, May 14, 2020, https://www.mcny.org/story/antonia-pantoja-organizer-and-activist-new-yorks-puerto-rican-community.

20. *Aspira of New York, Inc., v. Board of Education of City of New York* 394 F. Supp. 1161 (S.D.N.Y. 1975), https://law.justia.com/cases/federal/district-courts/FSupp/394/1161/1415173.

21. William G. Milán and Shirley Muñoz-Hernández, "The New York City Aspira Consent Decree: A Mechanism for Social Change," *Bilingual Review/Revista Bilingue* 4, no. 3 (September–December 1977): 169–79.

22. These raids were ended at MALDEF's request to then-INS Commissioner Leonel Castillo, a Carter appointee. See Michael A. Olivas, *No Undocumented Child Left Behind: Plyler v. Doe and the Education of Undocumented Schoolchildren* (New York: New York University Press, 2012). See also John Powell, "*Plyler v. Doe*: The Education of Undocumented Alien Schoolchildren in Texas, 1975–1982" (PhD diss., Southern Methodist University, 2022), https://scholar.smu.edu/cgi/viewcontent.cgi?article=1019&context=hum_sci_history_etds.

23. Michael A. Olivas, "The Story of *Plyler v. Doe*: The Education of Undocumented Children and the Polity," in David A. Martin and Peter H. Schuck, eds., *Immigration Stories* (Perry, MI: Foundation Press 2005).

24. Linda Greenhouse, "Court's Ruling on Illegal Alens a Doubtful Precedent," *New York Times*, June 17, 1982.

25. Mark Alexander Ortiz, "Cinematic Inclusivity," *Historical Studies Journal* 36 (Spring 2019): 1–21, https://spl.cde.state.co.us/artemis/ucdserials/ucd5410internet/ucd54102019internet.pdf.

26. Motley Deakin, "The Milagro Beanfield War (review)," *Western American Literature* 10, no. 3 (Fall 1975): 249–250, https://muse.jhu.edu/article/529165#.

27. David Steinberg, "Producer Envisions Cultural Message," *Albuquerque Journal*, March 13, 1988.

28. UnidosUS, "1995–2009 Alma Awards Highlights," YouTube, April 29, 2010, video. 9:47, https://www.youtube.com/watch?v=baMYSWwAomo.

29. See, for example, this iconic performance by the emerging singer David Archuleta at the 2009 ALMA Awards: https://www.youtube.com/watch?v=vZN7hBq7bBo.

30. See, for example: Lisa Navarrete with Charles Kamasaki, "Out of the Picture: Hispanics in the Media," National Council of La Raza, August 1994, https://unidosus.org/wp-content/uploads/1994/08/1404_file_OutofPic.pdf.

31. To take just one topic, see recent UnidosUS products on civil rights and racial equity: https://unidosus.org/issues/civil-rights-and-racial-equity.

32. Jacqueline Trescott, "Smithsonian Faulted for Neglect of Latinos," *Washington Post*, May 11, 1994.

33. Bob Menendez, "Menendez: National American Latino Museum Will Be Built," news release December 21, 2020, https://www.menendez.senate.gov/newsroom/press/menendez-national-american-latino-museum-will-be-built.

34. See Friends of the National Museum of the American Latino on LinkedIn, https://www.linkedin.com/company/friends-of-the-national-museum-of-the-american-latino-inc.

35. National Museum of the American Latino, "¡Presente! A Latino History of the United States," 2022, https://latino.si.edu/exhibitions/presente.

The Power of Stories

36. Miranda Mizariegos, "A New Exhibit Takes Visitors Closer to the National Museum of the American Latino," *NPR*, June 22, 2022, https://www.npr.org/2022/06/18/1105847319/a-new-exhibit-takes-visitors-closer-to-the-national-museum-of-the-american-latin.

37. Jennifer Schuessler, "Smithsonian's Latino Museum faces Political Headwinds Before a Brick is Laid," *New York Times*, September 23, 2023, https://www.nytimes.com/2023/09/23/arts/latino-museum-american-smithsonian.html.

38. See "Civil Rights and Racial Equity" page at UnidosUS' website, https://unidosus.org/issues/civil-rights-and-racial-equity for some of these analyses.

39. Jonah Winter and Raul Colon, *Roberto Clemente: Pride of the Pittsburgh Pirates* (New York: Atheneum Books, 2008).

40. Nicole Acevedo, "Roberto Clemente Book Removed from Florida Public Schools Pending Review over Discrimination References," *NBC News*, February 10, 2023, https://www.nbcnews.com/news/latino/roberto-clemente-book-removed-florida-public-schools-rcna70081.

41. Nicole Acevedo, "Roberto Clemente Book Approved for Use in Florida Public Schools Following Review for Discrimination References," *NBC News*, February 22, 2023, https://www.nbcnews.com/news/latino/roberto-clemente-book-florida-discrimination-review-approved-rcna71771.

42. Francísco E. Balderrama and Raymond Rodríguez, *Decade of Betrayal: Mexican Repatriation in the 1930s,* rev. ed. (Albuquerque, NM: University of New Mexico Press, 2006).

43. See excerpt here: Barbara Koppel, Director, *The Gumbo Coalition*, official trailer, https://www.youtube.com/watch?v=FfJclVJ2DY4.

44. Gregory Nava, director of, among many other films, *El Norte* and *Selena*, https://www.imdb.com/name/nm0622695.

45. Alejandro G. Iñárritu won back-to-back Oscars for *The Birdman* and *The Revenant*, see: https://www.imdb.com/name/nm0327944.

46. Episode guide for *Leguizamo Does America*, IMDb, https://www.imdb.com/title/tt27202182.

47. CNN Travel, "First Look at 'Eva Longoria: Searching for Mexico,'" https://www.cnn.com/shows/eva-longoria-searching-for-mexico.

48. For a sneak peek at what's to come, readers are advised to take in the exhibit "¡*Presente*!: A Latino History of the United States," at the Smithsonian National Museum of American History or via a virtual tour; see: National Museum of the American Latino, https://latino.si.edu/exhibitions/presente.

CHAPTER 20

E Pluribus Unum
Out of Many, [We Are] One

Sindy M. Benavides

We draw our strength from the very despair in which we have been forced to live. We shall endure.

—Cesar Chavez

In 1968, the Kerner Commission report concluded that our society was "separate and unequal." The commission's farsightedness is clearly visible more than 50 years later with the increased political polarization of our country, with the most notable example being the January 6, 2021, attack on our U.S. Capitol and democracy. Today we can clearly see the "continuing polarization of the American community, and, ultimately, the destruction of basic democratic values."[1]

In the last 5 decades, a significant number of programs have been created, and eliminated, to address the racial disparities impacting communities of color. Among the most notable is the integration of public schools. Although *Mendez v. Westminster* integrated schools in California in 1947 and *Brown v. Board of Education* integrated schools across the country in 1954, desegregation occurred at a slow pace and with varying timelines by state.

As we seek to highlight key policy recommendations, it is also important to highlight leaders who led ahead of their time as examples of courageous actions taken to create cultural and policy changes. On the issue of integration of schools, a great example is that of Republican governor Linwood Holton of Virginia, who in 1970 voluntarily placed his children, including future Virginia first lady Anne Holton, in the Richmond Public Schools system, which had a significant Black student population. Due to his actions and approach, Governor Holton was penalized for the rest of his political career.

In addition, the type of courage displayed by the Kerner Commission should be highlighted in today's political context because working on commonsense solutions, instead of advancing one's political career, is no longer the norm and could instead advance one's political retirement. What we are seeing from our federal legislative branch is chaos, with the ousting of the speaker of the House, Kevin McCarthy, the first speaker in American history to be removed from this post. "Healing our Divided Society" continues to be a key priority as rhetoric and division have been pervasive. It is not clear that Americans are further apart from each other than we've been in the past, given the historical context in past decades where the voices of non-white communities were not included.[2]

Notably, what has not changed is that national domestic programs, until the Infrastructure Investment and Jobs Act (2021) under President Biden, are still severely underfunded while a significant of revenue is still going to the Department of Defense as was the case in 1960 when taxpayers were funding a war. In fact, today many in Congress are turning their back on the most vulnerable populations in America by putting forth proposals that seek to cut Social Security and Medicare, bedrock programs that help our older population, while also seeking to restrict the Supplemental Nutrition Assistance Program (SNAP) eligibility requirements. Today, many American families are still recovering from a worldwide pandemic and increasing inflation rates with the issues of economy/jobs, housing, and health care still top of mind.

Although there have been advancement and upward economic mobility in the last few decades, Latinos and communities of color have experienced a ping-pong effect on key policy issues impacting their everyday lives, including access to opportunities, with a few steps forward and many more steps being taken back. These include the economy, representation, access to the ballot box, and immigration.

THE INVISIBLE 20%

According to the U.S. Census, as of July 1, 2022, the Hispanic population represented 63.9 million or 19% of the total U.S. population, making it the nation's largest racial or ethnic minority. In comparison, in 1970, only "9.1 million persons of Spanish origin were reported."[3] Although Latinos fuel population growth and will be 68% of all growth from 2020 to 2060,[4] Latinos are largely invisible in decision-making roles both in the private and public sector. Simply put: Although it is clear we exist, our contributions are not acknowledged and our work, as the backbone of many industries, is not valued. Policies shaping our nation and states must be inclusive in the development of policies that impact this growing community that is now nearly one-fifth of our population.

The Hispanic population grew by 50% or more from 2010 to 2020 in 517 of the 1,685 counties with 1,000 or more Hispanics, according to the 2020 Census.[5] Among all 3,140 U.S. counties in 2020, Latinos accounted for a quarter or more of the total population in 311 of them, including 101 where they were the majority.[6] Latinos are the present and future of America. The success of Latinos is the success of America.[7]

Yet as a country, we are missing the mark in providing access to equal opportunities. Before diving in, first, we must understand that there are parts of our (Latino) history that are not reconciled with facts. As Charles Kamasaki explains in *Immigration Reform: The Corpse That Will Not Die*:

> Under the Treaty of Guadalupe Hidalgo, which ended the Mexican-American War of 1848, most of what is now Texas, New Mexico, Arizona, California, Colorado, Utah and Nevada was acquired by the US ... Following the war, according to the conventional narrative, while

there were [sic] might have been unfortunate examples of discrimination against Mexicans and Mexican Americans, these were "casual," even isolated, and never approached anything resembling that faced by African Americans. In this narrative, Latinos resemble "white ethnic" immigrants like the Italians and Southern Europeans of the late nineteenth and early twentieth centuries, destined to face only modest levels of temporary discrimination that eventually were overcome by the country's commitment to equality of opportunity. The notion that native-born Latinos faced significant ongoing discrimination was not widely accepted in progressive circles.[8]

We must then begin with the untold story of Latinos in America, which includes pervasive discrimination, lynching, and guarantees that were never fulfilled to them under the Treaty of Guadalupe Hidalgo as U.S. citizens of this country. Acknowledgement of our contributions will not occur until there is an accurate history of our own community's identity-based discrimination, including the amount of oppression and racism faced by Latinos in our country today.

We also must understand that Latinos are the embodiment of endurance and survival, even when treated as the invisible. The pandemic highlighted the importance of Latinos as "essential workers" in key industries, with four in five Latinos having to leave their home to work and get paid. Latinos continue to work in key sectors within the food industry including as farmworkers and the meat packing plants. In addition, Latinos are in key positions within the health sector, often in the frontlines, interacting directly with the public.

Given the lack of inclusion even in conversations, Latinos are not only invisible, but also neglected and abandoned.

#REPRESENTATIONMATTERS

In a country that is ever more diverse, it is important to have inclusion and accurate representation in both the public and private sector. I want to highlight some advances as well as the opportunities to ensure our voices are present at the local, state, and federal levels.

Latinos in Government and Elected Office

On June 25, 2021, President Biden signed an Executive Order on Diversity, Equity, Inclusion, and Accessibility in the Federal Government. The Executive Order reaffirmed that our country is at its strongest when our public servants reflect the full diversity of the American people.[9] Over a 10-year period, from fiscal year 2011 to fiscal year 2021, the Government Accountability Office found that while the proportion of Hispanic federal employees increased by 1.4% over the decade, the overall percentage remained below 10%, roughly half of Latino representation in the overall U.S. civilian labor force.[10] In the Federal Equal Opportunity Recruitment Program (FEORP) report for fiscal year 2020, the percentage of Latinos in the workforce comprised 9.4%, nowhere near parity of our current overall demographic representation.[11]

In elected office, of the 500,000 elected positions available across the country, Latinos occupy 2% of these positions, or 7,087.[12] It is important to highlight that there are 61 Latino

Members in the 118th Congress, 11.27% of the total membership and nine more members than in the 117th Congress.[13] In addition, key findings from the NALEO Educational Fund report include a considerable increase in Latino representation across all levels of government. "Between 2001 and 2021, the number of Latino U.S. Representatives, state officials, judicial and law enforcement officials, and special district officials each more than doubled."[14] Although we have seen continuous growth in Latinos running for office and getting elected, we have much work ahead to ensure equitable representation at all levels of our government to enable Latinos to occupy these very important policymaking positions. As we continue to build the political bench, it's important that political institutions invest in Latinos rather than sideline them, as a factor used to measure their potential and ability to win their campaign is their ability to fundraise. Institutions must do more to build the pipeline and ensure that Latino candidates are connected to high-dollar networks and other institutions that may be able to support their campaigns.

Latinos in Television and Film

According to Latino Donor Collaborative in the "2022 Latinos in the Media Report," Latinos purchased 29%, or $2.9 billion, of all box office tickets in 2019. Yet in 2022, Latinos were only 3.1% of lead actors in shows, 1.5% of showrunners, and 1.3% of directors.[15] The gap between the Latino consumer proportion, economic impact, and Latino representation in the industry is abysmal.

There are some glimmers of hope, including seeing Latinos in leading roles such as America Ferrera in *Barbie*, which claimed the number one box office spot for 2 weeks in a row.[16] The television and film industry are instrumental in raising awareness and setting cultural trends domestically and globally. For Latinos "to be" and imagine what is possible, Latinos must see themselves represented in diverse roles in Hollywood. Equally important is for the general public to understand that Latinos are Americans, can lead in any role, and can portray any character, because we are racially diverse and can act as the girl next door or be the leading comic superhero, as we saw in *Blue Beetle*.

In the years ahead, it will be critically important that private media companies assess their own leadership structures, investments made in films created and directed by Latinos, and investments made in films where Latinos are in key leading roles. In addition, it's important to assess the progress made in key diversity, equity, and inclusion programs to understand if Latinos are increasing in parity to their demography and consumer base or if it's a mirage disguised under broader numbers.

THE NEW WAVE OF OPPRESSION: LIMITING ACCESS TO THE BALLOT BOX

As Latinos and other communities of color have increased in population numbers and eligible voters, Jim Crow laws that limit, structurally, our ability to access the ballot box have also increased. According to the Pew Research Center, in the 2022 midterm elections, there were 34.5 million Latinos who were eligible to vote, an increase of almost 4.7 million since 2018.[17] One important question we all must ask is why our ability to vote is being restricted when the will and action of the people are a fundamental value of our democracy.

Nationally we have seen key provisions of the Voting Rights Act limited. One of those decisions, *Shelby County v. Holder*, eliminated the use of preclearance, which meant that states no longer had to get federal approval of new voting rules. At the state level, we have seen states with growing numbers of eligible Latino voters, like Texas and Florida (among many others), enact laws that make it harder to vote. In some states, according to Brennan Center research, new voting rules have increased the racial gap in voter turnout.[18]

Although so many civil rights groups at the national and state level have come together in litigation, lawsuits can be costly and may take years. It is also a defensive approach rather than a proactive approach.

POLICY RECOMMENDATIONS

One of the largest areas of opportunity is to continue building coalitions that are diverse and include national and state-based organizations. There must be a multitier advocacy approach at the federal and state level due to the current makeup of the U.S. Supreme Court. Congressional action is needed to establish a new law that protects the right to vote for every citizen of this country.

Among the bills to build momentum around are The Freedom to Vote Act. As explained by the Brennan Center for Justice:

> The Freedom to Vote Act shores up the freedom to vote and strengthens American democracy. It sets baseline national standards to protect voting access and make it harder for partisans to manipulate elections. It creates new protections for election officials and workers, prohibits partisan gerrymandering, and blunts the problem of dark money. These and other key provisions all draw from best practices in the states.

In addition, other historic legislation to garner support for are the John R. Lewis Voting Rights Advancement Act, which would restore and update the Voting Rights Act's protections against racial discrimination in voting, and the For the People Act, which would expand voting rights, overhaul our campaign finance system, and make our democracy more inclusive.

As we look at legislation, it's especially critical to highlight redistricting. It's important to continue building momentum to make redistricting independent to keep self-interest and partisan gerrymandering from occurring. At its core, there should be transparency and public participation, which enables both individuals and grassroots organizations to advocate and bring the voices of the community to the map-drawing process.[19]

ECONOMIC OPPORTUNITY

According to the Bureau of Labor Statistics Projections, 78% of labor force growth over the next 10 years is projected to be Hispanic. Lucy Pérez accurately points to the lost economic opportunity when you take into account that Latino workers are underpaid, less likely to have nonwage employer benefits, and are disproportionately vulnerable to disruption. There is a $288 billion annual disparity in income compared with non-Latino White workers. The implication of this is that if wages for Latino workers were 35% higher, an additional 1.1 million Latinos could join the middle class.[20]

Economic gaps persist, although Latinos are present in the labor market, create small businesses, and are consumers. Latinos continue to be severely neglected, though we start more businesses per capita than any other racial or ethnic group in the United States.[21] Furthermore, as noted by Dan Stangler, "between 2007 and 2019, based on U.S. Census Bureau data, the number of Latino-owned *employer* businesses grew by 34%. The number of White-owned businesses, meanwhile, fell by 7% during that time period."[22]

It is important to highlight that the "new will" in the Executive branch has centered on building systems that seek to include the most underserved, including Latinos. On January 20, 2021, President Biden's first day in office, he signed Executive Order 13985, Advancing Racial Equity and Support for Underserved Communities Through the Federal Government. This historic executive order charged the federal government with advancing equity for all communities, including those that have long been underserved and it addresses the systemic racism in our federal government policies and programs.[23]

Equally notable is President Biden's commitment to increase federal contracting with small, disadvantaged businesses to 15% over 5 years. The trickle effect of the president's actions will be felt decades after, especially as the SBA is releasing contracting data that is disaggregated by race and ethnicity, which serves as a baseline for evaluating government-wide performance within each of the socioeconomic categories. By putting benchmarks and having disaggregated data, the public is able to see if, in fact, the mandates of the executive order will be fulfilled for all communities.

In the private sector, it is also noteworthy to highlight the 2022 State of Latino Entrepreneurship, which gives concrete data on lack of access to capital for Latinos:

> Latino-owned businesses seeking loans from national banks have stronger business metrics than White-owned businesses, yet have lower approval rates for loans over $50,000. At the time of application for business loans from national banks, LOBs have similar, if not better, qualifying indicators than WOBs on average. These include a gross revenue that is three times larger than WOBs, similar business and personal credit scores as WOBs, and lower outstanding debt than WOBs. Nevertheless, LOBs have substantially lower approval rates than WOBs when applying for larger loans ($50,000 or more), and higher rates of approval for small loans (less than $50,000).[24]

SOLUTIONS

To address the invisibility of Latinos in America, we should increase research and conduct polling on Hispanic ethnicity that should include a question around race and color, focused on how Latinos of various phenotypes are perceived by our society at large. In addition, it's important that data collection by the federal government is desegregated by race and ethnicity. In December 2021, the U.S. Small Business Administration disaggregated its data, which allows for transparency and further accountability, as only 1.8% of the 2020 fiscal year federal contracting went to Hispanic-owned small businesses, even as Latino-owned businesses grew in the last 2 decades.

Latinos are highly entrepreneurial and hardworking, but they require access to capital, powerful networks, and information. As programs are being developed in the federal government, it's important to reach the community by having dedicated coaches and navigators who can provide information on how to start a business for rising entrepreneurs and scale businesses for current business owners in both English and Spanish. A potential area of collaboration could be with the Stanford Latino Entrepreneurship Initiative, which operates the SLEI Education Scaling Program, a 9-week immersive program that provides business owners with education, enhanced networks, personal mentorship, and a better understanding of how to access and manage capital to scale their businesses.

Including dedicated funding to ensure that the information is accessible in multiple languages is critical, particularly in reaching English-limited communities. Dedicated funding for translations and developing culturally competent information should not be an afterthought, but rather seen as an investment to create and grow businesses.

Expanding investment in Latino businesses is critical in both the public and private sector, which requires access to capital. In addition, as was noted above, Latinos are denied loans at a higher rate than their white counterparts, which makes it even more difficult to start businesses in emerging sectors like artificial intelligence (AI). It's also important to establish collaborations and partnerships. The private sector should be investing at a higher rate in Latino-led venture capital (VC) firms that in turn are investing in other Latino businesses. These collaborations create stronger networks and may have the ability to address the needs of multigenerational businesses that are seeking to scale, merge, or develop equity.

IMMIGRATION

The United States of America is a nation of immigrants. Since the birth of our country, we have seen how immigrants gradually move up America's social ladder, reaching for their own American dream while shaping our economic standing around the world. According to the U.S. Census, the nation's foreign-born population is projected to rise from 44 million people in 2016 to 69 million in 2060, growing from 14% to 17% of the population. In historical context, the previous historic high was in 1890 when almost 15% of the population was foreign born.[25]

Immigration has always been a contentious issue. As noted by President Kennedy, "Immigration, or rather the British policy of clamping down on immigration, was one of the factors behind the colonial desire for independence. Restrictive immigration policies constituted one of the charges against King George III expressed in the Declaration of Independence."[26]

For decades, America has continued to follow the Immigration and Nationality Act of 1952, which codified our national laws on immigration. However, what is often so perplexing is that our own policymakers and the general public don't understand how our immigration laws must be updated to meet the shortage of labor and position the United States as a country of innovation in a world that is becoming ever more connected.

There is no question that permanent congressional action is needed. Latino Members of Congress must be a part of any immigration deal. To the detriment of our most vulnerable community, if there is no federal congressional action, we will continue to see a state-by-state approach and a wave of governors outdoing themselves by trying to enact some of the most egregious laws in modern times, including enabling local law enforcement to enforce immigration laws or, as we saw in Florida, enacting laws that prohibit individuals from "certain countries of concern" from purchasing property.[27]

It's also important to highlight specific actions that have created change. As it pertains to Temporary Protected Status (TPS), created under the Immigration Act of 1990, as of March 31, 2023, there were approximately 610,630 people with TPS living in the United States.[28]

> Under 8 U.S.C. § 1254a, DHS, in consultation with other federal agencies, may designate a country (or any part of a country) for TPS if (1) there is an armed conflict that prevents the safe return of nationals from that country; (2) there has been an environmental disaster in that country that substantially disrupts living conditions in the area affected; or (3) there are "extraordinary and temporary conditions" in the foreign country that prevent alien nationals from safely returning. An alien from a country designated for TPS may be permitted to remain and work in the United States for the period in which the TPS designation is in effect, even if the alien had not originally entered the United States lawfully.[29]

In the executive branch, the Department of Homeland Security can continue to expand TPS, as we saw in September 2023 when this program was updated to include nearly 500,000 Venezuelans. This program allows immigrants to legally work, support their families, and find stability in their new home. It allows for individuals coming from dangerous countries to emerge from the shadows to enrich and strengthened the fabric of America.

POLICY RECOMMENDATIONS

In *Figures of the Future*, Dr. Michael Rodriguez-Muniz highlights "demodystopias," which build narratives to instill fear and renders the "non-white" populations as a threat to the status quo, white dominance.[30] As we look at the immigration debate, it's important to understand that the portrayal of foreign-born immigrants as the "other" and the perpetual "guest" is important to track, through research, as it shapes the narrative of how new Americans are perceived. We must be ever vigilant of the anti-Hispanic, anti-Asian, anti-immigrant rhetoric employed by white supremacy groups that instill bigotry and racist stereotypes, and seek to dehumanize entire segments of our populations.

There must also be an acknowledgement that America was built on immigration policies that are discriminatory—enacting laws, like the National Origins Act that impacted specific nationalities, set a cap on immigration, and established a discriminatory national-racial quota.[31] As we look toward the future, we must enact national laws that serve our national interest and reflect our values of human dignity, respect, and equality. Congressional action focused on farmworkers, Dreamers, and the 11 million undocumented immigrants should be the center of any proposal moving forward. Although many politicians have built their careers as immigration hardliners by focusing just on the "wall" or the "border," this is shortsighted and a short-term approach to a policy issue that has been untouched for nearly 3 decades and demands a real solution.

In addition, climate change–related disasters like Hurricanes Eta and Iota, violence in countries like Honduras, and high crimes in El Salvador displace populations and continues the flow of migration north. Redesignating the "Ramos" countries, including Honduras and El Salvador as well as others, can resolve the litigation, protect current TPS holders, and prevent additional litigation from anti-immigrant states. This would allow for nearly 2 to 3.5 million people who are already in the Unites States but arrived after the last designation to be eligible for TPS protection and work permits.

CONCLUSION

As we look ahead, there are issues that due to their direct impact on Latinos need to be exposed and further discussed. One such issue includes gun violence, as some of the deadliest mass shootings in recent history have occurred in Latino communities, along with an increase in firearm violence. In 2020, gun violence killed 5,003 Hispanic Americans, a record number that averages to 13 people per day.[32] We must be able to look at the issue of gun violence from a broader lens, including it being an issue of health equity and its impact on education and housing.

As we, the Latino and immigrant people, seek to build a way forward, it is important that we elevate our perspective. We must first do some internal assessments to ensure we too have not become oppressors, particularly as we examine race, nationality, and language within our own communities. As a pueblo that has for far too long survived by overcoming and enduring, we deserve the opportunity to be free, seen, acknowledged, and have the ability to thrive in a country that has for so long been our home. For we too are American.

NOTES

1. John Herbers, "Panel on Civil Disorders Calls for Drastic Action to Avoid 2-Society Nation," *The New York Times*, March 1, 1968.

2. Michael Dimock and Richard Wike, "America Is Exceptional in the Nature of Its Political Divide," Pew Research Center, November 13, 2020.

3. U.S. Census Bureau, "We the American Hispanics," 3.

4. EthniFacts.com, U.S. Census Projections, n.d.

5. Jeffrey S. Passel, Mark Hugo Lopez, and D'Vera Cohn, "U.S. Hispanic Population Continued Its Geographic Spread in the 2010s," Pew Research Center, February 3, 2022.

6. Lucy Pérez et al., "The Economic State of Latinos in America: The American Dream Deferred," McKinsey & Company, December 2021, 13. See Exhibit E2 chart, p. 13: https://www.mckinsey.com/~/media/mckinsey/featured%20insights/sustainable%20inclusive%20growth/the%20economic%20state%20of%20latinos%20in%20america%20the%20american%20dream%20deferred/the-economic-state-of-latinos-in-america-v2.pdf

7. Passel et al., "U.S. Hispanic Population Continued Its Geographic Spread in the 2010s."

8. Charles Kamasaki, *Immigration Reform: The Corpse that Will Not Die* (Simsbury, CT: Mandel Vilar Press, 2019), 43.

9. The White House, "Executive Order on Diversity, Equity, Inclusion, and Accessibility in the Federal Workforce," June 25, 2021.

10. Erich Wagner, "Diversity in the Federal Workforce Has Improved Slightly over the Last Decade: But Latino Representation Among Federal Employees Continues to Lag Behind a Nationwide Benchmark," *Government Executive*, November 21, 2023, https://www.govexec.com/oversight/2023/11/diversity-federal-workforce-has-improved-slightly-over-last-decade/392213/.

11. A recommendation here is that the Office of Personnel Management (OPM) update the Hispanic Employment Statistical Report as the last report on the OPM website is from FY2018.

12. NALEO Educational Fund, "NALEO Educational Fund Highlights Record Number of Latino Elected Officials in 2021," January 12, 2022.

13. Congressional Research Service, "Membership of the 118th Congress: A Profile," Report R47470, April 21, 2024, 8.

14. NALEO Educational Fund, "NALEO Educational Fund Highlights Record Number of Latino Elected Officials in 2021."

15. Latino Donor Collaborative, "The 2022 LDC Latinos in Media Report," n.d., 10.

16. Toni Gonzalez, "The Significance of America Ferrera in Barbie," LatinaMediaCo, August 8, 2023.

17. Anusha Natarajan and Carolyne Im, "Key Facts About Hispanic Eligible Voters in 2022," Pew Research Center, October 12, 2022.

18. Kevin Morris, Peter Miller, and Coryn Grange, "Racial Turnout Gap Grew in Jurisdictions Previously Covered by the Voting Rights Act," Brennan Center for Justice, August 20, 2021.

19. Daniel I. Winter and Andrew Garber, Brennan Center for Justice, "Pass the Freedom to Vote Act," July 17, 2023, https://www.brennancenter.org/our-work/research-reports/pass-freedom-vote-act; Brennan Center for Justice, "Redistricting," n.d. https://www.brennancenter.org/issues/gerrymandering-fair-representation/redistricting

20. Lucy Pérez et al., "The Economic State of Latinos in America: The American Dream Deferred," McKinsey & Company, December 2021, 9.

21. Lucy Pérez et al., "The Economic State of Latinos in America: The American Dream Deferred," McKinsey & Company, December 2021, 12.

22. Dan Stangler, "Why Latino Entrepreneurs Are Growing Rapidly—And How They Can Grow Even Faster," *Forbes*, March 3, 2023.

23. The White House, "Fact Sheet: President Biden Signs Executive Order to Strengthen Racial Equity and Support for Underserved Communities Across the Federal Government," February 16, 2023.

24. Barbara Gomez-Aguinaga et al., "2022 State of Latino Entrepreneurship," Stanford Latino Entrepreneurship Initiative, February 2023.

25. Jonathan Vespa, Lauren Medina, and David M. Armstrong, "Demographic Turning Points for the United States: Population Projections for 2020 to 2060," U.S. Census Bureau, 3–4.

26. John F. Kennedy, *A Nation of Immigrants*, reprint ed. (New York: Harper Perennial, 2008), 37.

27. American Immigration Lawyers Association, "Florida Enacts Laws Imposing Significant Nationality-Based Restrictions on Ownership of Property by Individuals from 'Foreign Countries of Concern,'" AILA Doc. No. 23052305, May 23, 2023.

28. American Immigration Council, "Temporary Protected Status: An Overview," n.d., https://www.americanimmigrationcouncil.org/research/temporary-protected-status-overview.

29. Congressional Research Service, "Termination of Temporary Protected Status for Certain Countries: Recent Litigation Developments," CRS Legal Sidebar LSB 10541, last updated March 8, 2023.

30. Michael Rodriguez-Muniz, *Figures of the Future* (Princeton, NJ: Princeton University Press, 2021), 32.

31. Kennedy, *A Nation of Immigrants*, xiii.

32. Allison Jordan, "Gun Violence Has a Devastating Impact on Hispanic Communities," Center for American Progress, November 1, 2022.

CHAPTER 21

Kerner Commission Report
21st-Century Native American Perspective

Judith LeBlanc

STANDING ROCK: A MOMENT OF CIVIL UNREST

In the fading light of late September 2017, I strolled through the prayer camp nestled along the banks of the Missouri River in North Dakota. The sun's golden rays painted the landscape, enveloping thousands of our people who had gathered there, embodying the spirit of "water protectors."

The air was thick with the scent of food cooking over open fires, while laughter and the joyful sounds of children and dogs filled the air. Some played basketball, others tended to the horses, and there was even talk of a little "shopping" at the giveaway tent. Despite the warmth of the evening, the looming cold North Dakota weather served as a reminder that change was on the horizon. Yet, amidst it all, there was a profound sense of wholeness, a peace that etched itself into my being and remains with me to this day, guiding me through uncertain times.

Our history did not begin in 2017 at the Standing Rock Sioux Reservation, but it was there that our future took root. The Standing Rock Sioux Tribe waged a legal battle to safeguard their water supply from the looming threat posed by the Dakota Access Pipeline. Despite concerns the city of Bismarck raised over its water supply, the federal process pushed through permits against the Tribes' objections.

Driven by young activists and fortified by the wisdom of Oceti Sakowin elders representing nine Lakota, Dakota, and Nakota peoples, over 10,000 individuals converged at the prayer camp to resist the pipeline's construction. Their rallying cry, steeped in traditional Indigenous values and prayer, echoed around the world, sparking a global solidarity movement in support of Standing Rock's sovereign right to protect their water supply and sacred places.

This magical movement moment illuminated the urgent necessity of an Indigenous worldview that honors the interconnectedness of all living beings and seeks to live in balance with the natural world. It disrupted prevailing narratives about Native peoples in the 21st century, dispelling centuries-old myths and weaving a new narrative grounded in ancestral responsibilities.

As we stood united at the prayer camp, we joined hands with other movements for social justice, amplifying our voices in a chorus of change. Our collective action wasn't just about protecting the Missouri River; it was a testament to our intertribal belief systems, rooted in our sacred responsibilities to our Mother Earth and all its inhabitants.

Our time at Standing Rock was more than just an act of civil resistance; it was a profound awakening of awareness—an acknowledgment of our shared ancestral responsibilities. Urban and reservation Natives converged, driven by a sense of urgency and possibility rooted in our intertribal traditional values.

Standing Rock was our Montgomery Bus Boycott, our lunch counter sit-in—a declaration of our ancestral responsibilities in a world grappling with the climate crisis, economic insecurity, systemic racism, and threats to democracy and Tribal sovereignty.

Though labeled by some as "civil unrest," Standing Rock was, at its core, an act of love—a testament to the enduring power of collective action and the Native people's resilience in the face of adversity.

THE KERNER COMMISSION IN CONTEXT

Over 50 years ago, the Kerner Commission cited numerous grievances as triggers for civil unrest. Among them were discrimination in policing practices, the justice system, and consumer credit practices, inadequate housing and public assistance programs, high unemployment, and the exclusion of communities of colors from the democratic process."[1] It reviewed the current and historical roots of the frustration that erupted in the uprising in cities across the country.

The Civil Rights Movement earlier in the1960s and the outpouring of frustration in 1967 fueled a "magic movement moment," and sparked grassroots organizing across many communities. In 1968, the American Indian Movement (AIM) emerged in Minneapolis, Minnesota, representing a critical juncture for Native activism nationally. AIM's inception was intertwined with organizing and protests within the Black community, the Chicano and Puerto Rican communities, among women and LGBTQ+ people, and alongside the antiwar movement.

Despite the landmark legislation of the Civil Rights Act in 1964 and the Voting Rights Act in 1965, alongside the Great Society domestic programs. daily life for Black, Native, and other communities of color remained largely unchanged. The urban uprisings reflected the mounting hopelessness, powerlessness, and anger within these communities.

Over two hundred Native individuals convened in Minneapolis during the launch of AIM, frustrated by enduring discrimination and decades of oppressive federal Indian policies. "Frustrated by discrimination and decades of federal Indian policy, they came together to discuss the critical issues restraining them and to take control over their own destiny."[2] The Kerner Commission, tasked with addressing economic insecurity, deepening inequality, racist violence and policing, and threats to democracy, only mentioned American Indian communities once in their report. This stark omission underscored a broader oversight regarding the roots of discrimination and racism.

Since the arrival of colonial settlers, Native peoples have have attempted to coexist in dignity, but faced violent land dispossession, imprisonment, slavery, and militarism. Race has been used to divide and conquer, enabling the expropriation of land and power.

Rather than the simplistic notion of "two societies, one black, one white—separate and unequal," the reality was and is a growing multiracial society divided between the "haves" and "have-nots."

The commission's oversight regarding the American Indian experience underscores a broader blind spot on the role of economic and political systems in perpetuating divisions. Today, racial wealth disparity and income inequality are at their highest levels in 75 years, highlighting the urgent need to address systemic injustices and forge a path toward a more equitable society.[3]

BRIEF HISTORY OF FEDERAL POLICY

Then and now, Native people confront discrimination, income inequality, and the racial wealth gap. It is coupled with the historic denial of treaty and legal rights as sovereign nations. To comprehend the history of federal policies impacting Native American peoples today, one must grasp their unique relationship with the United States, shaped by a complex web of treaties, laws, and federal interventions.

With the arrival of European colonizers in 1492, Natives began a struggle that continues to the present day to have the right to self-govern and maintain their cultural traditions and practices, and to be treated as equals. In different periods of the development of the continent's economic and political systems, different policies emerged with one constant theme: removal, erasure, and denial of treaty rights.

During the Treaty Period, spanning the late 1700s to the late 1800s, the U.S. government ratified and entered over 300 treaties with sovereign Native American nations. The treaties acknowledged the nations' inherent sovereignty and established formal nation-to-nation agreements. However, they were frequently ignored, disregarded, and violated, which resulted in more encroachment of Indigenous lands and the loss of Tribal autonomy.[4]

In the Removal Era, from the 1830s to 1870s, the Indian Removal Act was passed by Congress in 1830. This piece of legislation reflected the government's ideological expression and pursuit of removing Native communities from their lands by every means possible. Forced relocations disrupted traditional ways of life, culture and language and often severed ties to sacred lands.[5]

The Allotment and Assimilation Period, spanning from the late 1800s to the 1940s, was an attempt to force Native people to abandon their communities to cut off connections to culture, values, and traditional practices. The bill instituted breaking up collective living areas into family plots, destroying the fundamental structure of Native tribal collective living.

In the Tribal Reorganization Era, from the 1930s to the 1960s, the government attempted to reverse the damaging effects of the allotment system and promote tribal self-governance. Many tribes faced challenges in reclaiming their traditional governance structures. The majority of tribes were forced into adopting constitutions that mirrored Western-style governance.[6]

The Termination Period, from the 1960s to the 1990s, saw federal policies aimed at ending the federal trust relationship with Native American tribes, absolving their responsibilities to fulfill treaties threatening tribal sovereignty and cultural continuity.

Finally, the Self-Determination Era, emerging in the 1970s, was a response to the growing magic movement moment of the Civil Rights and Native Rights Movements. The Self-Determination Era continues today, and tribes are successfully advocating for the right to play their traditional role as caretakers of Mother Earth, including sacred places that were taken or desecrated by fossil fuel industries or climate change. Tribal and Native communities are asserting their inherent rights to self-determination and sovereignty in the face of ongoing challenges and threats.

AMERICAN INDIAN REALITIES AT THE TIME OF THE KERNER REPORT

Conditions of Reservations

Tribal communities were left behind in terms of development and investment. They were much more likely to die from the flu or pneumonia. Infant mortality was several times higher than elsewhere in the nation. The life expectancy of American Indians in the 1950s was 44 years. For white Americans, it was 70 years.[7]

Reservations have been poor since they were created in the mid-1800s. With each successive federal policy, they seemed to become only smaller and poorer.[8] Throughout the 1960s, American Indians were the nation's poorest minority group and deprived of all economic opportunities.

Indian Termination Policy

The U.S. government adopted a new approach toward reservations during the 1950s and 1960s. They shifted their focus from containing reservations to encouraging Native Americans to relocate to urban areas. This meant the government ended treaties and agreements recognizing Native Nations as sovereign entities. The idea was that moving tribal citizens to cities would provide them with better education and employment opportunities, rather than fund the programs on reservations, compelling community and family separation and integration to address the Indian Problem. This led to the passage of the Indian Termination Act (House Resolution 108) in 1953, a series of laws and policies based on simply ceasing the federal–Tribal relationship.[9]

The termination policy aimed to end the recognition of Native tribes as sovereign nations and give all matters of Tribal affairs to the states. Government officials at the time believed that by assimilating Native Americans into mainstream society, they would become less reliant on federal assistance and contribute to the nation's economic growth and stability.[10]

Effects of Relocation

Over 100,000 Native Americans moved from their reservations to cities, where they faced discrimination, poverty, and isolation. They were incentivized with a job and housing, but the people behind this plan didn't realize how different Native people and urban cultures were. For many, city life felt completely unfamiliar, like a foreign country, because in many ways it was.

By the early 1960s, it was clear that these policies were creating a new group: the urban Indian poor. Many urban Indians found themselves trapped between two worlds, one culture and life on the reservation and one within poor inner cities.[11]

The flawed assumption that our society was divided into "two societies, one black, one white—separate and unequal" meant that the policies in place were driving Natives into the same places across the United States, which were already rife with frustration and powerlessness over continued racial injustices. This convergence between Native and African Americans in these urban areas provided a common ground for shared experiences of systemic oppression and disenfranchisement

Being together with Black and other communities of color in these urban areas sparked rebellion and resistance. They stood up against the unfair treatment, demanded things to change, and wanted equality and respect. In this united effort against injustice, their voices became louder and stronger. They fought for their rights and dignity, showing incredible strength in difficult times. Their coming together showed that people from different backgrounds can stand together and fight for a more just world.

Urban Indians helped lead many of the uprisings for treaty rights in the 1960s and 1970s. American Indians were subject to systemic racism plus stripped of their legal right to land, language, and culture, and denied their treaty rights. The uprisings and protests were a recognition of their status as sovereign citizens of their nations. They acted to fulfill their ancestral responsibilities.

It's a powerful reminder of the resilience and determination of communities in the pursuit of justice and equality.

"The Forgotten American"

The release of the Kerner Commission's report findings grabbed national attention. The report highlighted the deep-rooted racial disparities that exist in America, particularly in terms of access to education, housing, and employment opportunities. While the nation was grappling with these issues, American Indians were also struggling with their own set of challenges. They were often overlooked and neglected, leading to their status as the "Forgotten American," as President Lyndon Baines Johnson had pointed out in his message to Congress in 1968.

The struggles of American Indians were often ignored by the mainstream media, even though they were facing a multitude of issues, including poverty and racism. inadequate health care, and limited access to education and employment opportunities. They were also dealing with the loss of their lands, languages, culture, and traditions, which further added to their crisis.

As the country was coming to terms with the Kerner Commission's findings, it was becoming increasingly clear that American Indians were also in dire need of resources to address their issues. The challenges that Native communities faced were unique and required a different approach to be resolved.

In his May 1968 speech, President Johnson said, "The words of the Indian have become our words—the names of our states and streams and landmarks. His myths and his heroes enrich our literature. His lore colors our art and our language. For two centuries, the American Indian has been a symbol of the drama and excitement of the earliest America. But for two centuries, he has been an alien in his own land."[12]

President Johnson's remarks shed light on the dire circumstances and tragic situation of Native communities. In his speech, he cited stark statistics that revealed the extent of the impact of systemic racism and the denial of treaty rights. Among these statistics, Johnson highlighted that thousands of American Indian families resided in unsanitary and dilapidated dwellings, with some forced to live in huts or even abandoned automobiles. Unemployment rates among Native Americans soared close to 40%, representing more than 10 times the national average, while half of Indian schoolchildren dropped out before completing high school—a rate double the national average.[13]

These disparities were not confined to reservation lands; urban areas also bore witness to the struggles of migrating Native populations, many of whom found themselves ill-equipped for urban living. In Minneapolis, Ojibwe women shared couches and living room floors. As the number of migrants grew, they organized the first American Indian Center in the United States with many more to follow across the country. The Minneapolis Indian Center continues to be a hub of services, food, culture, and intertribal events and sports. They respond to the needs of the community, such as providing support for the community in the aftermath of the George Floyd murder.

President Johnson's term "Forgotten Americans" resonates with us; it captures the harsh truth that Native communities are often an afterthought in the eyes of the government and broader society. We find ourselves struggling for basic recognition and resources, pushed to the margins of a narrative that fails to acknowledge our rightful place as stewards of this land.

Yet, despite the challenges we face, our spirit remains unbroken. We continue to assert our identity, reclaim our heritage, and demand justice for past wrongs. The term "Forgotten Americans" serves as a rallying cry, reminding us of the importance of standing together, amplifying our voices, and reclaiming our rightful place in American history and society.

The Need for Change

The Indian termination policies of the 1950s sparked a movement of Indigenous resistance. Reservation and urban Native populations began coming together, forming the "Red Power" protest movement of the 1960s. It led to the occupation of Alcatraz, which was the catalyst for direct action. It was inspired by the broader Civil Rights Movement of the 1960s and sought to address the injustices and discrimination faced by Native Americans and push for greater Tribal self-determination and control over their lands and resources.

Some of the key organizations associated with the Red Power Movement included the American Indian Movement (AIM), the National Indian Youth Council (NIYC), and the urban communities who organized urban Indian community centers in Minneapolis, Chicago, San Francisco, and Seattle, to name a few. Militant direct actions were organized, which included the occupation of Alcatraz Island, the Bureau of Indian Affairs takeover by the Trail of Broken Treaties Caravan, and the occupation of Wounded Knee, to name a few. The Tribal-led campaigns to regain fishing rights in the Northwest and Midwest compelled landmark legal decisions bolstering sovereignty and treaty rights, creating regulations and law that still protect the Native right to fish on unceded treaty land and water.

The Red Power Movement played a crucial role in bringing attention to the issues that Native Americans faced. The movement welcomed anyone who wanted to help bring a balance of power by organizing protests, marches, and other actions to draw attention to these issues and demand change. As a result of the movement's efforts, several important laws were passed that recognized and protected Native American rights. One such law was the Indian Self-Determination and Education Assistance Act of 1975.

The Kerner Report, released in 1968, marked a pivotal moment in addressing the systematic racial disparities that plagued this country. It underscored the blatant inequities in access to education, housing, and employment opportunities. It shed light on the deep-rooted issues and realities of discrimination and injustice. However, despite its significance, it fell short of recognizing and addressing the systemic issues faced by American Indians.

In its analysis, the Kerner Report overlooked the historical trauma stemming from hundreds of years of policies that continue to reverberate through Indian Country. A more cross-cultural analysis was needed at the time to fully grasp the intricacies of the challenges faced by American Indians and to formulate effective solutions that respect and uplift Tribal sovereignty and cultural identity.

THE SITUATION TODAY

The world is in turmoil. In 2024, nearly half the global population is preparing to elect their national governments. The antidemocratic movement has been gaining momentum and is causing many problems in the United States. This movement is pushing false narratives about democracy, elections, the economy, people of color, and immigrants, and it is leading to a rise in threads of hate crimes. In fact, in October 2023, the Federal Bureau of Investigations reported the highest number of hate crimes ever recorded.[14]

The COVID-19 pandemic has also widened the gap between the "haves" and the "have-nots." The cost of college and essential living expenses has increased, making it even harder for those struggling financially. Congress has been fighting to protect family protection programs, but it has been an uphill battle. Unfortunately, essential programs that address childhood hunger and Medicare coverage have been terminated, making things even harder for those who are already struggling.

Public opinion reflects a growing concern about racism in society. Gallup Poll data spanning from 2001 to 2021 indicates a widespread belief that racism is worsening. The Kerner Commission's conclusion regarding the causes of the 1960s riots and violence, attributing them to "white institutions and racism, exacerbated by police brutality," remains contentious, especially among white individuals. Their perceptions of government responses and remedies vary widely, with Black respondents showing more sympathy toward the commission's findings.[15]

In Native communities, a new wave of leaders inspired by their ancestors' struggles is emerging. Water protectors and allies disrupted the dominant narrative about Native Americans and their political engagement, similar to the Civil Rights Movement in the

1960s. Secretary Deb Haaland's confirmation as the first Native women leader of the Department of the Interior (DOI) marks a transformative moment, echoing the significance of Shirley Chisholm's election as the first Black woman in Congress in 1969.[16]

Secretary Haaland's confirmation as the first Native woman in the federal government's executive branch was not the end goal—it altered the landscape for our ongoing organizing efforts, much like the experiences of the Black community. In her first year, Secretary Haaland convened a commission to study the impact of the racist, misogynistic term for Native women on over 650 federal geographical locations. Many locations were named in earlier centuries while our land was being violently expropriated. The long-term psychological impact of racist stereotypes in place names, athletic team mascots, statues, or flags is well-documented.[17]

Representation in governance is crucial for a truly multiracial democracy. The election of the first Native women to Congress in 2018—Deb Haaland (New Mexico) and Sharice Davids (Kansas)—reflects our growing political engagement. Haaland's historic appointment has spurred record numbers of Native candidates to run for office and has increased grassroots involvement in the electoral process.[18] Our political engagement is part of the long arc of achieving Tribal sovereignty and expanding democratic engagement despite the harsh economic and social conditions. Political empowerment and representation are the key links in restoring the constitutional rights of sovereignty and freedom from discrimination.

RECOMMENDATIONS

Embracing an Indigenous Framework for Guidance

> Western civilization, unfortunately, does not link knowledge and morality, but rather, it connects knowledge and power and makes them equivalent.
>
> —Vine Deloria Jr.

For us, governance isn't just about making decisions about who gets what and when; it's about honoring the interconnectedness of all living beings and our responsibility to future generations. Our traditional teachings emphasize the importance of balance and harmony with nature, recognizing that our actions today shape the world our children and grandchildren will inherit and that the cycle is a sacred obligation to act in ways that will benefit them.

When we talk about enriching policy recommendations from an Indigenous perspective, it's about more than just creating laws and regulations that are transactional or close the gaps between the "haves" and "have-nots." It's about weaving together the threads of our collective stories, experiences, and struggles to create justice and equity for collective well-being now and for our descendants.

The urgency of knowing where we come from isn't just a matter of historical curiosity; it's a call to action. It's a reminder that our journey as Native people is not confined to the pages of history books but continues to unfold in the present moment as we walk toward the future. It's about regaining our rightful place as sovereign nations and citizens, asserting our inherent and legal rights to self-determination, cultural revitalization, and environmental stewardship.

Walking the path of Indigeneity means walking with humility, courage, and resilience. It means standing tall in the face of adversity, rooted in the knowledge that our ancestors walked this same path before us, and they've led us, but so far, but now we lean on the same prayers and teachings to continue. It means embracing the richness of our cultural heritage. We are charged to weave our traditional understandings with Western advances, never privileging one over the other.

Incorporating the Indigenous framework into Western ways of thinking fosters dialogue, collaboration, and makes room for other perspectives to be heard. It benefits all of humanity. We must consider how an Indigenous framework will enrich policymaking and address challenges faced by all races and backgrounds.

Government Fulfilling Responsibilities to a Multiracial Democracy

The government has a fundamental responsibility to uphold the principles of a multiracial democracy. This means ensuring representation on all levels of government through a robust democratic system of governance. We need policies that invest in fair elections and regenerative economic development while recognizing the sovereignty of Indigenous peoples and communities of color who have faced historical injustices.

In his 1967 address to the nation, President Johnson highlighted the need to address ignorance, discrimination, poverty, and lack of opportunities to build a decent society. He emphasized the importance of rebuilding Tribal nations and repairing the damage caused by historical injustices:

> The only genuine, long-range solution for what has happened lies in an attack—mounted at every level—upon the conditions that breed despair and violence. All of us know what those conditions are: ignorance, discrimination, slums, poverty, disease, and not enough jobs. We should attack these conditions—not because we are frightened by conflict, but because we are fired by conscience. We should attack them because there is simply no other way to achieve a decent and orderly society in America.[19]

The Kerner Commission was formed to determine what measures the federal government should take to ensure that the United States is a just and inclusive society for everyone, regardless of their race. One answer is that the federal government should enforce regulations that guarantee that elections are conducted in a way that allows full participation from all members of society, including Native communities, communities of color, and low-income people. This is not only a political issue but also a social one. Investing in our communities begins to answer the extraordinary crisis global problems for the well-being of future generations.

Native American Voting Rights Act (NAVRA)

The Native American Voting Rights Act (NAVRA) is a crucial piece of proposed legislation aimed at addressing the unique challenges faced by Native American voters, including barriers to registration, identification requirements, problems of access to polling places, and language barriers. By enacting NAVRA, the federal government would take a significant step toward rectifying historical injustices and ongoing systemic barriers hindering Native Americans' full participation in the democratic process. By setting a baseline standard of access, NAVRA would prevent the perpetuation of discriminatory policies and practices that have historically denied the right to Native voters on reservations.

"We have to address ongoing discriminatory policies at the state and local levels," Native American Rights Fund staff attorney Jacqueline De León (Isleta Pueblo) said. "We need a federal policy that sets a baseline of access and prevents continuing abuses."[20]

Vine Deloria Jr., a prominent Lakota theorist in American Indian politics, emphasized the importance of sovereignty as the cornerstone of Native federal policies. He argued that without focusing on sovereignty, voting rights and civic engagement alone would not advance Native rights. Deloria's theories significantly influenced Native movement building, notably building a coalition around the Standing Rock Tribe's movement to stop the Dakota Access Pipeline and, as observed, in the 2020 elections, where many Native individuals supported policies now implemented by the Biden administration.

Deloria envisioned a democracy that supports the evolution of sovereignty into a "constituent power," giving Native nations greater control over their destinies and promoting self-determination. This evolution of sovereignty's interpretation, he believed, would benefit society by addressing systemic barriers to Tribal self-determination, racial equity, and economic equality. According to Deloria, the evolution of sovereignty's interpretation would benefit society in several ways. For one, it would transform the systems that have historically hindered Tribal self-determination, racial equity, and economic equality by empowering Native nations to have more control over their own affairs and could help to address some of the inequalities that all minorities have faced for generations.

Even though Tribal nationhood and treaty rights are still not fully realized, the movement for Native rights has made significant progress over the years. One notable example of this is the recognition of Native Americans as dual citizens of both Native nations and the United States. This recognition has helped establish conditions that make it easier for Native Americans to assert their rights and assert their cultural identities in a society that has long marginalized and oppressed them.

The Kerner Commission looked back at discrimination and economic exclusion patterns that were different for European immigrants. Their conclusion fell short because it did not weave in the impact of the systemic nature of racism that affected Native people or immigrants from Latin America, Africa, or Asia. At the heart of federal policy development should be the recognition of sovereignty and the establishment of reparative pathways for Native, Black, and other communities of color impacted by systemic racism and economic inequality. Only through such concerted efforts can we address the injustices of the past and work towards a more equitable future.

In an essay in *Smithsonian Magazine*, Alice George notes that "the commission argued that the crush of [European] immigrants occurred when the industrialization boom was creating unskilled jobs more quickly than they could be filled. On the other hand, African-Americans arrived [in urban areas] as industrialization wound down and the supply of unskilled jobs plummeted. Also, racial discrimination limited African-Americans' ability to escape from poverty."[21]

For Native people, ensuring structural reforms and government policies that strengthen self-determination and sovereignty will have an impact. In every era of government policies, the central focus was the denial of treaty rights as the tool to promote racism, discrimination, and economic inequality—to splinter Natives from Black, white, and other communities to protect the power of "the haves." Sovereignty is one of the central threads that must be woven into creating a multiracial democracy. Policies, practices, and laws must be geared to meeting the needs of the whole while recognizing the legal and moral status of Native nations as political, cultural, and legal entities.[22]

Free, Prior, and Informed Consent

The federal government has committed to a nation-to-nation relationship with Tribes. Still, it often ignores consultation on proposals or regulation changes, leaving Tribes with no alternative but legal action to force inclusion in the decision-making process. In January 2021, President Biden issued a presidential memorandum to all agencies, requiring plans for consultation with Tribes on legislation, plans, and policies.[23]

Native and Tribal communities should be included in all decisions that affect their lives, land, and resources as part of an inclusive multiracial democracy rather than just being consulted. The United Nations Declaration on the Rights of Indigenous People (UNDRIP) establishes the international standard for the basic needs of Indigenous communities and how governance can be in the right relationship with those responsibilities. UNDRIP states that "all peoples have the right to self-determination" and "all peoples have the right to freely pursue their economic, social and cultural development."[24]

Using Free, Prior, and Informed Consent (FPIC) as the operational principle for Tribal Nations and Native Hawaiian relations would begin a new era of federal government policy. Although the political climate is not conducive, we are in the early stages of a new era. In December 2023, the DOI announced new regulations for implementing the Native American Graves Protection and Repatriation Act (NAGPRA). The new regulation requires FPIC; prioritizes Indigenous knowledge of Tribes and Native Hawaiians (NHO) on repatriated objects; requires consent from descendants, Tribes, and NHOs for activities involving human remains; and sets a 5-year deadline for museums and federal agencies to update their inventories.[25]

Regenerative Economic Development

Investments and resources are crucial now, just like the Kerner Report emphasized in 1968. There is a growing trend of public and private investments that cater to the needs of Native communities and contribute to regenerative economic development. An Indigenous framework guides the most successful projects in Indian Country. However, we need to aim at achieving self-determination beyond immediate needs.

Traditional values prioritize the well-being of extended families and the collective community, including the land and natural world. By providing assistance that strengthens traditional belief systems and practices, we can promote self-determination and economic security. However, Native communities also face intersecting challenges related to health care, education, housing, and employment. For example, limited access to quality health care and education perpetuates cycles of poverty, while inadequate housing options contribute to overcrowding and instability. Recognizing and addressing these intersecting challenges is crucial for fostering holistic development and promoting a culture of abundance within Native communities.

Local and national Native groups are emerging as centers to fulfill this possibility. For instance, the NDN Collective announced in January 2023 that they had awarded $7.9 million to 200 grantees through the Collective Abundance Fund.[26] This initiative aims to build Indigenous wealth as defined by Indigenous people, with a focus on homeownership and repair, business development, and support for a reliable livelihood through mechanisms like debt relief, education, and skills development.

Addressing the systemic challenges faced by Native communities requires collaborative efforts between public and private sectors. This could involve partnerships between government agencies, philanthropic organizations, and Native-led initiatives to leverage resources, expertise, and networks for maximum impact. Adopting a coordinated approach that integrates public and private investments is essential for achieving sustainable solutions and advancing the goals of self-determination and economic security within Native communities.

Philanthropy

Philanthropy needs to step up and fill the resource gaps left by the federal government's failure to support Native nations and communities of color. Unfortunately, philanthropy has fallen short in Indian Country. A 2019 study by Native Americans in Philanthropy (NAP) and Candid found that only 0.4% of total annual funding from large U.S. foundations went to Native American communities and causes from 2002 to 2016.[27] One initiative, Native Voices Rising, champions self-determination and values-led investment in Indian Country. It gathers contributions from funders and distributes them through regional committees of tribal and Native community leaders and young activists. These decisions prioritize traditional values, practice-based evidence, and the fight against systemic racism.

Philanthropy needs support to become more connected to Native communities to engage in appropriate methods for funding communities versus funding one individual or one organization. The Indigenous value of community and collective well-being is the guide for effectiveness in Indian Country. The process has begun, with more Native leaders addressing funder gatherings, more Native-led research, and data about conditions and possibilities for nation-building in the 21st century. Unfortunately, the antidemocratic movement is chipping away at the minimal progress. In a recent survey of program officers, many spoke of fear-based retreats on centering systemic racism with a focus on Black, Native, and other communities. An article in *The Chronicle of Philanthropy* analyzed the results of 100 executive directors, program officers, and other philanthropy members interviewed on the status of investing in Black and Brown communities. The study revealed, "Emboldened by the Supreme Court's ruling [in 2023] against affirmative action in college admissions, conservative extremists have embarked on a campaign that characterizes anything directly supporting Black or Brown people as anti-white and potentially illegal. Some leading grantmakers are responding by running scared."[28]

The possibility of antidemocratic organizations taking legal action against foundations is beginning to interrupt the process of democratizing the political system and civic engagement at the grassroots level. And the false narrative is being reinforced "that such work is divisive, discriminatory, or illegal." The NDN Collective and other Native groups leading the drive to Indigenize economic development and ensure the democratic right of sovereignty will stall. The *Chronicle* authors continue: If philanthropy becomes preoccupied "with fears about liability, philanthropy misses a far larger and more immediate danger: These concessions accelerate right-wing narratives, thwart effective community action, and jeopardize meaningful progress toward racial justice."[29]

Public and private funding have challenges ahead. The sources of the challenges continues to be the same sources that sparked the uprisings in Black and Native communities in the 1960s and 1970s: economic insecurity, deepening inequality, racist violence and policing, and threats to democracy. Indigenous and traditional leaders and community organizers, younger and older, are in another new magic movement moment. The Standing Rock civil resistance prayer camp to stop the Dakota Access Pipeline has inspired, informed, and activated a movement that understands the need to be engaged in the electoral arena and be guided by the long-term goal of the recognition of sovereignty. The new movement is grassroots-based and includes traditional, elected Tribal leaders and grassroots community organizers. It moves with a values-driven strategy derived from the legacy and experiences of our ancestors.

The vision of the new movement sees the necessity of allies in action to respond to the manifestations of systemic racism in every community and the broad crisis problems of the natural world and human existence. Our traditional belief systems show the way to lead for the good of Mother Earth and all of humanity. Indigenous values are medicine in the fierce contention for political power to either reinforce or change the systems that caused the uprisings. Uprisings have occurred all through history. We need governance that strengthens, expands, and defends democracy for our collective well-being and the future of the natural world and humanity.

NOTES

1. National Museum of African American History and Culture, "The Kerner Commission," n.d. https://nmaahc.si.edu/explore/stories/kerner-commission.

2. Gale Family Library, "American Indian Movement (AIM): Overview," Minnesota Historical Society, last updated December 20, 2023, https://libguides.mnhs.org/aim.

3. American Compass, "A Guide to Economic Inequality," 2017, 4–8, https://americancompass.org/wp-content/uploads/2022/10/AC-Atlas-Inequality_Final-1.pdf.

4. Beth DiFelice, "Indian Treaties: A Bibliography," *Law Library Journal* 107, no. 2 (2015): 248–65, https://www.aallnet.org/wp-content/uploads/2018/01/Vol-107-no-2-2015-10.pdf.

5. Boughaba Charaff Edine and Selkhan Ismail, "The Removal Act and Ethnic Cleansing of the Indigenous" (PhD diss., Kasdi Merbah Ouargla University, 2022).

6. Scudder Mekeel, "An Appraisal of the Indian Reorganization Act," *American Anthropologist* 46, no. 2 (1944): 209–17, http://www.jstor.org/stable/663080.

7. Max Nesterak, "Uprooted: The 1950s Plan to Erase Indian Country," *APM Reports*, November 1, 2019, https://www.apmreports.org/episode/2019/11/01/uprooted-the-1950s-plan-to-erase-indian-country.

8. Nesterak, "Uprooted."

9. Charles F. Wilkinson and Eric R. Biggs, "The Evolution of the Termination Policy," *American Indian Law Review* 5, no. 1 (1977): 139–84, https://doi.org/10.2307/20068014.

10. Bryan Newland, "Federal Indian Boarding School Initiative Investigative Report," Bureau of Indian Affairs, May 2022, https://www.bia.gov/sites/default/files/dup/inline-files/bsi_investigative_report_may_2022_508.pdf.

11. Robert A. Trennert, "Review," review of *Termination and Relocation: Federal Indian Policy 1945–1960*, by Donald L. Fixico, *American Indian Quarterly* 12, no. 2 (1988): 151–52, https://doi.org/10.2307/1184320.

12. Lyndon B. Johnson, "Special Message to the Congress on the Problems of the American Indian: 'The Forgotten American,'" The American Presidency Project, May 6, 1968, https://www.presidency.ucsb.edu/node/237467.

13. Johnson, "Special Message to the Congress on the Problems of the American Indian."

14. Michael Lieberman, "New FBI Hate Crime Report Sparks Concern, Prompts Action," Southern Poverty Law Center, October 24, 2023, https://www.splcenter.org/news/2023/10/24/new-fbi-hate-crime-report-sparks-concern-prompts-action.

15. Gallup, "Race Relations," n.d., https://news.gallup.com/poll/1687/race-relations.aspx.

16. Robert Maxim and Randall Akee, "What Deb Haaland's Historic Nomination as Interior Secretary Means for Indigenous Peoples," Brookings, December 18, 2020, https://www.brookings.edu/articles/what-deb-haalands-historic-nomination-as-interior-secretary-means-for-indigenous-peoples.

17. U.S. Department of the Interior, "Interior Department Completes Removal of "sq___" from Federal Use," September 8, 2022, https://www.doi.gov/pressreleases/interior-department-completes-removal-sq-federal-use.

18. Gabriel R. Sanchez, "What Might We Expect from Native American Voters in the Upcoming 2022 Election?," Brookings, December 16, 2021, https://www.brookings.edu/articles/what-we-might-expect-from-native-american-voters-in-the-upcoming-2022-election.

19. Lyndon B. Johnson, "The President's Address to the Nation on Civil Disorders," The American Presidency Project, July 27, 1967, https://www.presidency.ucsb.edu/node/238062.

20. Jessica Douglas, "6 Things You Should Know About the 2021 Native American Voting Rights Act," *High Country News*, September 10, 2021, https://www.hcn.org/articles/indigenous-affairs-law-6-things-you-should-know-about-the-2021-native-american-voting-rights-act.

21. Alice George, "The 1968 Kerner Commission Got It Right, But Nobody Listened," *Smithsonian Magazine*, March 1, 2018, https://www.smithsonianmag.com/smithsonian-institution/1968-kerner-commission-got-it-right-nobody-listened-180968318.

22. David Myer Temin, "Custer's Sins: Vine Deloria Jr. and the Settler-Colonial Politics of Civic Inclusion," *Political Theory* 46, no. 3 (2018): 357–79, https://www.jstor.org/stable/26504285.

23. White House, "Memorandum on Tribal Consultation and Strengthening Nation-to-Nation Relationships," January 26, 2021, https://www.whitehouse.gov/briefing-room/presidential-actions/2021/01/26/memorandum-on-tribal-consultation-and-strengthening-nation-to-nation-relationships.

24. Department of Economic and Social Affairs Indigenous Peoples, "Free Prior and Informed Consent—An Indigenous Peoples' right and a good practice for local communities—FAO," United Nations, n.d., https://www.un.org/development/desa/indigenouspeoples/publications/2016/10/free-prior-and-informed-consent-an-indigenous-peoples-right-and-a-good-practice-for-local-communities-fao.

25. U.S. Department of the Interior, "Native American Graves Protection and Repatriation Act Systematic Processes for Disposition or Repatriation of Native American Human Remains, Funerary Objects, Sacred Objects, and Objects of Cultural Patrimony," *Federal Register*, December 13, 2023, https://www.federalregister.gov/documents/2023/12/13/2023-27040/native-american-graves-protection-and-repatriation-act-systematic-processes-for-disposition-or.

26. NDN Collective, "Collective Abundance Fund," n.d., https://ndncollective.org/collective-abundance-fund.

27. Native Americans in Philonthropy and Candid, "Investing in Native Communities," 2019, https://www.issuelab.org/resources/35493/35493.pdf.

28. Lori Villarosa, Ben Francisco Maulbeck, and Gihan Perera, "Racial Justice Programs Under Fire: Foundations Are Running Scared When They Should Double Down," *The Chronicle of Philanthropy*, February 6, 2024, https://www.philanthropy.com/article/racial-justice-programs-under-fire-foundations-are-running-scared-when-they-should-double-down.

29. Villarosa, Maulbeck, and Perera, "Racial Justice Programs Under Fire."

CHAPTER 22

United Against Hate
How Asian America Is Standing Up

George Huynh

INTRODUCTION

The United States of America holds itself to high standards. After all, we call ourselves the "land of the free, and the home of the brave." Even so, it does not feel that all of us are free, as large swaths of our population face oppression stemming from centuries of inequality. Although the United States is home to diverse communities, it is not immune to intolerance, including anti-Indigenous, Islamophobic, antisemitic, anti-Black, anti-Latinx, or homophobic discrimination, to name a few.

It is for those reasons, along with the rise in anti-Asian hate, that I would like to share my perspective as a Vietnamese American millennial and the current executive director of the Vietnamese American Initiative for Development (VietAID), home to the first community center and community development corporation founded by Vietnamese American immigrants and refugees in 1994.

Though I feel far from an expert in sociopolitical matters concerning the Vietnamese American community today, let alone the Asian American and Pacific Islander (AAPI) community, I recognize still the importance of speaking up and sharing my reflection on the 1968 Kerner Commission Report. Although I was born well after the Kerner Commission Report was written, I am able to write today thanks to several brave people who encouraged me and who inspire me today.

Thank you to the Eisenhower Foundation for welcoming my submission in their 2024 update to *Healing Our Divided Society*.[1] It is a great privilege to share this space with a number of inspirational community organizers, thinkers, and trailblazers across the country.

ASIAN IMMIGRATION TO AMERICA

The first Asians arrived in America in 1587, known as Luzonians, or Filipinos from Luzon Island, in the Philippines.[2] These individuals were slaves and indentured servants aboard Novohispanic ships sailing between modern Mexico and Asia. In 1763,

Filipino slaves and indentured servants aboard a Spanish galleon escaped and established the first Asian American settlement in Louisiana. Contrary to popular belief, the first Asian immigrants were not the thousands of Chinese immigrants who flooded into San Francisco in 1849 during the California Gold Rush, peaking at 20,000 immigrants in 1852, or 30% of the 67,000 immigrants that year alone, who contributed to the local economy.[3] Or the 12,000 Chinese immigrants who constructed the railroad from 1865 to 1869. They risked their lives especially during harsh winters and perilous working conditions, in laying the foundation for Americans not just for economic prosperity, but for fairer wages and improved labor conditions.[4] Although they brought skills, newly arrived immigrants from Asia took on jobs operating restaurants and laundromats due to language barriers and racial discrimination.[5]

Since setting foot on U.S. land in the 16th century, Asians have been seen as threats to American society; not just foreigners, but also leeches, or spies for the very governments that they fled.

The Chinese Exclusion Act of 1882 banned immigration by laborers, and made it more difficult for non-laborers, or white-collar professionals including academics and researchers, to gain entry based on their ethnic origin.[6] Subsequently, the Geary Act in 1892 and later the Immigration Act of 1924 established the 1890 Census as the basis for admitting new immigrants, at a rate of 2% of each nationality's 1890 numbers. Before that, the Barred Zone Act of 1917, spurred by World War I, established literacy tests to further restrict immigration to the United States.[7]

During World War II, many Americans distrusted citizens of Japanese ancestry, fearing that they might carry out espionage on behalf of the Japanese government.[8] As a result, beginning in 1942, over 127,000 Japanese Americans were detained in internment camps indefinitely. While the war raged on, American media spread racist propaganda, as *Life* magazine shared "How to Tell Japs from the Chinese."[9] These generalizations of skin color and facial characteristics only fed into stereotypes permeating through American minds. Even though in this particular instance the Chinese were depicted in a positive light, Asian Americans not conforming to these individuals' appearances—or worse, appearing more Japanese—would bear the brunt of hysteria. Although all interned Japanese Americans would be released at war's end, this legacy of discrimination would only lead to greater anti-Asian sentiment.

Although all exclusion acts were repealed after 1943, the yearly quota remained at 105 immigrants annually until the Immigration Act of 1965. Effective July 1, 1968, the limit increased to 170,000 members from outside the western hemisphere, with admission prioritized for the skilled and those seeking political asylum.

Perhaps coincidentally, 1968 was also when the Kerner Commission Report was published. The report focuses particularly on the history of blacks in American society and details the ongoing "disorders" or protests, especially those that occurred in the summer of 1967. The conclusion that "Our Nation is moving toward two societies, one black, one white—separate and unequal," reverberates today.

Our nation is evolving into a landscape of diverse societies, delineated by differences in political ideologies, spanning across generational and racial divides, influenced by cultural and religious affiliations, marked by distinctions in access to health care and education, and stratified between the rich and the poor. As we see the middle class decimated by the rising cost of living and interest rates, the gap between the haves and have-nots continues to widen.

MY FAMILY'S STORY

The first wave of Vietnamese Americans came following the fall of Saigon in April 1975. My father, Dũng "David" Huynh, served in the Vietnam War alongside the South Vietnamese and the U.S. Army. He spent 5½ years after the fall of Saigon in a re-education camp. Upon his release in 1980, he was granted political asylum in the United States for his service.

My parents arrived in America in 1992; my mom gave birth to my sister in 1993, my brother in 1994, and me in 1996. I am proud to be Vietnamese American, the son of two Vietnamese refugees. I am indebted to my parents, who sacrificed their worlds so that my siblings and I would have a better future. And while it didn't always feel inevitable, thanks to consistent governmental support, excellent public schools, and affordable public housing, we are well on our way to health and stability. For the antipoverty programs set in motion by the Kerner Commission report, we are blessed and grateful.

It is important to note that following the Immigration Act of 1990, skilled immigrants were heavily favored in the admission process, thereby boosting the percentage of Asians employed in high-skilled occupations. My family was not a part of this skilled immigrant group. Neither of my parents finished high school in Vietnam. They did, however, push us all to do so in the United States. My siblings and I attended the top public exam schools in the city through Boston Latin Academy and Boston Latin School. In 2017, my brother became the first in our family to graduate from college, earning a bachelor's in chemical engineering from the University of Massachusetts–Amherst, and a year later I followed suit with a bachelor's in political science from Yale.

PLACEMAKING WITHIN INSTITUTIONS

When Donald Trump was elected in 2016, the darkest clouds loomed over Yale's campus in New Haven, Connecticut. Class became a space for students and professors alike to commiserate, to unpack the future and ruminate on the possibility that a single individual could turn back the clock and reverse decades and even centuries of historic civil rights victories. It had been less than a year since protests in support of black student activists and free speech debates stirred across campus when I and many other Asian Americans were figuring out if and how we could support them.

We were also people of color, so why did we feel stuck in the middle? Where was our place in the "March of Resilience?" In the discourse of racial injustice?

It was in New Haven where I grappled with my racial and socioeconomic identity and confronted vast disparities between the haves and have-nots. I experienced inclusivity, but also exclusivity, based on my low-income background. For most of my college years, I could not help but feel like a diversity applicant. I carried daily doubts about whether I would have been admitted without my stories of financial hardship. And somehow that felt unfair to other high schoolers who may have outperformed me academically.

Fortunately, I found a brother in my roommate Jacob, a white kid hailing from Abingdon, Virginia. We bonded over sports, politics, and losing our fathers at a young age. I found not just solace but joy in the Vietnamese Students Association, where I served as co-president; in student government on the Yale College Council; and in my residential college, where I took part in intramural sports and learned nightly at dinner. It was in those moments of connecting with my close friends from diverse backgrounds that I felt accepted and cared for. It is in these affinity spaces where I had difficult conversations and felt the most comfortable.

INCREASINGLY VISIBLE

Today, with a total of 24 million people in the country comprising 7% of the total American population, the Asian American and Pacific Islander (AAPI) population is the fastest growing in the nation, with an expected increase to more than 40 million individuals by 2060.[10]

The AAPI community inhabits a peculiar place in society today: Not white enough to be Caucasian, yet not universally recognized as people of color despite histories of immigration and injustice.

The model minority myth, or the belief that Asian Americans have greater success than other minorities due to their law-abiding nature and hard work, persists, and has in large part driven up rates of anti-Asian hate during the years following COVID-19.[11] The term model minority was first coined in 1966 and remains commonly referenced today.[12]

Take the story of Vincent Chin, a Chinese immigrant, who was beaten to death in 1982 by two white men amid growing resentment stemming from rampant layoffs in the auto industry.[13] Chin was the adopted son of two Chinese immigrants, who became citizens because Chin's father had served in World War II. Chin was an industrial draftsman by day and a waiter at a Chinese restaurant on the weekends.

As the U.S. auto industry faltered, including at the Chrysler plant at which Chin worked in Detroit, Michigan, plant supervisor Ronald Ebens and recently laid-off Michael Nitz assaulted Chin, a scapegoat for the flourishing Japanese imports. His murderers never spent a day in jail.

Chin's case became the catalyst for the modern Asian American civil rights movement and the founding of numerous pan-Asian grassroots community organizations and legal advocacy groups across the United States. His story has become all too familiar for the AAPI community, which grapples with the consequences of his demise, and sometimes with the lagging pace of change and seeming futility of organizing.

For centuries, Asian Americans have been seen as other, treated with a sense of scorn. And not just East Asians or Southeast Asians. Post-9/11, backlash against Muslims, Sikhs, Arabs, and South Asians increased dramatically.[14] The United States implemented laws such as the Patriot Act to investigate anyone it suspected of terrorism and ultimately to protect our nation further. However, it also exacerbated scrutiny and surveillance of the aforementioned communities and anybody perceived to be part of these groups.[15]

The emergence of a novel coronavirus, or COVID-19, from Wuhan, China, has only exacerbated these feelings of hatred toward Asian Americans in the United States today. According to the Center for the Study of Hate and Extremism, between March 2020 and March 2021, rates of anti-Asian hate increased by 339% nationwide, including by 343% in New York City and 567% in San Francisco.[16] Thankfully, according to the FBI, data released in 2023 shows a decrease of 33% in anti-Asian hate crimes between 2021 and 2022.[17] It is yet to be seen if this trend will continue, as it may be part of the cyclical pattern. The highest rate of hate crime incidents, still, is against Black Americans. We must continue to address this epidemic together in solidarity with other marginalized communities.

Mainstream media has captured esteemed Asian American individuals like martial arts icons Bruce Lee and Jackie Chan; in modern professional sports, Tiger Woods, Michelle Kwan, and now Jeremy Lin, Naomi Osaka, Nathan Chen, and Suni Lee; entertainers in Bruno Mars, Ali Wong, Daniel Dae Kim, Lucy Liu, Jason Momoa, Mindy Kaling, Ke Huy Quan, and George Takei; and writers in Amy Tan and Viet Thanh Nguyen. We are also fortunate to have greater representation in government and business than ever before, with elected officials in Boston Mayor Michelle Wu and California Representative Ted Lieu, and leading businessmen like Joe Tsai of the Brooklyn Nets.

CONFRONTING CHALLENGES

Despite the AAPI community's growing numbers, issues facing the AAPI community the issues it faces remain under the radar. The AAPI community continues to be pigeonholed into a handful of categories. We continue to face challenges owing to racial discrimination. Aside from some unpleasant and erroneous stereotypes, such as being submissive, unathletic, science and math geniuses, unempathetic, and otherwise robotic, Asians have been cast as the model minority: Work hard and put your head down like the Asian does, and you will not have problems in America. This is negative not only for our other BIPOC communities but also for Asians who may not excel in school or have an interest in stereotypically "Asian" matters. Failure to conform to familial or societal expectations often leads to lower self-esteem and turmoil over self-identity.[18]

Even with these success stories, we must boost representation of Asian Americans in leadership positions. In a 2022 study by the National Institutes of Health, researchers found that "Asians/Asian Americans represented 32.6% of the scientific occupations at the non-leadership or staff level, but only 17.5% of the general leadership level (a difference of 15.1%)."[19]

For the individuals who feel invisible, this cuts deep. Many carry the weight of these stereotypes, trauma, and expectations from older generations to assimilate and achieve success in America.[20] There is a stigma of experiencing mental health. People of all ages, especially youth, are burdened with guilt and shame for expressing these thoughts to their elders, who have made so many sacrifices and gone through horrific trauma.

Especially in immigrant families, it should be the norm to prioritize self-care. Perhaps a positive byproduct of COVID-19 is that the whole world was forced to pause. To slow down and breathe. To prioritize our health and wellness over excellence or income. But now that the world has seemingly gone back to "normal," we have found ourselves stuck in patterns of complacency and rigidity.

According to the CDC and the U.S. Department of Health and Human Services, Office of Minority Health, in 2019, suicide was the leading cause of death for the AAPI community, ages 15 to 24.[21]

Women in the AAPI community, who feel pressure to conform to family expectations of having a family as well as a career, are particularly at risk for low self-esteem and depression. However, Asians remain reluctant to use mental health services and as the Office of Minority Health posits, "In 2018, Asian Americans were 60 percent less likely to have received mental health treatment relative to non-Hispanic whites."

In reaching out only to friends and families, Asians are depriving themselves of professional help. By establishing therapy from a licensed professional as a necessity and treating mental illness in the same way we view physical illness, we will destigmatize mental health crises as a weakness.

We must educate ourselves on this valuable information. To increase our mental health and well-being. To prevent suicide. To care for one another. Too many lives are at stake.

Although Asian Americans have a lengthy history in America dating as far back as 1587, we have been seen as the perpetual foreigner. No matter how much time we have spent here, we remain outsiders in our own country. This includes folks who have served in the military, who have built their businesses here, who have raised their families here. Language barriers have perpetuated such wrongdoing and discrimination.

For many immigrants, learning English is just not attainable. The adult brain, while more developed, is less able or unwilling to change with age. After age 10, the likelihood of reaching native-level fluency drops drastically.[22] Coupled with limited time and resources, fluency becomes a more distant goal. Language barriers limit access to education, employment, and social services for some Asian Americans.

Despite all these challenges, we refuse to back down—or to let the model minority myth be a racial wedge between ourselves and blacks. As people of color, it is on us to challenge stereotypes. As legendary Chinese American activist Grace Lee Boggs showed us through her advocacy efforts across racial lines in Chicago and Detroit, Asian Americans are stronger when we organize in solidarity with BIPOC communities who have been economically and politically disenfranchised.[23]

BUILDING EQUITABLE REPRESENTATION AND COLLECTIVE POWER

In the summer of 2023, the Supreme Court struck down affirmative action, ending race-conscious admissions to American universities.[24] This seemingly created more division among Asian Americans: Those in support of affirmative action see it as a means to address historic and systemic inequalities, while those in opposition see it as a threat to their chances of admission. By overturning affirmative action, fewer students of color, particularly Black, Indigenous, and Latinx students, will be admitted to top universities.

This decision, while it may result in an uptick of AAPI students at select schools, where they are already overrepresented, ultimately harms everyone, especially those who have been disproportionately impacted by systemic injustices.

Universities are increasingly offering Asian American studies courses, as they recognize the rich, diverse history that each of our native backgrounds brings.

By boosting representation in media, in nontraditional fields such as nonprofit work, government, and media, we can grow our collective power and advocacy. Although one should be valued just for being, we know that it is not how things go.

In Massachusetts, we recognize the vast disparities that exist among ethnic groups within the Asian diaspora today in the United States. In the summer of 2023, Massachusetts passed the Data Equity Bill (H.3115), which disaggregates data by ethnicity, not just within the AAPI community, but also other communities of color. As noted in a recent press release by the Asian Pacific Islander Civic Action Network (APIsCAN), of which VietAID is a member, in conjunction with the Asian American Legal Defense and Education Fund (AALDEF), "The new law mandates the Commonwealth of Massachusetts to collect, organize, and assemble public data on major ethnic groups, of which each major Asian group—including but not limited to Chinese, Japanese, Filipino, Korean, and Vietnamese—composes more than 466,000 Asian American residents living in the state. Breaking down data into subgroups for all races helps to understand the diverse experiences and needs of different ethnicities."[25]

Income inequality is growing most rapidly among Asian Americans.[26] According to the Pew Research Center, in 2018, Asians in the top 10% of the income distribution earned 10.7 times as much as Asians in the bottom 10%. As of 2019, Indian American households earned a median income of $119,000, the highest of any ethnicity.[27] Burmese American households earned $44,400, the lowest of any ethnicity. Taking a snapshot of 2019 still, the figure is $69,800 for Vietnamese American households and $81,600 for Chinese American households. Overall, the median income for an Asian American household is $85,800; this is slightly higher than the median income for all American households, which is $79,745. It is important to acknowledge that Asian Americans have varying levels of income, education, and well-being owing to our unique histories in this country.

All across the country, we must observe the material differences in health outcomes and life circumstances for our Asian American groups. That we are not a monolith but vastly diverse means that there are many individuals and groups among us who may need specialized support from government and community agencies. For many Southeast Asian refugees, assimilating to American life has been far from easy. In fact, due to their resettlement into cities of concentrated poverty and gang violence, "Southeast Asian refugees are at least three times more likely to be deported on the basis of an old criminal conviction, compared to other immigrants."[28]

In Boston, we are proud to have elected the first woman, first Asian American mayor in our city's history. But that is just the start. In this city, we collaborate. We recognize the contributions of organizers before us, from Dr. Martin Luther King, Jr., to the late Mel King.

In March 2023, dozens of nonprofit leaders within the AAPI community gathered at the Boston Foundation to begin crafting a rapid response plan in the wake of two separate assaults on our AAPI community members in the neighboring town of Quincy at the end of 2022. We grappled with questions about who should be involved, from law enforcement to government agencies to our own organizations, and how. We walked away perhaps with more questions than answers. We left also with greater resolve and heightened urgency to shield our community from harm. There is never a place for hate. Random acts of violence breed distrust, instability, and paranoia. Nobody should feel unsafe when they walk outside their door.

In Fields Corner, Dorchester, the largest and most diverse neighborhood in the city, we are building collective power through networks such as the Fields Corner Crossroads Collaborative, pulling together eight community-based organizations including the Dorchester House and VietAID. Through sharing resources and info to affect day-to-day and systems change. We believe in the power of the individual. In challenging systems that are outdated or no longer serve us.

As a community development corporation, VietAID strives to alleviate poverty and build affordable housing—to make Dorchester a home for all of us, rich or poor. In providing bilingual, bicultural preschool education, youth leadership development, senior day care, and case management services, we welcome in people of all ages. Although historically our work has been focused on the Vietnamese community, we are embedded in a multicultural neighborhood and welcome folks from diverse backgrounds into our community center space and our housing developments. As we celebrate our 30th anniversary in 2024, we aspire to grow our collective programming, restore and upgrade our building, and ultimately make our community more just and resilient—environmentally, economically, socially, civically, and politically.

Growing up at the Dorchester Youth Collaborative (DYC), I was exposed to other teens of color. I was taught by some incredible people in Emmett Folgert, Vinh Bui, Natalie Nguyen Woodruff, Maria Knight, Greg Hill, and Kenny Johnson, who despite looking so different, have so much more in common. DYC was a place where brothers and sisters of African, Cape Verdean, Latinx, and Vietnamese descent came together. Emmett, who is white, always says, "Your skin shade or ethnicity can never make you a devil—or protect you from becoming one." No matter what you look like, doing good or evil depends on your actions. And we all have a choice.

DYC is where I got much of my childhood education on building relationships, coalitions, and confidence. And despite being so small and soft spoken, I had a voice. In advocating for kids like myself, coming from homes with single parents and little financial means, I wanted to make a difference in the lives of others. We garnered hundreds of thousands of dollars for our teen center, for violence prevention and intervention. DYC was more than a hangout space, it was a second home, a safe haven where we learned invaluable skills, and perhaps most importantly, where we built lifelong relationships.

MOVING FORWARD

Sure, we have made progress since 1968. Morally and materially, in a country where growth is treasured, there is ample reason to have hope. America is far from its potential as an integrated society. We must rediscover the desire to improve individually and collectively and as a nation with grace and humility.

We should look to neighboring Canada to glean lessons on how to approach race relations. In 2019, Canada's government implemented an antiracism strategy, investing $45 million into their national antiracism strategy plan from 2019–2022.[29] Of that, $30 million was set aside for community-based projects to address racism. Owing to their national policy of multiculturalism dating back to 1971 and their inclusionary efforts today, *U.S. News & World Report* ranks Canada as the most racially equitable country in the world.[30]

It will take more than public–private partnerships to do good. It will take individual leaders in our community. Those driving the work and shaping hearts and minds on the ground level.

Our generation is no longer tolerating discriminatory behavior against victims of systemic injustice. The modern workplace seeks out diversity, equity, inclusion, and belonging training and workshops. In promoting equitable hiring and promotion practices, we can begin to rectify systemic practices of wrongdoing. We must continue with this momentum. Speak up. Join forces. Condemn injustice. Break the status quo. Celebrate differences and welcome opposing opinions.

Within the AAPI community, it is not enough to advocate among ourselves, and not only when it's expeditious. It's imperative that we show solidarity with black, Indigenous, and other people of color, to build relationships with one another and white allies, and to continue fighting for change—especially when it's difficult. Across generational lines, Asian Americans are adopting a more open-minded approach toward advocacy. Millennials and Gen Z especially refuse to maintain the generational practices of distrust and paranoia toward other communities of color. Instead, they—we—view others sharing values and ideals as friends in the fight against oppression.

We all share responsibility in advancing justice for our fellow Americans and future generations.

I'm proud to be working toward equity and justice in following in the footsteps of many lofty visionaries. I'd like to share some well-known quotations that inspire me and will continue to inspire generations to come.

As Dr. Martin Luther King Jr. said, "Darkness cannot drive out darkness: only light can do that. Hate cannot drive out hate: only love can do that."[31]

During these times when the news is overwhelmingly negative (and there is so much of it), we must think positively. Let's continue to call each other in and to move with compassion. Dream big but go small. One step at a time.

Start with love.

Love yourself. Love your friends and family. Your neighbors. Your enemies. They need it most.

Grace Lee Boggs tells us, "Love isn't about what we did yesterday; it's about what we do today and tomorrow and the day after."[32]

This is no time to sit back.

It begins with us. And we have to do it together. *Juntos. Cùng nhau.*

NOTES

1. Fred Harris and Alan Curtis, eds., *Healing Our Divided Society* (Abilene, KS: Eisenhower Foundation and Philadelphia: Temple University Press, 2018).
2. Kirby Aráullo, "The First Asian American Settlement Was Established by Filipino Fishermen," History.com, updated April 17, 2024, https://www.history.com/news/first-asian-american-settlement-filipino-st-malo.
3. Ellen Terrell, "Chinese Americans and the Gold Rush," Inside Adams Blog, The Library of Congress, January 28, 2021, https://blogs.loc.gov/inside_adams/2021/01/chinese-americans-gold-rush/.
4. U.S. Department of Labor, "Hall of Honor Inductee: The Chinese Railroad Workers," n.d., https://www.dol.gov/general/aboutdol/hallofhonor/2014_railroad.
5. Library of Congress, "Struggling for Work," n.d., https://www.loc.gov/classroom-materials/immigration/chinese/struggling-for-work.
6. National Archives and Records Administration, "Chinese Exclusion Act (1882)," n.d., https://www.archives.gov/milestone-documents/chinese-exclusion-act.
7. Immigration History, "Immigration Act of 1917 (Barred Zone Act)," Immigration and Ethnic History Society, n.d., https://immigrationhistory.org/item/1917-barred-zone-act/.
8. National Archives and Records Administration, "Japanese-American Incarceration during World War II," n.d., https://www.archives.gov/education/lessons/japanese-relocation#background.
9. Campus Writing Program, "WWII Propaganda: The Influence of Racism," University of Missouri, n.d., https://cwp.missouri.edu/2012/wwii-propaganda-the-influence-of-racism/.
10. U.S. Department of Commerce, "The White House Initiative on Asian Americans and Pacific Islanders," n.d., https://www.commerce.gov/bureaus-and-offices/os/whiaapi.
11. Victoria Namkung, "The Model Minority Myth Says All Asians Are Successful. Why That's Dangerous," *NBC News*, March 21, 2021, https://www.nbcnews.com/news/asian-america/model-minority-myth-says-asians-are-successful-dangerous-rcna420.
12. Asian American Pacific Islander Coalition (AAPIC), "Model Minority," University of California San Francisco, n.d., https://aapicoalition.ucsf.edu/model-minority.
13. Zinn Education Project, "June 19, 1982: Vincent Chin Beaten to Death in Hate Crime," n.d., https://www.zinnedproject.org/news/tdih/vincent-chin-hate-crime.
14. Neil G. Ruiz, Carolyne Im, and Ziyao Tian, "Asian Americans' Experiences with Discrimination in Their Daily Lives," Pew Research Center, November 30, 2023, https://www.pewresearch.org/race-ethnicity/2023/11/30/asian-americans-experiences-with-discrimination-in-their-daily-lives.
15. Institute for Social Policy and Understanding, "The USA Patriot Act: Impact on the Arab and Muslim American Community," 2024, https://www.ispu.org/wp-content/uploads/2017/07/the-usa-patriot-act_farid-senzai.pdf.
16. Kimmy Yam, "Anti-Asian Hate Crimes Increased 339 Percent Nationwide Last Year, Report Says," *NBC News*, February 14, 2022, https://www.nbcnews.com/news/asian-america/anti-asian-hate-crimes-increased-339-percent-nationwide-last-year-repo-rcna14282.
17. Federal Bureau of Investigation, "FBI Releases 2022 Crime in the Nation Statistics," news release, October 16, 2023, https://www.fbi.gov/news/press-releases/fbi-releases-2022-crime-in-the-nation-statistics.
18. Mental Health America, "Communities of Asian American and Pacific Islander Descent," n.d., https://www.mhanational.org/asian-pacific-islander.
19. Caroline Goon et al., "Examining the Asian American Leadership Gap and Inclusion Issues with Federal Employee Data: Recommendations for Inclusive Workforce Analytic Practices," *Frontiers in Research Metrics and Analytics* 7 (2022): 958750, 6, doi:10.3389/frma.2022.958750.

20. Mental Health America, "Communities of Asian American and Pacific Islander Descent."

21. Office of Minority Health, "Mental and Behavioral Health—Asian Americans," U.S. Department of Health and Human Services, n.d., https://minorityhealth.hhs.gov/mental-and-behavioral-health-asian-americans.

22. Jamie Ducharme, "Why It's So Hard to Learn Another Language After Childhood," *TIME*, May 2, 2018, https://time.com/5261446/language-critical-period-age.

23. Kaitlin Smith, "Remembering Grace Lee Boggs," Facing History, May 16, 2022, https://www.facinghistory.org/ideas-week/remembering-grace-lee-boggs.

24. Nina Totenberg, "Supreme Court Guts Affirmative Action, Effectively Ending Race-Conscious Admissions," *NPR*, June 29, 2023, https://www.npr.org/2023/06/29/1181138066/affirmative-action-supreme-court-decision.

25. AALDEF, "Massachusetts Passes Data Equity Bill," news release, August 10, 2023, https://www.aaldef.org/press-release/massachusetts-passes-data-equity-bill.

26. Rakesh Kochhar and Anthony Cilluffo, "Income Inequality in the U.S. Is Rising Most Rapidly Among Asians," Pew Research Center, July 12, 2018, https://www.pewresearch.org/social-trends/2018/07/12/income-inequality-in-the-u-s-is-rising-most-rapidly-among-asians.

27. Abby Budiman and Neil G. Ruiz, "Key Facts About Asian Origin Groups in the U.S.," Pew Research Center, April 29, 2021, https://www.pewresearch.org/short-reads/2021/04/29/key-facts-about-asian-origin-groups-in-the-u-s.

28. SEARAC, "Immigration," n.d., https://www.searac.org/programming/national-state-policy-advocacy/immigration.

29. Government of Canada, "Building a Foundation for Change: Canada's Anti-Racism Strategy 2019–2022," last modified June 23, 2021, https://www.canada.ca/en/canadian-heritage/campaigns/anti-racism-engagement/anti-racism-strategy.html.

30. *U.S. News & World Report*, "Best Countries for Racial Equity," n.d., https://www.usnews.com/news/best-countries/best-countries-for-racial-equity.

31. Martin Luther King, Jr., "'Loving Your Enemies,' Sermon Delivered at Dexter Avenue Baptist Church," November 17, 1957, transcript of audio recording, https://kinginstitute.stanford.edu/king-papers/documents/loving-your-enemies-sermon-delivered-dexter-avenue-baptist-church.

32. Grace Lee Boggs and Scott Kurashige, *The Next American Revolution: Sustainable Activism for the Twenty-First Century* (Oakland, CA: University of California Press, 2012).

Part II

HOW TO CREATE NEW WILL?

Dr. King, Economic Justice, and Moral Fusion

CHAPTER 23

Reviving the Heart of Democracy

Rev. William Barber II

As part of their training in medical school, doctors learn how to deliver bad news in a way that their patients can both hear it and still be able to do what's necessary to address the problem. If all a patient hears is bad news, they may give up in despair. If, on the other hand, a patient does not face the truth of their diagnosis, they will never get the treatment they need. Doctors have to learn how to deliver a dire diagnosis without forestalling hope for a better future. It's not an easy thing to do.

If patients need a doctor who can tell them hard truths in a way that helps them not give up, nations need something similar when they have to face the painful realities of their shared life. In 1968, the Kerner Commission said that America was "moving toward two societies... separate and unequal." It was a difficult diagnosis then, and in many ways the pathology it named has only further metastasized in our body politic. Despite some actions that have demonstrated the potential for real progress, the policies of the past 4 decades in the United States have largely served to hollow out the middle class and facilitate a growing gap between superrich elites and poor and low-income Americans. At the same time, culture wars that exploit religious faith have pitted Americans against one another, distracting the people who could unite for transformative change from the issues that matter most while making them think they have nothing in common with people who face many of the same day-to-day challenges they do.

As I watch what is happening in American public life, I am convinced that now, more than ever, America has a heart problem. Five interlocking injustices block the arteries of our common life: poverty, racism, ecological devastation, militarism, and the distorted moral narrative of religious nationalism. As many chapters in this book attest, any one of these injustices can be understood as a major impediment to the promise of life, liberty, and the pursuit of happiness. But they do not exist in isolation; they intersect, like plaque in an artery, and threaten to quench the life of our body politic.

We are not without hope, but we fool ourselves if we think we can pursue a better future without facing the root causes of our national strife. These interlocking injustices create real pain for tens of millions of Americans—140 million of whom are poor and low-income; 80 million uninsured or underinsured; upwards of 3 million who wake up every day and can buy unleaded gas but can't buy unleaded water for their homes. Religious nationalism, which depends on division, promotes Islamophobia, anti-Semitism, homophobia, attacks on women's rights, and gross distortions of our moral traditions. The original Kerner Commission was convened because leaders in

Washington wanted to understand why uprisings were happening in African American communities across the United States. In a sense, the answer was simple: People can only take so much before the energy goes somewhere. The widespread social costs of policy violence in this nation will either explode in chaos or be directed toward movements that transform our shared life.

Our problem is not a lack of resources. Our problem is not that we lack solutions to the social problems that ail us. As this report makes clear, we know many things we can do, and we have the resources to do them. Our problem is a lack of political will. We have a heart problem, and until we face this diagnosis, we have no hope of reviving the heart of democracy.

I do not despair in the face of this diagnosis because I spend time among poor and low-income Americans who suffer the most from our lack of will, but nevertheless demonstrate a determination to come together and reconstruct America. In my tradition, there is a scripture that says, "The stone that the builder rejected has become the chief cornerstone." Just as formerly enslaved people joined hands with poor white farmers during the Reconstruction era that followed America's Civil War and people of every race came together in a Second Reconstruction during the 20th century's civil and women's rights movements, folks who have experienced rejection in America are uniting to build a Third Reconstruction today. They are showing us the way toward a new will to become the nation we have never yet been. As the historian Peniel E. Joseph writes, "Today's Reconstructionists have a vision for multiracial democracy that might astonish even [Frederick] Douglass, [Ida B.] Wells, and [W.E.B.] DuBois. Black women, queer folk, poor people, disabled people, prisoners, and formerly incarcerated people have adopted the term abolition . . . and now use it to refer to a broad movement to dismantle interlocking systems of oppression."[1] We do not need a sophisticated study to uncover the secret formula that might allow us to build a new will in America. We need only heed the wisdom of our moral traditions and our history to learn from the "rejected stones" who are already leading us.

I want to outline seven lessons we can learn from today's Reconstructionists that promise a way toward reviving the heart of American democracy. I don't mean to suggest that these lessons can be extracted from the leadership and embodied wisdom of the directly impacted people who are showing us the way. We do not need the people and organizations that are used to being in charge to simply adopt these strategies. We need to build a movement with leaders who embody these principles at the center, and we all need to commit ourselves to following them toward freedom and equality for all of us.

WE NEED AN ANALYSIS THAT ACKNOWLEDGES THE DEPTH OF THE PROBLEM

When I was part of relaunching the Poor People's Campaign of 1968 on its 50th anniversary in 2018, consultants who work on campaign messaging discouraged us from using the word "poor." "Americans don't want to identify as poor, even if they are struggling," they told us. "Maybe try to find another way to name the challenge people face."

This is what the consultants told us. But as I traveled through the Black Belt of Alabama, to the borderlands in El Paso, Texas, through the hollers of Appalachia, and down the sidewalks of Skid Row, I met people who not only know they are poor, but also know they are silenced by their poverty. People who are organizing to abolish poverty in the richest nation in the history of the world are not ashamed of being poor; they are ashamed of a nation that refuses to acknowledge them.

According to the official poverty measure, an individual is not "poor" in the United States today if they earn $14,000 a year. This is the measure the federal government uses to say that some 40 million Americans are poor, and almost all antipoverty programs—publicly and privately funded—use this measure to identify where they should allocate resources. But the official poverty measure in the United States is a lie—in fact, it is a damned lie. I am a preacher, and I do not curse easily. But Jesus and the prophets teach us to curse death-dealing lies, and America's poor have taught me that the way we measure poverty in this country keeps tens of millions of people in the shadows.[2]

The truth is, more than 60% of people in the United States live paycheck to paycheck, and nearly half of Americans are poor or low income. There is not a single county in the United States where someone working fulltime at the minimum wage can afford to rent a basic two-bedroom apartment. Most of us struggle to get by while the wealthiest Americans and the corporations they own earn record profits. Tax policy over the past 4 decades has redistributed the largest amount of wealth from working people to the top 1% since plantation owners stole the lives and labor of the people they enslaved.

In the face of a crisis like this, it is too simplistic to suggest that our nation's problems are the result of a single politician or political party. Yes, Donald Trump has charismatized the old myths of racial division, but he did not create them. And Republicans have not been alone in promoting the neoliberal vision of "limited government" that has created the widening inequality in American life. The analysis of left versus right and progressive versus traditional is too simplistic to name America's heart problem. We need a deeper analysis, and people who have been pushed into the shadows are standing up and demanding that their experience matters in our shared life.

WE NEED MORAL LANGUAGE

To deny the existence of poor and low-income Americans is not simply an oversight. It is evil, just as it is evil for racist policies to deny the humanity of Black people and for anti-immigrant rhetoric to deny the humanity of refugees at our borders. Today's Reconstructionists press us to reclaim the sharp language of prophetic moral leaders to shock the heart of the nation. Our political slogans are too puny for the evil we face. We need moral language to revive the heart of democracy.

Like Frederick Douglass and the abolitionists of the 19th century, we can draw on the prophets of our shared religious traditions. Douglass understood that, when so many were using Christian faith to prop up and defend slavery, it was important to remind people that a prophetic cry for justice is at the heart of their religious commitments. Likewise today, as sociologists increasingly point to the influence of white Christian nationalism on the extreme polarization of American public life, we need to reclaim the Bible's language about love, justice, and mercy.

Yet America is a pluralistic society, and our moral vision has never been rooted in a singular, exclusive religious tradition. As movements issue a moral challenge to the evil we face, it is equally important that we draw on the constitutional language of justice and the need for equal protection under law. Just as Dr. King said he was going to call America to "be true to what she put on paper," today's Reconstructionists point to America's stated commitments to "establish justice" and "form a more perfect union." We are leaning into the logic of the Declaration of Independence, which suggests that a "long train of abuses" necessarily compels people to make demands of their government and, if they are not met, to reconstruct their government in such a way that the demands can be met.

This moral language isn't simply about persuading others to see things as we see them. It is also about coming to understand ourselves as equal agents in the formation of a just society. It is essential to the work of democracy, and we cannot address our heart problem without it.

What's more, a new moral language is needed to break through the false dichotomies that America's culture wars have created. When we understand that moral and religious language was co-opted in the late 1970s to push back against the gains of the civil and women's rights movements through the Moral Majority and the broader "religious right," we can see clearly how the divisions that are so obvious in our society today are not new. They are simply unveiled and amplified. Even more importantly, though, moral language helps name how these manufactured divisions are designed to distract us from the policy decisions that create a real and consequential divide between those who have more than they will ever need and those who live with their backs against the wall. These are the "separate and unequal" Americans that the original Kerner Commission sought to address, and we must keep our focus on this division today. We cannot be distracted by politicians who want to talk about book bans, "parents' rights," or whether history makes children feel guilty. Moral language helps us to challenge those same leaders to address the low wages, lack of access to health care, and declining life expectancy that characterize reality for the nearly half of Americans who are poor or low income today.

WE NEED A MORAL LINKING OF ISSUES

How is it possible that a relatively small minority of elites have been able to successfully subvert the will of the majority in a democratic society? This is a fundamental question of our political moment, and today's Reconstructionists are answering it with an "intersectional" analysis that is rooted in the fusion history of America's Reconstruction movements.

In 2007, after I was elected to lead the North Carolina NAACP, I visited with the leadership of every organization in the state that was committed to working on a justice issue. As I listened to them, I always asked the same question: who is blocking you from getting what your constituency wants? In every meeting, I heard the same list of organizations and politicians. So I started asking a second question: If these folks are cynical enough to stand together against all of us, shouldn't we be smart enough to come together and form a united front for the issues we're concerned about?

This wasn't an original insight. I was trying to put into practice what I had learned about fusion politics in North Carolina's history. While most Americans know that federal Reconstruction lasted for a brief decade after the Civil War, until President Rutherford B. Hayes removed federal troops from the South, a lesser-known piece of our Reconstruction history is that Black Republicans and white populists formed fusion coalitions across the South that continued to exercise political power in some places until the end of the 19th century. These coalitions were possible because people with different interests recognized that the former plantation class was against all of them, so they joined together to share power. In my home state of North Carolina, it took a violent coup to break the power of the Fusion Party, which controlled the municipal government in Wilmington in 1898.

What was true in the late 19th century is even truer today: It's all connected. The same policies that negatively affect poor and low-wealth people in Alabama also hurt poor and low-wealth people in Appalachia. The design of the Southern Strategy and the culture wars has been to constantly give people who might unite against elite interests reason to fight one another. So-called "wedge issues" are designed to split up the majority that does not benefit from the preferred policies of the richest among us. But today's Reconstructionists are reclaiming the only strategy that has even defeated the exploitation of elite interests. They are building fusion coalitions across the dividing lines of racial identity and issue areas.

WE NEED A POLICY FRAMING THAT RECOGNIZES THE DEATH MEASURE OF POLITICAL DECISIONS

One of the startling realities of recent data analysis is that life expectancy is on the decline in the United States, but we must look closer to understand the root cause of unnecessary death. Despite the fact that the United States throws out more food than is needed to feed every hungry person and has more cutting-edge developments in health care than any other nation—and despite our GDP growing exponentially in recent years—a study at the University of California–Riverside found that poverty is the fourth-leading cause of death in America.[3] Poor people can expect to die 12 or 13 years sooner than rich people in the United States, with the death rate gap between rich and poor increasing by 570% since 1980.[4]

In a series on declining life expectancy, the *Washington Post* reports that "The United States is failing at a fundamental mission—keeping people alive."[5] The United States has a significantly lower life expectancy than other nations with similar economic development. "America is increasingly a country of haves and have-nots, measured not just by bank accounts and property values but also by vital signs and grave markers." Dying prematurely, the *Post* found, has become the most telling measure of the nation's growing inequality.

This death measurement indeed is telling. It paints a picture of a country that has the resources to raise wages, end homelessness, expand health care, and invest in child care and other needed resources to help struggling families, but refuses to do so. It demonstrates a society (with Congress as the spear tip) that keeps proposing cuts to health care, food assistance, education, and more, even after policy experts have shown that such cuts result in suffering and death.

Today's Reconstructionists are refusing to let the debate about antipoverty programs or access to health care be reduced to an ideological difference between "big government" and "small government." They are reframing the policy debate in terms of life and death. Ironically, to exploit the wedge issue of abortion, culture warriors have spent decades and billions of dollars to try to persuade religious people that the narrow agenda of extremists is "pro-life." The counties represented by these so-called "pro-life" politicians, however, have seen some of the most dramatic increases in unnecessary death. The survivors of this assault on our common goods are increasingly naming the political agenda they are fighting as "policy murder." Their framing invites us to establish a death measure for every piece of public policy that is undermining the nation's commitment to "life, liberty, and the pursuit of happiness."

WE NEED CULTURAL ARTS TO INSPIRE RESISTANCE

When we look back at movements to reconstruct American democracy, they are not only marked by moral analysis, powerful articulation of the moral issues at stake, and compelling actions that engaged the masses. These movements are also peppered with songs, poetry, and visual arts that inspired people to believe that change was possible.

The spirituals, written and composed by enslaved people, were introduced to America during the First Reconstruction by the Fisk Jubilee Singers. Poets like Langston Hughes articulated the longings of millions when he wrote in the early 20th century, "America never was America to me, / And yet I swear this oath—/ America will be!" During the Second Reconstruction, when young people became nonviolent foot soldiers on the frontlines of the battle for democracy in the South, they took songs they had learned growing up in church and rewrote them as "freedom songs." When they faced racist sheriffs' deputies, they sang, "Ain't gonna let nobody turn me round." When they got on buses as integrated pairs to face inevitable violence and possible death, they sang, "Hallelujah, I'm a traveling / down freedom's main line!"

As today's Reconstructionists engage the cultural arts, we aren't simply inserting a song here and there in our public programs, nor are we just using the name recognition of celebrity artists to draw crowds to our events. We are, instead, drawing on the long tradition of resistance art in America and in our moral traditions. Activist artists and theomusicologists are writing and creating new pieces to convey the moral message we are lifting up in our actions. We are speaking the truth, singing the truth, and using art to help people imagine the future they cannot yet see.

RECOVER THE MORAL LEVERAGE OF OUR VOTES

We cannot deal with the heart problem we face in America without a mass mobilization of poor and low-wealth voters alongside everyone who wants to reconstruct democracy.

Indeed, I believe that the poor people are the new swing voters who can ultimately shift the political calculus in our common life. Here's why: Poor and low-income people make up a third of the U.S. electorate—more than 40% in swing states.[6] But almost no one in politics talk to poor and low-income voters because they are what the demographers call "low-propensity voters."

Rarely do we ask, however, why poor and low-income people are not voting. As I have walked alongside movements across this land, it's clear that poor people know something is wrong and have a vested interest in working for change. But they have not had many politicians from either party who have been willing to speak directly to them for decades. Most Republicans have assumed that everyone does well when "the economy" is doing well, while Democrats have preferred to talk about the "middle class." Meanwhile, GDP has continued to rise while fewer and fewer people enjoy the promises of the American Dream.

Many poor and low-income people have not voted in recent elections because they don't see anyone running to represent them. At the same time, however, massive voter suppression and election subversion campaigns have been conducted over the past decade in every statehouse controlled by a Republican majority. Through gerrymandering, voter purges, voter ID requirements, and cutbacks to voter access programs, incumbents in some of the poorest states in the nation are trying to make it more difficult to vote. Many have rightly pointed out that these policies are racist because they are descendants of the Jim Crow system and because they both target and disproportionately impact Black people. But they do not only impact Black people. Voter suppression is also making it more difficult for poor people, women, Native Americans, the disabled, and young people to vote. While these policies often target Black people, they diminish democracy for all of us.

In the midst of this reality, today's Reconstructionists are raising an alarm among poor and low-income eligible voters of every race. Our message is clear: They wouldn't be fighting us this hard if they didn't understand our power. It is essential that all of us who want to create a new will and revive the heart of American democracy also understand our power. In many parts of this nation, we still have more eligible voters sitting on the sidelines than active voters backing either side in political races. This means if we organize and mobilize poor and low-income voters, they have the power to be decision-makers in every election. We must reclaim the moral leverage of a movement that votes, continues to organize, and then keeps showing up to vote again.

RECOVER THE MORAL COMMITMENT TO LONG-TERM STRUGGLES

Finally, the directly impacted people who are leading today's movements for a Third Reconstruction understand that this is not a time for microwave movements. Activism is not a weekend avocation or a pastime for students who have been reading about an interesting social issue. Whether people are directly impacted by poverty, racism, a lack of access to health care, the denial of equal protection under the law, voter suppression, militarism, or ecological devastation, the new Reconstructionists are building coalitions that understand we are engaged in the work of building a new world together. Yes, the needs are urgent. And, at the same time, they demand a long-term commitment to build out the coalitions, formation programs, sustained analysis, and community networks that will make it possible for us to not only sustain a struggle for justice but also become the kind of society we want to see in the world.

We cannot think in terms of one march, one email, or one tweet. We have to make a long-term commitment to change. Like the 19th-century abolitionists who worked to get people to freedom even as they petitioned for a political end to slavery that they knew they might not live to see, we must learn to take care of one another and help one another toward freedom even as we imagine and demand an end to poverty, hunger, mass incarceration, discrimination, and inequality. Only by taking the long view can we have the resilience and determination to continue the work that is necessary to revive the heart of democracy.

I have a friend whose husband is living today, but he had a heart problem some years ago. When he experienced a heart attack at home, an ambulance came and the EMTs started CPR. They checked his vital signs, and it was clear that his heart still wasn't beating. They got out the paddles and shocked him. But he didn't come back. So one of the old paramedics said, "Shock him again."

Even still, there was no pulse. So that same paramedic said, "Hit him again." My friend, his wife, cried out, "He's not gone yet!" She told me the story afterward, how this persistent paramedic just wouldn't give up. "I've been out here too long," he told her. "Just because there's a flatline doesn't mean a life is finished."

When my friend told me the story, she was so glad that somebody who came to her house that day knew enough to say, "Shock him one more time!"

It is not easy or pleasant to face the fact that America has a heart problem—that we have, in fact, flatlined for so long now that some people have given up hope on the possibility of democracy. But as bad as things are, I'm so glad that there are movements today bringing people together to say, "Shock the heart of this nation one more time."

The Reconstructionists who came before us fought too hard, sacrificed too much, and achieved too much with far less than we have for us to give up now. We've got to shock the heart of this nation one more time.

Too many people's lives, both here and around the globe, depend on us righting our ship of state and fulfilling the promise of liberty and justice for all. We've got to shock the heart of this nation one more time.

The possibilities of our children's children and the viability of our fragile planet are simply too precious for us to give up now. It's time to shock the heart of this nation one more time.

Others have come before us to show us the way. We do not have to imagine what Reconstruction might look like from scratch. But it is our time now. We are the ones we have been waiting for. If we stand and do what is in our power to do, I know there is a Power greater than us—a Force beyond all our efforts to know and name—that can take out our heart of stone, as the prophet Ezekiel said it, and give us a heart of flesh. When we each do our part, we will find the shock we need to revive the heart of our democracy and become the America we have never yet been.

NOTES

1. Peniel E. Joseph, "How Black Americans Kept Reconstruction Alive," *The Atlantic*, November 13, 2023.

2. I challenge this lie in my book with Jonathan Wilson-Hartgrove, *White Poverty: How Exposing Myths About Race and Class Can Reconstruct American Democracy* (New York: Liveright, 2024).

3. David Danelski, "Poverty Is the 4th Greatest Cause of U.S. Deaths," UC Riverside News, April 17, 2023, https://news.ucr.edu/articles/2023/04/17/poverty-4th-greatest-cause-us-deaths.

4. Joel Achenbach et al., "An Epidemic of Chronic Illness Is Killing Us Too Soon," *Washington Post*, October 3, 2023, https://www.washingtonpost.com/health/interactive/2023/american-life-expectancy-dropping.

5. Achenbach et al., "An Epidemic of Chronic Illness Is Killing Us Too Soon."

6. Shailly Gupta Barnes, "Waking the Sleeping Giant: Poor and Low Income Voters in the 2020 Elections," Poor People's Campaign, October 2021, https://www.poorpeoplescampaign.org/waking-the-sleeping-giant-poor-and-low-income-voters-in-the-2020-elections.

CHAPTER 24

An Email and an Epistle for American Democracy

Cornell William Brooks

The Kerner Commission released its report only weeks before I had racial justice seared into my consciousness as a boy. As a 2nd grader in Anacostia, Washington, DC, I recall being told to go home from school because of some kind of disturbance. I later learned that someone my parents admired, the Rev. Dr. Martin Luther King, Jr., was assassinated. "Assassinated" was a word I did not understand, but I later associated with sadness, rage, and flames. Soon after Dr. King was killed, buildings were burned, stores were looted, some died, more were hurt, and even more were arrested in cities across America. I learned as a child that sorrow, anger, and injustice constitute an accelerant for unrest, like gasoline on a fire. More than a half century later, America is again on fire—even as the flames of outrage, anger, and sorrow have dimmed after the massive George Floyd protests in 2020, where 26 million people took to the streets in the largest and most geographically, generationally, and racially diverse demonstrations in American history.[1] Only to be followed by angry, sorrow-laden, and yet hope-inspired protests after the police homicides of Ahmad Arbury, Elijah McClain, Breonna Taylor—with the hashtags and homicides continuing even as this chapter goes to print.[2]

Accordingly, this chapter is written with the urgency of a digital email demanding action and a biblical epistle beseeching contemplation. This essay is not the analytic product of a disinterested social scientist, but an email and an epistle written by a practitioner of justice-making and a professor of social justice whose beloved students at Harvard and across the country study democracy while remaking it. Most of my students, millions of Americans, young people, and I are deeply concerned that America is on fire with the rising temperatures (and sea levels) of climate change, with an existential deadline on the planet. We are equally concerned about the less obvious fact that our country is aflame with racial divisions that are an existential threat to American democracy itself.

The modest words of this email and epistle seek to extinguish these fires and bridge the divisions to a future for an American multiracial democracy that is an inspiring model for the world. By model we do not mean arrogant American exceptionalism, only a challenge to ourselves to learn from our past and the world itself to make a democracy prosperously just for everyone. Accordingly, this chapter sets forth seven requirements for a multiracial democracy and seven strategic principles to build the will to achieve such an America.

Presciently, the Kerner Commission concluded that America was at risk of becoming a nation divided: Black and white, separate and unequal.[3] In this third decade of the 21st century, America is not merely split into unequal racial halves but being fragmented into multiracial pieces. African Americans are no longer the largest ethnic group, Hispanics are,[4] with both 24% of Black and 24% of Brown Americans facing stark discrimination in employment.[5] In a racially balkanized America, predictably, Black Americans face the most and most violent hate crime, but with Asian Americans, immigrants, Muslims, and Jews all being victims as well in recent spikes.[6]

Indeed, hate crimes are a visible violent enactment of the metaphor of the flames of racial animus. As such, these crimes represent a literal threat to the physical safety and well-being of our democracy. Relatedly, the January 6th insurrection was a physical threat to our democracy. Police officers were assaulted, members of Congress fled for their lives, and military and law enforcement reinforcements were called into action. And while the peaceful transfer of power took place, it is easy to imagine otherwise. The insurrection, however, was far more than a physical threat to American democracy.

The insurrection as an existential threat to democracy was animated and stoked by racism. From racially gerrymandered congressional districts that polarize the electorate, to Russian election interference that racially weaponized social media to further divide voters, to racially engineered voter suppression, the insurrectionists went to our nation's capital to take back their country from Black people and their allies.

If America is to become a just multiracial democracy, there are seven requirements and seven strategic principles to advocate for such a democracy. I propose we honor the 250th anniversary of the Declaration of Independence by laying the foundation for such a democracy by July 4th, 2026.

The requirements for a multiracial democracy through a Second American Founding include abolition of the Electoral College, compulsory or universal voting, an end to generational voter suppression, the eradication of racial voter suppression, carceral emancipation for citizenship, the democratization of artificial intelligence for democracy, and healing our history with reparations.

The first following the Civil War and the second being the Civil Rights Movement, during which the Kerner Commission released its report. That being said, the first two Reconstructions were attempted in a country that was not only Black and white, but demographically and predominantly so. That is most certainly not the case today. As such, America needs not so much a third Reconstruction as literally a Second Founding. America in the second decade of the 21st century looks nothing like America of the 19th century of the first Reconstruction. The multiracial coalitions of the 1870s were largely biracial. Today, such a multiracial coalition would be racially reductionist. Accordingly, a 21st-century multiracial democracy requires a new civic infrastructure. A Second Founding of America requires a new foundation.

Among those requirements is the abolition of the Electoral College. Harvard Kennedy School scholar Alex Keyssar argues that the Electoral College has been unrepresentative and flawed from conception.[7] As such the Electoral College represents voices of blocks of states, not the distinctive democratic voices of a multiracial, multiethnic, and multigenerational America—as would be the case with the direct election of the president.

As well as an end to the Electoral College, the right to vote should be universal and constructively compulsory, that is, less of a legal minimum and more of a civic maximum. According to the scholar Gilda Daniels, the Constitution minimally interprets the right to vote as a series of "thou shall nots."[8] The Fifteenth Amendment essentially says thou shall not impinge the right to vote based upon race, color, or previous condition of servitude; the Nineteenth Amendment, thou shall not restrict the vote based upon gender; the Twenty-Sixth Amendment, thou shall not limit the youth vote based on age (setting the national standard at 18 years); and finally the Snyder Act, thou shall not engage in racial discrimination against Native Americans exercising the right to vote.[9]

Each of these amendments and this legislation represent voter protection in the form of discrimination prohibition; there is no affirmative right to vote in the U.S. Constitution. The practical consequence of this is that the American electorate is often left to defend itself from voter discrimination, with or without the support of elected officials. Massive amounts of money are spent monitoring and protecting elections by civil rights groups without the government having an affirmative responsibility to not only protect the right to vote but maximize voting. If voting were treated like jury duty, that is, as both a right and a responsibility, citizens would be expected and modestly incentivized to vote. Were America like, say, Australia, where voting (per se, not voting for any candidate or party), is compulsory, we could imagine a country where voter turnout is at least 80%.[10] Accordingly, voter turnout rather than voter suppression would be the norm for all Americans and certainly for oft-excluded Black, Latino, Native American, disabled, and young voters.

Before and after universal voting, a just multiracial democracy needs the protection of legislation like the John R. Lewis Voting Rights Advancement Act barring racial discrimination in voting and restoring the ability of the Justice Department to bring affirmative litigation to protect the right to vote at the first appearance of voter suppression[11] under the Voting Rights Act of 1965. The Justice Department lost the ability to affirmatively protect the right to vote with the *Shelby v. Holder* Supreme Court decision.[12] This is important because the late legal scholar Lani Guinier described African Americans as the proverbial canaries in the coal mine.[13] This is to say that African Americans are often the first and worst victims of voter suppression; their discrimination is emblematic of the discrimination that other voters face. To ensure that everyone's vote is protected, we must first and foremost secure the right to vote for those most vulnerable.

As with racial voter suppression, an increasingly racially diverse and younger electorate must be protected against generational voter suppression. College campuses are often split into congressional districts to gerrymander the youth vote. Moreover, students often face an array of impediments to vote simply because they are young: confusing voter registration, inaccessible polling places, and de facto poll taxes.[14] As my students and I have discovered in our work with the Andrew Goodman Foundation, to combat youth voter suppression in both predominately White institutions (PWIs) and Historically Black Colleges and Universities (HBCUs), the youth vote is underprotected and the Twenty-Sixth Amendment underlitigated. Legal, philanthropic, and civic resources must be devoted to not only turning out the youth vote but protecting it as well.

The civic infrastructure of American democracy may well crumble unless we find the means by which to harness rather than be harmed by the power of technology. Most obviously, artificial intelligence threatens to not merely disrupt but potentially degrade our democracy. Technologists are already warning us about the potential for misinformation and disinformation, the capacity of large language programs to deceptively write laws that human voters may or may not sanction,[15] as well as the ability for AI to personalize digital communication to deceive voters.[16]

It's important for America to affirmatively instrumentalize artificial intelligence in service of democracy rather than cowering in indecision apprehensive of it being weaponized against democracy. The scholar Bruce Schneier has written that while there is a current monopoly on programs like ChatGPT, we can well imagine government investing in AI that promotes civic education coalition building, and even collaboration on public policy issues and concerns. Microsoft and Google need not have a monopoly on tools like ChatGPT. What if America had a public option for AI in service to the citizenry, similar to a public option in health care—with investment.[17] While technology may be agnostic as to its use, a 21st-century multiracial democracy demands that we be affirmative as to how it could be used to better democracy.

A demographic fraction of American democracy and a civic percentage of the electorate is invisible. Like Ralph Ellison's *Invisible Man*,[18] there are literally millions of Black, Latino, and poor men who are locked away in America's prisons and jails and as such ineligible to vote, find it difficult to vote after release, and are politically out of sight and out of mind. In the same way economists don't count prisoners among the unemployed, elected officials don't count those who don't vote because of felony disenfranchisement or their inability to get to the polls. When it comes to the franchise the word "felon" erases the word "citizen" or "voter."

Accordingly, America must engage in what I term Carceral Emancipation for Citizenship. It is not enough to treat 2 million Americans in prison as criminals in need of rehabilitation, America must treat them as imprisoned people in need of emancipation for citizenship. If under the Thirteenth Amendment involuntary servitude is prohibited "except as punishment for crime," then the nation has a responsibility, at a minimum, to literally emancipate those subject to involuntary servitude and restrictions on their citizenship. Accordingly, the millions who are disenfranchised as consequence of felony convictions or being in prison, on parole, or on probation should have the right to vote fully restored. Moreover, justice-involved citizens must be accorded not only the same rights as other citizens but also be subject to the same civic expectations as other citizens—that is to say, voting and civic participation are treated as pillars of rehabilitation. Moreover, the right to vote should not be preconditioned on former prisoners paying fines, fees, and/or court costs.

If poll workers are the doorkeepers to voting, police are the gatekeepers to America's prisons and the carceral state. To emancipate citizens who have been incarcerated, it is not enough to address people coming out of prisons, America must also address policing as driving incarceration and violence. Young Black men are 21 times more likely to be killed at the hands of the police than their White counterparts.[19] A Black man has a 1 in 1,000 chance of being killed by the police, so much so that police homicide is a leading cause of death.[20] Violently over-policing law-abiding innocent citizens because they are stereotyped as criminal suspects makes those citizens second class citizens whose lives, votes, and rights matter less.

Carceral emancipation means freeing Black communities from policing that has killed the innocent from Elijah McClain to Breonna Taylor and led to mass incarceration.

Specifically, this means the legislative removal of qualified immunity, the legal shield that ensures police can't be prosecuted for misconduct, violence, and even murder. As well as the elimination of qualified immunity, policework must be limited to public safety that can only be done by law enforcement. Nuisance stops, low-level traffic enforcement, and mass prosecution of misdemeanors must end. Police are but one public safety tool. Quality schools, engaged teachers, well-lit and landscaped streets, public health professionals,[21] and good employment are also tools.

Lastly, we must heal our history to have a future as a just democracy. America can never be a multiracial democracy with a history that is unacknowledged, banned, and ignored in ways that rob many of intergenerational wealth. The distinguished labor economist William "Sandy" Darity and independent scholar Kirsten Mullen have comprehensively described the ways in which America through chattel slavery, Jim Crow, contract mortgages, the convict leasing system, and redlining has imposed a racial wealth gap between White America and African Americans of $10–12 trillion.[22] The legal, public policy, and historical evidence is well-documented and yet underread and ignored. Trying to create or even sustain an enduring democracy with the victims of racial theft and the unwitting beneficiaries of theft standing side by side without discussing the theft is intellectually disingenuous and morally duplicitous.

There are those who contend that healing our history and ensuring our future with reparations is a nonstarter as it is politically radical and fiscally unprecedented. My Harvard Kennedy School colleague Linda Bilmes and I demonstrate in a forthcoming paper that there is a norm in government practice, history, and policy that says when citizens are harmed through no fault of their own, government steps in to make them whole. We call this norm "reparatory compensation." When a farmer loses a crop to an act of nature, the government will often subsidize the loss of the crop. When a veteran loses a limb, whether in battle or on base, the government will often compensate the service member. Even when employees work for a failing company, the government protects them against the loss of their pensions. After reviewing scores of government programs, my colleague and I demonstrate that government has the expertise, experience, and resources, as in millions and even billions of dollars, to compensate for nonracial harms. These routine compensated nonracial harms are analogous and sometimes identical to the racial harms suffered by Black Americans through a history that extends into the present.[23]

Recently, partially in response to our work, nearly half of all state attorneys general[24] and the Commission for Reimagining the Economy of the American Academy of Arts and Sciences have called for compensating Black World War II veterans who were discriminatorily denied G.I. Bill benefits.[25] America can start with aging Black World War II vets as a first step to redressing her racial history.

A multiracial democracy demands that we heal the past in order to heal the future. This means not merely checks and cost estimates but creating a reparations commission to collect the untold stories, repressed memories, and unspoken testimonies to help America heal.

This bold agenda for a 21st-century multiracial democracy is within reach if we employ strategic principles of advocacy. After having spent 30 years as a civil rights prosecutor, ordained minister, and NAACP president and CEO, I came to the Harvard Kennedy School to teach and as importantly learn public leadership and social justice with young people. Together, we created a unique intergenerational and interdisciplinary social justice clinic, the William Monroe Trotter Collaborative for Social Justice. I developed and tested a set of advocacy principles for this clinic. These seven principles can be used to build the will to realize our democracy agenda.

The first of these principles is Moral Ambition. It's not enough to be pragmatic and practical to realize the Second Founding for a multiracial democracy. Simply being practical and pragmatic may increase the sense of agency people have, but not necessarily inspire them to use that agency. In it is important to be morally ambitious with goals that inspire, convict, and compel. All we need to do is recall the great Pauli Murray, who even as a Howard University Law School student in the 1940s illustrated moral ambition. Murray argued in class that lawyers could defeat the doctrine and creed of Jim Crow, "separate but equal," in 10 years. Her all-male professors and all-male classmates derided the preposterous idea of the lone woman at the law school. She, nevertheless, set forth a strategy for defeating Jim Crow in a term paper, which laid the foundation for the subsequently successful argument that "separate was inherently unequal." After graduation, a group of Methodist church women, not lawyers, contracted her to turn her term paper into a pamphlet on segregation.[26] Murray instead turned the paper into a textbook that became known as the bible of state segregation laws.[27] When Thurgood Marshall and NAACP lawyers prepared to argue *Brown v. Board of Education*, they used her term paper, textbook, and legal theory to change American history by defeating Jim Crow.

The lesson here is clear: We begin with a morally ambitious agenda. Accordingly, we need not be timid about the need to rebuild the civic infrastructure of our country to support a robust democracy.

Second, one of the ways in which we can advance this Second Founding is by describing this endeavor not as a frantic response to an existential threat but an existential opportunity. In other words, it's not a matter of continually being on defense against threats to this democracy but seizing a generational opportunity to reposition our democracy for a future far better than the founding fathers or our forebears could even have imagined. Focusing on this generational opportunity gives us a reason to focus on youth with a sense of urgency. Urgency without this sense of opportunity debilitates agency. To simply say we must act quickly under penalty of severe consequences may leave the public unsure and enfeebled. To say, however, we must act quickly to avert grave consequences and to embrace generationally unprecedented opportunity may infuse the public with civic confidence and empowerment.

Third, now is the time to use a principle I term an Empowering Hermeneutic History. The legal scholar Derek Bell wrote a parable about the power of history. In the *Chronicle of the Slave Scrolls*, Bell a historical fable in which African Americans, after mediating on the accounts of their enslaved forebears, begin to excel in ways that defy the expectations of white supremacy.[28]

In the same way rabbis, priests, imams, and ministers used biblical history to morally inspire, history can be used as a tool of advocacy to realize our agenda. Theologians use a concept called hermeneutics or the science of interpretation. Rather than merely read suppressed and ignored histories as a recitation of facts, events, and dates, we must interpret our histories in ways that empower our democracy. Applying an Empowering Hermeneutic of History enables citizens not only to read the dry Byzantine provisions of the Voting Rights Act, but to reflect on the courage of a young John Lewis to find the strength to advocate for an end to youth voter suppression and a beginning of universal voting. This Empowering Hermeneutic of History should guide all of our advocacy efforts.

This Hermeneutic of History is evident in Martin Luther King's well-quoted and underread "I have a dream" speech. King quotes the Gettysburg Address, Declaration of Independence, and the National Anthem.[29] He reinterprets each of these romanticized notes of American history as a song to be sung to fuel the fight for racial justice and freedom. We must strategically employ history to sustain what will be difficult and even dangerous advocacy.

As important as history is in this effort, so too is the principle of Morals and Money, Ethics and Economics. Quite often economic arguments for policy are made, with ethical arguments made on the side—if at all. The most powerful arguments are often ones that conjoin the economic and empirical with the moral and narrative. From prison closures to reductions in juvenile incarceration, we have seen time and time again arguments for giving people a moral second chance with arguments for reducing the cost of mass incarceration. Another example of the applications of the Morals and Money principle is the campaign I led in New Jersey to allow people with criminal records to compete for jobs without having to check a box inquiring as to whether or not they had been arrested and/or convicted of a crime. The successful campaign to ban the box in New Jersey[30] and the subsequent federal legislation illustrates what happens when you marry moral and money arguments. Accordingly, we must ask what are the economic and ethical costs of not having a just multiracial democracy? What are social externalities, the hidden social costs borne by vulnerable and invisible?

Related to the principle of Morals and Money is the principle of Sacred Texts and Secular Scholarship. It is not enough to use academic studies or reports to make the case. Whenever possible, we must seek ways to relate the results of studies to the values of sacred texts, for those for whom this is important and relevant. For example, 10 years before the Kerner Commission, Drs. Mamie and Kenneth B. Clark used their famous doll experiment to demonstrate the pernicious effects of segregation in *Brown v. Board of Education*. Few Americans actually read the study indicating that segregated Black children often selected an identical White doll over a Black doll, when asked which is better. Nevertheless, many people saw the picture of Kenneth Clark holding up dolls and having the Black child point to the White doll as being better.[31] The picture, an Instagram image of its day, confirmed for many religious people the evils of segregation in terms of the scripture. If all children are created in the image of God, the *Imago Dei*, it would be not unconstitutional but immoral to convince segregated children that their image of themselves is inferior. The study and the pictures not only illustrated a legal point for the Supreme Court, but a moral point in the court of moral opinion. We should do no less.

To create the will for our democracy agenda, we can employ the principle of Youth as Generationally Disruptive Technology. In the same way telephones and digital cameras made the Kodak cameras of old obsolete or Uber and Lyft disrupted the taxicab industry, youth represent generationally disruptive technology for social movements. Accordingly, youth often accelerate the pace, elevate the demands, and expand the Overton window of what's possible in movements. For this ambitious democracy agenda, youth must be so engaged.

Kimberlé Crenshaw among others has advanced social justice well beyond the academy by helping many to understand that injustices don't represent separate points of vulnerability but often overlap in a Venn diagram of injustice and identity.[32] One human being may bear the brunt of multiple injustices on various points of identity gender, race, class, etc. It's important for us to use that understanding of multiple identities and overlapping injustices to build shared empathy and narrative. We must communicate that we are more than a nation of segmented grievances, but a community grounded on a moral canon and the civic compact. In other ways, we must describe our efforts with an intersectional analysis and shared undergirding vision.

Lastly, I conclude that such an agenda is only possible if it is predicated on a sense of hope. Had the formerly enslaved Harriet Tubman compared the 70 slaves or so she freed on the Underground Railroad[33] to the 4 million enslaved,[34] she might have given up. Her hope and leadership were not based on the dire math of reality, but on a calculation of faith. Hope is not empirically demonstrated; it is morally chosen. An American multiracial democracy befitting her citizenry may be built with a strategy, but its foundation is our hopes.

NOTES

1. Lara Putnam, Erica Chenoweth, and Jeremy Pressman, "The Floyd Protests Are the Broadest in US History—and Are Spreading to White, Small-Town America" *Washington Post,* June 6, 2020.

2. Rich McKay, "Factbox: People of Color Whose Deaths Inspired Wave of U.S. Protests." *Reuters,* June 26, 2020.

3. U.S. National Advisory Commission on Civil Disorders, *The Kerner Report: The 1968 Report of the National Advisory Commission on Civil Disorders* (New York: Pantheon Books, 1988).

4. Eric Jensen et al., "2020 U.S. Population More Racially and Ethnically Diverse Than Measured in 2010," U.S. Census Bureau, August 12, 2021.

5. Camille Lloyd, "One in Four Black Workers Report Discrimination at Work," Gallup, January 12, 2021.

6. Federal Bureau of Investigation, "Hate Crime in the United States Incident Analysis," 2022.

7. Alexander Keyssar, *Why Do We Still Have the Electoral College?* (Cambridge, MA: Harvard University Press, 2020).

8. Gilda Daniels, "Democracy's Destiny," *California Law Review* 109 (June 2021), https://doi.org/10.15779/Z38BG2HB3Q.

9. Norman J. Ornstein, "Lift Every Voice: The Urgency of Universal Civic Duty Voting," The Brookings Institution and The Ash Center for Democratic Governance and Innovation, Harvard Kennedy School, 2020.

10. Ornstein, "Lift Every Voice."

11. Andrew Garber, "Pass the John R. Lewis Voting Rights Advancement Act," The Brennan Center, September 19, 2023, https://www.brennancenter.org/our-work/research-reports/pass-john-r-lewis-voting-rights-advancement-act.

12. *Shelby County v. Holder,* 133 S. Ct. 2612 (2013).

13. Lani Guinier and Gerald Torres, *The Miner's Canary: Enlisting Race, Resisting Power, Transforming Democracy* (Cambridge, MA: Harvard University Press, 2003).

14. Yael Bromberg, "Youth Voting Rights and the Unfulfilled Promise of the Twenty-Sixth Amendment," *University of Pennsylvania Journal of Constitutional Law* 21, no. 5 (2019): 1105.

15. Bruce Schneier, Henry Farrell, and Nathan E. Sanders, "How Artificial Intelligence Can Aid Democracy," *Slate*, April 21, 2023, https://slate.com/technology/2023/04/ai-public-option.html.

16. Nathan E. Sanders and Bruce Schneier, "Just Wait Until Trump Is a Chatbot," *The Atlantic*, April 28, 2023, https://www.theatlantic.com/technology/archive/2023/04/ai-generated-political-ads-election-candidate-voter-interaction-transparency/673893.

17. Schneier et al., "How Artificial Intelligence Can Aid Democracy."

18. Ralph Ellison, *Invisible Man* (New York: Vintage International, 1995).

19. Ryan Gabrielson, Eric Sagara, and Ryann Grochowski Jones, "Deadly Force, in Black and White," *ProPublica*, October 10, 2014.

20. Michael A. Robinson, "Social Justice Implications for Black Men's Health: Policing Black Bodies," in *Black Men's Health: A Strengths-Based Approach Through a Social Justice Lens for Helping Professions*, ed. Yarneccia D. Dyson, Vanessa Robinson-Dooley, and Jerry Watson (Cham, Switzerland: Springer International Publishing, 2022), 169–179.

21. Birmingham Public Safety Task Force and William Monroe Trotter Collaborative for Social Justice, Harvard University, "Reform and Reimagine Birmingham Public Safety 2021," December 10, 2020, https://birminghamwatch.org/wp-content/uploads/2020/12/Reform-and-Reimagine-Birmingham-Public-Safety.pdf.

22. William A. Darity, Jr. and A. Kirsten Mullen, *From Here to Equality: Reparations for Black Americans in the Twenty-First Century* (Chapel Hill, NC: The University of North Carolina Press, 2020).

23. Linda Bilmes and Cornell William Brooks, "Recognizing Reparations as Regular and Routine: The Implications for Black Americans of U.S Precedent, Norms, and History," *The Russell Sage Journal of the Social Sciences*, forthcoming.

24. Office of the Attorney General, "AG Campbell Leads Bi-Partisan Call on Congress to Pass GI Bill Restoration Act, Grant Benefits to Black World War II Veterans and Their Families," news release, Mass.gov, July 26, 2023, https://www.mass.gov/news/ag-campbell-leads-bi-partisan-call-on-congress-to-pass-gi-bill-restoration-act-grant-benefits-to-black-world-war-ii-veterans-and-their-families.

25. Commission on Reimagining the Economy, "Advancing a People First Economy," American Academy of Arts and Sciences, November 2023, 52–54. The author, as a member of the Commission on Reimagining the Economy, urged the commission to address the racial wealth gap of Black World War II veterans through "reparatory compensation," estimating and addressing harms through a variety of government compensatory programs. Reparatory compensation is the subject of a forthcoming paper by the author and Harvard Kennedy School professor Linda Bilmes.

26. Rosaline Rosenberg, *Jane Crow: The Life of Pauli Murray* (New York: Oxford University Press, 2017).

27. Pauli Murray, ed., *States' Laws on Race and Color* (Athens, GA: University of Georgia Press, 1997).

28. Derek Bell, *And We Are Not Saved: The Elusive Quest for Racial Justice* (New York: Basic Books, 2008), 215–38.

29. Martin Luther King, Jr., and James Melvin Washington, *A Testament of Hope: The Essential Writings of Martin Luther King, Jr.* (New York: Harper & Row, 1986), 217–20.

30. Pamela Varley and Cornell William Brooks, "Strategic Moves & Tough Choices: The Campaign Behind New Jersey's 'Ban the Box' Law," Harvard Kennedy School Case Program, June 30, 2020, https://case.hks.harvard.edu/strategic-moves-tough-choices-the-campaign-behind-new-jerseys-ban-the-box-law.

31. "Brown v. Board and 'The Doll Test,'" Legal Defense Fund, November 9, 2023, https://www.naacpldf.org/brown-vs-board/significance-doll-test.

32. Kimberlé W. Crenshaw, "Race, Gender, and Sexual Harassment," *Stanford Law Review* 1241 (1991): 1467.

33. Erin Blakemore, "Why Harriet Tubman Risked It All for Enslaved Americans," *National Geographic*, October 18, 2019, https://www.nationalgeographic.com/history/article/harriet-tubman-risked-everything-enslaved-americans.

34. Aaron O'Neill, "Black and Slave Population 1790–1880," Statista, February 12, 2020, https://www.statista.com/statistics/1010169/black-and-slave-population-us-1790-1880.

Persuasion, Democracy, and Voter Rights

CHAPTER 25

Values, Villain, Vision
Messaging to Mobilize Our Base and Persuade the Conflicted

Anat Shenker-Osorio

INTRODUCTION: SAY WHAT YOU'RE FOR AND CALL OUT THE OPPOSITION

If we want to "heal our divided society"[1] and "make good the promises of American democracy to all citizens,"[2] we must instill in people a desire to take and sustain action for progressive policies and candidates.

Over a decade of evidence garnered through surveys, randomized controlled trials, field experiments, and, more importantly, real-world campaigns for progressive issues and candidates, has brought to light a set of consistent messaging principles for mobisuasion: In other words, mobilizing our base and persuading the conflicted for our causes and candidates.

The first among these is Say What You're For. All too often progressive messaging relies upon negation, from "immigrants are not taking our jobs" to "we do not have voter fraud" to "tackling climate change will not harm our economy." Much like Nixon declaring "I am not a crook" made viewers suspect him of criminality, negations lend airtime and therefore credence to what we're attempting to refute. In addition, we tend to offer negative demands, such as stop voter suppression, end mass incarceration, ban fracking, and so on. These fail to paint the "beautiful tomorrow"—offering people a sense of what the world would be like were our policies to be put into practice.

At the same time, we must convey a critical contrast between our proposition and the opposition—clearly indicating what's on the line if those who seek to silence voices, restrict votes, and pervert values gain power.

Right now, our most common explanations for inequities—the gap between rich and poor, health disparities, "Black people were admitted to jail at more than four times the rate of White people,"[3] and so on—simply describe how outcomes differ between groups. This is all what and no why. These formulations leave it up to the audience to fill in the cause. But instead of accurately seeing structural forces at play, people all too readily blame individuals for their plight and are moved against progressive solutions. For example, whites hearing about racial disparities in deaths from COVID-19 were more likely to believe the government was doing too much for pandemic relief.[4] And when penal institutions were presented as having more Black inmates, white respondents favored more punitive measures.[5]

In short, when we fail to make clear that a problem is person-made, it becomes challenging or even impossible to demand it be person-fixed. When we fail to correctly identify who is responsible, we risk feeding the all-too-ready assumption that the people experiencing poor outcomes are the ones responsible for this.

For the purposes of promoting the Kerner Commission's aims, we must make clear for our audiences how our present-day divisions emerged, name who is deliberately blocking effective solutions, and unpack how they're able to thwart what continue to be majoritarian preferences. In short, we cannot create public will for a fairer, freer, more just America unless we correctly identify what impedes that will.

The very idea that our society "is divided" suggests this arose from the ether; that we are somehow drifting apart like continents breaking away from what was once Pangea. Further, this gives credence to the troubling idea that "both sides" are equally responsible, and that asking people to respect pronouns or rein in police violence is somehow akin to seizing the basic rights and freedoms of targeted groups.

In fact, stoking and exacerbating divisions is a political strategy authoritarian leaders pursue in order to claim and hold onto power. While the selected scapegoats differ and the phrases used to shame and blame them come in many forms, all authoritarian leaders know that the quickest route to an "us" is railing against a "them," a vital precursor to obfuscating plans to destroy democracy and rule only for the already wealthiest and most powerful few.

We see this in Orbán's Hungary, where Roma people are vilified and denied justice.[6] We saw it in the main slogan of the Brexit campaign, which vowed to "take back control" over immigration.[7] And we watched Brazil's Bolsonaro rail against "gender ideology" and lambast LGBTQ+ people to seize power.[8] It's no surprise that an ever-present authoritarian faction in America has continued to carry the tiki torch to advance what once justified enslavement of people from Africa and Native genocide, which became Jim Crow, Nixon's Southern Strategy, the Tea Party, and now the MAGA Movement.

Fortunately, we have hope-inducing examples to follow of not merely overcoming the politics of cruelty, but of making the absolute most of a very narrow governing majority and implementing policies to shore up democracy, address inequality, and improve life for people of all races, backgrounds, and genders. Arguably, the most comprehensive domestic example of this comes from Minnesota.

THE "MINNESOTA MIRACLE": REBUFFING RIGHT-WING RACE BAITING TO ACHIEVE PROGRESSIVE GOVERNANCE

In 2016, Donald Trump came within roughly 45,000 votes of winning Minnesota[9]—the best a Republican had done at the top of the ticket in this state since Ronald Reagan in 1984.[10] Minnesota Republicans saw in this landmark performance an opportunity to amass greater power utilizing the time-honored Right-wing populist strategy: divide in order to conquer.

A largely white state with a recognizable Somali American population, thanks to the immigrants who first settled there before the 1980s, joined by refugees fleeing civil war in the early 1990s, Minnesota seemed fertile terrain for nurturing the Republican seeds of anti-Black race-baiting, anti-refugee xenophobia, and anti-Muslim fearmongering. On cue, state Republicans, who seized control of the state senate and held the house in 2016, accelerated attacks about Somali-run day care centers, accusing them of funneling funds intended to subsidize child care into suitcases full of cash sent to Africa to finance terrorism.[11] Right-wing media in the state had their typical field day spreading these stories, stoking and exacerbating fear of this "other" in order to increase their political power by promising to protect "real Minnesotans" from this threat.

This tried-and-true dog whistle strategy, using racially coded invectives to evoke and provoke grievances among whites against people of color, proved integral to Trump's success in the state and beyond it. Indeed, Trump unofficially entered the political arena by sowing doubts about President Obama's origins and faith. And Trump doubled down on this when he officially launched his bid for presidency, riding his golden elevator into the bowels of xenophobia against Mexican Americans, with talk of "illegals" and promises of a border wall. In this, Trump dialed up the volume on standard Republican phrases like "welfare queens" and "inner-city crime," language that conveys that Black and Brown people cause harm to "hard-working Americans" (read: white people) without actually ever naming racial categories.

Yet 2016 was the election where pundits penned seemingly endless op-eds attributing Hillary Clinton's loss to her having spoken too openly and frequently about race. Perhaps most famously, Mark Lilla penned the piece[12] that would become its own genre—finger wagging about the limitations and dangers of what was once called "political correctness," renamed "identity politics" and now recast as "cultural issues" or "wokeness."

Both nationally and in Minnesota, this argument played out not merely in media but became the very heart of hand-wringing over how to regroup and reorient after seeing the Midwestern "Blue Wall" crumble. The diagnosis offered was that "working-class voters," who to hear pundits tell it aren't just white but generally male, were turning against the Democratic Party and progressive policies. The standard advice—an echo of similar guidance called "triangulation" in Bill Clinton's era and "popularism" today—was to moderate our message, silence any talk of purportedly polarizing issues like race and policing, immigrant rights, and abortion, and stick to universally beloved economic promises.

To be sure, the advice that engendering support for progressive policies and politicians requires championing only poll-tested issues like lowering prices and creating jobs seems logical. Why wouldn't you say only the things that nearly everyone likes and no one outright hates? However, this approach continuously fails in practice because it ignores the realities of how people come to judgments, what's required to change their minds, and what inspires them to take and sustain necessary actions to achieve policy victories.

First, not talking about race is great advice, unless your issue is race. And when you're attempting to "reverse the exploitation of Americans by the privileged and the rigged system" and "expose and advocate against the denial of exploitation,"[13] it is. Second, in reality, there are no race-neutral issues. While one could argue for things like more funding for public education, securing voting rights, or providing affordable housing without naming race, opponents of these endeavors will always bring race into the picture.

Indeed, as Ian Haney López has laid out, the true purpose of the dog whistle politics strategy is to impugn people of color in order to undermine belief in government itself.[14] The precise evidence-based policies that the Kerner Commission championed are portrayed as wasteful government "handouts" to the "undeserving," tacitly coded as people of color, unfairly seized from "hardworking taxpayers," who we're meant to understand are white. Opponents of these measures convince voters that we cannot have universal benefits like labor protections, free public education through university, or single-payer health care because there is no "us." Instead, there is a "them," who do not merit any public benefits.

Fortunately for Minnesota, decades of organizing and robust multiracial coalition building left them clear-eyed and ready to effectively address the racially divisive messaging that Republicans had long pumped out.

During the 2016 campaign, organizers knocking doors in rural Minnesota documented a repeated pattern. When they would show up touting progressive economic policies—from creating quality jobs to making child care more affordable—voters would register approval. But their enthusiasm would falter as they trotted out Right-wing talking points about immigrants coming for those employment opportunities or stealing those child care funds. In short, economic promises—desirable as they were—could not withstand the Right-wing storyline blaming immigrants, and Somalis more specifically, for the troubles of "real Minnesotans."

Rather than fall into despair, state leaders from Faith in Minnesota, Education Minnesota, SEIU Minnesota, and Our Minnesota Future joined in on a national project taking shape that would become what we now call the Race Class Narrative (RCN).

In 2018, this research project[15] began thanks to the efforts of *Dog Whistle Politics* and *Merge Left* author Ian Haney López, who approached me to help craft and test messaging to settle the tiresome debate about whether to speak exclusively of racial issues or center our political appeals in race-neutral class rhetoric. Haney López and I teamed up with Heather McGhee, at that time the president of Demos, and began qualitative and quantitative exploration with Lake Research Partners and Brilliant Corners nationally and within California, Indiana, Ohio, and, of course, Minnesota. In this, we worked alongside SEIU's Racial Justice Center with communications director Tinselyn Simms. Anika Fassia steered this whole process—from research design to dissemination of findings.

Over the course of 10 focus groups and five surveys, we found that messaging fusing together race and class didn't merely best standard opposition rhetoric. It out-performed status quo Left-wing approaches that eschew mention of race among voters across racial groups.[16] Minnesota took this even farther, conducting an 800-person canvassing field experiment. Voters were shown a real Republican flyer replete with racially coded invectives and then one of two rebuttals; one was race neutral and the other utilized the newly crafted RCN approach. "Among white respondents, a majority agreed with the initial dog whistle script. When these respondents were shown the class-only progressive flyer and asked which candidate they would select, 55% stuck with the racially divisive politician, and 44% shifted to the progressive candidate. But for those shown the race-class message, the numbers flipped. Only 43% stayed with the conservative candidate while 57% switched to the progressive who addressed race and class together."[17]

In 2020 retesting, we validated these previous findings and found RCN more effective with voters of color and white voters than race-only storylines that argue for equality and justice without addressing class-based economic inequities; the same held true for various experiments run independently by pollsters and academics as well as our own further testing.[18]

RCN moved those with mixed feelings on questions of racial justice, economic policymaking, and the role of government toward more progressive views across the board. At the same time, among respondents in agreement with us on the broad spectrum of progressive values and policies, it increased their desire to take action and abated their cynicism, helping them believe that we could come together to make the improvements in our society that the Kerner Commission championed.

This "engage the base and persuade the middle" approach is integral to RCN. Our strategy rests upon the belief that turnout is persuasion, because if your base won't carry the message, the middle will not hear it. Our efforts to create a better world do not enjoy the luxury of endless advertising budgets. We must have our choir singing from the same songbook to ensure that the congregation hears the joyful noise and goes out to convert new adherents.

RCN uses a tried-and-tested messaging architecture. We shorthand this as Values, Villain, Vision. It begins, not with a recitation of the many problems we confront, but rather an evocation of a shared value with an explicit mention of race or whatever dimension of division the opposition is bringing to the fore. This shared value is our opening *say-what-we're-for* salvo.

The value named is selected on the basis of the issue to be discussed and explicitly names race, class, gender, geography, and/or faith—depending on the axis of division the opposition is promoting. For example, a campaign to raise wages we could say, "No matter what we look like or what's in our wallets, most of us believe that people who work for a living ought to earn a living." An effort to promote universal single-payer care would kick off with "Whether we're Black or white, Latino or Asian, Native or newcomer, if someone we love is ill or injured we want them to have the very best care without going bankrupt to get it." And a campaign to dismantle state restrictions on voting would begin, "Across race and places, in America we believe that voters pick our leaders, our leaders do not pick their voters."

In fact, the original Kerner Commission report employed this RCN-style opening, saying "it was time to make good the promises of American democracy to all citizens—urban and rural, white and black, Spanish-surname, American Indian and every minority group."[19]

After we name a value relevant to the task at hand and insist it is shared across races, places of origin, zip codes, and/or genders, we move to articulating the problem we're confronting. And do so naming the perpetrators who created it.

As mentioned earlier, the first step to solving any problem is recognizing its origins. Unfortunately, the nearly ubiquitous unsourced problem statements we tend to write, like "voting rights are under attack," "democracy is eroding," or "our Nation is moving toward two societies, one black, one white—separate and unequal,"[20] eclipse from view the actors behind these outcomes. Attacks on the franchise aren't of origins unknown. Our nation is not a fertilized egg dividing. People do things; and when these things harm other people, it is absolutely critical we make clear the culprits behind these misdeeds.

Thus, in RCN messaging, we call out these culprits in the Villain sentence after our opening Value. Returning back to the example offered on raising wages, this second sentence could read as follows: "But today, a handful of corporations and the politicians they pay for are holding down wages, while they point the finger at Black people, new immigrants, or people struggling to make ends meet, so we'll look the other way while they hoard profits from the wealth our work creates."

In addition to making clear there's a who behind our struggles, an effective Villain call out does two other things. First, it exposes the right's strategy of deliberate division and scapegoating: it narrates the dog whistle, making visible and thus less effective how opponents of equality obfuscate their aims by blaming some "other" for the harms they wreak upon us. If they can convince you that José, standing in front of Home Depot soliciting day labor, powerless to set public policy, is "taking your job," you'll fail to notice that Jeff Bezos actually did this deed. If they can recast their efforts to restrict voting under the guise of "election security," by inventing false claims about fraud, we will look the other way while Black folks in urban centers are made to stand in line for hours to exercise their most fundamental freedoms.

And, second, the Villain sentence tells us not just what the bad guys are up to but why they engage in their nefarious aims. Above, their motivation was listed as "hoard profits." A Villain sentence for a health care message would also indicate not only what opponents are doing but underscore the desires behind it. For illustration—"But a wealthy and powerful few divide us based on what we look like, where we come from or who we love so they can keep refusing to pay what they owe in taxes to ensure all of us have the care our families need."

While the two examples offered here provide a profit-seeking backstory, as is fitting for the respective issues they address, an equally effective explanation is the pursuit of power by unscrupulous politicians. Especially when we're advocating for realizing our democracy or confronting injustices in things like policing and immigration policy, the more accurate way to convey what the right is up to is to describe their quest to seize or maintain control. Thus, in a message for voting rights, this second sentence would say, "But today MAGA Republicans want to claim and hold power by taking away people's freedoms to pick our own leaders based on what we look like or where we live. They know that they cannot win by courting more voters and so they attempt to keep us from voting."

Finally, an RCN message ends by addressing what we most often see is our core obstacle to moving audiences to action. As public polling and ballot initiatives often prove, our opposition is not the opposition itself, but rather cynicism. It's not that people do not believe our ideas are right but rather they feel that they are not possible. Most Americans want more affordable health care, better wages and working conditions, equitable voting, quality schools for all, commonsense gun reforms, clean air and water, and so on. But since they feel these aims are unlikely to come to fruition, why bother giving up absolutely precious time and energy to lost causes?

This final Vision sentence paints the aforementioned "beautiful tomorrow." In this, we strive to sell the brownie and not the recipe; meaning that we do not expect the name of our policy to entice people but rather we lure them by narrating the outcomes the policy will deliver. Thus, for example, "paid family leave" becomes "you're there the first time your newborn smiles" and "voting rights" turns into "you decide who governs in your name" or "you have a hand in the rules that determine your future."

A concluding Vision sentence for raising wages would say, "By joining together we can rewrite the rules so all of us can earn a good living and live a good life." And for voting it could say, "By demanding our leaders pass the Freedom to Vote Act, we can make this a place where 'we the people' includes all of us, no exceptions."

RCN works for both issue-specific messages, as we've just explored, and also to craft an overarching narrative. Coming back to Minnesota, we found that a particularly resonant opening value was group harmony and the vision centered on the Golden Rule.

Minnesota's strength comes from our ability to be there for each other—to knit together people from different places and of different races into a community. For this to be a place of freedom for all, we cannot let a greedy few and the politicians they fund divide us based on what someone looks like, where they come from, or how much money they have. It's time we talk to each other and stand up for anyone getting bullied or shut out by ugly rhetoric. We must pick leaders who honor the Golden Rule, treating others as they want to be treated. Together, we can make Minnesota a place where freedom and community are for everyone, no exceptions.[21]

A full narrative, no matter how well crafted, does not a winning campaign make. This is why, from its inception, RCN has operated on what we call a three-legged stool model to build public will for causes and candidates. Leg one is building the choir: that is, getting disparate groups from across a state or issue area to agree to repeat the same message. It cannot be repeated enough how critical repetition is. Messages that are more familiar to audiences are routinely rated as more credible, convincing, and positive. This is because hearing something we already know creates cognitive ease—our brains are able to predict what comes next without effort. This, again, is why we focus so much on animating our "choir."

The second leg is writing the songbook. In essence, undertaking research to arrive at a winning message—of the variety shared above—that will move conflicted voters and engage the base, ideally inspiring them to want to repeat our message.

Finally, we have the mounting the multimedia production leg—that is creating digital ads, memes, events, radio announcements, collateral materials, visible swag, and so on to put the messaging in people's faces over and again.

Thus, once we completed the original RCN research, we created a branded campaign for the 2018 election called Greater Than Fear, with the tagline "in Minnesota we're better off together."[22] The name was an intentional nod to "Greater Minnesota," the phrase used to name the rural parts of the state. This was the locus of the opposition's efforts to stir up fear and so we directed our overarching brand straight at it. The tagline was an affirmative callback to Senator Paul Wellstone's saying, "We all do better when we all do better," which we were surprised to hear focus group respondents in the state offer up routinely.

We created a Greater Than Fear messaging guide[23] for use by all of the organizations in the coalition. This means we had a message repeating the branding to argue for driver's licenses for undocumented immigrants, one for increasing funding to public schools, another advocating for wage hikes, and yet another pushing back at anti-Muslim invective. We trained thousands of organizers in this messaging and had them do their electoral canvassing in Greater Than Fear shirts.

We made digital and radio ads, full-color posters, bus ads, and printed materials. When Trump came to Rochester, Minnesota, we held a Greater Than Fear rally in lieu of an anti-Trump march, which would have simply given him more airtime. We created a "Dogs Against Dog Whistling" social media avatar that folks used to clap back at Right-wing race baiting and a dog-related GOTV event. During the Republican debate, we provided a "dog whistle" bingo card, to inoculate folks against their standard invectives by showing we could predict beforehand precisely what they'd say. In short, we found ways to amplify this branding and messaging in every way that we could.

In 2018, progressives swept the executive races—including a very tense attorney general race for Black Muslim Democrat Keith Ellison—flipped the Minnesota House and won two U.S. senate seats (there was a special election to fill Al Franken's vacated spot.)

This same mighty coalition kept meeting weekly to decide which messages to amplify in between elections. Then, over the pandemic summer of 2020, George Floyd was murdered by Minneapolis police and Republican Minnesota Senate Majority Leader Paul Gazelka asked, "Where's the apology to the moms out in the suburbs scared to death about what's happening all around them, and seeing the glowing fire in Minneapolis–St. Paul?"[24]

Greater Than Fear no longer seemed an apt sentiment given how real and understandable fear was among Black Minnesotans. Thus, while organizers kept using the RCN messaging framework, they selected We Make Minnesota as the 2020 overarching brand. And we developed a public safety message called Fund Our Lives.

In response to Gazelka's obvious attempts to pit "suburban moms" against people of color demanding justice within the Twin Cities, Faith in Minnesota developed an "I am a suburban mom" campaign wherein women of all races recorded videos declaring their desire for real safety and an end to police violence, and challenging the perception of who really lives in the suburbs and what they believe. As ever, we used an RCN framework to declare what we are for and push back against opposition efforts to divide, scapegoat, and sow fear.

Despite the enormous strain of COVID-19, the horrific distress of police brutality, and the challenges of the mass reckoning for racial justice birthed in Minnesota in 2020, progressives once again prevailed in the election.

These seasoned campaigners delivered again in 2022, finally achieving a Democratic trifecta by flipping the Minnesota House despite the predictions of a "red wave." Once again, Keith Ellison faced a challenging attorney general race, given not merely his race and faith but his key role in bringing Derek Chauvin to trial and achieving an extraordinarily rare conviction against a police officer. Right-wing operatives threw every standard "law and order" trope at this race and still did not prevail because campaigners in Minnesota have mastered how to put forward an affirmative values-based narrative that calls out the other side for their politics of cruelty and entices a multiracial coalition to come together for better.

With a one-seat majority, between January and May of 2023, Minnesota Democrats passed 15 pieces of progressive legislation, including protecting abortion rights, providing free school meals, legalizing driver's licenses for undocumented people, increasing transit funding, codifying voting rights, and granting paid family and medical leave.[25] These lawmakers were able to pass this astonishing sweep of laws—despite their narrow margin in government—because they had campaigned explicitly on a platform of racial and economic justice. They did not come into office offering a Republican-lite version of leadership. Voters chose them expecting to have progressive policy outcomes.

Minnesota may be the most comprehensive example of adopting effective messaging and truly implementing it. But it's far from the only one. Wisconsin, Michigan, and Pennsylvania also participated in RCN research and implementation, developing their own multiracial coalition to carry out effective messaging and help flip these states in 2020 and retain Democratic control in 2022. Indeed, the track record of wins from school board races to senate campaigns spans across the country and even to the UK and Australia.[26]

CONCLUDING THOUGHTS: IF YOU WANT PEOPLE TO COME TO YOUR CAUSE, BE ATTRACTIVE

As Toni Cade Bambara said, "The role of the artist is to make the revolution irresistible." So too, I would argue, is the role of the activist. We must convey how the policies we seek to implement will make people's families, communities, and futures truly desirable. If we want people to come to our cause, we must be attractive—that is, provide a compelling vision that draws them in.

And, at the same time, we cannot forget that politics—and any effort to change public policy absolutely requires entangling ourselves in politics—isn't a game of solitaire. Our audiences do not hear only from us. They are subjected to the unending race-baiting and fearmongering of our opposition. Thus, what we tell people must provide a clear origin story for present-day problems they know all too well, and rebuff, or ideally inoculate against, the opposition's tale of who is to blame.

Finally, we must keep in mind that a message that no one hears is, by definition, not persuasive. A message is like a baton that must be passed from person to person. Thus, where we're often admonished that we're simply "preaching to the choir," the choir is where the good trouble, to use John Lewis's phrase, starts. And without them singing in harmony we cannot move the congregation to convert new participants to our cause.

NOTES

1. Fred Harris and Alan Curtis, eds., *Healing Our Divided Society: Investing in America Fifty Years After the Kerner Report* (Abilene, KS: Eisenhower Foundation and Philadelphia: Temple University Press, 2018).

2. Harris and Curtis, *Healing Our Divided Society*.

3. Julie Wertheimer, "Racial Disparities Persist in Many U.S. Jails," Pew Trusts, May 16, 2023, https://www.pewtrusts.org/en/research-and-analysis/issue-briefs/2023/05/racial-disparities-persist-in-many-us-jails.

4. Allison Harell and Evan Lieberman, "How Information About Race-Based Health Disparities Affects Policy Preferences: Evidence from a Survey Experiment About the COVID-19 Pandemic in the United States," *Social Science & Medicine* 277 (2021): 113884, https://pubmed.ncbi.nlm.nih.gov/33845391.

5. Rebecca C. Hetey and Jennifer L. Eberhardt, "Racial Disparities in Incarceration Increase Acceptance of Punitive Policies," *Psychological Science* 25, no. 10 (2014), https://doi.org/10.1177/0956797614540307.

6. Bernard Rorke, "Orbán Steps Up the Hate and Seeks a 'Robust Social Mandate' for Antigypsyism," European Roma Rights Centre, February 14, 2020, http://www.errc.org/news/orban-steps-up-the-hate-and-seeks-a-robust-social-mandate-for-antigypysism.

7. Stuart Gietel-Basten, "Why Brexit? The Toxic Mix of Immigration and Austerity," *Population and Development Review* 42, no. 4 (2016), 673–680, https://www.jstor.org/stable/44132229.

8. Andrea Dip, "'Gender Ideology'—A Fantastical and Flexible Narrative," Heinrich Boll Foundation, September 27, 2022, https://us.boell.org/en/2022/09/27/gender-ideology-fantastical-and-flexible-narrative.

9. Office of the Minnesota Secretary of State, "2016 Election Results," https://www.sos.state.mn.us/elections-voting/election-results/2016/2016-general-election-results.

10. Aaron O'Neill, " Minnesota's Electoral Votes in U.S. Presidential Elections 1860–2020," Statista, June 21, 2022, https://www.statista.com/statistics/1130583/minnesota-electoral-votes-since-1860.

11. FOX 9 Minneapolis-St. Paul, "Somali Community Leaders Respond to Fox 9 Daycare Fraud Report," *Fox 9*, May 18, 2018, https://www.fox9.com/news/somali-community-leaders-respond-to-fox-9-daycare-fraud-report.

12. Mark Lilla, "The End of Identity Liberalism," *New York Times*, November 18, 2016, https://www.nytimes.com/2016/11/20/opinion/sunday/the-end-of-identity-liberalism.html.

13. Eisenhower Foundation, "Healing Our Divided Society at the United Nations," March 1, 2023.

14. Ian Haney López, *Dog Whistle Politics: How Coded Racial Appeals Have Reinvented Racism and Wrecked the Middle Class* (New York: Oxford University Press, 2015).

15. We Make the Future Action, "About the Race Class Narrative," n.d., https://www.wemakethefutureaction.us/history-of-the-race-class-narrative.

16. ASO Communications and We Make the Future Action, "Memo: The Race Class Narrative," n.d., https://www.wemakethefutureaction.us/resources-documents/2021-rcn-memo.

17. Ian Haney López, Anat Shenker-Osorio, and Tamara Draut, "Democrats Can Win by Tackling Race and Class Together. Here's Proof.," *The Guardian*, April 14, 2018, https://www.theguardian.com/commentisfree/2018/apr/14/democrats-race-class-divide-2018-midterms.

18. López et al., "Democrats Can Win by Tackling Race and Class Together."

19. The National Advisory Commission on Civil Disorders, *Report of the National Advisory Commission on Civil Disorders* (Washington, DC: U.S. Department of Justice, Office of Justice Programs, 1968).

20. Harris and Curtis, *Healing Our Divided Society*.

21. Lake Research Partners et al., "Race-Class Narrative: Minnesota Dial Survey Report," May 2018, https://www.demos.org/sites/default/files/publications/LRP%20Report.Race-Class%20Narrative.Minnesota.C3.2018.05.23.pdf.

22. https://greaterthanfear.us

23. Greater than Fear, "Messaging Guide," n.d., https://69k.939.myftpupload.com/wp-content/uploads/2020/01/GreaterThanFear_MessagingGuide_Print_11x8.5_horizontal.pdf

24. Desmond Declan, "Gazelka Demands Apology to Minesotans, Suburban Moms," Bring Me the News, June 6, 2020.

25. Caroline Cummings, "2023 Minnesota Legislative Session Ends. See What Bills Passed," *WCCO News*, May 20, 2023, https://www.cbsnews.com/minnesota/news/session-nears-end-a-look-at-what-bills-have-passed-and-whats-still-left-on-the-table.

26. ASO Communications and We Make the Future Action, "Winning with the Race Class Narrative," https://asocommunications.com/messaging_guides/winning-with-the-race-class-narrative/.

CHAPTER 26

A New North Star to Lead Us to a Representative Democracy That Is Just and Equitable for All

LaTosha R. Brown

> Imagination is more important than knowledge. For knowledge is limited to all we know and understand, while imagination embraces the entire world, and all there ever will be to know and understand.
>
> —Albert Einstein

As we begin the 21st century, the call for reimagining U.S. democracy becomes more urgent than ever. The America of today is a mosaic of cultures, ethnicities, genders, and perspectives that far exceeds the scope envisioned by the original framers. To truly embody the principles of justice and equality, a re-examination of the democratic framework is essential. This chapter aims to provide a historical analysis of the origins of U.S. democracy, highlighting the need for reimagining it to better represent the diverse and pluralistic nature of America today. It is hard for America to move forward in its evolution as a society if we keep looking back. America needs our imaginations.

Reimagining U.S. democracy also necessitates rectifying historical injustices perpetuated by the original framers of the Constitution. Initiatives such as reparations for descendants of slaves, recognition of Indigenous sovereignty, and gender equality measures are essential steps toward overhauling the imbalances that have persisted for centuries. A forward-looking democracy must grapple with its past to pave the way for a more equitable future.

The foundation of the United States of America lies in the principles enshrined in its Constitution, penned by the original framers who laid the groundwork for the nation. However, as we navigate the complexities of the 21st century, it becomes imperative to critically examine and reimagine U.S. democracy to ensure justice for all, not just a privileged few. The original framers, visionary in their own right, undoubtedly had brilliant minds, and crafted a document that laid the groundwork for a new form of governance by way of the U.S. Constitution.

However, it is essential to acknowledge the historical context in which they operated. The late 18th century was marked by deeply entrenched inequalities, with slavery and the subjugation of women prevalent.

The framers, largely comprising white, affluent men, were products of their time, and their perspectives were inevitably influenced by their social status. Bound by the limitations of their time, perspectives often skewed toward the white male elite. While seeking to establish a democratic republic, they were limited in their vision of inclusivity. They largely ignored the pre-existence of the Indigenous peoples inhabiting the land for centuries. Additionally, the infamous Three-Fifths Compromise is another stark example, reducing enslaved individuals to mere fractions of a person for representation purposes, left out of the political process, reinforcing the notion that some were more equal than others. The omission of their voices and the absence of considerations for their rights devalued from the start non-white men.

Hence the exclusion of marginalized groups, such as the Indigenous peoples, women, and African Americans, in the foundational documents that conceptualized "America's form of Democracy," means that they do not capture the diverse fabric of the America of today and fails to encapsulate the principles of justice and equality for all.

As society has evolved, it is crucial to challenge the notion that the framers' perspectives should be the sole point of reference for shaping U.S. democracy. The world has evolved, and so must our democratic ideals. Looking back with rigid adherence to an outdated worldview inhibits progress and hinders the establishment of a truly just society. Since this framework was flawed from the get-go, as society continues to evolve in the 21st century, we need a new North Star to guide us to a sustainable democracy for all. Challenging the sole point of reference provided by the original framers is not a dismissal of their contributions but a recognition that the principles they espoused must evolve to meet the needs of a diverse and dynamic nation in the 21st century.

EMBRACING AND CELEBRATING DIVERSITY

The 21st century demands a democracy that reflects the diversity and pluralism inherent in the American identity. The concept of rights has evolved since the 18th century, with an expanding understanding of human rights encompassing issues such as LGBTQ+ rights, environmental justice, and economic equity. By acknowledging the perspectives of all citizens, irrespective of their race, gender, socioeconomic background, or sexual orientation, we move closer to a system that is truly just and inclusive. Representation in political offices, decision-making bodies, and policy formulation must be reflective of the rich tapestry that is America today.

Reimagining U.S. democracy requires a dynamic approach that adapts to contemporary notions of rights and justice, recognizing that the original framers could not have foreseen the challenges and aspirations of a multiethnic society's aspirations shaped by the implications of persisting technological improvements.

To fulfill the promise of justice for all, a democratic framework that embraces diversity, addresses historical injustices, and adapts to contemporary ideals is essential. We must see diversity and inclusion as strengths of this nation and simultaneously as gifts toward progress and expansion of thought.

INDIVIDUAL FREEDOMS SUPPORT THE COMMON GOOD

A sustainable democracy aims to create a society that is just, equitable, and inclusive for all, with emphasis on the word *all*. From the original framers' perspective, "all" did not include non-white men. The bedrock of democracy has long been built upon the principles of individual freedoms, which creates an unsustainable tension with the principle of preserving the "common good."

There is a growing concern that this emphasis on personal liberties is leading to a fallacy in the very foundation of democratic ideals. While individual freedoms are undeniably crucial, an exclusive focus on them can erode the principles of democracy and majority rule, tilting the balance toward a system that prioritizes self-interest over the common good.

Firstly, the overemphasis on individual freedoms can foster a sense of hyper-individualism, where citizens prioritize their personal liberties at the expense of collective well-being. Democracy, by its nature, requires a delicate balance between individual rights and the common good. However, as the emphasis on personal freedoms intensifies, there is a risk of neglecting the interconnectedness of society. This individualistic mindset may result in policies and actions that benefit a few at the detriment of the broader community.

Moreover, the fallacy lies in the potential distortion of the democratic principle of majority rule. Democracy is not merely about protecting the rights of the individual but also ensuring that the decisions made reflect the will of the majority. A democracy built solely on individual freedoms can lead to a scenario where the desires of the few outweigh the needs of the many, as authors Daniel Ziblatt and Steven Levitsky have argued.[1]

This subversion of majority rule can undermine the very essence of democracy, as it risks concentrating power in the hands of a privileged minority rather than reflecting the diverse perspectives of the populace.

Furthermore, the fallacy becomes evident in the erosion of the social contract that underpins democratic governance. In a democracy, citizens willingly surrender certain individual freedoms for the greater good, trusting that the system will work toward the betterment of society. However, an exaggerated focus on personal liberties can disrupt this social contract, as individuals may resist necessary collective actions, such as taxation for public services or adherence to regulations designed to protect the community and the planetary ecosystem.

The erosion of democratic principles is also evident in the widening socioeconomic disparities that can result from an exclusive emphasis on individual freedoms. When individual freedoms are prioritized without considering their impact on the common good, it can lead to policies that exacerbate inequality. The wealthy few may exploit their freedoms to amass more resources and influence, leaving the majority disenfranchised and undermining the very notion of equal representation.

To address this fallacy, it is essential to strike a nuanced balance between individual freedoms and the common good. Democracy thrives when it ensures that personal liberties are protected within a framework that prioritizes the well-being of the entire society and the ecosystem in which it thrives. This involves recognizing the interconnectedness of citizens and understanding that safeguarding the common good is not antithetical to individual freedoms but rather a necessary condition for their meaningful existence.

The fallacy of democracy built solely on individual freedoms lies in the potential erosion of democratic principles and majority rule. A healthy democracy requires a delicate equilibrium between individual liberties and the collective good. Failing to strike this balance risks distorting the essence of democracy, concentrating power among the few, and undermining the principles of equal representation and majority rule that are at its core. It is imperative to recalibrate our understanding of democracy to ensure that it remains a system that serves the interests of the many while respecting the rights of the individual.

PARTICIPATORY DEMOCRACY AND ACCOUNTABLE ELECTED OFFICIALS

As we see it today before our eyes, the devolution of government with elected officials breaching the social contract of representation for partisan politics. At its core, democracy thrives on the principles of representation, accountability, and the protection of individual freedoms. However, when elected officials deviate from a commitment to democratic ideals, it undermines the very essence of participatory democracy. Elected officials serve as the voice of the people, entrusted with the responsibility of translating citizens' diverse perspectives into policies that reflect the collective will. When officials abandon their commitment to democratic ideals, they risk becoming detached from the needs and aspirations of the electorate. This detachment erodes the foundation of representation, leading to decisions that prioritize personal interests or partisan agendas over the common good.

Participatory democracy is the cornerstone of the United States' political system, emphasizing the active involvement of citizens in decision-making processes. Having U.S. elected officials who are not dedicated to democratic values is antithetical to the fundamental principles that sustain a thriving democratic society.

Citizens should be able to expect their elected officials to act ethically, responsibly, and with utmost transparency. Officials who do not adhere to these democratic principles foster a culture of distrust and cynicism among the electorate. Without accountability, citizens lose faith in the democratic process, believing that their participation and votes no longer hold the power to shape a government that truly represents their interests. Officials who abandon these principles may endorse policies that infringe upon individual freedoms, discriminate against certain groups, or undermine the rule of law. This not only weakens the fabric of democracy but also jeopardizes the very rights that participatory democracy seeks to protect.

Having U.S. elected officials who are not committed to democratic ideals poses a direct threat to participatory democracy. The pillars of representation, accountability, transparency, protection of individual freedoms, and a level playing field are crucial for the functioning of a healthy democratic society. When elected officials deviate from these principles, the very essence of democracy is compromised, and the democratic process becomes a mere facade. It is imperative for citizens to remain vigilant and hold elected officials accountable.

MORE EQUITABLE DISTRIBUTION OF POWER

Given this erosion of democratic ideals in elected officials, relying solely on partisan political parties to distribute power in the United States poses significant risks as well to the foundations of participatory democracy. Political parties, while instrumental in shaping the political landscape, should not be the exclusive gatekeepers of power. A healthy participatory democracy requires a broader distribution of power that includes mechanisms for direct citizen engagement and checks on concentrated political influence.

By nature, political parties are inherently driven by their own interests and agendas. While they play a crucial role in aggregating and representing diverse views, they can prioritize partisan goals over the broader interests of the populace for party elites rather than addressing the nuanced needs and concerns of the entire citizenry. This concentration of power within parties leads to a disconnect between elected officials and the people they are meant to represent.

Furthermore, the exclusive dominance of a two-party system limits the spectrum of political ideas and stifles alternative voices. This diminishes the richness of democratic discourse and hampers the representation of minority perspectives. A truly participatory democracy should encourage the flourishing of diverse ideologies and provide avenues for smaller parties, citizens, and independent candidates to contribute to the political dialogue.

REMEDY DISPROPORTIONAL REPRESENTATION

The two-party system contributes to one of the fundamental flaws of the Electoral College: its propensity to misrepresent the true will of the American people. The system allocates electoral votes based on the number of congressional representatives and senators in each state, creating an imbalance that overemphasizes the influence of less populous states. In the 21st century, the United States is characterized by an increasingly diverse population with varied perspectives and needs. However, the Electoral College does not effectively reflect this diversity. Partisan candidates tend to focus their campaigns on battleground states based on the party agenda, often neglecting the concerns of minority communities in noncompetitive states. This lack of inclusivity undermines the democratic ideal of representing the interests of all citizens, irrespective of their background.

In the 21st century, the disparities in state populations have reached unprecedented levels. The current system allows a minority of voters in less populous states to have a disproportionate impact on the outcome of presidential elections. This results in a situation where the weight of a vote varies significantly depending on the state of residence, leading to a skewed representation of the electorate. As a result of this incongruence, the principle of equal representation for the states (in the Electoral College and the Senate) dilutes the democratic value of one person, one vote. The electoral power of citizens residing in densely populated states is diminished, contributing to an inherent injustice in the electoral process.

POLITICAL REPRESENTATION SHOULD REFLECT THE POPULATION

The Electoral College has failed to adapt to demographic shifts and changing societal dynamics. The system perpetuates a winner-takes-all approach in most states, discouraging candidates from reaching out to diverse constituencies. As a result, certain demographics, particularly minority groups, are often marginalized in the electoral process. Moreover, the winner-takes-all system in many states stifles third-party candidates, further limiting the range of voices heard in the electoral arena. This lack of inclusivity and representation impedes the ability of the Electoral College to serve as an accurate reflection of the nuanced political landscape in the 21st century.

In today's time, the U.S. Electoral College stands as an antiquated institution that no longer serves the democratic ideals it was intended to uphold. Population misrepresentation, demographic inadequacy, and an inability to adapt to technological advancements collectively render the system irrelevant for the modern electorate. The United States must embark on a reevaluation of its electoral processes to ensure that they accurately reflect the diverse voices and political will of the nation. Whether through reform or the adoption of alternative systems, it is imperative to embrace mechanisms that align with the democratic principles of equality, representation, and inclusivity in the evolving landscape of American politics.

ESTABLISHING A DEPARTMENT OF DEMOCRACY

To find a new North Star to guide us to a sustainable democracy that can perfect this union, America must not rely on the assumption either that we have exhausted democratic ideals or that our systems are infallible, but we must recognize that there is a need to structurally reform all systems that are the antecedent of the original framers' intention. The assaults on our democracy are executed by those who are unwilling to detach from that intention and embrace a new reality for which America has evolved.

In recent years, democratic ideals that have long been considered sacrosanct are facing an onslaught from various quarters. Authoritarian regimes, disinformation campaigns, cyber warfare, and internal divisions threaten to erode the democratic fabric that the United States holds dear. The parallels with the aftermath of 9/11 are striking, as the nation responded decisively to protect its homeland. The post-9/11 era saw a paradigm shift in national security priorities, necessitating a comprehensive and coordinated response to safeguard the homeland. The response, the establishment of the Department of Homeland Security in the aftermath of the 9/11 attacks, serves as a precedent for the creation of what I propose: a "Department of Democracy." In a similar vein, the contemporary threats to democracy demand a centralized and focused effort to protect and reinforce democratic institutions.

Similarly, the establishment of a Department of Democracy is now crucial to counter the multifaceted threats imperiling the democratic principles upon which the nation was founded. The Department of Homeland Security demonstrated the effectiveness of a coordinated response to diverse and evolving threats. Likewise, a Department of

Democracy would serve as the epicenter for coordinating efforts across various agencies and departments to address the nuanced challenges posed by both external and internal forces seeking to undermine democratic principles. The establishment of a Department of Democracy is not just a proactive response to contemporary challenges but a crucial step in fortifying and sustaining democracy in the United States. Drawing inspiration from the creation of the Department of Homeland Security after 9/11, this new department would serve as the vanguard in protecting democracy from external and internal threats. By adopting a comprehensive mandate that includes electoral integrity, countering disinformation, promoting civic education, and addressing systemic issues, this federal office would ensure that the democratic ideals cherished by the nation remain resilient and enduring in the face of evolving challenges.

Now, more than ever, the United States must demonstrate its commitment to democracy by establishing a dedicated entity to safeguard its core principles. Domestic challenges, including rising polarization, extremism, and erosion of trust in democratic institutions, contribute to the internal weakening of democratic ideals. The Department of Democracy would play a pivotal role in fostering national unity, promoting civic education, and addressing the root causes of polarization, ensuring that democratic values remain resilient in the face of internal and external divisions. A dedicated Department of Democracy would be equipped to thwart these external threats, fortifying the nation's defenses against attempts to undermine the democratic will of the people by fostering an informed and engaged citizenry that is critical to the sustainability of democratic values.

The Department of Democracy should take a lead role in implementing robust cybersecurity measures, conducting audits, and collaborating with states to fortify election systems against external interference. Ensuring the integrity of elections is paramount to a functioning democracy. Combating disinformation requires a multifaceted approach, including public awareness campaigns, media literacy initiatives, and collaboration with tech platforms. A Department of Democracy must not only address immediate threats but also tackle the systemic issues that undermine democratic ideals. This includes addressing socioeconomic inequalities, promoting inclusivity, and reinforcing democratic institutions to withstand the pressures exerted by divisive forces.

STRENGTHENING AND SECURING THE RIGHT TO VOTE

As a national advocate, I have worked through my organization, Black Voters Matters, to secure the right to vote under the John Lewis Voting Rights Advancement Act (VRAA).[2] Throughout history, the struggle for voting rights has been a relentless march toward inclusivity and equal representation. The Fifteenth Amendment to the U.S. Constitution, ratified in 1870, declared that the right to vote shall not be denied or abridged on the basis of race, color, or previous condition of servitude. Similarly, the Nineteenth Amendment, ratified in 1920, extended voting rights to women. These amendments were not temporary measures but enduring statements of equality and justice.

The legacy of constitutional amendments that expanded voting rights serves as a testament to the permanence of these fundamental liberties. The right to vote, once extended to a group of citizens, should not be subject to expiration dates or the capricious winds of political change. Embracing this legacy requires acknowledging that voting rights are not privileges to be doled out intermittently but integral components of a democratic society that demand permanence.

In the crucible of democracy, the right to vote stands as a sacred pillar, an unyielding foundation upon which the edifice of a just and representative government is erected. Yet the precarious nature of this right, subject to the whims of legislative renewals and proposals, undermines the very essence of a government by the people, for the people. This debate forcefully contends that the right to vote should not be a transient privilege but a permanent, unassailable right for all citizens in the United States. The time has come for an unwavering commitment to the principles of democracy, casting aside the shackles of legislative uncertainty that currently surround this fundamental right.

MAKING VOTING RIGHTS A PERMANENT RIGHT

The current landscape of voting rights in the United States is marred by a disconcerting fragility, characterized by the need for periodic legislative renewals. The Voting Rights Act of 1965, a seminal piece of legislation that aimed to dismantle barriers to voting, has been subject to amendments and renewals over the years. The very fact that a right as fundamental as voting requires constant reaffirmation raises questions about the steadfastness of the democratic foundations upon which the nation is built.

The periodic renewal of voting rights legislation exposes the process to partisan maneuvering, creating a precarious situation where the right to vote becomes a bargaining chip in the political arena. This vulnerability undermines the principle that voting is a universal right, transcending party lines and affiliations. A permanent right to vote would insulate this fundamental democratic tenet from the ebb and flow of political tides.

The uncertainty surrounding the permanence of voting rights fosters an erosion of public trust in the democratic process. Citizens must be assured that their right to participate in the democratic discourse is not contingent upon the shifting sands of political negotiations. A permanent right to vote provides a bedrock of confidence, fostering a resilient belief in the democratic ideals that form the backbone of the nation.

RESTORING VOTING RIGHTS FOR THE FORMERLY INCARCERATED

In the 21st century, upholding the democratic value of inclusivity is paramount for those who have been incarcerated. Championing the full participation of formerly incarcerated individuals in democracy is not just an act of justice, it is a commitment to building a more inclusive and robust democratic society. Restoring full citizen rights to formerly incarcerated individuals is a crucial step toward achieving this ideal. Democracy thrives when all voices are heard, and all citizens have the opportunity to actively participate in shaping their communities. By immediately reinstating the rights of those who have served their sentences, we reaffirm the principles of rehabilitation and second chances, essential elements of a just and progressive society.

Denying voting rights to formerly incarcerated individuals perpetuates a cycle of disenfranchisement and undermines the very foundation of democracy. Excluding this segment of the population perpetuates systemic inequalities and inhibits the collective growth of society. Embracing the reintegration of formerly incarcerated individuals into the democratic process not only promotes fairness and equity but also fosters a sense of civic responsibility.

THE IMPERATIVE OF A CONSTITUTIONAL AMENDMENT: FORTIFYING DEMOCRACY AGAINST BACKSLIDING

To secure the permanence of voting rights for all citizens in the United States, the most potent and enduring solution lies in a constitutional amendment explicitly enshrining this fundamental right.

A constitutional amendment would provide an impregnable fortress against any attempts at backsliding on the principles of democracy. It would elevate the right to vote to a position beyond the reach of political machinations, ensuring that the bedrock of representative government remains unshaken by the tempests of partisan interests. Instead, such an amendment should reflect the evolving values of a democratic society, which acknowledges that the right to vote is not static but must adapt to the changing demographics, perspectives, and aspirations of the nation. This adaptability is essential for a democracy to thrive and remain true to its foundational principles.

The right to vote is the heartbeat of a vibrant democracy, pulsating with the essence of citizen participation and representation. The current paradigm of legislative renewals exposes this fundamental right to the vicissitudes of political expediency, threatening the very essence of democratic governance. A call for the permanent enfranchisement of all citizens in the United States through a constitutional amendment is not a radical proposition; rather, it is a resounding declaration of commitment to the principles that define the nation.

The historical precedents set by constitutional amendments, the imperative of adapting to evolving notions of equal protection, and the need to fortify democracy against backsliding all underscore the urgency of this proposition. The right to vote, once granted, should not be a fleeting privilege but a permanent fixture in the mosaic of American democracy. It is time to cast aside the ephemeral nature of legislative renewals and embrace a vision where the right to vote is as enduring as the democratic ideals upon which the United States was founded.

IT IS OUR HUMANITY AND NOT OUR POLITICS THAT WILL SAVE US

If America is truly to see itself as one nation under God, it is important to recenter itself as a nation rooted in love and not fear, a nation committed to centering the love of humanity in every policy priority and policy decision that we make. We must find a new North Star that will give us hope, inspire our imaginations to evolve as a nation, and elevate the edict of sisterhood/brotherhood. We cannot move forward unless we see each other, the people, as the most important and precious resource in our nation. We must shift the paradigm from profit over people and see ourselves as more than subjects of a nation; instead, we must see ourselves as founders of a new nation. An America that is most just, more equitable and more peaceful. It requires that as citizens we must also make a seismic shift in how we see ourselves as our brother's/sister's keeper, understand that individual freedom cannot be at the expense of impeding the freedom and safety of others and most importantly, commit to love and care for the least of these—a universal principle found across all faiths, as its moral compass. Our politics will not save us, but our humanity will.

I believe the United States, a mosaic of cultures, beliefs, and dreams, is poised to re-center itself by embracing the richness of its diversity. Legislation, with its stern countenance and ink-stained pages, may attempt to codify behaviors and norms, but it falters when faced with the boundless expanse of love. Love is a force that knows no boundaries and cannot be confined within the rigid framework of rules. It flourishes in the spontaneous, the unrestrained expressions of the heart that transcend the limitations imposed by the written word. It is not a legislative command but a harmonious call to recognize the beauty in our differences, to celebrate the kaleidoscope of identities that paint the canvas of our nation.

As we traverse the ever-evolving landscape of our shared existence, let us not be confined by the limitations of legal decrees. Instead, let us embark on a journey of the heart, where the moral compass of compassion guides us toward a center where love, unencumbered by laws, can flourish in the radiant tapestry of our collective humanity.

Yet, as we navigate the vast landscape of humanity, we find a sanctuary in the notion of recentering our shared existence. In the United States, a nation forged in the crucible of diversity, we discover the opportunity to rekindle the flame of our shared humanity. To recenter is not to shackle the spirit but to liberate it from the burdens of prejudice, bias, and discord.

The intricate dance of empathy, compassion, and understanding is the choreography that guides us toward the center of our collective being. Legislation may not decree love, but it can create the conditions that foster a society where the love of humanity is centered, in all its myriad forms, and can bloom and prosper freely.

In the symphony of voices that echo through the American landscape, there is an invitation to listen, to understand, and to acknowledge the shared humanity that unites us all.

Recentering humanity is an endeavor that transcends the constraints of legal doctrines. It beckons us to engage in the dance of compassion, to extend a hand in solidarity, and to weave a narrative that values the inherent worth of every individual. As we embark on this collective journey, we discover that the true legislation of the heart lies not in statutes but in the unspoken bonds that connect us all. The promise of recentering humanity in this country will be a testament to the enduring spirit of a nation that strives for a more perfect union. It is an acknowledgment that love, in its purest form, cannot be legislated but can be cultivated through the fertile soil of understanding and acceptance.

NOTES

1. Daniel Ziblatt and Steven Levitsky, *Tyranny by the Minority* (New York: Crown Books, 2023).
2. Andrew Garber, "Pass the John R. Lewis Voting Rights Amendment Act," Brennan Center for Justice, September 19, 2023.

CHAPTER 27

Calling In as Compassionate Activism

Loretta J. Ross

> We are people of the United States. We are also all citizens of the world. Together we must work together for the common good of the whole world. All stakeholders must be involved in this. Safe food, a healthy earth, small farm agriculture, a living wage are concerns of all of us. Ordinary citizens should not be simply observers in crucial decisions that affect everyone. Openness and transparency are essential for democracy. We all need the spiritual freedom to be able to listen to one another and engage in constructive dialogue. . . . Without a culture of basic human rights, especially economic rights, the human family does not have the minimum essentials necessary for human life.
>
> —Benjamin J. Urmston, S.J., *Blueprint for Social Justice*

A lot of people seem to have given up on the concept of democracy in America. According to the Pew Research Center in September 2023, 65% of Americans reported they were exhausted by the bitter partisanship that makes it seem that nothing can be done to turn the country's malaise around. Disgusted disengagement is even more acute for young people who understandably believe that politicians lack the political will to address existential issues like racial and gender injustice, climate change, gun violence, immigration, and economic inequality. Using angry red/blue polarization rhetoric as a pathway to power, conservative politicians have purposefully divided us from each other.

America is at an inflection point, either striding eagerly forward to take on the challenges of the 21st century or lurching fearfully backwards, reinscribing the white supremacist domination of the 19th century, as if all progress toward human rights in the 20th century can be totally revoked. To paraphrase a quote often attributed to Upton Sinclair: "It is difficult to get a country to understand injustice when profits depend on not understanding it." The people who profit from the dysfunction of democracy do not seek evidence-based solutions, because social cooperation does not serve their electoral or financial interests. Yet they have the biggest microphones provided by a compliant, profit-seeking media ecosystem, more dedicated to staying in business than in journalism. No wonder people are fed up and feel overwhelmed.

Many of us toggle between outrage and panic as we witness how people feel so alienated from each other. It takes a lot of emotional energy to be "woke" and pay close attention to things that violate our moral standards but appear beyond our ability to fix. We watch our loved ones and communities pull apart in a different directions in ways that often don't make sense to us. Our society encourages cynicism and apathy because our economic and social problems appear to overwhelm our coping abilities. Most people just want to hunker down and ignore the firestorms of racism, bigotry, ignorance, and corruption.

It does not have to be this way.

I believe that more people want our country to be better than those who profit from the chaos. Not everyone who disagrees with progressives and liberals is an enemy. The presumed red/blue political divide is more complicated than a simplistic analysis explains. The recent state-level electoral victories protecting abortion rights in conservative states prove that demonizing and labeling people simply because of their presumed political affiliation or racial or gender identities is not a sophisticated strategy to gain the power to prevent human rights violations.

How can we develop our compassion for each other so that we develop the political will called for in the Kerner Report? How can we build bridges to convince people not give up on this fledgling democracy? A civil rights proverb comes to mind: When the world feels like an uncleanable mess, just start cleaning where you are.

Among the many possibilities for defenders of democracy and human rights, I believe in the power of calling people *in* instead of calling them out as one compassionate activist strategy to bridge the political divide. Calling in has the potential to help us navigate conversations we thought were impossible or difficult. It can bring together people who share a desire to make our democracy work, to improve the lot of every American, and to build a brighter future for those of us who want to do better and need help figuring out how. Many people are thirsty for different ways of relating to other people with whom they disagree. By coming together through calling in, we can help our country develop the political will to fix our broken dialogues.

Unfortunately, instead of a collaborative calling in culture, we're immersed in a punitive calling out one that pits us against each other, preventing efforts to develop the collective power to build the political will to emerge from this dystopian quagmire. Calling out is the act of publicly shaming someone for something they've said or done to correct them or hold them accountable for the harm they've caused. The ultimate calling out is canceling someone, a form of social exile that can cost people their jobs or at least their reputations.

Call-out and cancel culture began to be identified as a problem only when people previously silenced by the power structure started standing up against those who abuse their power. Calling out quickly became a form of organized mass outrage through the virality of the Internet, such as the Black Lives Matter movement against police brutality or the #MeToo campaign that identified men who improperly denigrated and violated women. Regardless of political affiliation, call-out/cancel culture has become the weapon of choice to hold people accountable for social transgressions. Both calling out and canceling are aided by social media algorithms that generate massive profits from social discord because of financial models that benefit from angry users.

But the consequences of a call-out cancellation are not evenly distributed. For example, many more leftist professors are fired than conservative ones. While the Republican Party has embraced moral shamelessness and anarchic violence as political virtues, the Democratic Party is more vulnerable as it scrambles to defend democratic norms and institutions against Trumpism while not mimicking the hypocrisy of the Republicans. Al Franken resigned for sexual improprieties while Matt Gaetz stayed in office and defenestrated his own Republican leadership.

Conservatives want a monopoly on the power to control people's behaviors or knowledge, like book banning, outlawing abortion, or costing an NFL athlete like Colin Kaepernick his job because he protested police brutality. But they also want to be victims and perpetrators at the same time when they accuse liberals and progressives of being sensitive "snowflakes" trying to language police them or hold them accountable for corruption and opportunism. One shouldn't have to explain basic decency and kindness to grown people, but here we are.

The war on education by conservatives is not a recent phenomenon. Conservatives don't want educators to teach history because they want to repeat it. From failing to teach about what happened to Native Americans, to the revisionist history of the Civil War, to the Scopes Monkey trial, to teaching that the struggle against white supremacy ended with Martin Luther King's death, education is another form of politics just as diplomacy is another form of war by another means.

The recent attacks on college presidents at Harvard, MIT, and the University of Pennsylvania foreshadow conservative attempts to attack the diversification of higher education and America overall. Regrettably, two of the presidents resigned, with Claudine Gay's brief 6-month tenure at Harvard becoming a symbol of the conservative movement's campaign against diversity, equity, and inclusion policies in academia, corporations, and the government. For every step forward toward justice and inclusion, conservatives launch a furious backlash to halt any progress.

When politicians betray their oaths of office or pander to the worst elements of our society, call-outs are appropriate ways to democratize power. Sometimes called "accountability" culture or "consequence" culture, people identify behaviors, policies, or words that harm people, even if these things were tolerated before (like sexual harassment) or the victims weren't permitted to punch back (like police brutality). The power of collective outrage can be used to punish those who may have previously gotten away with problematic or criminal behaviors.

Yet call-outs can also be used inappropriately. As writer Andrea Gibson says, "Great politics don't necessarily equate to compassionate people. I've encountered a number of politically progressive humans who act enthusiastically cruel. I've also known a ton of wonderful people who had terrible politics simply because they hadn't yet been exposed to new ways of thinking."[1] Call-outs can result in preventing potential, proven, or problematic allies from working together to defend democracy. The futile pursuit of political purity or language policing is frequently more destructive than productive, and often results in a cannibalistic frenzy of self-defeating political posturing.

People often resort to call-outs because they don't know how to have productive conversations with people with whom they disagree and from whom they are different. Most people are also not very good at self-reflection and examining the beliefs they want to impose upon others. Instead of seeking out dialogue and understanding, they confuse constructive criticism with angry public shaming. The poisonous call-out culture pours gas on the social fires and convinces many people that we're up against implacable forces, and the struggle is simply not worth it because failure is inevitable.

Calling In as Compassionate Activism

The hostile environment created by excessive calling out demotivates many people who then disengage from the human rights movement to avoid guilt-driven performative activism. Because of our censorious attitudes, we risk telling people to hate the very thing that could bring them joy and hope: cooperating with others who want to defend democracy.

The call-out culture is not the fault of individuals, but the practices of individuals. Let me explain. The fault lies with an inadequate educational system in which people are not taught to distinguish between opinions and facts, and too few people know how the government and our electoral democracy actually work.

Our civil institutions like religious and community organizations are weakened and fail to teach the basics of cooperatively living in a pluralistic society with compassion and empathy. If people do not share a common set of facts or trust in their fellow citizens, it is difficult, if not impossible, to develop the political will to effectively implement the recommendations of the prophetic Kerner Report or what we've learned in the 56 years since it was written.

I don't agree that it's futile to work against injustices and immorality. Another choice is available. The question is not whether we do the work but how. Our compassion deficit, bipartisan despair, and numbing apathy can be replaced with hope, optimism, and transformation to change our relationships, organizations, and culture through understanding why instead of calling each other out, we should learn how to call each other in.

I believe people can be taught how to increase their emotional intelligence to change this gladiatorial culture that damages our relationships and our society. We can learn to strengthen the empathy space within ourselves and avoid shaming and blaming people with our unrestrained anger. We can choose to turn conflicts into conversations and learn to have joy in working with others—even those we didn't think we need—to achieve undivided justice. We can build the power and the political will to build the democracy we deserve and that was promised to us.

Learning calling-in techniques expands our emotional bandwidths, so that we understand our options instead of defaulting to fighting with each other. We must not turn people off who want change but are repelled by the toxic arrogance of the call-out culture. We can build conversational containers to achieve accountability in respectful yet radical relationships. We must improve our ethical and emotional processes by changing the antisocial aspects of our culture into a healthier one for all. As Dr. Martin Luther King, Jr. said, "For we are deeply in need of a new way beyond the darkness that seems so close around us."[2] It's not easy, but it's worth doing.

But first, let me tell you how I got here.

Being homeless is unlike any other feeling in the world. There is compounded trauma from living on the street in a poor neighborhood where your neighbors also worry about eviction and homelessness. Perhaps fearing they might be next, people avert their eyes, when they might have spoken in my pre-homeless times. While I was pleasantly surprised by the unexpected kindness of many people, I was also disappointed by those who gave me their judgmental gaze instead of a dollar. They walked around me in wide circles like I was radioactive.

I offer this brief vignette from my life because times of extreme crisis can also be times of exciting opportunities, a kairotic moment. I learned this in my twenties. My extended community and family helped me turn my life around so that I'm now a tenured professor at an elite university teaching about white supremacy in the age of Trump. I'm privileged to use my experience to offer valuable life lessons to young people, not as a scold, but hopefully as a mentor offering guidance through love and respect.

As a college professor, I have a choice: To protect students from the truth or teach them about it. Educators can't do both at the same time. One of the topics I teach is about the Kerner Commission report, and the missed opportunity America had to turn itself around by fully embracing democracy instead of white supremacy, which has been the eternal contradiction in the heart of our country since its founding. As civil rights scholar Vincent Harding wrote, "We are citizens of a country that does not exist."[3] Because of our convictions, each generation of human rights activists has struggled to achieve the ideals of America, willing them into existence. Now, the country stands on the precipice of either collapse or regeneration.

As the storm clouds of authoritarianism—a.k.a. fascism—again loom over our nascent democracy, it's more necessary than ever to assure ourselves of our power to create change, and not simply be victims of those who profit from others' misery. In 1967, Hannah Arendt wrote that truth is fragile and can be lost to the "onslaught of power."[4] That has been the fate of the Kerner Commission report.

Black feminist bell hooks wrote:

> Dominator culture has tried to keep us all afraid, to make us choose safety instead of risk, sameness instead of diversity. Moving through that fear, finding out what connects us, reveling in our differences; this is the process that brings us closer, that gives us a world of shared values, of meaningful community.[5]

I include some of my personal story because the jagged experiences of my life could have made me bitter, resentful, or envious of those who didn't suffer like I did. Instead of anger and hate, learning about radical love from mentors like Reverend C. T. Vivian and Shulamith Koenig filled me with hope and strengthened my resilience. After fighting hate groups like the Ku Klux Klan alongside Reverend Vivian and Anne Braden in the 1990s, I became motivated by optimism for the possibilities of change.

Reverend Vivian often said, "If you ask people to give up hate, then you must be there for them when they do." I learned that when I dehumanized others, I was really dehumanizing myself. Understanding radical love means accepting that my past pain does not require permanently shutting doors on those with the power to hurt me. Radical love is an unconditional love that is not motivated by what someone else can do for me, but what I can do for others. It is fueled by compassion, integrity, and honesty. Eventually, I learned what I was really doing for the past 50 years was building coalitions by calling people in. This is how we build political will.

The phrase "calling in" was originally coined in 2013 by Ngọc Loan Trần, a Việt/mixed-race trans writer who explained,

> I picture "calling in" as a practice of pulling folks back in who have strayed from us . . . a practice of loving each other enough to allow each other to make mistakes, a practice of loving

ourselves enough to know that what we're trying to do here is a radical unlearning of everything we have been configured to believe is normal.[6]

Loan offered a pathway to help build the human rights movement we so desperately need. Calling in speaks to peoples' love for justice and desire for positive social change. Human rights means taking democracy very seriously by living it, debating it, and teaching about it. Calling in begins with healing our relationships with ourselves and others. It gives those doing the calling in an opportunity for self-reflection and correction. It leads to alliances that make inclusion and collaboration the norm. Building a calling-in culture enables us to use our collective strengths to help heal the planet. On the other hand, calling out compromises our potential strengths and unity.

Loan's essay transformed how I saw many of the techniques and lessons I had stumbled upon over the decades. These weren't just tools for calling in myself and understanding my own relationship with hate, insecurity, and anger. They were tools that the movement of progressive and liberal allies needed to value and put into practice.

Calling in begins with healing our relationships with ourselves and others, which requires radical forgiveness and radical love. And it grows from there. It leads to alliances that make inclusion and collaboration the norm. As I looked back, I realized that all of the successful social justice organizations and movements I'd been a part of had been able to succeed because they adopted the tenets of calling in before we had a term for these practices.

Respectfully listening to the stories that people tell and understanding the experiences behind why different people choose to use different words is a calling-in practice of human solidarity, rather than a reason to condemn someone for having different perspectives. Calling out often increases the suffering of those who are already hurting. It's actually difficult to call someone out—an act of symbolic violence—when we respect their human rights and honor their differences. That's why it's so easy to call people out when we are out of alignment with our integrity and values, when we forget to be kind. We can say what we mean and mean what we say, but we don't have to say it mean. That's a choice.

When we practice calling in, we are sensitive to our pain and the despair of others even as we struggle to make sense of everything that is going on. Many of us yearn to be part of something bigger than ourselves that gives our life meaning. It is not enough to be correct, we must take correct action because we are stronger when we work together using our differences as strengths instead of reasons to separate. We can refuse to accept the status quo of injustices because of our skin color, sexual orientation, gender identity, class, ability, or other condition. We have more questions than answers, and we want to figure it out with others. Through calling in, we can demonstrate our belief in the power of joy, transformation, and healing for ourselves and our world.

Calling in requires us to invest in each other as members of the human rights movement. It is not an identity-based practice but an opportunity for everyone to self-reflect, apologize, repair, and change behavior. By remembering the bigger picture in our fight for democracy, calling in encourages a spirit of inquiry and curiosity and radical generosity. Through active, loving listening practices, we can discover how much we have in common with those we have previously seen only as opponents.

We can learn how to deal with harm caused by racism, sexism, etc., without creating more harm. We cannot protect human rights by violating them. Our goal is to build a human rights–based society where inclusion, not exclusion, is the norm, and not just an ideal. This requires bringing more people into the human rights movement and creating a welcoming, fun, and informative atmosphere for them to grow and cooperate with others. We must disrupt all oppressive spaces and not replicate a system of domination, neglect, and brutality. This means that our processes are as important as our outcomes and that we must invite everyone to learn how to overcome internalized oppression by using compassionate strategies for ourselves and our communities. We can hold people accountable through forgiveness and respect while appreciating their humanity and believing we all have the capacity to change.

All of our call-outs must be about justice, not the power to intimidate others. We misuse call-outs when we set up situations that exclude others based on identity or political perspectives. We should seek to build community with others to interrogate the structures and practices of injustice. We should not be afraid of power, because we need power to end human rights violations. This also means avoiding hardening our victim status and failing to grow beyond what's happened to us. We want power shared across communities with principles of justice and equity. Power should be exercised with appropriate accountability measures. Power should be viewed as a resource that anyone can practice sharing and that can be delegated through democratic processes and structures.

To practice calling in, we must be strategic, because our purpose is to build the power and political will to bring people together for positive social change. To be strategic, we have to practice the following skills:

- Don't assume perfect unity is necessary for effective collaboration.
- Assess which conflicts are worth engaging through what means and to what end. Pick your battles!
- Remember the long arc by adding the dimension of time in situations of high stress (e.g., go for a walk, ask for a break).
- Use accessible language to communicate even if there are still points of disagreement.
- Strive to understand and to be understood, not just to be heard.
- Keep your eye on the prize and don't be deflected.
- Practice active listening skills.

To develop strategies that build unity instead of breaking it, we can:

- Prioritize unity over winning an argument.
- Let go of minor offenses.
- Not assume you don't have allies—allies don't need to share your identity.
- Work to make sure strategies are consistent with the mission and/or organizational values.
- Be inclusive instead of exclusive.
- Anticipate consequences and conflicts.

- Proactively assume trauma will show up but don't allow it to run things.
- Reinterpret challenges as opportunities for growth.

To invoke bell hooks again, we must remember that to be committed to justice we must believe that ethics matter, that it is vital to have a system of shared morality. I believe that calling in practices for the human rights movement in the 21st century will be as important as nonviolent strategies were for the Civil Rights Movement in the 20th century: a statement of our values and how they are demonstrated through our commitment to build the Beloved Community.

NOTES

1. Andrea Gibson, "The Cost of Call-Out Culture," https://andreagibson.substack.com/p/the-cost-of-call-out-culture.

2. Dr. Martin Luther King, Jr. "'Beyond Vietnam,'" The Martin Luther King, Jr. Research and Education Institute, April 4, 1967, https://kinginstitute.stanford.edu/king-papers/documents/beyond-vietnam.

3. Marian Wright Edelman, "Dr. Vincent Harding's Call to Make America America," *Huffington Post*, May 30, 2014, https://www.huffpost.com/entry/dr-vincent-hardings-call_b_5420247.

4. Hannah Arendt, "Truth and Politics," *The New Yorker*, February 18, 1967, https://www.newyorker.com/magazine/1967/02/25/truth-and-politics.

5. bell hooks, *Teaching Community: A Pedagogy of Hope* (New York: Psychology Press, 2003).

6. Ngọc Loan Trần, "Calling IN: A Less Disposable Way of Holding Each Other Accountable," BGD, December 13, 2013, https://www.bgdblog.org/2013/12/calling-less-disposable-way-holding-accountable.

Media, Evidence, and Misinformation

CHAPTER 28

When Our "Truth-Tellers" Won't Tell Us the Truth

Looking Back at the Kerner Commission Report and Ahead to a Transformed Media Landscape

Ray Suarez

Talk to people working inside U.S. newsrooms, and the observation that the news business is in crisis seems almost trite, a detail so obvious it should not come as a surprise to anyone in our vast constituencies stretching from Point Barrow, Alaska, to Key West, Florida.

Yet outside the business, among our readers, listeners, and viewers, that same crisis may be felt but little understood. Its severity only breaks into the public consciousness when yet another newspaper closes its doors, or a well-known journalism brand announces yet another round of big layoffs.

In 2023 and 2024, layoffs rocked newsrooms across broadcast, print, and online media, bringing deep cuts to CBS News, *The Los Angeles Times*, *The Washington Post*, *Vox*, CNN, Vice Media, NBC News, and *Sports Illustrated*. The story of the news business in the United States, throughout the 20th century and into the 21st, is a long saga of economic and technological disruption, along with regularly shifting regulatory boundaries for the broadcast news industry.

What's happening now is different.

Even as the population expands, the audiences for news products is shrinking. (The Census Bureau estimated the U.S. population at the time of the Kerner Commission report at approximately 200 million, compared to some 335 million today.[1] The latest Census estimates the population over 18 years of age at 258 million people.[2]) From the 1960s to the 1990s, American newspapers sold more than 60 million copies on weekdays, and Sunday circulation peaked at over 60 million in the 1990s. In the 21st century, the audience for newspapers has dropped like a rock, on weekdays and Sundays, falling to just over 20 million.[3]

There was a dream of somehow finding a way to rebuild the jet while at cruising altitude over America, and creating a soft digital landing with profits and audiences intact. That has not come to pass. From the biggest legacy media companies to the smallest community outlets, from revered brands to brash startups, the business has wrestled with the transition from historical business models built around printing presses and airwaves to digital transmission, turning dollars of legacy media investment into dimes of digital revenue.

There are two important differences between the American media landscape of the Kerner Commission era and the country today. Now, many more contestants are fighting for eardrums and eyeballs, breaking mass audiences into smaller, discrete pieces of mosaic tile. Critically, while outlets struggle to capture your attention, the public's trust for the news industry has tumbled over the last half century to the lowest ever measured. The news business is not alone. In many respects, declining trust for the news business mirrors the waning deference toward and confidence in many other pillars of American life: the courts, medicine, the police, the public schools.

However, after starting from a lower base of trust during the tumult of the 1960s, newspapers and broadcasters have now plunged even further below many other institutions, and are now trusted by just single-digit percentages of Republicans (and larger, but still minority shares of independents and Democrats).[4]

A healthier news industry, with an intact business model, might have been able to negotiate the challenges of a rapidly changing technological and regulatory environment and retain audiences and trust. Instead, the ravages of the modern marketplace are weakening an already depleted body: hedge funds buy up newspapers and strip their assets and decimate their staffs; broadcasters watch their audiences abandon them for on-demand products yielding less reliable profits; and an aggressive, well-funded disinformation industry rises to capture enthusiasm, attention, and clicks.

In the 2020s, the news industry is a punch-drunk fighter trying to see the country through eyes swelling shut and trying to speak to its audiences through a fat lip and busted teeth. In 1968, the legacy media spoke to America from an Olympian height, through television and radio networks, wire services, newspaper chains, independent dailies, and weekly magazines. In the 21st century, big media struggles to remain relevant to a vast and diverse audience. In the second half of the 20th century, that same business took its immense power and reach for granted, and its accumulating deficiencies made it fail at a critical moment.

The smoke was still clearing in Black ghettoes across America when Lyndon Johnson appointed the governor of Illinois, Otto Kerner, to chair a commission examining all aspects of the two hot summers the country had just endured. Long pent-up rage had exploded out of 150 cities, and in a perfect illustration of the gulf between Black and white America, many Americans had no idea why.

It should tell you plenty about America in 1968 that an 11-member presidential commission chosen to examine the origins of Black unrest in America had two Black members, one a Republican from Massachusetts. Perhaps that is a rant for another day. One of the areas of national life singled out for examination by the commission, along with employment, policing, and residential segregation, was the news media. In the aftermath of riots before and after the killing of Martin Luther King, Jr., the performance of the people who were supposed to be the eyes and ears of people far from the action was found to have only made the problems worse. It was hard to imagine a more simple, straightforward, and damning assessment:

"We have found a significant imbalance between what actually happened in our cities and what the newspaper, radio and television coverage of the riots told us happened."

It got worse.

"We found that the disorders, as serious as they were, were less destructive, less widespread, and less a black-white confrontation than most people believed."

In short, the people who, by consensus, were relied upon to gather and transmit the truth to waiting readers, listeners, and viewers did not tell the people the truth at a critical time in the life of the country. When the times demanded an information environment that would help citizens not only understand the moment-to-moment events but their wider meanings and implications in order to do the work of being a citizen, Americans were let down. Implicitly given the assignment of informing a continent-sized country of the events that created the realities of its national life, the news business, in print, audio, and on-screen, was found to have failed the American public. To its great credit, the commission's investigators reviewed thousands of newspaper articles, radio and television reports, and found systemic problems:

—a tendency to sensationalize
—credulous repetition of information from official sources
—collapse of longstanding problems into a Black vs. white framing
—generations-long failure to report on the realities of Black life in the United States

These failures, the commission concluded, tended to have a synergistic effect, cross-pollinating and compounding their severity. The asymmetry of understanding got us to the late 1960s with a country that knew little of the realities of Black life in America, and a Black population, at the time more than 20 million out of 200 million,[5] convinced the national media were part of a white "power structure" in America ignorant of their lives and hostile to their interests.

At this distance, as America looks back over its shoulder at the world of 1968, it is easy to forget how Johnson-era America was still early in the process of tearing down the walls of law and custom that kept Black America separated from mainstream life. We were just a few years away from the civil rights legislation that tore away the last legal remnants of Jim Crow. We were much less than a decade from the actual integration of public schooling (as opposed to their legal dismantling supposedly begun with the 1954 *Brown* decision by the Supreme Court), which saw previously rigidly segregated school districts dig in their heels in what was called "massive resistance."

National brands refused to open businesses in Black commercial districts in urban America, which had the unintended effect of allowing Black-owned businesses to hold off the coming tidal wave of massively capitalized brands that would eventually rush in and swamp their small canoes. Isolation had created a parallel society. There were separate chambers of commerce, professional associations, publications, debutante balls, theatrical circuits, fraternal organizations, personal care products, and clothing brands. City Hall, to the degree that its presence was felt in the ghetto at all, provided too few jobs (even as white populations dwindled), trained too few Black police officers, assigned too few Black principals and schoolteachers to local public schools, and provided too few recreational opportunities in some of the densest, oldest neighborhoods of aging cities.

By 1968, 2 full decades of government-subsidized white flight and suburban growth had not only changed the spatial arrangements of race, but intensified the class dimensions of American life as well. Right after the World War II, Black and white Americans in center city neighborhoods were more likely to know, and live near, people richer and poorer than themselves. Global economic meltdown followed by world war meant little new housing had been built anywhere in urban America for almost 20 years. It was not unusual for big chunks of America's urban giants, New York, Chicago, Philadelphia, to have local housing vacancy rates of 1–2%.[6] With demobilization and a social slingshot effect of postponed marriages and childbirths, and government programs creating a new class of Americans, the brief era of widely shared social burdens quickly began to end.

If the commissioners found that the media had failed to hold up a mirror to society and remind us how much we had become strangers to each other when urban riots burned through the country, it is hard to imagine what a 21st-century report would say about the way media encourages and intensifies that estrangement. As Jim Bishop chronicled in his landmark book *The Big Sort*, we have built a nation of strangers brick by brick, in decades of furious self-sorting that left millions of rank-and-file Americans less able to believe others were different from themselves because they were simply less likely to know them, or encounter them.

The Kerner Report indicted the media for missing the story of the widening chasms in American life in 1968. By the 2020s, the media, enabled by technological change, accelerated by the algorithmic ability to create intensely customized private realities, has moved from observer to cause, from chronicler to partner in widening social divides.

Earlier in my career, I was very critical of the unwillingness of my own business to take the people who consumed our information to places that were challenging, ideas that were uncomfortable, to tell them stories that upset easily accepted, but false, notions about American life. Since so much of the revenue stream of the information business was based on bringing people into the room and keeping them there, there was a paradoxical disincentive to tell people anything they didn't want to hear. We were society's truth-tellers, but structured the business in a way that made being popular more important than being honest, and entertaining more profitable than being informative.

As the cratering of trust continued, the nature of the challenge changed as well: When the business was willing to take on entrenched interests, expose hidden wrongdoing, tell audiences dismaying and discouraging truths, it was more likely to do so for the consumption of self-selected audiences, to narrower audiences that came to the act of reading, watching, and listening news that confirmed its beliefs.

Geography, economics, and history, the sheer weight of the last 60 years, conspire to make newsrooms reinforcers and transmitters of well-worn ideas about race and class. America's biggest metropolitan areas are vast territories, with a massive city at their heart, and huge numbers of smaller municipalities clustered around them for hundreds of square miles. As Los Angeles, Chicago, New York, and Philadelphia metros got bigger, their broadcast news and newspaper staffs got smaller.[7] The attention reporters could give county councils on the edge of the metropolitan area, mayors of small cities, budget and zoning battles in growing municipalities far from downtown was limited by the number of journalists deployable across half a dozen counties, often in multiple states.

Even as crime was dropping across America, local news coverage devoted to crime remained level, or increased.[8] A world of mayhem came to TV screens on the late local news, shot by crews dispatched by assignment desks glued to police scanners downtown. Drug busts, murder scenes, the aftereffects of vandalism, and spinning police lights at the scenes of multiple-car fatal accidents train a distorted lens on the complicated and challenging life of a metropolitan area. The daily lives of suburban viewers, craved by advertisers for their disposable income, were often ignored, in favor of the easily collectible images of tumult and urban dysfunction much closer to "home," the downtown newsroom. As staffs dwindled and expensive far-flung bureaus closed, "covering" a metropolitan area of 8 or 9 million people with two reporters on duty was a deepening fantasy.

However, this syndrome creates something much more serious than mere "misimpression." Policymakers are sensitive to public fears, even if those fears may be misplaced, or exaggerated. Some of the responsibility for persistent fear of crime—even as crime was dropping like a rock across America—must be laid at the doors of newsrooms driven by crime coverage, and the way the work of politicians is reported to the public.

At the end of decades of this kind of coverage, the table was set, the mold was secure. Cities were "dangerous" even as they got safer every year, suburbs "safe" even as they got more dangerous. Constrained resources solidified the unspoken association between Black and Brown people, cities, and crime. This makes it inevitable that a shortcoming identified by the Kerner Report in 1968, an overreliance on official narratives to shape what the public understands about the daily realities faced in metropolitan America, gives tremendous power to already amplified "big voices" in the culture. Required to file as soon as possible, or make air today, a stenographic press no longer has the time needed to check what it is told. It is forced to "pass along" what it hears, unable to verify it before telling the public.

No longer seeing its own information business as trustworthy, the public surrenders to the loudest and most persistent voices in the room, rather than ones that have earned credibility from steady and persistent digging for facts. The commissioners saw a problem in 1968 when they found in crisis coverage "many of the inaccuracies of fact, tone and mood were due to the failure of reporters and editors to ask tough enough questions about official reports, and apply the most rigorous standards possible in evaluating and presenting the news. Reporters and editors must be sure that descriptions and pictures of violence, and emotional or inflammatory sequences of articles, even though 'true' in isolation, are really representative and do not convey an impression at odds with the overall reality of events."

That might not seem like a lot to ask. It appears to be a bedrock principal that might be handed down in a college course called "Introduction to Journalism." Over the arc of decades, as the power to credibly define the world has leached out of news institutions and pooled up instead in unlikely and widely distributed places, this fundamental baseline may be gone as well. It has left us with a society unable to understand real risk, and less able to reckon with real threat.

One afternoon while gathering interviews for a book on urban America, I interrupted a woman watering her lawn to talk about life in her Chicago neighborhood. Years of declining crime rates preceded our chat, and we were standing in what already had long been one of the statistically safest areas in the whole city. Not much had changed around the place we stood, she reported. But when I asked her what the biggest problem in the area was, she didn't hesitate for a second. "Crime," she said. She had not been touched by it. Nor had her neighbors. But a dystopian vision came to her TV screens every night, reinforcing her sense of danger, threat, disorder. Lived experience and close observation of the world literally just outside her door had offered little reassurance, and could not compete with media-delivered danger. When I reminded her that the place where we stood was the safest place in the city, she shot back, "You still have to worry about it." I thought, but did not say, "If you still have to be that worried, maybe you should move."

Fast forward to 2020. America once again could sit in front of the television and consume endless hours of danger and disorder. This time, however, malign forces could magnify unfolding events, pressing down the gas to create impressions of even more chaos.[9] By the time cars were burning and stores being looted in that pandemic summer of 2020, a lot had changed in the operating maps of the world that live between Americans' ears. Social media had created new trust networks. Information provocateurs chipped away at the authority of the news business to define and quantify events and their scale. From a thousand miles away, an online poster could modify aerial photographs of Washington, DC, streets lit by mercury vapor streetlamps, and declare to thousands of strangers, "Downtown DC is burning." That photo could then be picked up by thousands more, and spread to hundreds of thousands more. Months later, clad in camo and army surplus "tactical gear," January 6 marchers outside the United States Capitol could tell me one of the reasons they had come was to reclaim the city from the violence and destruction of the summer just past.

One woman watering her lawn, convinced of persistent threat in an objectively safe place, is sad. Thousands of angry men convinced unknown, unidentifiable forces had burned down large sections of the seat of government is something more like a tragedy. Similar magnified scenes of chaos in Minneapolis, Portland, and elsewhere were regularly heard after January 6 as explanation, and justification for, the insistence that the crowds that breached the Capitol and caused injury and millions of dollars in damage should face no punishment.

Of course, this is not every reporter, or every newsroom, or even every day. However, a shrinking "news hole," filled by a shrinking staff, framed by a scaffolding provided by a shrinking number of advertisers has made the output of the news industry less vital to audiences, as the world only gets more complicated, and demands more mastery of the facts by an audience faced by rising challenge. This is the crux of the modern challenge: The world demands a better-informed citizen, consumer, voter, taxpayer, PTA member, commuter, and neighbor. The gush, the swollen river of stuff flowing to laptops, smartphones, and televisions creates the illusion of sufficiency.

On any given day, you can easily find multiple sources for more facts about more things than were ever available to average citizens ever in the history of the world.

. . . Mickey Mantle's batting average in the 1954 World Series.

. . . The height of Mt. Kilimanjaro.

... The average May Day temperature in Shanghai.

... The amount the U.S. government needed to borrow in 2023 to pay all of the country's bills.

... The distance covered by monarch butterflies in their annual migration. It's all there. What might have taken a whole afternoon in a reference library, you could probably run down in 5 minutes using the phone in your pocket. (Except for Mantle's batting average; 1954 was his first year in the Major Leagues and the Yankees did not make it to the World Series.)

The information tsunami does not make us smarter.[10] When news organizations and researchers give rank-and-file citizens general knowledge and current events quizzes, they have a weaker grasp of events, a shakier mastery of science and geography than they did a generation ago. Decades of buck-passing did not take us where we might have wanted to go. National news organizations closed foreign bureaus, sure the wire services and syndication services would pick up the slack. Regional newsrooms did not fear cutbacks in suburban bureaus and staff because local outlets would serve hyper-local, parochial interests. Legacy outlets could safely cut back on providing various kinds of coverage because people who really wanted it would go online to find it. All the while, they buy out newsroom veterans, cut editors, and ask everyone on the vast conveyor belt bringing "content" to waiting audiences to do more, with less, and for less. It is the logic of production applied in many other fields of endeavor, sure, but the public's right to know seems to be more important than the shrinking chocolate bar or the next cheapest place in the world to make sneakers.

The news business and the public were engaged in a long breakup, and seemed not to want to acknowledge it. Like a long-married couple drifting apart, the silences growing longer, the casual mistrust growing deeper, until finally neither could remember why they were still together.

A large part of the public bailed out quietly, without rancor, taking advantage of the gradual shift in the power relationship between provider and customer.[11] As if to say, "You, newscasters, will no longer be able to tell me I have to wait until the top of the hour to hear a newscast. I, the listener, can punch one up whenever I like. You, layout people and editors, will no longer direct my eye to this column on that page to signal to me that you have decided this is the most important story. I will decide which story is important to me. I will direct your website to send me the stories I am interested in, on the topics I am interested in."

The news business, a shrinking crowd of desperate pleasers, made it possible for you to be your own assignment editor, your own layout staff, your own program director, your own executive producer. The spell is broken. For every one who still uses the product (only now on their own terms), the numbers would indicate there is an even larger group of adults who have decided to do without us all together. Alienated from what it dismissed as an elite industry endlessly condescending, this group still traffics in information. Only now the sources are not those authorized by training and the folkways of the news business to speak with authority. This new audience decides for itself who has authority.

That new information economy is taking us to some strange places in the 2020s. Millions of people tell opinion researchers they believe at least part of the web of stories that involve a shadowy network of the world's rich and powerful kidnapping and trafficking children not only for their sexual gratification but to drink their blood to maintain their youth.[12] These fantastic propositions include the one that Donald Trump is still president of the United States, and battling these dark forces behind the scenes, and that Joe Biden has been dead for years and is being portrayed in his rare public appearances by an actor.

Large portions of the public have told pollsters in recent years they believe pictures they see on broadcast news and stories in the newspapers are simply made up, invented, nothing but contrivances.[13] Charismatic television hosts have convinced large numbers of people that the young victims of horrific school shootings, or the panicky crowd gunned down at a concert in Las Vegas, were actors. Are not really dead at all. Their stunned and grief-stricken relatives? Actors.[14]

The technological revolution that has enabled the seeker to put a finger on all the world's knowledge has also made it possible for the motivated fabulist to show photographic "proof" of actors at crime scenes, complete with names and résumés. The erosion of trust in the news business allowed a dangerous new business to rise, a parallel universe of misdirection and deceit. Almost half a century ago, the Kerner Commission concluded a dangerous gulf had been allowed to arise between American communities. That gulf, the commission insisted, had been midwifed by a news industry ridden with stereotype, casual and lazy in its reporting. The commission found when talking to Black residents of highly segregated areas, "the newspapers are mistrusted more than the television. This is not because television is thought to be more sensitive or responsive to Negro needs and aspirations, but because ghetto residents believe that television at least lets them see the actual events for themselves."

The commissioners never could have imagined the revolution about to sweep an already unmoored American news business in the form of artificial intelligence. So-called "deepfakes," AI-generated characters and video sequences are already here. Office holders, activists, and journalists themselves are bracing for national elections that may yet be marred by simulations of events that never happened, including statements that politicians never made, breathlessly narrated by reporters who never existed. A business that enjoyed a solid relationship with its public, determination to fight back, and the resources fit for the battle might at least make it a fair fight. Reports are already coming in from other places in the world where deepfakes and AI are already starting to influence voters.

If that happens in the United States, the public will not be entirely blameless. A public that has begun to regard being told the truth as option rather than imperative leaves itself vulnerable to the opportunistic infection of disinformation. A public that has embraced a reflexive, unearned distrust of any source that delivers information contradicting already held conviction is an electorate ripe to be misled. It is possible to hear an outlandish conspiracy theory and be mystified. How could anyone believe the Super Bowl is fixed as part of an elaborate plot to re-elect an incumbent president? How could anyone believe microchips are being hidden in vaccines to enable the control of vast numbers of Americans through signals from 5G cell phone towers?

There have always been popular delusions. Before broadcasting, before widespread literacy, such notion had to be passed from person to person. It was hard, and slow, to inject these ideas into the bloodstream of the widest possible public. Printing sped the movement of ideas. Photography, radio waves, television, motion pictures, all accelerated the speed at which ideas could jump from place to place. Now the Internet has floored the accelerator, making it possible for even the most outlandish notions to pick up a bit of DNA from here, a stray piece of virus from there, to pick up speed and potency and appeal.

A news business that can no longer command attention, that no longer speaks with authority, that can safely be ignored and ridiculed, has created space for the malign and the merely misled. Conspiracy theories, even the zaniest ones, make a kind of sense. You must remember that human beings are unstoppable meaning-making machines. Given the bits and scraps of the truth that may at first seem an unrelated jumble, people will impose order on a random collection of stuff. The age of conspiracy is the predictable response to an information ecosystem that does not propose to offer a coherent view of the world.

Back when the vast majority of American televisions were tuned to programs distributed by just three companies, and most adults read a newspaper, and those newspapers created a consensus view of the world, you might say Americans "knew the same things." Granted, there was variation. There were political tendencies and tribalism, sectional and cultural loyalties. The newsstand in a big metropolitan area might have been stuffed with papers that catered to slightly different interests, but knowing the same things meant they didn't fall along too wide a continuum.

The Kerner Commission looked at the way the news business covered urban unrest in 1967 and 1968 and saw a business unresponsive to community needs and irresponsibly handling the dynamite of racial and economic difference. It called for care and discretion, fairness and responsibility, because the news business held a privilege and unrivaled place in American society.

Fast forward 6 decades, and you see a media system unimaginable by the dozen worthies who went to work to understand America's seasons of tumult. Today, anyone can appoint themselves a journalist. The tools of creation and distribution are cheap, easy to use, and widely available. Anyone who decides for themselves to acquire some basic skills can turn themselves into a videographer, a reporter, a photographer, a documentarian, or an information activist. For all that, fewer people make a full-time living as a journalist in America in 2024 than did at the turn of the century.[15] Consider for a moment how much greater the sheer volume of "stuff" there is in the pipeline, a steady stream of information, impressions, ideas, and idiocy beamed to your eyes and ears, pushing and shoving for precious slivers of your attention. More things are "knowable" than at any time in the history of the world, yet so much more of it seems tentative, less-than-solid. It took decades and a bewildering and unpredictable set of social trends, inventions, and outcomes to get us here. It's going to take a long time to get us out.

The truth business has to take the measure of its opponents in the untruth business. It's going to take resources and training and a real understanding of the stakes. The Kerner Commission put it pretty well: "We believe that to live up to their own professed standards, the media simply must exercise a higher degree of care and a greater level of sophistication than they have yet shown." They asked a lot in 1968, having seen how critical good journalism was to the health of a society in good times and bad. We cannot ask less of ourselves today as producers and consumers of one of society's most vital products, reliable information.

Just as the Kerner Commission gave specific recommendations for improving the work of the news business and avoiding a repeat of the urban riots of the 1960s, I have advice for my business. Given the gathering trends in the public and private sector, I would hope to see the following in pushing back against the degradation of our national and international media landscape:

1. More not-for-profit corporations, and fewer billionaire saviors. The news business has had enough time to assess the effectiveness of both. The not-for-profit media sector deals with the headwinds of rises and dips in available cash, but relieved of the burden of making money far exceeding what it takes to cover the news and pay the bills, has done outstanding, award-winning work. Billionaire saviors, on the other hand, sometimes bring new infusions of cash and optimism, only to eventually succumb to the pressure for profit that has served the business so poorly in recent years. Huge layoffs at Patrick Soon-Shiong's *Los Angeles Times* and Jeff Bezos's *Washington Post* have been sobering reminders that the guys on white horses still want, still need to make money. I'd rather be doing NPR and *ProPublica*'s journalism for the next 20 years than that of ABC News or the trashed and denuded *Chicago Tribune*.
2. Cross-training, and raising up the workforce of the future. A nimble, multiplatform, cross-trained workforce needs to know how to write compelling prose, take great pictures, and edit crisp audio. More and more news organizations demand skills that once were the siloed province of specialists. Remaining employed will require even more. Not just wide curiosity, always an essential, but a foundational understanding of a broad array of the disciplines that shape what we think of as "news," like economics, public health, politics, geography, ecology, and demographics. Be deep in a few, and wide enough to capably cover many.
3. Artificial intelligence to the rescue! Though journalists are rightly frightened about what AI may mean to the future of the newsroom, it may also bring promise. Machine learning programs are already acting as sorters, helping news consumers choose between reliable, factual reporting and some of the supercharged lying and distortion that wears journalism's respectable clothes. With all the legitimate terror about deepfakes, doctored photographs, computer-generated audio putting words in the mouths of prominent figures, AI also has the capacity to speed research, relieve drudgery, and aid the public in sorting out what's true and what's not.
4. Local, local, local. Along with the absolutely vital defense of journalistic norms at the international and national level, local news must be healthy. The market orientation of much of America's for-profit journalism led to greater and greater consolidation, and the withering of many local news outlets. A local school board debate, a zoning controversy, the siting of a waste transfer station . . . all won't make national newscasts or the pages of *The Wall Street Journal*. Those issues dictate the way of life in communities across America, and create the context for developing the muscles of civic engagement. New models for local news are being created right this minute by public media, which has assigned itself the task of filling the vacuum created by the loss of thorough, consistent, hyperlocal news coverage.

5. Talk to reporters! It may seem obvious, but journalists making inquiries in order to establish the facts in a story they are covering can't be shunned. Especially if you want to be covered thoroughly and fairly, you should not duck reporters. Worst of all is hiding essential truths, dealing in half-truths, or avoiding them all together and then complaining after the fact about mistakes, or not being covered fairly.
6. Reviving a reverence for the truth. This is probably a tough ask. Valuing work that is dogged, and complete, and factual over work that is merely entertaining would help move the market needle toward getting a different range of product. Officials and citizens should not refuse to talk to reporters and then complain about inaccuracies after the fact. In much the same way, it is tough to ignore the rigorous, choose to gorge on cheap informational calories, and then complain that "no one's doing serious work anymore." Marketplaces for goods, and information, respond to customer preferences.

In short, we all have a role in creating a better information ecosystem. Customers and consumers, practitioners, and the institutions that sponsor the creation of the work all have a role to play in creating better journalism. Let's keep our fingers crossed that it's not too late to create a better marketplace.

NOTES

1. US Census Bureau, "Estimates of the Population of the United States to October 1, 1968," November 19, 1968, https://www2.census.gov/library/publications/1968/demographics/P25-410.pdf; U.S. Census Bureau, "Quick Facts," n.d., https://www.census.gov/quickfacts/fact/table/US/LFE046222.

2. Stella U. Ogunwole et al, "Population Under Age 18 Declined Last Decade," U.S. Census Bureau, August 12, 2021, https://www.census.gov/library/stories/2021/08/united-states-adult-population-grew-faster-than-nations-total-population-from-2010-to-2020.html.

3. Sarah Naseer and Christopher St. Aubin, "Newspapers Fact Sheet," Pew Research Center, November 10, 2023, https://www.pewresearch.org/journalism/fact-sheet/newspapers.

4. Lydia Saad, "Historically Low Faith in U.S. Institutions Continues," Gallup, July 6, 2023, https://news.gallup.com/poll/508169/historically-low-faith-institutions-continues.aspx.

5. Claudette E. Bennett et al., "We the Americans: Blacks," U.S. Census Bureau, September 1993, https://www.census.gov/library/publications/1993/dec/we-01.html.

6. Becky Nicolaides and Andrew Wiese, "Suburbanization in the United States After 1945," *Oxford Research Encyclopedia of American History*, April 2017.

7. Mason Walker, "U.S. Newsroom Employment Has Fallen 26% Since 2008," Pew Research Center, July 13, 2021, https://www.pewresearch.org/short-reads/2021/07/13/u-s-newsroom-employment-has-fallen-26-since-2008.

8. Josh Gramlich, "What the Data Says About Crime in the U.S.," Pew Research Center, April 24, 2024, https://www.pewresearch.org/short-reads/2020/11/20/facts-about-crime-in-the-u-s; Daniel Romer, Kathleen Hall Jamieson, and Sean Aday, "Television News and the Cultivation of Fear of Crime," *Journal of Communication* 53, no. 1 (2003): 88–104, https://doi.org/10.1111/j.1460-2466.2003.tb03007.x.

9. Roudabeh Kishi and Sam Jones, "Demonstrations and Political Violence in America: New Data for Summer 2020," ACLED, September 3, 2020, https://acleddata.com/2020/09/03/demonstrations-political-violence-in-america-new-data-for-summer-2020.

10. Tom Infield, "Americans Who Get News Mainly on Social Media Are Less Knowledgeable and Less Engaged," *Trust Magazine*, November 16, 2020, https://www.pewtrusts.org/en/trust/archive/fall-2020/americans-who-get-news-mainly-on-social-media-are-less-knowledgeable-and-less-engaged.

11. Naomi Forman-Katz, "Americans Are Following the News Less Closely Than They Used To," Pew Research Center, October 24, 2023, https://www.pewresearch.org/short-reads/2023/10/24/americans-are-following-the-news-less-closely-than-they-used-to.

12. PRRI, "New PRRI Report Reveals Nearly One in Five Americans and One in Four Republicans Still Believe in QAnon Conspiracy Theories," press release, February 24, 2022, https://www.prri.org/press-release/new-prri-report-reveals-nearly-one-in-five-americans-and-one-in-four-republicans-still-believe-in-qanon-conspiracy-theories.

13. Amy Mitchell et al., "Many Americans Say Made-Up News Is a Critical Problem That Needs To Be Fixed," Pew Research Center, June 5, 2019, https://www.pewresearch.org/journalism/2019/06/05/many-americans-say-made-up-news-is-a-critical-problem-that-needs-to-be-fixed.

14. Dave Collins, "Sandy Hook Witnesses Testify About Alex Jones' Hoax Claims," *AP*, September 13, 2022, https://apnews.com/article/shootings-texas-violence-school-connecticut-96345da42248bdc70c12653d1a46ff9a.

15. Stephen Waldman, "The Journalist Population," Report for America, June 28, 2021, https://www.reportforamerica.org/2021/06/28/the-journalist-population.

CHAPTER 29

"Little Brother Is Watching Big Brother"
The Flawed Media Lens on Policing and Racism

Julian E. Zelizer

The Kerner Commission was extremely critical about how the media covered urban unrest.[1] While the sections of the commission report about policing and economic hardship captured much of the attention—both at the time and in our historical memory—the members had tough words to say about how largely white reporters understood and analyzed the violence that had erupted in the summer of 1967. "Lacking other sources of information," the commission declared, "we formed our original impressions and beliefs from what we saw on television, heard on the radio, and read in newspapers and magazines. We are deeply concerned that millions of other Americans, who must rely on the mass media, likewise formed incorrect impressions and judgments about what went on in many American cities last summer."[2]

To be sure, there had been many pivotal moments when the national media had been instrumental in capturing the ways that police authorities could turn against Black Americans simply trying to exercise their rights. In several high-profile clashes, such as Birmingham, Alabama, in May 1963 or Selma, Alabama, in March 1965, the footage that reporters aired of police attacking law-abiding citizens who were protesting for civil rights created shock and awe, in both cases generating support for national civil rights legislation. As two distinguished historians of journalism argued, "The civil-rights revolution in the South began when a man and the eye of the television film camera came together, giving the camera a focal point for events breaking from state to state, and the man, Martin Luther King Jr., high exposure on television sets from coast to coast."[3]

But with the relationship between ordinary policing, racism, and urban violence, where the conflict was not as explicit as what happened in Birmingham in 1963, the problem was that white reporters, regardless of their talent, didn't have much sense of what the experience of being a Black American in the city was like. Most of them had not been continually harassed by police authorities. Most had not lived in communities where the persons who were supposed to provide protection acted as threats. Most had not lived in areas of the country where families were trapped by pervasive discrimination as job opportunities disappeared. Most did not understand what it felt like to be on the bottom end of racial hierarchies that were entrenched through local and state institutions. "Television coverage," the commission said, "tended to give the impression that the riots were confrontations between Negroes and whites rather than responses by Negroes to underlying slum problems." This kind of coverage had generated great distrust of the news. The commission quoted one person interviewed as having said: "The average black person couldn't give less of a damn about what the media say. The intelligent black person is resentful at what he considers to be a totally false portrayal of what goes on in the ghetto. Most black people see the newspapers as mouthpieces of the 'power structure.'"[4]

The solution, according to the commissioners, was to diversify the newsroom and to provide more permanently assigned reporters to cover urban and racial affairs. The changes had to also include editors, producers, commentators, and more. The vision was that by changing who covered the news, particularly with more Black reporters, the news industry would better its understanding would be of the dynamics on the ground. Black reporters would be able to grasp why arrests had sparked such massive confrontations and the ways in which police created hostile climates for residents. Even for a commission that paid an unusual amount of attention toward institutional racism, the confidence that diversification itself could offer an elixir to these problems was rooted in the liberal ethos of the 1960s that was behind the major legislation passed by Congress. The commission made other recommendations, including the creation of a private, non-profit Institute of Urban Communication that would serve as a clearinghouse to train journalists on urban issues, recruit and place Black journalists, review the performance of how the media covered racial issues, improve relations between the press and the police, produce research, and bolster coverage of all urban affairs. "Along with the country as a whole," the commission lamented, "the press has too long basked in a white world, looking out of it, if at all, with white men's eyes and a white perspective. That is no longer good enough. The painful process of readjustment that is required of the American news media must begin now. They must make a reality of integration—in both their product and their personnel."[5]

There was progress over the coming decades. Newsrooms, and to some extent television and radio studios, started to look more like America. The diversification of the workforce did offer greater perspective on the issues that were shaping America, not only with regard to race but gender and ethnicity as well (although non-white reporters remained a small percentage of the overall labor force).

Following the 1960s, there were more reporters who were trying to pay more attention to the way that race manifested itself in local, state, and federal institutions, as the commission had recommended. Alice Travis, a graduate of Immaculata College who grew up in the home built by her grandfather, hosted the syndicated show "For You . . . Black Woman," which first went on the air in 1977. Inspired to go into journalism by the Kerner Report, Travis's show was groundbreaking, as it featured a Black female host who tackled questions that were relevant to persons like her. "The media and its lack of coverage dealing with racial issues was also held responsible for creating the problems outlined by the commission," she recalled, "That wasn't lost on white news managers who were forced to acknowledge the need to bring diversity to their historically white newsrooms. The Kerner report opened the door of opportunities that had been unfairly closed to Black journalists for too long." Other shows went on air featuring Black reporters and dealing with issues that affected the community, such as *Black Journal* on public television and *Say Brother* on WGBH-Boston.[6]

Ultimately, however, traditional reporters were limited in that much of what happened with policing happened outside the public eye. The encounters that caused so much friction happened when nobody was around. Accounts to reporters often pitted citizens accused of wrongdoing with police authorities who were still generally trusted. Cameramen and photographers were rarely on hand to capture the sorts of harassment and violence Black citizens faced.

The real breakthrough in coverage of institutional racism in policing arrived as a result of technology—technology that became accessible to average citizens who could capture and then transmit what the racial experience was like. This was not something envisioned by the commission, though the effects were what had been hoped for.

The first major breakthrough were handheld camcorders. This technology allowed individual Americans with no expertise to record video of live events, then stored on the cassettes of the machines. Whereas in Chicago in 1968, the violence of police against antiwar protesters reached the nation through television network reporters, in the 1980s and 1990s professionals were no longer needed.[7] In 1988, Clayton Patterson videotaped police attacking activists in Tompkins Square Park, New York, who were there to protest a new curfew. Tompkins Square had become a site for many homeless New Yorkers who had been squeezed out of an increasingly expensive home market dominated by co-ops and condos. "I was good at catching cops doing bad things," Patterson explained.[8] A local network picked it up. As a result of the video, prosecutors indicted six police officers. The story was broadcast by national shows such as *Oprah Winfrey Show* and CNN. When speaking to Oprah, Patterson said, "This is a revolutionary tool. Little brother is watching Big Brother."[9]

More dramatic was Rodney King in 1991. On March 31, a 31-year-old immigrant from South America named George Holliday filmed four police on the LAPD attacking Rodney King, a Black American man who had been pulled over for speeding. Standing on his balcony, Holiday videoed the violence on his Sony Handycam. The video recorders had come on the market in 1985, quickly overtaking Sony's earlier Betamax technology. The technology had been around for over a decade, but by the middle of the 1980s, Sony had figured out how to make a machine that was light, effective, easy to use and relatively cheap compared to older efforts. It could literally be held with one hand, compared to older, bulkier cameras that were placed on the shoulder. Holliday then sent the tape to a local television news show, which purchased it for $500. The broadcast aired 81 seconds of the dramatic film. Cable news picked up the material and played it repeatedly throughout their news cycle. Americans rewatched the videotape many times, shocked and horrified about what was taking place. Many who had seen the grainy footage assumed that the police would be found guilty by the courts. Despite King's size and efforts to get up, it seemed very clear that the officers had unloaded an excess of violence against him. But in the courtroom, which had been moved from Los Angeles to the more conservative Simi Valley, the jurors saw things differently. They returned with "not guilty" verdicts. All four policeman were let go. On the night of the verdict, South Central erupted in 5 days of unrest (which came to be known as the Los Angeles Riots of 1992), likewise captured in gory detail by television crews that used new kinds of cameras that could be put on helicopters to film what was happening on the ground. The coverage of the riots themselves included more of an examination of a connection with the police wrongdoing, as opposed to coverage in the 1960s, which blamed the "rioting" on "riffraff" and "outside agitators" rather than an outburst of anger about racism. The phraseology of "rioting" over "unrest" or "rebellion" created normative assumptions about what was happening.[10]

Cable television news, which took off when CNN first went on the air in June 1980, proved to be another important factor in giving attention to racist police violence. Once networks such as CNN, Fox News (1996) and MSNBC (1996) were operational, they created a 24-hour news cycle that was in constant search for content and unincumbered by the kinds of time limitations that traditional networks had once contended with in the era of 30-minute evening news shows. Online journalism, which gradually supplanted physical print journalism, also found itself with more "space" to cover a broader range of stories, including moments when police were caught doing wrong to Black and Latino Americans. The platforms created opportunities for citizens or reporters who found evidence of unjust police violence to garner some attention for their stories.

Nonetheless, despite these changes much of the revelation of violence depended on traditional pathways of discovery and investigation, without the kind of video image that had driven the Rodney King scandal. In 1999, for instance, the investigation into four plainclothes officers (all of whom were acquitted) in New York's Street Crime Unit who fired 41 rounds at an unarmed Amadou Diallo, a 23-year-old Guinean student, unfolded without video evidence. Diallo had reached into his pocket to pull out identification; the officers said they believed that he was taking out a gun. It was often left to the realm of culture to garner attention for what this sort of police racism looked like. Films such as Spike Lee's *Do the Right Thing* (1989) or Bruce Springsteen's song "American Skin (41 Shots)" offered the most vivid window into what Black Americans experienced when nobody was looking. A substantial number of songs, such as Geto Boys "Crooked Officer" (1993), in the flourishing world of rap music did more than anyone else to keep this subject in the public limelight.

Then came the smartphone. In 1992, the computer giant IBM had introduced the first version of what would come to be known as the "smartphone." Unlike the mobile phones introduced in the 1980s by Motorola, the Simon Personal Communicator allowed users to enjoy a touch screen as well as numerous features such as email communication and a calendar. Compared to current technology, the machines remained rudimentary.[11] In 2000, the first smartphone was connected to the Internet, in 2002 the Blackberry 5810 was introduced to the market, and in 2007 Apple launched the iPhone. In 2010, the iPhone 4 included the first front camera capable of recording videos. Though Samsung's Omnia HD had included video recording when released in 2009, the ease of using the iPhone and the quality of the videos was better than before. Other phones soon followed, and video cameras quickly became a regular feature of the devices that millions of Americans were carrying around in their pockets. As prices dropped with competition increasing, more persons were able to buy these machines. City and suburban streets were filled with people who had the ability at any moment to pull out their phone and record what was going on around them.

The smartphone became a powerful tool for recording police violence. On July 17, 2014, for instance, 22-year-old Ramsey Orta recorded the arrest of Eric Garner in Staten Island for selling illegal cigarettes. The arrest quickly took a lethal turn, as the police placed Garner in a choke hold. With Orta's smartphone capturing the scene, the police kept choking Garner as he could be heard pleading that he couldn't breathe. Garner would then die in police custody. Orta gave his video to the *New York Daily News*, and the videos were quickly disseminated throughout the media. The video led to protest and calls for justice. The video of officer Daniel Pantaleo, who would be fired from his job, resulted in efforts to ban the use of choke holds. "I can't breathe," protesters would chant.

By the second half of the 2010s, the videos would find audiences even when the local or national media was focused on other stories. The advent and expansion of social media outlets such as Facebook (2004) and Twitter (2006) allowed users to post their own images, unedited and unfiltered, and thereby inject them into the national conversation. Applications such as Signal were important so that protesters could share images and video without fear of surveillance and retribution. The speed with which this material could "go viral" nationally and internationally was breathtaking. Very often, the videos, recorded on smartphones, that were placed on these sites spread rapidly and then led television and print reporters to cover the incident. As a result, there were a number of moments when police violence against Black Americans became a major focus of conversation, with more people than ever witnessing the kind of harassment and random violence that the Kerner Commission had reported on in 1968. The #BlackLivesMatter movement was built on top of the foundation of these videos as their demands for bold police reform—which included shifting funding away from police departments toward other kinds of services—depended on the recorded evidence smartphones were providing. With each new video came another round of protest and push for reform.

Online journalism also increased the range of specialized news outlets, including sites that were devoted to covering race. *The Root*, created in 2008, vastly expanded after 2015 when it was purchased by Univision Communications and has provide some of the most hard-hitting stories on issues of racial injustice. In 2020, the *Grio* provided a television network and website also devoted to news and culture about Black Americans.

These all became platforms through which Americans learned, on May 25, 2020, that police in Minneapolis, Minnesota, murdered 46-year-old George Floyd, who was suspected of using counterfeit bills. On a video recording of the attack, Americans could see Officer Derek Chauvin shoving his knee into Floyd's neck for 9 minutes and 29 seconds. As he could be heard saying "I can't breathe," Floyd died. Darnella Frazier, a 17-year-old high school junior, filmed the entire event. Frazier posted it to Facebook and Instagram. She typed in a caption: "They killed him right in front of cup foods over south on 38th and Chicago! No type of sympathy </3 </3. #POLICEBRUTALITY." The video went viral. It was a stunning contrast to the official news release from the police department that read: "Man Dies After Medical Incident During Police Interaction." Frazier's recording belied this misleading headline. "Seriously, read it again knowing what we know," CNN anchor Jake Tapper told his viewers.[12] The video spread at a moment when there was heightened attention to social media as Americans were locked in their homes as a result of the pandemic, clinging to the virtual world for interconnection. Protests took place all over the country, often the first time that many Americans left their homes. Unlike most cases, this time there was justice. Two of the police were convicted and sent to jail.

One of the iconic images from these months would be protesters, holding their cellphones up high with the camera aimed in front of them, confronting police with their weapons and barricades.

The cumulative impact of the citizen videos, combined with the platforms of social media and cable news, was dramatic. The amount of coverage given to police violence was much greater than anything experienced before the 1970s, when the issue had generally remained a subject for civil rights activists and local reformers. By the time that Joe Biden started his presidency in 2021, the topic had become one of the major flashpoints in debates about racial justice. Although there was a strong backlash by "law and order" advocates claiming that the videos distorted stories and that activists were ignoring the real value of what law enforcement did, the issue of racial police violence had moved front and center to the ongoing conversations about race relations in the United States. Amateur videos greatly enhanced the interest and ability of mainstream news organizations to cover the issue. The video evidence provided a strong rebuke to government and police leaders who denied that these were serious problems—or that these kinds of incidents happened at all. The sheer number of stories contradicted familiar claims that such violence was merely a result of "bad apples" and didn't represent any kind of systematic problem. The concept of institutional racism gained new hold in mainstream coverage of policing.

The discussions extended beyond policing. An entire cottage industry of books and articles on the "carceral state" gained widespread attention. Writers such as Michelle Alexander provided penetrating explorations of the ways that private prisons, drug sentencing guidelines, and other factors disproportionately affected the non-white community.[13]

But even the new era revealed major problems and limitations. Despite all the shifts in coverage and trials generated by video evidence of police racism, progress has remained limited at an institutional level.[14] Many officers continue to escape accountability. Large-scale institutional reform in policing has been minimal. Attacks on efforts to "defund the police" have gained significant strength, even pushing a more sympathetic Democratic Party away from the kinds of changes that would be needed to ensure Black Americans did not have to face these threats on a regular basis.

Some of the problem has to do with the modern media ecosystem itself. Despite changes that addressed some of the concerns expressed by the Kerner Commission, the national media remains flawed. A bias toward sensationalism and commercial incentives focuses many networks and print outlets on the images of violence rather than the structural problems that allow them to happen. Producers and editors are often eager to devote more resources to showing, and replaying, the videos of the attacks than on much dryer discussions about how to transform law enforcement so as to diminish these moments. Insufficient attention to rules, organization, procedure, and institutions has created space for backlash efforts which insist that all reformers aim to do is make the streets less safe. Civil rights advocates also note that the interest in these videos can have the unintended effect of objectifying the Black body in ways that enforce and strengthen racist sentiment within the national culture.

The quick attention span culture of the newsroom, and its consumers, also hurts. While there have been numerous flashpoint moments when the nation is focused on the problems of policing, everyone tends to quickly move on. The news cycle thirsts for the new and has the tendency to shift from one story to the next within days if not hours. One major natural disaster or outrageous presidential statement has the capacity to turn reporters away from acts of racism toward something else. This makes it extremely difficult for reformers to keep attention on the topic. Given that institutional reform takes time, the short attention span makes it hard to sustain the kind of public support that would be needed to overhaul law enforcement.

The limitations of the modern media have also made it difficult to focus attention on other questions that concerned the Kerner Commission, including inequality, poverty, and the permanent economic dilapidation of certain pockets of the nation. These are the kinds of issues that receive minimal coverage in the media. There are many reasons for the absences, from the economic interests of the major companies that produce the news to the difficulty of sustaining viewers and readers on these kinds of stories. In a culture that privileges snapshot sensationalism, reporting about the structures that impact our lives has been left to scholars whose work has been able to break into the mainstream.[15]

The news industry itself has been in a period of serious crisis that threatens to weaken its ability to impact public opinion. Many news organizations have been struggling to survive. Local television shows and publications have shut down. National networks such as CNN and MSNBC have undertaken drastic cost-cutting measures to survive declining viewership and commercial revenue. Social media sites such as Facebook and X have lost some of the confidence they once inspired as avenues to disseminate news, with revelations about the practices of the ownership undermining public trust in their ability to serve as a true, unfiltered "public forum." The political polarization of the news industry, where commercial incentives still remain strong, has created siloed worlds of information that make it almost impossible to "shock" the system. Every news story, whether that be the video of a Black American being killed by a policeman or the efforts to tackle a deadly pandemic, are absorbed into the red and blue world of politics. Americans believe different sets of facts, listen to different voices of information, and stick to fundamentally different world views about how to address problems. The fault lines within our news media keep getting worse and erode the potential for important stories to breakthrough in ways that can lead to reform.

As more news shifts to platforms such as TikTok, the challenges will only become magnified. According to the Pew Research Center, an expanding portion of the electorate, including adults, is starting to obtain their news from this platform The share of adults obtaining their news from TikTok has risen to 14% in 2023 from 3% just 3 years earlier.[16] The effects are already apparent. Some analysts, for instance, speculated that the disconnect between strong national economic data and the sour views of younger Americans resulted from the impression given by TikTok messages about what some have called the "Silent Depression."[17] The difficulties posed in reporting on news about race and policing will be equally difficult as this and other social media sites tend to thrive on emotional information that can go viral rather than the most substantive data. Former DNC Chairwoman Donna Brazille warned that social media algorithms thrived on amplifying "the most incendiary thing out there."[18] To be sure, the appeal of these platforms to younger Americans has the potential to keep core issues related to race front and center. But the news will have to be handled with great care given the bias of the technology.

The most inspiring recent coverage of policing has resulted from nonprofit journalistic organizations that have started to take form in recent years. This, many agree, has become the most exciting component of modern journalism. These organizations have been able to raise money to fund long-term investigative reporting and retain the ability to deal with important and controversial issues that might not be lucrative when it comes to advertising or the world of shares and retweets. For example, the Marshall Project, a nonprofit news organization founded in 2014 devoted to the criminal justice system, has produced a series of important stories about these issues. *ProPublica*, created in 2007, has also released a number of pathbreaking pieces on issues such as the counsel poor American defendants are granted in the Mississippi courts and a massive expose of police violence in Indiana.[19] In Houston, a new nonprofit news startup called the American Journalism Project received over $20 million in 2022 to launch one of the largest regional efforts to bring back high-quality local journalistic coverage. The *Texas Tribune*, a member-funded, nonprofit newspaper founded by Evan Smith and Ross Ramsey, has been generating considerable excitement with its high-quality reporting and vision of revitalizing local journalism.

These kinds of nonprofit news organizations offer an excellent path to tackle some of the shortcomings that have prevented the press from doing better in their coverage of these issues. The investment in long-term investigative work offers the best path toward work that will deal with systematic structural and institutional questions at the heart of racism in policing rather than focusing primarily on dramatic and horrifying episodes of violence devoid of this context. Government subsidies would be extremely useful for other forms of journalism, including grants to support the work of nonprofit institutions. The United States has been a laggard relative to comparable nations in supporting the media. The historian Victor Pickard has proposed the creation of a "public media fund" of $30 billion, financed through taxes on media organizations and through other kinds of revenue streams, that could be used to support noncommercial journalism initiatives. As recent precedent, Pickard pointed to New Jersey, where the state government allocated money for the "Civic Information Consortium, that supports local media." Just as important, he writes, there has been long-standing precedent within the United States—including federal subsidies to the postal system, which transported newspapers, in the 18th century as well as the Public Broadcasting Act of 1967—to provide these types of subsidies. Many other comparable, democratic countries such as England and Canada have invested substantially in outlets that provide high-quality reporting.[20]

There is also an urgent need to support recent efforts to combat disinformation. At Stanford University, the History Education Group was created by researchers in 2021 to design interventions that can help to push back against disinformation. Funded through the National Science Foundation, the initiative aimed to rebuild trust in the media. The goal was be to create programs that can be adapted by classrooms around the country. Unfortunately, this and other programs have come under attack from conservative legislators such as Ohio Republican Jim Jordan, and universities have been feeling pressure to scale back for fear of losing federal dollars.[21] It will be important in the coming years that there is strong pushback against these efforts to pressure institutions into cutting back operations that can offer vital steps forward in civics education.

Some of the changes in the media will depend on the willingness of private commercial companies to adjust their own practices, even when there is economic risk. Internal change will be enormously difficult, since the problems within the industry have tended to push executives toward the lowest common denominator. Ever since the news shifted from being a public service on a commercial platform to an entirely commercial enterprise, all the wrong incentives have remained strong. The instinctive response to the struggles facing the industry have been for platforms to offer more sensationalism rather than to invest in higher-quality reporting. Broadcasting, social media, and online publishing are being driven by the chase for advertising dollars, subscribers, and clicks, all of which pushes news outlets toward facilitating and strengthening the kind of intense division that stimulates viewers and readers to tune in. It isn't working. Those who lead within this industry need to consider revamping their product. The answer to the economic struggles facing the industry won't come from doing more of the same but, rather, from doing new things better. There are some examples of what the medium can still accomplish. The magazine *Bolts*, for instance, has been producing first-rate work on the intersection of race and issues such as gerrymandering and voting rights. The U.S. edition of *The Guardian* has taken the industry by storm, receiving strong praise for its wide-angle coverage of domestic American politics. *The American Prospect*, with its explicitly liberal perspective, publishes some of the most thoughtful and analytical pieces on politics within a larger context.[22] From the conservative perspective, *National Affairs* has done the same, elevating the conservative discourse well above brethren in mainstream sites. While it will remain impossible to control the kind of information that goes out to the public, given the ease of spreading information on social media, the major networks and online platforms will continue to have disproportionate influence on the tenor of the industry.

Perhaps more problematic than the nature of and constraints on the press, however, has been the basic problem that the Kerner Commission revolved around: the ways in which institutional racism was deeply entrenched in the body politic. Although the commission rightly recognized that media coverage of these problems mattered very much and that more sophisticated reporting would help shed light on why urban unrest frequently took place around policing, the commissioners underestimated just how much the racist foundations of the United States could survive exposure. Police institutions are built around multiple layers of organization that protect officers from being punished or held accountable—from unions whose priority is to protect members to government officials who do not want their communities portrayed in a negative light. The forces of reaction against #BlackLivesMatter have proven to be fierce, becoming a central talking point for many politicians in the Republican, and even Democratic Party. Tackling the institutional roots of racism has continued to be much more controversial and challenging than addressing legal segregation and voting rights (though here too, racial justice has been under attack).

We certainly would not want to turn back the clock to where the news media was at the time of the Kerner Commission. As a whole, the industry has changed in important ways, giving much more attention over the decades to the problems that commissioners discovered in their tours of the cities, but for which they had to rely on the testimony of local citizens and officials who had witnessed the problems firsthand. Now, racial police violence has been documented, discussed, and elevated into a problem that is recognized as serious in scale and scope.

The limits of what the media can do, and the challenges that we face in the years ahead, are tragic. While the news media since the 1960s has been able to show in much more detail the profound ways in which racism impacts our law enforcement system, we remain and will remain a nation that is "separate and unequal" as a result of white racism until our citizens make institutional reform a top priority. The only way to actually make America great will be for our government officials to reconfigure our basic models of policing so that law-abiding Black Americans don't have to walk the streets afraid that one day they might be a victim captured on video and transmitted around the world.

NOTES

1. I explore some of these themes in "The Media and Race Relations," in *Healing Our Divided Society: Investing in America Fifty Years After the Kerner Report,* eds. Fred Harris and Alan Curtis (Philadelphia: Temple University Press, 2018), 374–384.

2. Julian E. Zelizer, ed., *The Kerner Report: National Advisory Commission on Civil Disorders,* Revised Edition (Princeton, NJ: Princeton University Press, 2016), 316.

3. Alexis C. Madrigal, "When the Revolution was Televised," *The Atlantic,* April 1, 2018.

4. The Kerner Report, 373–375.

5. The Kerner Report, 389.

6. Maya S. Cade, "She Was Oprah Before Oprah," *New York Times,* October 17, 2023.

7. For the best discussion of television, the protests, and the conventions, see Heather Hendershot, *When the News Broke: Chicago 1968 and the Polarizing of America* (Chicago: University of Chicago Press, 2023).

8. *Vice,* "Clayton Patterson on Covering the Tompkins Square Riot of '88," July 3, 2021.

9. Emily Raboteau, "The Long, Vital History of Bystander Recordings," *The New Yorker,* August 11, 2016.

10. Elizabeth Hinton, *America on Fire: The Untold History of Police Violence and Black Rebellion Since the 1960s* (New York: Liveright, 2021).

11. Doug Aamoth, "First Smartphone Turns 20: Fun Facts About Simon," *TIME,* August 18, 2014.

12. Azi Paybarah, "How a Teenager's Video Upended the Police Department's Initial Tale," *New York Times,* April 20, 2021.

13. Michelle Alexander, *The New Jim Crow: Mass Incarceration in the Age of Colorblindness* (New York: New Press, 2000).

14. Brennan Center for Justice, "State Policing Reforms Since George Floyd's Murder," May 21, 2021.

15. See, for examples, Matthew Desmond, *Poverty, by America* (New York: Crown, 2023); Naomi Klein, *The Shock Doctrine: The Rise of Disaster Capitalism* (New York: Metropolitan Books, 2007); Richard Rothstein, *The Color of Law: Forgotten History of How Our Government Segregated America* (New York: Liveright, 2017).

16. Katernina Eva Matsa, "More Americans Are Getting News on TikTok, Bucking the Trend Seen on Most Other Social Media Sites," Pew Research Center, November 15, 2023.

17. Jeanna Smialek and Jim Tankersley, "Want to Know What's Bedeviling Biden? Tik Tok Economics May Hold Clues," *New York Times,* November 17, 2023.

18. Carly Thomas, "Bill Maher Shares His Concerns on 'Real Time' About the Way Information is Spread on TikTok," *Hollywood Reporter,* November 18, 2023.

19. Caleb Bedillion, "Mississippi Courts Won't Say How They Provide Lawyers for Poor Clients," *ProPublica,* September 17, 2023; Ken Armstrong, "Another Police Office Pleads Guilty to Punching Handcuffed Man," *ProPublica,* April 14, 2023.

20. Victor Pickard, *Democracy Without Journalism? Confronting the Misinformation Society* (New York: Oxford University Press, 2019), 136–163.

21. Naomi Nix, Cat Zakrzewksi, and Joseph Menn, "Misinformation Research Is Buckling Under GOP Legal Attacks," *Washington Post,* September 25, 2023.

22. Perry Bacon, "7 News Outlets Reimagining Political Journalism in Smart Ways," *Washington Post,* May 23, 2023.

CHAPTER 30

Race and Media in a Polarized Society

Robert Faris

In 1968, the Kerner Commission condemned American news media coverage of race relations as marred by "sensationalism, inaccuracies, and distortions" and concluded that the media "failed to report adequately on the causes and consequences of civil disorders and the underlying problems of race relations."

News media in America has undergone drastic changes since that time, and while there are positive signs of progress in the past half century, where progress has occurred it has been frustratingly slow, and elsewhere coverage of race in America has deteriorated. Websites promoting White supremacy have taken root online, talk radio shows broadcast negative stereotypes of minorities, and thinly veiled racist content is not uncommon on news and opinion shows on cable television. While many in America are now better informed and more attuned to race-related issues than in the 1960s, many are now regularly exposed to more distorted and inaccurate portrayals of the lives and challenges of minorities in America, and some to open racism and xenophobia.

Perceptions and opinions about race and identity are the primary division in American politics,[1] and this division is sustained by media structures that evolved to serve the political factions engaged in this fight. Here I describe how promoting misinformation about the state of racism in the United States is a key—perhaps essential—narrative element that holds together the conservative movement and that this served as an important motivating factor in the formation of Right-wing media. Additionally, many journalists acting in good faith and according to the prevailing standards of objective media have helped to perpetuate misleading narratives about the role of race in American politics.

Opinions and perceptions of race in America are embedded in the political, social, and media structures that have evolved since the time of the Kerner Commission and become entrenched in our highly polarized society. To speak of "the media" as a coherent set of institutions and actors is no longer a useful abstraction, and to consider the opportunities and impediments for better informing citizens about race in America, we must grapple with the splintering of media into different factions, operating by different rules, serving different ends, and presenting profoundly different takes on the ongoing role of racism in America.

Radio, television, and newspapers still play a vital role in American media systems, but the profusion of digitally mediated news and social media offers news consumers far greater choice in where and how they get their news. Audiences now play a larger role in filtering, curating, and amplifying stories and narratives that resonate with them. There is still some validity to the notion that coverage of news is dictated by a set of agenda-setting elites, but with the shifts in the media landscape, news leaders have considerably less influence over the way Americans understand and interpret political and social events. The biggest structural change in American media has been the separation of the public sphere into two distinct media and information systems.

Although many decades in the making,[2] the emergence of a separate media system designed to serve conservatives in America accelerated in the 1980s with the launch of Rush Limbaugh's radio show. Limbaugh, perhaps the most influential figure in Right-wing media, set the tone for this emerging sector, using racism, xenophobia, and misogyny to attract an audience of predominantly working-class White listeners attracted to his confrontational style, hyper-partisanship, and sensationalistic diatribes against liberals.[3] Fox News, launched in 1996, rose to become the most viewed cable news network in America by attracting a decidedly conservative partisan audience. The marquee stars of Fox News including Bill O'Reilly, Sean Hannity, Glenn Beck, Tucker Carlson, and others have fueled racial divisions and activated racial resentment. Like many conservative media sources, Fox News has generally been careful to avoid explicit racism, relying instead on dog whistles and coded language. This allows them to cater to audiences with strong ties to White identity while not offending conservatives who do not want to be a party to explicit racism.

The emergence of conservative media as a distinct counterpoint to traditional media outlets facilitated the cleavage of audiences into opposing media spheres. But viewing American media as a polarized system without also recognizing the stark asymmetry overlooks a central factor that defines and shapes American media, politics, and race relations. The media organizations that are favored among those in the center and left of the political spectrum are predominantly grounded in the journalistic norms and practices developed in the 20th century along with the professionalization of journalism and its valuing of the pursuit of accuracy and objectivity. Here I use the term "objective media" to refer to those that follow these norms, to emphasis the juxtaposition to "partisan media"—those media organizations with a stronger commitment to making a partisan case over a comprehensive, fair, and accurate rendering of the facts.

Conservative media, developed as a counterpart to what was perceived as a liberal bias in media, was conceived of and has thrived as a distinctly partisan enterprise. This means that Right-wing media is more insular than traditional media in that it gains no traction outside of conservative audiences. Relatedly, the ideas and perspectives that garner the most attention in conservative media are more extreme, catering to a narrow range of news consumers.[4] With partisan coverage comes a greater use of sensationalistic storylines and content that induces emotional responses and outrage.[5] Partisan media is also more vulnerable to the spread of misleading and false narratives. Researchers have consistently found misinformation to be more prevalent in Right-wing media than in the center and left. The root of this issue is not one of media literacy, education, or moral character. Left to their own devices, liberal audiences are just as prone to favor stories that satisfy partisan urges. The attraction to partisan talking points and the vulnerability to believing falsehoods is inherently human and can be found across the political spectrum. The difference is that the partisan content is a relatively small part of media coverage in the center and left and is overshadowed and constrained by the coverage of journalists and legacy media organizations committed to objectivity, while in conservative reaches of the media ecosystem, partisan media is the product.

Underlying these well-documented and easily observable differences in media behavior are different media cultures and norms that govern the behavior of actors and shape the reporting and narratives that garner attention. In objective media, the path toward advancement for journalists is getting it right and applying critical coverage to all without fear or favor. Fabricating stories or intentionally misleading audiences is grounds for dismissal. This, of course, does not prevent mistakes, but the norms, incentives, and systems of accountability are intended to promote accuracy and objectivity, and to correct errors. In contrast, partisan media is guided by the needs and exigencies of social identity: highlighting and crafting narratives that hold together the collective, advance the in group, and diminish the out group. In this environment, there is no upside to telling hard truths unless they are recognized as playing a greater role in serving the needs and strength of the community.

It is difficult to overstate the influence that these fundamentally different media paradigms have on the relationships among politicians, media, and citizens. In the objective paradigm, media serves as a check on the behavior of politicians by reporting on their poor governing choices, unmet promises, and false claims. The relationship between politicians and media is often antagonistic and media take great pride in holding public officials to account. In this paradigm, citizens are exposed to criticism of the leaders they have backed and are subject to disappointment and dissonance when they learn that they have been misinformed or let down. In the partisan media paradigm, media serves more as a mouthpiece for the political coalition, backing the leaders in conflicts against the other party and shoring up support among partisans. Criticism of in-group leaders is generally about whether they are sufficiently loyal to the cause. This could be related to differences in the party platform and adherence to the overarching party narrative.[6] Consistently missing from this equation is accountability journalism, holding political leaders accountable for their performance. This political information environment tolerates and rationalizes extreme political behavior as exemplified by the antidemocratic and authoritarian speech and actions of Donald Trump and his supporters. As columnist Jamelle Bouie describes the dynamics: "The key issue for conservative voters and conservative media isn't whether a Republican politician can pass legislation or manage a government or bridge political divides; the key question is whether a Republican politician is sufficiently committed to the ideology, whatever that means in the moment."[7]

Another key feature of this asymmetrically polarized environment is that Democrats can more easily support Republican positions and defend making compromises with Republicans. Indeed, they may be rewarded for this if it is framed in the public discourse as working toward the greater good rather than just a loss to the other side and a betrayal of the cause. Yet Republicans have no incentive to compromise with Democrats and every incentive to thwart any Democratic initiative. If Democrats are in favor of a government program to improve health, fix bridges, or enhance competitiveness, Republicans will be opposed. If liberals seek to acknowledge and address systemic racism in this country, they can be assured of Republican opposition and count on Right-wing media to argue why it is harmful for the country. The future of government action to address economic and racial disparities in the United States with bipartisan support is not promising.

Many have pointed to the scourge of disinformation and hate on social media and the perils to our democracy and governance systems as more people turn to untrustworthy sources of information to understand the world. This is a legitimate concern that appears to be only getting worse. The recent changes at X (formerly Twitter) have included the reversal of efforts to purge the platform of disinformation and abusive content as well as welcoming back many prominent users who had been booted from the platform for spouting hateful speech, including White supremacists.[8] While acknowledging the problems, we should not exaggerate the role of technology in the spread of bad information. The problems with disinformation and the distorting influence of partisan media predate the Internet and tend to be most acute in conservative media both online and off.[9] Were the Internet alone the source of the problem, we should see a more uniform problem across the political spectrum. And while social media is vulnerable to manipulation, it is often embedded in broader media ecosystems with shared sources of information, authorities, and epistemic standards.

Just as our political behavior is guided by our social identity, the way in which we obtain and process new information—political or otherwise—is a social process.[10] Our understanding of the world is more fundamentally a function of our political identity and less a matter of individual discernment.[11] What we know and believe depends in large part on the media systems that we opt into, media systems that filter, curate, and amplify stories and narratives, that elevate certain voices and media organizations over others, that determine who serves as an authoritative voice, and decide what constitutes knowledge. This is particularly salient in our highly polarized political environment where trust in media is highly correlated with party affiliation.[12] The most trusted sources of news and political information for one side are viewed as untrustworthy by other. This means that partisans are effectively buffered from being influenced by media from the other side. Spending more time with opposing views will not fix this, as it is not a question of exposure as much as processing and interpretation. Politically engaged citizens are made aware of what the other side is saying, as this is now a core part of reporting the news, whether on the left, center, or right. The media reports and arguments from the other side are repackaged, critiqued, and contextualized, and, as needed, are discounted and refuted.

A rather depressing but likely accurate depiction is that many White Americans are aligned with the conservative movement through simple ethnocentrism[13] and are informed by a media system that has evolved to rationalize, justify, and reinforce this social affiliation and to defend against any evidence and facts that might weaken this commitment. Changing partisan hearts and minds through more effective journalism is not impossible but faces deeply entrenched institutional obstacles.

In 1968, the Kerner Commission report notably stated that "Our Nation is moving toward two societies, one black, one white—separate and unequal." Addressing racial disparities remains unresolved. A distinct but related divide in our society has come into sharper focus compared to the 1960s. We have come to occupy two distinct epistemic systems that promote and disseminate fundamentally different information and perspectives about the nature of race relations in the country. The prevailing attitude among Republicans is that structural racism is not an issue and hence any efforts to address the persistent problems associated with racism are misguided and unwarranted. This attitude, in fact, may be necessary to maintain the current coalition on the right. The dominant view among Democratic voters, including most White Democrats, cuts in the opposite direction. These views on race in America reflect the prevailing narratives in their respective media spheres, one of unfinished work to address the oppression that has held back Black advancement, and one that depicts efforts to understand and address racial biases as an unjust distraction from and impediment to addressing the problems of all Americans.

Following the election of Barack Obama in 2008, attitudes about race in America have only become more polarized and more salient. The election of a Black president prompted a backlash by many White Americans.[14] The autopsy conducted by the Republican National Committee in the aftermath of Mitt Romney's loss to Barack Obama in 2012 recommended that the party reach out more to minority voters. The party instead moved in the opposite direction as Donald Trump won the party nomination and the 2016 general election by conducting a racially divisive campaign that activated and exploited White identity. Studies show that high levels of racial resentment proved to be the factor most associated with support for Trump.[15]

The rise of Trump was both a cause and a consequence of a more highly racialized political climate. It is also true that he found a niche in a party that has fostered racial divisions for many decades, predating even the political upheaval of the Civil Rights Movement of the 1960s and the many chapters that followed, such as Nixon's Southern strategy, Ronald Reagan's invocation of welfare queens, Gingrich's reference to Obama as the food stamp president, and the Willie Horton ads featured in the 1988 George H. W. Bush campaign. A Pew Research Center study shows that the divide in opinions about race in America widened further in the 4 years of the Trump presidency. When asked whether it is a lot more difficult to be a Black person than a White person in this country, 74% of Biden supporters agreed versus 9% of Trump voters. The big shift was among Democrats, which increased from 44% to 74% in 4 years. Agreement among Trump supporters fell from 11% to 9%.[16]

The issue of race was always close to the forefront in the 2016 election. A core question that has animated media coverage and academic research is whether Trump's base was motivated more by economic stagnation or racial resentment. Sides, Tessler, and Vavreck make a strong case that racial attitudes among Whites are a stronger factor than economic anxiety when evaluated separately.[17] Cramer argues that when considering perceptions of deservingness and injustice, economics and race are not separable.[18] It is not difficult to see how the two are intertwined and how economic stress might activate ethnocentrism.

Heather McGhee describes how White-run governments in the South drained public pools and dismantled public services rather than open them up to Blacks.[19] She lays out how attitudes about race distort attitudes about public policy by fostering zero-sum thinking, and how this became a catalyst to change opinions about economic policies. Essentially, White backlash provided support for the Reagan-era free-market push that cut programs that benefited Black families. The merging and distortion of culture and economics has long been a part of conservative politics and reinforced by media coverage. The public grievances of the Tea Party movement that emerged in 2009 were ostensibly focused on government debt. Yet researchers found that the members of the movement were not distinct in their concern over public borrowing but were religious social conservatives who were overwhelmingly White and "had a low regard for immigrants and blacks long before Barack Obama was president, and they still do."[20]

There is a compelling reason that conservatives benefit from a political dividing line defined by culture—essentially race and religion—rather than economic inequality more broadly. The conservative movement in America as currently constituted relies on a coalition of social conservatives, largely White and Christian, and small government, fiscally conservative voters. Baked into this coalition is a potentially disruptive conflict over economic policy, pitting working-class voters who are disillusioned with neoliberal economic policies against those advocating for drastic cuts to government programs that benefit the poor and working class. As long as the culture wars remain at the forefront of political debates, it is easier to ensure that economic policies and outcomes are viewed through the distorting lens of race and identity. This strategy is manifest in the manufactured controversies related to race, such as opposition to teaching critical race theory in American schools. Similarly, we see increasing attacks on educational programs that cover race and growing opposition to diversity, equity, and inclusion programs.[21] Perspectives on race are a potential source of tension within the conservative movement between those who favor overt racial conflict and those who prefer to say it is not about race. The rhetorical cover for this is to argue that bringing up the history of racism in America is itself the source of racial conflict, a stance that is tied to the notion that racism is no longer an important issue in the country. Continuing political fights that exploit the biases and attitudes of White identifiers, while also offering a measure of deniability for those who are uncomfortable with a focus on race, will help to sustain the conservative coalition.

Adam Serwer offers a trenchant and insightful critique of the role that media has played in helping Americans to avoid an uncomfortable reckoning with racism in American life and politics.[22] He writes: "But even as once-acceptable forms of bigotry have become unacceptable to express overtly, white Americans remain politically dominant enough to shape media coverage in a manner that minimizes obvious manifestations of prejudice, such as backing a racist candidate, as something else entirely." He argues that the incentive in media to describe racism as something else spans the political spectrum: "The argument for the innocence of Trump's backers finds purchase across ideological lines: white Democrats looking for votes from working-class whites, white Republicans who want to tar Democrats as elitists, white leftists who fear that identity politics stifles working-class solidarity, and white Trumpists seeking to weaponize white grievances. But the impetus here is not just ideological, but personal and commercial. No one wants to think of his family, friends, lovers, or colleagues as racist. And no one wants to alienate potential subscribers, listeners, viewers, or fans, either."

Telling the truth about race in America is tied to telling the truth about economics and class, and the electoral success of conservative America depends on avoiding this. As we look toward possible solutions, there is no clear path toward reform from within partisan media as long as attempts by media organizations to moderate will result in smaller audiences and financial loss and if individual efforts are more likely to be met with punishment than reward. This collective-action problem in partisan media means that we need to look elsewhere for effective responses.

A natural place to look for help would be in regulatory changes, perhaps following the lead of European countries that outlaw hate speech and require Internet companies to be more aggressive in limiting harmful speech.[23] Regulatory responses in the United States, however, will be limited by the country's deeply held commitment to free speech and the reliance on the marketplace of ideas to deal with problems related to political speech. This is unlikely to change, particularly in the current political and legislative environment. There is dissatisfaction with the status quo, and calls for action come from both sides of the aisle, but there is no consensus over the nature of the problem or what needs to be done. Liberals tend to favor expanding efforts to curtail disinformation and harmful speech while conservatives tend to favor fewer restrictions on speech.

There are incremental regulatory steps that would help. Requiring greater transparency of Internet companies into content moderation practices would improve our ability to craft better responses and would provide an incentive for companies to deal with harmful speech more effectively.[24] Ensuring that researchers have access to data will promote greater public accountability.[25] Another possible step would be to remove liability protections for Internet companies that encourage online abuses and do not make a reasonable effort to address online harms, which could be enacted without stipulating where lines are drawn in making content moderation decisions.[26] Enhanced regulation can help to chip away at the most egregious forms of disinformation and harmful speech while still allowing private companies to decide what is and is not appropriate on their platforms—an imperfect system with no obviously better alternatives.

An area where positive change is possible is in strengthening the segments of media that are committed to objective reporting. On the media production side of the equation, there is much work to be done to improve the level of public discourse over issues of race and equity in America. We need more and better coverage of race and equity issues. This will require greater investments in media organizations devoted to this mission, such as the Marshall Project and *The Root*, among others. It will also require more progress in hiring and promoting minority journalists and leaders in large media organizations.

One significant step within the reach of those who seek to find solutions would be to reduce the laundering of propaganda through objective media, limiting the ability of partisan media to set the media agenda, and countering the framing of real-world events in misleading ways. Just as partisan media is vulnerable to disinformation, objective media has been guilty at times of validating and amplifying partisan propaganda. One example of this is the way that the Trump campaign in 2016 effectively hacked the institutional playbook of election coverage in his favor; media coverage related to Trump skewed toward immigration, a topic that Trump pushed, and coverage related to Clinton focused on her emails, a topic that arguably led to her defeat.[27]

This ties into an active debate about how to fairly and accurately cover the actions and provocations of conservative politicians. Central to this debate is the way in which objectivity is understood and operationalized. Wesley Lowery, a proponent of change, frames the issue in the following way: "Since American journalism's pivot many decades ago from an openly partisan press to a model of professed objectivity, the mainstream has allowed what it considers objective truth to be decided almost exclusively by white reporters and their mostly white bosses. And those selective truths have been calibrated to avoid offending the sensibilities of white readers. On opinion pages, the contours of acceptable public debate have largely been determined through the gaze of white editors."[28]

In practice, neutrality has been used as a stand-in for objectivity. Covering the arguments from both sides of political disputes has its merits, but is not the same as objectivity. When respected media organizations provide both sides of an argument, they risk lending credence to false narratives and thereby misleading readers. Letting readers draw their own conclusions based on the facts is appealing, but research has shown that balanced coverage can distort public discourse.[29] Completing the transition away from balance toward objectivity will not be simple. Clearly stating the facts while remaining impartial may be impossible in our asymmetric political environment. Without the anchor of neutrality and balance, the pursuit of objectivity requires discernment and judgment, straying into more subjective ground in the pursuit of objectivity. A challenge for media will be to give a full and fair consideration to the perspectives of all sides of political events while not allowing partisan media to set the media agenda and in a way that helps their readers accurately evaluate the veracity of political arguments. It is unclear how different media organizations will settle on this issue, but it bears the potential to significantly change how race and power are covered, perhaps for the better.

None of this is going to get any easier. The American media industry is likely to undergo further major changes in the coming years. Covering the costs of investigative reporting will continue to challenge this vital part of covering current events while producing content using AI becomes increasingly more viable. One aspect to monitor is the technology race in which watchdogs use AI-generated content to detect content introduced by malicious actors while malicious actors use the same technologies to elude detection. Of likely greater importance will be how humans adapt their standards and tools of quality control to the use of these tools. One possible outcome is that the advent of more automated reporting and curating of information will result in greater reliance on human systems and expertise to separate fact from fiction and a further distancing between those media paradigms that try to get things right and those that put more emphasis on producing effective partisan talking points. Another key question deserving of attention is how these changes will influence the ability of media organizations to successfully maintain and attract new audiences, particularly younger people,[30] and whether this will facilitate a further splintering of media audiences and erosion of trust in media. The questions of how to improve public understanding of political and social events in an asymmetrically polarized world, and, at the core, how to fully and accurately report on issues of race and identity, are still unresolved.

NOTES

1. Lee Drutman, "How Race and Identity Became the Central Dividing Line in American Politics," *Vox*, August 30, 2016, https://www.vox.com/polyarchy/2016/8/30/12697920/race-dividing-american-politics.

2. Nicole Hemmer, *Messengers of the Right: Conservative Media and the Transformation of American Politics* (Philadelphia: University of Pennsylvania Press, 2016).

3. Alex Shephard, "Rush Limbaugh Made America Worse," *The New Republic*, November 28, 2023, https://newrepublic.com/article/161405/rush-limbaugh-racist-sexist-conservative-media-worse.

4. Yochai Benkler, Robert Faris, and Hal Roberts, *Network Propaganda: Manipulation, Disinformation, and Radicalization in American Politics* (New York: Oxford University Press, 2018).

5. Jeffrey J. Berry and Sarah Sobieraj, *The Outrage Industry: Political Opinion Media and the New Incivility* (New York: Oxford University Press, 2013).

6. In *Network Propaganda*, we describe this dynamic as the propaganda feedback loop.

7. Jamelle Bouie, "The Only Questions to Ask About These House republicans," *New York Times*, October 20, 2023, https://www.nytimes.com/2023/10/20/opinion/house-republicans-jordan-gaetz-greene.html.

8. David Gilbert, "Elon Musk Is Turning Twitter Into a Haven for Nazis," *Vice*, November 29, 2022, https://www.vice.com/en/article/n7zm9q/elon-musk-twitter-nazis-white-supremacy.

9. R. Kelly Garrett and Robert M. Bond, "Conservatives' Susceptibility to Political Misperceptions," *Science Advances* 7, no. 23 (2021): eabf1234.

10. It is long recognized that for most people, their primary political attachments are not to particular policies or ideologies but to social groups. Philip E. Converse, "The Nature of Belief Systems in Mass Publics," *Critical Review* 18, no. 1–3 (2006): 1–74. (Originally published in David E. Apter, ed., *Ideology and Discontent* (London: Free Press of Glencoe, 1964), 206–261.)

11. Donal P. Green, Bradley Palmquist, and Eric Schickler, *Partisan Hearts and Minds: Political Parties and the Social Identities of Voters* (New Haven, CT: Yale University Press, 2004).

12. Mark Jurkowitz et al., "U.S. Media Polarization and The 2020 Election: A Nation Divided," Pew Research Center, January 24, 2024, https://www.pewresearch.org/journalism/2020/01/24/u-s-media-polarization-and-the-2020-election-a-nation-divided.

13. Donald R. Kinder and Cindy D. Kam, *Us Against Them: Ethnocentric Foundations of American Opinion* (Chicago: University of Chicago Press, 2010).

14. Michael Tesler, *Post-Racial or Most-Racial? Race and Politics in the Obama Era* (Chicago: University of Chicago Press, 2020); Jamelle Bouie, "How Trump Happened," *Slate Magazine*, March 13, 2016, https://www.slate.com/articles/news_and_politics/cover_story/2016/03/how_donald_trump_happened_racism_against_barack_obama.html.

15. John Sides, Michael Tesler, and Lynn Vavreck *Identity Crisis: The 2016 Presidential Campaign and the Battle for the Meaning of America* (Princeton, NJ: Princeton University Press, 2019).

16. Pew Research Center, "Voters' Attitudes About Race and Gender Are Even More Divided Than in 2016," September 10, 2020, https://www.pewresearch.org/politics/2020/09/10/voters-attitudes-about-race-and-gender-are-even-more-divided-than-in-2016.

17. Sides et al., *Identity Crisis*.

18. Katherine Cramer, "Understanding the Role of Racism in Contemporary US Public Opinion," *Annual Review of Political Science* 23, no. 1 (2020): 153–69, https://doi.org/10.1146/annurev-polisci-060418-042842.

19. Heather McGhee, *The Sum of Us: What Racism Costs Everyone and How We Can Prosper Together* (New York: One World, 2022).

20. David E. Campbell and Robert D. Putnam, "Crashing the Tea Party," *New York Times*, August 17, 2011, https://www.nytimes.com/2011/08/17/opinion/crashing-the-tea-party.html.

21. April Simpson, "Diversity, Equity and Inclusion in the Crosshairs in GOP-Controlled States," Center for Public Integrity, March 10, 2023, https://publicintegrity.org/education/diversity-equity-and-inclusion-in-the-crosshairs-in-gop-controlled-states.

22. Adam Serwer, "The Nationalist's Delusion," *The Atlantic*, November 17, 2017, https://www.theatlantic.com/politics/archive/2017/11/the-nationalists-delusion/546356.

23. Chris Riley, "EU Advances Groundbreaking Law for Online Platforms - U.S. Lawmakers Should Pay Attention," R Street Institute, December 14, 2020, https://www.rstreet.org/commentary/eu-advances-groundbreaking-law-for-online-platforms-u-s-lawmakers-should-pay-attention.

24. Susan Ness, "Platform Regulation Should Focus on Transparency, Not Content," *Slate Magazine*, December 2, 2020, https://slate.com/technology/2020/12/platform-regulation-european-commission-transparency.html

25. Coalition for Independent Technology Research, https://independenttechresearch.org.

26. Danielle Keats Citron, "How to Fix Section 230," *Boston University Law Review*, 103, no. 3 (2023): 713–61, https://www.bu.edu/bulawreview/files/2023/10/CITRON.pdf.

27. Benkler et al., *Network Propaganda*.

28. Wesley Lowery, "A Reckoning Over Objectivity, Led by Black Journalists," *New York Times*, June 23, 2020, https://www.nytimes.com/2020/06/23/opinion/objectivity-black-journalists-coronavirus.html.

29. Maxwell Boykoff and Jules Boykoff, "Balance as Bias: Global Warming and the US Prestige Press," *Global Environmental Change* 14, no. 2 (2004): 125–36, https://doi.org/10.1016/j.gloenvcha.2003.10.001.

30. Nic Newman, "Young People Are Abandoning News Websites—New Research Reveals Scale of Challenge to Media," The Conversation, June 13, 2023, https://theconversation.com/young-people-are-abandoning-news-websites-new-research-reveals-scale-of-challenge-to-media-207659.

CHAPTER 31

Toward a More Evidence-Based Policy Agenda

Justin Milner

INTRODUCTION

Social progress in America has never been linear. It can feel sometimes that our journey is akin to looking through a kaleidoscope. In one view, our nation has witnessed remarkable advancements since the era of the Kerner Commission. For instance, the dramatic strides in educational attainment at the high school and college levels, life expectancy, and decreasing poverty levels represent important steps forward.

However, when you twist the kaleidoscope to its side a bit, the words of the Kerner Commission's report, penned over half a century ago, remain strikingly relevant today. Persistent issues like racial disparities in economic opportunities and the widening wealth gap signal the vast divide in the American experience. A justice system that incarcerates millions of Americans and disrupts the lives of millions of others, with dramatically disproportionate effects for Black Americans, has only worsened since the Kerner Report. Moreover, the recent surge in social activism highlights ongoing struggles for equity and justice, mirroring past calls for societal reform.

As much as ever, we know that we must do better in order to minimize injustice and maximize opportunity in our country. And to improve the lives of Americans, we have to figure out what works. This goal—one that falls under the heading of evidence-based policy—accords with the aims of the Kerner Commission. At the heart of their findings was a simple yet profound directive: amplify what works in addressing social issues and minimize ineffective approaches. This objective remains as pertinent as ever.

The good news: In the last several decades, we have made real progress on the pursuit of a more evidence-based policy agenda. The public and nonprofit sectors see the value of data more than ever. We are starting to create proof points of how we can test and learn more about how to improve lives of kids, families, and communities and to build a stronger research base upon which to build an outcomes-oriented social policy agenda. However, the reality is that too few Americans—especially those from disadvantaged communities—benefit from these advances.

This chapter aims to offer a brief synopsis of the state of evidence-based policy in the United States and offer a way forward. First, it will detail a few examples of where we have advanced on evidence-based policymaking in recent years. Next, it will outline a few areas of social policy where progress in evidence-building has taken hold. Finally, it will argue that we need to move toward the next frontier of evidence-based policy, finding a way to scale proven programs and insights to more significantly move the needle on social outcomes in the United States.

ADVANCEMENTS IN EVIDENCE-BASED POLICYMAKING

At its core, evidence-based policy focuses on the use of rigorous research methods to build credible evidence about "what works" and direct resources toward effective interventions.[1] The theory of change behind evidence-based policy is deceptively simple: harness data to design interventions and policies to improve outcomes; collect and analyze data to evaluate whether the interventions deliver such outcomes (and, often, at what cost); and use the insights and findings from the evaluation to inform policy, program, practice, and budget decisions.[2] In reality, none of these steps is simple.

In recent years, there has been a notable escalation in the commitment to rigorous evaluation within the realms of public and philanthropic funding, marking a significant development to support evidence-based policymaking. This heightened investment underscores a growing consensus on the value of causal research, particularly randomized controlled trials (RCTs), in shaping effective social policies. The number of RCTs across all fields has increased dramatically in the last 30 years.[3] The philanthropy Arnold Ventures alone has funded over 120 RCTs of social programs in the last 10 years.[4]

In this realm, causal research, particularly RCTs, stands as a gold standard. RCTs offer several advantages, including robustness in establishing causality, replicability, and clarity in outcomes. Of course, these methods are not without limitations. Not all situations lend themselves to randomization, RCTs often grapple with external validity issues and mask variation in average treatment effects, and they may not capture the nuanced complexities of real-world scenarios.[5] But they often provide the clearest lens by which to establish impact and offer a stronger sense of confidence about what works. By prioritizing such empirical methodologies, funding entities are helping to build a more scientifically grounded policy landscape, where interventions are not only theoretically sound but also empirically validated for real-world impact.

This trend toward rigorous evaluation signifies a paradigm shift toward a more evidence-driven approach in addressing complex social issues. The approach reflects an evolving understanding that policy effectiveness hinges on data-driven and empirical insights. The last 20 years have seen important steps to build stronger data systems, design interventions rooted in stronger theory, and test and learn about their efficacy. A few developments are worth highlighting in particular.

Evidence Act. The Foundations for Evidence-Based Policymaking Act of 2018, commonly known as the Evidence Act, marked a significant legislative milestone.[6] The law built upon the Government Performance and Results Act of 1993 (GPRA), which helped initiate evidence building at the federal level by creating a performance planning and reporting framework.[7] The bipartisan Evidence Act mandates federal agencies to develop and implement evidence-building plans, significantly enhancing the role of empirical data in policy formation. A critical component of the Evidence Act is its focus on open data access, designed to facilitate transparency and enable comprehensive policy analysis by various stakeholders. Additionally, the act mandates the appointment of chief evaluation officers in federal agencies. These officers are responsible for integrating rigorous evaluation methods into program development and execution, ensuring that government interventions are grounded in robust empirical evidence. This requirement represents a systematic effort to bridge the gap between research and practical policy implementation.

While some of the potential of the Evidence Act has taken hold, full implementation still has not taken place, much like GPRA.[8] Some of the main limitations have been a lack of capacity within agencies and Office of Management and Budget to develop and implement guidance on how to fulfill requirements of the act. Further, agencies generally lack the resources required—and were never guided clearly by the Evidence Commission—to support the tasks and duty expectations related to the act.[9]

Learning Agendas. As part of the Evidence Act, most major federal agencies were required to develop learning agendas. These documents represent roadmaps for articulating and answering key questions that are relevant to the programs, policies, and regulations of an agency. Over 20-plus agencies have developed learning agendas to guide their work, and the Evaluation Officer Council currently shares all the plans on a public website, a significant step forward in opening up agencies to be more transparent about the direction of their research aims.[10] As others have noted, it is likely that the process of developing the agendas is as valuable as the products and can ideally strengthen relationships between producers and potential users of evidence.[11]

Tiered-Evidence Grantmaking. Tiered-evidence grantmaking is a systematic approach to funding social programs and interventions based on the strength of evidence supporting their effectiveness. This model typically categorizes programs into tiers, with the top tiers representing interventions with the strongest, most rigorous evidence, often derived from methods like RCTs. The goal of tiered-evidence grantmaking is to allocate funding more effectively by prioritizing programs that have demonstrated significant impact, thereby increasing the likelihood of achieving desired outcomes in various social sectors.[12] Tiered-evidence programs have taken hold across at least five programs and have allocated billions of dollars through the framework.[13] The models are not without fault. In discussing the passage of the Families First child welfare law, Fitzsimmons stated that the tiered approach they included was a "ladder without lower rungs, leaving many organizations without the ability to climb it" and that without creating "space for joining and ascending, and relying instead on the established and dominant, we limit our ability to develop new solutions to our most pressing challenges."[14] Finding ways to complement the evidence-building components of tiered grantmaking alongside technical assistance for organizations to ascend is an important future aspiration. That said, as the GAO noted, "the lessons agencies have learned in implementing tiered evidence grants could be applied to other federal grant programs that use evidence and evaluation requirements as a condition for receipt of federal grant funds."[15]

Evidence Clearinghouses. Evidence clearinghouses have emerged as important summative tools to reflect the state of knowledge in social science, from research from tiered grantmaking and elsewhere. They serve as repositories that compile, assess, and disseminate research findings on the efficacy of various programs and policies. By providing centralized access to evaluated and rated programs and interventions, clearinghouses like the What Works Clearinghouse in education and the Home Visiting Evidence of Effectiveness in health care can play a role in guiding decision-making. They offer policymakers and practitioners a consolidated, accessible source of information, enabling informed choices about which interventions to implement or fund. The rigor in these clearinghouses' methodologies for reviewing and rating evidence—which, admittedly, vary quite a bit—ensures that only interventions backed by substantial empirical support are recommended, helping at least to inform policy decisions.

In reality, evidence clearinghouses also present very real limitations. One significant challenge is ensuring the comprehensiveness of the evidence they compile. Given the vast scope of research conducted across various policy areas, it can be challenging to include and update all relevant studies, potentially leading to gaps in the information provided. Additionally, the criteria used to assess the quality of evidence can vary, leading to inconsistencies in how different interventions are evaluated and compared. Another limitation is the potential for a lag between the latest research findings and their incorporation into the clearinghouse, which can affect the timeliness of the information available to policymakers and practitioners. Lastly, while these clearinghouses are invaluable for understanding what works, they often provide less insight into how programs can be effectively implemented in diverse contexts, which is a critical component of scaling interventions successfully.[16]

EXAMPLES OF EVIDENCE BUILDING IN KEY POLICY DOMAINS

Beyond the larger areas of movement in evidence-based policymaking, there have also been important advancements through the accumulation of evidence. Below, a few of those areas are highlighted as examples of key endpoints of investments in research: the identification of programs, policies, and interventions that have demonstrated efficacy in rigorous evaluation in multiple places. While this type of replication remains rare, it is a reminder that it is in fact possible to reach this point.

Sector-Based Employment Strategies

One area is in sector-based employment strategies. In the past, there have been many attempts to develop job training programs that are both relatively cost-effective and deliver meaningful impacts for low-income individuals. Research often found that the programs could help people get jobs, but that their earnings were not appreciably greater.[17] However, in recent years, rigorous evaluations have identified sector-based models—where people received trainings for high-demand jobs in existing sectors like health, IT, and manufacturing—that have driven significant long-term earnings increases for job seekers without 4-year college degrees. With the support of government and philanthropic funders like Arnold Ventures, a number of programs have all undertaken long-term RCTs of their programs and have shown such models can be effective.

The programs do not look exactly the same, often focus on different industries, and have different types of support. For example, the program Year Up provided 6 months of full-time skills training in the IT and financial services sectors, followed by 6-month internships; Project Quest focused on a range of supports to help complete training programs at community colleges; Per Scholas, as part of the WorkAdvance study, focused on largely in-house IT training across 15 weeks. Despite the variation, these programs can move the needle in important ways. A review of the evidence of such programs found that they can help participants gain entry in higher-paying jobs in key sectors with higher wages.[18] For these programs, participants were found to earn significantly higher earnings than their control counterparts. And over time, these differences add up. Further, in terms of policy relevance, these programs were also found to be cost effective. For example, a cost-benefit analysis of Year Up found net benefits of $38,484 (mainly from the large participant earnings gains) that substantially outweigh the net program costs of $23,135.[19]

Pre-K–12 Learning

Another area where the evidence base has advanced in recent years is in tutoring. Longstanding educational disparities between and within socioeconomic groups were only magnified over the course of the pandemic. The scope of learning losses since 2020 have been dramatic, particularly within high-poverty schools.[20] One promising approach to address such gaps has been the provision of additional supports such as tutoring. A recent metanalysis of 90-plus RCTs on tutoring found that such programs can have substantial positive impacts on learning with a pooled effect size that is the equivalent of a student advancing from the 50th percentile to nearly the 66th percentile.[21] The analysis found that the effects of programs were strongest when they included teachers or paraprofessional tutors, started in earlier grades (though this was not true for some of the most effective programs), and took place during the school day.[22]

A few high-dosage programs are particularly notable and have been able to demonstrate impact through multiple studies. One program, Saga Education, has proven effective for older youth, an especially challenging population. Saga generally assigns students to a 1-hour tutoring session every day as part of their regular class schedule, taught by paraprofessionals (to help lower the overall cost and increase the scalability of the program). Over the course of the year, those students who received tutoring (treatment-on-treated) found significant impact, with students demonstrating between 1–2 more years of math learning than their counterparts. The tutoring also increased GPAs of students and reduced incidence of math failure.[23] The exciting takeaway that Guryan and colleagues found is that "it is possible to substantially improve academic skills by accounting for the challenges of individualizing instruction—among other things—and that these strategies can be effective even when implemented in traditional public high schools to broad, representative samples of students."[24]

Toward a More Evidence-Based Policy Agenda

Another space with significant ongoing research and some emerging evidence is education technology. As computers and personalized learning become increasingly integrated into classrooms, it will become even more important for schools to invest in programs that are actually effective rather than the latest fad. One survey found that computer-assisted learning programs have "enormous promise" and that 20 out of 30 programs undergoing rigorous evaluation via RCT reported significant positive effects, with the strongest effects found in math-oriented programs.[25] One such program is ASSISTments. Across multiple RCTs, ASSISTments has demonstrated an ability to improve math scores for kids in middle school. The latest study—which shared initial findings in mid-2023—found that the program had a positive impact on student learning in the long term, helped close achievement gaps between white students and students of color, and benefitted more those students whose schools had a higher percentage of students from economically disadvantaged backgrounds.[26] More good news: The program costs less than $100 per student. As schools continue to face challenges, tutoring and ed tech will be places that decision-makers will likely turn in the future, highlighting the importance of figuring out what works best.

Higher Education

In the sphere of higher education, a significant shift is occurring in how institutions support student success. Historically, higher education systems have grappled with challenges like access, retention, and graduation rates, particularly for underrepresented and low-income students. While traditional approaches have had varying levels of impact, recent years have seen a growing emphasis on evidence-based programs.

The Accelerated Study in Associate Programs (ASAP), pioneered by the City University of New York (CUNY), stands as a groundbreaking model in the higher education landscape. Launched in 2007, ASAP's primary aim is to expedite the completion of associate's degrees within 3 years. The program addresses key barriers faced by low-income and underrepresented students in higher education. It offers a comprehensive support package that includes financial assistance, such as tuition waivers for those eligible for financial aid and free textbooks, alongside dedicated academic and career advising. Additionally, the program mandates full-time enrollment, recognizing the correlation between full-time study and higher graduation rates. This holistic approach is designed not only to alleviate financial burdens but also to provide a structured, resource-rich educational environment conducive to student success.[27]

The program's results through rigorous evaluation have been impressive. Two well-conducted RCTs—one with a sample of 896 students at CUNY community colleges, the other with a sample of 1,501 students at three Ohio community colleges—have found that the program increases college graduation rates significantly (44% versus 29% in Ohio). Just as impressive, the long-term evaluation—funded by Arnold Ventures—found a statistically significant 11% ($1,948) increase in average annual earnings in the sixth year after random assignment ($19,573 in the treatment group versus $17,626 in the control group).[28] Further, results from an adaptation of the program targeting students in 4-year colleges to support bachelor's degree completion also delivered significant impacts.[29]

Another program, Bottom Line, delivers one-on-one guidance and support, starting from the college application process and extending through to college graduation. An RCT found Bottom Line produced an 8 percentage point increase in the likelihood of earning a bachelor's degree within 6 years after random assignment (i.e., 5 years after expected high school graduation).[30] In the social policy sector, we should consider these results to be blockbuster and worthy of focus and continued attention.[31]

THE NEXT FRONTIER OF EVIDENCE-BASED POLICY

To this point in the chapter, I have outlined ways in which the evidence-based policy has advanced and offered a few areas where knowledge accumulation has been strongest. The Evidence Act, strategic grantmaking, and an overall growing research base of programs demonstrating impact via rigorous evaluation are important steps forward. And yet, the next frontier of evidence-based policy—continuing to find ways to synthesize, replicate, implement, and scale the insights and programs that we have learned can drive outcomes this past 15 years—may represent the most important and most challenging. Researchers have detailed the complexity of scaling even proven interventions.[32] Others have found that when programs are scaled, they suffer from "voltage drops," losing efficacy as the intervention expands to greater populations.[33]

Given what the field has learned, there are several critical steps that will be especially important to develop a scaling agenda to improve outcomes for kids, families, and communities in the coming years. The rest of this chapter will focus on core recommendations that may be especially useful for funders, philanthropic and public, to advance such efforts.

RECOMMENDATION #1: CONTINUE TO INVEST IN BUILDING THE SUPPLY OF EVIDENCE

First, we need to invest more persistently in building a robust supply of evidence. Central to this endeavor is the commitment to funding and building a stronger culture of testing and learning.

To realize our vision for impactful and efficient social policies, it is crucial that government significantly increases its investment in rigorous evaluation. A practical and transformative approach would be to allocate, for instance, 1% of all grant funding designated for social programs specifically to research and evaluation methods.[34] Such a dedicated funding stream would catalyze a deeper understanding of program effectiveness, fostering a culture of continual learning and adaptation in social policy implementation. Moreover, the reinvigoration of the Social Innovation Fund, with a renewed focus on scaling evidence-based programs through a tiered-evidence approach, could be another vital step. This relaunch would not only support the growth of proven initiatives but also encourage the meticulous evaluation of emerging programs. The emphasis on tiered evidence would ensure that funding is judiciously directed toward programs at varying stages of development and evidence, thereby maximizing the impact of federal dollars. In essence, a substantial increase in evaluation funding is more than a financial commitment—it is a pledge to ensure that social policies are not only well-intended but also empirically validated and genuinely effective in addressing the complex challenges faced by our communities.

Beyond financial support, policymakers and funders should also be more strategic about building a culture of testing. One effective strategy in this regard is the incorporation of variation in policy and program delivery. Seeking out variation through randomization, differentiated rollout, and interrupted time series analyses offers valuable opportunities to examine "what-if" scenarios and establish counterfactuals. This approach is crucial in determining whether and how different groups are impacted by specific services or interventions. Implementing such variations can present practical and ethical challenges, particularly concerning the equitable distribution of services and support.

These challenges must be weighed against the ethical implications of not rigorously testing programs. History has shown that some well-intentioned interventions, like Scared Straight or DARE, may have negligible or even adverse effects.[35] Without thorough testing, we risk perpetuating ineffective or harmful practices. As Manzi states, the goal of our research investments should be to construct a "mountain of pebbles"—an accumulation of insights from numerous, smaller-scale RCTs rather than solely seeking the more elusive transformational insights.[36] He advocates for making constant testing a foundational aspect of government, agency, and nonprofit operations, seeking incremental improvements that collectively contribute to significant advancements in social policy. This approach, while challenging, is essential for ensuring that policies and programs are genuinely effective and beneficial for the communities they aim to serve.

RECOMMENDATION #2: DEVELOP CONCENTRATIONS OF RESEARCH TO ADVANCE PRACTICAL KNOWLEDGE

Building on the first recommendation, we should seek out ways to create concentrated investment areas to deepen our understanding of effective interventions across various policy domains. This approach acknowledges the need for a broader exploration of "what works" in social policy, and that no single solution can address the myriad of challenges faced by diverse populations. The heterogeneity of target populations necessitates a multifaceted approach, as different groups have distinct needs and respond differently to various interventions. Similarly, the diversity in policymaker approaches and the array of needs within communities demand a range of strategies.

Therefore, we need to find ways to go deep on key issues. This concept of building a comprehensive evidence base aligns with the analogy of creating a mosaic, as described by Gugerty and Karlan.[37] In this context, each study or intervention contributes a small yet crucial piece to the larger picture. While individual studies may not immediately precipitate sweeping policy changes, collectively they contribute incrementally to a clearer, more comprehensive understanding of effective policy measures. This gradual process of knowledge accumulation is essential for developing nuanced and impactful policies.

Reflecting on specific examples above such as high-dosage tutoring and sectoral training, it becomes evident that concentrated investments in these areas have significantly advanced our understanding of effective strategies in education and workforce development—and lend more easily to scaling. These examples illustrate how targeted investment in specific domains can yield valuable insights, guiding policymakers toward more effective and tailored interventions.[38] Such concentrated efforts in diverse domains are vital for advancing our collective knowledge and enhancing the efficacy of evidence-based policymaking.

RECOMMENDATION #3: REPLICATE, REPLICATE, REPLICATE

The third recommendation, intrinsically linked to the second one, emphasizes the critical role of replication in evidence-based policymaking. Replication serves as a key mechanism to bolster our confidence and certainty in the effectiveness of various interventions, providing evidence of generalizability across conditions.[39] It addresses the inherent variability in the impacts of any single program demonstration and mitigates the limitations of relying on isolated research findings. In light of the "replication crisis" of the last 15 years—a period marked by several studies failing to replicate in follow-up research—the importance of this recommendation becomes even more pronounced.[40] This crisis raises significant concerns: If research findings are not consistently replicable, how can we reliably advance our knowledge about what works across different settings?

It's important to acknowledge the challenges associated with replication, including the time and costs involved, the potential for change within the programs themselves, and issues like system shifts and leadership turnover. Despite these valid concerns, the pursuit of replication remains a cornerstone in our efforts to build a reliable and robust evidence base, essential for advancing our understanding of effective social policies. The response to this challenge should not be a retreat from replication efforts but a deeper engagement with them. One proposal for incentivizing replication is the creation of an Evidence Fund that provided matching support for state and local organizations that were compelled to replicate programs with proven effects in new settings.[41] Such a fund could help jumpstart more replications.

It's imperative to identify and support programs and interventions that demonstrate efficacy across multiple contexts. The example of the Accelerated Study in Associate Programs (ASAP) above serves as a pertinent case in point, where replication efforts have been instrumental in validating its effectiveness across different educational contexts. Further, recent work suggests that establishing rigorous methodological standards both initially and during replication phases can significantly enhance the likelihood of replicating effects in new settings.[42] Others have advocated for three to four well-powered replications of original studies to obtain more precise estimates of impact.[43] Ultimately, this approach necessitates a reconsideration of the incentives for replication in academia, policymaking, and philanthropy.

RECOMMENDATION #4: DESIGN STUDIES WITH SCALE IN MIND

The fourth recommendation emphasizes the necessity of designing studies with an explicit focus on scalability. The design of social programs and policies necessitates a fundamental shift in perspective: From their inception, they should be conceived and structured with scalability as a central goal. This approach requires a departure from traditional program design, which often focuses on short-term efficacy within controlled, small-scale environments. As highlighted by Al-Ubaydli and colleagues, a key to successful scaling lies in anticipating and planning for the challenges and dynamics of expanding a program to a broader context. They write that they we should flip "the traditional knowledge creation model, calling on scholars to place themselves in the shoes of the policymakers whom they are trying to influence."[44]

In practice, this means that researchers and policymakers should collaborate from the outset to envision how a program might be implemented on a larger scale. It involves anticipating the potential challenges and opportunities associated with scaling up during the initial design phase of the study. This collaboration should consider various factors, including the diversity of target populations, potential changes in implementation costs, and how the intervention might interact with different environmental variables. Embracing this type of heterogeneity to test different variants of the program could be crucial for creating interventions that are not just successful in a limited context but have the potential to bring about substantial, widespread change.[45] To support this work, funders can push researchers and practitioners to clarify their scaling approach at the outset.

Additionally, stakeholder engagement can be an important part of this process. Involving practitioners, policymakers, and community members in the design phase can offer critical perspectives on the practical aspects of scaling an intervention. Their input can help ensure that the study is grounded in real-world applicability and is responsive to the needs of those it aims to serve.[46]

RECOMMENDATION #5: PRIORITIZING RESEARCH TRANSPARENCY AND INTEGRITY THROUGH OPEN SCIENCE

The fifth recommendation underscores the critical importance of research transparency and integrity in the field of evidence-based policymaking, advocating for the adoption of open science principles. Open science refers to practices such as making data, materials, and the research process accessible and transparent to the public and other researchers. This approach fosters a research environment where collaboration, verification, and innovation can achieve a level of integrity essential to building accurate knowledge. It is particularly crucial in giving realistic estimates of impact and avoiding the overpromising of results. Additionally, the risks associated with low-powered studies are more discernible via practices that emphasize transparency and replicability, ensuring that research findings are both reliable and generalizable.[47] The evidence clearinghouses could be a particular useful way to drive these open science best practices, if adopted.[48]

Another powerful tool of research transparency is the importance of pre-analysis plans (PAPs). A PAP is a document where researchers outline their study design, hypotheses, and analysis plan before they begin data collection. This practice serves as a safeguard against "p-hacking," where researchers intentionally or unintentionally manipulate data to find significant results. Yokum and Bowers elucidate distinct ways in which a PAP can bring utility to the research process. The most apparent benefit is its role in preventing the manipulation of data and research questions, thereby addressing issues related to publication bias. PAPs also encourage good project management practices by requiring researchers to meticulously plan their studies in advance. This level of planning can be especially beneficial when thinking about scaling, as it involves key decision-makers in the research process from the outset, thereby aligning research questions with practical policy needs and building demand for future research findings.[49]

Embracing open science and practices like PAPs is vital for advancing the field of evidence-based policymaking. They enhance the credibility and utility of research by ensuring that studies are conducted and reported with the highest standards of transparency and integrity. This approach is not just about maintaining scientific rigor; it's about building trust in research findings among policymakers, practitioners, and the public. By committing to these principles, the research community can ensure that the insights and knowledge gained from studies are robust, replicable, and truly informative for policy development and program implementation. It is critical to give realistic estimates of impact. DellaVigna and Linos found that a sample of published literature on behavioral nudges estimated an average effect size of 33.5% (or 8.7 percentage point increase) whereas the average effect size of government nudges—essentially taking those nudges to scale—was 8% (or a 1.4 percentage point difference).[50] They attribute an important part of that difference to selective publication—that is, only studies that find positive impacts find their way into a journal. The takeaway should not be that government nudges don't work, it should be that we have to be realistic with regard to our expectations of just how effective they might be, especially at scale. Greater commitment by funders and researchers to principles of open science will help lead the way on that issue.

RECOMMENDATION #6: INVEST IN BUILDING—AND TESTING— A STRONGER EVIDENCE ECOSYSTEM

Improving the supply and quality of research is only one side of solving the scaling of evidence equation. How can we augment the assimilation of research findings into policy decisions, making these findings not only accessible but also actionable for policymakers? Our current understanding indicates that the integration of policy research into actual policymaking is disappointingly limited, and it is clear that the impact of policy research is complex and challenging to quantify.[51]

The policy process is not a simple technical or transactional process, but rather a complex one dependent on political agendas, institutional conditions, and individual beliefs and motivations.[52] Supports—both inside and outside of government—are often required to help understand the real-world demands of policymakers, demonstrate the real-time value of data, advocate for research and evaluation, and translate evidence to address timely challenges. To surmount some of these challenges, funders should look to intermediary organizations to play a "connective tissue" role to translate and connect research to decision-makers. These groups help by translating academic research into formats that are easier for decision-makers to understand and use. They also provide tools and examples that make it simpler to apply the latest research in real-world settings, ensuring that science actually informs public services and leads to better outcomes.

The Office of Evaluation Sciences in the General Services Administration is a strong example of an internal translation office that has the capacity to help identify research opportunities and connect to important policy outcomes.[53] The office comprises an "interdisciplinary team that works across the federal government to help agencies build and use evidence" and has worked with dozens of federal agencies.[54] J-PAL North America is an example of an external organization that works as a close intermediary between policymakers, practitioners, and researchers. They have helped to develop and launch dozens of RCTs on topics of high relevance to a wide range of policy domains.[55] Another model that has proven valuable, particularly in education, are research-practice partnerships (RPPs). These are collaborations that "promote educational improvement and transformation through engagement with research."[56] While understanding of their impact is still emerging, RPPs have shown some promise in helping to inform the design and implementation of interventions to improve student outcomes.[57]

A forward-looking promising avenue for addressing the research-to-policy gap lies in the potential of generative artificial technology (AI) models. It is easy to envision a future where decision-makers, or their staff, access an adaptive AI portal to query a key policy issue. Imagine a platform where questions like "What are the most effective tutoring programs?" or "How can we effectively tackle the homelessness crisis in our city?" are answered with research-backed, actionable insights. The feasibility of this vision is bolstered by emerging initiatives that reflect elements of this approach. For instance, the "living evidence" model—which aims to ensure that systematic reviews and other evidence syntheses are continually updated to reflect the most up-to-date evidence—is starting to take hold in health and other policy domains.[58] We are only on the precipice of these alternative approaches to research synthesis and translation, but developing tools that are grounded in rigorous research and are practical enough to provide actionable guidance to future policymakers should be a priority of funders interested in supporting a scaling agenda.

Importantly, as we explore these different modes of connecting research to policymakers and practitioners, we should maintain our vigilance with regard to testing and learning. As above, we should seek out variation and opportunities to rigorously evaluate—ideally through randomization—the ways in which we provide supports, test new modes of communication, and employ tools to support more evidence-based decision-making. The frontier of developing rigorous evidence around scaling is wide open.

CONCLUSION

As we look ahead to future volumes of updates to the Kerner Commission report, I expect (hope!) that there will always be a chapter devoted to the role of evidence-based policy in the table of contents. The reason is simple: Building knowledge through research to inform decisions and improve the lives of kids, families, and communities in America is an evergreen process.

Envisioning a New Will for social progress, it is imperative to place evidence-based policymaking at the forefront. This New Will emphasizes not only the development of research on policies informed by evidence, but also a committed shift toward rigorously evaluating and scaling programs that demonstrably improve social outcomes. Central to this will is an epistemic humility, an acknowledgement that our current understanding is not infallible, coupled with an unwavering optimism in our ability to innovate and improve through testing and learning. Together, this philosophy champions a New Will of experimentation, where rigorous testing and learning become the bedrock of policymaking.

To actualize this vision, it is crucial to align these efforts with the dynamic landscape of policy and the real-world needs of policymakers. By doing so, we not only refine how research informs policy but also set the stage for more effective and impactful policy decisions. This approach is not just a theoretical ideal; it is a practical necessity for addressing the complex social challenges of our time.

The path ahead is one of action and urgency, where the lessons of the past and present converge to illuminate a future where social programs are not just hopeful endeavors but embodiments of measurable, sustainable progress. As we gaze through the kaleidoscope of America's evolving story, a steadfast commitment to evidence-based policymaking can be a guiding prism, refracting our efforts into a clearer, more equitable vision for the nation's future.

NOTES

1. Jon Baron, "A Brief History of Evidence-Based Policy," *The ANNALS of the American Academy of Political and Social Science* 678, no. 1 (2018): 40–50.

2. EBPC (Evidence-Based Policymaking Collaborative) "Principles of Evidence-Based Policymaking," Urban Institute, August 1, 2016.

3. Christiaan H. Vinkers et al., "The Methodological Quality of 176,620 Randomized Controlled Trials Published Between 1966 and 2018 Reveals a Positive Trend but Also an Urgent Need for Improvement," *PLOS Biology* 19, no. 4 (2021): e3001162, https://doi.org/10.1371/journal.pbio.3001162.

4. See Arnold Ventures, "Summaries of Research Grants," n.d., https://www.arnoldventures.org/summaries-of-rct-grants.

5. Angus Deaton, and Nancy Cartwright, "Understanding and Misunderstanding Randomized Controlled Trials," *Social Science & Medicine* 210 (2018): 2–21.

6. See H.R.4174, Foundations for Evidence-Based Policymaking Act of 2018, 115th Congress, https://www.congress.gov/bill/115th-congress/house-bill/4174.

7. Government Accountability Office, "Evidence-Based Policymaking: Practices to Help Manage and Assess the Results of Federal Efforts," July 2023, https://www.gao.gov/assets/gao-23-105460.pdf.

8. Jerry Ellig, "Ten Years of Results from the Results Act," Mercatus Center at George Mason University Working Paper No. 10–21, May 1, 2010, http://dx.doi.org/10.2139/ssrn.2485602.

9. Data Foundation, "Evidence Commission After 5 Years: A Progress Report on the Promise for a More Evidence-Informed Society," 2022.

10. See Evaluation.gov, "Evidence Plans," n.d., https://www.evaluation.gov/evidence-plans/learning-agenda.

11. Kathryn Newcomer, Karol Olejniczak, and Nicholas Hart, "Learning Agendas: Motivation, Engagement, and Potential," *New Directions for Evaluation* 2022, no. 173 (Spring 2022): 63–83.

12. Erica Poethig et al., "Supporting Access to Opportunity with a Tiered-Evidence Grantmaking Approach," Evidence-Based Policymaking Collaborative, August 2018.

13. Government Accountability Office, "Tiered Evidence Grants: Opportunities Exist to Share Lessons from Early Implementation and Inform Future Federal Efforts," September 2016, https://www.gao.gov/assets/gao-16-818.pdf.

14. See Kelly Fitzsimmons, "Moving Beyond the "Tier-anny of Evidence" to a More Equitable Approach," Project Evident, February 22, 2022, https://projectevident.org/news/tieranny-of-evidence.

15. Government Accountability Office, "Tiered Evidence Grants."

16. See Alex Neuhoff, "The What Works Marketplace: Helping Leaders Use Evidence to Make Smarter Choices," Results for America, April 2015, http://results4america.org/wp-content/uploads/2015/04/WhatWorksMarketplace-vF-1.pdf.

17. Richard Hendra et al., "How Effective Are Different Approaches Aiming to Increase Employment Retention and Advancement?," MDRC, April 2020.

18. Lawrence F. Katz et al., "Why Do Sectoral Employment Programs Work? Lessons from WorkAdvance," *Journal of Labor Economics* 40, no. S1 (2022): S249–S291.

19. David Fein and Samuel Dastrup, "Benefits That Last: Long-Term Impact and Cost-Benefit Findings for Year Up," Office of Planning, Research, and Evaluation, Administration for Children and Families, U.S. Department of Health and Human Services, March 2022.

20. Dan Goldhaber et al., "The Consequences of Remote and Hybrid Instruction During the Pandemic. Research Report," Center for Education Policy Research, Harvard University, May 2022.

21. Andre Joshua Nickow, Philip Oreopoulos, and Vincent Quan, "The Impressive Effects of Tutoring on PreK-12 Learning: A Systematic Review and Meta-Analysis of the Experimental Evidence," EdWorkingPaper: 20–267, https://doi.org/10.26300/eh0c-pc52.

22. See J-PAL, "The Transformative Potential of Tutoring for PreK-12 Learning Outcomes: Lessons from Randomized Evaluations," n.d., https://www.povertyactionlab.org/sites/default/files/publication/Evidence-Review_The-Transformative-Potential-of-Tutoring.pdf.

23. See Roseanna Ander et al., "Boosting Academic Performance through Individualized Tutoring in Chicago Public High Schools," J-PAL, n.d., https://www.povertyactionlab.org/evaluation/boosting-academic-performance-through-individualized-tutoring-chicago-public-high.

24. Jonathan Guryan et al., "Not Too Late: Improving Academic Outcomes Among Adolescents," *American Economic Review* 113, no. 3 (March 2021): 738–65.

25. Maya Escueta et al., "Education Technology: An Evidence-Based Review," NBER Working Paper 23744, August 2017.

26. Mingyu Feng, Kevin C.-W. Huang, and Kelly Collins, "Technology-Based Support Shows Promising Long-Term Impact on Math Learning: Initial Results From a Randomized Controlled Trial in Middle Schools," WestEd, June 2023.

27. See Social Programs That Work Review, "Evidence Summary for Accelerated Study in Associate Programs (ASAP)," Arnold Ventures, April 2023, https://evidencebasedprograms.org/document/cuny-asap-evidence-summary.

28. Gilda Azurdia and Katerina Galkin, "An Eight-Year Cost Analysis from a Randomized Controlled Trial of CUNY's Accelerated Study in Associate Programs," MDRC, July 2020.

29. Jing Zhu, Michael Scuello, and Diana Strumbos, "Evaluation of Accelerate, Complete, Engage (ACE) at CUNY John Jay College of Criminal Justice," City University of New York and Metis Associates, April 2023.

30. See Social Programs That Work, "Bottom Line," October 27, 2021, https://evidencebasedprograms.org/programs/bottom-line.

31. See Michael Friedrich, "A Life-Changing Impact," Arnold Ventures, June 21, 2023, https://www.arnoldventures.org/stories/a-life-changing-impact.

32. Stefano DellaVigna, Woojin Kim, and Elizabeth Linos, "Bottlenecks for Evidence Adoption," Working Paper 30144, National Bureau of Economic Research, June 2022.

33. John A. List, *The Voltage Effect: How to Make Good Ideas Great and Great Ideas Scale* (New York: Currency, 2022).

34. See Results for America, "9 Ways to Make Federal Legislation Evidence-Based: 2019 What Works Guide for Congress," February 1, 2019, http://results4america.org/wp-content/uploads/2019/02/What-Works-Legislation-2019-9-Ways-to-Make-Legislation-More-Evidence-Based.pdf.

35. Donald F. Ketl, "Programs Like D.A.R.E. and Scared Straight Don't Work. Why Do States Keep Funding Them?" *Governing*, May 21, 2018.

36. Jim Manzi, "A Mountain of Pebbles: Effectively Using RCTs in the Public and Nonprofit Sectors," in *Next Generation Evidence: Strategies for More Equitable Social Impact*, eds., Kelly Fitzsimmons and Tamar Bauer (Washington, DC: Brookings Institute Press, 2024).

37. Mary Kay Gugerty and Dean Karlan, "Ten Reasons Not to Measure Impact—and What to Do Instead," *Stanford Social Innovation Review* 16, no. 3 (2018): 41–47, https://doi.org/10.48558/2A2K-0K07.

38. See the Evidence Review syntheses at https://www.povertyactionlab.org for strong examples of the outputs of concentrated research investments.

39. Brian A. Nosek and Timothy M. Errington, "What is replication?," *PLoS Biology* 18, no. 3 (2020), e3000691.

40. Colin F. Camerer et al., "Evaluating Replicability of Laboratory Experiments in Economics," *Science* 351, no. 6280 (2016): 1433–36.

41. See Arnold Ventures, "A Proposal to Focus Social Spending on Proven, High-Impact Programs: The 'Funding Match for Evidence' Demonstration," December 2020, https://evidencebasedprograms.org/document/funding-match-for-evidence-demonstration.

42. John Protzko et al., "High Replicability of Newly Discovered Social-Behavioural Findings Is Achievable," *Nature Human Behaviour* 8 (2024): 311–19.

43. Omar Al-Ubaydli et al., "How Can Experiments Play a Greater Role in Public Policy? Twelve Proposals from an Economic Model of Scaling," *Behavioural Public Policy* 5, no. 1 (2020): 2–49.

44. Al-Ubaydli et al., "How Can Experiments Play a Greater Role in Public Policy?"

45. Dilip Soman and Nina Mažar, "The Science of Translation and Scaling" in *Behavioral Science in the Wild,* eds. Nina Mažar and Dilip Soman (Toronto: University of Toronto Press, 2022), 1–19.

46. Rebecca Maynard, "How Researchers Can Make the Evidence they Generate More Actionable," in *Next Generation Evidence: Strategies for More Equitable Social Impact*, eds. Kelly Fitzsimmons and Tamar Bauer (Washington, DC: Brookings Institute Press, 2023).

47. Katherine S. Button et al., "Power Failure: Why Small Sample Size Undermines the Reliability of Neuroscience," *Nature Reviews Neuroscience* 14, no. 5 (2013): 365–76.

48. Evan Mayo-Wilson, Sean Grant, and Lauren H. Supplee, "Clearinghouse Standards of Evidence on the Transparency, Openness, and Reproducibility of Intervention Evaluations," *Prevention Science* 23, no. 5 (2021): 774–86.

49. David Yokum and Jake Bowers, "The Value of Pre-Analysis," in *Next Generation Evidence: Strategies for More Equitable Social Impact*, eds. Kelly Fitzsimmons and Tamar Bauer (Washington, DC: Brookings Institute Press, 2023), 295–305.

50. Stefano DellaVigna and Elizabeth Linos, "RCTs to Scale: Comprehensive Evidence from Two Nudge Units," *Econometrica* 90, no. 1 (2022): 81–116.

51. Kate Williams and Jenny M. Lewis, "Understanding, Measuring, and Encouraging Public Policy Research Impact," *Australian Journal of Public Administration* 80, no. 3 (2021): 554–64.

52. Martha Fedorowicz and Laudan Y. Aron, "Improving Evidence-Based Policymaking: A Review," Urban Institute, April 2021.

53. Elizabeth Linos, "Translating Behavioral Economics Evidence into Policy and Practice: A Report for the National Academies of Sciences, Engineering, and Medicine," 2023.

54. See Office of Evaluation Services, https://oes.gsa.gov.

55. See J-PAL, n.d., https://www.povertyactionlab.org/evaluations.

56. Caitlin C. Farrell et al., "Practice Partnerships in Education: The State of the Field," William T. Grant Foundation, July 19, 2021.

57. Caitlin C. Farrell et al., "Learning at the Boundaries of Research and Practice: A Framework for Understanding Research–Practice Partnerships," *Educational Researcher* 51, no. 3 (2022): 197–208.

58. Tari Turner et al., "Living Evidence and Adaptive Policy: Perfect Partners?," *Health Research Policy and Systems* 21, no. 135 (2023).

The Visual Arts, Monuments, and the Performing Arts

CHAPTER 32

Carry History, Hold Truth
Art in the Public Realm

Rocío Aranda-Alvarado, Margaret S. Morton, and Lena Sze

> History and culture are interrelated, yet there is no common understanding of what the American story is—we don't share an understanding of what our past is.
>
> —Kevin Young, poet and Director of the Smithsonian National Museum of African American History and Culture

Wars rage across our globe, in Sudan, Congo, Ukraine, Gaza. In our country, divisions over identity and nationalism roil civic spaces and set parameters on public discourse and dialogue, driving deepening Islamophobia, anti-Semitism, misogyny, and racism. We are living in a time of political and cultural movements to erase history and deny diversity through a combination of book bans, restriction on rights, including reproductive rights and free expression, and the strict legislation of people's gender and sexuality. The simple idea that an un-representative media and arts landscape in the United States created a legacy of invisibilization, dehumanization, and marginalization is fundamentally connected to the Kerner Commission report based on the National Advisory Commission on Civil Disorder.

The 1968 Kerner Report to President Lyndon Johnson revealed that racial uprisings across many cities were in fact fueled by hatred and systemic racism against Black communities by White Americans. Media and journalism, the report suggested, needed more representative writers, editors, and producers of color who understood the conditions plaguing the lives of Black Americans and their communities. The report also urged the federal government to dismantle discriminatory practices in education, employment, policing, and the criminal justice systems, and to improve housing, education, employment, and social services for Black communities. The report represented an unprecedented analysis of the root causes of the racial uprisings, including the history of the enslavement of Africans. President Johnson accepted the report, but he did not take official action on its conclusions.[1]

Now, nearly 60 years after it was released, the Kerner Report powerfully demonstrated how systems of exclusion, starting with slavery, shaped inequality in the lives of Black Americans through the Great Migration to the west and north. The legacy of that report lives on today in our current inequitable systems that disadvantage people by race, class, gender, and disability.

In parallel with this larger structural inequality, so too historically have our systems of creative production privileged the telling of stories of European-centric white communities through various forms of expressive culture. Art, stories, and narratives define our culture by holding a mirror up to our society. Artists and storytellers carry our history and express truths in their work in ways that reach broader audiences and touch people in meaningful and transcendent ways. Artists and storytellers also hold cultural power that leads us to view the Kerner Report through a similar lens. The report underscored the deficit of reflective coverage of the press and media as a critical contributing factor in the urban rebellions across U.S. cities between 1964 and 1967 from Watts to Detroit to Newark, New Jersey. As the Kerner Report made plain, fewer than 5% of the people employed by the news business in editorial jobs in the United States were Black. Media systems of the time were fed by reporters and producers who, as the Kerner authors wrote: "reported and wrote from the standpoint of a white man's world . . . and a white press that repeatedly reflects the biases, the paternalism, the indifference of White America." Black communities did not see themselves in the stories about American life told by the American press. There is perhaps no more powerful reflection of what can happen when there is a lack of representative storytelling rooted in inequitable and segregated social, economic, and political conditions.[2]

The histories and stories of Black communities, and similarly by extension those of Indigenous, Latinx, and Asian American communities, had not been told in U.S. media and journalism nor in popular culture, the stages of theaters, the walls of museums. On top of the absence of reflective media, journalism, arts, and culture, true and comprehensive histories of Black Americans were not understood, rendered, and taught as part of the history of the United States, an especially sobering irony as Black Americans and other marginalized communities contributed so much to the formation of distinctly American economic systems and cultures.[3] One of the legacies of the Kerner Report is a simple and yet radical call to arms to reflect the full American story. Artists and culture bearers have historically played a large role doing just that even as they have long been undercapitalized and underseen.

The question we ask today is: How do we empower artists to speak truth about the human condition, continue their work, and build a future vision for a country that is inclusive of all and that is premised on building a multiracial and feminist democracy? Many of us intuitively understand the power of art to shift dominant or one-dimensional narratives and to reckon with history, create new narratives, speak truth to power as it were. Yet in this article we also seek to demonstrate the interplay between culture and community power, and specifically to outline ways that artists and art are documenting history and culture and advancing issues of unity across communities and justice for all.

The Kerner findings made plain how incomplete representation of stories and truths about Black Americans (and, by extension, other communities of color) reproduces social harm. This dearth of knowledge about various component communities of our society diminishes knowledge of history in general, while also impacting race relations and even leading to the mistrust and disinformation that characterizes our media systems and cultural discourses today. Artists, with their elevation of cultural expression, help us reckon with our complicated American history, true histories of Black Americans, Latinx, Asian, and Indigenous Americans, and ultimately with who we are. Doing so not only honors their humanity, but is critical to understanding how their experiences have shaped our country and how we might make a future shared by diverse peoples.

History holds countless powerful examples of cultural campaigns aimed at shifting the public's imagination, opinion, and knowledge. The United States has already seen art interventions aimed at elevating and validating "culture" for political purposes. We suggest that new partnerships with a multitude of artists, culture bearers, and creatives holding relevant creative practices can reckon with history in more tangible ways by engaging directly with community and the public at large. Moreover, these kinds of artworks and art practices help build the new will to achieve the goals of the Kerner Report.

In this chapter, we take four different moments in post-Kerner American history to illustrate our points. First, that culturally specific institutions and funding initiatives that came out of the Kerner moment (1960s and 1970s) were not just examples of artists and culture bearers asserting their power as an addendum to the political projects of their communities but that in founding institutions, spaces, and artist collectives, they were performing essential political work to advance rights and justice. Second, that artists learned to hone a robust set of artistic practices in the 1980s that were fundamentally political and activist in nature and orientation. At the moment that the neoliberal consensus was starting to calcify when Reagan's and Thatcher's politics of austerity came down, these artists provided a window into imagining and living out an alternative set of values. Third, the culture wars that extended from the late 1980s until the post-9/11 moment taught artists and communities potent ways of negotiating with and resisting state power and provided a trenchant defense of the rights to life, freedom, and expressive culture by marginalized and politically targeted minority communities. And finally, the last 10 years has witnessed a flourishing of creative interventions, artist-driven activism, public art, monuments, narrative change, and other forms of public reckoning in the face of a vicious assault on the rights of so many Americans. We end the chapter with a five-point plan suggesting that, among other items, governments and philanthropy provide deep resourcing in artist-led, community-responsive institutions and that we provide support for opportunities for artists and activists to work together on the pressing issues of Kerner's day and today, from inequitable systems of education to criminal justice.

BUILDING INSTITUTIONS

Across the country, in the wake of the Civil Rights and anti-war movements, artists and activists began working together to create the change they wanted to see. Inspired by the ideals of the Black Panther Party, Latinx groups like the Young Lords Party and the Brown Berets were formed, as was the umbrella Asian American radical political and arts space known as Basement Workshop. These groups provided social and health services to their communities, organized protests against police brutality, and advocated for access to jobs and education. Forged from the fires of 1965 and 1967, artists responded by supporting these movements for justice with music, theater, and art. In turn, this activism supported the flourishing of community-based cultural institutions. Communities developed local art spaces that would be responsive to their artists and their concerns. The Charles H. Wright Museum of African American Culture in Detroit was founded in

1965. This was followed in quick succession by the creation of the Wing Luke Museum of the Asian American experience in 1967 in Seattle, the Studio Museum in Harlem (1968), Taller Boricua and El Museo del Barrio (1969) in New York, Galería de la Raza (1970) in San Francisco, and Self-Help Graphics (1970) in Los Angeles, among many others that continued to be created throughout the 1980s and into the 1990s.

The neighborhood museum movement, the mural arts movement, and the community-based arts activism of the 1960s and 1970s in the United States were attempts to intervene in political processes that disadvantaged communities of color—largely without cultural institutions or archives addressing ethnic or race-specific histories and the resources to move their populations out of the degraded social, political, and economic conditions that the Kerner Commission confronted. These multicultural movements sought to challenge the bias, built into and inherited over generations, that culture was composed of European high art forms and "masterpieces," rather than non-European "artifacts." From the mid-1960s to the mid-1970s, municipal governments in big cities like Chicago and New York City began to be responsive to the cultural activity and organizing happening in Black and Brown communities from the New York City then-Department of Parks, Recreation and Cultural Affairs sponsoring the Harlem Cultural Festival in 1969 to the establishment of independent departments of cultural affairs that began to provide public funding for the first time for artistic activity across communities and cities that had seen Kerner-era racial rebellion and economic unrest.

In addition, artists organized among themselves, protesting their lack of representation in mainstream organizations. First to organize was the Black Emergency Cultural Coalition, created in 1967 by a group of 75 African American artists protesting the content of the *Harlem on My Mind* exhibition, and the complete lack of representation of Black artists in the exhibition. Other activist groups were spurred by the race protests across the country and also by the U.S. involvement in wars in Southeast Asia, and the burgeoning feminist movement. The most active was New York's Arts Workers Coalition and its arm known as the Black and Puerto Rican Caucus, in 1969. The coalition focused their efforts on demanding political and economic reforms at the Museum of Modern Art, the Metropolitan Museum of Art, and the Whitney Museum of American Art. Demonstrations were organized at the entrances of these institutions with signs protesting a lack of representation in both exhibitions and collections.

Protest culture made its way into the works of artists working during this time and expressed its solidarity in many ways. Faith Ringgold, for example, created and gifted a painting in 1971 for incarcerated women at New York's Rikers Island jail facility. The work, "For the Women's House," incorporates images of women at work in various roles, including as bride, mother, laborer, construction workers, police officer, professor, and scientist, underscoring the feminist perspective she brought to the art of her time, insisting on figurative narratives that provided maximum clarity and impact.

ART AS ACTIVIST PRACTICE

This kind of activism continued throughout the 1980s and 1990s, centering various causes and communities. Like their predecessors of the 1960s and 1970s, artists continued to respond to the effects of police brutality. A salient example comes from the work of Jean-Michel Basquiat, who brought attention to the violent death of Michael Stewart at the hands of New York City transit police with his work *Defacement* (1983). The title can refer to many experiences of Black people and artists working during this time, as well as to conceptions of the burgeoning graffiti movement and of the artists who led it as defacers of property.

Indeed, seeing Stewart's life in the aftermath of his beating, coma, and his eventual death, Basquiat was known to have repeated frequently, "It could have been me." At the trial of the six transit police officers in 1985, all were acquitted. This pattern of violent fatalities at the hands of police who act with impunity continues and therefore continues to be recorded and acknowledged by artists. They eloquently memorialize the victims in various media, but particularly in paintings and public art, as in the renowned portrait of Breonna Taylor by Amy Sherald that circulated widely through exhibitions and reproductions.

Government inaction and disdain for victims of the AIDS epidemic led to the birth of ACT UP in 1987. Early on, science focused exclusively on the gay white male population and purposefully excluded known cases of AIDS in Black men.[4] AIDS activists also focused on White gay populations until the founding of the Black AIDS Institute in 1999. The artistic activism in response to this invisibilization can be found in the works of many visual artists, including Nyland Blake, Derek Jackson, Kia LaBeija, Glenn Ligon, and Kalup Linzy, among many others, but also, as artist–activists argued, in the music of the era, including House music and its attendant Ballroom culture.[5] Ballroom activism, in particular, supported LGBTQ+ youth and individuals through the creation of chosen families and homes that all were invited to inhabit and call their own. The ballroom houses become the primary source of information and education on safe sex practices for Black and Latinx youth and young adults overlooked by the mainstream health industry.[6]

In 1986, the Guerrilla Girls published their poster "ONLY 4 COMMERCIAL GALLERIES IN N.Y. SHOW BLACK WOMEN. ONLY 1 SHOWS MORE THAN 1." The feminist group formed in 1984 in response to the International Survey of Painting and Sculpture exhibition at the Museum of Modern Art, which of 169 artists included only 13 women.[7] From their inception, the anonymous artists who participated in Guerilla Girls were concerned with the lack of racial and gender equity in the art world. They produced posters targeting dealers, curators, museums, galleries, critics, and artists, citing art market data taken directly from the most respected sources in order to lay bare the racism and patriarchy entrenched in the art world. The activists adopted the names of deceased artists to maintain their anonymity and paid homage to Black women artists through names like Meta Warrick Fuller, Romaine Brooks, and Alma Thomas. The public nature of this artistic activism was particularly important, as denizens of the elite art world would arrive at work in the SoHo neighborhood, which was filled with the posters of data proving the inherent inequities of the art industry. The women extended their public reach with billboards, bus ads, magazine spreads, protest actions, letter-writing campaigns, and even broadsheets placed in the bathrooms of major museums.

Activism had been a central feature of earlier historical periods from the political work of the Mexican muralists of the early 20th century to the Black Arts Movement that corresponded with the Kerner Report, and certainly when ethnic-specific cultural institutions were forged as part of various communities' political organizing. However, in the moment of intense neoliberal revanchism during the Reagan/Bush years, the valence of this activism changed from being located in cultural institutions and groups and became more rooted in individual and collective artistic practice, perhaps because of the ways in which "Arts and Culture" (capital a and c) were increasingly enfolded into the problematic systems of resourcing whereas individuals operating at the then-margins of society, e.g., gay and queer artists, Black artists, women artists, chafed at the yawning silence of the crises that were killing their communities, including AIDS, police and state violence, and gender-based violence. The artist–activists of the 1980s and 1990s became increasingly entrepreneurial in a sense, highly mobile, adaptable, and working in the forms of graffiti, wheat-pasting, zines, performance, and site-specific installations during those times that in many ways required those pastiche and participatory forms.

THE "CULTURE WARS"

With strong echoes in today's climate, the culture wars from the mid-1980s through the 1990s were fought on campuses in the form of educational curricula and faculty hires. More broadly, it was fought within arts public funding bodies, in the press, and in Congress most famously with Senator Jesse Helms's broadsides against funding the NEA because of artists Andres Serrano and Robert Mapplethorpe. It was all intended to show how the representational was tied to the material. As Carole Vance argues in an essay: "The fundamentalist attack on images and the art world must be recognized . . . as a systematic part of a Right-wing political program to restore traditional social arrangements and reduce diversity. The right wing is deeply committed to symbolic politics, both in using symbols . . . and in understanding that, because images do stand in for and motivate social change, the avenue of representation is a real ground for struggle."[8]

For Right-wing critics on the attack during that culture wars moment, identity was about claims to being pro-American and ascribing to a particular form of religious Christian evangelism. Helms famously opined that "[Serrano] is not an artist. He is a jerk. And he is taunting the American people, just as others are."[9] For NEA-funded artists and their allies and supporters, "identity" was about claims to multiple identities simultaneously, without the depoliticizing effect of empty calls for pluralism. For Senator Helms, famous for his extreme anti-LGBTQ+ views, his calls for segregation, and his vigorous defense of the Confederate flag, and his associates, artists' aesthetics and products needed to follow a formula of "Americanism," one in which critique and difference could not only not be expressed but also could not be. Following an unsurprising course, Helms was also one of a small minority of senators in 1988 who voted against the reparations and redress bill that passed Congress and was signed by Reagan to compensate survivors of the Japanese American "internment" (now often referred to as incarceration or concentration camps) during World War II, a decades-long advocacy effort led by Japanese Americans, many of whom served in the U.S. military, and propped up by a multiracial contingent of supporters. The consistent narrative for defunding the NEA, barring any public health educational materials "promoting homosexuality," preventing funding for reparations for Japanese Americans, and valorizing the Confederate flag as a symbol of "American history" relied upon a single and narrow interpretation of what it means to be "American," one premised on a history of racial violence, state oppression, and stigmas attached to being racial, ethnic, and sexual minorities.

The Reagan administration, marked by racialized fights over welfare, crime, and the specter of the AIDS crisis and the culture wars of the 1990s cast a long shadow into the start of the 21st century and in many ways laid the groundwork for the art and organizing to emerge after the events of September 11, 2001. There was already a template for collectivist reimagining and appropriation of texts, slogan, documents, and images to create new art and for asking the core questions during a time of panic and fear. Visible Collective/Naieem Mohaimen created installations, lectures, performances, and videos making "visible" the ways in which the "war on terror" made specific people and populations both hypervisible and invisible, i.e., the racialized face of a manufactured "terrorist" threat and undocumented, criminalized working-class immigrants who often bore the brunt of so-called post-9/11 policies (2004–2007).[10] Along similar lines, during that moment, artists Chitra Ganesh and Mariam Ghani created the *Index of the Disappeared*, a long-term project to collect and create an archive of those detained and/or deported in the United States and globally.[11]

One chapter of the culture wars of the 1970s and 1980s ended with the National Endowment for the Arts losing its authority to directly support artists, except in more narrow programmatic forms. It is an enduring lesson of how public government officials use artists and culture for political means, through narrative tropes and leveraging religion and identity to score political points. This controversy does offer the instructive takeaway that elected officials have employed the narrative power of art to awaken the public's opinion and dialogue. The question is, how do policy advocates and artists, working with government and communities, more effectively deploy art and narratives to advance civic engagement, build concrete narratives about truth and culture, and advance the goals of a multiracial feminist democracy?[12]

ART INTERVENTIONS IN THE PUBLIC REALM

Extreme polarization, weakened institutions, and the rise of violent rhetoric and political action have characterized the last decade in the United States. There has also been during this time a real flourishing of creative interventions, artist-driven activism, and an expansion of public art and public forums for art. The public realm now includes the Internet, public art, monuments, narrative change, and other forms of public reckoning. Criminal justice reform advocates are beginning to see value in integrating systems-involved community members and artists in shaping policy and changing narratives about crime and incarceration through initiatives like the Art for Justice Fund.[13] This 6-year time-limited fund partnered criminal justice activists with artists to disrupt mass incarceration and advance new narratives about safety.[14]

In this climate of extreme political repression, we've also been witness to campaigns, rooted in historical truth, by artists to shift the public's imagination. Spurred by the toxic and racist rhetoric of the 2016 presidential election, artists Hank Willis Thomas and Eric Gottesman formed the artist collective For Freedoms, which aims to center artists' voices in public discourse, broaden what participation in democracy looks like, and initiate a larger conversation about the role of art in local, national, and global politics. Their practice includes collaboration with artists across the country, the commissioning of large-scale billboards, and creating public and civic dialogues at art and cultural venues.[15]

Monuments are part of America's DNA. One of the most durable examples of public monuments heroicizing political projects and values is the postbellum "Lost Cause" drive, in which thousands of monuments to Confederate figures (one estimate is 1,747) were mounted in states in the South and beyond by organizations like the United Daughters of the Confederacy or local governments with the ultimate goal of reinterpreting the loss and lessons of the Civil War and valorizing leaders and soldiers of the South. Those monuments collectively performed an important role, teaching Southerners and Americans about the so-called righteousness of the Confederate cause. Following the recent rise of the Black Lives Matter movement, and a rash of police shootings of unarmed Black men, the United States saw concerted momentum to change that landscape of outmoded public monuments that celebrate historic figures reflecting White supremacy, the Confederacy, and the general over-representation of White male historical military figures as "heroes."

In 2015, the racial massacre of nine Bible study parishioners at Emanuel African Methodist Episcopal Church in South Carolina helped deepen public awareness of monuments and symbols of the Confederacy. In 2021, a collective action by the group #TakeEmDownNOLA successfully influenced the removal of the Jefferson Davis monument in New Orleans but could only do so under the cover of night. There were many such efforts across the United States to remove, deaccession, or move monuments to museums, given the new will to change the public symbolic landscape. Efforts to remove from the public landscape the monuments of America's violent past included, for example, taking down the Confederate flag from the South Carolina statehouse.

Prompted by this deeper public scrutiny of monuments, since 2012 the public art/history studio Monument Lab has done strategic work with community, artists, educators, and public agencies to rethink approaches to public engagement and memory. Monument Lab defines a monument as "a statement of power and presence in public" and includes its support for The More Up Campus in Montgomery, Alabama. Artist Michelle Browder acquired a historical site associated with J. Marion Sims (for generations, Sims was honored as the so-called "father of gynecology" despite his horrific experimentations on enslaved women). Browder's *The Mothers of Gynecology* is dedicated to conversations, art, and history preserving the legacy of slavery, Black women's maternal health, and reproductive justice. Since 2022, the Mellon Foundation has been leading transformative work to ensure that the U.S. monuments landscape "more completely and accurately" represents all our histories. The Mellon program's formidable scope of reach includes large-scale national monuments such as Irei, memorializing the more than 125,000 individuals of Japanese ancestry unjustly imprisoned in U.S. War Relocation Authority Camps during World War II, to new forms of historic storytelling as created by the Movers and Shakers' Kinfolk project that imagines immersive monuments of Black historical figures using augmented reality (AR) that is layered onto existing physical monuments.

In addition to the new landscape of monuments, artists and cultural institutions continue to pose striking questions about the health of our democracy and have engaged in provocative and essential work in the civic realm more broadly. The Japanese American National Museum (JANM), a Smithsonian affiliate located in Little Tokyo, Los Angeles, was founded more than 40 years ago to tell Japanese immigrant and Japanese American stories as an assertion or reclamation of those stories as part of American history. JANM integrates arts and culture programming into its core programmatic and exhibitions work.

Finally, the pandemic's disproportionate impact on communities of color and the racial reckoning with the systems of racial exclusion spurred by George Floyd's murder, is a glaring reflection of Kerner's unfulfilled promise. At the same time, the pandemic awakened us all to the deep needs of and precarity of the economic condition of artists. Important responsive initiatives include USA Artists leading the largest relief effort providing direct relief for artists; the Mellon Foundation's Creatives Rebuild New York guaranteed income initiative for artists in New York State; and the example of artist Carrie Mae Weems, who passionately worked to inform and educate people of color about the COVID-19 virus by targeting cities across the country with posters: "Resist Covid Take 6!"

CONCLUSION

Creatives may be the most underutilized asset in the progressive movement.... When artists tell new stories, they can shift the culture and make new politics possible—cultural strategy is about understanding that fact and empowering artists to do what they do best.

—Jeff Chang, historian, journalist, and critic

In this chapter, we see how artists play a leadership role in responding to systems of injustice, and in shaping new visions. Through their vision and practice, they have forged spaces and institutions, advanced their forms of political practice, and utilized the public realm in inventive and expansive ways. These moments don't just arrive after the Kerner Commission report, they were shaped and must be understood in relation to Kerner because artists—like many in their communities—sought to dismantle fundamentally and historically unjust systems and deploy these specific approaches toward building cultural power.

Art and cultural content are vital elements of social impact alongside mass media and popular culture. Investments in culturally specific art, engaged with community, are an important focus for public policy advocates, government, and philanthropic leaders committed to building the policy changes still critically urgent 55 years after Kerner. We know that artists with justice in their sights have always worked to empower communities, and we offer exemplary efforts in multiple sectors that amplify this work because investing more deeply in these forms has greater potential to catalyze culture change and advance justice for all. Below is a shortlist of recommendations about how to build the new will to enact the still urgent recommendations of the Kerner Report through art, artists, and cultural strategies.

(1) Invest in evolving forms of public art and new narratives honoring culture, expression, and history.

> Specifically, we must support underresourced municipal and other government-sponsored public art programs and dynamic public art organizations across the country. Examples include the Public Art Fund's enlivening of public spaces to Creative Time's recent collaboration with Charles Gaines in creating a slave ship in the form of moving chains; New York City's Percent for Art program collaborates with city agencies to embed art into public capital projects, including the planned installation at Prospect Park honoring Shirley Chisholm by artists Amanda Williams and Olalekan Jeyifous; and SPARC, one of the most important public art organizations centering community, founded by Judith Baca in Los Angeles in the 1970s. Foundations are leading inventive investments in the public realm: Bloomberg Philanthropies' Public Art Challenge supports collaborations between mayors and artists in addressing community challenges, and the Mellon Foundation's transformational work to reimagine monuments that reflect all communities and untold history.

(2) Showcase public art that includes artists creating narrative change for social justice and artists creating in the immersive space.

> The public realm includes not just physical symbols visible to the public but also organizations and collectives shifting narratives in other ways. For instance, IllumiNative, a Native woman–led racial justice organization, builds power by increasing Native people's visibility and the political activations organized by the aforementioned For Freedoms; the Pop Culture Collaborative funds pop culture creatives from TV and music, to gaming and zines, as well as research around narratives of people of color, immigrants, refugees, Muslims, and Indigenous people, especially those who are women, queer, transgender, and/or disabled; and the Center for Cultural Power trains social justice advocates and artists in countering negative narratives that drive injustice.

> Pioneering artists working at the intersection of technology and creativity are bringing the issues of justice to new, younger audiences in more direct ways. Artists are using their practice to reveal, as Joy Bwolomwini does, the risks of emerging technology and racial profiling. The interdisciplinary *American Artist* uses video, installation, new media, and writing to assess the history of contemporary culture as well as notions of futurism. Organizations such as Movers and Shakers are using AI and VR to reposition historic figures, and the School for Poetic Computation is exploring the intersections of code, design, hardware, and theory.

(3) Resource art spaces and museums that recognize their civic value for building cultural power.

> An increasing number of museums and arts spaces are advancing power, history, and truth telling by investing in Afro-descended, Latinx, Indigenous artists and curators and

stories more deeply and directly. They are using space more boldly to present work, to educate the public about voting rights and issues of civic importance. We must hold up those arts spaces and museums that are brave and inventive in activating their space for civic engagement and public discourse, and who are bringing the history of unseen communities and culture to life. Studio Museum in Harlem is a beacon for the cultivation of Black and African contemporary artists across the globe, and, under Thelma Golden's leadership, also training curators of African and Latinx descent now working across the United States. Alabama's Equal Justice Initiative (EJI) employs a mixture of storytelling and visual art to document the history of America's racial oppression against Africans, an effort aided by artists like Kwame Akoto-Bamfo's narrative depiction of the treacherous Middle Passage and the death of the 1 to 2 million children, men, and women; and its National Memorial for Peace and Justice, designed by Mass Design Group, also plainly narrates the story of the nation's criminal and undocumented lynchings.

Institutions like the Metropolitan Museum of Art are reimagining the use of their spaces to expand the civic space and visibility of art, from Lauren Halsey's majestic roof installation inspired by the Temple of Dendur to its installation on its building facade of Wangechi Mutu's larger-than-life bronze goddesses. In Detroit, the non-collecting Museum of Contemporary Art of Detroit prioritizes resources around programming, support for living artists, and presentation of emerging artists; and in 2015, the Cranbrook Art Museum enlivened the city's public spaces when artist Nick Cave curated citywide installations of his iconic *Soundsuits* from dance performances to partnerships with LGBTQ+ youth to marching bands. Museums are also partnering with artists to bring history to life, including the Mississippi Museum of Art's A Movement in Every Direction: Legacies of the Great Migration exhibition. The Whitney Museum of Art so beautifully narrated the journey of the Mexican Muralists, from the landscape of the Mexican Revolution to its influence on the great American artists of the 20th century.

(4) Forge new impactful partnerships between policy and rights advocates, artists, and cultural workers.

The deep-seated systemic challenges raised by the Kerner Commission confronted inequity and exclusion across education, economic opportunity and fair housing, and beyond. While there have been ongoing and major strides across all of these areas, there is still so far to go in undoing deeply segregated public education and housing, and continuing disparity across employment and economic opportunities. The lens of artists and cultural workers already committed to fighting for the change we wish to see can be illuminating for policy advocates and galvanizing for the work.

The aforementioned Art for Justice Fund has demonstrated the power of partnering criminal justice advocates with artists in working to ensure more reasonable criminal justice sentencing. The fund's legacy has inspired important platforms led by impacted artists, including poet Reginald Dwayne Betts's Freedom Reads organization, working to resource libraries in prisons across the United States, and the Center for Art and Advocacy, forged by artist Jessie Krimes to help impacted artists cultivate their practice through mentorship and technical assistance. Similarly, the Ford Foundation's Reclaiming the Border Narrative, a collective initiative among immigrant rights advocates, the National Association of Hispanic Journalists, and the National Association of Latino Arts, has contributed to an archive at the University of Arizona to comprise art, stories, and content that reflects the truth and dignity of the impacted individuals and families during this tumultuous era.

Finally, New York City's Public Artists in Residence (PAIR) is an artist residency program that embeds artists in city government to identify and implement creative solutions to pressing civic challenges.[16] Inspired by the first city artist in residence at the Department of Sanitation, Mierle Laderman Ukeles, PAIR partners artists with individual agencies as diverse as the Department of Education and the Department of Correctional Services.

The unfinished business of the Kerner Commission and its warning of the harm wrought by overlooking representative journalism and media is especially prescient in today's conditions where misinformation flourishes and polarization both disallows civic engagement and creates further polarization. Through history, we see the tenacity of artists to counternarrate and to disrupt injustice with their art and their fearless activations, and by creating spaces and institutions. We urge government and philanthropy to work together more strategically to partner with artists and visual arts organizations committed to activating public spaces, arts spaces, museums, the Internet, and varied forms of popular culture, and integrate into society works that penetrate all our histories; that advance and strengthen truthful civic knowledge; and that encourage the multiracial feminist democracy of our dreams.

NOTES

1. The National Advisory Commission on Civil Disorders, *Report of the National Advisory Commission on Civil Disorders* (Washington, DC: U.S. Department of Justice, Office of Justice Programs, 1968), 91.

2. The Kerner Report, 203.

3. Until the second half of the 20th century, American history, after all, was generally told from the perspectives of white Europeans and their descendants centered around the "discovery" of America in 1492. The prevailing story America told about itself valorized the discovery of a country already inhabited; it glossed over, or worse, justified, the domination, forced displacement, and slaughter of Native Americans, the kidnapping, enslavement, and trafficking of African and African Americans, and the state-sanctioned exclusion and racial animus confronted by Chinese migrants and their descendants, among other instances of systemic and persistent oppression.

4. Gretchen Gavett, "Timeline: 30 Years of AIDS in Black America," *Frontline*, PBS, July 10, 2012, https://www.pbs.org/wgbh/frontline/article/timeline-30-years-of-aids-in-black-america. The Centers for Disease Control and Prevention publishes their *Morbidity and Mortality Weekly Report* on a mysterious illness related to pneumonia on June 5, 1981, but omits the two Black patients who were similarly diagnosed, https://www.cdc.gov/mmwr/preview/mmwrhtml/june_5.htm.

5. Tom Kerr, "A History of Erasing Black Artists and Bodies from the AIDS Conversation," *Hyperallergic*, December 31, 2015, https://hyperallergic.com/264934/a-history-of-erasing-black-artists-and-bodies-from-the-aids-conversation.

6. Emily A. Arnold and Marlon M. Bailey, "Constructing Home and Family: How the Ballroom Community Supports African American GLBTQ Youth in the Face of HIV/AIDS," *Journal of Gay & Lesbian Social Services* 21, no. 2–3 (2009): 171–88, https://doi.org/10.1080/10538720902772006.

7. Guerrilla Girls, "An Interview from Our New Book, *Confessions of the Guerrilla Girls*, Published in 1995," 1995, https://www.guerrillagirls.com/confessions_interview.

8. In Philip Yenawine, Marianne Weems, and Brian Wallis, eds., *Art Matters: How the Culture Wars Changed America* (New York: New York University Press, 1999), 230.

9. "Comments on Andres Serrano by Members of the United States Senate," *Congressional Record*, May 18, 1989, https://home.csulb.edu/~jvancamp/361_r7.html.

10. Susette Min, "Tonal Disturbances: Works on Paper by Jenny Perlin and Visible Collective," *Social Text* 26, no. 1 (2008).

11. Ronak K. Kapadia, *Insurgent Aesthetics: Security and the Queer Life of the Forever War* (Durham, NC: Duke University Press, 2019).

12. Isaac Kaplan, "Censorship, 'Sick Stuff,' and Rudy Giuliani's Fight to Shut Down the Brooklyn Museum," *Artsy*, December 23, 2016.

13. Art for Justice Fund, https://artforjusticefund.org.

14. The impact of the Art for Justice Fund was far-reaching. At the end of its work in June 2023, its impact achieved various cash bail reforms in several states, bans on juvenile life without parole in nine states, and restoring voting rights for formerly incarcerated Floridians. Its acclaimed MoMA PS1 2020 exhibit "Marking Time: Art in the Age of Mass Incarceration" featured impacted artists work in museums across the country, advancing narratives on injustice and alternatives to mass incarceration.

15. For an example of a billboard, see https://louisville.edu/art/exhibitions/all/new-monuments-for-freedoms-make-america-great-again.

16. NYC Cultural Affairs, "Public Artists in Residence (PAIR)," n.d., https://www.nyc.gov/site/dcla/publicart/pair.page.

CHAPTER 33

Healing Toward New Will

Claudia Peña

> Interbeing is the understanding that nothing exists separately from anything else. We are all interconnected. By taking care of another person, you take care of yourself. By taking care of yourself, you take care of the other person. Happiness and safety are not individual matters. If you suffer, I suffer. If you are not safe, I am not safe. There is no way for me to be truly happy if you are suffering.
>
> —Thich Nhat Hanh, *How to Fight*

Nary an artist does not day and night dream of a better world. As a casual viewer, we can take in the beauty of any particular piece. But upon further conversation with the artist, we learn more about each thought and decision, where their dreams for that better world are woven into the fabric of the art piece. Dreams beget dreams and so it becomes incumbent upon us as viewers to add our own imagination to the world the artist created. Hence, we become artists too, in conversation with the original piece and its creator.

This was the lucid dream that became For Freedoms (FF). In 2016, the culmination of a series of conversations between friends was an art performance. As a response to the polarization taking place in the nation, artists Eric Gottesman, Hank Willis Thomas, Michelle Woo, and Wyatt Gallery founded the first artist-led super PAC. The goal was to model what politics could, and perhaps should, look like: irreverently inserting themselves in the political process, encouraging conversations about who belongs, contemplating the role of creativity in leading the nation, and questioning everything. FF was born of this desire to explore every aspect of human expression. Where some might draw a distinction between politics and art, many know a good politician benefits from knowledge of "performance." And a visual artist who seeks to sell their work in the art market benefits from knowledge of "politics." Blurring these lines is exactly the kind of output the super PAC sought. If artists sat at more tables, we would likely solve more issues more effectively. Certainly, more humanely.

THE EVOLUTION OF FOR FREEDOMS

When the *Report of the National Advisory Commission on Civil Disorders* came out in 1968, Dr. Kenneth B. Clark made the insightful observation that report after report was "the same moving picture re-shown over and over again, the same analysis, the same recommendations, and the same inaction." The authors of the report earnestly hoped everything they'd learned (though admittedly not much were "new" learnings) would effect an end to "destruction and violence" should the recommendations be heeded.

Just as updates to the report have been handed off to new researchers and scholars over time who help build on the original vision, For Freedoms evolved from a super PAC to a C4 and eventually, to nonprofit. The mission has likewise evolved, though at its core, it is always about artists modeling and inspiring civic engagement. One example is how FF diversified and increased the platforms from which artists can be heard/seen/felt by taking to the public realm. In accessing billboards as a space for exhibition, FF wrested back territory from consumerism and placed it back into the public discourse. Instead of using billboards to sell products, that public space is used to sell ideas. Or at the very least, to pose thoughtful questions that lead to a plethora of ideas through dialogue.

During the initial crowd-sourced "50 State Initiative," For Freedoms collaborated with artists across the nation to put billboards up in every state of the union, including Washington, DC, and Puerto Rico. One such billboard (Figure 33.1) used the famous photograph by Spider Martin, titled *Two Minute Warning*, documenting civil rights marchers on the Edmund Pettus Bridge facing Alabama state troopers on what became known as "Bloody Sunday." The addition of the text "Make America Great Again" made for a controversial piece. The media was confused and people from across the political spectrum had questions. What did the artists mean? Were they insinuating that America was "great" during the Civil Rights Movement? Before? Which side of this showdown was the "great" side—the protesters or law enforcement? Was this billboard in reference to a sitting president? Or Ronald Reagan, Bill Clinton, Barack Obama—all who uttered these lines in past speeches? Or was the slogan from Octavia Butler's 1998 novel *Parable of the Talents* where a dictator president sets about on a modern crusade of sorts? These four simple words garnered so many questions and questions tend to lead to conversation. Thus, the billboard was a complete success in that people were inspired to think critically. This is the power of visual art.

That power stems from the fact that artists impact reality just as much as reality impacts art. For Freedoms took inspiration from Norman Rockwell's paintings that depicted FDR's Four Freedoms in 1943. FDR spoke of our rights to Freedom of Speech, Freedom of Worship, Freedom From Fear, and Freedom From Want, and Rockwell's paintings portrayed each of these in the style of photorealism. In 2018, FF updated these paintings through a series of photographs. Where Rockwell's paintings portrayed mostly White people, and as the nation looks markedly different in 2018 than it did in the 1940s, the remix of the photographs/paintings ensured more of the diversity of the United States was captured through race and ethnicity, religion, (dis)ability, and certainly a wide range of spiritual paths (see Figure 33.2). The updated photographs invite the viewer to consider that everyone, regardless of demographic, has a right to the four freedoms.

As the organization continued along its path, it developed a set of values to help guide the work both internally and externally. As a group of artists building together, and as a constant collaboration, few are the days where there is no disagreement. FFs is an anti-partisan artist organization—specifically because being partisan has proven to be fairly harmful—but even the way "anti-partisan" is defined in the organization will

Figure 33.1. An FF Billboard

Figure 33.2. Norman Rockwell painting contrasted with a *TIME* magazine cover.

take different directions depending on who you ask. In fact, I am writing this chapter about For Freedoms and yet, many of my colleagues would likely disagree with some of my analysis and interpretations. This is an important part of our work—the multiplicity of perspectives and ideas.

But by seeking out larger values together, the amoeba-like collective can move steadily toward something bigger, even if that journey is not the same narrow path for everyone. For example, one value is to promote nuanced stories and being visionary as opposed to reactionary. When we open ourselves to nuance, we can more easily steer clear of overgeneralizations and judgmental perspectives. Taking time to not merely react but to construct a vision and work toward that means we spend our time and energy on our own

Figure 33.3. Our Values

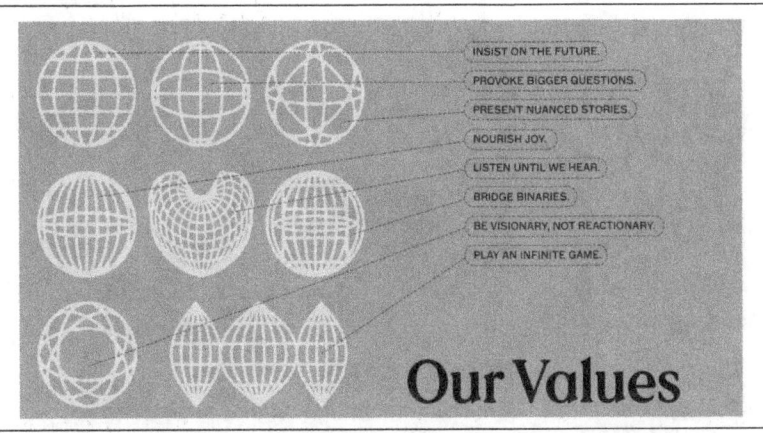

[Figure showing wireframe globe illustrations with labels:]
- INSIST ON THE FUTURE.
- PROVOKE BIGGER QUESTIONS.
- PRESENT NUANCED STORIES.
- NOURISH JOY.
- LISTEN UNTIL WE HEAR.
- BRIDGE BINARIES.
- BE VISIONARY, NOT REACTIONARY.
- PLAY AN INFINITE GAME.

Our Values

narrative and not someone else's. These are guides on how to interact with each other as FF creates together. And the values (Figure 33.3) serve as guides in how the organization relates to the world and orients toward the art they create. It is a blueprint for anyone who would like to add their dreams to these.

In 2020, an ASL interpreter FF worked with helped the team recognize they were moving toward four new freedoms. From FDR's original four freedoms, FF expanded them toward awakening, justice, healing, and listening. These four freedoms overlap and are in constant relationship with one another (Figure 33.4). Digging deep into each one, FF creates what is referred to as "invitations" related to the freedoms so that other artists can iterate as well. Each generation has the responsibility to advance the lessons from their ancestors and to further efforts toward equality, equity, and liberation for everyone. The evolution of the four freedoms is to be expected in order to create new will.

These moments of significant change in the FF sphere are a result of constant collaboration and, thus, constant calibration. As new artists enter the space, fresh ideas reinvigorate the dream and add color to more fully form the big picture.

After dancing with Awakening in 2020–2021, struggling with Justice in 2022–2023, FF is delving deep into Healing and Listening in 2024. Healing is in the zeitgeist. Across the world, people in every discipline are discussing the impacts of trauma and a plethora of healing modalities. Indigenous people are seeking healing through their own ceremonies and movements such as NDN Collective's LANDBACK. Black people are making use of various healing methods such as Tricia Hersey's Nap Ministry and also movements such as that of Reparations. Friends everywhere are seeing therapists. Women are refusing to take the blame. People are learning to say "no." And artists continue to speak truth. Paul Robeson said, "Artists are the gatekeepers of truth. We are civilization's radical voice."

One truth that is clear is that unaddressed trauma or lack of healing causes harm. In the small ways we watch some children lash out to hurt someone when they are in pain, we also know nation-states will attack another sovereign nation as a result of being in pain. It happens on the individual scale, as well as from family to family, organization

Figure 33.4. The New Four Freedoms

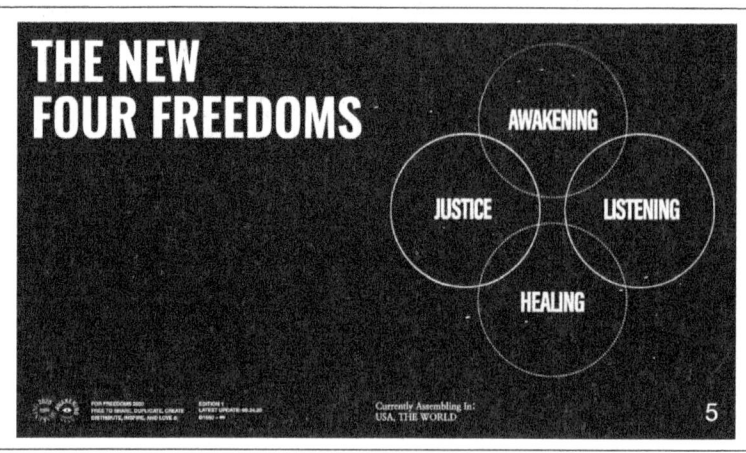

to organization, and government to government. As the saying goes, "hurt people hurt people." In the United States, systems of oppression such as ableism, transphobia, patriarchy, and racism have wreaked havoc on everyone.

A specific issue I am interested in is the effect of the systems that denied huge swaths of people in the United States inclusion, people who were overwhelmingly left out of civic participation for most of its history. Generally, only White men with property were allowed to vote initially and everyone else was excluded including slaves, women, most Jews and Catholics, and Indigenous people. For decades and even centuries, some of these groups of people were completely disenfranchised. It has only been a handful of decades where all citizens regardless of race, gender, and (dis)ability in the United States have had their right to vote protected. Even then, as mass incarceration has been one of the greatest voter disenfranchisement projects ever, there are arguments to be made that the United States is still not a true democracy. However, overwhelmingly, millions more people can vote now who could not for the majority of this country's history. And because these people's voices were not counted for so long, the United States has weaker voter turnout than most developed nations. According to the Pew Research Center, in the 2020 elections, though there was a surge in voting, the United States ranked thirty-first out of the 50 countries surveyed regarding voter turnout.

This fact often leads to allegations of voter apathy. Marketing for voter engagement leans heavily on guilting people into participating by pointing toward how many people died to secure the right to vote. Or perhaps the marketing schemes tap into people's feelings of civic duty in the JFK "ask not what your country can do for you—ask what you can do for your country" vein. I believe it is not voter apathy that leads to such low turnout, but voter pain. Among other realities, such as voter suppression, we know people experience pain from a system that explicitly denied them participation and has done little to be accountable.

HEALING IS NEEDED

To the extent possible, people need to heal their relationship with the state and their government to feel like they can engage civically. Art can do that. Artists like Amelia Winger-Bearskin, whose work digs into Indigenous values of cocreation; Miguel Luciano, who makes work about his dual relationship with Puerto Rico and the United States; and Muna Malik, whose work touches on journeys of migration. These artists face the traumas that leads to healing and in turn, makes room for people to civically engage.

The Kerner Commission report made the connection between the uprisings and grief. Much of that grief has been explicitly about the death of loved ones such as Martin Luther King, Jr. and Eric Garner. But some of the grief is about loss of opportunity, loss of land, loss of language, loss of dignity, loss of access—much of this resulting from government policy. New will comes from facing things head on, accountability, and the ability to ameliorate pain. We have ushered in a new era of candor that invites honesty and action around gender pronouns, toxic masculinity, the perils of hypercapitalism and climate change, and trauma and healing. These are all things Gen Z does not shy away from as have generations past. They have experienced the dangers of sweeping things under the rug, putting on a brave face, and keeping dirty laundry a secret. With this type of integrity and righteousness, not only will we have new will, we will generate the exact flavor of will we need to catapult our nation past good ideas and good intentions, into a reality worth bragging about.

For Freedoms believes in "inviting everyone in" because each person is an artist. While some people do not yet understand themselves in this light, we know that the more people tap into their Creativity and Imagination, the more quickly we will move into a more balanced and egalitarian reality. Artistry in every industry is left untapped until people awaken to the truth—the Creator created us to create. And upon that awakening, new will shall be abundant.

CHAPTER 34

Art as Translation

Carlton Mackey

For me, the role of the artist is to translate the longings of the hearts of the people. This is what I understand as my mandate. This is the weight of what this moment in time—this moment of fracture, unrest, and uncertainty—means to me and my understanding of my function as an artist.

I believe people often turn to artists to help them make sense of what is going on in the world around them through the lens of their own perspective. People also often lean on artists to represent them and to speak on their behalf in ways they may not feel empowered to. In the absence of artists who assume these roles, the media, which function as the interpretative voice of the world, can have a gaslighting effect on those experiencing the acute impact of oppression. Their disconnect from those reporting on the world from the outside can feel like psychological manipulation, sowing self-doubt and confusion. This is in fact a tool to gain more power and control—distorting reality and forcing one to question their own judgment and intuition.

Therefore, the role of the artist as translator is concretized not just by the creation of art but by the rootedness of the artist in the communities themselves. It is their proximity to the very pangs of racism and the everyday awareness of the realities of what it means to do more with less. My definition of community is not limited to neighborhood or geographic region. My definition of community is "those with whom we struggle for justice." The artist who emerges from within the community then is both the griot and the activist. We, as artists, have a unique responsibility to proclaim the expressed desires of the communities we are part of and to channel their righteous rage into liberating expression. This must be the wellspring from which art comes to be the true vehicle for transformation.

ON THE OTHER SIDE OF STRUGGLE

But I believe that fully unleashing the transformative power of art comes not only from its authentic emergence from within the community and its reflecting back to the community a view of itself in its moment of crisis, but also from offering the community a vision of what it has the power to become. It must foster a love of self and love of the community that believes in what both are worthy of becoming on the other side of the struggle.

It is here that Emory Douglas, the indomitable information minister of the Black Panther Party, emerges as a lodestar, casting a profound influence on my understanding

Art as Translation

of this idea. Douglas's work within the Black Panther Party, especially as the chief illustrator and art director for *The Black Panther* newspaper, stands as a testament to the power of visual storytelling in the pursuit of justice.

A TOOL FOR ACTIVISM

Douglas's art was not merely an aesthetic expression; it was a potent tool for activism. His bold, graphic illustrations served as a visual voice for the Black power movement, capturing not only the struggles but also the resilience and aspirations of Black communities in America. Through the pages of *The Black Panther*, he painted a vivid picture of not only resistance to power from the outside of the community but of pride, unity, and the presence of power within the community. These are themes that resonated deeply with my artistic ethos. The rawness of Douglas's imagery, the unapologetic celebration of Black identity, and the fearless confrontation of systemic oppression leaves an indelible mark on my creative ethos. It was not just about art for art's sake; it was about leveraging art as a weapon against injustice.

The Black power movement, with Emory Douglas as one of its visual architects, was a radical call for self-determination and empowerment. Douglas should continue to be noted for his ability to distill complex sociopolitical issues into visually arresting images. It was a masterclass in the symbiotic relationship between art and activism.

The more I immerse myself in the world of Emory Douglas's creations, the more I can understand the transformative potential of art to not only reflect the community's voice—its struggles alongside its hopes and passions—but art's ability to shape narratives.

SHAPING NARRATIVES

The Black Panther Party's newspaper was not just a publication; it was a revolutionary manifesto etched in ink and paper, challenging perceptions, and demanding change. My understanding of Douglas's ability to communicate the urgency of the Black power movement through compelling visuals met the killing of Michael Brown in Ferguson, Missouri, as a crucible—a moment that galvanized me into action. In response to the painful images and the collective grief that echoed across the nation, I founded Black Men Smile. This was not just a reaction; it was a deliberate act of defiance against the narratives that sought to reduce Black identity, particularly Black male identity, to tragedy.

Black Men Smile emerged as a celebration, a resistance, and a testament to the revolutionary power of Black joy. It started with a simple hashtag—#blackmensmile—and has organically evolved into a vibrant, crowd-sourced archive of over 115,000 images and a community of nearly 100,000 followers on Instagram. The movement became a sanctuary, a space where Black men could authentically celebrate themselves in a world that often sought to diminish their humanity.

Creating this platform for resistance, reflection, and renewal gave me a deeper understanding of the emotional landscape carved by Douglas in the Black power movement. As did Douglas, I recognized the transformative potential of positive representation.

Black Men Smile became a declaration—a narrative crafted in pixels in an ever-growing landscape that leveraged the power of social media as a tool for movement makers but became real through the formation of communities built on shared experiences pushing back against the prevailing narratives of victimhood.

In resonance with the words of Alice Walker that "Resistance is the secret of Joy," this movement was not just about smiling for the camera; it was a collective act of defiance, a reclaiming of agency in the face of adversity. It was a deliberate effort to showcase the multifaceted nature of Black identity, countering the one-dimensional portrayals that often dominated mainstream media—the same media that functioned to gaslight our communities about the realities of their struggle. Black Men Smile, in its essence, was a visual manifesto that hoped, in its own way, to leverage visual narratives to echo the spirit of the Black power movement—a testament translating the longings of the hearts of the people through the revolutionary power of art.

ART AND SPIRITUALITY

Arturo Lindsay, an artist known for his profound exploration of the intersection between art and spirituality, emphasizes the transformative potential of this connection. Lindsay's work delves into the spiritual dimensions of the human experience, drawing inspiration from African diasporic traditions and the cultural practices of the Gullah people. Through his art, Lindsay seeks to evoke a sense of the sacred, inviting viewers to engage with the spiritual aspects of life. In a similar vein, James Baldwin, a prominent figure in literature and civil rights activism, acknowledged the inherent connection between art and spirituality. Baldwin's writings often grapple with profound existential questions and the search for meaning, particularly in the face of oppression. Both Lindsay and Baldwin recognize that art has the capacity to tap into the deepest recesses of the human soul, offering a space for introspection, connection, the exploration of broader societal values, but most importantly, the compulsion for freedom and liberation.

The intersection of art and spirituality, as understood by Lindsay and Baldwin, becomes another transformative force in society. Art that engages with spirituality becomes a vehicle for fostering resilience, empathy, and interconnectedness. It encourages individuals to embark on an inward journey, exploring their thoughts and emotions in the context of broader societal challenges. The Kerner Report's vision of societal transformation encompasses not only structural changes but also a cultural shift, and the confluence of art and spirituality contributes to this shift by nurturing a sense of shared purpose alongside communal well-being.

This intersection takes on profound significance in my role at the High Museum of Art, where I co-lead an initiative named OASIS alongside my colleagues in the education department. OASIS is a unique program centered on the convergence of art, presence, and contemplative practice. Within OASIS, we take spirituality seriously, recognizing it as a primary meaning-maker and a crucial element in engaging with art and creativity.

OASIS encompasses three activations in the museum, featuring movement-based practices like yoga or tai chi, sound healing experiences with instruments like sound bowls, and a conversation series led by me titled "Seeing with Spirit." This series facilitates casual and thoughtful conversations connecting art and spiritual practices. Each month, I engage with a faith, spiritual, or contemplative practitioner, exploring a specific work of art and delving into the ways that art invites deeper reflection into their contemplative practice. The guest speakers come from diverse backgrounds, including a Yoruba priestess, a Tibetan Buddhist monk, and thinkers from Christian, Jewish, and Muslim traditions.

The connection between art and spirituality serves as a powerful avenue for introspection, self-discovery, and communal healing. In times of societal fractures, individuals seek connections, meaning, and renewal, and these can be particularly expressed amid differences in faith or religious beliefs. What's remarkable is witnessing people not only come together across these differences but also use art as a portal for discussing and understanding these differences. By avoiding proselytizing about their religion and instead offering interpretations of a work of art through the lens of their faith, the guest speakers create a space for dialogue. The program's structure acknowledges that the guest speaker is not an authority on the art, fostering an environment where participants feel permission to interrogate the work through the lens of their own faith. This dialogue becomes a rare and enriching space where people talk about usually divisive topics, and art becomes the sounding board for these conversations.

Art, with its capacity to evoke emotions and provoke thought, seamlessly aligns with the spiritual practices guiding individuals toward inner balance and a broader perspective on their place in the world. Furthermore, the OASIS program's emphasis on mindfulness practices is particularly relevant in an era marked by heightened anxiety, often attributed to the pervasive influence of social media. Recognizing the need for practices that cultivate presence, awareness, and mental well-being, OASIS positions the museum as a sanctuary for mindfulness. Participants can temporarily disconnect from the chaos of the external world and engage in activities that promote tranquility and self-reflection.

The deliberate confluence of art, spirituality, and mindfulness within OASIS serves as a strategic response to contemporary societal challenges. It acknowledges that fractures in society extend beyond the structural (racism) and economic, reaching into the spiritual and mental realms. By creating a space that encourages holistic well-being, we may contribute to the "new will" by fostering resilience, empathy, a sense of interconnectedness . . . and an ability to speak beyond boundaries.

ART, TRANSFORMATIVE EDUCATION, AND SOCIAL JUSTICE

In the realm of transformative pedagogy, as illuminated by bell hooks in her groundbreaking work *Teaching to Transgress*, art emerges as a powerful catalyst for societal transformation. hooks advocates for an educational approach that challenges existing norms, fostering critical thinking, inclusivity, and a profound engagement with knowledge. Art, in this context, becomes a dynamic tool for transcending conventional boundaries in the learning process. It encourages students to explore diverse perspectives, question established systems, and, importantly, connect their learning to broader societal issues. The intersection of art and education, as envisioned by hooks, not only shapes individual perspectives, but, I propose, may contribute to the collective construction of the "new will," echoing the aspirations articulated in the Kerner Report. By integrating artistic expression into the educational fabric, students are not only exposed to different modes of creativity but, with art, may also be encouraged to become active participants in shaping a society that values equity, empathy, and transformative change. This intersection is the grounding for the Arts and Social Justice (ASJ) Fellowship Program.

In 2020, amid a groundswell of national attention to racial and social injustice after the killing of George Floyd and building on my belief in the power of art to affect positive social change, this program was born. The idea came together that summer out of conversations between me and Kevin Karnes, associate dean for the arts in Emory College. We talked about how Emory can engage meaningfully with our city in this unfolding moment of crisis, and about what we could learn from Atlanta's artists, many of whom have been working tirelessly toward racial and social justice their whole careers.

"What drew us together is our shared faith in the power of art to open spaces for conversation, community-making and collective action," says Karnes. "We believe that those things are urgently needed if we are to emerge from this moment in a way that is whole, and, we hope, better than how we lived together before."

The fellowship pairs artists with classes ranging from business to biology, from creative writing to computer science, from the School of Math and Science to the School of Medicine. Selected from a pool of nearly 100 applicants, the inaugural cohort of Arts and Social Justice Fellows showcases some of the most celebrated and vibrant threads of artistic creativity in the city.

Participating faculty members work alongside their partnered ASJ Fellows to design creative projects that reflect racial or other inequities. The projects are embedded into existing courses and brought to fruition by students within the framework of those classes.

One example was the pairing of professional actor and playwright Garrett Turner and award-winning journalist Hank Klibanoff for the writing course Georgia Civil Rights Cold Cases, which centered in part on the history of the 1906 Atlanta race massacre.

Liz Greene, a senior at Emory in 2020, one of 16 students in this class, found herself delving into this historical tragedy. In a stark parallel to the context of the Kerner Report, this dark episode retained a disturbingly contemporary relevance. Before taking this course, however, Greene had never heard of this gruesome event—a violent upheaval that unleashed around 5,000 white men rampaging through downtown Atlanta. The aftermath was horrific, with Black-owned businesses vandalized, and Black residents subjected to hanging, stabbing, bludgeoning, and shooting. The 3-day chaos left 25 Black Atlantans dead, and countless homes and businesses in ruins, with none of the perpetrators facing conviction. Reflecting on the course, Greene emphasized its profound impact, acknowledging the visceral reminder it provided that the struggle against such injustices has persisted for generations, underscoring the substantial distance yet to be covered. However, for Greene and her peers in Emory's Georgia Civil Rights Cold Cases course, this tragic uprising evolved beyond a somber footnote in Atlanta's history.

Utilizing art as a medium for memory, imagination, and empathy-building, she and her classmates immersed themselves in the untold human stories of the oppressed and the oppressors. They achieved this by crafting and performing scripts that depicted their imagined scenarios, embodying the thoughts, feelings, and emotions of that fateful day in 1906 and drawing connections to similar emotions experienced today.

Emma Kantor, an Emory senior studying creative writing and film, says melding historical research and storytelling through the Georgia Civil Rights Cold Case course required "digging deep to understand hour-by-hour what happened that night." "A lot of this class was uncovering stories that aren't widely understood," she says. "Learning about the 1906 Atlanta massacre made me think about what is happening right now that won't be widely understood—how history can be presumed and lost and found."

Each month throughout the semester, the full cohort of faculty, ASJ Fellows, and their students gather to learn about each other's work, and to exchange ideas across the university about the arts and social justice. The semester concludes with a public unveiling and citywide conversation to consider collectively the completed art-based projects and the questions they raise.

Bringing these ASJ Fellows together with a group of scholars—whose courses challenge traditional thinking about the intersection of race, public health, and business—will advance and offer critical nuance to the public dialogue about these issues, as well as prepare college students to face these issues with courage and compassion as they encounter them in the real world. This approach aligns with the Kerner Commission's call for comprehensive policies and cultural shifts and highlights the transformative power of art as a vehicle for transformative education, as bell hooks describes, and its integral role in fostering the collective determination or the new will needed for societal renewal.

NAVIGATING LEGACY: MONUMENTS, NAMES, AND THE UNIVERSITY LANDSCAPE

In 2021, the president of Emory University created a commission tasked with reassessing the names and legacies associated with historic buildings on campus. I had the pleasure of serving on that commission. This initiative, born out of a broader national dialogue on historical monuments, echoes the unique challenges faced by communities in the South regarding monuments honoring Confederate figures.

Debates about the fate of Confederate monuments and memorials across the United States highlight a crucial aspect of societal memory. The decisions we make regarding these monuments determine not only how we remember the victims of past horrors but also whose memories we value and venerate. It's a profound consideration—deciding whose lives and legacies matter, and it shapes our collective understanding of history. Ultimately the Commission was tasked to generate a report to the president with recommendations for what the university should do regarding buildings named after former presidents, board members, and donors whose legacies may be intertwined with racist ideologies.

Chairing the commission was an Emory law professor who created a framework where we created a report that emphasizes the need for circumspection, acknowledging the challenge of judging historical eras through the moral lens of the present day. It recognizes that named buildings have become part of the institution's history and that preserving or removing these names has implications for future generations. The commission's charge echoes the broader national discourse on contested monuments, calling for a nuanced approach that considers not only the historical actions of the individuals but also their impact on the university's values. This approach aligns with my broader commitment to ethical engagement and social justice, bringing artistic sensibility to bear on questions of institutional memory and representation.

In the discourse around Confederate monuments, there's a prevalent focus on what should be torn down, but the chair's vision advocated for a broader conversation about who and what we should be building up. Chairing this commission was Dr. Fred Smith, whose specialized research at the Emory School of Law delves into the interests and rights of African ancestors, exploring the legal frameworks designed to protect the memories of the dead from exploitation and degradation. Legal rights to a decent burial, rules against destroying gravesites, and civil rights laws banning discrimination after death reflect the important take that we can leverage of our nation's seeming interest in human dignity, memory, and legacy.

The legal framework he offered would extend to our thinking about monuments. Currently, there exists a substantial imbalance between monuments honoring colonizers, enslavers, and Confederates compared to memorials dedicated to the colonized, captured, and controlled. This disparity not only harms the living but also perpetuates an assault on the memories of the dead victims of police killings, public lynchings, enslavement, land confiscation, and other atrocities. It denies them the ability to leave a legacy and shape our collective memory.

To address this inequality and contribute to a more just and egalitarian society, we must actively invest in monuments and memorials that uplift the memories and legacies of those historically marginalized. Drawing inspiration from initiatives like Europe's Stolpersteine or Bryan Stevenson's Legacy Museum and the National Memorial for Peace and Justice or The Stolen Lives Quilt, we can create spaces that commemorate the lives and mourn the deaths of those who have been overlooked by traditional monuments.

Moving forward on a path to greater equality and justice, we should allocate more resources to knowing and celebrating the names, stories, memories, and legacies of individuals who have been historically marginalized. This commitment aligns with the broader vision of the Naming Honors Committee, where our recommendations for the university became not only to reassess existing names but to actively contribute to building a university environment that fosters inclusivity, intellectual rigor, and a commitment to justice.

This endeavor, in any context across the world, is not without challenges, as it requires navigating the delicate balance when dealing with historical legacies, especially in a university setting, where tradition often holds significant weight. The acknowledgment that past contributions have been historically unrecognized due to systemic racism underscores the need for prudence in celebrating legacies. As I contributed to this complex and transformative process, my artistic sensibility was a guiding force.

Again, art has the power to provoke thought, challenge norms, and invite reflection. In my specific context of university naming and as it relates to broader conversations about monuments in general, it becomes a tool for prompting a reconsideration of legacies, a medium for engaging with history critically, and a means for envisioning a future that aligns with the values of justice and equity.

RECOMMENDATIONS FOR CHANGE

The Kerner Commission's stark warning of "two Nations, one black, one white—separate and unequal" remains tragically relevant. In the spirit of bridging this divide and fostering inclusivity, the following five recommendations embrace the transformative power of art. Advocating for policy recommendations is not just a prescription for change; it is anchored in my belief in the profound potential of art to shape societies. These recommendations reflect the multifaceted impact art can have on societal structures, and span five key domains—neighborhoods and communities, education, diversity and inclusion, collaboration beyond borders, and science and technology. However, the implementation of these policies is not without challenges and requires a nuanced approach to navigate potential complexities.

EDUCATION POLICIES—ART AS A BRIDGE TO EDUCATION

- Integrated Arts Curriculum: Revise educational frameworks to include mandatory arts education from an early age. Embed the arts across various subjects, not just isolated to art classes, allowing students to explore historical events through drama, interpret scientific concepts through dance, and delve into social issues through creative writing. This holistic approach fosters critical thinking, emotional intelligence, and problem-solving skills, while nurturing respect for diverse perspectives and experiences.
- Artist-in-Residence Programs: While my experiences have been more so in higher education, inviting artists to reside in K–12 schools for extended periods fosters an atmosphere of creativity and innovation. This can be particularly valuable in districts that don't have art programs or full-time art teachers. Artists can collaborate with core subject teachers to develop project-based learning experiences, mentor students, and provide real-world exposure to various art forms.
- Arts-Focused Summer Programs: Implement subsidized summer arts programs offering intensive workshops and mentorship opportunities for students from low-income backgrounds. These programs can bridge educational gaps, identify, and nurture young talent, and provide safe spaces for self-expression, equipping youth with valuable skills and a sense of empowerment during a particularly challenging time when school is out.

COMMUNITY ENGAGEMENT POLICIES—REVITALIZING COMMUNITIES THROUGH PARTICIPATORY ART INITIATIVES

- Neighborhood Arts Labs: Establish community art centers equipped with resources and professional guidance. These labs could offer free or subsidized workshops in various art forms, from visual arts and music to dance and

filmmaking. Community residents would have the agency to help shape workshop themes, ensuring content reflects their experiences and aspirations. This empowers self-expression, fostering a sense of ownership and identity within the community. Collaborative public art projects can emerge from these labs that reflect the community's voice.
- Collaborative Public Art Projects: Allocate funding for murals, sculptures, or performance pieces created collaboratively by artists and community members. This encourages dialogue, breaks down social barriers, and transforms public spaces into living testimonies of shared identities and local narratives.
- Mobile Arts Caravans: Utilize mobile units equipped with art supplies and technology to reach more rural and underserved neighborhoods lacking access to dedicated arts spaces. These caravans, like the community-centered arts labs, can provide creative outlets for youth, spark intergenerational engagement, and celebrate cultural diversity. In addition to providing art access, these mobile units can also help bridge the digital divide by bringing access to technology—an ever-increasing component of artistic creation.
- Community Tech Labs: Establish accessible community tech labs equipped with computers, specialized software, and high-speed Internet. These labs would offer free or subsidized training programs in digital art forms like animation, 3D modeling, coding for interactive installations, and augmented reality design. This direct engagement addresses the specific needs and challenges faced by marginalized communities, ensuring equitable access to the empowering world of digital art.

LOCAL AND INTERNATIONAL COLLABORATION POLICIES—AMPLIFYING DIVERSE AND MARGINALIZED VOICES

- Develop a robust online platform that serves as a dynamic hub for connecting artists and art organizations worldwide. This platform could facilitate networking, knowledge sharing, and collaborative project development, creating fertile ground for cross-cultural artistic expression. Imagine a digital space where indigenous artists from South America connect with electronic music producers in New York, or where a Japanese manga artist collaborates with a street artist from Nairobi on a virtual installation exploring themes of climate justice. The platform could also host a comprehensive digital archive showcasing the artistic expressions of diverse communities and marginalized groups globally. This would ensure greater visibility and accessibility to cultural treasures often relegated to the periphery, promoting mutual understanding and appreciation of differences.
- Drawing inspiration from the impactful work of Hank Willis Thomas and the For Freedoms project, which engaged over 200 artists across the United States in creating billboards addressing pressing social issues, sparking dialogue, and igniting local activism, the platform would foster local and international collaborations tackling social justice issues and advocating for human rights.

Imagine a global photography project documenting the experiences of refugees around the world, or a collaborative mural painted by youth activists from conflict zones, their shared artwork becoming a powerful symbol of solidarity and hope. This sort of platform could provide space for more than art to be exchanged. It could also include tactics and strategies for organizing and encourage a deeper appreciation for both the similarities and important differences across movements for justice.
- The platform could also support smaller-scale community-based projects, connecting local artists with international counterparts to share traditional art forms, cocreate performances, and develop educational workshops. This grassroots approach ensures diverse voices are not drowned out by larger initiatives, fostering cultural exchange and empowerment at the community level.

These recommendations go beyond a mere call for change; they invite a collective reflection on values, and present practical ideas for creating spaces where art becomes a catalyst for inclusive, transformative, and interconnected communities.

CONCLUSION

As an educator and artist, I bear witness to the power of resilience and creativity. I see my commitment to personal growth and transformation as a continuation of the legacy of those who came before me. The resonances of the Kerner Report still echo from the past but point to the realities of our present condition that extend beyond the classroom and the canvas. My work at the intersections of academia, community engagement, spirituality, and policy advocacy converge to strengthen my conviction in the transformative capacity of art as a catalyst for enduring societal change.

Guided by influences of artists such as Emory Douglas, James Baldwin, Arturo Lindsay, bell hooks, and pivotal societal moments, I hope my journey contributes to a narrative committed to amplifying marginalized voices. From the birth of the Black Men Smile movement in response to the tragic death of Michael Brown to initiatives within higher education to work at the High Museum of Art at the intersection of art and spirituality, alongside an exploration of the complexities of historic monuments within the context of Emory University, these elements serve as crucial components in my commitment to not only arts advocacy, but also to reevaluating and reshaping historical narratives, acknowledging the importance of circumspection in honoring legacies consistent with present values.

Art, in its myriad forms, isn't merely a medium of expression; it's a force for social change. It has the potential to move beyond reflecting the present to envisioning a future of strength and resilience. The policy recommendations, ranging through education, community engagement, and collaboration, offer a future vision for the transformative potential of art on a societal scale.

This is a call to action—beacon for a collective endeavor extending to all those recognizing the profound impact that art can have on shaping societies. May it become a movement—a promise to make the transformative power of art sustainable beyond this moment, crafting a communal narrative of unity, understanding, and enduring joy. As we step away from this exploration, may the remnants, like those of the original report, remain—a living testament to the belief in the revolutionary power of creativity—a force that, when harnessed for societal good, can genuinely change the world. It certainly has changed me.

CHAPTER 35

Regenerating the Body of Culture

brooke smiley

I take space for pause—and listen. Body, give me hope. I feel my midline, a place of balance among so many differences within me. I am whole and many parts together, even among all the storms and all the history. The body strives for homeostasis. It gives me hope because there is a chance for two sides to come together and meet, amongst all the different systems, tissues, and intelligence—and if that can happen in my own body and is happening in each of our bodies, then that gives me hope for how we can come together as a community of cells, cells of a larger body. We are all nature—no matter how separate or isolated or divided our current culture teaches us or asks us to perform. We have choice in how we meet ourselves here, and one another.

There is a growing awareness for the need of body and earth-based healing experiences. Performing arts are being redefined and support is growing for sustainable practices that nourish not only public spaces but artists living beyond mere survival. To do more than survive, to find comfort in the body, one can begin exploring curiosity. Our ability to be curious revitalizes capacity for expression and connection, not just as individuals but as a body of culture. Funding structures have hiccuped as our field grows. Meanwhile Native artists and organizations are innervating sustainable, resilient funding ecosystems to begin to meet the abundance transpiring among civic-engaged performing arts projects. We are not just making performance, but regenerating land stewardship. We include budget lines for Native partnership fees, transforming who has access to art making and what communities have a voice and are benefiting as a part of our evolving culture.

REVALUING BODY AND EARTH

The ability to encourage listening in one's body is nurtured when in relationship with the earth. The earth meets us in our experience of being parts to a greater whole. When there is access to earth, rocks, water, fire, and land, and all that live in and amongst and underneath, there is access to what nourishes us on a cellular level. Our ancestors are here. Our life force is regenerated here. These elements are all teachers, beings with their own consciousness. As Derrick Jensen points out when naming Indigenous concepts of interrelatedness while tipping the "Great Chain of Being" (scala naturae), animals, plants, and rocks hold intelligence beyond any hierarchical representation we can conceive of.[1]

When we come into relationship with intelligence and histories other than our own, it brings out a truth, it cultivates relationship.

I acknowledge my intention is continually in service to my body learning how to be safe in relationship. I am invested in this care so I can better offer spaces of relative safety to others, and be able to protect myself when I notice this absence of capacity in the room. I acknowledge that my safety is shaken when coming into visibility, and that I am not alone in this inherited generational fear.

I feel in my body a 𐓏𐓟𐓶𐓘, a desire to do my best and be strong, to not give up. It has taken perseverance in broadening my practices to be able to show up and learn when in relationship. These practices include dance and somatic movement education, and also sustainable building methods, specializing in superadobe. A big part of my learning has focused on how to cultivate safety when meeting my own story, my family's stories, my friends' stories, and trusting in a rhythmic pacing of toward and away, digesting how my story relates with anyone else who has ever left their homelands out of safety or survival.

My grandfather is Osage. When he was 8, he was removed from his mother and father's home after she died, and much was silenced about what he saw, felt, and experienced. Like many families that dissolved overnight, choices were made to survive. He eventually joined the Navy, coming out to California in the late 1920s, along with numerous Osages. This time in our collective history is known as the "Reign of Terror" and is the basis for Martin Scorsese's most recent film *Killers of the Flower Moon*, featuring Lily Gladstone, Leonardo DiCaprio, and Robert De Niro.[2] So many Osages left during this time that there are now Northern and Southern California Osage groups who gather annually as a way of connecting with our culture, sharing fellowship and conversations vital to us. There is a separation from those who were able to remain on the Osage Nation homelands with real respect for who was able to continue our cultural practices. This is apparent in the In'Lonschka ceremonial dances where families no longer have benches, camps, and family songs because of this loss of contact.

In my journey of reconnection I have been received in ways well beyond what I ever had imagined or dreamed, encouraging that there is space for hope and healing, for truth and love to replace fear and harm.

My evolving relationship with dance and movement, earth and family, community and 𐓏𐓘𐓻𐓘𐓻𐓘 Osage culture has contributed to the pulsation of safety in my expression, empowerment, and service. As a Native person who grew up outside of my homelands, and as one of many Native people who are healing from generational trauma, violence, and forced diaspora specific to the U.S. government, addressing safety in public discourse and art experiences is foundational. Everyone's base level is unique. Investing in practices that provide space for difference, do not assume, and are active in consent with ways to check in and make a new choice is vital.

There are layers to our developing nervous system that carry us throughout life and inform our body's capacity for participation, expression, connection, and art making. These are deeply reflected in our life force and ability to rebound from unexpected challenges. The very first foundational layer is to survive. To do more than merely survive, one may begin to adjust toward comfort in the body, somewhere, somehow. This ability to move toward comfort can be in relation to oneself, an animal, a form of expression, an environment, language, an idea, or another person. This can lead to discovering a sense of bonding. Bonding is deeply regulating on a cellular level. Bonding is sustained comfort. This may be evident when looking toward consensual desires for touch, whether it is with the places on the earth you are in contact with now, or adjustments toward comfort while falling asleep horizontal in bed at night. The space for choice to adjust toward comfort generates a possibility for bonding. And bonding grows an opportunity for deep relaxation and restoration in the parasympathetic nervous system. This returning back to balance, or homeostasis, can occur both inside the body and also grows to be outside of oneself, forming a resonance of trust. It is only when we are able to do more than survive, adjust toward comfort, enter the possibility for bonding, that we ever have a chance to meet the last phase of becoming curious.

Curiosity is the foundation for learning something new. Curiosity is when there is enough safety in the body to explore beyond what we already know. In the perceptual-response cycle, there are nine stages our nervous systems experience that influence our capacity to experience something new, or experience the same information differently.[3] This somatic knowledge has been developed by Bonnie Bainbridge Cohen, a somatic visionary and longstanding practitioner who developed Body Mind Centering® with the integral network of community members from babies to elders. Together, this teaching of embryology, experiential anatomy, and repatterning continues to grow much like an organism, with applications and approaches evolving with new people, circumstances, and communities.

The perceptual-response cycle begins with preconceived expectations. This is what one expects to have happen before anything actually happens. This is based upon what

Figure 35.1. *Huddle*, Simone Forti.

Simone Forti, *Huddle*, 1961. Performance. 10 min. The Museum of Modern Art, New York. Committee on Media and Performance Art Funds. © 2018 The Museum of Modern Art, New York. Guided by brooke smiley, performed at Cal Earth, 2018. Photo: © 2018 Alexis Story Crawshaw.

previous perceptions one has of their past experiences. History can and does repeat itself in our bodies daily. This then moves into presensory motor focus, which is an ability to choose which incoming stimuli to pay attention to or absorb. Depending on what we choose to experience, we may be missing a great deal of all that is present, as in trauma patterns. This cycle goes further into the patterning of who we are and why we are this way, ending right back to the beginning again with underlying questions: Where in all of this is there space for choice? Where is there space to learn and experience something new?

If my ancestors chose invisibility and silence out of safety and survival, imagine the underlying tones of fear to be seen for who one actually is in the world, in one's fullness, in one's identity, in one's culture. How is this fear embodied and passed forward in our cells from one generation to the next? Being Native today, being an artist who acknowledges the confusion inside the perceived fear of not wanting to be seen—there is a recognition of trauma, there is a recognition of complexity.

To include the people of the land whose ancestors were systematically isolated, violated, murdered, and forced to relocate necessitates an acknowledgement of complexity. If we are invited to the table, we aren't coming with the same nervous systems. We are growing and reaching curiosity through expression, art making, and meeting what wants to be made visible, to be healed. Art experiences have healing at the root of each stage, be it with laughter and comedy of the phenomenal TV series *Reservation Dogs*, directed by Sterlin Harjo with an all-Native cast and crew, or language revitalization with ways of uplifting languages and stories of the land.

REVITALIZING ART/EXPRESSION/CULTURE

Performing arts are growing to include social practice, place-based community processes to invite a deeper connection to one another, culture, and the land. The stakes are high for those who invest in the unknown. For those who make their choice to invest in listening to community needs and valuing process. The challenge is real when in relationship with a society whose priorities are taught through languages that omit most meaning and nuance. In a world of measured outcomes, defined successes, artists fill in the gaps of what is missing, inventing new ways of relating, seeing, and being. Those who are valuing difference are shifting the foundations of how we relate not just with ourselves, with one another, with our earth, and our histories, but globally, and interstellar.

The performing arts are unique. They can connect social justice, education, and sciences because they specifically bring us into relationship with the body. Arts inspire the process of discovering one's voice, our autonomy, and also our interconnectedness. How a country values the arts and its artists informs the value systems for society, establishing how and where we come together. What language is used determines so much about that invitation.

In the Osage language, 70% of all words are verbs. Movement is a big deal. Not acknowledging that things are moving and in relationship with something else erases more than half of our language. Erasing half of our language erases a sensitivity to what and how we are in relationship. It erases what we value, diminishes our way of acknowledging connection, perceiving, being alive, and changing in the world. Our Osage language is primarily based on two things: proximity and movement, and we share this ratio with many other Native languages. Proximity is how near or far one thing is to something else. Movement or positionality is how one is in relationship to something else that is moving or in a certain orientation.[4] The English language, however, is almost entirely the opposite, 70% are nouns and 30% are verbs.

In Osage, there is no name for the cardinal directions, like West. There is only a word for where the sun rises or where the sun is going down on the horizon. When you take away acknowledging that there is a horizon and one is in relationship with it, when you take away that there is a sun that is always moving, then there is only a name, or a noun, like the West. Similarly, taking away how one is in connection with others, in connection with the world erases the lens of relationship, but more importantly the safety that can be drawn from recognizing I am not alone. I am not in isolation. I am part of a greater whole that is moving.

Beginning with language, there are inherent differences in the way Native people perceive and express in the world, unique to each tribe, each family, and each person. Language is the backbone for how one communicates, informing our shared experiences, and defining our choices. It highlights what is valued, seen, and given voice to. It also values what is being dismissed. For all Native people, speaking their language incurred violence, and no longer became an option during colonization. Many Native languages were lost in this way as it was illegal to speak or dance until the 1978 American Indian Religious Freedom Act was passed. Consider, if your language is illegal, what does that do to one's body? To the generations of bodies that come after? How can expression ever be empowered again? How many generations does it take, as United Nation honoree Marc Bamuthi Joseph describes, to "heal forward"?[5]

Separation from expression, repression of natural response, cultivates disease. Thankfully our generation is in a bodily revolution that is not just based in language revitalization, but in all forms of expression including the performing arts. How is worldview considered in Western performing arts? What education is taking place to widen the field?

Western performing arts are known to include dance, music, theater, opera, poetry, circus, puppetry, magic, improv, and comedy, deriving from lineages and methods that began in Greece in the 6th century B.C. Looking to these fields today, how are artists who are of a different descent, who inherently embody a different way of living in the world, meeting this moment? Many artists are developing methodologies for societal transformation, for reconnection with community. What Western performance was utilized for is changing. Even the term *performing arts* no longer speaks to what artists are successfully pulling off, what we are capable of, and the structures of support we are revolutionizing to generate safety, connection, and belonging into a healthier body of culture.

Leilehua Lanzilotti is a contemporary Kanaka Maoli (Native Hawaiian) composer/ multimedia artist and 2022 Pulitzer Prize finalist, who centers community and sustainability in their work. Awarded with the Native Arts and Cultures 2023 SHIFT Transformative Change and Indigenous Arts, Lanzilotti is partnering with Te Ao Mana in generating community-centered practices that includes free hula, language education, and cultural workshops leading up to their new opera project, *Liliʻu*. It tells the story of when Queen Liliʻuokalani was imprisoned and the power of the songs she composed.[6] Lanzilotti is seeding the ecology of sustainability through residencies to first learn more about community needs and responding in alignment.

This space to come together through language and culture and celebrate the diaspora is a contemporary study in resilience: Hawaiians are being sustained financially while creating an opera that is about resilience. The heart of the artistic work is reflected in the structure of the project itself in creating resilient ecosystems.

Indicative of contemporary Native arts culture is the capacity to span many fields. What are examples of multidisciplinary, collaborative performing arts projects today?

EARTH.SPEAKS

EARTH.SPEAKS is a land-based public art project aimed at healing through the community creation of earth markers, guided with trauma-informed Body Mind Centering® somatic movement education and multisensory movement scores. This project grew as an integral next step when land is returned back to a tribe, or to begin the conversation of bringing land stewardship back into Native leadership in national parks, monuments, and forests.

Rooting in risk and love, this project enlivens art experiences as both diplomacy and education. It recenters public spaces and who they serve by guiding creative processes with Native and non-Native communities, uplifting the complexity of contemporary Native identity across generations. It uplifts the collaborative creation of embodied earth markers and multisensory dance performances to remap our worlds.

The first iteration of EARTH.SPEAKS, ámanikyatumeʼɵvi, or "Resting Hand" (2023), was made in collaboration with the Southern Ute Tribe while I was an artist in residence with Green Box Arts in Green Mountain Falls, Colorado. This was the first time I connected how I first move in a space to inform the design. I was dancing after it had snowed, and I could see my pathway. This path became repetitive, and I saw that my footprints created a design (see Figure 35.2). After discussion and visiting the site with Southern Ute Cultural Preservation officer Cassandra Atencio, this evolved to become a circle of earthen benches with the creek running through the middle, a resting hand with the water flowing back toward the center of the heart (Figure 35.3).

These earthworks, varying in scale, are built by hand, repurposing materials of war—earth, sandbags, barbed wire, and water—and utilizing them for peace. This technique called superadobe comes from earth architect Nader Khalili,[7] who was tapped by NASA for these innovative, human-focused earth buildings that incorporate primitive technology with contemporary safety standards.

The emergence and building of these earth markers empowers Native individuals, centers Native individuals in community, and literally rebuilds these relationships by hand. Much of how we as Native people have been and are currently portrayed is in the past tense. I believe this is a real opportunity for the Native community to have agency in how we are portrayed and the unique gifts we have to share, centering our relationship with the earth. This work orients Native artistic practice in the conversation of social

Figure 35.2. Movement Footprint

brooke smiley, Movement Footprint, EARTH.SPEAKS, March 2023. Green Mountain Falls, CO. Green Box Artist in Residence.

Figure 35.3. EARTH.SPEAKS. ámanikyatumeʼevi, or "Resting Hand," 2023

brooke smiley, EARTH.SPEAKS, May 2023. Green Mountain Falls, CO. Green Box Artist in Residence. Photo: © 2023 Dave Wolverton.

services and curates sustainable opportunities to imagine, create, and build, while generating visibility, education, and art in our most sacred spaces.

The second iteration took place in Spring of 2024, and partners with Bioneers Native Youth Leadership Program, Lawrence Hall of Science, and the Muwekma Ohlone Tribe in what is known as Berkeley, California. It is supported by the National Endowment for the Arts and California Arts Council. Throughout 2024 and 2025, I aim to build three more earthworks, with organizations in Missouri, Oklahoma, and California.

My goal for the next decade is to utilize the EARTH.SPEAKS project to activate local body and land-based art processes to repair relationships within Native communities and with non-Native people. Uplifting deeper histories of the land, making visible and creating access for the First Peoples of these lands will provide healing for our bodies and with one another. The dream is to partner with national monuments, parks, and forests, generating new belonging not only with the land but in the bodies.

EARTH.SPEAKS is one of several Native-led art projects based in community that will nurture Native and Indigenous presence and history, uplifting Native culture with a visual artifact for future generations to return to.

Through the exceptional producing team at Sozo Impact, this project actively invites partnerships with arts organizations, national monuments, parks, and forests, Indigenous Tribes, and trusted leaders in these lands with deep ties to community members.

RE-INDIGENIZING LAND STEWARDSHIP/NATIVE LEADERSHIP/PLACES OF BELONGING

What if public land stewardship included Native leadership? How might our evolving culture benefit with the history and knowledge in connection to land? How might this inspire Native youth programs that centered around arts and education? What if spaces were designed and built by Native people for Native people on these lands? How might the regeneration of the Indigenous cultural body regenerate the body of all of our cultures?

As Native peoples, we do not have access to our most sacred lands. Some are privately owned, and others are now national monuments. Our younger generations are growing up without a sense of belonging or connection and stories are being lost. We have an opportunity to create a cultural shift in terms of Native visibility and presence.

Theater performances that also meet the impossible task of generating belonging through community connection include the transformative plays *We the People* by Ty Defoe (Oneida and Ojibwe) and Larissa Fasthorse (Sicangu Lakota) and *Where We Belong* by Madeleine Sayet (Mohegan). These works address belonging on a broader scale and how to build relative safety by orienting towards education, healing, and expression.

There is evidence and hope for the future of democracy. It is in the connections we make as humans, and the practices of care we cultivate beyond the politics that may try to divide us.

The *Lili'u* and EARTH.SPEAKS projects are some of many Native and Indigenous examples that show why including Native leadership in public land stewardship is of benefit to ecological and cultural diversity. The impact of Native-forward works that bring Native bodies back into relationship with sacred lands like our national monuments, parks, and forests is a revolutionary step in changing the public discourse around contemporary Native identity and the integrity and sustainability of our relationship with lands.

RE-EDUCATING PARTNERSHIPS AND FUNDING STRUCTURES

As the absolutely incredible Quita Sullivan (Montaukett/Shinnecock) aptly called out:

> "Changing starts with who is making decisions."[8] Funding is beginning to emerge, but the urgency to develop structures of sustainable support is not always from an indigenous perspective.

Leading and modeling sustainability deserve to be as much a part of my work as anyone else's. A way to begin doing this now is to reevaluate the value systems in your annual budget, in your project budgets. Include partner fees for the Native tribe on whose land you are creating work; invite them to be a part of your process to learn who they are, what their needs are, and how your project may contribute. Provide funding to them for talking with you; relationship building is a budget line. Include Native leadership in your board. Provide Native community members with parking passes if you're at an institution on their homelands. The most important part of a land acknowledgement is the accountability piece. Ask, what am I doing now to uplift Native people and community members' needs? How can I show up to this in the arc of a 2-, 5-, 10-year plan?

Artists reveal how to be in relationship through long trust-building processes, through collaborative projects that listen to community needs from more than one voice. Artists are learning how to do more than survive in a culture dominated by quickness, reproduction, and product. We are generating our own systems of sustainable support for one another, and inviting funders on board, because funding structures have long failed us. Organizations leading this shift in leadership include:

- First Nation Performing Artists, or FNPA, is an Indigenous-led initiative that "makes visible, public, and transparent the urgent decolonizing work the performing arts field."[9] Emily Johnson (Yup'ik) and Ronee Penoi (Laguna Pueblo/Cherokee) are co-leads in the working consortium, alongside a wide network of Native advisors and participants. This initiative is creating an ecosystem with an annual convening, and providing three tracks that actively gather people in community with education for producers, venues, and institutions, as well as relationship building and networking tracks with opportunities for Native artists to meet, share experiences, and communicate needs.

- New England Foundation for the Arts, who through their grant-funding structures are promoting a "human-centric"[10] approach that recognizes artists, also need opportunities to network with their peers, engage with other funders, and build financial acuity.
- During the pandemic, when venues were breaking agreements with individual artists, Creating New Futures, a "Working Guidelines for Ethics & Equity in Presenting Dance & Performance" and "Creating New Futures: Phase 2, Notes for Equitable Funding from Arts Workers" was developed.[11] These two visionary models greatly educated how to come into right relationship when the risks are high for individual artists, and was made with several Indigenous people leading the conversation.
- Larissa Fasthorse (Sicangu Lakota) and Ty Defoe (Oneida and Ojibwe) have been monumental in generating the unique success of establishing Western Arts Alliance's Advancing Indigenous Performance (AIP) program with Native Launchpad awards. Their consulting company Indigenous Direction, alongside the incredible WAA Executive director at the time, Tim Wilson, and dream team of Scott Stoner and Indigenous Performance Production's Andre Bouchard, aided in its emancipation. Heartfully, the program manager was Ed Bourgeois (Mohawk).

How can you or your organization be of service to your community, or meet the Native community's evolving needs? Ask. Provide a line in your budget devoted to relationship building. Hire a Native consultant to educate you and grow your relevance, sustainability, and cultural health. What if our country's art budget was equal to the military budget? In a world volatile with war, what is the status of our cultural defense?

CULTURE AND FUTURE HOMEOSTASIS

Engage the artists who are centered in discovery, learning, play, and process. Not knowing the outcome is a key factor when inciting change, when learning what can be discovered. The work that needs to be done is bridging access back to nature, back to land. This invites a rich history beyond the settler colonial story.

Inviting Native leadership has been proven to bring homeostasis to the earth body (see Figure 35.4). What if we viewed "natural resources" not as sites of extraction and capitalism, but as sacred teachers of natural phenomena, intelligence, and consciousness? What if artists of our time gave our bodies the chance to orient around the earth, to listen, and build new footprints that change the directions in why and how we come together? To rest, to explore, to play, to move beyond surviving, into the possibility of finding curiosity, not only in our bodies, but in the world is what we can move into, in relationship with each other—this is moving toward a balanced future in arts and art making.

Figure 35.4. Opening Circle, Body Mind Centering® Association conference "Self and Other"

Opening Circle, Body Mind Centering® Association conference "Self and Other," hosted by brooke smiley in partnership with the Coastal and Santa Ynez bands of Chumash Indians. UC Santa Barbara. Photo by Alexis Story Crawshaw.

NOTES

1. Derrick Jensen, *The Myth of Human Supremacy* (New York: Seven Stories Press, 2016).

2. This movie was originally based on the book by David Grann, but the script was changed dramatically after coming into relationship with the Osage Nation during the filming process. The movie now incorporates a scene from Charles Redcorn's book *A Pipe for February*, which shares our history from an Osage perspective.

3. The perceptual-response cycle is taught in the course Senses and Perceptions, one of many Somatic Movement Educator (SME) courses, developed by Bonnie Bainbridge Cohen and the School for Body Mind Centering®. I completed the SME training with teachers Mary Lou Seereiter, Amy Matthews, Reva Hazeltine, Wendy Hambidge, and Mark Taylor in 2018.

4. This derives from my current Osage language class with Wakonze Chris Cote in Verbs I, offered by the Osage Nation in Fall 2023.

5. Marc Bamuthi Joseph, "How Can the Performing Arts Heal Our Divided Society," Kerner and Healing Convening, October 4, 2021, https://www.youtube.com/watch?v=ty0CUAz3MGQ.

6. Leilehua Lanzilotti, *Liliʻu*, n.d., https://leilehualanzilotti.com/liliu.

7. Cal Earth, https://www.calearth.org.

8. Mike Scutari, "'You Have to Actually Change.' A Major Theater Funder's Quest to Diversify Its Decision-Making," *Inside Philanthropy*, September 11, 2023.

9. First Nations Performing Arts, "Intent," n.d., https://www.firstnationsperformingarts.global/intent.

10. Scutari, "'You Have to Actually Change.'"

11. Creating New Futures, "Working Guidelines for Ethics and Equity in Presenting Dance and Performance" and "Notes for Equitable Funding from Arts Workers" (public documents), n..d., https://drive.google.com/drive/folders/1B6bbiFTBP1UAvt9qFchr7nLUndh7zorA

CHAPTER 36

The Art Will . . . A Musing on Life in the Performing Arts
A Case Study for NEW WILL

Lisa Richards Toney

WILL means to do something despite the challenges that ensue. At least, that is how I think about it. As simple as it sounds, I am left wondering how this simple, only four-letter, unisyllabic word exerts a massive energy to stir the rise of a nation but without follow-through can transform burgeoning hope into a blunder of festering FEAR. We have all seen what can happen when fear takes hold.

I experience fear as an emotional response to something that is endangering. But danger is subjective, as what is deceitfully dangerous to me might be beautifully revelatory to someone else. But how did fear become the emotional response to something unknown and thereby the unknown was to be feared?

Let's jump to culture. If you believe, as I do, that culture is simply a way of life represented within a community and that it reverberates from a set of values that guide us in what and who to praise and despise, then you may also believe that encountering something unknown or countercultural can be perceived as dangerous and trigger a fear response. I have never known the ego to be wired to sit willingly in the discomfort of fear—our bodies are not designed that way, I don't think (ever heard of fight or flight response?). I've never known culture, as it also serves to promote an embodiment of pride, to be wired that way either. The mixing, then, of fear and pride is an absolute danger.

And so, it's no wonder that we block, lock out and lock up, distort, restrain, and even kill that which we don't know or understand; that which can't be contained—that which we fear.

Does WILL stand a chance up against FEAR? Be honest. No.

Take the 1968 Kerner Report,[1] the groundbreaking study commissioned by the government on race relations in the United States. From my view, the key issues that it aimed to address and with its recommendations resolve—racial inequality, criminal justice reform, economic disparities, and political representation—remain ever-present. It's been half a century, yet we are still experimenting with how to solve these issues, which, based on my experience, have an even greater and more vehement complexity in the context of today's society. What is it that we fear? That we will be found out to be citizens of stolen land and fearful of examining the truth of what we feared? That we must confront how we have behaved and who we have become? Unless we have the will to change our trajectory, I fear that we will continue with this mockery of what the Kerner Report aimed to achieve. The dismantling of the impacts of systemic racism, I feel, will require more than the constitution of who we are and who we pride ourselves to be. After all, if you ask me, we have been constructed from fear and it has usurped our will.

So, there you have it; fear won.

But wait, as this life is far from over and the ancestors have not had their say! To me it's a shame that we have fought for the better part of the last 55 years to move the pin on some of the most important issues facing the preservation of human dignity, but in some ways, we may be worse off now. Based on what I see on both sides of the political aisles and in between, the report's directives have not succeeded in inspiring a strategy that the masses would follow, because the personal constitution from which the masses are presently operating is more than flawed; it's downright perilous. I would like to see a new paradigm that catalyzes change by inspiring a more urgent will to overcome the catastrophes of our own making and their devastating spiraling effects.

I absolutely believe that the performing arts are a powerful tool to advocate for change. I also believe that the circumstances that have led to where we find ourselves today can be addressed through economic empowerment and social mobility efforts such as investments in community arts centers, theaters, music, and dance programs, and by ensuring those investments reach our most vulnerable communities. I have vivid memories of walking the halls of the penitentiary at Riker's Island to get to the classroom of incarcerated youth that looked forward to my weekly drama classes where I guided them to pen a new vision for themselves using the dramatic form. I don't know what happened to those youths, but I do know, by the sheer excitement many had when we worked together, they had seeded hope. Then there were the students from an alternative high school in New York who would come to see morning productions of *Manchild in the Promised Land*, performed by Joseph Edward, who recreated the Claude Brown character who struggled to find his path in a land that held little promise despite what our foremothers and forefathers were told. Nonetheless, he discovered his own will to persist and it was out of the mouths of babes an articulation of comparisons between life then (in the 1950s in Harlem) and life now. The theater experience was equally artistically sound and educationally astute, in that it invited the youth to experience the arc of change that the Claude character made despite the lack of promise that surrounded him. Many spoke vulnerably as they recounted aspects of their own lives and made promises for redirection.

Both of these experiences make a compelling case for increased support to artists and arts organizations serving people with harsh life circumstances and helping them to excavate the context and influences of their circumstances as well as to advocate for solutions that they can buy into. These are social advocacy and social justice stories just as much as they are arts stories. Spending time excavating through, with the dramatic form as canvas, it became clear to me that the life circumstances of the youth at the juvenile detention center and of those who were considered on their last leg of hope at the alternative school, were partially due to the dichotomization of the life paths of the haves and those who aren't even sure if they are worth longing to have. This dichotomy is sustained by that dangerous mix of fear and false pride. But if we could act on the evidence that what was exchanged during the theater experience was far from ephemeral, and instead a seeding of NEW WILL for each of us who are part of our own version of a marginalized community to excavate beyond the gatekeeping that has provided our narratives up until now, using the tools the arts offer to excavate our authenticity and restore empowerment, we could engender NEW WILL to change.

Even though I have not spent the better part of my life's work focused on solving the magnitude of systemic societal ills that plague us, the kernel of my life's work in the arts compels my musing on how the performing arts can build a personal constitution of creativity and free expression that empowers individuals to be their best version of themselves. That's my expertise. How we get to this place of empowerment that inspires one with the WILL to follow through on whatever they believe their conviction to be (solving the social ills of our time, as the Kerner Report urges) is where the magic lies and where the attributes of confidence, communication skills, collaboration, empathy, and understanding become actualized. Although one might not completely transcend race, power, or privilege, in my view, once the attributes have taken hold, one has more than they need to soar; my experience has taught me that one can dismantle the posturing that weighs down progress.

I am led to ponder these questions:

1. What is it about the constitution of the performing arts that counters banality and a lack of WILL?
2. How do performing arts inspire those of us endeavoring for a changed society to embody the WILL to fulfill the transformational change?

Here is my story. . . .

I was only 6 when I first encountered it. I know that because I remember what my mom insisted that I wear. We were headed to the Kennedy Center to see *Annie*, the hit musical at the time, and I guess it was all the rage—the obligatory navy and white two-piece sailor suit dress with the giant red bow. I can remember the tilted walk down the center aisle to the middle of the orchestra section of the opera house at arguably the most esteemed national treasure dedicated to the performing arts. In my mind's eye, I can still see the hundreds of children, mostly girls, all dressed up just as I was. Some even wore the obligatory sailor suit dress, just like me. I fit right in.

Fitting in wasn't something that came natural to me. I was shy. I was very tall for my age, which, to me, made me annoyingly lanky, and my perception was confirmed when I looked at myself in any mirror. I didn't hate myself; I just didn't understand myself nor how to go about figuring me out. I had good friends at school, but in crowds or with people I didn't know, I felt awkward. In those moments, I felt disconnected from my body as if I was on the outside staring at myself, critiquing what I saw. Looking back, I can see how that sense of disconnection was a form of anxiety that would be the steady pinching that tried hard to chip away my chance at confidence. If you'd asked me then, I would have insisted that it was everyone—in the entire theater—who was also looking at me. The imagined critical stares brought forth insecurities I wouldn't confront until many years later.

The Art Will ... A Musing on Life in the Performing Arts

By then I was 12 and finally mustered the courage to attempt what I had been longing for. Prior to then, I was too shy and too self-critical to become a dancer. I was also somewhat fixated on an unattainable bigness of what I thought a dancer was, without the courage to get out of my head and at least try to be her. Those years felt like I was being held back by an unexplainable force—like how I felt when the opera house curtain fell, reminding me that the theatrical experience was ephemeral. While everyone else jumped up to leave, and Annie and the other characters had clearly exited the stage, I was immovable—still utterly mesmerized from the music, the dancing, the expressiveness, the orchestra, and the lights—the spectacle of it all—and an emotionality that found its way 'cross the footlights and into my core being. It kind of took a hold of me; I was frozen in my seat. Eventually, after some prodding from my mom and my realization that the place was nearly empty, I released my freeze and stood up. As I reluctantly walked up the aisle to exit, it hit me that, in my fixated state, I had conjured up something like nothing I'd experienced before. No matter how ephemeral the play itself had been, what I left with was mine to keep and no one could take it from me.

After some time, I connected the dots. I realized that what I had conjured up and taken with me from the theater had been an imagined version of myself but as full as my 6-year-old self could ruminate. In my mind's eye, I could see that I was still tall, maybe not so lanky though, and I was fierce. I envisioned myself a dancer leaping across the stage and somehow, I transformed into the orchestrator for all things connected to the production. Without knowing it, my mind was desperately trying to make sense of the order of operations for all those things—something people in my field find themselves still contemplating. Days, months, and years would pass, and my memory of that day remained fresh, allowing me to linger and just imagine. I felt most connected to myself during those dream states. I was on the inside and liked what I saw, what I felt—I had no reason to wander outside. I was in my happy place, musing a prayer that would one day awaken me to what I could become.

Remember, it would be 6 more years before I found my WILL to act on this journey of becoming. The act of becoming was a verb, a space of motion that guided me in embracing all parts of myself and staying connected to what I found. I found myself. It was maybe the first time in my life that I began to truly understand and like myself for who I was—maybe because it somehow made clearer who I was becoming.

I was now on my way. It hadn't even been a week into my schedule of rehearsals for the student-devised production *Save Our Children*, which featured an amalgamation of creative and out-of-the-box artistic expression, a compassion for what inner-city communities were facing, and culturally affirming rituals that drove us to be the courageous change agents we wanted for our communities. I could feel my transformation. Little did I know that my artistic process would be my go-to nourishment for this WILL I had to be somebody. Even though I came from a good family and had high expectations placed upon me, this was Washington, DC, in the late 1980s/early 1990s; it was rough! It was the height of street violence among Black youth alongside the "war on drugs"; it was as if they were synonymous. Some of my castmates who were close to the vine of said wars found solace and direction through their participation in that production—they were the children and their time spent endeavoring in that performance saved them, literally. Evidence. I remember some of them retuning later in the fall to start dance, voice, and drama classes and check out the fuss everyone was making over the upcoming production—and soon, there was another production and another—and we all had roles and we each had a purpose. The arts saved us.

Looking back, that period brought forth a body of artistic expression that could have easily become the canon for the empowerment of Black youth. It was all made possible by the formidable Carol Foster, the founder and artistic director of the DC Youth Ensemble. With her, I spent 5 years immersed in the performing arts and was afforded a myriad of opportunities to train and perform. Though I was not the castmate fighting to stay clear of the messiness of the streets, I had my own war that had yet to cease its fire—fighting my mess of low self-esteem. Anxiety would become something I'd learn to live with, and I'd learn tactics to not let it stop me from achieving my goals. Mrs. Foster and especially my mother, Phoebe Richards, deserve the credit when it comes to the push I needed and the environment I needed to grow confidently into the woman I am today.

When I think back on those formative years, most of which were spent in dance and drama studio spaces or on the stages of community theaters and in audiences of wherever for whatever I could muscle a ticket to attend, I am in awe of the positive lessons from those years and how they show up in my life today. Like most of us, when we look back, we have enough hindsight to wrap our experience with a bow—and tie it tight and neatly store it in our memories. My memories of those years and the arts experiences that filled them are not distorted with a rosy filter, but rather something vaster like life itself. Growing up in an arts community, I experienced both well-intentioned self- and community-serving opportunities that marked purposeful life lessons along my journey. I liken it to a grounding from which I could soar in any direction, whether it be the arts or something else if I was willing to put in the work. I had proven to myself that I could sit in the discomfort of hard things (both my anxiety and the unrelenting discipline that the performing arts required), and I could equally find and elicit joy for myself and my community. What stands out about those experiences is that I had space to dream—the space to develop an authentic confidence that would carry me through. And it also showed me that I had the passion, grit, creativity, discipline, and humility—the stuff that WILL is made of—to become somebody that 6-year-old me, who once sat frozen, mesmerized, and in awe of it all would have been proud to be.

I tell my story to show how the arts encouraged my own self-exploration and how my experiences were foundational to the self-confidence, courage, and staying power that I needed, helping me to find the will to move forward in the arts despite the reality that I would not pursue a professional dance career. Instead, my vision for how I would participate in the arts expanded. I would not have become the president and CEO of the Association of Performing Arts Professionals without the will to imagine myself anew. While not everyone can make a living shrouded in the beauty, challenge, and discovery that is the performing arts, everyone can be inspired by the lived experiences of artists and arts leaders. By way of form and function, the performing arts inspires a WILL to lean in with an openness to what is both beautiful and ugly, and sometimes all at once. From there, we are challenged to courageously imagine for ourselves a new WILL that anyone would be proud to shout from the rooftops and tell the world: the arts are serious business, for the arts change lives!

What's missing from my story is a relaying of the times I spent on my soapbox (giving persuasive speeches, leading graduate-level lectures, or stating my opinions boldly at my own family's holiday dinner table) insisting, pleading, and not letting the naysayers get a word in edgewise, to express the connection between the performing arts and the social woes of the time. And I didn't suffer fools. Looking back, I can admit that all that vigor may have been amplified by fear that I wouldn't be able to make a career for myself if I couldn't convince people that what I was saying was true, that they should care about the arts just as much as I do. Somehow the lines had blurred, and my own self-worth was wrapped up in my plea for their caring. Sure, it was well within my right to express my opinion, but I would fervently keep talking (not a breath in between) for fear that any space of silence would be an opening for me to be criticized and subsequently have probable cause to doubt myself and the life I was feverishly trying to build. Although I learned to sit in this discomfort, I didn't like the hollow feeling that made me into a shell of myself—disconnected and on the outside—unable to quiet the voice inside of me that willingly joined the barrage. It could take days to recover. Days plus a round of pep talks from my mom or a mentor to be reminded that my experience would prove the haters wrong. My experiences in the arts were anything but frivolous; in fact, they were just the opposite—they were so very serious.

But, after many years of this—this seriousness—I felt limited by it, too—limited by the policies and codes where the word "arts" was there but the true meaning of the word was becoming increasingly hard to find. I didn't care for the stuffy seriousness and I resented the fluffy frivolity. I certainly didn't want to spend my career shuffling between these two worlds that rarely could find middle ground. Plain and simple, I embodied so much more.

The performing arts is a welcomed relief from the temporal solutions of the past, those which have been too exact, too fixed, and not fluid enough, too steady and not dynamic enough; too contrived and not wildly authentic at all—not sustainable at all. What we have been reluctant to admit is that sustainability encompasses a flexibility to "exist beyond artificial boundaries of titles or departments, each of which are more about training and tracking, than problem-solving and innovating."[2] A new WILL accepts that the intrinsic value of the arts diminishes artificial boundaries and is more open to collaboration and deep exploration, which can yield actual solutions. For when we ignore the inevitable—that change is the only constant—we risk the trappings of irrelevance quicker than we care to admit. We forget that policy is only one step on the continuum, and in my view, it is arguable if it should be the first.[3]

So, if you ask me, it's not the Kerner Report—and its policies—that has failed, it's the lack of WILL that has failed. If we could apply the values of the performing arts, I am confident we could scaffold an innovative and accessible paradigm that, while revered for its malleability, has just enough container to carry forth the urgent conviction that the report incites.

As it stands now, we can map almost every issue area that the Kerner Report outlines to a litany of contemporary crises. While I am no expert on the process from which the solutions emanated, it is clear to me that the results have not had the indelible impact for which was intended. We need NEW WILL.

The arts, intrinsically and extrinsically, give us a new lens through which to create process and to inspire solutions. My experience in the performing arts has shown me how it taps into a personal, guttural, almost spiritual connection that activates all the faculties of reasoning—including emotional intelligence—permitting us to be open to new ways of thinking. Just take the word *create*—which means to bring into existence—and the implication that something is being born that was not already there; talk about taking a risk! And to think about the optimal conditions for such risk-taking, for birthing something new, my thoughts don't quite match up to the image of dusty annals of pronouncements. Creation begs to be free, dynamic, and vibrant by awakening all the faculties of reasoning to form a holistic expression. For me, inherent in creation is an open space to fail without time wasted on judgment, but rather an expectation to get back up and try again. It's the activation of the liminal space that takes its time to burgeon into something shrouded in love, in acceptance, in understanding. It's more than a masterpiece as it's not limited by an expectation or obligation, nor simply a feeling or a desire. But it's hardly about dichotomies, for that's not creation at all.

As I see it, even the best solutions will stifle if they sit too much in the canisters of bureaucracy. It's not that policies are inherently problematic, but policies alone are inherently fixed, and what's needed for us to achieve the goals as articulated in the Kerner Report goes well beyond a right and wrong, or one-dimensional, framing. This is a job for the sixth dimension! I believe that the arts as the NEW WILL can get us there.

My experiences have reinforced my belief that inherent in looking to the arts for NEW WILL is the acknowledgment that solutions need to be adaptable to the dynamic nature of society and a holistic appreciation for the diverse set of economic and sociopolitical factors that frame and impact one's culture and one's environment, and thus the ease or dis-ease with which one exists in the world. Much of what I am suggesting requires a commitment to make cultural competencies part of the rubric for success. It also requires collaboration, which means sharing space with the stakeholders long and often enough to engender an equitable playing field that draws one from the outside (where the focus is inevitably analyzing and criticizing) to the inside; that begs one to understand and empathize to ensure an authentic space and motivation to help seed change. I am reminded of the courageous SAG-AFTRA artists and arts workers who valued themselves enough to strike and stand up to the powers that be and demand changes to multiyear contracts. Their WILL can be lauded, not just in our field, but in our society—our fight for equity is not just an arts fight but also a social justice fight that the world can learn from.

Delving deeper in this story, we come to understand that artists occupy a space in our society that, for many, they've had to first imagine and then create for themselves. In that process, they have had to grapple with their own will, to persist or not, and if they've come out on the side of a will to persist, they did so through a rubric that was flexible enough to hold risk—the trial and error, both joy and pain—and then the qualities that would birth the creation itself—trust, patience, courage—that evolve from the conviction to persist. For the artist, WILL is personal! It's not just the job or profession of the artist to create, it's their life blood to survive. The work of an artist welcomes curiosity and thrives when the response incites differing points of view and multiple interpretations and applications. Putting forth those values in the context of finding solutions to the issues raised in the Kerner Report, the arts level the playing field for whose voice matters.

The examples also teach us that we must amplify the contributions of artists in the context of equity, and, should we invite their participation, we must take care to protect them as culture bearers from the cut-throat daggers that have been mocked as due process, and in the process rips the soul from ever knowing. Our culture bearers, griots, soothsayers, our mothers and fathers of memory must be respected for the geniuses they are. Take, for example, Harlem Stage and their commitment to provide a platform for artists of color, particularly Black artists whose talents have been marginalized, to show both their critique and their vision for excellence. More than leaders, I see artists as magic-makers who enable our connection to more authentic cultural ways of knowing. Some are dramatists who do the work to peel back the curtain for all to see (and sometimes hold up the mirror for us to see ourselves) how we even got into this mess. Others encourage us to take a step into their vision by suspending our disbelief long enough to awaken our senses to take in the raw experience of that which has been created. When the arts experience goes well and the audience is in full applause, we are reminded that it was worth the wait or the investment or the inconvenience because it forever lives in one's mind's eye or wherever one's dreams take hold to inspire imagining forward. The urgency that it stirs is the beginning of new will and a way forward.

There are many examples, for the arts have been here all along; it's not new to know of our impact, but to be open enough to welcome our place at this table of questioning and solving, I will say that, on behalf of the performing arts community, I gladly accept. In looking at my life's work and the legacy I hope to leave for the next generation of arts workers and dreamers, I am inspired that the thing that saved me is considered as a paradigm to save the world. Its impenetrable connection between the mind, body, and soul to form a more perfect constitution is genius. And if a genius can't settle us down here on Earth to truly create a more perfect union of less racial injustice, less economic inequality, less poverty, our living may as well be in vain. Here, right now, is our chance to get it right.

NOTES

1. The National Advisory Commission on Civil Disorders, *Report of the National Advisory Commission on Civil Disorders* (Washington, DC: U.S. Department of Justice, Office of Justice Programs, 1968).

2. Alberta Arthurs and Michael F. DiNiscia, eds., *Are the Arts Essential?* (New York: New York University Press, 2022).

3. Arthurs and DiNiscia, *Are the Arts Essential?*

Index

Aamoth, Doug, 362n11
Abdullah, Hatem O., 161n8
Abortion as wedge issue, 204, 298, 317, 323, 338
Abrams, Zara, 204n26
Accelerated Study in Associate Programs (ASAP), 385, 388
Acevedo, Nicole, 246nn40–41
Achenbach, Joel, 297nn4–5
"Achievement gaps," 53–54, 58
Ackerman, Spencer, 15n25
Activism and art, 402–404, 419
ACT UP, 403
Adams, Char, xxn16
Aday, Sean, 351n8
Adultification of Black youth, 137–138
Advancement Project, 65
Advancing Indigenous Performance (AIP) program, 438
Affirmative action, 17, 45, 87–91, 206–207
  fairness, concept of, 92–94
Affirmatively Furthering Fair Housing (AFFH) mandate, 176, 179, 182
Affordable Care Act, 7, 205, 228
Afif, Iman N., 161nn7–8
AFL-CIO, 79n32
Aguilera, Cristina, 245
Ahmed, Farida B., 221n15
Akee, Randall, 270n16
Akoto-Bamfo, Kwame, 409
Aladangady, Aditya, 150n41
Albert, Dustin, 136n24
Alcatraz Island protests, 268
Alexander, Michelle, 364n13
Alexander v. Sandoval, xviii
Alfonso, Y. Natalia, 29n43
Alliance for Educational Justice, 65
Alliance for Quality Education (AQE), 69
Alper, Mariel, 150n49
Alpert, Geoffrey P., 110n7
Alsan, Marcella, 203n21
Al-Ubaydli, Omar, 388n43, 389n44

American Climate Corps, 99, 100
American Compass, 264n3
American Educational Research Association, 54n12
American Federation for Children, 75
American Federation of Teachers (AFT), 77n26, 77n28, 79n31, 81n35, 82n37
American Immigration Council, 259n28
American Immigration Lawyers Association, 259n27
American Indian Movement (AIM), 264, 268
American Indian Religious Freedom Act (1978), 433
American Indians. *See* Native Americans
American Latino Media Arts (ALMA) Awards, 245
The American Prospect, 367
American Psychiatric Association, 135nn13–14
American Psychological Association, 81, 135nn13–14
American Public Health Association, 208
American Rescue Plan Act (2021), xvi–xvii, 5–6, 7, 8, 57, 58, 76
"American Skin (41 Shots)" (Springsteen), 362
AmeriCorps, 96, 97, 99
Ander, Roseanna, 384n23
Anderson, Chloe, 150n46
Anderson, James D., 86n7
Andrew Goodman Foundation, 304
Annenberg Inclusion Initiative, 242
Annual Statistical Supplement, 24n7
Anwar, Shamena, 149n37
Aponte, Mari Carmen, 245
Appelbaum, Binyamin, 30n49
Aranha, Anil N. F., 214n3
Aráullo, Kirby, 278n2
Arbury, Ahmad, 302
Archer, Deborah, 133n3
Arenberg, Samuel, 7n19
Arendt, Hannah, 340n4
Arias, Elizabeth, 221n12
Armstrong, David M., 258n25
Armstrong, Ken, 366n19
Armstrong, Martin, 30n52
Arnold, Emily A., 403n6
Arnold Ventures, 381n4, 384, 385n27, 388n41

448

Index

Aron, Laudan Y., 390n52
Arteaga, I. A., 54n9
Art for Justice Fund, 405nn13–14, 409
Arthurs, Alberta, 445nn2–3
Artificial intelligence (AI), 176–177, 179, 180–181, 258, 304–305, 354, 356, 377, 391
Artiga, Samantha, 200n3, 242n8
Arts and culture
  art and activism, 419
  artists, role as translators, 418–428
  diversity and representation, 400–410
  in public realm, 405–407
  recommendations for policymaking, 408–410, 425–427
  and spirituality, 420–421
  and will to change, 440–447
Arts and Social Justice (ASJ) Fellowship Program, 422–423
Asante-Muhammad, Dedrick, 173n21
Ashford, Grace, 151n62
Asian American Legal Defense and Education Fund (AALDEF), 284n25
Asian American Pacific Islander Coalition (AAPIC), 281n12
Asian American populations
  challenges, 282–283
  COVID-19 pandemic and hate crimes, 281–282
  current situation, 281–282
  equitable representation, 283–285
  future recommendations, 285–286
  immigration to America, 278–280
  model minority myth, 281
ASO Communications, 318n15
Aspen Institute, 98
  Forum for Community Solution, 99n10
ASPIRA (advocacy organization), 243–244, 243n18
#AssaultAtSpringValley report, 65
ASSISTments, 385
Atencio, Cassandra, 434
Atwell, Matthew, 99nn10–11
Augmented reality (AR), 406
Augustine, Lindsay, 174n32
Automated Valuation Models, 172
Avery, Beth, 151n56
Aviles, Gwen, 242n10
Ayscue, Jennifer, 54n11
Azurdia, Gilda, 385n28

Ba, Bocar A., 114nn17–18
Baca, Judith, 408
Bacon, Don, 103
Bacon, Perry, 367n22
"Bad apple" analogy, 124–125

Bahn, Kate, 37n4
Bail, 150. *See also* Incarceration
Bailey, Marlon M., 403n6
Bailey, Nikitra, 178n41
Baker, Bruce, 82n38
Baker, Doug, 232n39
Bakke decision (1978), 90
Balderrama, Francísco E., 246n42
Baldwin, James, 127, 127n21, 420, 427
The Ballad of Gregorio Cortez (film), 245
Bambara, Toni Cade, 323
Bannon, Steve, 14
Barber, William J., 104n24
Barbie (film), 255
Bard Prison Initiative, 151
Barksdale Reading Institute, 78
Barnes, Katherine Y., 124–125, 125n14
Barnes, Shailly Gupta, 299n6
Barnett, Bernice McNair, 89n22
Barnum, Matt, 75n12, 82n36, 83n40
Baron, Jon, 381n1
Barrón-López, Laura, 14n24
Barry, Celeste, 148n33, 151n55
Bartlett, Robert, 172n14
Basquiat, Jean-Michel, 403
Bauer, Tamar, 389n46
Bay Area Regional Health Inequities Initiative (BARHII), 218n8
Bayer, Patrick, 149n37
Beard, Jessica, 161n8
Bebinger, Martha, 150n49
Beck, Glenn, 371
Becker, Gary S., 12n9
Beckett, Katherine, 146n26
Bedillion, Caleb, 366n19
Bell, Derek, 307, 307n28
Bell, Kristen, 149n37
Benkler, Yochai, 371n4, 376n27
Bennett, Antoine, 102
Bennett, Claudette E., 349n5
Berg, Nate, 172n17
Berger, Sam, 17n38
Berkowitz, Seth A., 229n36
Berner, Ashley, 242n12
Berry, Christopher, 192n16
Berry, Jeffrey J., 371n5
Berwick, Donald, 208
Berzofsky, Marcus, 150n49
Be the Change, 98
Betsey, Charles, 41n20
Betts, Reginald Dwayne, 409
Bezos, Jeff, 356
Bhutta, Neil, 64n4, 173n18–20

Bias
  appraisal bias and housing, 169–170, 172–173, 174, 177
  in criminal justice system, 137–138, 146, 148–151
  in medical care, 204
  in policing, 125, 128, 203
Biden, Joe, 28, 57, 100, 109, 148, 231–232, 273, 354, 374
  American Rescue Plan Act (2021), 5–6, 7, 8
  child care policy, 8
  Council of Economic Advisers, 5
  debt cancellation, 7
  economic policy, 6, 15–16
  Executive Order 13985, 257
  Executive Order on Diversity, Equity, Inclusion, and Accessibility, 254
  racial justice policy, 16–17
Biden v. Nebraska, 17
Biggs, Eric R., 265n9
The Big Sort (Bishop), 350
Bilmes, Linda, 306n23
Bioneers Native Youth Leadership Program, 435
Bipartisan Workforce Pell Act, xix
Birmingham Public Safety Task Force, 306n21
Bishop, Jim, 350
Bivens, Josh, 43n29, 232n39
Black Arts Movement, 403
Black community
  Black-owned small businesses, 7
  health insurance, 7
  in low-wage occupations, 37
  maternal mortality, 7
  unemployment rates, 39–40
  union representation, 45–46
Black Emergency Cultural Coalition, 402
Black Journal (public television program), 360
Black Lives Matter (BLM) movement, 14, 17, 110–111, 144, 187, 190, 337, 367, 406
Black Men Smile movement, 419–420, 427
Black Panther Party, 418–419
Black Voters Matters, 332
Black youth
  adultification of, 137–138
  adult prosecution of, 133, 135–137, 139
  bias in perception of, 137
  in criminal justice system, 133–138
  cultural stereotypes of, 133–135
  dehumanization of, 137
  incarceration of, 143–152
  recommendations to improve criminal justice system, 138–140
Blake, Jamilia J., 138n33
Blake, Nyland, 403
Blakemore, Erin, 309n33

Blakinger, Keri, 151n52
Bloom, Laura Begley, 30n50
Blue Beetle (film), 255
Blueprint for Addressing the Maternal Health Crisis, 7
Blumstein, Alfred, 143n1
Bocian, Debbie Gruenstein, 175n36
Body awareness and earth-based healing, 429–438
Body-worn cameras, 112
Boger, John Charles, 86n3
Boggs, Grace Lee, 283, 286n32
Bolsonaro, Jair, 316
Bolts (digital magazine), 367
Bond, Christopher, 103
Bond, Robert M., 373n9
Bonhomme, Raphael, 78
Bor, Jacob, 203n20, 220n9
Boshara, Ray, 220n10
Boston Foundation, 284–285
Boston Planning & Development Agency, 201n7
Bottom Line program, 386
Bouie, Jamelle, 372n7, 374n14
Bourgeois, Ed, 438
Bowers, Jake, 389–390, 390n49
Bowie, Chet, 143n3, 144n12
Boykoff, Jules, 377n29
Boykoff, Maxwell, 377n29
Braden, Anne, 340
Braga, Anthony A., 115n21, 118n37
Brandeis, Louis D., 232n42
Bratton, Bill, 116
Brazil, 316
Brazille, Donna, 365
Brennan Center for Justice, 256, 257n20, 364n14
Bridgeland, John M., 99nn10–11
Bridgeman, Anne, 75n6
Brilliant Corners, 318
Brittain, John, 58n25
"Broken windows" theory, 116
Bromberg, Yael, 304n14
Bronson, Jennifer, 150n49
Brookings Institution, 87, 146, 163–164
Brooks, Cornell William, 306n23, 308n30
Brooks, Rick, 175n36
Brooks, Romaine, 403
Brooks, Rosa, 115n20
Browder, Michelle, 406
Brown, Claude, 441
Brown, David W., 7n20
Brown, Madeline, 207n41
Brown, Michael, 14, 144, 203, 419, 427
Brown, Michael K., 165n18
Brown v. Board of Education (1954), xvi, 73, 88–89, 243, 252, 307, 308
  progress in following decades, 74

Index

Buchanan v. Warley, 171n10
Budiman, Abby, 284n27
Buggs, Shani A., 116n25
Bui, Vinh, 285
Build Back Better Framework, 100, 182
Bump, Philip, 134n11
Burciaga, Rebeca, 89n20
Bureau of Justice statistics, 111
Bureau of Labor Statistics (BLS), 39nn6–7, 39n9, 39n12
  projected labor force growth, 256–257
Burnham, Linda, 13n18
Burns, Kalee, 5nn4–5
Bush, George H. W., 374
Bush, George W., 28
Bustamante, Alí, 17n41
Butler, Octavia, 413
Button, Katherine S., 389n47
Bwolomwini, Joy, 408

Cable Communications Policy Act (1984), 27
Cade, Maya S., 360n6
Caldwell, Alicia A., 75n12
"calling in" vs. calling out, 336–343
  "calling in," creation of term, 340–341
  skills and strategies, 342–343
Cambridge, Massachusetts, 127–128, 128n25
Cameras, body-worn, 112
Camerer, Colin F., 388n40
Campaign Zero, 203n17
Campbell, David E., 375n20
Campisi, Natalie, 27n28
Campus Writing Program, 279n9
Canada, racial equity, 286
Cancel culture, 337. *See also* "Calling in" vs. calling out
Cannon, Jill S., 54n10, 229n35
Capitalism, critiques of, 22–23
Carceral Emancipation for Citizenship, 305–306
Career and technical education (CTE), 77, 79, 82
Carey, Kevin, 75n11
Carlson, Tucker, 371
Carr, Peggy, 57
Carson, E. Ann, 143n3, 143n8, 144n15, 144n16, 144nn11–13, 146n28
Carter, Jimmy, 25
Carter, Prudence L., 51n1, 53n6
Cartwright, Nancy, 381n5
Carver-Thomas, D., 56n19
The Case for Big Government (Madrick), 30
Cashin, Sheryll, 91n32
Castilla, Emilio J., 115n24
Castillo, Leonel, 244n22
Castro, Joaquin, 242

Cauffman, Elizabeth, 136n23
Cave, Nick, 409
CCRC Staff, 151n57
Cedillo, Dominic, 242n13
Cell phone video, 112
Center for Art and Advocacy, 409
Center for Cultural Power, 408
Center for Education Policy Research (Harvard University), xvii
Center for Responsible Lending (CRL), 178
Center for the Study of Hate and Extremism, 282
Center for the Transformation of Schools (UCLA), 63
Centers for Disease Control and Prevention (CDC), 175n37, 220n10, 221n11, 221n16, 225n22, 225n23
The Century Foundation, 221n14, 223n20
Chadwick, Andrew, 28n32
ChalleNGe, 96
Chan, Jackie, 282
Chang, Jeff, 407
Change. *See also* Policymaking
  contemporary situation, power rebalances, 15–16
  impetus to/will for, 213–233, 440–447
  need for, 268–269
  obstacles to, 111–113, 376–377
Channel, Jacob, 175n35
Charles H. Wright Museum of African American Culture, 401–402
ChatGPT, 79, 305
Chauvin, Derek, 322, 363
Chavez, Cesar, 252
Chein, Jason, 136n24
Chen, Nathan, 282
Chen, Yiyu, 57n21
Chenoweth, Erica, 302n1
Chesney, James D., 233n5
Chetty, Raj, 201n9, 220n9
Child care policy, 7–8, 58, 297–298, 318
Child labor, 23
Child Tax Credit (CTC), xviii, 5, 76
Child Trends, 56–57
Chin, Vincent, 281
Chinn, Juanita J., 225n24
CHIPS and Science Act (2022), 15, 100, 176
Chisholm, Shirley, 270, 408
Chiwaya, Nigel, xviiin16
Choi, Ann, 174n34
Chokshi, Dave A., 220n9
The Chronicle of Philanthropy, 274–275
Chronicle of the Slave Scrolls (Bell), 307
Cilluffo, Anthony, 284n26
Cisneros, Henry G., 241n3
Citizens United decision, 103
Citron, Danielle Keats, 376n26

City Year, 98
Civic Enterprises, 99
Civic Information Consortium, 366
Civilian Climate Corps (CCC), 100
Civilian Conservation Corps (CCC), 100
Civil Rights Act (1866), 186, 189, 189n13
Civil Rights Act (1870), 186
Civil Rights Act (1964), xviii, 40, 43, 264
Civil Rights Act (1968), 188
Civil Rights Cases, 186–187nn1–2
The Civil Rights Road to Deeper Learning, 57–58
Clark, Kenneth B., xxii, 308, 412–413
Clark, Mamie, 308
Clemente, Roberto, 246
Climate change, 29
  climate injustice, 172
Climate Power, 15n33
Clinton, Bill, 13, 27, 247, 317
Clinton, Hillary, 317
Coalition for Independent Technology Research, 376n25
Cogburn, Courtney D., 220n10
Cohen, Bonnie Bainbridge, 431
Cohen, Jacqueline, 143n1
Cohn, D'Vera, 253n5
College Advising Corps, 98
Collins, Dave, 354n14
Collins, Kelly, 385n26
Collyer, Sophie, 76n15
Colon, Raul, 246n39
The Color of Law (Rothstein), 53, 188
Commission on Reimagining the Economy, 306n25
Community schools, 59, 80, 82
Confederate flags, 404–405
Confederate monuments, 406, 423–424
Congressional Hispanic Caucus, 242
Congressional Research Service, 255n13, 259n29
Conspiracy theories, 353–354, 355
Consumer Financial Protection Bureau, 175n38
Converse, Philip E., 373n10
Conway, Erik M., 22n1, 29n44
Cookson, Peter W., 58n25
Cooper, Alexia, 146n21
Cooper, Matthew, 144n15
Coppola, Francis Ford, 248
Copps, Michael, 28
Cornyn, John, 103
Corporal punishment, 65. *See also* Schools
The Corps Network (TCN), 96, 97, 98, 100
Costigan, Amelia, 229n31
Cote, Wakonze Chris, 433n4
Covert, Bryce, 13n12

COVID-19 pandemic, 29, 56–57
  and anti-Asian racism, 281–282
  and crime rates, 157–165
  Hispanic community, 242
  and housing crisis, 173n23, 175
  and inequities, 200, 214, 269
  recession, 37
Cowan, Josh, 75n10
Cowan, Ruth Schwartz, 24n8
Cowen, Tyler, 30
Cox, Chelsey, xin1
CPI Inflation Calculator, 24n15
Cramer, Katherine, 373n18, 374
Cranbrook Art Museum, 409
Crane, Jasper, 25
Credit markets, 171–172
Credit scoring, 169
Crenshaw, Kimberlé W., 309n32
Crifasi, Cassandra K., 116n25
Crime
  community-based interruption efforts, 139–140
  crime rates, 133–134
  homicide rates, 145–146, 147
  juvenile crime, 134–135
  post-COVID-19 pandemic, 157–160
  "superpredator" theory, 134–135
  violence post-COVID-19 pandemic, 157–165
Crime Bill (1994), xx
Criminal justice system
  and bias, 137–138
  pretrial detention, 150
Critical thinking, 79, 421, 425
Croninger, R., 56n20
"Crooked Officer" (Geto Boys), 362
Crowley, Mary, 137n27
Culture wars, 293, 296–298, 404–405
Cummings, Caroline, 323n25
Current Population Survey, BLS, 39n9, 39n12, 39nn6–7
Currie, Elliott, 163n13
Curtis, Alan, 214n3, 241nn2–3, 278n1, 315nn1–2, 319n20, 359n1

Danelski, David, 297n3
Daniels, Gilda, 304, 304n8
Darity, William A., Jr., 12n8, 306, 306n22
Darling-Hammond, Kia, 57n22
Darling-Hammond, Linda, 52n2, 55n13, 56n16, 57n22, 74–75, 74n4, 75n7
Dastrup, Samuel, 384n19
Data Foundation, 382n9
Davenport, Paul, 150n40
Davids, Sharice, 270
Davis, Angela J., 149n38

Index

Davis, Elizabeth, 111n9, 149n34
Deakin, Motley, 245n26
Dean, Mike, 102, 102n18
"Death measurement," 297–298
Deaton, Angus, 381n5
de Brey, Cristobal, 87n8
Declan, Desmond, 322n24
deCourcy, Katherine, 37n5
Defacement (Basquiat), 403
DeFelice, Beth, 264n4
Defoe, Ty, 436, 438
De León, Jacqueline, 272
DellaVigna, Stefano, 386n32, 390, 390n50
DeLong, Brad, 15n27
Deloria, Vine, Jr., 270, 272
Democracy Index 2022, 30
Demos (think tank), 318
De Niro, Robert, 430
"Department of Democracy," 331–332
Deregulation, 25–27
Derenoncourt, Ellora, 37n4, 226n28
DeSantis, Ron, 75
Desegregation, 51–52, 54, 74
Design It for Us, 81
DeSilver, Drew, 440n1
Desmond, Matthew, 365n15
DeVos, Betsy, 75
Dewey, John, 213, 213n1
Di, Qian, 172n13
Diallo, Amadou, 362
DiCaprio, Leonardo, 430
The Dick Cavett Show, 127
Digest of Educational Statistics (NCES), 87
Dilulio, John, 134–135
Dimock, Michael, 253n2
DiNiscia, Michael F., 445nn2–3
Dionne, E. J., 30, 30n49
Dip, Andrea, 316n8
Disinformation/misinformation, 304–305, 331–332, 366, 373, 376
Diversity
   art, representation in, 400–410
   embracing and celebrating, 327–328
   in police profession, 114–115
   richness and strength of, 334–335
   diversity, equity, and inclusion (DEI) programs, xviii
Divito, Emily, 15n29
Dobbin, Frank, 115n24
Dog Whistle Politics, 318
Domestic Policy Council, 230n38
Donato, Rubén, 88n17
Donheiser, Julia, 75n8
Donnelly, Ellen A., 150n44
Donnelly, Michael, 102

Donohue, John, 41n19
Dorchester House, 285
Dorchester Youth Collaborative (DYC), 285
Do the Right Thing (film), 362
Douglas, Emory, 418–419, 427
Douglas, Jessica, 272n20
Douglass, Frederick, 130, 131n31, 294, 295
Downen, Robert, 17n44
Downpayment assistance (DPA) models, 178. *See also* Homeownership
Downpayment Toward Equity Act, 178
Draut, Tamara, 219n17
DREAMers, 14
Driscoll, Anne K., 221n13
Driving Equality Act (Philadelphia), 149
Drug offenses, 146, 148
Drug treatment, 150–151
   medication for opioid use disorder (MOUD), 150–151
Drutman, Lee, 370n1
DuBois, W.E.B., 294
Ducharme, Jamie, 283n22
Duster, Chandelis, 17n43
Dyson, Yarneccia D., 305n20

Earned Income Tax Credit (EITC), 228, 229
Earth-based healing, 429–438
EARTH.SPEAKS (public art project), 434–436
East Harlem Youth Agenda for the Eighties, 98
Ebens, Ronald, 281
Eberhardt, Jennifer, 316n5
Economic climate, current, 231–232
Economic Policy Institute, 45n32, 232n42
EdChoice, 75
Edelman, Marian Wright, 340n3
Edine, Boughaba Charaff, 264n5
Edison Electric Institute, 25
Edley, Christopher, Jr., 128n24, 129n26
Education. *See also* Higher education; Schools
   conservative opposition to, 338
   evidence-based programs, 384–385
   public education, 75–76, 81–84
   racial inequities, 51–53
   school finance reform, 53
   teachers, collective bargaining, 82
   teacher shortages, 82
   transformative, 421–423
Educational Opportunity Project (Stanford University), xvii
Edward, Joseph, 441
Edwards, E., 146n27
Edwards, Frank, 110n7
Einstein, Albert, 326
Eisenhower, Dwight D., 23n6

Eisenhower, Edgar Newton, 23
Eisenhower Foundation, 117n35, 278, 317n13
Electoral College, 303, 330–331
Electricity in rural areas, 24
Elementary and Secondary Education Act (ESEA) (1965), 51, 74
Ellig, Jerry, 382n8
Elliot, Stuart W., 59n27
Ellison, Keith, 322
Ellison, Ralph, 305, 305n18
El Museo del Barrio, 402
Ely, Danielle M., 221n13
Ember, Sydney, 28n36
Emergency School Aid Act (1972), 51–52
Emory University, 423, 427
Employment. *See* Jobs
Empowering Hermeneutic of History, 307–308
ENOUGH Act (Maryland, 2024), xiii
Entrepreneurship, 7, 258
Environmental injustice, 172
Epstein, Rebecca, 138n33
Equal Credit Opportunity Act (1974), 176, 178n43
Equal Employment Opportunity Commission (EEOC), 41n25
  budget and staffing, 40–43, 45
Equal Employment Opportunity Committee, 89
Equity Inclusion and Enforcement Act, xvii–xix
Errington, Timothy M., 388n39
Escueta, Maya, 385n25
Esparza, Moctezuma, 245
Esposito, Michael, 110n7
EthniFacts, 253n4
Eurocentrism, 400n3
Evans, Ariel, 12n6
Evans, Christopher, 65n6
Every Student Succeeds Act (ESSA), xvii–xviii, 58–59
Evidence Act (2018), 381–382, 386
Evidence-based policymaking, 318, 380–392
  higher education, 385–386
  preK-12 education, 384–385
  recommendations, 386–391
  sector-based employment strategies, 383–384
Evidence-Based Policymaking Collaborative (EBPC), 381n2
Evidence clearinghouses, 383
Experiential learning, 78–80

Fabelo, Tony, 55n15
Fair and Just Prosecution, 150
Fair Housing Act (1968), 176, 178, 182, 188–189
Fair Housing Assistance Program, 176
Fair Housing Trends Report, 174
Fair Isaac Corporation (FICO), 169n1
Fair Labor Standards Act (FLSA), 36–37, 44–45

Fairness Doctrine, 26
Fairplay for Kids, 81
Fair Sentencing Act (2010), 148
Faris, Robert, 371n4
Farrell, Amy M., 124n12
Farrell, Caitlin C., 391nn56–57
Farrell, Henry, 305n15
Farrie, D., 56n17
Fassia, Anika, 318
Fasthorse, Larissa, 436, 438
Favro, Tony, 139n36
Feagin, Joe R., 89n22
Federal Bureau of Investigation (FBI), 13n11, 148n32, 282n17, 303n6
Federal Communications Commission (FCC), 26–27
Federal Deposit Insurance Corporation (FDIC), 26
Federal Equal Opportunity Recruitment Program (FEORP), 254
Federal Housing Administration (FHA), 70, 174
Federal Housing Finance Agency, 174
Fedorowicz, Martha, 390n52
Fein, David, 384n19
Feiveson, Laura, 76n20
Feng, Mingyu, 385n26
Fenton, Justin, 111n11
Ferrera, America, 255
Feuer, Michael, 92nn34–35
Fields Corner Crossroads Collaborative, 285
Fifteenth Amendment, 304, 332
Figures of the Future (Rodriguez-Muniz), 259
Finkelhor, David, 139n35
Firearm injuries, 157–158, 160, 161–162
First Nation Performing Artists (FNPA), 437n39
First Step Act (2018), xxi, 148, 150
Fisher, Abigail, 91
Fisher I decision (2013), 91
Fisher II decision (2016), 91
Fisk Jubilee Singers, 298
Fitzsimmons, Kelly, 382n14, 389n46
Fixico, Donal L., 266n11
Fletcher, Arthur, 90
Florant, Aria, 16n36
Flores, Ely, 102, 102n19
Floyd, George, 16, 109, 113, 122, 129, 144, 202–203, 302, 322, 363, 422
Flynn, Andrea, 13n10
Folgert, Emmett, 285
Foner, Eric, 100n12
Food and Nutrition Service, 228n30
For Freedoms (artist collective), 405–406, 408, 412–417
"Forgotten Americans," 267–268
Forman, James, Jr., 114n18, 152n65
Forman-Katz, Naomi, 353n11

Fortenberry, James Dennis, 163n10
For the People, 150
Fortune 500 companies, 27n25
Forum for Community Solutions, 98
Forward Thinking, 137n31
Foster, Carol, 444
Foundation for Economic Education, 25
Foundations for Evidence-Based Policymaking Act (2018), 381–382
Fourteenth Amendment, 186, 193
Fox, Bryanna, 110n7
Fox, Liana, 5nn4–5
Fox, Zach, 172n12
FOX 9 Minneapolis-St. Paul, 317n11
Fox News, 371
Franken, Al, 322, 338
Frankenberg, Erica, 54n11
Franklin, Ben, 131, 131n31
Frazier, Darnella, 363
Free, Prior, and Informed Consent (FPIC) principle, 273
Freedom Reads, 409
Freedom to Vote Act, 256
"Free Market Project" (University of Chicago), 25
Free markets, failure of, 28–29
Friedman, Milton, 25
Friedrich, Michael, 386n31
Fuller, Meta Warrick, 403

Gabrielson, Ryan, 305n19
Gaetz, Matt, 338
Gaines, Charles, 408
Gale, Rebecca, 229n34
Galea, Sandro, 220n9
Gale Family Library, 263n2
Galería de la Raza, 402
Galkin, Katerina, 385n28
Gallup poll data, 269n15
Ganesh, Chitra, 405
Garber, Andrew, 261n19, 304n11, 332n2
Garces, Liliana M., 90n31
Garcia, Kim, 242n7
Garland, Merrick, 109
Garner, Eric, 203, 362–363, 417
Garnett, Keshia, 229n31
Garraty, John Arthur, 100n12
Garrett, R. Kelly, 373n9
Gateway to College, 98
Gavett, Gretchen, 403n4
Gay, Claudine, 338
Gazelka, Paul, 322
General Services Administration, Office of Evaluation Sciences, 391
George, Alice, 272n21

George Floyd Justice in Policing Act, 109
Georgia Civil Rights Cold Case course, 422–423
Gerardi, Kristopher, 173n23
Geronimus, Arline T., 204n28
Gerstle, Gary, 13, 13n13
Geto Boys, 362
Ghandnoosh, Nazgol, 143n9, 144n14, 147nn29–30, 148n33, 151n55, 151n58, 151n61, 152n65
Ghani, Mariam, 405
G.I. Bill (1944) benefits, 70, 306
Gibson, Andrea, 338, 338n1
Gietel-Basten, Stuart, 316n7
Gilbert, David, 373n8
Gillespie, Jonathan, 55n15
Gillham, Patrick F., 86nn1–2
Gillibrand, Kirsten, 103
Gillon, Steven M., 5, 88n12
Gilman, Nils, 13, 13n19
Gingrich, Newt, 102, 374
Gladstone, Lily, 430
Glass-Steagall (Banking Act of 1933), 26
Gleason, Joseph, 241n1
Goff, Phillip Atiba, 137–138, 138n32
Golden, Thelma, 409
Goldhaber, Dan, 384n20
Goldhammer, Arthur, 76n19
Goldin, Jacob, 5n3, 7n18
Goldstein, Joel K., 89n20
Golland, David Hamilton, 90nn28–29
Gomez-Aguinaga, Barbara, 257n24
González, Gilbert C., 243n15
Gonzalez, Sarah, 14n23, 134n7
Gonzalez, Thalia, 138n33
Gonzalez, Toni, 255n16
Goodell, Sarah, 229n37
Goodison, Sean, 114n16
Goodman, Melody, 171
Goon, Caroline, 282n19
Gottesman, Eric, 405, 412
Gould, Elise, 8n27, 37n5
Government, appropriate role of, 22–31
Government Accountability Office, 381n7, 382n13, 382n15
Government Performance and Results Act (1993), 381–382
Graham v. Florida, 136n19
Gramlich, Josh, 351n8
Gramm-Leach-Bliley Act (1999), 26
Grange, Coryn, 256n18
Grann, David, 430n2
Grant, Glenn A., 150n47
Grant, Sean, 389n48
Grantmaking, tiered-evidence, 382–383
The Grapes of Wrath (Steinbeck), 245

Gratz v. Bollinger (2003), 90, xviiin18
Graves, Lucia, 28nn37–38
Gray, Freddie, xi, xiv, 203
"Great Chain of Being" (Scala Naturae), 429–430
Greater Than Fear election slogan, 321–322
Great Recession (2008–2012), xvi, 56, 175, 175n31
Great Society programs, xi, 51, 76–77
   opposition and pushback, 53–56
Green, Donal P., 373n11
Greene, D. M., 56n18
Greene, Liz, 422
Greenhouse, Lind, 244n24
Greytak, E., 146n27
TheGrio (television network/website), 363
Gross, Neil, 110n4, 112n13, 115n23
Gross, Samuel R., 124–125, 125n14
Gross, Terry, 64n2
Gruening, Ernest, 24n16, 24nn11–13
Grutter v. Bollinger (2003), 90–91
Guerrilla Girls, 403, 403n7
Gugerty, Mary Kay, 387n37
Guinier, Lani, 89n23, 304, 304n13
Gumas, Evan, 204n24
Gunja, Munira, 204n24, 205n32
Guryan, Jonathan, 384n24
Guth, Madeline, 150n51

Haaland, Deb, 270
Hager, Eli, 143n5
Hahn, Robert, 135n12
Hakel, Milton D., 59n27
Haldar, Sweta, 150n51
Hall, Garrett, 205n37
Halsey, Lauren, 409
HALT Fentanyl Act, 151n60
Hamad, Rita, 229n37
Hambidge, Wendy, 431n3
Hamilton (musical), 248
Haney López, Ian, 318, 318n14, 319nn17–18
Hannity, Sean, 371
Hansen, Michael, 87n9
Hanson, Caroline, 7n22, 7n26
Hanson, Jarrod, 88n17
Hanushek, Eric, 83
Harding, Vincent, 340
Harell, Alison, 316n4
Harjo, Sterlin, 432
Harlan, John Marshall, 186–187
Harlem Cultural Festival, 402
Harlem on my Mind (exhibition), 402
Harper, Shaun R., 86n6
Harris, David A., 123n5, 124n11
Harris, Fred, 214n3, 241nn2–3, 278n1, 315nn1–2, 319n20, 359n1

Harris, J. John, 88n16
Hart, Nicholas, 382n11
Harvard University, xviii, 91
Hate crimes, 269, 282, 303
Hayes, Rutherford B., 297
Hazeltine, Reva, 431n3
Head Start, 54, 74, 228
Healing Our Divided Society (Harris & Curtis), 241, 278
Health. *See also* COVID-19 pandemic; Public health
   "death measurement," 297–298
   health care policy, 7
   Healthy People 2030, 215n6, 222n19
   inequities in health outcomes, 200, 221–227
   infant/maternal mortality, 203–204, 221–225
HealthCare.gov, 99nn8–9
Heckman, James (J. J.), 41n19, 54n9
Helms, Jesse, 404
Hemmer, Nicole, 371n2
Hendershot, Heather, 361n7
Hendra, Richard, 383n17
Herbers, John, 252n1
Hermann, Alexander, 173n24
Herrera, Santiago, 30n47
Hersey, Tricia, 415
Hetey, Rebecca C., 316n5
Higher education
   benefits of, 202
   diversity/inequities, xviii, 74, 87, 93, 338
   evidence-based policymaking, 385–386
   financial aid, 52
High Museum of Art, 420, 427
Hill, Greg, 285
Hill, Latoya, 200n3, 242n8
Hillsdale College, 75n13
Himmelstein, David U., 201n9
Hinh, Iris, 75n9
Hinton, Elizabeth, 110n1, 362n10
Hiring Opportunities Coalition (HOC), 101
Hispanic/Latino populations
   government representation, 254–255
   population growth, 253–254
   in television and film, 255
   terminology, 241n4
Historically Black Colleges and Universities (HBCUs), 62
Historical Survey of Consumer Finances, 64
History Education Group (Stanford University), 366
Hjalmarsson, Randi, 149n37
Hoffman, Kelly M., 203n22
Holliday, George, 361
Holt, Jennifer, 27n19, 27nn29–30
Holton, Anne, 252
Holton, Linwood, 252

Index

Homeownership. *See also* Housing crisis
  and American Dream, xvi
  downpayment assistance (DPA) models, 178
  first generation homebuyer programs, 177–178
  homeownership gap, 173
Home Owners Loan Corporation (HOLC), 174
Home Visiting Evidence of Effectiveness, 383
Homicide. *See* Crime
Hood, J. Larry, 90n30
hooks, bell, 340, 340n5, 421–422, 427
Hoover, Herbert, 23
Horton, Willie, 374
Horwitz, Robert Britt, 28n32
Hostetter, Martha, 203n22
Housing Choice Vouchers (HCVs), 179, 180
Housing crisis, 173. *See also* Homeownership
  appraisal discrimination, 174
  "black twins" in Chicago, 190–191
  housing inequities, 188
  housing policy, 6
  mortgage lending discrimination, 174–175
  real estate discrimination, 174
  recommendations for justice, 175–182
  redlining, 174–175, 178, 188, 306
  renters, 192
  segregation, 170–171, 172–175
  small-area fair market rent standards (SAFMRs), 194
  voucher programs, 194
Housing Crisis Response Act, 182
Howard, Jacqueline, 203n23
Howard University, 89
Howell, Elizabeth A., 225n24
Howell, Junia, 174n31
Hoyert, Donna L., 204n24, 221n14
Hoynes, Hilary, 229n37
Huang, Kevin C.-W., 385n26
Hughes, Joe, 76n16
Hughes, Langston, 298
Hughey, Matthew, 86n5
Huie, Stephanie A. Bond, 226n26
Hungary, 316
Hunt Institute, 77n27
Hureau, David M., 116n25
Huynh, Dũng "David," 280

Iftikar, Jon S., 91n33
Illuminative (racial justice organization), 408
Im, Carolyne, 255n17, 281n14
Immigration
  Asian American, 278–280
  policy concerns, 258–260
  Somali populations in U.S., 317
  vilification of immigrants, 317

Immigration Act (1990), 259, 280
Immigration and Nationality Act (1952), 258
Immigration and Naturalization Service (INS), 244
Immigration History, 279n7
Immigration Reform (Kamasaki), 253–254
Iñárritu, Alejandro G., 248n45
Iñárritu, González, 248
Incarceration rates, 143–152, 305–306
  challenges and obstacles, 151
  racial inequities, drivers of, 147–151
  recent trends, 144
  and voting rights, 333–334
Inclusive Communities Project, Dallas, Texas, 194
"*Index of the Disappeared*," 405
Indian Self-Determination and Education Assistance Act (1975), 269
Indian Termination Act (1953), 266
Indigenous peoples. *See* Native Americans
Inequities. *See also* Poverty; Racial inequities
  appraisal discrimination, 174
  community health framework to reduce, 217–219
  health outcomes, 200, 221–227
  homeownership gap, 173
  homicide rates, 157–159
  housing bias and real estate discrimination, 174
  Latinos in workforce, 256–257
  mortality rates, 225–227
  mortgage lending discrimination, 174–175
  policy-based solutions to health disparities, 228–230
  socioeconomic, 151
  wealth gap, 173, 226
Infant/maternal mortality, 203–204, 221–225
Infield, Tom, 353n10
Inflation Reduction Act (2022), 7, 15, 100, 164, 176
Infrastructure Investment and Jobs Act (2021), 58, 100, 164, 176, 253
Ingram, Emily, 101n17
Ingram, Erin S., 99nn10–11
Institute for Social Policy and Understanding, 282n15
Institute of Urban Communication, 360
Internal Revenue Service, 17
Internet, monopolization of, 27
Intrator, Jake, 170n5
Invisible Man (Ellison), 305
Ipsos (market research firm), 77n25
Irving, Doug, 76n22
Ismail, Selkhan, 264n5

Jackson, C. Kirabo, 53n4, 82n39
Jackson, Derek, 403
Jackson, John H., 68n9
Jamieson, Kathleen Hall, 351n8
January 6 U.S. Capitol attack, 252

Japanese American National Museum (JANM), 407
J.D.B. v. North Carolina, 136n26
Jensen, Derrick, 429–430, 429n1
Jensen, Eric, 303n4
Jeyifous, Olalekan, 408
Jim Crow era, 88–89
Job Corps, 99
Jobs. *See also* Youth unemployment
  job creation, 39–40, 46
  job training programs, 383–384
  minimum wage policy, 36–39, 44–45
  unemployment, 6, 39–40, 41, 46, 162–164
Jobs for the Future, 98
John Jay College of Criminal Justice, 146
John Jay College Research Advisory Group, 146n23
Johns Hopkins Police Department, 129
Johns Hopkins University School of Education, 242
Johnson, Emily, 437
Johnson, Frank, 189
Johnson, Kenny, 285
Johnson, Lamar K., 214n3
Johnson, Lyndon B., 51, 76n23, 110, 188, 267–268, 267n12, 268n13, 271n19
  Executive Order 11365, 86, 123
  at Howard University, 89
Johnson, Rucker C., 52, 52n3, 53n4, 74, 74n5
Johnson, Thaddeus L., 143n5
Johnson, Tonika, 190–191
Johnston, William R., 80n33
Jones, Alexi, 150n43
Jones, Candice, 140n38
Jones, Cynthia E., 150n44
Jones, Nikole Hannah, 66
Jones, Ryann Grochowski, 305n19
Jones, Sam, 352n9
Jones v. Mayer, 189nn11–12
Jordan, Allison, 260n32
Jordan, Jim, 366
Joseph, Marc Bamuthi, 433, 433n5
Joseph, Peniel E., 294, 294n1
Joyce, Kathryn, 76n14
J-PAL North America, 384n22, 391, 391n55
Jurkowitz, Mark, 373n12
Just Action (Rothstein & Rothstein), 190, 191–192, 195
Juvenile Justice and Delinquency Prevention Act (JJDPA), xxi

Kaiser Permanente, 208–209
Kalev, Alexandra, 115n24
Kaling, Mindy, 282
Kam, Cindy D., 373n13
Kamasaki, Charles, 241n1, 245n30, 253–254, 254n8
Kandra, Jori, 232n39
Kang, Cecilia, 28n36
Kantor, Emma, 423
Kantor, Harvey, 74n3
Kapadia, Ronak K., 405n11
Kaplan, Isaac, 405n12
Karlan, Dean, 387n37
Karnes, Kevin, 422
Karoly, Lynn, 54n10
Katz, Lawrence F., 384n18
Katznelson, Ira, 89n27
Keffer, Sarah, 88n15
Kegler, Scott R., 157n1, 160n3
Kelling, George L., 116n26, 118n36
Kelly, Mary Louise, 173n25
Kennedy, John F., 258, 258n26, 260n31
  Executive Order 10925, 89
Kent, Ana Hernàndez, 220n10
Kerner, Otto, 86, 348
Kerner Commission
  background and overview, 11–12
  creation of, xi–xii, xv, 51, 86, 348–349
  diversity, lack of, 199
  goal of, 123
  loving framework, 66–72
  new Great Society, 73–84
  race equity and racial justice, 17–18
  research and methodology of, 110
Kerner Report, 51, 179–182n39
  challenges of accepting, 293–294
  criticism of media coverage, 370
  on deep-seated racism and Eurocentrism, 399–400
  EEOC budget and staffing, 40–43, 45
  evidence-based policies, 318
  exposure of inequities, 133
  future recommendations, 44–46, 57–59
  job creation and unemployment, 39–40, 46
  minimum wage, 36–39, 44–45
  "New Will," xii–xiii, 73, 294, 391–392, 417, 421–422, 440–447
  recommendations on housing and finance, 169–170
  Richard Nixon's opposition, 16
  union membership and representation, 43–44, 45–46
  use of racial terms, 123n1
  on "white society," 187–190
Kerr, Tom, 403n5
Kerry, John, 103
Ketl, Donald F., 387n35
Keynesian economic frameworks, 25
Keyssar, Alexander, 303n7
Khalili, Nader, 434
Khullar, Dhruv, 220n9
Killers of the Flower Moon (film), 430

Index

Kim, Daniel Dae, 282
Kim, Woojin, 386n32
Kinder, Donald R., 373n13
King, Ledyard, 134n9
King, Martin Luther, Jr., 6, 87–88, 104, 110, 188, 205n29, 284, 286, 308n29, 339n2
   assassination of, 302
   Poor People's Campaign, 11–12
King, Mel, 284
King, Rodney, 122, 203, 361–362
Kishi, Roudabeh, 352n9
Klein, Ezra, 16n35, 18n47
Klein, Naomi, 365n15
Klein, Sarah, 203n22
Klibanoff, Hank, 422
Kliff, Sarah, 29n45
Kluckow, Rich, 144n11, 144n15
Knight, Maria, 285
Koch, Charles, 31
Kochhar, Rakesh, 284n26
Koenig, Judith Anderson, 59n27
Koenig, Shulamith, 340
Kohler-Hausmann, Issa, 110n5
Konczal, Mike, 12n6, 15n29, 16–17, 16n37
Koppel, Barbara, 247n43
Korte, Lara, 207n43
Kowalski, Amanda E., 7n20
Krimes, Jessie, 409
Krishnakumar, Priya, 148n32
Kulish, Nicholas, 29n45
Kunz, William M., 28n33
Kurashige, Scott, 286n32
Kushner, Jared, 28
Kutateladze, Besiki, 137n27
Kwan, Michelle, 282

LaBeija, Kia, 403
Ladson-Billings, Gloria, 89n21
Lagasse, Jeff, 209n47
Lake Research Partners, 318, 321n21
Lakritz, Talia, 27n31
Lambie-Hanson, Lauren, 173n23
Lanfear, Charles C., 160n5
Lang, Lucy, 149n37
Lanzilotti, Leilehua, 433–434, 434n6
Lash, Martha, 88n19
Latino Donor Collaborative, 255n15
Latino/Hispanic populations. *See* Hispanic/Latino populations
LatinoJustice, 244
Lau v. Nichols, 244
Lawrence, Elizabeth M., 202n15
LEAD, Los Angeles, 102
Leading Health Indicators (LHIs), 221–227

League of United Latin American Citizens (LULAC), 243
Learning agendas, federal agencies, 382
Leatherby, Lauren, 114n19
Lee, Alexandre, 170n3
Lee, Bruce, 282
Lee, Edmund, 28n35
Lee, Hedwig, 110n7
Lee, Spike, 362
Lee, Suni, 282
Lee, Yee Hee, xxn32
Legal Defense Fund, 308n31
Leguizamo, John, 248
Leguizamo Does America (television program), 248
Leonard, Jonathan S., 41nn21–22
Leonhardt, David, 15n30
Leovy, Jill, 111n12
Leung-Gagne, M., 55n14
Levitsky, Steven, 328, 328n1
Lewis, Jenny M., 390n51
Lewis, John R., 189, 256, 304, 308, 323
Lewis, Kristen, 98n7
Li, Wei, 175n36
Liberalism, racial, 12–15
Library of Congress, 279n5
Lichstenstein, Nelson, 13nn14–15
Lieberman, Carl, 111n8
Lieberman, Evan, 316n4
Lieberman, Michael, 269n14
Lieu, Ted, 282
Light, Michael T., 143nn6–7
Ligon, Glenn, 403
Lilla, Mark, 317n12
Limbaugh, Rush, 371
Lin, Jeremy, 282
Lindsay, Arturo, 420, 427
Linos, Elizabeth, 386n32, 390n50, 391n53
Linzy, Kalup, 403
Lipsky, Michael, 113n14
Lipton, Eric, 28n36
List, John A., 386n33
Literacy, 77–78
   literacy tests and immigration, 279
Liu, Jane, 43nn27–28
Liu, Lucy, 282
Livingston, M. D., 65n7
Lloyd, Camille, 303n5
Loan Trần, Ngọc, 340–341, 340n6
Lofstrom, Magnus, 149n35
Lofton, Holly, 201n10
Long, Heather, 64n3
Longoria, Eva, 248
López, Gerardo R., 89n20
Lopez, Jennifer, 245

López, Jose, 244
López, Lidia, 244
Lopez, Mark Hugo, 253n5
López, Monxo, 244n19
López Green, Viviana, 241n1
Losen, Daniel J., 55n15
Lost Cause movement, 406
Love, Hannah, 163nn11–12, 164n16
Loving Cities Index, 68–69
Loving Communities Stimulus Package, 70–71
Lowery, Annie, 17n39
Lowery, Wesley, 376, 376n28
Lu, Han, 151n56
Lucas, Bailee, 163n10
Luciano, Miguel, 417
Luhby, Tami, 226n27
Lundstrom, Eric W., 160n4
Luong, C., 56n18
Lurie, Ithai Z., 7n18, 7n20

MacDonald, John M., 150n44
MacDorman, Marian F., 225n24
Mach, Jennifer, 233n5
Mackenbach, Johan P., 220n9
Mackevicius, Claire L., 82n39
MacLaury, Judson, 89n24
MacLean, Nancy, 30, 31n53
Madland, David, xxn29
Madrick, Jeff, 30, 30n48
Madrigal, Alexis C., 359n3
Madubuonwu, B., 146n27
MAGA Movement, 231, 316, 320
Magee, Lauren A., 163n10
Maier, Anna, 59n26
Major League Baseball (MLB), 125
Make America Great Again (MAGA) Movement, 231, 316, 320
Malen, B., 56n20
Malik, Muna, 417
Manchild in the Promised Land (Brown), 441
Mandel, Richard, 134n8
Mann, Catherine L., 207n42
Manzi, Jim, 387n36
Mapplethorpe, Robert, 404
Marijuana use, 146, 148
Markowitz, Sara, 229n37
Marmot, Michael (M. G.), 220n9, 226n29
Mars, Bruno, 282
Marshall, Thurgood, 243, 307
Marshall Project, 366, 376
Martin, David A., 244n23
Martin, Gregory J., 28n33, 28n35
Martin, Iman K., 225n24

Martin, Spider, 413
Martin, Trayvon, 14
Martin, William McChesney, 188n5
Martinez-White, Xiomara, 175n35
Maruschak, Laura M., 150n49
Marx, Gary T., 86nn1–2
Maslow's Hierarchy of Needs, 67
Massachusetts
 Fair Share amendment, 69
 Massachusetts Affordable Housing Alliance, 178
 school finance litigation, 56
Mass Design Group, 409
Massey, Douglas S., 170n5
Massoglia, Michael, 143nn6–7
Masterov, D. V., 54n9
Mastro, Elena Maker, 98n5
Maternal/infant mortality, 203–204, 221–225
Matsa, Katernina Eva, 365n16
Matthew, Dayna Bowen, 87n10
Matthews, Amy, 431n3
Maulbeck, Ben Francisco, 275n28, n29
Maxim, Robert, 270n16
Maye, Adewale, 36n1, 37nn2–3, 43nn30–31, 45n33, 46n34
Maynard, Rebecca, 389n46
Mayo-Wilson, Evan, 389n48
Mažar, Nina, 389n45
McCabe, David, 27n22
McCain, John, 27
McCarthy, Kevin, 252
McChesney, Robert W., 27n24
McClain, Elijah, 302, 305
McCrain, Josh, 28n35
McCubbin, Janet, 7n18
McDevitt, Jack, 124n12
McGhee, Heather C., 18n46, 202n13, 205nn30–31, 205nn33–35, 318, 373n19, 374
McInerney, Mark, 229n37
McKay, Rich, 302n2
McKernan, Signe-Mary, 14n21
McKinley, Jesse, 151n62
McLennan, Marsh, 76n18
McLeod, Morgan, 151n63
Meares, Tracey L., 115n21
Media coverage
 bias, 28
 Black exclusion from, 400
 conservative media, history of, 371–372
 coverage of urban unrest, 359–362
 failures of, 349
 media accountability, 138
 neutrality vs. objectivity, 377
 nonprofit journalism, 366

Index

and racial issues in contemporary society, 362–368, 370–377
  reform and transformation, 347–357
  at time of Kerner Report, 370
Medicaid, 7
  Healthy Opportunities Pilot, North Carolina, 208
Medina, Lauren, 258n25
Mehta, Jonaki, 149n39
Meija, Pamela, 242n7
Mekeel, Scudder, 264n6
Meko, Hurubie, 151n62
Melamed, Samantha, 149n35
Mellon Foundation, 406
Mendez, Felicitas, 242–243
Mendez, Gonzalo, 242–243
Mendez v. Westminster, 243, 252
Mendez v. Westminster: Desegregating California's Schools (film), 243n16
Menendez, Bob, 246n33
Menn, Joseph, 366n21
Mental Health America, 282n18, 282n20
Merge Left, 318
Metropolitann Museum of Art, 409
Mexican American Legal Defense and Educational Fund (MALDEF), 244
Michelmore, Katherine, 5n3
"Mijorities," 129, 129n27
Mikva Challenge, 98
The Milagro Beanfield War (film), 245
Milán, William G., 244n21
Milani, Katy, 12n6
Miller, Chris, 5n2
Miller, Doug, 229n37
Miller, Peter, 256n18
Miller, Stephen, 14
Miller v. Alabama, 136n20
Mills, Charles, 12n5
Milton Eisenhower Foundation, 129
Min, Susette, 405n10
Minimum wage policy, xix–xx, 36–39, 44–45
Minino, Arialdi M., 139n34
"Minnesota Miracle" (2016 election), 316–317, 318–319, 321–323
Miranda, Lin Manuel, 248
Misinformation/disinformation, 304–305, 331–332, 366, 373, 376
Mississippi Museum of Art, 409
Mitchell, Amy, 354n13
Mizariegos, Miranda, 246n36
Model Cities programs, 181
Moffitt, Terrie, 135n13
Mohaiman, Naieem, 405
Mohammed, Selina A., 220n10

Momoa, Jason, 282
Montejano, David, 243n14
Montialoux, Claire, 37n4
Monument Lab, 406
Monuments, 406
  Confederate monuments, 406, 423–424
Mora, G. Cristina, 242n13
Moral issues
  Empowering Hermeneutic of History, 307–308
  and justice issues, 296–297
  moral language, 295–296
  and voting rights, 298–299
Morello-Frosch, Rachel, 54n8
Morris, Edward W., 55n15
Morris, Jonathan S., 28n33
Morris, Kevin, 256n18
Morrison, Aaron, 151n59
Mortgage lending discrimination, 174–175. *See also* Housing crisis
Mosley-Johnson, Elise, 202n11
Moss, Emily, 202n14
The Mothers of Gynecology (memorial park), 406
Moule, Richard K., Jr., 110n7
Movers and Shakers' Kinfolk project, 406
Moving to Opportunity (MTO), 229
Mt. Pelerin Society, 25
Mueller, Tom, 205n36
Muhitch, Kevin, 151n58
Mullen, A. Kirsten, 306n22
Multiracial movements
  in Minnesota, 318, 322–323
  need for, 104–105, 302–303, 306–307
  representation in governance, 270, 271, 304
Mulvihill, Geoff, 150n50
Muncey, D., 56n20
Muñiz, Raquel, 88n15
Muñoz-Hernández, Shirley, 244n21
Murguía, Alfredo, 246–247
Murray, Paulie, 307
Museum of Contemporary Art, 409
Museums
  as community-based institutions, 401–402, 403
  and cultural power, 408–409
  and Hispanic experience, 246
  neighborhood museum movement, 402
Mutu, Wangechi, 409
Myers, John M., 27n19

NAACP, 243, 296, 307
NAEP (National Assessment of Educational Progress), 56, 57
NALEO Educational Fund, 254n12, 255, 255n14
Namking, Victoria, 281n11

Nap Ministry, 415
Narragon, Melissa, 174n28
Naseer, Sarah, 347n3
Natarajan, Anusha, 255n17
National Advisory Commission on Civil Disorders, 11n2, 62n1, 73n1, 146n18, 319n19
National Affairs, 367
National Alliance for Youth and Young Adult Advocates (NAYYAA), 100
National Apprenticeship Act of 2023, xix
National Archives and Records Administration, 279n6, 279n8
National Assessment of Education Progress (2022), 57
National Association of Hispanic Journalists, 410
National Association of Latino Arts, 410
National Association of Manufacturers (NAM), 25
National Association of Realtors, 175n39
National Association of Social Workers, 135nn13–14
National Bureau of Economic Research, 39n8, 39nn10–11
National Center for Education Statistics (NCES), 57
National Congress of American Indians, 98
National Council of Young Leaders, 98n4
National Council on Crime and Delinquency, 134n6
National Electric Light Association (NELA), 24–25
National Employment Law Project (NELP), 14n20
National Fair Housing Alliance (NFHA), 170n6, 171n11, 172n16, 174n33, 178
National Guard, xi
National Guard Youth ChalleNGe, 99
National Guard Youth Foundation, 98
National Housing Act (1949), 169n2
National Housing Trust Fund, 179
National Museum of African American History and Culture, 263n1
National Museum of the American Latino, 246nn34–35
National Policing Institute, 118n38
National Research Council, 143
National Science Foundation, 366
National Youth Employment Coalition (NYEC), 101
Native American Graves Protection and Repatriation Act (NAGPRA), 273
Native Americans
  contemporary situation, 269–270
  EARTH.SPEAKS art project, 434–436
  funding structures for arts and culture, 437–438
  history of federal policy, 265–266
  Indigenous concepts of healing, 429–430
  land stewardship, 436–437
  languages, 433
  Osage culture, 430–431

Osage language, 432–433
policy recommendations, 270–275
Red Power protest movements, 268–269
relocation of, 266–267
Standing Rock Sioux Reservation Protest, 263–264, 272
at time of Kerner Report, 264–265, 266–269
urban communities, 267
Native Americans in Philanthropy (NAP), 274n27
Native American Voting Rights Act (NAVRA), 271–272
Native Voices Rising, 274
Nava, Gregory, 248n44
Navarrete, Lisa, 241n1, 245n30
Nazaryan, Alexander, 52n3, 74n5
NCES Digest of Educational Statistics, 87
NDN Collective (advocacy organization), 274, 274n26, 275
NEA (National Endowment for the Arts), 404
Neal, Michael, 172n15
neighborhood arts labs, 425–426
neighborhood collective efficacy, 115–117, 118
neighborhood-level diversity, 284
neighborhood-level policing, 115–117
neighborhood-level segregation, 170, 171, 187–188, 190–192, 194–195, 350
neighborhood museum movement, 402
neighborhood schools, 75
neighborhood violence, 162–163
Neller, Seth, 7n19
Nellis, Ashley, 143n4, 144n17, 147n29, 164n17
Nelson, Anne, 28n39
Neoliberalism, 12–13, 16
Ness, Susan, 376n24
Nesterak, Max, 265nn7–8
Neuhoff, Alex, 383n16
Neuman, Susan B., 78n29
Newcomer, Kathryn, 382n11
New England Foundation for the Arts, 438
New Jersey, school finance litigation, 56
Newland, Bryan, 265n10
Newman, Nic, 377n30
Newsday, 193
Newton-Small, Jay, 14n22
"New Will"
  call for, xii–xiii, 73
  case study, 440–447
  creation of, 294, 391–392, 417, 421–422
Nguyễn, David Hòa Khoa, 91n33
Nguyen, Viet Thanh, 282
Nhat Hanh, Thich, 412
Nichols, Tyre, 203

Index

463

Nickow, Andre Joshua, 384n21
Nicolaides, Becky, 350n6
Nineteenth Amendment, 304, 332
Nitz, Michael, 281
Nix, Justin, 110n7
Nix, Naomi, 366n21
Nixon, Richard M., 16, 75, 90, 374
No Child Left Behind Act, 56
Nonprofit news organizations, 366
Nosek, Brian A., 388n39
Notice of Proposed Rulemaking (NPRM), 176n40
Novoa, Christina, 8n29
Nye, David E., 24n14, 24nn9–10
Nyrop, Kris, 146n26

OASIS (arts initiative), 420–421
Obama, Barack, 13–14, 205, 317, 374
 Executive Order 13684, 123
Ochoa, Erin M., 116n25
O'Donnell, Katy, 170n4
Office of Civil Rights, 58
Office of Evaluation Sciences, General Services Administration, 391n54
Office of Minority Health, 283n21
Office of Rights and Liberties (ORL), 128
Office of the Attorney General, 148n31, 306n24
Office of the Minnesota Secretary of State, 316n9
Ogunwole, Stella U., 347n2
Olejniczak, Karol, 382n11
Olivas, Michael A., 244nn22–23
Olmos, Edward James, 245
Olovsson, Conny, 29n42
100,000 Opportunities Initiative, 101
O'Neill, Aaron, 309n34, 316n10
Open science, 389–390
Opotow, Susan, 137n29
Oppel, Richard A., 114n19
Opportunity Youth (OY), 98–101
Orbán, Viktor, 316
O'Reilly, Bill, 371
Oreopoulos, Philip, 384n21
Oreskes, Naomi, 22n1, 29n44
Organization for Economic Cooperation and Development (OECD), 76, 200n5, 204
Ornstein, Norman J., 304nn9–10
Orozco, Cynthia E., 243n14
Orta, Ramsey, 362–363
Ortiz, Mark Alexander, 245n25
Ortíz, Vilma, 243n14
Osaka, Naomi, 282
Ostadan, Bahar, 110n6
Ou, S., 54n9

Our World in Data, 226n26
Owens, Major, 103

Palim, Mark, 174n29
Palmquist, Bradley, 373n11
Pang, Baobo, 30n47
Pantaleo, Daniel, 363
Pantoja, Antonia, 243–244
Papachristos, Andrew V., 116n25
Parable of the Talents (Butler), 413
ParentsTogether, 81
Parks, Rosa, 189
Parolin, Zachary, 58n23
Partners for Education at Berea College, 98
Passel, Jeffrey S., 253n5, 253n7
Pastor, Manuel, 53–54, 54n8
Patterson, Clayton, 361
Patton, Lori D., 86n6
Patton, Stacey, 134n10
Paybarah, Azi, 363n12
Payne-Patterson, Jasmine, 36n1, 37nn2–3
PDK International, 77n24
Pearman, F. A., 56n18
Pedrick, Keith Williamson, 89n25
Pell Grants, 151, 228
Penoi, Ronee, 437
Perera, Gihan, 275n28, n29
Pérez, Lucy, 253n6, 256–257, 256n19, 257n21
Perez-Sanz, Sarah, 242n7
Perry, Andre M., 176n26
Perry, Brea L., 55n15
Persico, C., 53n4
Personal Responsibility and Work Opportunity Reconciliation Act (1996), xv–xvi
Peterson, Dana M., 207n42
Pew Research Center, 255, 336, 365, 373n16, 374
Pfaff, John E., 152n65
Pfeiffer, Denise, 79
Pfingst, Lori, 146n26
Philadelphia Plan, 90
The Philadelphia Youth Network, 98
Philanthropy, need for, 274–275
Pickard, Victor, 26n18, 366, 366n20
Pickett, Justin T., 111n10
Piketty, Thomas, 29n46, 76, 76n19
Pinchot, Gifford, 24
Piño, Elizabeth, 160, 161n6
Piore, Adam, 28n39
Plessy v. Ferguson, 88, 243
Plyler v. Doe, 244
Podhorzer, Michael, 18n47
Poethig, Erica, 383n12
Police brutality, 203, 207

Police reform, 109–119
  collective efficacy, 117
  data collection/population benchmarking, 123–124
  "defund the police," 129, 129n28
  focused deterrence, 117–119
  innovations, effective, 113–119
  legislation, 113
  obstacles to, 111–113
  "place-based" predictive policing, 118
  procedural justice, 128–129
  "progressive prosecutors," 130
  qualified immunity, 208
  race and transparency, 122–131
  racism and media coverage, 359–368
  RRD Model, 125–126, 128, 131
  traffic stops, 149
Policymaking. *See also* Evidence-based policymaking
  arts and education recommendations, 425–427
  and death measurement, 297–298
  immigration, 259–260
  Latino representation, 257–258
  Native American issues, 270–275
  voting rights, 256
  will to change, 230–233, 440–447
Poor People's Campaign, 104, 294–295
Pop Culture Collaborative, 408
Popovich, Nadja, 172n13
Porter, Nicole D., 146n24, 151n63
Poverty, 294–295
  childhood, xvii–xviii, 51–52, 76
  concentration of, 54
  and "death measurement," 297–298
  ENOUGH Act (Maryland, 2024), xiii–xiv
  and health, 220–221
  political prioritization of, 96
  racial statistics, 104
  reductions following Child Tax Credit (CTC), 5–6
  and youth unemployment, 98–99
Powell, John, 244n22
Powell, Lewis, 90
Pre-analysis plans (PAPs), 389–390
Preschool, 54, 56, 58
President's Task Force on 21st Century Policing, 123nn3–4
Pressman, Jeremy, 302n1
Price, Gregory N., 86n4
Prindle, Gregory M., 28n32
Prison populations. *See* Incarceration rates
PRO (Protecting the Right to Organize) Act, 46
Procedural justice, 115
Progressive movements
  messaging, 315–323
  post-neoliberal economics, 15–16
  school finance reform, 56

Project Quest, 384
"Pro-life" movement, 298
ProPublica (nonprofit journalistic organization), 366
Prosecutors Alliance of California, 150
Protecting the Right the Organize (PRO) Act, xxii
Protest culture and art, 402–404
Protzko, John, 388n42
Public Allies, 98
Public Artists in Residence (PAIR), 410
Public Broadcasting Act (1967), 366
Public education
  federal role, 83
  privatization movement, 75–76
  staffing and resources, 81–84
Public health. *See also* COVID-19 pandemic
  community health framework, 217–219
  COVID-19 pandemic, 157
  definitions, 200
  future directions, 206–209
  Kerner Report on, 199–209
  maternal/infant mortality, 203–204, 221–225
  Medicaid expansion, 205–206
  mental health, 203
  poverty and health inequities, 220–221
  and racism, 202–206
  responses to trauma, 139
  Social Determinants of Health (SDOH), 214, 215–217, 228, 230
  and wealth gap, 201–202
  years of potential life lost (YPLL) and homicide, 159
Public Religion Research Institute (PRRI), 354n12
Puerto Rican diaspora, 243–244
Puerto Rican Legal Defense and Education Fund, 244
Pulp Fiction (film), 125
Punitive environments. *See* School discipline
Putnam, Lara, 302n1
Putnam, Robert D., 375n20

Qualified immunity, 208
Quan, Ke Huy, 282
Quan, Vincent, 384n21
Quarshie, Mabinty, 12n7
Quillian, Lincoln, 41n24
Quintero, Esther, 78n29

Raboteau, Emily, 361n9
Race Class Narrative (RCN), 318–321
"Race-neutral" politics, 14, 44, 91, 147–148, 193, 317–318
Racial inequities
  achievement gaps, 53–54
  contemporary situation, 62–64
  disciplinary procedures, 65–66

Index

in education, 51–53
Federal Government's role, 5
generational wealth, 64
graduation rates, 62–64
housing, 64, 173n22
school discipline, 55
school funding, 54–55
systemic supports, 64–65
wealth gap, 71, 76
Racial issues
credit markets, 171–172
criminal offenses vs. enforcement, 144–147
diversity in police profession, 114–115
housing segregation, 170–171, 174
incarceration, inequities in, 143–144
media coverage in contemporary society, 370–377
and police policies, 110–111
police reform and transparency, 122–131
wage gap, 41
wealth gap expansion, 173
Racial profiling, 124–125, 128
Racism
anti-Asian, 14
anti-Asian, surrounding COVID-19 pandemic, 281–282
anti-Latino, 14
Canada's approach, 286
costs of, 207
crime and cultural stereotypes, 133–137
and fear of crime, 133–134
history of in U.S., 87–88
media coverage of policing, 359–368
and public health, 202–206
structural/systemic, 12–13, 133, 246, 373–374
during Trump administration, 14–15
Raise the Wage Act (2023), xix–xx
Ramirez, Antonio, 102
Ramsey, Ross, 366
Randomized controlled trials (RCTs), 381, 387
Rapfogel, Nicole, 208n45
Ratcliffe, Monica, 88n19
Raudenbush, Stephen W., 116n29
Ray, Rashawn, xvin5
Reading instruction, 77–78
Reading Opens the World program, 78
Reading Universe project, 78
Reagan, Ronald, 13, 26–27, 75, 316, 374, 405
Real Solutions for Kids and Communities (AFT), 77
Reardon, Sean F., 64n5
Reclaiming the Border Narrative, 410
Reconstruction periods in U.S. history, 294, 297, 300
Rector, Ricky Ray, 13
Redburn, F. Stevens, 143n2
Redcorn, Charles, 430n2

Redford, Robert, 245
Redlining, 174–175, 178, 188, 306
Redmond, Nicole, 225n24
Redmond-Jones, D., 56n20
Red Power protest movements, 268–269
Reentry Employment Opportunities (REO), 99
Rehavi, M. Marit, 149n36
Rehkopf, David H., 229n37
Reich, Robert, 27n27, 232, 232n40
Reist, Kayla, 78n29
Renters rights, 6. *See also* Housing crisis
Reparations and redress
Black Americans, 207
Japanese Americans, 404
Report of the National Advisory Commission on Civil Disorders. see Kerner Report
Research-practice partnerships (RPPs), 391
Reservation Dogs (television series), 432
Restoring Racial Justice, 218n7
Results for America, 386n34
Reynolds, A. J., 54n9
Richards, Phoebe, 444
Ricketts, Lowell R., 220n10
Riley, Chris, 376n23
Riley, K. Jack, 146n26
Ringgold, Faith, 402
Rittenhouse, Kyle, 134
Ritzdorf, Marsha, 171n9
Roberto Clemente: Pride of the Pittsburgh Pirates (Winter), 246
Roberts, Aki, 114n17
Roberts, Chief Justice John, 91
Roberts, Hal, 371n4
Roberts, Neil, 12n5
Robeson, Paul, 415
Robey, Jason P., 143nn6–7
Robinson, Michael A., 305n20
Robinson-Dooley, Vanessa, 305n20
Rockwell, Norman, 413
Rodgers, William M. III, 41n23
Rodríguez, Raymond, 246n42
Rodriguez-Elliott, Stephen, 170n7
Rodriguez-Muniz, Michael, 259, 259n30
Roeder, Amy, 170n8
Roehrkasse, Alexander F., 143n6
Roe v. Wade, 204
Rogers, Hal, 103
Romer, Daniel, 351n8
Romney, Mitt, 374
Roosevelt, Franklin, 23, 26, 29
Roosevelt Institute, 16
The Root (online magazine), 363, 376
Roper v. Simmons, 135n14, 136nn15–18
Rorke, Bernard, 316n6

Rose, Geoffrey, 226n29
Rosenberg, Rosaline, 307n26
Rosenthal, Jill, 208n45
Ross, Cody T., 110n7
Ross, Marisa C., 116n25
Rothstein, Leah, 187n4, 188n10, 192n16
Rothstein, Richard, 53n5, 53n7, 187nn3–4, 188n6, 188n10, 192n16, 365n15
Rothwell, Jonathan, 174n26
Rowlands, D. W., 163nn11–12, 164n16
Roy, Ravi K., 27n23
RRD (Reason, Result, Duration) Model, 125–126, 128, 131
Rudolph, Linda, 208n46
Rufo, Christopher, 75
Ruíz, Claudia, 243n17
Ruiz, Neil G., 281n14, 284n27
Rumminger, Jana, 124n12
Russo, Charles J., 88n16

Saad, Lydia, 348n4
Sabol, William J., 143n5, 144n11, 144n15
Sadd, James, 54n8
Saga Education, 384
Sagara, Eric, 305n19
Sampson, Robert J., 116nn28–30
Sanchez, Gabriel R., 270n18
Sanders, Bernie, 27
Sanders, Nathan E., 305nn15–16
Sandidge, Rosetta F., 88n16
Sankin, Aaron, 170n7
Saving on a Valuable Education (SAVE), 6–7
Sawyer, Wendy, xxn31, 150n43
Say Brother (public radio program), 360
Sayet, Madeleine, 436
Schaeffer, Katherine, 76n21
Scham, Sandra Arnold, 89n25
Schermele, Zach, 17n40
Schickler, Eric, 373n11
Schieder, Jessica, 232n39
Schlefer, Jonathan, 30n49
Schleimer, Julia P., 160n5, 162n9, 163n15
Schneier, Bruce, 305, 305nn15–17
Schools. *See also* Education
  school choice, 13
  school discipline, 55, 65–66
  school finance litigation, 56
  school voucher programs, 75
Schott Foundation, 62, 68–69
Schuck, Peter H., 244n23
Schuering, Danile P., 27n19
Schuessler, Jennifer, 246n37
Schultz, Howard, 101
Schultz, Sheri, 101

Schultz Family Foundation, 101
Schwartzapfel, Beth, 151n52
Sciarra, D., 56n17
Science, open, 389–390
Scorsese, Martin, 430
Scott, A. O., 27n26
Scott, Elizabeth S., 136n21
Scuello, Michael, 385n29
Scutari, Mike, 437n8, 438n10
SEARAC, 284n28
Searching for Mexico (documentary series), 248
Sebastian, Thea, 146n23
Section 8 housing programs, 194–195
Seereiter, Mary Lou, 431n3
Segregation
  history of, 186–195
  housing, 170–171, 172–175
  school segregation, xvii–xviii
Seidman, Lila, 150n51
SEIU Racial Justice Center, 318
Self-Help Graphics, 402
The Sentencing Project, 146, 164
Serrano, Andres, 404
Service and Conservation Corps, 96, 97
Serwer, Adam, 375, 375n22
Sexton, Jared Yates, 87n11
Shakira, 245
Shapiro, Thomas M., 53n5, 88n18
Sharkey, Patrick, 117, 117nn31–34, 140n37
Shelby County v. Holder, xxi, xxin37, 256, 304, 304n12
Shellow, Robert, 110n2
Shelton, Ryan, 97
Shenker-Osorio, Anat, 319n17
Shepard, Dan, 175n35
Shephard, Alex, 28n39, 371n3
Sherald, Amy, 403
Sherman Anti-Trust Act, 23
Shipley, M. J., 226n29
Sides, John, 373n15, 373n17, 374
Siegel-Hawley, Genevieve, 54n11
Silver, Christopher, 171n9
Silver-Greenberg, Jessica, 29n45
Simmons-Duffin, Selena, 200n6
Simms, Tinselyn, 318
Simon, David, 229n37
Simon, Ruth, 175n36
Simon, Thomas P., 157n1, 160n3
Simpson, April, 375n21
Sims, J. Marion, 406
Sinclair Broadcast Group, 28
1619 Project, 16, 66
SkillUp Coalition for Employer Network, 101
Slansky, David Alan, 114n15

Index

Small business policy, 7
Smartphones, 362–363
Smialek, Jeanna, 365n17
Smith, David Livingstone, 137n30
Smith, Erica L., 146n21
Smith, Evan, 366
Smith, Fred, 424
Smith, Hannah R., 114n17
Smith, Kaitlin, 283n23
Smith, Lucille, 233n5
Smith, Peter, 175n36
Smith, Renée M., 13n16
Smitherman, Herbert C., 213n2, 214n3, 214n4, 233n5, n42
Smithsonian Institution, 245–246
Snyder Act, 304
Sobieraj, Sarah, 371n5
Social Determinants of Health (SDOH), 214, 215–217, 228, 230
Social Innovation Fund, 386
Social justice
and the arts, 408, 421–423, 432
Arts and Social Justice (ASJ) Fellowship Program, 422–423
beyond academia, 309
Social media, 80–81, 363
Soman, Dilip, 389n45
Soon-Shiong, Patrick, 356
Sotomayor, Sonia, xviii
Souljah, Sister, 13
Soundsuits (Cave), 409
Southern Christian Leadership Conference, 189
Southern Poverty Law Center, 269n14
Sozo Impact, 435
SPCPs (Special Purpose Credit Programs), 178
Spielberg, Steven, 248
Springsteen, Bruce, 362
Staff, Sonja B., 149n36
Standing Rock Sioux Reservation Protest, 263–264, 272
Stanford Latino Entrepreneurship Initiative (SLEI), 258
Stanford University, 11n3
Stangler, Dan, 257, 257n22
STASH program (Massachusetts Affordable Housing Alliance), 178
Statista, 104nn21–22
St. Aubin, Christopher, 347n3
Steger, Manfred B., 27n23
Stein, Judith, 13, 13n14
Steinbeck, John, 245
Steinberg, David, 245n27
Steinberg, Laurence, 136nn21–25
Stern, Nicholas, 29, 29n41
Stevenson, Adlai, 22

Stevenson, Bryan, 424
Stewart, Michael, 403
Stolberg, Sheryl Gay, 204n27
Stolpersteine projects, 424
Stoner, Scott, 438
Storytelling, power of, 241–248
Strength in Diversity Act, xviii–xix
Strickland, Kyle, 11n1, 16n34
Stripling, Sam, 7n19
Stronger Workforce for America Act, xix
Strumbos, Diana, 385n29
Student loan debt, 6–7, 17
Student Nonviolent Coordinating Committee, 189
Students for Fair Admissions v. Harvard (2023), xviii, 91
Studio Museum, Harlem, 402, 409
Substance Abuse and Mental Health Services Administration (SAMHSA), 146n25
Sullivan, Quita, 437
Sumner, Steven A., 157n1, 160n3
The Sum of Us (McGhee), 205
Supplee, Lauren H., 389n48
Supplemental Nutrition Assistance Program (SNAP), 228, 229, 253

Tabuchi, Hiroko, 172n13
Taft Hartley Act (1947), 25n17
Taifa, Nkechi, 208n44
Takei, George, 282
Takyar, Delaram, 117n31
Talk Poverty, 104n23
Taller Boricua, 402
Tan, Amy, 282
Tankersley, Jim, 365n17
Tannen, Johnathan, 170n5
Tapp, Susannah N., 111n9, 149n34
Tapper, Jake, 363
Tarantino, Quentin, 125
Taslitz, Andrew E., 128nn22–23, 129n26
Taueg, Cynthia, 233n5
Taylor, Breonna, 203, 302, 305, 403
Taylor, Mark, 431n3
Taylor-Thompson, Kim, 133n5
Teachers. *See* Education
Teaching to Transgress (hooks), 421–422
Tea Party movement, 14, 375
Telecommunications Act (1996), 26–27, 27nn20–21
Telles, Edward, 243n14
Temin, David Myer, 273n22
Temple, J. A., 54n9
Temporary Protected Status (TPS), 259
Terrell, Ellen, 279n3
Tesler, Michael, 373n15, 374n14
Tessum, Christopher W., 202n12
Texas, Medicaid expansion, 205–206

Texas Tribune, 366
Theoharis, Jeanne, 110n3
Thirteenth Amendment, 186, 189, 305
Thomas, Alma, 403
Thomas, Carly, 365n18
Thomas, Hank Willis, 405, 412, 426
Thomas, June Manning, 171n9
Thomas, Taylor Miller, 207n43
Thompson, Alex, 14n24
Thompson, Anthony C., 133n5
Thomson, Dana, 57n21
303 Creative LLC v. Elenis, xviii–xix
Tian, Ziyao, 281n14
Tibken, Shara, 170n7
Tiered-evidence grantmaking, 382–383
TikTok, 365
Timm, Jane C., 28n34
Title VII (Civil Rights Act, 1964), 40, 43
Torrats-Espinosa, Gerard, 117n31
Torres, Gerald, 304n13
Totenberg, Nina, 283n24
Trail of Broken Treaties Caravan, 268
Trauma
 of Black students, 65, 81
 and healing, 415, 417
 historical, 269
 and homelessness, 339
 public health response to, 139, 282
Travis, Alice, 360
Travis, Jeremy, 143n2
Trawalter, Sophie, 137n28
Treaty of Guadalupe Hidalgo (1848), 242
Tregle, Brandon, 110n7
Trennert, Robert A., 266n11
Trescott, Jacqueline, 246n32
Troiano, Emily, 229n31
Trump, Donald, xvi, xx, 14–15, 28, 109, 280, 295, 316–317, 354, 372, 374, 376
Tsai, Joe, 282
Tsang, Amie, 28n35
Tubman, Harriet, 309
Tucker, Whitney, 75n9
Turchan, Brandon, 118n37
Turner, Garrett, 422
Turner, Nicholas, 151n59
Turner, Tari, 391n58
Tuskegee Syphilis Experiment, 203
Twenty-Sixth Amendment, 304
"Two Minute Warning" (Martin), 413
Tyler, Tom R., 115n21
Tymas, Whitney, 137n27

Uggen, Christopher, 151n54
Ukeles, Mierle Laderman, 410

Underground Railroad, 309
Underwood, Bill, 151n61
Uneasy Peace (Sharkey), 117
Unemployment, youth. *See* Youth unemployment
Unemployment rates, 6, 39–40, 41, 46
 COVID-19 pandemic, 162, 164
UnidosUS, 242, 245, 245n28
Union membership and representation, 43–44, 45–46
United at Peace, 102
United Community Schools, 80
United Nations Declaration on the Rights of Indigenous People (UNDRIP), 273
United States
 "Department of Democracy," 331–332
 divisiveness, contemporary, 336–337, 370–377
 elected officials, accountability, 329
 governmental representation, disproportional, 330–331
 individual freedoms/common good, 328–329
 as multiracial democracy, 302–309
 need to restructure for justice, 326–335
 participatory democracy, 329
 power distribution, 330
 2016 "Minnesota Miracle," 316–317, 318–319, 321–323
Universities. *See* Higher education
University of California v. Bakke (1978), 90
University of Michigan Law School, 90–91
University of North Carolina, 91
Urban Institute, 178
Urmston, Benjamin J., 336
Urofsky, Melvin I., 89n26
U.S. Bureau of Labor Statistics, 101n14
U.S. Bureau of the Census, 241n6, 253n3, 347n1
U.S. Constitution
 Fourteenth Amendment, 186, 193
 Nineteenth Amendment, 304, 332
 original framers, 326–327
 Thirteenth Amendment, 186, 189, 305
 Thirteenth and Fourteenth Amendments, 186–187
 Twenty-Sixth Amendment, 304
 and voting rights, 334
U.S. Department of Commerce, 281n10
U.S. Department of Health, Education, and Welfare, 221n13
U.S. Department of Labor, 279n4
U.S. Department of the Interior, 270n17, 273n25
U.S. Government Accountability Office, 242n11
U.S. National Advisory Commission on Civil Disorders, 303n3
U.S. News & World Report, 286n30
U.S. Supreme Court
 affirmative action and voting rights, 206–207

Index

Alexander v. Sandoval, xviii
Bakke decision (1978), 90
Biden v. Nebraska, 17
Brown v. Board of Education, xvi, 73, 74, 88–89, 243, 252, 307
Buchanan v. Warley, 171n10
Citizens United decision, 103
Fisher I decision (2013), 91
Fisher II decision (2016), 91
Graham v. Florida, 136n10
Gratz v. Bollinger (2003), xviiin18, 90
Grutter v. Bollinger (2003), 90–91
J.D.B. v. North Carolina, 136n26
Jones v. Mayer, 189nn11–12
on juvenile crime, 135–137
Lau v. Nichols, 244
Miller v. Alabama, 136n20
Plessy v. Ferguson, 88, 243
Plyler v. Doe, 244
on racial zoning, 171
Roe v. Wade, 204
Roper v. Simmons, 135n14, 136nn15–18
Shelby County v. Holder, xxin37, 256, 304n12
Students for Fair Admissions v. Harvard (2023), xviii, 91
303 Creative LLC v. Elenis, xviii–xix
U.S. Surgeon General, 81n34

Vachuska, Karl, 170n7
Vance, Carole, 404
Van Dam, Andrew, 64n3
Vargas, Nicholas, 242n13
Varley, Pamela, 308n30
Vavreck, Lynn, 373n15, 374
Venhuizen, Harm, 150n45
venture capital (VC) firms, 258
Vera's Motion for Justice, 150, 151n59
Vespa, Jonathan, 258n25
Vestal, Christine, 151n53
Vice, 361n8
VietAID, 285
Vietnamese American Initiative for Development (VietAID), 278
Villarosa, Lori, 275n28, n29
Vinkers, Christiaan H., 381n3
Violence. *See* Crime rates
Visible Collective, 405
Vivian, C. T., 340
von Hoffman, Alexander, 188n9
Voting rights, 206–207, 255–256, 303–304
    and constitutional amendments, 334
    Electoral College, 303, 330–331
    for formerly incarcerated, 333–334
    and moral issues, 298–299

Native American Voting Rights Act (NAVRA), 271–272
    strengthening, 332–334
    voter suppression, 304
Voting Rights Act, xxi, 206–207, 256, 264, 304, 333
Voting Rights Advancement Act (VRAA), 256, 304, 332

wage policy, xix–xx, 36–39, 44–45
Wagner, Erich, 254n10
Wagner, Pete, xxn31
Wakefield, Sara, 152n64
Waldman, Stephen, 355n15
Waldron, Hilary, 220n9
Walker, Alice, 420
Walker, Mason, 351n7
Walker, Samuel, 124n9, 125n15
Wallis, Brian, 404n8
Wanamaker, Marianne, 203n21
Warnock, Raphael, 178
War on Drugs, xx, 147–148, 208, 443
War on Poverty, 51–52
Warren, Rick, 22n3
Washington, James Melvin, 308n29
Washington Post, 297
Waters, Maxine, 178
Watson, Amy, 28n39
Watson, Jerry, 305n20
Watts riots, xi
Waxman, Olivia B., 17n45
Wealth gap expansion, 173
Weaver, Timothy, 13n17
Webster, Daniel W., 116n25
Weems, Carrie Mae, 407
Weems, Marianne, 404n8
Weiner, Daniel I., 261n19
Weis, Julia, 242n9
Weisburd, David, 115nn21–22, 118n37
Weizman, Shelly R., 151n53
Welfare reform (1996), 13
Wells, Ida B., 294
Wellstone, Paul, 321
Welner, Kevin G., 51n1, 53n6
We Make the Future Action, 318nn15–16, 323n26
Werfel, Daniel I., 17n42
Wertheimer, Julie, 315n3
West, Heather C., 144n15
Westen, Drew, 241n5
Western, Bruce, 143n2, 146n19, 146n22
Western Arts Alliance, 438
Whaples, Robert, 23n5
What Works Clearinghouse, 383
White, B. A. B., 54n9
White supremacy, 70, 340, 370

Whitney, Melissa, 124n10, 124n13
Whitney Museum of Art, 409
Wiese, Andrew, 350n6
Wike, Richard, 253n2
Wildeman, Christopher, 143n6, 152n64
Wilentz, Sean, 88n14
Wilkinson, Charles F., 265n9
Willen, Paul, 173n23
William Monroe Trotter Collaborative for Social Justice, 306n21, 307
Williams, Amanda, 408
Williams, Carmen, 97, 97n3
Williams, David R., 203, 220n10
Williams, Hosea, 189
Williams, Kate, 390n51
Williams, Nikema, 103
Williams, Reginald II, 204n24
Williams, Serena, 204, 204n25
Williamson, Jake, 174n29
Williamson, Vanessa, 71n10
Williams v. Wallace, 189n14
Willis, Larkin, 58n25
Wilson, Danielle, 5n4
Wilson, James Q., 116, 116n26
Wilson, Tim, 438
Wilson, Valerie, 40n18, 41n23
Wilson-Hartgrove, Jonathan, 295n2
Winger-Bearskin, Amelia, 417
Wing Luke Museum, 402
Winter, Jonah, 246n39
Withrow, Brian, 123–124
Withrow, Brian L., 124nn6–8
Wong, Ali, 282
Wong, Felicia, 11n1, 12n4, 15n28, 16n34
Woo, Michelle, 412
Wood, Betty, 88n13
Wooden, Ontario S., 86n6
Woodruff, Natalie Nguyen, 285
Woods, Tiger, 282
Woolhandler, Steffie, 201n9
Workers' rights, 23–24
Workforce Innovation and Opportunity Act (2014), xxi, 96, 99
Worlddata.Info, 30n51
World Health Organization, 214n5, 217n6
Wright, Dwayne Kwyasee, 88n15, 90n31

Wright, Marisa, 202n16
Wu, Michelle, 282
Wyatt Gallery, 412

Yam, Kimmy, 282n16
Yang, Jenny R., 43nn27–28
Yap, Maureen, 174n30
Year Up, 96, 98
Yenawine, Philip, 404n8
Yin, Leon, 170n7
Yokum, David, 389–390, 390n49
Young, Caitlin, 172n15
Young, Kevin, 399
YouthBuild USA, 96, 97, 98, 99, 102
Youth Formula Program (WIOA), 99
Youth PROMISE Act, xx–xxi
Youth unemployment
  media, role of, 103–104
  multiracial cooperation, need for, 104–105
  Opportunity Youth (OY), 98–101
  political momentum for, 102–103
  programs to combat, 96–98
  underserved groups, 101–102
  youth as advocates, 98
YPLL (years of potential life lost), 159
Yurukoglu, Ali, 28n33
Yzaguírre, Raul, 245

Zajacova, Anna, 202n15
Zakrzewski, Cat, 366n21
Zandi, Mark M., 229n35
Zeigler, Sara L., 28n40
Zelizer, Julian E., 188n8, 359n2
Zeng, Zhen, 150n42
Zhang, Michael, 27n31
Zhu, Jing, 385n29
Zhu, Linna, 172n15
Ziblatt, Daniel, 328, 328n1
Zillow, 173n25
Zimmerman, Emily, 201n8
Zimmerman, George, 14
Zimring, Franklin E., 116n27
Zinn Education Project, 281n13
Zoning. *See also* Housing crisis
  exclusionary, 170–171
  zoning reform, 192

About the Editor and Contributors

Alan Curtis is president and CEO of the Eisenhower Foundation. He was Crimes of Violence Task Force Co-Director on President Lyndon Johnson's National Violence Commission, Executive Director of President Jimmy Carter's interagency Urban Policy Group and Urban Policy Advisor to the Secretary of Housing and Urban Development. Dr. Curtis has testified before Senate and House committees; and served on many boards including the Congressional Human Rights Foundation and the American Academy of Political and Social Science. He has published in *The New York Times* and *Washington Post,* and has written or edited, among other books, *Criminal Violence; Locked in the Poorhouse; American Violence and Public Policy; Patriotism, Democracy and Common Sense;* and *Healing Our Divided Society.* He holds an AB from Harvard, an MSc from the University of London and a PhD from the University of Pennsylvania.

Michael Akinwumi is the chief responsible AI officer at the National Fair Housing Alliance (NFHA) where he is tasked with critical responsibilities, including the development and implementation of Responsible AI policies and guidelines that prioritize fairness, privacy, security, explainability, reliability, and non-algorithmic solutions. He provides strategic oversight and leadership, collaborating with senior management to advocate for ethical AI practices in housing and lending, and assess potential risks associated with AI use in housing and lending. Stakeholder engagement and education are part of his portfolio, involving interactions with both internal and external parties to gather input, educate employees, and ensure adherence to Responsible AI principles. Moreover, he represents NFHA in industry discussions, advocating for responsible AI practices and staying current with emerging regulations and ethical frameworks to educate providers of housing and lending AI products and services on the need for compliance and alignment with responsible national and global AI standards. Previously, he led governance engineering, recommender systems, and machine learning solutions for various sectors, such as fintech, banking, and insurance. He holds a PhD in Applied Mathematics from the University of Alberta and has multiple certifications and honors in data analysis and mathematical modeling. Dr. Akinwumi lives his belief that "only a life lived for others is worth living."

Rocío Aranda-Alvarado is an art historian and curator. She joined Ford Foundation in 2018 after serving as curator at El Museo del Barrio for nearly a decade. At Ford, she is a senior program officer on the Creativity and Free Expression team, focusing on support for arts and culture organizations across the United States. At El Museo, she presented visual arts and programming that reflected the history and culture of El Barrio, as well as the greater U.S. Latinx and Latin American diaspora. She organized exhibitions featuring emerging and established artists, including Presente! The Young Lords in New York, Museum Starter Kit for El Museo's 45th anniversary, and several versions of El Museo's biennial. From 2000 to 2009, she was curator at the Jersey City Museum, where she organized solo exhibitions of Chakaia Booker and Raphael Montañez Ortiz, and many group exhibitions. Rocío has lectured as an adjunct professor; consulted and curated independently on Latinx and Latin American art and culture; and published and advised, in both a scholarly and curatorial capacity, at various institutions. She earned her PhD in art history from the Graduate Center, City University of New York.

Anil N.F. Aranha, PhD, is associate director in the offices of Medical Education and Diversity and Inclusion with a joint faculty appointment in the Department of Internal Medicine at Wayne State University School of Medicine. His research interests include medical and public health education; food, nutrition, and health behaviors; social determinants of health; health disparities; geriatric health care; health care services and outcomes; patient satisfaction and medical intervention cost-effectiveness. He has published extensively in leading scientific journals and his publications comprise peer-reviewed articles and abstracts, book chapters, and research reports.

Nikitra Bailey serves as executive vice president at the National Fair Housing Alliance (NFHA). As a member of NFHA's senior leadership team, she leads the organization's Public Policy and Communications divisions and assists in managing Resource Development. Ms. Bailey develops and spearheads visionary, comprehensive policy, and communications strategies to implement NFHA's mission of eliminating all forms of housing discrimination and ensuring that everyone has decent, stable, affordable housing in well-resourced, opportunity-rich communities free from bias. She also provides thought leadership that supports over 200 member organizations; liaises with policymakers and other stakeholders; and works collaboratively with NFHA's departments, membership, and Board of Directors to promote housing equity and equitable opportunities. Ms. Bailey has authored numerous reports and articles on predatory lending's impact on people of color and women and is a frequent media contributor. She has provided expert testimony to Congress on a range of fair and affordable housing issues and reform of the Government Sponsored Enterprises. Ms. Bailey co-leads the Black Homeownership Collaborative's work stream on fair housing and consumer protection and is on the board of directors of the National Institute for Minority Economic Development and Consumer Reports. Ms. Bailey served on the Consumer Financial Protection Bureau Community Advisory Board from 2018–2021. She holds a JD from the University of Pittsburgh School of Law, and a BA from The Pennsylvania State University.

William J. Barber II, DMin, is President and Senior Lecturer of Repairers of the Breach and founding director of the Center for Public Theology and Public Policy at Yale Divinity School. A bishop with the Fellowship of Affirming Ministries, he has served as

About the Editor and Contributors

co-chair of the Poor People's Campaign: A National Call for Moral Revival since 2018. While serving as a pastor and the President of the North Carolina NAACP, he helped launch "Moral Mondays" in 2013.

Branville G. Bard Jr., DPA, currently serves as the Vice President for Public Safety and Chief of Police for Johns Hopkins University and Medicine. He is a reform-minded pracademic who is heavily influenced by the social and procedural justice movements. Dr. Bard is an expert on racial profiling, racially biased policing, and other topics where race and the criminal justice system intersect. He has previously served as the police commissioner for the City of Cambridge, Massachusetts, and as the chief of police for the Philadelphia Housing Authority Police Department. He began his career as a member of the Philadelphia Police Department, where he retired as a police inspector.

Sindy Marisol Benavides, a proud Honduran American, is the president and CEO of Latino Victory, a progressive organization dedicated to building Latino political power at the local, state, and federal levels. Sindy is a recognized national civil rights leader, with nearly 2 decades in the nonprofit sector. She has helped build organizations to scale from the bottom up through strategy development, governance, communication, partnerships, revenue development and outreach. She now devotes her career to public service, ensuring that countless young people, women, and immigrants have the same opportunity. She received her BA from Virginia State University in Petersburg, Virginia, where she graduated valedictorian of her class and studied Political Science with a minor in Spanish. She has also attended American University for her master's degree in International Affairs and is working on submitting her substantial research paper.

Jared Bernstein currently serves as the chair of the Council of Economic Advisers. Previously, Bernstein served as chief economist to then-Vice President Biden in the Obama–Biden Administration before joining the Center on Budget and Policy Priorities, where he served as a senior fellow from 2011–2021. A former social worker, Bernstein has a long and distinguished track record devising economic policies that expand opportunity for working Americans. Bernstein has previously served as Executive Director of the White House Task Force on the Middle Class and as an economic advisor to President Obama; prior to his service in the Obama–Biden Administration, he was a senior economist and director of the Living Standards Program at the Economic Policy Institute and served as Deputy Chief Economist at the U.S. Department of Labor under President Clinton. Bernstein received his bachelor's degree from the Manhattan School of Music, his masters of social work degree from Hunter College, and his PhD in social welfare from Columbia University.

Cornell William Brooks is Hauser Professor of the Practice of Nonprofit Organizations and Professor of the Practice of Public Leadership and Social Justice at the Harvard Kennedy School. He was awarded the HKS Innovations in Teaching Award. He is also the Director of The William Monroe Trotter Collaborative for Social Justice at the Kennedy School's Center for Public Leadership and the Visiting Professor of the Practice of Prophetic Religion and Public Leadership at Harvard Divinity School. Brooks is the former president and CEO of the National Association for the Advancement of Colored People (NAACP), a record-setting civil rights attorney, and a fourth-generation ordained minister.

LaTosha R. Brown is an award-winning visionary thought leader, institution builder, cultural activist and artist, and connector. She is a nationally recognized go-to expert in Black voting rights and voter suppression, Black women's empowerment, and philanthropy. LaTosha is the co-founder of Black Voters Matter Fund and Black Voters Matter Capacity Building Institute. These initiatives are designed to boost Black voter registration and turnout, as well as increase power in marginalized, predominantly Black communities. LaTosha is also the visionary, founder, and co-anchor of a regional network called the Southern Black Girls & Women's Consortium, a $100 million, 10-year initiative to invest in organizations that serve Black women and girls. The goal of the consortium is to create a new approach to philanthropy by allowing every component of the program, inception to execution, to be created by Black girls and women in the South. Ms. Brown has been the 2020 Hauser Leader at the Center for Public Leadership at Harvard Kennedy School, the 2020 Leader in Practice at Harvard Kennedy School's Women and Public Policy Program, and a 2020–2021 American Democracy Fellow at the Charles Warren Center at Harvard.

Erik M. Conway is a historian of science and technology living in Altadena, California. He completed his PhD from the University of Minnesota in 1998, with a dissertation on the development of aircraft landing aids. Currently, he works as the historian of the Jet Propulsion Laboratory, a unit of Caltech. He is the co-author with Naomi Oreskes of *Merchants of Doubt: How a Handful of Scientists Obscured the Truth on Issues from Tobacco Smoke to Climate Change*, and *The Big Myth: How American Business Taught Us to Loathe the Government and Love the Free Market*.

Elliott Currie, PhD, is professor of criminology, law, and society at the University of California, Irvine, and adjunct professor in the Faculty of Law, School of Justice, Queensland University of Technology, Australia. He is the author of many books on crime, delinquency, drug abuse, and social policy, and was a finalist for the Pulitzer Prize in general nonfiction in 1999. He is also a winner of the 2004 Book Award from the Benjamin L. Hooks Institute for Social Change.

Linda Darling-Hammond is the Charles E. Ducommun Professor of Education Emeritus at Stanford University and president of the Learning Policy Institute. She also currently serves as president for the California State Board of Education. She was executive director of the National Commission on Teaching and America's Future and was the leader of President Barack Obama's 2008 education policy transition team, as well as a member of President Joe Biden's education transition team in 2020. Among her more than six hundred publications are several award-winning books, including *The Right to Learn* and *The Flat World and Education: How America's Commitment to Equity will Determine our Future*.

Robert Faris is a researcher and writer whose work focuses on political communication and the role of networked media structures in shaping public discourse. Faris is currently an affiliate at the Berkman Klein Center for Internet and Society at Harvard University, where he served as research director for over a decade. Previously, he has held research positions at the Shorenstein Center on Media, Politics and Public Policy and the Center for International Development at Harvard. Faris holds a PhD from the Fletcher School of Law and Diplomacy at Tufts University.

Michael Feuer is dean and professor of Education Policy at the Graduate School of Education and Human Development, George Washington University. Feuer's research has focused on the economics of education, international comparative assessments, teacher preparation, inequality and academic opportunity, science policy, use of research to inform policy, philanthropy, and civics. Feuer consults to governments and research organizations in Europe, Israel, and elsewhere.

Nazgol Ghandnoosh, PhD, is the co-director of research at The Sentencing Project, an organization that advocates for effective and humane responses to crime that minimize imprisonment by promoting racial, ethnic, economic, and gender justice. She conducts and synthesizes research on criminal legal policies, with a focus on racial disparities, lengthy sentences, and the scope of reform efforts. In *The Lancet Infectious Diseases*, she explained why people serving long sentences for violent crimes should have been included in COVID-19–era decarceration efforts. Her report, "A Second Look at Injustice," is a comprehensive analysis of a growing, powerful tool to curb mass incarceration: second look policies, which enable extreme sentences to be reevaluated. She also serves on the District of Columbia Sentencing Commission.

Neil Gross is the Charles A. Dana Professor of Sociology at Colby College and a senior fellow at the Niskanen Center.

Matt Hughes is the director of editorial and narrative strategy at the Roosevelt Institute, where he leads the editorial team in the shaping and production of publications, op-eds, speeches, and newsletters. He worked on Roosevelt and the New Republic's *How to Save a Country* podcast and was previously a researcher in the office of Joseph E. Stiglitz at Columbia University. His work has been covered by *The New York Times, Politico,* and *Vox*. Matt holds an MPA in urban and social policy from Columbia University and a BA in economics and politics from New York University.

George Huynh is the executive director of the Vietnamese American Initiative for Development (VietAID). He holds a BA in political science from Yale. His background includes community organizing, teaching, nonprofit work, and government experience, from his time at the Dorchester Youth Collaborative, Boston Public Schools, the Volunteer

Lawyers Project, and the City of Boston. He has served under three Boston mayors as their liaison to Fields Corner and the Vietnamese community citywide, then later to Dorchester.

John H. Jackson is president and CEO of the Schott Foundation for Public Education, where he leads the Foundation's efforts to ensure a fair and substantive opportunity to learn for all students regardless of race or gender. Under his leadership, Schott transitioned to a public fund that supports movement building, cross-sector collaboration, and pro-public education narratives as both a funder and advocacy partner. Previously, Dr. Jackson served as national director of education and chief policy officer of the NAACP from 2000–2007 and as Senior Policy Advisor in the Office for Civil Rights (OCR) at the U.S. Department of Education under the Clinton administration.

Judith Le Blanc is a citizen of the Caddo Nation. She has been the executive director of Native Organizers Alliance (NOA) for 8 years. She leads a national Native training and organizing network that supports tribes, traditional societies, and community groups, urban and reservation, in organizing grassroots political power to achieve Native sovereignty and racial equity for all. Judith is a board member of the Movement Strategy Center and chair of the board of the NDN Collective. She currently serves on the Environmental Justice Working Group, convened by U.S. Representatives Raul Grijalva and Barbara Lee. Judith was a 2019 Roddenberry fellow. In 2022, she was a resident fellow at the Institute of Politics at the Kennedy School of Harvard University.

Carlton Mackey is assistant director of Education, Community Dialogue, and Engagement at the High Museum of Art in Atlanta, Georgia. Mackey is also the co-creator/co-director of the Emory University Arts and Social Justice Fellowship Program. The Arts and Social Justice Fellows program brings leading Atlanta artists into Emory classrooms to help students translate their learning into creative expressions of activism in the name of racial and social justice. Formerly, Mackey codeveloped and served as director of the Ethics and the Arts Program at the Emory University Center for Ethics and was a lecturer in Emory's Department of Film and Media. Mackey created Black Men Smile, a viral social media hashtag and multifaceted platform for amplifying the revolutionary power of Black joy. Mackey's work blends a unique combination of social consciousness, creativity, scholarship, and social connection to create powerful impressions that invite new discovery and personal transformation.

Adewale A. Maye is a policy and research analyst with the Economic Policy Institute's Program on Race, Ethnicity, and the Economy. He studies the root causes of racial economic inequality in order to advance inclusive and restorative policy solutions that build equity. His research interests are centered at the intersection of labor economics, the political economy, and structural racism. Prior to joining EPI, Adewale was a policy analyst with the Center for Law and Social Policy (CLASP), where he focused on expanding workers' rights on issues including paid leave, paid sick days, and fair scheduling, as well as advocating for broader economic justice initiatives that impact marginalized communities, such as student loan debt cancellation and labor standards enforcement.

About the Editor and Contributors

Justin Milner is executive vice president for Evidence and Evaluation at Arnold Ventures, a philanthropy working to improve the lives of all Americans by pursuing evidence-based solutions to our nation's most pressing problems. Prior to joining Arnold Ventures, he was vice president of the Research to Action Lab at the Urban Institute, where he led a team focused on policy research and translation. In previous roles, Justin worked at the Annie E. Casey Foundation, the U.S. Department of Health and Human Services, and as a kindergarten teacher. He holds an MPA from Princeton University and a BA from Yale University.

Margaret S. Morton is the senior program advisor for the Mellon Foundation's Presidential Initiatives: Imagining Freedom, the Monuments Project, and Puerto Rico. She collaborates closely with the Presidential Initiatives staff and grantees on all aspects of the office's grantmaking. Margaret has supported public funding and grantmaking for the Arts and other forms of creative expression for 20 years. Most recently, she led the Ford Foundation's Creativity and Free Expression program investments in the arts, media and journalism in the United States, and documentary film across the U.S. and nine international regions. Margaret also supported New York City's public funding for the arts and cultural sector, as general counsel and deputy commissioner of the Department of Cultural Affairs. Prior to her work in philanthropy, Margaret served as counsel on the Senate Judiciary Committee's Subcommittee on the Constitution and as legislative counsel to New York City's Deputy Mayor for Criminal Justice, in roles that advanced civil rights legislation, criminal justice reforms and alternatives to incarceration. Margaret's passion for the arts is marked by prior service on the Art Law Committee of the New York City Bar Association; board membership on the Theater Development Fund; and currently, as an Advisor to SMU's Data Arts center, which provides evidence-based insights on the U.S. arts and cultural sector. Margaret earned her juris doctorate from Georgetown University Law Center and her bachelor of arts degree from Barnard College, majoring in American History and Dance.

Janet Murguía is president and chief executive officer of UnidosUS, the largest national Hispanic civil rights and advocacy organization in the United States. Murguía has sought to strengthen UnidosUS's work and enhance its record of impact as a vital American institution by amplifying the Latino voice on issues affecting the Hispanic community, such as education, health care, immigration, civil rights, and the economy. Murguía began her career in Washington, DC, as legislative counsel to former Congressman Jim Slattery. She later worked at the White House, ultimately serving as deputy assistant and director of legislative affairs to President Bill Clinton. After serving in the Clinton administration, Murguía was deputy campaign manager and director of constituency outreach for the Gore/Lieberman presidential campaign. Before joining UnidosUS, Murguía was executive vice chancellor for university relations at the University of Kansas (KU). She received three degrees from KU: a BS in journalism, a BA in Spanish, and a JD from the School of Law.

Naomi Oreskes is the Henry Charles Lea Professor of the History of Science and affiliated professor of Earth and Planetary Sciences at Harvard University. An internationally renowned scientist and historian, she is a leading voice on the reality of anthropogenic climate change and the history of efforts to undermine climate action and scientific truth. Oreskes is an author of nine books and over 150 scholarly and popular articles. Her opinion pieces have appeared around the globe, including in *The New York Times*, *The Washington Post*, *The Times* (London), and the *Frankfurter Allgemeine*. In 2015, she wrote the Introduction to the Melville House edition of the Papal Encyclical on Climate Change and Inequality, *Laudato Si*. In 2018, she became a Guggenheim Fellow, and in 2019 was awarded the British Academy Medal.

Claudia Peña is the executive director of For Freedoms, an artist-led organization that models and inspires creative civic engagement to awaken a national political identity around listening, justice and healing. She is also on faculty at UCLA School of Law and in the Gender Studies department. Claudia is the founding codirector of the Center for Justice at UCLA, home of the Prison Education Program, which creates innovative courses that enable faculty and students to learn from, and alongside, participants who are currently incarcerated. Claudia writes from her own voice and the lens of For Freedoms. For Freedoms is rich with perspectives, ideas and interpretations, and this chapter reflects just one such angle.

Lisa Rice is the president and CEO of the National Fair Housing Alliance (NFHA), the nation's only national civil rights agency solely dedicated to eliminating all forms of housing discrimination and ensuring equitable housing opportunities for all people and communities. NFHA is also the trade association for over 170 member organizations throughout the United States that work to eliminate barriers in the housing markets and expand equal housing and lending opportunities. NFHA provides a range of programs to affirmatively further fair housing including housing and community development, responsible AI, education and outreach, research, public policy and advocacy, training and consulting, and enforcement initiatives. Ms. Rice is a member of the Leadership Conference on Civil and Human Rights Board of Directors, Center for Responsible Lending Board of Directors, FinRegLab Board of Directors, JPMorgan Chase Consumer Advisory Council, Mortgage Bankers Association Consumer Advisory Council, Freddie Mac Affordable Housing Advisory Council, Fannie Mae Affordable Housing Advisory Council, Quicken Loans Advisory Forum, Bipartisan Policy Center's Housing Advisory Council, and Berkeley's The Terner Center Advisory Council. She has received numerous awards including the National Housing Conference's Housing Visionary Award and was selected as one of TIME Magazine's 2024 "Closers."

Loretta J. Ross is a professor at Smith College in the Program for the Study of Women and Gender where she teaches courses on white supremacy, human rights, and Calling In the Call Out Culture. Loretta also is a recipient of a MacArthur Fellowship, Class of 2022, for her work as an advocate for reproductive justice and human rights. Loretta was the national coordinator of the SisterSong Women of Color Reproductive Justice Collective (2005–2012) and cocreated the theory of Reproductive Justice. Loretta was national codirector of the April 25, 2004, March for Women's Lives in Washington, DC, the largest protest march in U.S. history at that time. She founded the National Center for Human Rights Education (NCHRE) in Atlanta, Georgia, launched the Women of Color Program for the National Organization for Women (NOW), and was the national program director of the National Black Women's Health Project. One of the first African American women to direct a rape crisis center, Loretta was the third executive director of the DC Rape Crisis Center.

Leah Rothstein is coauthor, with Richard Rothstein, of *Just Action: How to Challenge Segregation Enacted Under the Color of Law*. Leah has worked on public policy and community change, from the grassroots to the halls of government. She has led research for local governments on reforming community corrections policy and practice, and has been a consultant to nonprofit housing developers, cities and counties, redevelopment agencies, and private firms on community development and affordable housing policy, practice, and finance. Her policy work is informed by her years as a labor and community organizer. Leah received a bachelor's degree from UC Santa Cruz and a master's in public policy from the Goldman School of Public Policy at UC Berkeley.

Richard Rothstein is the author of *The Color of Law: A Forgotten History of How Our Government Segregated America* (2017), and coauthor of its sequel, *Just Action: How to Challenge Segregation Enacted Under the Color of Law* (2023). He is the author of many other books and articles on race and education, most of which are listed on a web page at the Economic Policy Institute.

Zakiyah Shaakir-Ansari is interim co-executive director of the New York State Alliance for Quality Education (AQE), the leading statewide organization for educational justice in New York State. Zakiyah brings a wealth of knowledge on policy, organizing, and campaign strategy, leveraging the skills and experience she developed as a parent of eight New York City public school students and as a parent activist. Zakiyah has worked on a range of education justice issues including equitable funding, ending the school-to-prison pipeline, culturally responsive education, community schools, school governance reform and progressive revenues to fund schools—among others. In 2017, she was named one of *City and State* magazine's "25 Most Influential in Brooklyn."

Anat Shenker-Osorio is principal and founder of ASO Communications, host of the Words to Win By podcast, and principal of ASO Communications. She has led research for new messaging on issues ranging from freedom to join together in union to clean energy and from immigrant rights to reforming criminal justice. Anat's original approach through priming experiments, task-based testing, and online dial surveys has led to progressive electoral and policy victories across the globe. Anat delivers her findings packed in snark at venues such as the Congressional Progressive Caucus, Centre for Australian Progress, Irish Migrant Centre, Open Society Foundations, Ford Foundation and LUSH International. Her writing and research are profiled in *The New York Times, The Atlantic, Boston Globe, Salon, The Guardian,* and *Grist,* among others.

brooke smiley is a California-based Indigenous 𐒼𐒖𐓓𐒰𐓓𐒰 (Osage) interdisciplinary artist whose work uplifts the complexity of Contemporary Native Identity across generations through the collaborative creation of earth markers (sustainable outdoor structures and sculptures) and multisensory performances. With a background in dance, earth architecture, and indigenous justice, Brooke earned her MA from Trinity Laban, BFA from CalArts, and is a graduate of California Institute of Earth Art and Architecture (CalEarth). She specializes in Somatic Education from an Indigenous, Body Mind Centering® (BMC®), Somatic Experiencing® (SE®), social justice perspective, guiding anatomical, embryological, and elemental learning in connection to lineage and land, uplifting personal agency and difference. Her newest work, EARTH.SPEAKS, enlivens public art experiences as both diplomacy and education, Re-Indigenizing public spaces and who they serve by guiding creative processes with Native and non-Native communities, National Parks, and institutions worldwide.

Herbert Smitherman Jr. MD, MPH, is a Professor of Medicine at Wayne State University School of Medicine, Chief Executive Officer, Michigan AHEC, Southeast Regional Center (SERC), and president and CEO of Health Centers Detroit Foundation, Inc., the first Federally Qualified Health Center look-alike designated in Detroit, Michigan. He has practiced medicine in Detroit for the past 37 years. His research and expertise focus primarily on creating sustainable systems of care for urban communities.

Dorothy Stoneman, EdD, is founder and former CEO of YouthBuild USA, Inc., the support center for 260 YouthBuild programs in the USA, and 80 in 20 other countries. In YouthBuild, low-income unemployed young people ages 16 to 24 who left high school without a diploma enroll full time for 6 to 24 months to work toward their high school equivalency or diploma—while getting paid to build affordable housing for homeless and low-income people in their neighborhoods. A strong emphasis is also put on leadership development and civic engagement. Graduates are placed in jobs and/or college. Stoneman helped found and worked through 2022 with Opportunity Youth United, a national multiracial network of deeply engaged urban and rural young people. Among many awards, she received the John Gardner Leadership Award in 2000, a MacArthur Fellowship in 1996, and the Skoll Award for Social Entrepreneurship in 2007.

Ray Suarez is the host of the public radio program and podcast *On Shifting Ground*, produced by Commonwealth Club-World Affairs and KQED-FM. He has been a visiting professor of Political Science at NYU Shanghai, and the John McCloy Visiting Professor of American Studies at Amherst College. He is a graduate of New York University and the University of Chicago. Earlier in his career, Suarez was the host of the daily news program *Inside Story* from Al Jazeera America, Chief National Correspondent for The PBS NewsHour, and the host of *Talk of the Nation* from NPR. His recent podcast productions include two seasons of *Going for Broke*, produced with the Economic Hardship Reporting Project, and *The Things I Thought About When My Body Was Trying to Kill Me*, from Evergreen Podcasts, about cancer and recovery. Suarez' journalism has been recognized with two DuPont-Columbia Awards, an Overseas Press Club Award, the Ruben Salazar Award from UNIDOS-US, and UCLA's Public Policy Leadership Award for his reporting on urban America, among others.

Lena Sze, a writer and cultural worker originally from New York City is currently the Program Associate at the Ford Foundation's Creativity and Free Expression program area. She has worked at the NYC Department of Cultural Affairs, the Lower East Side Tenement Museum, and the Asian Arts Initiative, among other cultural organizations. Lena received her PhD in American Studies from New York University and has taught at Parsons / The New School, NYU, and Hunter College (City University of New York).

Kim Taylor-Thompson is professor of law emerita at New York University School of Law. She serves as the Chair of the Board of the Equal Justice Initiative and the Public Welfare Foundation. Her scholarship focuses on the distorting effects of race on the experience of justice. She served on the MacArthur Foundation Research Network on Law and Neuroscience and the Adolescent Development Working Group. She founded the Criminal Justice Program at the Brennan Center for Justice. She earned her JD from Yale Law School and her BA from Brown University.

Lisa Richards Toney is president and CEO of the Association of Performing Arts Professionals (APAP). She is a committed arts leader working to advance the performing arts industry throughout North America. In September 2023, Lisa was named among industry luminaries to the first NYC Live Entertainment Industry Council by New York Mayor Eric Adams. She was also named one of "The Next 50" as part of the 50th anniversary celebration of the John F. Kennedy Center for the Performing Arts. With more than 20 years in the field, she holds an MA from New York University and a BA from Spelman College as well as fellowships from the Vilar Institute of Arts Management at the Kenney Center and The Thomas J. Watson Foundation.

Randi Weingarten is president of the AFT, a union of 1.75 million people who work in education, healthcare, and public services. The AFT is dedicated to the belief that every person in America deserves the freedom to thrive. Prior to her election as AFT president in 2008, Weingarten served for 11 years as president of the United Federation of Teachers, representing 200,000 educators in the New York City public school system. She taught history at Clara Barton High School in Brooklyn from 1991 to 1997, where she helped her students win several awards debating constitutional issues. Weingarten holds degrees from the Cornell University School of Industrial and Labor Relations and Cardozo School of Law. She practiced law at Stroock & Stroock & Lavan. She is involved in the Democratic National Committee, J Street and other civic organizations. Weingarten resides with her wife Rabbi Sharon Kleinbaum in New York City.

Michelle A. Williams, ScD, is a renowned epidemiologist, an award-winning educator, and a widely recognized academic leader. She recently stepped down as dean of the faculty at the Harvard T. H. Chan School of Public Health after 7 years and is currently spending a sabbatical year as a visiting professor at Stanford University. Following her sabbatical, she will return to the Harvard Chan School as the Joan and Julius Jacobson Professor in Epidemiology and Public Health. Prior to becoming dean, she was professor and chair of the Department of Epidemiology at the Harvard Chan School and program leader of the Population Health and Health Disparities Research Programs at Harvard's Clinical and Translational Sciences Center. Her research places special emphasis in the areas of reproductive, perinatal, pediatric, and molecular epidemiology. She has published more than 520 scientific articles and was elected to the National Academy of Medicine in 2016. In 2020, she was awarded the Ellis Island Medal of Honor and recognized by *PR Week* as one of the top 50 health influencers of the year.

Valerie Wilson, PhD, is a labor economist and director of the Program on Race, Ethnicity, and the Economy at the Economic Policy Institute in Washington, DC. Dr. Wilson has testified before Congress on racial disparities in unemployment and earnings and was keynote speaker for the regional Federal Reserve Banks' series on Racism and the Economy: Focus on Employment. Prior to joining EPI, Wilson served as Vice President of Research at the National Urban League Washington Bureau in Washington, DC. In 2022, she was President of the National Economics Association, and in 2023, she was elected to become a fellow of the National Academy of Public Administration.

Dwayne Kwaysee Wright is an assistant professor of Higher Education Administration and the director of Diversity, Equity, and Inclusion (DEI) Initiatives at the Graduate School for Education and Human Development within George Washington University. Dr. Wright's research and social activism seek to advance educational opportunity and equity for all students, particularly those historically oppressed and marginalized in American society. A first-generation college and professional student, Dr. Wright earned his Doctor of Philosophy in Higher Education from Pennsylvania State University in 2018. He also holds a Juris Doctor from the Pennsylvania State University Dickinson School of Law (Penn State Law), a Master of Education from Penn State's College of Education, and a Bachelor of Arts in Political Science from The Norfolk State University (an HBCU). He is currently licensed to practice law in New York and New Jersey and is pursuing a Master of Business Administration/Graduate Certificate in Non-Profit Management at the George Washington University School of Business.

Felicia Wong is president and CEO of the Roosevelt Institute, where she directs the organization's mission, vision, and strategy in pursuit of a high-care, low-carbon economy that works for all. She was the U.S. representative on the G7 Economic Resilience Panel in 2021, served on the Biden–Harris administration transition advisory board, and currently serves as vice chair of the Treasury Advisory Committee on Racial Equity.

Julian E. Zelizer is a *New York Times* best-selling author and has been among the pioneers in the revival of American political history. He is the Malcolm Stevenson Forbes, Class of 1941 Professor of History and Public Affairs at Princeton University, a CNN political analyst, and a regular guest on NPR's "Here and Now." He is the award-winning author and editor of 25 books, and the winner of the D.B. Hardeman Prize for the Best Book on U.S. Congress, awarded by The Lyndon Baines Johnson Foundation.